UNDERSTANDING HUMAN BEHAVIOR IN ORGANIZATIONS

UNDERSTANDING HUMAN BEHAVIOR IN ORGANIZATIONS

Wendell L. French

Fremont E. Kast

James E. Rosenzweig

School of Business Administration
University of Washington

1817

HARPER & ROW, PUBLISHERS, New York
Cambridge, Philadelphia, San Francisco,
London, Mexico City, São Paulo, Singapore, Sydney

Sponsoring Editor: Jayne L. Maerker
Project Editor: Mary G. Ward
Text Design: Michel Craig
Cover Design: Hudson River Studio
Text Art: Vantage Art, Inc.
Production Manager: Jeanie Berke
Compositor: Ruttle, Shaw & Wetherill, Inc.
Printer and Binder: R. R. Donnelley & Sons Company

UNDERSTANDING HUMAN BEHAVIOR IN ORGANIZATIONS

Library of Congress Cataloging in Publication Data

French, Wendell L., 1923–
Understanding human behavior in organizations.

Includes index.
1. Organizational behavior. 2. Psychology,
Industrial. I. Kast, Fremont Ellsworth, 1926–
II. Rosenzweig, James Erwin, 1929– . III. Title.
HD58.7.F74 1985 158.7 84-28980
ISBN 0-06-042186-X

85 86 87 9 8 7 6 5 4 3 2 1

CONTENTS

PREFACE

Human behavior in organizations is an inherently fascinating subject. We are all members of various organizations and frequently wonder what causes people to behave the way they do. Why are some organizations successful in accomplishing their goals *and* providing a high level of satisfaction for individual participants, whereas other organizations are ineffective and much less satisfying? This book provides insight with regard to this question. It is concerned with understanding the behavior of people in an organization context. This understanding is based on a body of knowledge stemming from the behavioral sciences. The book is concerned with the application of this knowledge to specific behaviors occurring in an organizational context—*organizational behavior.*

> Organizational behavior is a field of study based on research, observation, and theory. It is concerned with analyzing and understanding the attitudes, feelings, perceptions, motives, and behavior of people in an organizational context. Its primary goals are improved individual and organizational performance and increased participant satisfaction.

This book is dedicated to helping you *understand* more about human behavior in organizations. But, it is much more. It is also directed toward helping you *predict* how people will behave in different group and organizational contexts. As a manager, and as a member, it is important to be able to predict accurately how people will behave in certain situations. For example, how will employees respond to a new performance evaluation and compensation program? How will the new computerized information system affect both the performance and satisfaction of individuals? Astute, skillful managers develop the ability to anticipate and predict human behavior in their organizations.

The book is also directed toward helping you *influence* the behavior of people in organizations. This is particularly important for managers, who, as leaders, must be able to influence the behavior of people toward the accomplishment of group goals. Much of the discussion will be directed toward improving your *skills* as a future manager. These four goals are pursued concurrently throughout this book:

1. Helping you to understand human behavior in organizations.
2. Helping you to predict human behavior in organizations.

3. Helping you to influence human behavior in organizations.
4. Helping you to develop your managerial skills.

This book relies heavily on developments in the behavior sciences—in particular the fields of organizational behavior, organization theory, and organization development. The concepts presented are founded in the theory and research findings from these fields. However, it is more than this. It is also based on developments in and understanding of applications in actual organizations. Only part of the knowledge about human behavior in organizations can come from theoretical concepts and academic research. A great deal of knowledge is developed through ongoing managerial practices and experiences. Throughout this book the theory/research orientation is integrated with the practice/application orientation of organizational behavior.

Organizations of all types have many similar characteristics and functions. They have goals, technologies, structures, human relationships, and managerial activities. The systems approach is used to help understand organizations and, more specifically, human behavior in them. However, we are becoming increasingly aware that each organization develops its own internal culture (ways of operating) and climate (ways that participants perceive things). Managers of organizations develop philosophies about how to perform their roles and how to deal with people—their styles of action. Management style is the distinctive manner in which a manager behaves as constrained by organizational culture and guided by personal philosophy. Organizational culture and managerial style have significant effects on two fundamental issues involved in every work organization. We need to develop organizations that are effective and efficient (productive) and that also provide a climate appropriate to the well-being of their human participants. Throughout this book we will "keep in mind" these two major issues of organizational productivity and quality of work life. They are not mutually exclusive, managers should always recognize their importance and interdependence. Recent studies of excellent organizations (in terms of long-run performance) suggest that one thing they have in common is a high regard for and continuing attention to their human resources.

We will not be content in this book to describe and discuss history or current issues and practices. Such material will be covered in order to provide perspective, but the emphasis will be on change and improvement. One of management's most difficult tasks is dealing with transitions. However, success in such endeavors can lead to high personal satisfaction.

Out of a great deal of material and a large number of topics concerning human behavior in organizations we have attempted to select issues that are most relevant to you for achieving the four goals cited above—understanding, predicting, influencing, and skill building. The book is organized in a logical way to help you in your learning. It looks at (1) individual, (2) interpersonal, intragroup, and intergroup, and (3) systemwide aspects of organizational behavior. Each chapter starts with a series of short incidents from real life that illustrate the issues to be covered. At the end of each chapter there is a section entitled *So*

What? Implications for You. These are key generalizations that are discussed from two perspectives: (1) as a member of an organization and (2) as a current or future manager. There is also a section at the end of each chapter entitled *Learning Application Activities* that provides learning activities that you can do individually, in small groups, and in the total class. They are directed toward applying the knowledge that you have gained from reading the chapters. You are asked to use the concepts gained from the text as a knowledge base for experiencing and reflecting on reality-oriented exercises, cases, and field observations. You can use them to develop your ability to apply ideas and to develop your managerial skills. Through this process you can become more actively involved in your learning process.

We want to thank our students and colleagues who have helped in the development of this book. Students provide the testing ground for determining the importance, interest, and understandability of concepts and ideas. They also participate in field testing the learning application activities. Academic colleagues, through their books and journal articles, provide most of the conceptual ideas and research findings. Finally, practicing managers are directly concerned with the application of theory stemming from organizational research. They provide the final testing ground for ideas coming from the behavioral sciences. Feedback from organizational experience is essential for validating and generalizing managerial guidelines. Nothing is as practical as a theory that works.

Wendell L. French
Fremont E. Kast
James E. Rosenzweig

PART ONE

INTRODUCTION

Part One is designed to set the stage for the entire book. It is a first step toward understanding the nature of organizations and their importance in our lives. It introduces conceptual tools for studying human behavior in organizations that will be used throughout the book.

Chapter 1 starts with a series of short vignettes illustrating various human issues in organizations. Some of them show successful ways of managing human resources; others illustrate ineffective management. The field of organizational behavior is defined and related to other behavioral sciences. Some of the most frequently encountered issues, problems, and dilemmas in organizational behavior are discussed.

The systems view is presented in Chapter 1 as a framework for understanding organizations and their functions. Organizations are composed of five key subsystems: (1) the goal- and value-related; (2) the technical; (3) the psychosocial; (4) the structural; and (5) the managerial. Within this framework, we will address two fundamental issues: the need to develop organizations that are effective and efficient (productive); and the need to develop a climate appropriate to the well-being of participants in those organizations. The chapter will conclude with an outline showing how subsequent sections relate to the systems model.

1

Overview of Human Behavior in Organizations

LEARNING OBJECTIVES

After reading this chapter you should be able to:

1. Have a better understanding of the nature of organizations and recognize their pervasiveness.
2. Define organizational behavior and give examples of "people problems" in organizations.
3. Understand how dealing effectively with human factors is an important managerial skill.
4. Identify several individual/organizational dilemmas, such as productivity and quality of work life.
5. Outline a framework for studying human behavior in organizations.

TROUBLE AT ATLANTIC LIGHT AND POWER

Steve Osborn, general manager of Atlantic Light and Power, was facing a very difficult, unpleasant problem. Rather shy and retiring, he was trained as an engineer and had risen through the ranks without formal management training. He preferred to focus his time and talents on the technical aspects of running the electric utility and let his immediate subordinates deal with the other problems. So far, this approach had proved successful. His department heads had substantial autonomy and he was not bothered with many of the personnel-related problems. He tried to be available for individual consultation, but he did not believe in the need for any kind of regularly scheduled group meetings to discuss problems.

However, a serious matter had arisen that demanded his attention. Without prior warning, he had been notified that the local electrical workers union was filing a grievance against one of his department heads, Glen Connelly. This was a critical matter. Except for top management, all of the utility's employees were union members. A major conflict with the union could be disastrous.

Looking over a copy of the grievance that had been given him by the company lawyer, he could scarcely believe his eyes. The Glen Connelly he knew had been with the company for only two years but in that time had done a superlative job with the rate studies and analytical work required of him. He had taken on many responsibilities and would often work at night using his home terminal, which was hooked up by telephone to the company's main computer. He was unmarried and devoted most of his energy to the company. Steve had always liked Glen. They shared similar backgrounds and had many common interests.

As he reviewed the union complaints against Glen, Steve felt as if he were reading about a stranger. "Moody," "arrogant," "quick-tempered," "irrational," "harrassing": these were some of the adjectives used to describe the man. Steve knew that Glen had had a conflict with the State Energy Office over some new federal regulations, but it was difficult to deal with environmentalists. Still, the list of incidents involving Glen was extensive: "Screamed at terminal operator . . . ridiculed employee in front of others . . . violation of union agreement by refusing employee necessary sick leave . . . threatened to fire employee for laughing . . . asking employee harrassing questions concerning personal life . . ." Steve had to admit that the allegations were clear and well documented, leaving little question in his mind as to their authenticity.

Steve leaned back in his chair to reflect. He was depending on Glen to prepare the utility's case for a hearing before the Public Utility Commission concerning a critically needed rate increase. However, he could hardly ignore the complaint, considering the power the union wielded over the utility. He wished he were fishing.

MANAGEMENT VS. LABOR

Last Year's Walkout of Air Traffic Controllers Was Spurred by More Than Just Economic Grievances

When some 11,000 air traffic controllers walked off their jobs in an illegal strike in the summer of 1981 and were subsequently fired and debarred from future federal jobs by President Reagan, national attention focused on a dramatic new instance of conflicts between management and labor. According to a recently completed ISR survey of the striking controllers and their nonstriking counterparts and supervisors, last year's strike actually grew out of pervasively harsh and indifferent organizational management.

The traditional economic motives such as better pay, better benefits, and shorter work weeks were not the prime movers in the controller walkout, according to ISR's David G. Bowers. Although that summer's strike was called by the Professional Air Traffic Controllers' Organization (PATCO), it was bred in and precipitated by the deteriorating conditions created by the Federal Aviation Administration's own organizational and management practices, Bowers says.

POOR MORALE

The findings showed that morale was very poor among air traffic control personnel at all levels of the organization, from the bottom to the top. FAA personnel in 15 of the 25 job classes sampled for the study gave overall ratings to their job environments that were significantly more negative than the national norms.

A very telling indicator of internal FAA problems, according to Bowers, was the finding that both the striking controllers and the current FAA employees (nonstriking controllers, technicians, team supervisors, and managers) produced comparatively similar—and mostly negative—assessments of their own jobs. This finding figured largely in the task force conclusion that wide-ranging changes in management style and philosophy are needed within the FAA.

AUTOCRATIC STYLE

Bowers also found evidence of extensive disagreement within the organization on the appropriateness of specific management styles and practices. FAA employees holding managerial positions gave relatively high approval to an autocratic, no-questions-asked style of management, while the generally younger technicians and controllers—strikers and nonstrikers alike—strongly rejected such a style.

"A less directive and bureaucratic style would have buffered the problem of the strike," Bowers says, "and a participative style would have solved it."

Inequitable treatment by supervisors and worker perceptions of management as rigid, autocratic, punitive, and uncaring led most of the individual strikers to their walkout decision. Bowers reported peer pressure apparently played little or no role in those decisions. The areas of greatest discontent among the striking controllers were indicated by their very low ratings of the FAA on the following: concern for individual workers' well-being, talent, and motivation; fair possibilities for rewards such as recognition, better pay, and promotion; practical, effective organization of workloads with clear-cut decision-making processes and goals; positive, encouraging attitudes among supervisors; and overall job satisfaction.

"Workers felt that ability had little to do with promotion," Bowers says, "and that individuals often were moved up because they became too old to handle the traffic on the boards or because they were favorites of the local managers."

Source: Institute for Social Research, *ISR Newsletter*, Autumn 1982 (Ann Arbor, Mich.: The University of Michigan), p. 3. Reprinted by permission.

ACUTE STRESS

In the course of the study, the task force found evidence of what Bowers terms a "peculiar and acute form of stress" among the air traffic controllers, brought on by such situations as traffic overloads or near misses of mid-air collisions. These stressful episodes, unlike more common sources of job stress, apparently have a cumulative effect over time, Bowers says. The longer a controller stays on the board, the greater becomes his or her buildup of stress.

"Burnout," which Bowers defines as a disabling level of stress in a worker, was evident in only about 5 percent of the controller population overall. But burnout affected fully two-thirds of the controllers with 15 to 20 years of experience.

Most of these problems at the FAA prevailed prior to the strike and probably still do, well into the months following the walkout, Bowers says. The persistence of problematic conditions and deteriorating personnel relations led the three-member task force to conclude that the FAA "seems headed toward more people-related problems in the future." The task force recommended a wide-ranging set of management reforms whose major focus was on improving employee/management interactions.

BILL'S BOATHOUSE

Bill's Boathouse was different from all the other restaurants for which Karen had worked. While in college she had partially supported herself by working as a waitress in a number of fast-food service outlets and restaurants. She started at Bill's right after receiving her degree in elementary education from the university. Teaching positions were not available and Karen took the job of waitress and hostess "just temporarily." That was six years ago. During this time, she had also worked at Bill's other two restaurants—one located in Hawaii and the other in Phoenix—but they were not quite the same as the Boathouse.

Bill's was located on the waterfront and had done exceptionally well. The volume for lunch was substantial, serving primarily the business community and assorted boaters. In the evening, the crowd was quite diverse: many families, younger people in their 20s and 30s, and some out-of-towners. Bill's had established an excellent reputation for quality food and beverages and was clearly the place to go.

It was hard to know just what made Bill's different. The owners/managers seemed to have a high degree of respect for all the employees. Most of the workers were similar to Karen—college graduates in fields where there were limited career opportunities. Some were currently in school, working on advanced degrees. The employees all took pride in providing excellent service. There was much less bickering than in other places where Karen had worked. In fact, there seemed to be a great deal of cooperation. If anyone was rushed or had other difficulties, the others pitched in to help.

The owners seemed to emphasize team spirit and group relationships. They held membership in various athletic clubs to which all employees had access. They sponsored various teams and individual events, such as 6-kilometer runs. The special Bill's Boathouse sweatshirts were very popular with employees and customers. The luncheon shift employees had brunch together at 10:00 A.M. each day and there was a good deal of outside socializing.

The general respect for employees showed itself in many ways. On more than one occasion the owners had supported the employees when customers were unreasonable or unruly. The customer was "always right," but only to a point. Employees were not expected to grovel and sacrifice their self-respect. At the same time, employees who were guilty of dishonesty or didn't pull their weight were soon terminated. Bill's seemed to have high expectations for all employees and gave support in return.

Karen made good money from gratuities. But this didn't seem to be as big an issue here as at other restaurants. In the course of their work, waitresses and bartenders become quite skilled at sizing up customers based on the potential tip. In some restaurants, Karen knew certain types would be labeled as deadbeats and given inferior service. At Bill's all customers were treated well. Karen prided herself on providing prompt and courteous attention to customers, even when she knew the potential for a large tip was low.

Bill's had achieved the reputation as the best place in town to work. Whenever there was an opening, several hundred people applied. Current employees often had friends who wanted to work at Bill's. Karen and the others were very careful to recommend only people who they knew were qualified and who would get along well at Bill's. What made Bill's different? Karen wasn't certain, but she did know that it was an excellent place to work and that it also seemed to be very profitable for the owners.

A GIFT FOR DELTA

Some Happy Employees at Delta Want to Buy a Big Gift for the Boss

BY MARGARET LOEB

Staff Reporter of *The Wall Street Journal*

ATLANTA—In its third fiscal quarter, ended March 31, Delta Air Lines ran up an $18.4 million loss, its biggest ever. But that didn't keep the airline from giving its employees an unexpectedly generous pay raise of some 8.5% in September.

Ginny Whitfield, a flight attendant, and others were impressed. "A bunch of us were sitting around one day saying how wonderful this company was," she says. "So someone said, 'Let's buy them an airplane.' "

A $30 million Boeing 767 airplane, no less.

"WE'LL ACCEPT IT"

With two other flight attendants, Ginny Whitfield organized a campaign to raise the purchase price from Delta's 36,000 employees, who are nonunion. With this week's paychecks, the employees will be asked to sign a pledge card voluntarily committing 2.5% of one year's pay to the airplane purchase. Delta has 20 Boeing 767s on order. The employees' gifts would pay for the first one to go into service.

Delta officials emphasize that the idea is entirely the employees', not Delta's, but "if they buy the jet, I guarantee you we'll accept it," a spokesman for the airline says. At Delta headquarters, he says, "Everybody is just a wee bit overwhelmed."

It remains to be seen whether employees will pledge enough money. The campaign organizers expect 80% of the employees to go along, and that should be enough to provide the needed $30 million. In any case, Delta will get whatever money does get pledged.

SOME RESERVATIONS

Some employees already have responded favorably to the idea of buying Delta an airplane.

Source: *Wall Street Journal,* 28 September 1982, p. 29.

"I think this is fantastic," says Ken Mabry, a Delta mechanic. "I've never been so excited in my life about giving back a portion of my salary." He figures his pledge toward the airplane purchase will cost him about $875 of his $34,000 yearly earnings.

But a reservations clerk in Miami says, "I think it would be a real drain on the employees to have to pay out that money. I think it's a nice gesture, but I don't have that much money. The company can get a loan. The company already has budgeted for it."

QC CIRCLES AT TOYOTA

QC circles are small groups of plant workers who voluntarily organize regular meetings to study ideas and methods of quality control and conduct joint technical studies. The QC circles aim, quite simply, to solve problems in the work process and to help workers derive greater satisfaction from their jobs. Satisfaction comes in various forms: from accomplishing a task, from having a contribution recognized, from improving skills, and from achieving personal growth.

Workers are encouraged to strive towards these satisfactions both as individuals and as members of a team, working to create a cheerful, rewarding work environment. Toyota's interest in QC circles doesn't come from a desire for short-term profits; in fact, in-company evaluations of QC activities rarely include discussions of how improvements may have increased profits. The company's QC evaluations tend to emphasize worker enthusiasm, project success, and how well everyone is participating.

The QC circles consist of a group of workers headed by a leader. They may work on two, three, or more projects at the same time. In such cases "mini" QC circles are formed, and sometimes "joint" circles of members from two or more circles, to work together on the same project.

QC circles do not limit themselves to product-quality concerns. Themes emphasized in recent years include product quality, cost, maintenance, safety, air and water pollution, and alternative resources.

Source: "Quality Control at Toyota Motor Corporation," *The Wheel Extended: Toyota Quarterly Review,* Special Supplement no. 11 [July-September 1982], p. 11. Reprinted by permission.

INTRODUCTION

These incidents appear to have little in common. They are about different organizations: an electric utility, airport control towers, a restaurant, an airline, and an automobile manufacturer. The people have quite different professions and tasks. Yet, there is a common thread running through the vignettes. They all deal with people working in organizations and how they act under different circumstances. They illustrate the importance of human factors in small groups and in large organizations.

The vignettes suggest varying degrees of success in dealing with the human aspects of organizations. In *Atlantic Light and Power,* Steve Osborn was facing a difficult problem with his department head, Glen Connelly, who appeared to have a high level of technical competence but was sorely lacking in managerial skills. The *Management vs. Labor* vignette illustrates a situation in which there was a high level of conflict between the air traffic controllers and their management. In contrast, most employees at Delta Air Lines have developed strong loyalty to their company and many were willing to give back some of their earnings to help the company prosper. *Bill's Boathouse* also presents a climate that maximized both employee motivation and satisfaction and organizational performance. *QC Circles at Toyota* illustrates how one company has systematically used small groups to accomplish the company's purposes and to increase motivation and satisfaction.

Dealing effectively with human resources is certainly one of management's most important and difficult functions. Many managers, particularly those with several years of experience, tell us that their most difficult problems are human-relations issues. Understanding human behavior in organizations and developing managerial skills for dealing more effectively with people are the primary goals of this book.

Why should you be concerned with understanding human behavior in organizations? With so much to be learned about the economic and technical aspects of business—accounting, finance, marketing, and production—why devote valuable time to studying a subject as "soft" as organizational behavior? The answer is that understanding human behavior and managing human resources effectively are of vital importance to organizations. There is substantial evidence that "people problems" are being considered a serious practical concern in managerial circles. Box 1.1 is a selection of article titles taken from prominent publications read by practicing managers. They reflect a wide variety of issues, all of them relating to the human aspects of organizations. Readership surveys indicate that managers want to understand behavior in their organizations and to develop their own skills for dealing with people.

In this chapter we will provide an overview of the book via the following topics:

Pervasiveness of Organizations
The Field of Organizational Behavior
The Nature of Organizations

PERVASIVENESS OF ORGANIZATIONS

Organizations are an important part of our lives. Think of the number of organizations that directly affect you. College, athletic or social groups, and family are examples. But what about the hosts of others: the stores where you shop, the government agencies in your community, the doctor's or dentist's office, your auto insurance agency, the local public utilities? These organizations affect you, both in terms of services received and your own pocketbook. Looking to the future, you will in all likelihood be employed in one or more organizations where you will spend a large portion of your time for many years to come. Your work organizations will have a profound effect on your career and life satisfactions.

In modern society, both the number and complexity of organizations have

BOX 1.1
WHAT DO MANAGERS READ?

"Improving Productivity and Job Satisfaction"
"Quality of Life: The Role of Business"
"Human Values and Leadership"
"Matching the Individual and the Organization"
"Human Resource Planning: Managerial Concerns and Practices"
"How to Improve the Performance and Productivity of Knowledge Workers"
"Leadership: A Beleaguered Species?"
"Sex Stereotyping in the Executive Suite"
"The High Cost of Discrimination"
"Doing Away With the Factory Blues"
"Young Workers: Are They Getting Worse?"
"Dealing With the Aging Work Force"
"Gray Power: Next Challenge to Business"
"Worker Participation: Contrast in Three Countries"
"Dual Careers—How Do Couples and Companies Cope with the Problems?"
"The Design of Work in the 1980s"
"Power is the Great Motivator"
"Participative Management At Work"
"Can Behavioral Science Help Design Organizations?"

increased significantly. During the nineteenth century, most people had contact with only small organizational units, such as the family and those operating in the immediate community. During the twentieth century, there has been a phenomenal growth in the number, size, diversity, and complexity of organizations: from large-scale businesses, unions, hospitals, schools, governmental agencies, to multinational corporations. The growth of these organizations and their pervasive effect on our lives make it imperative that we develop a better understanding of the kinds of complex social systems they represent.

This book is about human behavior in organizations. Because you will belong to many organizations, the book speaks to a substantial area of your life. Understanding the dynamics of organizational life; identifying the key variables that enhance effective performance in organizations; and simply becoming adept at getting along with others: all will be important for your future success. A mastery of knowledge and skills can be of great practical value as you attempt to achieve your personal goals and gain lasting satisfaction from organizational memberships.

People Problems in Organizations

The ability, effort, and performance of people are important variables in determining whether any organization achieves its goals. Although technical, financial, and other resources are important, it is the human resource that makes the system function. At the same time, there are many problems associated with these human resources. How can we select, train, motivate, organize, lead, and compensate people to ensure effective and efficient performance in meeting organizational goals while at the same time encouraging and helping them to achieve personal satisfactions? This is management's most difficult challenge.

Organizations are social systems composed of people working together to accomplish goals. Because the human element is such a vital ingredient, managers will always be faced with people problems. It is inevitable that when people work together, many personal, interpersonal, group, and organizational issues arise. There is of course no way to prevent or cure all of these people-related problems. Indeed, attempts to eliminate all such conflict would lead to a sterile organization. Human problems exist in every social system and effective managers learn that they are a natural, ongoing part of organizational life. In fact, one of the reasons for being a manager is to deal with such issues.

Organizations are investing a great deal of money to help managers cope with people problems. Over the past several decades there has been a significant increase in the popularity of management seminars and training programs directed at understanding behavior in organizations. In terms of number and size, such management development programs seem to be more prevalent than seminars dealing with economic and technical problems. Box 1.2 indicates the wide variety of seminar topics. These are not programs directed at college students; they are specifically developed for practicing managers and are in response to a *real need* to understand more about human behavior. Business and other organizations are well aware that the human side of their enterprises requires continuing attention

BOX 1.2
SAMPLE TITLES OF MANAGEMENT DEVELOPMENT SEMINARS AND WORKSHOPS

Women Managers and Their Human Resource Responsibilities
Motivation and Effective Performance
Organization Development: A Team Approach to Improving Organizations
Stress: Its Implications for Individuals and Organizations
Leadership and Management Training
Team Building
Intergroup Relations
Human Resources/Career Management Workshop
Organizational Feedback and Leadership Style
Situational Leadership
Developing Supervisory Leadership Skills
Assertiveness Training for Managers
Interpersonal Skills Lab

and study. Human-resource development within organizations includes many vexing issues, but it also provides challenging opportunities which, if met, can lead to a great sense of satisfaction for managers and employees alike.

Understanding Human Behavior in Organizations—Two Perspectives

Throughout this book, two perspectives are elaborated: that of a member and that of a manager in the organization. The book is designed to provide useable guidelines for increasing your effectiveness in both contexts. Its purpose is to increase your knowledge and understanding of how organizations operate. As an organization member, it is important to develop insights into characteristics and key processes that affect you. As a manager, gaining a broad knowledge is an even more vital issue. It is incumbent on you as a manager to develop substantial understanding of human behavior within an organizational context *and* to develop skills for dealing with behavioral issues.

In order to emphasize this dual-perspective, we provide a section at the end of each chapter that summarizes the generalizations concerning the topics covered and the implications for personal action from the viewpoint of: (1) a member of an organization and; (2) a current or future manager.

THE FIELD OF ORGANIZATIONAL BEHAVIOR

This book is concerned with the study of the behavior of individuals and groups in the context of organizations. We advocate the use of the term *human behavior in organizations* to describe this area of study. However, you will frequently find,

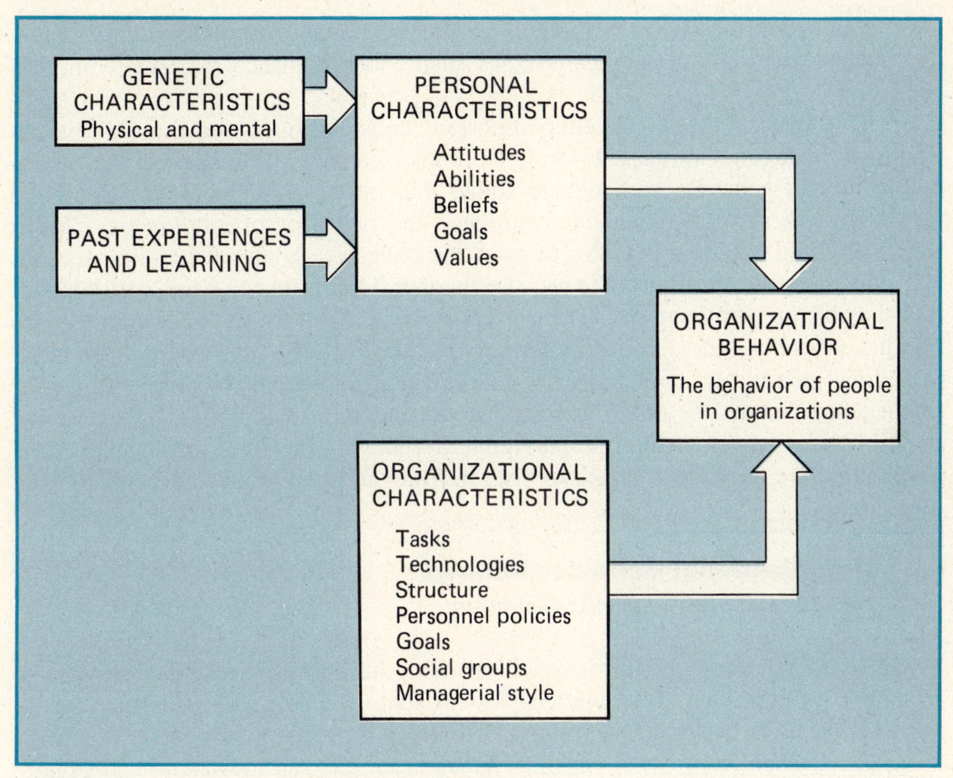

FIGURE 1.1 A Model of Organizational Behavior

here and in the literature, the term *organizational behavior* or *OB* used to represent this field.

The equation

$$\text{Behavior} = f(P, E)$$

where *P* is personal characteristics and *E* is environment provides a fundamental basis for understanding organizational behavior. Human behavior is a function of the personal characteristics of the individual *and* the environmental context. Test this concept against your own personal experiences. Have you ever found yourself in a new and strange situation in which you were quiet and passive? Yet that same evening, when you were with a group of close friends, you were the life of the party. Same person but different situation; consequently, your behavior was quite different.

Figure 1.1 provides an elaboration of this concept specifically related to organizational behavior. Your personal characteristics are based on inherited genetic factors plus all of the past learning experiences that have shaped your personality. You bring these personal characteristics into the organizational situation, which, in turn, affects the way you think and act. Contextual factors such as the nature of the task, the technology present, organizational structure, management style, and personnel policies also have a direct influence on your behavior.

This figure suggests another important consideration, one that will be developed throughout this book. One of the key managerial functions is to understand human behavior and to help shape that behavior to meet organizational goals. In other words, managers *influence* the behavior of employees. This is inevitable and essential in order to meet the collective goals of the organization. In influencing or altering behavior, the manager can affect the personal characteristics of the employees by trying to improve abilities (training) or by trying to modify attitudes (persuading). Alternatively, the manager can change the organizational context by modifying the task, structure, system of compensation, or management style. In other words, change and improvement in behavior can result from either changing the individual or changing the situation. Usually, it is most effective to make changes in both in order to elicit improved behavior and performance.

Organizational Behavior Defined

We are ready for a specific definition:

> Organizational behavior is a field of study based on research, observations, and theory. It is concerned with analyzing and understanding the attitudes, feelings, perceptions, motives, and behavior of people in an organizational context. Its primary goals are improved individual and organizational performance and increased participant satisfaction.

The field of organizational behavior emphasizes both research and practice. It attempts a scientific study of the behavior of individuals and groups in the context of organization. It also addresses the practical tasks of helping people to achieve greater satisfaction in their organizational lives and aiding those in management to become more effective in dealing with human resources.

It is the *organizational context* that gives the field a unique thrust, differentiating it from other related disciplines. People behave in many different contexts—home, school, church, workplace, athletic team. The situation can be solitary (alone) or social (with one, several, or many others). The purposes for being in an organizational context can also vary from earning a living to campaigning for a favored political candidate to playing poker. In the study of organizational behavior, we examine that large segment of our life activities occurring in organizational settings.

Relationship to Other Behavioral Sciences

OB is a behavioral science. It combines parts of the disciplines of psychology, sociology, and anthropology. Behavioral science in general emphasizes the development of theoretical concepts, empirical research, and applications concerning human behavior in all contexts. It is also concerned with predictions about human behavior. OB, then, with its specific aim of understanding behavior in organizational contexts, represents one of the *applied* behavioral sciences and is a primary foundation for the practice of management.

Psychology is the scientific study of behavior (animal and human) in all its contexts. As the field has grown, it has divided into many areas of specialization. *Social psychology* is the subfield that seeks to understand individual human behavior in a social context. It is the study of the *individual-in-society*: how individual behavior is shaped, influenced, and determined by the presence of other people. Many of the concepts from social psychology are applicable to organizational behavior.

Sociology is the scientific study of human behavior in groups; it is the study of social relations and interactions and the study of products of these relations, such as social norms, roles, and institutions. The field of sociology has also become specialized and two subfields deal with many of the same phenomena as organizational behavior. *Industrial sociology* deals with the patterns and structures arising out of work groups and the *sociology of complex organizations* deals with the dynamics and structures of organizations *per se*. Many of the concepts from these fields are appropriate to the study of organizational behavior.

Anthropology is the scientific study of the human race and of evolving civilizations. *Social anthropology* is a subdiscipline that focuses on culture as reflected in customs, values, habits, attitudes, and institutions. Organizational issues such as systems of authority are studied in the context of families, tribes, or larger groupings. The theories and concepts emanating from anthropological research provide a foundation for understanding human nature and behavior in organizational contexts.

The field of organizational behavior does not stand alone. It is an applied behavioral science that draws concepts and research findings from many fields. However, as an applied field, organizational behavior is vitally concerned with the utilization and application of knowledge in practical organizational situations. The acid test of the field is how well the concepts can be applied over time in living organizational situations to improve both performance and participant satisfaction.

Issues, Problems, and Dilemmas in OB

OB faces questions of varying complexity and generality. Many are framed explicitly in the chapter topics and subtopics of this book. However, we will introduce a sample of such questions here so as to give an overall sense of the task facing the student of contemporary organizations.

Why do people work?
What motivates people and what discourages them?
What kinds of interactions enhance the quality of work performance and the sense of individual satisfaction?
How much decision-making participation for subordinates makes sense in terms of solution quality and participant acceptance?

What is the effect of leadership style on performance?
How do beliefs, values, attitudes, biases, and stereotyping tendencies affect human behavior in organizations?
What are the dynamics of status- and role-systems in organizations?
What are the consequences of group behavior on individual motivation and satisfaction? On organizational performance?
How should cooperation and competition be balanced in organizations?
What are some of the causes of communication breakdowns between people, subunits, and levels in organizations?
Can, and should, work teams learn how to diagnose and modify their group cultures?
Are there effective ways to manage conflict in organizations?
What is the effect of personnel policies and practices on motivation?
What are the consequences of perceived inequity, injustice, or unfairness in an organization?
Do different tasks and technologies call for different leadership styles?
What is the effect of organizational "climate" on motivation and productivity?
How can organizations become more efficient in terms of ability to compete in world markets and still become more humane?
How can we view organizational phenomena so that we orient ourselves toward solving rather than culprit hunting?
How can we do a better job of diagnosing and managing our own interpersonal and group relationships?

THE NATURE OF ORGANIZATIONS

Organizations are contrived social systems; they are created, maintained, and frequently disbanded by people. They often have a life of their own, beyond that of any individual member; Hughes Tool Company continues without Howard Hughes, Getty Oil Company without J. Paul Getty, and the Federal Bureau of Investigation without J. Edgar Hoover. The vast array of existing organizations might suggest a state of affairs where few characteristics are shared. Yet, we can find certain common threads running through all organizations.

Open Systems in Interaction with Environment

Organizations are open systems in interaction with their environment. A system is an organized unitary whole composed of two or more interdependent parts, components, or subsystems and delineated by identifiable boundaries. Organizations, as open systems, receive inputs, transform these inputs in certain ways, and return outputs to their environments. The business organization receives inputs of materials, money, and human resources, performs transformational functions on them that add some measure of utility, and returns the product or service to the market place.

Systems theory provides a conceptual scheme that helps us understand organizations and, more specifically, the patterned human behavior that constitutes organizational life. Using systems concepts we can define an organization as:

1. A *subsystem of its broader environment* that is
2. *Goal-oriented* (people with a purpose) and that includes
3. A *technical subsystem* (people using knowledge, techniques, equipment, and facilities),
4. A *structural subsystem* (people working together on integrated activities),
5. A *psychosocial subsystem* (people in social relationships), all coordinated by
6. A *managerial subsystem* (people planning and controlling the overall endeavor).

Although the definition is elaborate, it provides a concept of organization that fits all types. The social group planning a party at the club possesses these characteristics, as does the doctor's office and the gasoline service station. General Electric and the United Nations, while obviously much more complex, possess these characteristics to no less a degree.

The Systems View of Organizations

Any organization can be viewed as an open, sociotechnical system composed of a number of subsystems, as illustrated in Figure 1.2. An organization is not exclusively technical or exclusively social. Rather, it is an ongoing structuring and integrating of human activities around various technologies: people using technologies to accomplish organizational goals.

The internal organization can be viewed as composed of several major subsystems. The organizational *goals and values* are important in determining the nature of activities and the general climate. The organization as a subsystem of society must accomplish certain goals that are endorsed by the broader society. The organization performs functions for society and, if it is to be successful, it must conform to social requirements.

The *technical* subsystem refers to the knowledge required for the performance of tasks. By organizational technology we mean the techniques, equipment, processes, and facilities used in the transformation of inputs into outputs. The technical subsystem is determined by the goals of the organization and varies according to the task requirements. For example, the technology for producing home computers differs significantly from that used in an oil refinery or hospital. The technology frequently prescribes the type of organizational structure and the psychosocial system attending it.

Every organization has a *psychosocial* subsystem, which consists of the human resources—individuals and groups in interaction. It consists of individual

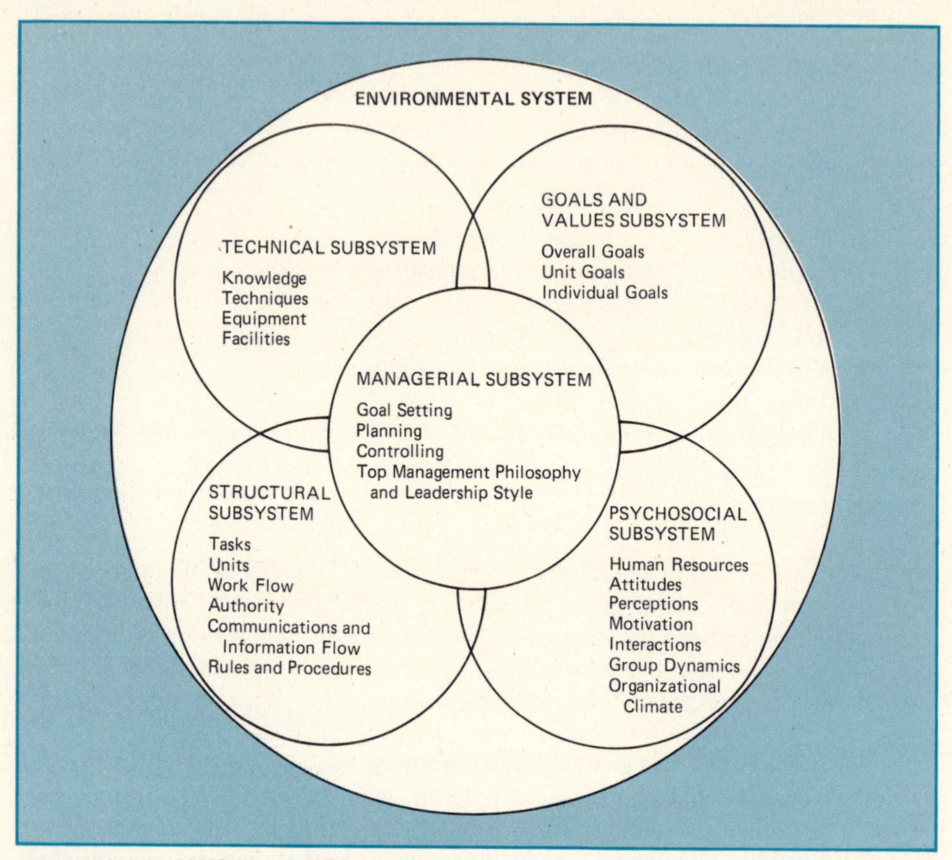

FIGURE 1.2 Key Organizational Subsystems

behavior and motivation, norms, systems of influence, and group dynamics. It is also affected by the sentiments and feelings, values, attitudes, expectations, and aspirations of the people in the organization. This subsystem is, of course, affected by external environmental forces as well as by the technology, tasks, and structures of the internal organization.

The organization's *structure* provides for formalization of relationships between the technical and the psychosocial subsystems. It involves the ways in which the tasks of the organization are divided (differentiation) and coordinated (integration). In the formal sense, structure is set forth by hierarchical charts of the organization, by position and job descriptions, and by rules and procedures. It is reflected in patterns of authority, communication, and work flow.

The *managerial* subsystem spans the entire organization by relating the organization to its environment, setting the goals, developing strategic and operational plans, designing the structure, and establishing control processes. It is the vital force in linking the other subsystems together.

The systems view provides a basic model for describing and understanding

all types of organizations. It will be used as a frame of reference throughout this book.

Other Characteristics

There are some additional characteristics of organizations that are particularly relevant in the study of organizational behavior:

- Inherent in organizations is a division of labor (different people doing different things) and a hierarchy of authority (some people directing the activities of others).
- Although individuals form organizations, an organization is a collectivity. We cannot understand organizational behavior by focusing exclusively on the individual.
- Organizations possess some characteristics and relationships not found in other human collectivities. For example, families and social gatherings may not have formal superior subordinate relationships, elaborate division of labor, or an explicitly established structure.
- Two essential organizational functions are communication and coordination. Because different parts of the organization perform separate tasks, some means must be found for putting the parts back together, for integrating the diverse activities. This integration is termed coordination; it occurs through communication.
- Many organizational phenomena are spontaneous, unplanned, and often unpredictable. These *intervening* or *mediating* phenomena emerge because of the interactions of people and groups with the structure and processes of the organization. They may be predictable to some extent, but they are not a result of some direct cause-and-effect operation like giving an order and getting a compliance. Rather, they are phenomena that occur *between* an order and its planned outcome. Resentment, excuse-making, and sabotage fall into this category.
- Individual members have different perceptions of the reality of the organization. Each member has limited organizational views or horizons based on such things as experience, position, task, level, and place in the communication network. The real organization exists in the collective minds of all participants.

Our six-point definition of organizations and the supplementary characteristics listed above suggest the boundaries of a special field of study. We are not concerned with behavior in general, nor even human behavior in general. We are concerned with human behavior in organizational contexts, and primarily behavior in the context of the work organization.

KNOWLEDGE AND PRACTICE

Although it is helpful for every member to have some understanding of organizational behavior, it is the manager who has the most direct opportunity to use this knowledge. Research has shown that managers spend most of their time on direct, interpersonal, verbal communication; that is, in direct interaction with subordinates and others. The ability to describe, diagnose, predict, and prescribe behavior in organizations is essential for managerial success.

Because of wide individual differences and variations in organizations, it is impossible to derive ironclad laws, absolute principles of organizational behavior. What holds true for some individuals in specific circumstances may not hold true for others. In a sense, every situation is unique. However, there do appear to be patterns of relationships among the variables that are important to understand.

Contingency Views

Throughout this book we will stress applications in specific situations. Contingency or situational views focus on the interrelationships among key variables and subsystems in organizations. They suggest, for example, that different leadership styles are appropriate in different situations. This approach emphasizes the role of the manager as diagnostician, pragmatist, and artist.

An underlying assumption of the contingency view is that there should be a congruence between the organization and its environment and among the various subsystems, including the human resources. A primary managerial function is to maximize this congruence. The contingency view suggests that there are appropriate managerial approaches for different types of organizations, and that their application will lead to greater effectiveness, efficiency, and participant satisfaction. Contingency concepts are particularly useful when thinking about human behavior in organizations. People vary and react differently to particular situations. For example, some people are motivated primarily by monetary rewards, whereas for others achievement and recognition are more important. For some people, a directive leadership style works best, while others respond better with a nondirective leader. The need for contingency thinking becomes even more pronounced when we consider that a given individual might respond quite differently in two different situations.

The field of organizational behavior should be viewed in terms of contingencies rather than absolutes. There are no universal principles that work for all individuals and all organizations. However, contingency views can suggest the managerial actions most appropriate for specific situations. Effective management of people requires a good understanding of general concepts of human behavior, the ability to diagnose individuals and situations, and the skill to act in a flexible, effective manner. Systems and contingency concepts do not guarantee managerial success. They do facilitate more thorough understanding of complex situations and increase the likelihood of appropriate managerial actions.

PRODUCTIVITY AND THE QUALITY OF WORK LIFE

Two fundamental issues are involved in the study of human behavior in work organizations: the need to develop organizations that are effective and efficient (productive) and the need to provide a climate appropriate to the well-being of the human participants. Our organizations have to be productive if they are to meet the needs of society. There has been a gradual decline in the rate of growth of productivity in the United States over the past decade. This has had adverse consequences in terms of inflation, low growth of real income, and deteriorating competitive positions in relation to other countries. Effective and efficient organizations are essential to our society and to each of us individually. Without efficient businesses, schools, hospitals, and other such organizations we would revert to the kind of subsistence living that has characterized vast populations through much of the world's history.

Even though there have been major economic and social advances, many problems remain in the quality of work life. There is evidence that many people feel a growing dissatisfaction with their work experiences (see Box 1.3). This is not necessarily because the situation has become worse; rather, it is because human aspirations for a better existence—and, in particular, a more rewarding work life—have moved further into the realm of the expected. Throughout this book we will focus on the twin issues of organizational productivity and quality of work life. They are by no means mutually exclusive, and managers must learn to recognize the important bearing each has on the other.

BOX 1.3
QUALITY OF WORK LIFE IN ORGANIZATIONS

Many observers are concerned these days about the quality of work life in organizations, about organizational productivity, and about possible changes in the work ethic of people in contemporary Western society. Indeed, there has been a clamor in the popular press of late that we are in the midst of a major "work ethic crisis" that has its roots in work that is designed more for robots than for mature, adult human beings. . . .

People today want jobs that allow them to use their education, that provide "intrinsic" work satisfactions, and that meet their expectations that work should be personally meaningful. No longer will people accept routine and monotonous work as their legitimate lot in life.

According to this line of thinking, we have arrived at a point where the way most organizations function is in direct conflict with the talents and aspirations of the people who work in them. Such conflict manifests itself in increased personal alienation from work and in decreased organizational effectiveness.

Source: J. Richard Hackman, "The Design of Work in the 1980s," *Organizational Dynamics,* Summer 1978, pp. 3–4. Adapted by permission of the publisher. © 1978 by AMACOM, a division of American Management Associations, New York.

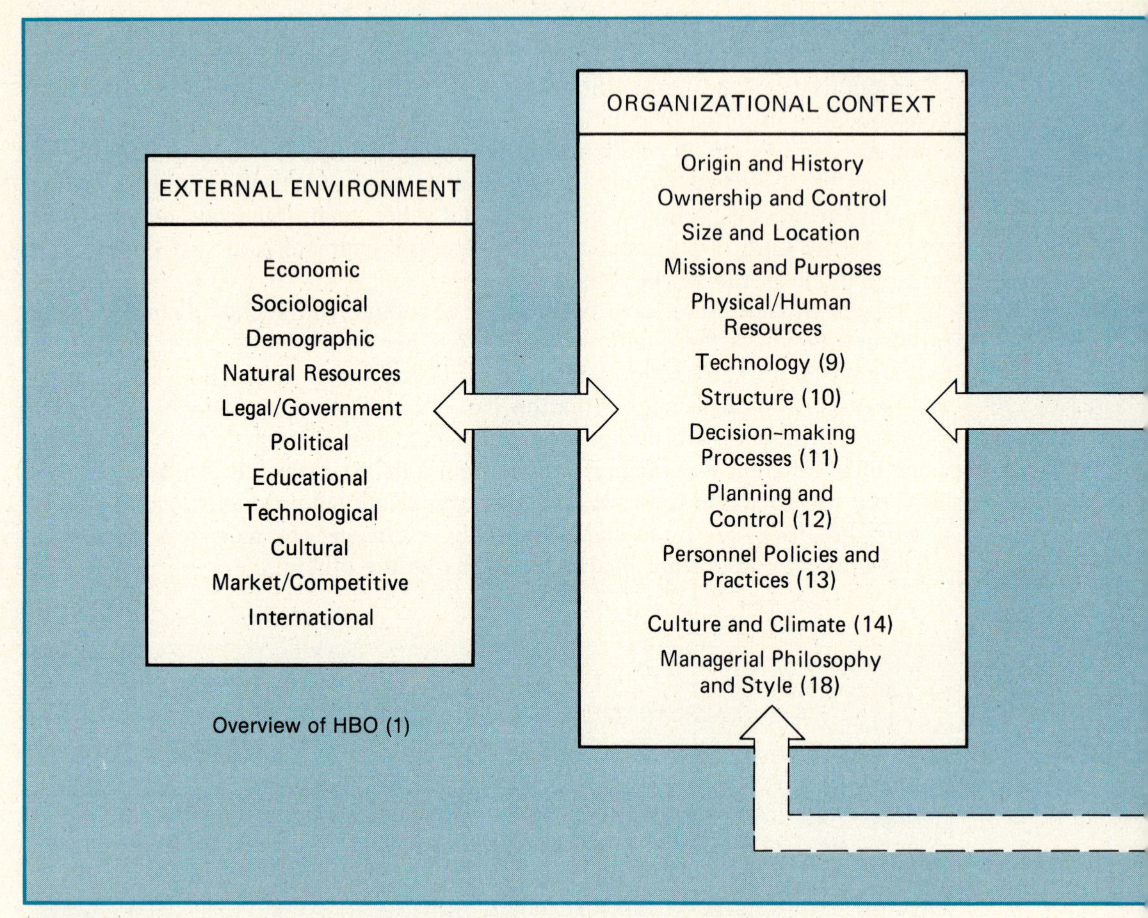

FIGURE 1.3 A Framework for Studying Human Behavior in Organizations

Our Beliefs, Attitudes, and Values

Although we will try to be objective, our beliefs, attitudes, and values will inevitably influence what we say in this book, and we wish to be explicit about some of them at the outset. We believe, for example, that the ultimate purpose of organized effort should be to improve the quality of human life. Any degrading or dehumanizing practices in the service of efficiency constitutes a misplaced emphasis on means over ends. We place a high value on human growth and satisfactions in the organizational context.

But this is not to deny the importance of organizational effectiveness and efficiency. What, for example, would our medical care be like without laboratories, pharmaceutical suppliers, schools, clinics, and hospitals? Where would food come from if it were not for the organization and technology represented by the modern farm, the food-processing plant, the shipping and distribution centers?

Even though some of us may occasionally long for the simple life in which

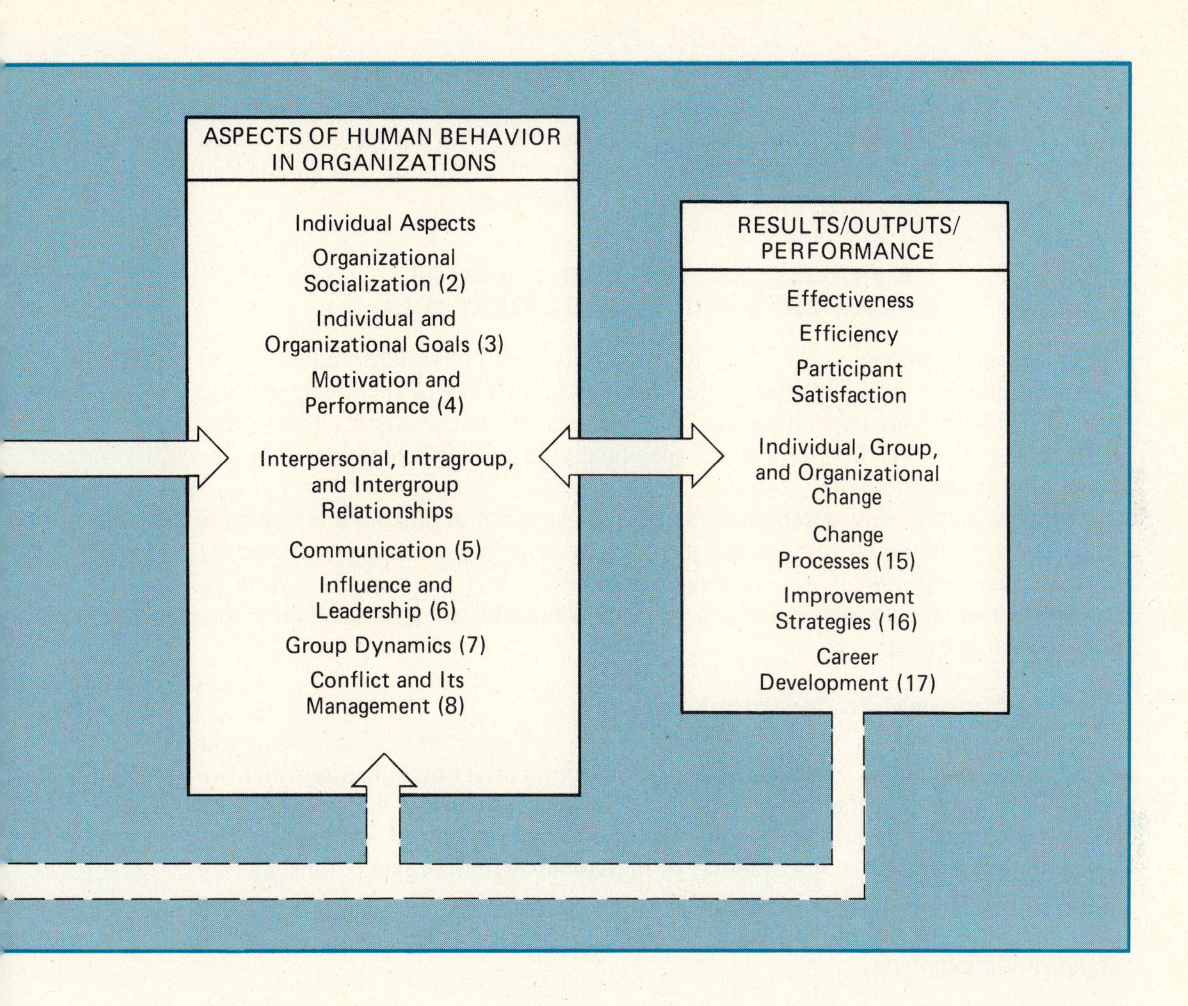

we grow our own food and build our own lodging, we would be quick to rely on the manufacturers of axes, needles, cloth, and salt—and on our neighbors. And these elementary wants would soon give way to desires for chain saws (and from there to sawmill lumber), sewing machines, store-bought clothes, and packaged foods. And radios, and symphonies, and art, and automobiles, and jet aircraft, and street lights, and television. Modern men and women need organizations, and we want them to be effective and efficient. We want lumber to be cut in regular dimensions, automobiles to work and to be safe, airplanes and ski lifts to carry us without crashing, steaks to be cooked to specification, stockings that don't run, and physicians' prescriptions to cure. These things do not come about by magic. They require people working together effectively.

Thus, it is axiomatic for us that organizations should pay attention to human values while at the same time committing themselves to productivity and innovation. As we shall show, a great deal of research suggests that these matters are not mutually exclusive, and that optimal organizational effectiveness requires deliberate and careful attention to both the people of the organization and the tasks to be performed. So we want organizations to be both people-centered and production-centered. We do not subscribe to the cynical attitude that claims that one must always be pursued at the expense of the other.

A FRAMEWORK FOR THE STUDY OF HUMAN BEHAVIOR IN ORGANIZATIONS

Organizational behavior is the study of the activities of individuals and groups in organizational settings. In order to develop our knowledge of this field, we first need to identify the most important organizational characteristics that affect participants. We can then look more specifically at human behavior within this contextual framework.

Figure 1.3 presents a general model for the study of organizational behavior and serves as the major framework for this book. The major components are: (1) the external environment; (2) the organizational context; (3) aspects of human behavior in organizations; and (4) the results, outputs, and performance of organizational activities.

The External Environment

Organizations do not exist in isolation; they are open systems in interaction with their environment. Many environmental factors affect organizations and the behavior of people in them. For example, the general level of education in the outside population determines the types of skills available and also affects the personalities, aspirations, and abilities of individuals within organizations. In this book we will not attempt to consider these environmental forces in isolation, but they will enter into the discussions as they relate to the specific behavior of organization members.

Organizational Context

The context is comprised of the basic characteristics that set the stage for organizational activities and the processes by which people and groups interact. An organization's origin and history, as well as its ownership and control, have an important influence on many activities. Size, location, technology, structure, and mission also give each organization its uniqueness. Other important determinants of, and constraints on, human behavior in an organization are its modes of decision making, planning, and control and its overall personnel policy and practice. We will consider these variables in terms of their effect on the internal organizational context within which human behavior occurs.

Aspects of Human Behavior in Organizations

People do not come into organizations as blank slates, unblemished wax to be molded to organizational requirements. Each of us has a personality shaped by our heredity and past experiences. We have attitudes, perceptions, and ways

of behaving. We are motivated to satisfy certain needs and have skills and aspirations. Nor do we ever become totally immersed within the organization; a substantial part of our lives remains outside if we are to remain emotionally healthy. In a sense we are all part-time members of any organization and retain a separate identity. Obviously, people are the essence of any social organization and we need to recognize variable individual behaviors as key factors.

But an organization is a social system and not just a collectivity of individuals. These interpersonal and social relationships are the focal points for the study of human behavior in organizations. We will consider *individual factors* in conjunction with *interpersonal, group,* and *intergroup* relationships and broader, *system-wide* characteristics. Separate chapters will be devoted to consideration of key topics within these major areas: organizational socialization, the interplay of individual and organizational goals, motivation, communication, leadership, group dynamics, and cooperation and conflict.

Results/Outputs/Performance

Organizations do not exist without purposive activities. They must *do something* that results in various types of outputs. They might turn out motorcycles, chewing gum, well patients, educated students, or any number of other goods and services. They may perform these activities effectively, efficiently, and with a high degree of participant satisfaction. In effect, these outputs are the *results* of organized activity. No study of organizational behavior is complete without looking at the issues of performance and output.

But, we are not concerned with short-term output only. We are also interested in *development* processes; that is, building a better organization that allows individuals, groups, and the total organization to maximize their potentials and to improve performance over the long run.

PLAN OF THE BOOK

The book is composed of the following five parts:

Part One: "Introduction" is an overview of organizational behavior.
Part Two: "The Individual and the Organization" begins by looking at the socialization process as it relates to organizations

(Chapter 2), followed by a discussion of the integration of individual and organizational goals (Chapter 3). It concludes with a discussion of motivation and performance (Chapter 4).

Part Three: ''Interpersonal, Intragroup, and Intergroup Relationships'' concentrates on several fundamental aspects of human behavior in organizations; communications (Chapter 5); influence and leadership (Chapter 6); group dynamics (Chapter 7); conflict and its management (Chapter 8).

Part Four: ''Effect of Organizational Factors on Human Behavior'' focuses on system-wide aspects of organizational behavior. It gives separate treatments of the most important organizational variables affecting human behavior: technology (Chapter 9); structure (Chapter 10); decision-making processes (Chapter 11); planning and control systems (Chapter 12); personnel policies and practices (Chapter 13); and culture and climate (Chapter 14).

Part Five: ''Individual, Group, and Organizational Change'' is concerned with the practical application of the concepts developed throughout the book to individual and organizational change and improvement. It starts with change processes (Chapter 15), followed by improvement strategies (Chapter 16). It then looks at issues of individual career development (Chapter 17) and concludes with a discussion of the effect of managerial philosophy and style (Chapter 18).

Vignettes

You will note that each chapter starts by presenting a series of cases, short vignettes, or incidents that serve as real-life illustrations of issues to be covered. Many of these vignettes are taken from experiences reported by our university students and by participants in various management development programs. Others are taken from newspapers and other current publications; some are from our personal experiences. They all represent brief scenes from organizational life and take place in many different contexts. We hope they will arouse your interest to learn more about human behavior in organizations. We urge you to (1) develop your own vignettes of organizational experiences, (2) relate the text material to your experience, and (3) share your reflections with your peers. There is a great deal to be learned from astute observations of actual behavior in organizations.

SO WHAT? IMPLICATIONS FOR YOU

At the end of each chapter there is a section taking its title from that conventional practical response to new explanatory models—the ''so what?'' Rather than provide the traditional chapter summary, we thought it would be more useful to review key generalizations and help you relate them to your individual situation as a potential or actual member of a work organization, or as a future or current manager.

While your first position out of school may not be managerial, there are many concepts applied to human behavior that will find direct relevance to your working membership in any organization. As you progress in your career, assuming greater responsibility for the actions of others, a shift in perspective will be required of you for which you can prepare yourself. You will of course find that no generalization can be applied wholesale to every organization. The "implications" section invites you to take the subtle journey from theory to practice.

LEARNING APPLICATION ACTIVITIES

A section under this title will appear in each chapter with exercises that you can do individually, in small groups, and/or in the total class. They are directed toward applying the knowledge that you have gained from reading the chapters.

Here, we will recommend that you write a short vignette reflecting your own personal experience with the subject matter. This can be a useful exercise; it is another way of bringing your personal experiences to bear on the conceptual material, and vice versa. We will also suggest that you reflect further on the selected vignettes presented at the beginning of each chapter. You might want to act out the roles in a particular vignette in a simulation of a real situation. We also recommend that you observe real organizations and talk with employees. It is important that you see the applicability of the concepts from the book in real situations.

We frequently suggest that you share observations, reflections, and findings with small groups or the total class. In our experience, learning about human behavior in organizations and developing skills in managing human resources is often enhanced by sharing ideas with others. In this sense, learning is a social as well as an intellectual experience.

Additional Learning Resources

In writing this book we faced a dilemma. Should we attempt to present all of the concepts and research findings related to the subject with complete references to the literature? Or, should we present the ideas in a more popularized, readable fashion? The first approach could lead to a book written like most academic journal articles or Ph.D. dissertations—thorough, but ponderous and dull. The second approach might appear to be written from the top of our heads, with scant support from the research literature. We hope we have chosen a judicious compromise between these two approaches.

We have reviewed the literature and research related to the subject matter of each chapter and have alluded to some of the more significant contributions. Obviously, there is a great deal more written concerning any one of these issues. References are provided, where appropriate in the text, to sources of additional information on specific subjects and the cited materials are listed at the end of each chapter. Our goal was to develop an interesting, readable book that will be relevant to your organizational experiences, but one based on a thorough background of relevant knowledge from the literature and research in the behavioral sciences.

REFERENCES

Hackman, J. Richard. "The Design of Work in the 1980s." *Organizational Dynamics,* Summer 1978, pp. 3–4.

Loeb, Margaret. "Some Happy Employees at Delta Want to Buy a Big Gift for the Boss." *Wall Street Journal,* September 28, 1982, p. 29.

"Management vs. Labor." Institute for Social Research, *ISR Newsletter,* Autumn 1982, p. 3.

"Quality Control at Toyota Motor Corporation." *The Wheel Extended: Toyota Quarterly Review,* Special Supplement no. 11 (July–September 1982), p. 11.

PART TWO

THE INDIVIDUAL AND THE ORGANIZATION

The individual is a fundamental unit of analysis for the study of any organization. Understanding individual goals, attitudes, motivation, and behavior sets the stage for consideration of groups and organizational characteristics in later sections of the book.

Chapter 2 looks at the issues involved when an individual becomes a member of an organization. In the socialization process, the person enters into an unwritten psychological contract: the party of the second being the organization. Entry is an important period in the development of high performance standards and effective adaptation for both the person and the organization.

In Chapter 3 goals are considered from three perspectives: environmental, organizational, and individual. The setting of goals, the performance of tasks, and achieving satisfaction are considered in relation to one another. Potential conflicts between goals are discussed, as well as means by which management can deal with these problems when they occur.

Chapter 4 deals with motivation and performance. It considers why people expend effort and how managerial skills can help them tap their own sources for renewed activity. A model of the overall process of motivation is presented using the concepts of effort, performance, and satisfaction.

2
Organizational Socialization

LEARNING OBJECTIVES

After completing this chapter you should be able to:

1. Define in your own terms the concept of organizational socialization.
2. Recognize the significance of the unwritten psychological contract made between the individual and the organization.
3. Appreciate the importance of the early phases of the socialization process for career development and future performance.
4. Utilize concepts of organizational socialization in your own career planning and development.
5. Understand why managers should develop policies and practices that make the socialization process more effective for the organization and more satisfying for the individual.

THE FIRST DAY

Nancy Armstrong was back home from the first session in Mrs. Rossi's kindergarten class at Evergreen Elementary School. It had been a very long day, beginning at 7:30 A.M. when she waited to catch the 8:00 school bus. Her older brothers and playmates had told her a great deal about school and she had anticipated this day all summer. She arrived at school to find 25 of her future classmates and a few parents—all strangers. Nancy secretly wished that her mother were there, but she also was proud that she was toughing it out alone. Some of the other children, even several boys, were hanging onto their parents and crying to go home. Mrs. Rossi seemed very nice and after assigning them seats, she passed out books, crayons, and other materials. After lunch they played several games.

Time went by so fast that Nancy had a hard time telling her parents all that had happened. She had become lost going from the school bus to her room. One of the boys had pushed her while they were lining up for the snack. She had sat next to Sara Chin and they played together while waiting for the bus home. It had been an exciting day, not exactly what she expected. She looked forward to tomorrow with enthusiasm and a little apprehension.

ONWARD WASHINGTON

Allen Henderson had recently been elected to his first term as a United States congressman. He was busy winding up his affairs as mayor of Central City and getting organized for the family move to Washington, D.C. Election to Congress was the greatest thing that had ever happened to him. Ever since law school, he had had aspirations for a national political career but he had not expected it so soon. He was only 31, but ex-congresswoman Elizabeth Swenson had retired and he was the right person in the right place at the right time to appeal to the voters. He had worked hard campaigning and when the favorable election returns came in, the enthusiasm of his campaign workers during the victory celebration seemed to charge him with energy. Now, after all the excitement, he had to face the reality that he was actually going to the nation's capital.

Of course he had met a number of congressmen and senators in his term as mayor, but this was different. Now he was joining the club. He had strong feelings about changing national policies, particularly on environmental issues and helping cities. But he was realistic in recognizing that a freshman congressman might not have much influence. He wanted to get good committee assignments—where the action started. He was enthusiastically waiting for the start of the 98th congressional sessions but he still didn't quite believe that he would be a part of it.

SAN FRANCISCO HERE I COME

Carol Komoto had just received a telephone call from the manager of the San Francisco branch of a national CPA firm offering her a position. She had been waiting for the call and accepted immediately. She had completed her degree in accounting and passed the CPA examination on the first try. A number of other CPA firms had interviewed her, but this was her first choice and she was very pleased.

Now, however, she was having some second thoughts and some questions. The move to San Francisco was going to be different than anything she had known. She had lived at home and in the dormitories while at the university and had grown up in the local community. Being away from her family and friends would be new for her but then, San Francisco had its compensations. It really sounded exciting. She was really more apprehensive about this being her first professional job. Carol felt fairly confident about her accounting knowledge, but she was not very clear about what her first assignment would be. The fact that there would be an initial training program was a comfort, but she also was a little impatient to work directly with clients. And finally, she wondered how she would fit into the branch. When she had visited the branch, the manager and others in the office seemed nice, but all of the CPA's were men and she wondered how they would react to a woman colleague. Would they give her the same responsibilities and opportunities as the male trainees? Would they be reluctant to send her out of town alone on an assignment? How would clients accept a woman CPA? Well, she would have to wait and see, but she couldn't help but wonder.

A REAL BUST

Richard Grayson was shaken. He had just completed teaching his first class at Eastern University and it had been a shambles. He had been hired directly after receiving his MBA as instructor in marketing. The past three months had moved very fast for Richard and his family. He really had not thought much about teaching as a career but when Dean Peterson of Eastern was interviewing, Richard had signed up. Although the interview went well, he was quite surprised when the dean called the following week offering him the position. He accepted immediately. But, he was anxious and had reservations about his ability. He had never had any teaching experience, nor had he taken any courses in instructional methods. The only thing he had to go on was his own experiences as a student in observing the teaching methods of his professors.

After packing the car and rented trailer he moved from California to New York four weeks before the beginning of the fall semester. Unfortunately, he was about the only one on campus—it was summer vacation and the other instructors were gone. He was assigned to teach four marketing classes in the day program and one class in sales management during the evening. He was shocked when he received the class list for his evening session. Among the registrants were a number of sales managers and sales personnel from several larger companies in the area. Frankly, Richard was scared. How could he, a recent MBA graduate and only 24, teach a group of experienced people anything about sales management? Sure, he had several classes in the field, but his only experience had been selling newspapers—and not very successfully at that.

The class met his worst expectations. It was scheduled for two hours. He was nervous, but did manage to use 30 minutes taking roll, making up a seating chart, and passing out the assignments. In the next 15 minutes he told the class everything he had planned for the entire two-hour session. In the next 30 minutes he covered all the subject matter he had planned for the entire course and finally let them go early with a half-hearted, "See you next Wednesday." Driving home, Richard was convinced he was a failure. What was he going to do next Wednesday night and for the next 15 weeks? Even worse, he still had to face the four daytime classes. He needed help, but didn't know where to turn. He even thought about packing up the trailer and returning to California. "The first day out and I am already a bust. Who needs it anyhow!"

INTRODUCTION

These are people facing highly individualized life situations. However, they are sharing the common experience of being a newcomer. Their behavior suggests similar attitudes and feelings. They share a sense of excitement, feel at least some apprehension, seek information about their environment, and face new roles and social relationships. Contrast their attitudes and behavior with a typical junior high school student who knows "everything about school," the long-established CPA, the octogenarian congressman, or the venerable old professor who is still using ten-year-old lecture notes.

The newcomer is involved in the process of *socialization*. It is a process that starts with birth and continues throughout a life-time. Although it also occurs in higher animals, it is much more intensive for humans, with their long biological and emotional maturation process. It is a most significant and remarkable process that transforms the raw material of a biological human into a social person. It helps the individual develop values, beliefs, and attitudes, reinforces appropriate behavior, and defines the role of the person in the social group. As the word implies, it is an interactive social process. In this chapter we will discuss the organizational socialization process under the following topics:

The Concept of Socialization
Interactions Between Individual and Organization
The Psychological Contract
Individual Requirements and Expectations
Organizational Requirements and Expectations
Sociocultural Factors in Organizational Socialization
Importance of Initial Job Socialization
Matching of Individual and Organization
Improving the Socialization Process
Diagram of Organizational Socialization Process
So What? Implications for You

THE CONCEPT OF SOCIALIZATION

"Socialization refers to the process by which persons acquire the knowledge, skills, and disposition that make them more or less able members of their society" (Brim & Wheeler, 1966, p. 3). We have all undergone this process many times. Certainly, significant socialization occurs during infancy and early childhood. We are born into this world with potential for a very wide range of behavior, but we learn from our parents and other close associates to behave within a narrower range that is customary and acceptable. We faced resocialization on entering the first grade, joining an athletic team or the scouts, matriculating into college, and learning our first job. With all of these early socialization experiences it might be thought that the adult should easily adapt to new social situations. However, as we saw above, neither the sophisticated and politically astute Congressman

Henderson, nor the bright and technically qualified CPA Komoto, nor the educated and ambitious instructor Grayson was any more immune to anxiety and doubt than our kindergartener Nancy Armstrong. Resocialization is a continuing part of human existence. The homemaker who has been devoted to the family faces resocialization to new life interests after the children leave. The retiree and his wife ("What am I going to do when he is underfoot all day long?") have to make major readjustments.

In two of the examples—those of the CPA and the congressman—we did not describe actual socialization but rather *anticipatory socialization*. Humans have the ability through reflective thought to act out social situations and social roles in their imagination. We can imagine what it is going to be like and may rehearse in advance the social roles we may have to embrace in the future. Little children play house; little leaguers envision life in the majors; business students may think of themselves as company presidents. "Anticipatory socializations is thus a fancy name for a variety of mental activities which include daydreaming, forecasting future situations, role rehearsing, and much more" (Clausen, 1968, p. 9). In this sense, anticipatory socialization entails self-socialization. It is likely that CPA Komoto has already envisioned her promotion to partner in the firm, and Congressman Henderson anticipated passage of nationally renowned legislation under his name (and, who knows, maybe someday the White House?). But, as the experiences of Instructor Grayson suggest, anticipation and reality don't always match. He may have envisioned himself as a brilliant and stimulating lecturer, but he turned out to be a flop. This suggests the importance of *self-image* in the socialization process. We will discuss this in more detail later.

Actual and anticipatory socialization are vitally important in all our lives. However, we can look in greater depth at one important segment, *organizational socialization*. In the near future you will be directly involved in this process when you leave college and start your working career. Eventually, as managers and professionals, you will be responsible for the socialization of newcomers and subordinates in your organizations.

Individual on the Boundary of the Organization

The individual joining any organization develops new values, attitudes, and behaviors appropriate for membership. The problems associated with entrance into and adaptation to work organizations are issues of adult socialization. In complex societies with rapid technological and sociological changes, it is impossible to socialize the young child to all future roles. Every individual must face continuing resocialization to new situations throughout his or her life.

One of the most important periods of adult socialization is when the individual is on the boundary of a new organization ready to become a member. Figure 2.1 illustrates the individual moving through the boundary to become a member. The diagram is simple but the process is complex. There is a great deal of difference between being an outsider looking in and being a full-fledged and accepted member. Most organizations select individuals who can become members—and require newcomers to behave in appropriate ways.

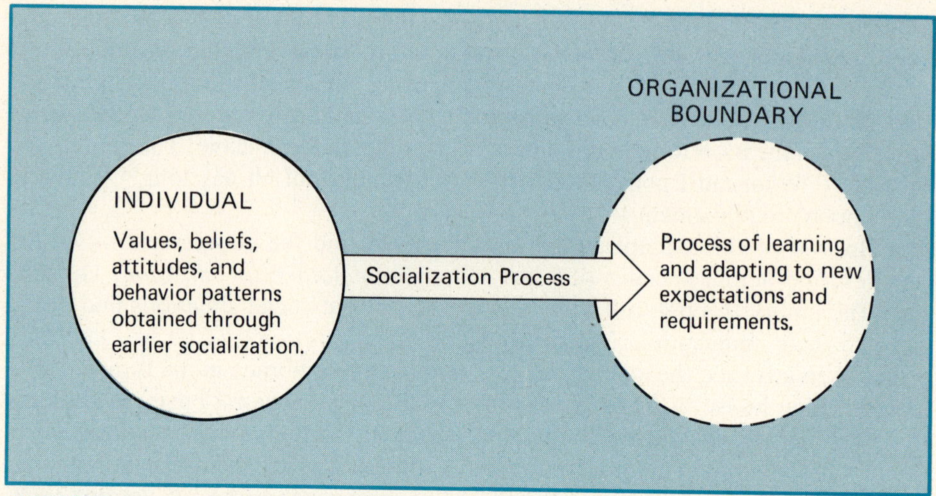

FIGURE 2.1 The Socialization Process

Organizational socialization—the process of becoming an accepted member—is a reciprocal process; the individual adapts, but so does the organization. Every time an organization takes in a new member, it, too, is subject to new influences increasing likelihood of change. For example, the opening up of business and other organizations to greater participation by women and minorities not only results in the need to socialize these groups, but also requires changes in the organizations themselves.

Self-image and Membership

Individuals hold a certain image of themselves when entering the organization. This undergoes changes as they interact with the organization and learn new tasks and roles. The new lawyer is likely to have a significantly different self-image after she has been in the law firm for six months than when she started. Organizational life has given her opportunities to test her knowledge and skills and to assess her own strengths and weaknesses.

Joining any organization means developing new involvements and relationships with other people. The person meets new people, participates in many informal groups, and is exposed to many interpersonal influences. Previous relationships established before entering the organization are often modified. How often have we heard, "Joe really has changed since he left college and went to work for a living. He certainly has become more serious. We don't have as much in common anymore."?

Membership often requires the development of new values appropriate to the position. To become a successful member, the individual must accommodate, at least to some degree, the goals, values, and practices of the organization. The young medical intern working in a hospital, for example, may modify his goals and values from those learned during his professional education. The new CPA, fresh from examinations in accounting theory and practice, may have to modify his approach significantly to fit actual organizational practices.

We have stressed here the initial process of integrating into the organization. But, just as in the world at large, the process is never complete. Later on the individual may be transferred, promoted, move to another organization, or even change careers. Technological and structural shifts may occur, task requirements may be modified, and social groups may change. All of these changes may require the resocialization of the person into a new situation.

BOX 2.1
ORGANIZATIONAL SOCIALIZATION

Work organizations offer a person far more than merely a job. Indeed, from the time individuals first enter a workplace to the time they leave their membership behind, they experience and often commit themselves to a distinct way of life complete with its own rhythms, rewards, relationships, demands, and potentials. . . .

Any organizational culture consists broadly of long-standing rules of thumb, a somewhat special language, an ideology that helps edit a member's everyday experience, shared standards of relevance as to the critical aspects of the work that is being accomplished, matter-of-fact prejudices, models for social etiquette and demeanor, certain customs and rituals suggestive of how members are to relate to colleagues, subordinates, superiors, and outsiders, and a sort of residual category of some rather plain "horse sense" regarding what is appropriate and "smart" behavior within the organization and what is not. All of these cultural modes of thinking, feeling, and doing are, of course, fragmented to some degree, giving rise within large organizations to various "subcultures" or "organizational segments". . .

Insofar as the individual is concerned, the results of an organizational socialization process include, for instance, a readiness to select certain events for attention over others, a stylized stance toward one's routine activities, some ideas as to how one's various behavioral responses to recurrent situations are viewed by others, and so forth. In short, socialization entails the learning of a cultural perspective that can be brought to bear on both commonplace and unusual matters going on in the workplace. To come to know an organizational situation and act within it implies that a person has developed some commonsensical beliefs, principles, and understandings, or in shorthand notation, a *perspective* for interpreting one's experiences in a given sphere of the work world.

Source: John Van Maanen and Edgar H. Schein, "Toward a Theory of Organizational Socialization," in Barry M. Staw [Ed.], *Research in Organizational Behavior* [Greenwich, Conn.: JAI, 1979], pp. 210–212. Reprinted by permission.

INTERACTIONS BETWEEN INDIVIDUAL AND ORGANIZATION

How many organizations are you a member of? How many affect your life in important ways? These are simple questions but require some thought. If you consider all organizations that have an influence, direct or oblique, on your life and behavior, the list would likely be in the hundreds and still probably would not be complete. For example, in driving to school (an organization of which you are a voluntary member) your behavior is influenced by the speed limit (a product of governmental institutions). If you are caught speeding, the State Highway Patrol and the courts will begin to loom large in importance.

Never the Total Person

Although we recognize that we are in constant interaction with organizations, we should remember that they never encompass the *total person*. Organizations are designed to accomplish specific purposes, and they engage only a segment of the person in accomplishing these objectives. They are most interested in the specific behavior that affects individual performance in meeting these goals. A person may be a champion bowler, a great husband and father, a card-carrying Republican, a member of the church choir, and a subscriber to *Playboy,* but these affiliations are likely to be irrelevant to the organization if his task is to put two bolts on the left front door of the cars coming down the assembly line. Managers are interested in having individuals adapt their behavior in organizationally relevant matters. Furthermore, the work situation requires that the individual shape a vast repertoire of potential behaviors to a narrow range of specific actions. It seeks to utilize only part of a person's skills and abilities.

Thus, there is always limited integration or socialization of the total person into the organization. "People who perform organizational tasks must be sustained by factors outside the organization. The organization is not the total world of the individual; it is not a society. People must fulfill other social roles; besides, society has shaped them in ways which affect their ability to perform organizational tasks. A man has a marital status, ethnic identification, religious affiliations, a distinctive personality, friends, to name only a few. . . . Daily, people come contaminated into the organization" (Perrow, 1970, p. 52). This does not mean, of course, that organizations, and particularly work organizations, are not important to their human participants. On the contrary they are becoming more, rather than less, important.

Never the Total Organization

Just as the organization never encompasses the total person, the individual does not comprehend and experience the total organization. The individual's "organizational horizon" is limited (Porter, Lawler, & Hackman, 1975, p. 115). People in organizations have limited perspectives of the total organization because of differences in hierarchical level, tasks assigned, departmental affiliations, and interpersonal contacts. Moreover, different people subject to the same organizational influences may have different perceptions. It is often startling for

BOX 2.2
THE IMPORTANCE OF ORGANIZATIONS

The psychological importance of the organization to the individual who works in it has increased in the last two generations. Radical changes in contemporary Western industrialized society have altered many of the ways in which people could satisfy their economic, social, and psychological needs. These changes have required people to find new ways of obtaining job security; new social devices for protection against injury, sickness, and death; modes of developing new skills, new forms of recreation, and new sources of support. Increasingly, people have found new devices for dealing with their reality problems through employment in organizations. . . . Affiliation with an organization in which a person works seems to have become a major device for solving the problems resulting from these economic, social, and psychological changes.

Source: Harry Levinson, *The Exceptional Executive: A Psychological Conception,* [Cambridge, Mass. Harvard University Press, 1968], pp. 27–29. Reprinted by permission.

professors who receive student evaluations of their courses to find vast differences among individual responses. Some students (hopefully many) may rate their course and instructor as excellent, while others (hopefully few) rate it a disaster. The same thing seems to occur when employee attitude surveys are taken. Workers performing the same task and receiving approximately the same rewards sometimes have significantly different perceptions about the leadership style and quality of the work environment. It is quite obvious that we perceive and react to new situations in different ways because of past socializations to life and our own personalities.

$B = f(P,E)$

We do not want to engage in the long-standing controversy over whether human behavior is a result of hereditary predispositions or environmental influences. Rather, we submit the equation: $B = f(P,E)$. Behavior is a function of the interaction between the person and the environment. The adult brings into the organization personal predispositions to behave in certain ways based on hereditary traits filtered through previous socialization processes. At the same time, the organization tries to provide an environment that will stimulate the person to behave in certain organizationally appropriate ways. Actual behavior is a result of the interaction of these forces.

This formulation helps us to understand how different people within the same organization have different perceptions and behave in different ways. Socialization is never absolute or complete for any participants—each retains an individual personality that makes him or her unique.

THE PSYCHOLOGICAL CONTRACT

A basic part of the socialization process is the development of a "psychological contract" between the newcomer and the organization. The psychological contract is not a written, legal document. Rather, it results from the process of reciprocation in fulfilling mutual expectations and satisfying mutual needs in the relationship between a person and the work organization. The key word here is process: "The psychological contract is unlike a legal contract in that it defines a dynamic, changing relationship that is continually being renegotiated. Often important aspects of the contract are not formally agreed upon—key organizational and individual expectations are sometimes unstated, as well as implicit premises about the relationship" (Kolb, Rubin, & McIntyre, 1979, p. 12).

The psychological contract covers the total range of expectations from the individual and the organization. The individual has expectations about what will be received over and above monetary compensation—satisfactory working conditions, career opportunities, appropriate status and role definition, challenging work, and fair treatment—as well as what must be given—time and energy, loyalty, willingness to accomplish organizational goals, and reasonable acceptance of authority. The organization in turn has many expectations of what it will receive from the employee and what it will give in return.

The early phases of socialization involve sorting out and defining the terms of this contract. Not all expectations, neither the individuals nor the organizations, can be met; there is explicit and implicit bargaining in which each side has to compromise. For example, the new employee may have high expectations concerning a challenging initial job assignment. However, there may be limitations on the availability of such jobs and the employee may have to settle for the prospect of advancing to such a position in the future.

The extent to which such bargaining is direct and open versus indirect and suppressed varies a great deal, depending on leadership styles and organizational practices. In some situations employees are encouraged to discuss their needs and expectations. In other organizations these subjects are taboo. The degree of conflict in the continual negotiations of the psychological contract obviously depends on the extent to which the new employee and the organization have mutual or compatible expectations. Because of limited information concerning these expectations prior to employment, the early socialization period is characterized by many adjustments and compromises.

Expectations

The psychological contract with its emphasis on the expectations of both the individual and the organization is closely related to expectancy models of human behavior. People have expectations about how their own behavior will affect future outcomes. The motivational force for the individual to engage in a particular behavior is a function of: (1) the expectations the person holds about what outcomes are likely to result from the behavior, and; (2) the values the individual places on the outcomes (Porter, Lawler, & Hackman, 1975, p. 56). For example, the new employee is motivated to expend effort if he expects such effort will lead to performance that is rewarded. Under this theory, effort→performance→rewards leads to satisfaction and continued motivation.

This expectancy model will be covered more completely in Chapter 4. However, it is important to recognize how important expectations are in the process of organizational socialization. Newcomers have certain expectations about how their own effort and performance will lead to personal rewards that contribute to their satisfaction. These may be modified substantially during the socialization process. For example, if the employee finds that good performance does not lead to valued rewards from the organization, then she may adjust her level of effort accordingly. The employee and the organization are in effect negotiating a new psychological contract based on these changed expectations.

INDIVIDUAL REQUIREMENTS AND EXPECTATIONS

It would be impossible to list all the expectations that individuals have of organizations. People are very different in these expectations and organizations vary in their ability or willingness to meet them.

Self-Concept

When joining an organization you are not just selling your physical and mental abilities. Like it or not, you are also bringing along your psychic self in the bargain. Your own self-concept plays a major part in the socialization process.

Self-concept is the way you perceive and judge yourself. It is your way of thinking about the kind of person you really are. Do you see yourself as a leader or follower? Do you have a high need for power, achievement, or social affiliations? Are you aggressive or passive? People have the unique capacity for thinking about their own behavior and their impact on others.

Self-concept is of vital importance in the process of organizational socialization. When the self-concept is compatible with one's organizational role and requirements, the person is likely to be motivated, oriented to task performance, and satisfied. However, when self-concept and organizational role are not compatible, then integration is difficult and motivation, performance, and satisfaction are likely to be low.

This does not mean that self-concept is totally fixed. Indeed, one of the important aspects of organizational socialization is the potential modification in your self-concept. The new intern on the emergency ward may find that he is really not as cool and unemotional as he thought and may seek a less-pressured career. The MBA graduate who thought of herself in passive terms may be thrust into a leadership position where she is effective and gratified.

Part of the organizational socialization process may be learning to develop a self-concept appropriate for the new situation. "Each of us learns to construct somewhat different selves for the different kinds of situations in which we are called on to perform, and for the different kinds of roles we are expected to take" (Schein, 1974, p. 339). It is unlikely that we can change our basic personalities and value systems substantially, but we can develop new social selves in terms of new attitudes, competencies, behavior patterns, and ways of relating to others in different situations. To some extent, we can redesign ourselves to fit the role requirements of new situations.

Individual Expectations from the Work Organization

People appear to have different expectations regarding their work lives. Studs Terkel reports on interviews with over 130 workers in all types of jobs. These interviews indicate the wide range of expectations, motivations, and satisfactions affecting people in work organizations. They present verbal portraits of how people feel about their job experiences. The evidence from these interviews—with accountants, auto workers, airline flight attendants, police officers, bank tellers—is that people in most occupations have expectations for their work lives that are not being fulfilled. Terkel evokes something of this disenchantment in describing his book: "It is about a search, too, for daily meaning as well as daily bread, for recognition as well as cash, for astonishment rather than torpor; in short, for a sort of life rather than a Monday through Friday sort of dying" (Terkel, 1974, p. xi).

There are many other evidences that people have increasing aspirations for their work lives. They don't want to work for money alone, but are seeking other satisfactions. We should not interpret this as indicating that there is wide-scale job dissatisfaction. Other research studies have found that many people have relatively high satisfaction with their work and would choose the same career if they had it to do over again. Rather, the issue seems to be that even though work life has improved, this improvement has not kept pace with aspirations.

ORGANIZATIONAL REQUIREMENTS AND EXPECTATIONS

The other party to the psychological contract is the organization, with its own complement of expectations. An organization is, by definition, a cooperative social venture, and it requires the integration and mutual adaptation of human activities; it cannot accommodate totally individualistic behavior. This is equally true for the family, the school, and the work organization. All three have certain expectations and requirements that must be balanced against individual expectations in the development of the psychological contract. The organizational side of the contract puts its emphasis on:

1. Achieving organizational goals that are different from the personal goals of individual members.
2. Having sufficient involvement, commitment, and initiative from organizational members.
3. Requiring individuals to take certain organizational roles.
4. Having people perform certain tasks effectively and efficiently.
5. Requiring participants to accept authority and to assume responsibilities.
6. Achieving the integration and coordination of activities.

7. Requiring adherence to policies, rules, and procedures.
8. Attaining responsiveness to leadership and influence.
9. Developing sufficient loyalty to maintain the organization as a social system.

The list could be much longer; however, it is sufficient to illustrate that the organization itself has expectations, requirements, and constraints that are different from, and often in conflict with, the expectations of individual members.

Organizational Climate

The requirements and expectations communicated by the organization blend together to form the organizational climate.

> Organizational climate is a relatively enduring quality of the internal environment of an organization that (a) is experienced by its members, (b) influences their behavior, and (c) can be described in terms of the values of a particular set of characteristics (or attributes) of the organization (Tagiuri & Litwin, 1968, p. 27).

It should be emphasized that climate is based on the characteristics of the work organization *as perceived* by the participants.

The newcomer develops a perception of the organizational climate through anticipatory socialization and in the early socialization process. This climate creates in the individual certain expectations and encourages certain values, attitudes, and modes of behavior that influence both task performance and perceived satisfaction (Payne & Pugh, 1976; Hellriegel & Slocum, 1974). We will consider organizational climate in detail in Chapter 14.

Learning Organizational Roles

One of the most important aspects of the socialization process is the learning of a new role for the individual. In a general sense every society ascribes various roles to its members. Roles are the expected behavior patterns for a specific position in a society or organization. We ascribe roles to children, students, workers, managers, and professionals such as doctors and lawyers. Given a particular position in a social group we tend to act out the role based jointly on the expectations of others and our own interpretations. Practically all social acts may be thought of as constituting role behavior in the sense that individual actors respond to expectations of others regarding their performance.

An organization is composed of a number of related roles. Many factors come into play in defining and assigning these roles: the nature of the tasks to be done; the degree of responsibility accorded; the order of levels in the hierarchy; the technical and interpersonal competencies required (Katz & Kahn, 1978, pp. 185–221). The newcomer is faced with the problem of learning not only a new personal role, but also the entire system of roles that influences the behavior of all other members in the organization.

BOX 2.3
WORK IN AMERICA

Significant numbers of American workers are dissatisfied with the quality of their working lives. Dull, repetitive, seemingly meaningless tasks, offering little challenge or autonomy, are causing discontent among workers at all occupational levels. This is not so much because work itself has greatly changed; indeed, one of the main problems is that work has not changed fast enough to keep up with the rapid and widescale changes in worker attitudes, aspirations, and values. A general increase in their educational and economic status has placed many American workers in a position where having an interesting job is now as important as having a job that pays well. Pay is still important: it must support an "adequate" standard of living and be perceived as equitable—but high pay alone will not lead to job (or life) satisfaction.

Source: *Work in America,* Report of a Special Task Force to the Secretary of Health, Education, and Welfare, [Cambridge, Mass.; MIT Press, 1973], pp. xv–xvi. © 1973. Reprinted by permission.

Many people in the organization have a share in influencing and prescribing the role of the newcomer. In the sometimes confusing world of organizations, the resultant prescriptions and descriptions are neither precise nor consistent. Different people will provide conflicting information. For example, the newcomer's superior may inform him about company rules and expected levels of performance, but the work group may press for an unofficial code prescribing shortcuts or maintaining output at less than the officially prescribed level. The boss may extol the importance of initiative but then check every move of the employee. The newcomer is subject to substantial role conflict.

Role conflict is not unique to work organizations; it occurs throughout life. The parent may have conflicts over the expectations of the work organization and family. The assembly-line worker may have conflicts between the role expectations of the company and the union. The lawyer may have conflicting role prescriptions from the Bar Association, the ACLU, the clients in her charge, and her own professional ethics.

Forced with contradictory demands, the newcomer in the organization has to come up with a self "role prescription" for how he or she will behave in a particular situation. This is a basic part of the socialization process.

SOCIOCULTURAL FACTORS IN ORGANIZATIONAL SOCIALIZATION

People coming into organizations are not like raw material inputs possessing rigid specifications. No amount of quality control and inspections will ensure that they are 99.99% perfect and uniform. They are individuals influenced by hereditary factors, previous socialization processes, and their other life experiences. In the socialization processes, organizations are working with highly variable, heterogeneous, and somewhat imperfect human resources. To the extent that individuals have faced significantly different acculturation processes in their earlier lives, they represent different inputs to the socialization process. Many studies have indicated that workers coming from different communities (rural versus urban), from different social classes, or who are in other ways differentiated by past socialization have different expectations, motivations, behaviors, and satisfactions. These groups represent subcultures that prepare people differently for functioning in work organizations. Looking at these subcultures may help us understand some of the problems that result from variations in social learning among societies or among subgroups within a society (Nord, 1976).

Influence of Subcultures

The phenomenon of sociocultural divergence can be illustrated by looking at two groups in the work force: women and minorities. We are born into two broad subcultures based on gender—male or female. There are obvious physiological differences, but how much these contribute to later differences in the behavior of men and women is the subject of much controversy. A good deal of evidence suggests that many dissimilarities occur because of different socialization processes for girls and boys. There appear to be rather clearly defined sex-role stereotypes for men and women (Broverman et al., 1972). The young girl or boy is socialized to match these stereotypes. Some of the major components of sex-role socialization are: (1) each society arbitrarily views a wide variety of personality characteristics, interests, and behaviors as appropriate for one sex or the other; (2) sex roles are systematically inculcated in individuals, beginning at birth, by parents, the educational system, peers, the media, religious institutions, and other informational sources; (3) individuals learn appropriate sex roles through role models and differential reinforcement; (4) sex roles form the core of an individual's identity or self image; and (5) in many societies the male role enjoys the higher status (Polk, 1974).

Stereotypical masculine traits (more logical, objective, aggressive, and ambitious as well as less sensitive, warm, and expressive) are often perceived to be more desirable for mature adults than stereotypical feminine characteristics (more emotional, sensitive, and expressive as well as less aggressive, objective, and logical). "Women are clearly put in a double bind by the fact that different standards exist for women than for adults. If women adopt the behaviors specified as desirable for adults, they risk censure for their failure to be appropriately feminine; but if they adopt the behaviors that are designated as feminine, they are necessarily deficient with respect to the general standards for adult behavior" (Broverman et al., 1972, p. 75).

This creates additional problems for women seeking to rise in the organizational hierarchy to managerial positions. The effective manager is seen to have those traits most closely associated with the masculine (and adult) sex role. The aspiring woman generally must assume some of these traits if she is to be successful in a managerial position. However, the more aggressive woman is often described as pushy, ruthless, and domineering. An aggressive man, behaving in essentially the same way, is called a "go-getter" or a "take-charge guy." If a woman behaves in the stereotypical feminine manner, she is likely to be considered overcautious, incapable of decisive action, and too emotional.

There are further indications that other factors in organizations contribute to the problem, such as differential recruitment of women to lower-level jobs that require dependence and passivity and excessive controls that give women less power (Acker & Van Houten, 1974). Taken together, past socialization into differentiated sex roles and conditions within organizations that reinforce these differences create unique problems of socialization—both for the woman and the organization. It takes much more than just saying, "We are opening the doors" to reach a successful accommodation.

Many minority groups face similar problems in organizational socialization. In the past, earlier socialization in many such groups—through family, education, peer groups—had prepared the individual to take lower-level jobs rather than professional and managerial positions. This is changing, but slowly. Many minorities have developed higher expectations and aspirations and more higher-level positions are being opened to them. However, problems of successful integration of the individual into the organization remain. For example, one study found that many blacks moving into positions that were traditionally jobs for whites only felt substantial apprehension. They anticipated more job difficulties (particularly ones related to their isolated racial position) than did their white counterparts. Managers were also initially apprehensive about their future performance and about conflicts that might arise.

> It is evident that the introduction of blacks into sensitive jobs created many strains for the managers, as well as on the new employees themselves. Initial apprehension, and subsequent relief when things turned out better than expected, has been a common theme in much of the social change witnessed during the last few decades. But a positive outcome is not inevitable. It depends on proper information and correct, determined action (Kraut, 1975, pp. 614–615).

It is very important for the organization and the manager not to fall into habits of stereotyping different subcultures. Many people associate certain personality traits with different groups in our society. Sometimes this is useful, but more likely we find that it blinds us to really understanding the individual as a unique human being. Often, with better information we find that there are not as many differences as we expected. For example, a recent comparative study of black and white managers in a number of large companies found that the self-concept, personal values, and strength of achievement, power, and affiliation needs between the two groups were not significantly different (Watson & Barone, 1976).

There is an additional key factor when considering the socialization process for women and minorities entering into new, higher-level positions in organizations. This is not only a process of change for the newcomer, but something requiring significant *resocialization* of existing members. Not only are we modifying the values, attitudes, and behavior of the new employee, we are also asking for substantial change on the part of others in the organization. This makes the process even more difficult.

Cross-cultural Comparisons

Early socialization processes deeply affect the expectations and behavior of a particular people. For example, in Japan the Nenko system of lifetime commitment to an organization is often associated with centuries-old behavior patterns and value orientations. This system is based on traditional Japanese values of respect for elders, the importance of family and group social systems, and mutual responsibility, loyalty, and collaboration. However, the Nenko system is not universal in Japan. It is used only in the larger enterprises and does not cover temporary employees and outside contract workers.

This system does appear to work well within the culture, but there are major questions about its appropriateness in other societies, such as the United States. The reverse of this is also true: many modern U.S. corporate practices are not easily transferred to other countries. This becomes particularly evident in multinational corporations operating in a foreign country. In the organizational socialization process for foreign nationals taking managerial roles in U.S. corporations abroad, we may find that we are requiring people to develop attitudes, values, and behavior patterns that are in conflict for the individual. The same problem may make itself felt among a certain group of American employees and managers in the coming decades. What will be the consequences of more people working for German-, Japanese-, or Arab-owned companies? Will there be major difficulties in organizational socialization for the American working in the U.S. for a company owned and directed from Tokyo?

As we develop more varied and complex organizations and recruit people from different subcultures, we can anticipate that the socialization process will become even more complex. Not only must individuals adjust, but the organization will have to adapt to the attitudes, beliefs, and behavior patterns that different people bring into the organization. We see an increasing possibility of having more diverse values, views, and even life styles among different participants and groups within organizations.

IMPORTANCE OF INITIAL JOB SOCIALIZATION

Some people believe that the period of early organizational socialization is not particularly important. The newcomer is there to get acquainted with the organization, to learn about the task requirements, and to size up the situation without too much involvement. The organization should look the newcomer over and really not expect much. The newcomer should play it cool and not make too many commitments to the organization.

There is very strong evidence that this approach is inappropriate for the individual and the organization. The first year is one of the most significant periods in the work career of the individual. The development of values, attitudes, and behavior patterns during this period strongly influences future career development.

Why is this so? There is a law of primacy which holds that the earlier an experience, the more important its effect because it influences how later experiences will be interpreted. The newcomer entering the organization is uniquely subject to new influences. When he enters the organization he is uncertain about the role that he will play and his concept of himself is thrown into question. Finding himself in a stressful and "unfrozen" situation, "he is motivated to reduce this stress by becoming incorporated into the 'interior' of the company. Being thus motivated to be accepted by this new social system and to make sense of the ambiguity surrounding him, he is more receptive to cues from his environment than he will ever be again, and what he learns at the beginning will become the core of his organizational identity" (Berlew & Hall, 1966, p. 210). This is the very period when recruits can best test their own self-concepts and expectations of organizational life. It is during this time when the most important components of the psychological contract will be negotiated, thus determining the new recruit's organizational commitment. This phase is particularly important for the young college graduate who is starting a career in a work organization. In a longitudinal study of 62 college graduates entering into a management training program, Berlew and Hall followed the careers of the trainees over a five-year period. The researchers hypothesized that "very early in his organizational career an individual will develop enduring attitudes and aspirations which will have important effects on his future behavior. Of particular interest is the early development of performance standards and job attitudes. From the moment he enters the organization, a new manager is given cues about the quality of performance that is expected and rewarded" (Berlew & Hall, 1966, p. 210). The major research question was whether the degree of challenge faced in the first year had an impact on later performance and success. The study confirmed that managers given challenging initial jobs with high expectations for performance were more successful in their later careers than those given less challenging jobs. They were socialized to have higher aspirations and performance standards. The moral seems to be that "success breeds success"; numerous other studies seem to confirm these findings (Buchanan, 1974). Newcomers should thus be given challenging but obtainable goals rather than "snap assignments." They should be involved in the establishment of these goals and be given honest feedback on performance.

The Organization Sizing Up the Individual

We have emphasized the importance of the initial socialization process in establishing the individual's values, expectations, behavior patterns, and achievement orientation. The other side of the coin is also apparent. It is during this period that other members of the organization are making key judgments about the personal characteristics, behavior, and performance of the new individual. Initial impressions (which may be based on limited evidence) are long lasting. Just as in Hollywood, there is a danger that the individual may become type-cast and it is often difficult to break out of this role in the future. The new instructor will often be judged by faculty colleagues as to classroom effectiveness early in her career. Quite often these perceptions are based on limited information, but they are enduring and difficult to change. The first day and the first few months really do count in the individual's organizational career.

MATCHING OF INDIVIDUAL AND ORGANIZATION

In view of the large variations in individual personality characteristics and the almost equally wide differences in organizational climates, it is understandable that there are many problems in appropriately matching and integrating the individual and the organization.

Frequently both the individual and the organization have some influence in the selection process. The corporation recruits, interviews, tests, and selects from a number of candidates. The individual investigates and evaluates various job opportunities. In some situations, the organization has the most say in the matching process, the individual, little. The present author remembers standing naked in line at the San Diego Induction Center and hearing the sergeant say: "Which do you want, the Army, the Navy, or the Marines?" The unspoken response, "None of the above," was decidedly not one of the choices. In other cases, neither the organization nor the individual has much say about who will be a member of the organization. This is typically true for the child entering a compulsory school system. It is also true for the inmate entering the correctional institution.

In most cases, however, there is the potential opportunity for selection and matching on the part of both the individual and the organization to increase the probability of more effective socialization and integration.

People React Differently to Organizations

Given individual differences and the variety of organizations, it is natural to expect people to react differently to organizational life. People who have a high need for security and a well-ordered life may find career satisfaction in a bureaucratic, structured organization. The postal system and some banks may provide the appropriate environment. Others would find them intolerable and would be completely frustrated. More adaptive and dynamic organizations may allow the individual greater autonomy and flexibility but require continual changes in roles, new behavior, and a high tolerance for uncertainty and ambiguity. Some people may thrive working on a short-lived project team for NASA or an aerospace company, but others would find it nerve-racking and develop ulcers.

An extensive study was conducted in a number of organizations that sought to examine the relationship between the external environment, the internal environment (organizational climate and design) and the sense of competency and satisfaction of organizational members. It was found that the appropriate fit between these three variables led to effective organizational performance *and* a high level of participant satisfaction and motivation. The study indicated the importance of matching the characteristics and values of individuals to the appropriate organizational environment, both external and internal. This obviously has important implications both for the organization's selection of people and for the individual's career decisions. A better match between individual characteristics and organizational requirements would obviously benefit both. The *contingency view* enunciated in the study's conclusion holds that there is no inherent conflict between the individual and the organization: "Rather than suggesting a dichotomy between organizational effectiveness and individual fulfillment, the contingency approach suggests that there can be a true integration of individual and organizational growth and development" (Lorsch & Morse, 1974, p. 144).

People Do Change Organizations

Socialization is a two-way process. It is fairly obvious to new parents, for example, that their lives have been changed significantly when they bring the first baby home from the hospital. And they continually modify their behavior as the infant passes through various stages of childhood. The teacher makes certain attitudinal and behavioral adjustments for each new class. The manager adapts to the new employee. All agents of socialization are therefore themselves subject to change as a result of this process.

The degree of change effected in organizations and in their agents of socialization is directly related to the novelty of the situation with which they are presented. The first child is much more likely to change the parents than the tenth. The young teacher is more likely to be changed than the veteran. However, even the long-established organization member may face a period of significant resocialization when presented with new circumstances. Examples of the introduction of women and minorities into higher positions in work organizations illustrate that the established managers also undergo major readjustments. The first women in the military academies were not only called upon to change themselves but occasioned substantial changes that affected other recruits and the entire organization.

Agents of socialization (parents, peers, teachers, managers, etc.) faced with different types of human inputs into the organization will themselves have anxieties and apprehensions about the process; they may behave much like the newcomer. They are facing a new social situation and to an extent are unfrozen from their past attitudes and behavior patterns. They, too, are more receptive at this time to informational inputs and cues about how they should perform their role as socializer.

Individualization is the reciprocal of socialization. While the organization is attempting to modify the individual to its requirements, "he in turn is striving to influence the organization so that it can better satisfy his own needs and his own ideas about how it can best be operated" (Porter, Lawler, & Hackman, 1975, p. 170). This individualization process is of vital importance to the long-term survival of organizations: particularly those facing rapidly changing environments and internal circumstances. It is one of the primary sources of organizational change and adaptation.

> The enterprise, if people did not pursue individualization attempts, would tend to become locked into a particular *modus operandi* encompassing an unchanging set of beliefs and norms. While this might be effective in the short run, the environment in which organizations operate is much too dynamic for this kind of rigidity to lead to success over the long run. Thus, individualization, aside from its functional properties for the psychological well-being of the employee, has potential survival value for the organization (Porter, Lawler, & Hackman, 1975, p. 170).

Obviously, the ability of individuals to influence the organization changes over time. They are likely to have greater influence as they move up the organizational hierarchy. However, even lower-level participants may have significant influence—frequently more than is recognized. For example, he or she may have technical expertise, control over information and resources, access to persons, and the power to give or withhold effort, interest, and commitment (Mechanic, 1962).

IMPROVING THE SOCIALIZATION PROCESS

There seem to be some broad generalizations coming out of studies of organizational socialization processes (Van Maanen & Schein, 1979). First, there is strong evidence that anticipatory socialization leads to higher expectations on the part of individuals about their organizational roles than can be fulfilled. There seems to be a downward adjustment of expectations and aspirations on the part of new members in the organization during their first year. This appears to be true for college graduates entering management training programs, for police trainees, and for many professionals (Van Maanen, 1975). High initial expectations leading to some disillusionment is the typical pattern.

This may be caused by many factors. The graduate business school that prepares its MBA graduates to fill high managerial positions later in their career may instill expectations that cannot be met until the individual has earned this position by performing basic tasks. Unrealistic expectations may also be created in many industrial jobs. For example, one large organization established a magnificent training facility for workers just joining the organization. The learning environment was ideal, the instructors capable, and the training program highly effective. Unfortunately, when the trainees were assigned to the gritty realities of the shoproom floor, many became disillusioned and quit. Turnover during the training program was extremely low, but nearly 50 percent left during the first year on the job.

With the opening of new positions to women and minorities we see many examples of unrealistic expectations on the part of both the individual and the organization. For example, when a university department hired its first black assistant professor it painted a rosy picture of academic life. The professor also put his best foot forward. However the department failed to specify clearly all of the expectations for teaching and research of a new assistant professor. Even more critical, it did not fully recognize the potential role conflicts that the new professor would face. His academic performance was evaluated solely on a basis of the traditional expectations of an assistant professor. The department did not provide effective collegial advice, coaching, and support in helping the newcomer adapt to the situation.

The professor in turn had difficulties in making the adaptation from graduate student to teacher and imposed unrealistic expectations on his students. Like so many new Ph.D.s, he tried to accomplish too much too soon in the classroom. The black professor felt isolated from his peer professors and disenchanted with his students. There was little feedback and encouragement during the socialization process. After two years, the black professor resigned, disillusioned and bitter. The department became uncertain about its commitment to equal opportunity. As in many cases of failure in the socialization process, both sides had contributed to the difficulties, and each could have helped improve the process.

The Individual Perspective—Realistic Career Planning

The individual should be realistic in recognizing that entering any organization entails some personal gains and some losses. Every adult resocialization process requires the abandonment of certain past values, attitudes, and behavior patterns that may have been part of the self-image cultivated by the individual. We should not expect the process to be easy.

During the selection process, the individual should obtain as much information as possible about the organizational climate and its effect on the definition of roles. Recruiters, in their zeal to attract the best new members, are not always the best source for this kind of information. A more objective appraisal may come from those who have recently joined the organization. This is not always easy to obtain (it is even more difficult to get information from those who were dissatisfied and left), but it is important to investigate longer-range career opportunities as well as immediate rewards, such as salary and fringe benefits.

Organizational Perspective—Initial Socialization

Certainly, more balanced recruitment and selection techniques can ease the socialization process. Some organizations have attempted to provide the prospective employee with more realistic job previews in the form of booklets, films, visits to the work site, and informal discussions that convey not only the positive side of organizational life, but some of the potential problems and frustrations as well (Hall & Hall, 1976; Wanous, 1980; Feldman, 1976). The recruiters fears that this might put off the better candidates have proven unjustified, and research indicates that turnover and dissatisfaction are significantly lower for people who have received realistic information and expectations.

Organizational socialization can be underdone, appropriately done, or overdone (Schein, 1968). If it is underdone it may lead to nonconformity, rebellion, and alienation on the part of the individual who rejects all the norms and values of the organization. The rebellious individual is dissatisfied with both himself and the organization. He may be fired or he may quit. The other extreme is oversocialization: where the individual totally conforms to the organization, unquestioningly perpetuating and demanding acceptance of existing goals, values, and practices. The goal of appropriate socialization should be to develop creative individualism where the person generally accepts the key goals, values, and norms of the organization but also retains the desire to seek changes and improvement.

Fortunately, there is growing attention to organizational socialization processes, both by researchers and practicing managers (Van Maanen, 1978). The importance of these processes is becoming more evident in terms of both organizational performance and human satisfaction.

DIAGRAM OF THE ORGANIZATIONAL SOCIALIZATION PROCESS

Figure 2.2 provides a summary diagram of the organizational socialization process. It starts with the past life experiences of the individual and the past experiences and practices of the organization. Clearly, these have a major influence on the process. The diagram suggests that both the individual and the organization bring a number of requirements, constraints, and expectations into the process. The socialization process requires significant adaptations on the part of both and results in the negotiation of a psychological contract. The outcome of the process may lead to two failures—alienation/rebellion or ultraconformity. Neither of these is desirable from either the individual's or the organization's standpoint. Creative individualism is the desired mean: the achievement of which has great importance for the career development of the individual and for the continued growth, change, and development of the organization.

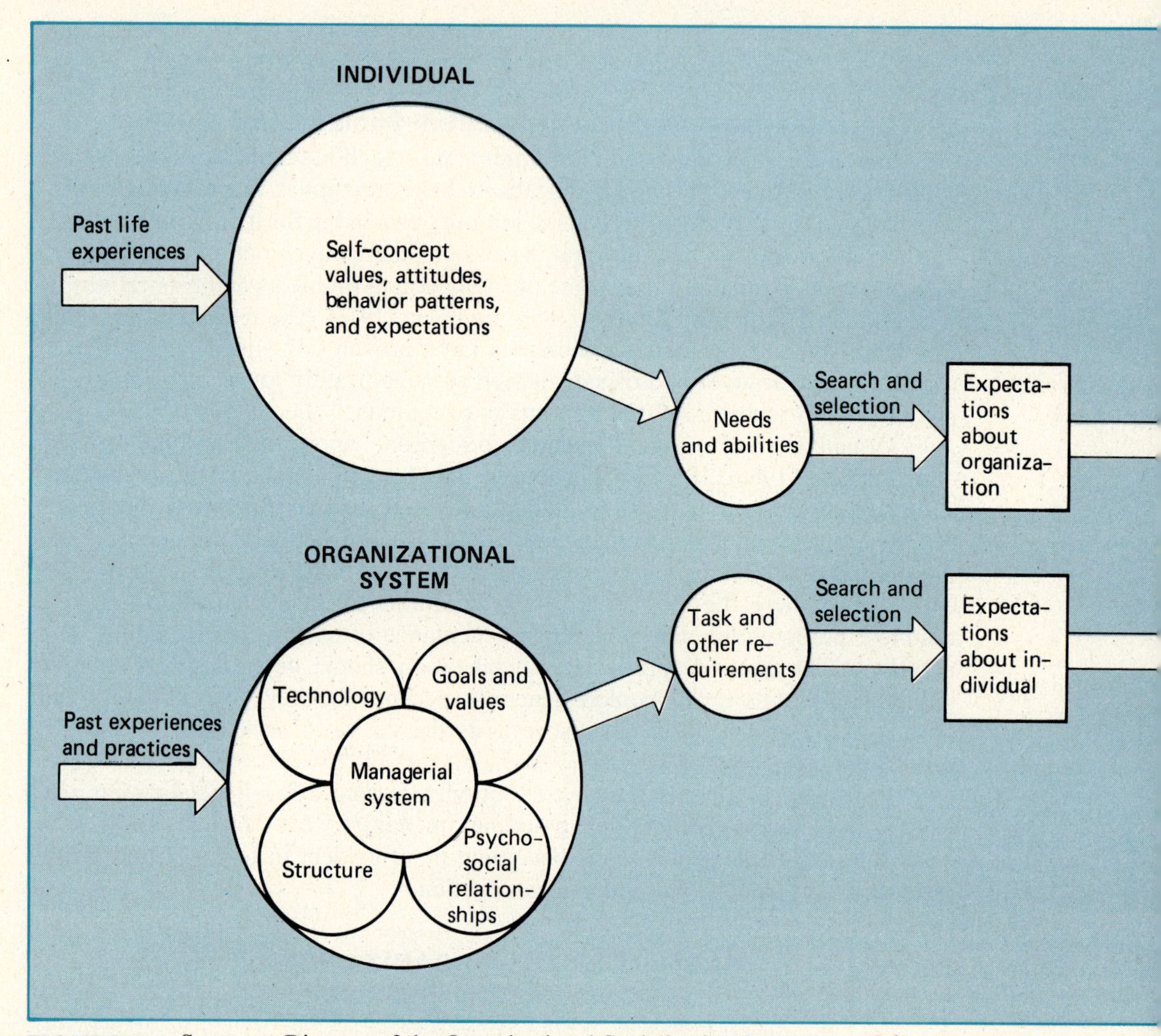

FIGURE 2.2 Summary Diagram of the Organizational Socialization Process

SO WHAT? IMPLICATIONS FOR YOU

As a Member in an Organization

Generalizations	Implications
1. People feel anxious and uncertain in new social situations.	1. Recognize that it is natural to feel anxious and uncertain joining an organization. You are not unique, others have similar feelings.

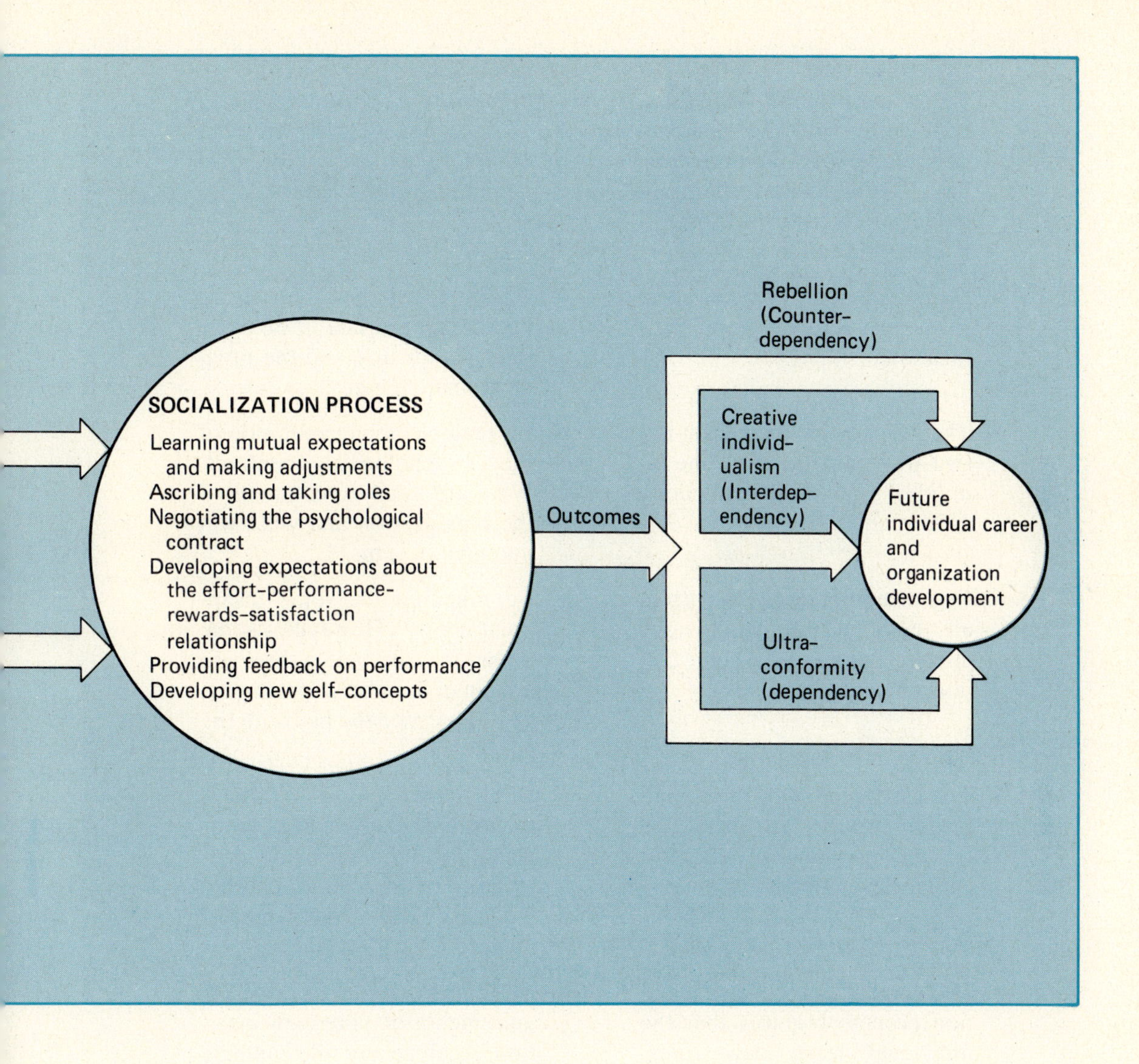

Generalizations	Implications
2. The anticipatory socialization process establishes your initial view of the organization.	2. Obtain as much accurate information about the organization and its climate as possible. Talk with current and past employees if possible and visit your potential work sites.
3. The individual's self-concept plays a major part in the so-	3. Think specifically about your self-concept. Does it match the

Generalizations	Implications
cialization process. When it is compatible with the organizational role and requirements, he or she is likely to be motivated, oriented to task performance, and satisfied.	organization requirements? Check your perceptions with others who will give you straightforward answers.
4. Certain personality types seem to fit best into different organizational situations.	4. To the extent possible, try to find an appropriate fit between your personality and the organizational climate.
5. The psychological contract is a two-way bargain. Both the individual and the organization have requirements.	5. Be realistic about your side of the psychological contract. What are your expectations of the organization and what will you give in return?
6. Organizations rarely live up to all the expectations of newcomers and there are some disillusionments.	6. Be prepared for some disappointments. However, some things may be better than you anticipated. Think positively. Try to balance the bad with the good.
7. The early phases of the socialization process are important for an individual's long-term career development.	7. Don't look for snap assignments. Find aspects of your new position that provide challenge. Try to obtain accurate feedback on your performance.
8. The organizational socialization process requires that the individual learn new roles. That some roles will conflict is inevitable.	8. Be realistic about the role requirements of your new position. Analyze any role conflicts that develop and try to reduce them with the help of your superior or others. Recognize your own perceptual limitations. When others have significantly different views of the organization, ask why. (Part of the difference may be *you* rather than the organization.)
9. The organizational socialization process can have several	9. Strive for creative individualism rather than total rebellion

Generalizations	Implications
outcomes; underconformity, ultraconformity, and creative individualism.	(better to leave) or absolute conformity (too high a price for you and for the organization).
10. During the individual's career he or she will be subject to continual resocialization.	10. Be responsive to the need to grow and change as you move into new positions and departments, assume managerial positions, and if it comes to it, change organizations.
11. People vary in degree to which they find satisfaction and self-fulfillment in their work organizations.	11. When embarking on a career it is important to think realistically about your life satisfactions in other than work activities. Work is important but it isn't everything. How will you develop a meaningful and well-balanced life from your career and other activities?

As a Current or Future Manager

Generalizations	Implications
1. The newcomer will have many uncertainties and anxieties about the work.	1. Recognize these feelings and empathize. It's easy to forget. Provide information and counseling to help the newcomer adjust.
2. Subcultural differences and past socialization may create variations in the expectations and behavior of newcomers.	2. As a manager you should be prepared to adjust to these variations. Don't expect to treat all people the same. Effective leadership means responding to individual differences.
3. More varied and heterogenous human inputs into organizations require more adaptive and creative socialization processes.	3. When utilizing a wider variety of people, such as women and minorities, you should be prepared to make personal and organizational adjustments. Don't assume that these newcomers will adapt totally to past practices.

Generalizations	Implications
4. Recruiters and managers frequently oversell the organization to newcomers. This can lead to disillusionment and frustration.	4. Don't oversell the organization. Provide realistic job previews. Tell both the good and the bad. Develop specific programs to provide this information.
5. There is evidence that certain personality types fit best into different situations.	5. Try to match the personality to organizational position. Don't hire the aggressive, achievement-oriented person to fill a routine role (or the reverse).
6. The socialization process is reciprocal; both the individual and the organization change.	6. Be prepared to change. Remember that over the long run the way most organizations remain dynamic and flexible is through the creativity and innovativeness of human resources.
7. A psychological contract is formed between the individual and the organization. It is in its most formative stages during the earlier period of socialization.	7. Think specifically about the psychological contract. What do you expect of the newcomer and what will you provide? Talk this over with him or her.
8. The early phases of work experience are very important for future performance.	8. To the extent possible, provide challenging assignments. At least strive to make some aspects of the job challenging. Let the employee help in designing challenging components.
9. Challenging, realistic goals and feedback on performance are especially important during the socialization process. The newcomer especially, wants to know, "How am I doing?"	9. Work with and help new employees set goals. Provide feedback on performance. (It is important to stress positive rather than negative feedback.) This may be done through a formalized management-by-objectives program, but it can also be done more informally through the manager interacting with employees.

Generalizations	Implications
10. Many people—immediate supervisors, peers, informal groups, and other managers—are involved in the socialization process.	10. Try to make effective use of other members to help in the socialization process. Encourage them to interact and provide feedback to newcomer. Work with others to establish a climate of support.
11. There are dangers in attempting to oversocialize the individual and to seek too much conformity.	11. You are not buying the total person. Try to keep the socialization process geared to pivotal issues. Remain flexible on other aspects.
12. Even the long-term manager doesn't see the total organization or the total person.	12. Recognize your own perceptual limitations. Be alert to inputs from newcomers (as well as others) that may provide alternative perception. Feedback on how the newcomer sees the organization can be valuable.
13. Organizational socialization processes are vitally important for both organization performance *and* human satisfaction.	13. Develop strategies for more effective socialization. Don't just go along with traditional, institutionalized, and often poorly thought-out programs. This is an area for careful planning.

LEARNING APPLICATION ACTIVITIES

1. Write a vignette, similar to those at the beginning of the chapter, that illustrates your experience with organizational socialization.

2. Use your imagination to complete the story of Carol Komoto in her first year in the CPA firm. Interview someone who has faced a similar experience. This will be especially useful if you are an accounting major.

3. What could Richard Grayson *(A Real Bust)* have done to minimize his difficulties during his socialization as a university instructor? How might he have prepared better for this experience?

4. Think about yourself as another person—different sex, race, age—and imagine your entry into a specific organization. For example, what might it be like to be the first woman in the United States Air Force Academy or the first male nurse in a hospital? What problems would you anticipate? What aspects would be appealing?

5. You have joined many groups and organizations and have been through the socialization process a number of times.

(a) Think about the psychological contract you "negotiated" with a specific organization and outline your expectations of the organization and its expectations of you.

(b) Evaluate how well your expectations have been met and how well you have fulfilled the organization's expectations of you.

6. Obtain information concerning the entry and orientation process for a specific organization. Contact the organization directly, visit your college placement center for information, or obtain information from a friend who is trying to find a job.

(a) What type of information does the organization provide the candidate?

(b) Do the company representatives provide a realistic job preview or are they overselling?

7. Consider the type of organization and the kind of job you want after you graduate.

(a) List your expectations for the general organizational climate.

(b) List your expectations for your first job.

8. *Step 1:* Write two brief scenarios, of several paragraphs each in which you describe: (1) an experience that you have had in being socialized into an organization; and (2) an experience in which you were involved in socializing another person into a group or organization.

Step 2: After you have written these scenarios, meet in groups of four to six to share your experiences. Discuss those factors that contributed to successful and unsuccessful socialization into organizations.

REFERENCES

Acker, Joan, and Donald R. Van Houten. "Differential Recruitment and Control: The Sex Structuring of Organizations." *Administrative Science Quarterly* 19 (June 1974): 152–163.

Berlew, David E., and Douglas T. Hall. "The Socialization of Managers: Effects of Expectation on Performance." *Administrative Science Quarterly* 11 (September 1966): 207–223.

Brim, Orville G., Jr., and Stanton Wheeler. *Socialization After Childhood: Two Essays.* New York: Wiley, 1966.

Broverman, Inge K., Susan Raymond Vogel, Donald M. Broverman, Frank E. Clarkson, and Paul S. Rosenkrantz. "Sex Role Stereotypes: A Current Appraisal." *Journal of Social Issues* 28/2 (1972): 59–78.

Buchanan, Bruce II. "Building Organizational Commitment: The Socialization of Managers in Work Organizations." *Administrative Science Quarterly* 19 (December 1974): 533–546.

Clausen, John A. (Ed.). *Socialization and Society.* Boston: Little, Brown, 1968.

Feldman, Daniel C. "A Practical Program for Employee Socialization." *Organizational Dynamics* 5/2 (Autumn 1976): 64–80.

Hall, Douglas T., and Francine S. Hall. "What's New in Career Management?" *Organizational Dynamics* 5/1 (Summer 1976): 17–33.

Hellriegel, Don, and John W. Slocum, Jr. "Organizational Climate: Measures, Research and Contingencies." *Academy of Management Journal* 17 (June 1974): 255–280.

Katz, Daniel, and Robert L. Kahn. *The Social Psychology of Organizations,* 2nd ed. New York: Wiley, 1978.

Kolb, David A., Irwin M. Rubin, and James M. McIntyre. *Organizational Psychology: An Experiential Approach,* 3d. ed. Englewood Cliffs, N.J.: Prentice-Hall, 1979.

Kraut, Allen I. "The Entrance of Black Employees into Traditionally White Jobs." *Academy of Management Journal* 18 (September 1975): 610–615.

Levinson, Harry. *The Exceptional Executive: A Psychological Conception.* Cambridge, Mass.: Harvard University Press, 1968.

Lorsch, Jay W., and John J. Morse. *Organizations and Their Members: A Contingency Approach.* New York: Harper & Row, 1974.

Mechanic, David. "Sources of Power of Lower Participants in Complex Organizations." *Administrative Science Quarterly* 7 (December 1962): 349–364.

Nord, Walter R. "Culture and Organizational Behavior." In *Concepts and Controversy in Organizational Behavior,* 2d. ed., pp. 197–211. Santa Monica, Calif.: Goodyear, 1976.

Payne, Roy, and Derek S. Pugh. "Organizational Structure and Climate." In Marvin D. Dunnette (Ed.), *Handbook of Industrial and Organizational Psychology,* pp. 1125–1175. Chicago: Rand McNally, 1976.

Perrow, Charles. *Organizational Analysis: A Sociological View.* Belmont, Calif.: Wadsworth, 1970.

Polk, Barbara Bovee. "Male Power and the Women's Movement." *The Journal of Applied Behavioral Sciences* 10 (Summer 1974): 415–431.

Porter, Lyman W., Edward E. Lawler III, and J. Richard Hackman. *Behavior in Organizations.* New York: McGraw-Hill, 1975.

Schein, Edgar H. "Organizational Socialization and the Profession of Management." *Industrial Management Review* 9/2 (Winter 1968): 1–16.

———. "The Individual, the Organization and the Career: A Conceptual Scheme." In David A. Kolb, Irwin M. Rubin, and James M. McIntyre (Eds.), *Organizational Psychology: A Book of Readings,* 2d ed., pp. 333–49. Englewood Cliffs, N.J.: Prentice-Hall, 1974.

Tagiuri, Renato, and George H. Litwin (Eds.) *Organizational Climate.* Boston: Division of Research, Graduate School of Business Administration, Harvard University, 1968.

Terkel, Studs. *Working: People Talk About What They Do All Day and How They Feel About What They Do.* New York: Pantheon Books, 1974.

Van Maanen, John. "People Processing: Strategies of Organizational Socialization." *Organizational Dynamics* 7/1 (Summer 1978): 18–36.

———"Police Socialization: A Longitudinal Examination of Job Attitudes in an Urban Police Department." *Administrative Science Quarterly* 20 (June 1975): 207–228.

Van Maanen, John, and Edgar H. Schein, "Toward a Theory of Organizational Socialization." In Barry M. Staw (Ed.), *Research in Organizational Behavior,* pp. 209–264. Greenwich, Conn.: JAI Press, 1979.

Wanous, John P. *Organizational Entry: Recruitment, Selection, and Socialization of Newcomers.* Reading, Mass.: Addison-Wesley, 1980.

Watson, John G., and Sam Barone. "The Self-Concept, Personal Values, and Motivational Orientations of Black and White Managers." *Academy of Management Journal* 19 (March 1976): 36–48.

Work in America, Report of a Special Task Force to the Secretary of Health, Education, and Welfare. Cambridge, Mass.: MIT Press, 1973.

3

Individual and Organizational Goals

LEARNING OBJECTIVES

After reading this chapter you should be able to:

1. Define goals and understand their functions.
2. Explain the importance of goals to individual behavior and organizational performance.
3. Understand the dynamics of goal-setting processes in organizations.
4. Discuss the relationships between goals, satisfaction, and performance.
5. Appreciate the nature of goal conflicts.

CLASS LIMITS

Bob Albright was upset. He needed the required course in organizational behavior, but the section of the class that he wanted was already full. He had a part-time job in the afternoon and tried to schedule morning classes. The advisor said the class was full, but that he might appeal to Professor Mary Garcia for special permission as an overload.

Bob attended the first day of class and then talked with Professor Garcia. There were five or six other students seeking admission to the class. Professor Garcia listened briefly to their stories, but then explained that there was a limit of 36 students and the class was already full. The class involved group discussions and projects designed for a moderate number of students. Besides, there were only 36 chairs in the room and they were occupied. The other students seeking admission left, but Bob stayed on to argue his case. He had to work to stay in school and needed the class for graduation. He even suggested that he would sit on the window sill if that would help. He gave it his best shot; Professor Garcia listened sympathetically, but she didn't give him permission to enter the class.

Bob recognized that further argument was fruitless, so he left grudgingly. "What kind of university is this anyway that it won't accommodate a little? Damned bureaucracy! I sure will be glad to get out of here!"

COME FLY WITH ME

Sally Toski graduated from college with a degree in sociology and joined International Airlines as a flight attendant. Her initiation into the world of airline travel began with an intensive six-week training program in all aspects of flight safety, service, and effective public relations with passengers. She was assigned a route between San Francisco and the Orient and found her job fascinating and challenging. After several years and additional training she was promoted to head flight attendant in charge of all activities in the cabin of the aircraft. She enjoyed this new position and received excellent performance reviews.

One of her responsibilities was to make reports on the probationary flight attendants assigned to her crew. She recognized the importance to the company of gathering information on every aspect of the probationary employees' work, including attitude, competence, relationships with other crew members, and customer satisfaction. However, Sally felt very uncomfortable giving anything less than a satisfactory rating to a new employee regardless of performance. She empathized with beginning employees and tended to make allowances for less than sterling performances.

About five months after her promotion, Sally was faced with the problem of reporting on a probationary employee, Margaret Murphy. Margaret evidenced little knowledge of how to perform her assigned duties and consequently slowed up the entire service. In addition, she had a noticeably poor attitude and was quite vocal in her complaints to co-workers about the demeaning nature of the work. She had little sympathy with passengers and Sally had to straighten out several misunderstandings. Sally clearly saw problems in Margaret's work attitude but she hesitated to turn in a really honest, negative performance report. After the six-month probationary period, Margaret became a permanent employee of the airline.

A GOAL CRISIS

In 1973, the National Tuberculosis and Respiratory Disease Association (TBRD) underwent a major reorganization to become the American Lung Association. Since the turn of the century, TBRD had been successful in obtaining contributions for Christmas Seals that helped "fight" tuberculosis. These monies were used for research and support of various sanitariums and for educating the public in preventive measures aimed at the dreaded contagion, "consumption." The programs were successful and helped significantly to conquer the disease, but this very success led to a goal crisis for the association.

With TB under control and the major goal achieved, was there a need for the organization to continue? The situation was similar to the change that the National Foundation for Infantile Paralysis experienced when the Salk vaccine was developed and used to combat polio. Although TBRD had accomplished its major goals, there was an existing organization that had been highly successful in receiving contributions. There were also a substantial number of people committed to the organization.

In 1973, TBRD announced its new "goal for action." It had decided to turn attention to other respiratory diseases such as emphysema, asthma, and lung cancer. To reflect this new goal, the name was changed to the American Lung Association. However, there was considerable confusion among the staff, volunteers, and public concerning this transformation. Under the old association, the goal had been clear—eradicate TB—and there was significant commitment to this goal. The new association had a much less precise goal and consequently had more difficulty in establishing a clear identity.

COME, LET US ALL SING TOGETHER

Community Church was in the process of choosing a new senior choir director. One of the selection committee members said, "I like Robert's high standards and his dedication to hard work. As a choir we really do like to sound good and it seems that he would help us accomplish this." The minister spoke up: "Since Robert said that he was a minister's son, we could expect that he would understand the goals of the church." Another choir member on the committee said, "Robert came to church last Sunday to hear the choir. I thought we sang rather well and I was surprised that he was so critical when we talked with him later. However, he did show good musical analysis so I imagine he knows what he is talking about and really could help us."

The decision was made to hire Robert and, at his first choir rehearsal, he spoke of his dedication to music. "I know your previous director. He is a good friend and a fine musician, but quite easygoing. I am not that way. When I am working, I work hard, and I expect you to do likewise while we are rehearsing. Socializing and talking are for other times." Robert had the choir spend a great deal of time on each musical phrase and demanded perfection. The minister and the music director heard comments from the choir members such as, "I am so tired of singing the same little bit over and over. Robert never lets us think for ourselves. He treats us like children." In one rehearsal, one of the altos turned around and whispered to the men singing behind her: "That really sounded good that time!" Robert saw her turn and snapped, "We've just wasted thirty seconds of rehearsal time!"

Time passed and members of the congregation stopped by after the services to tell the minister how much better the choir sounded and how polished they seemed. "Our new choir director certainly knows his business."

After several months, the music director and the minister met with Robert to discuss the progress of the choir. They both noted how well the choir was sounding and that the congregation had many favorable comments. However, they suggested that there were complaints from the choir members. Robert's frustration boiled over. "I can't understand their complaints. They're lazy and just don't want to work hard. They forget everything from one week to the next! They seem to think that rehearsal is a social session and don't really understand the importance of perfection in music."

The minister was in a dilemma. He knew that the choir was technically better than it had ever been. However, he was sensitive to the interpersonal conflicts and complaints that seemed to be pulling the choir apart. He had come to the church four years before when it was suffering a declining membership and had worked hard to restore the interest and good will of the congregation. He did not wish to see his efforts at rebuilding people's concern for each other torn to shreds.

LET THEM EAT MUSH

Mary Washington had recently graduated from the university with a degree in dental hygiene. She began working in her home town for Dr. Garrity, her family dentist. She had known him for a long time. In fact, he had encouraged her to go into dental hygiene and she looked forward to her new job. During the first few weeks, Mary began to realize that the training she received at the university was quite idealistic compared to the way Dr. Garrity ran his dental practice.

"Preventive dentistry" had received special emphasis throughout Mary's training. She had learned about the importance of giving patients complete and accurate information about their oral health so that they could take responsibility for preventing their own dental disease. She had also learned that 90 percent of the adult population has periodontal (gum) disease and that this causes far more tooth loss than dental decay. Mary felt professionally obligated to treat and educate her patients about the prevention of dental disease.

When Dr. Garrity discovered that Mary was spending fifteen minutes out of every hour in "non-service oriented" patient education he expressed the view that patients expected a full hour of "hands-on" treatment. He felt that trying to educate patients was a waste of time because the patients didn't care about preventing dental disease anyway.

Several weeks later, the receptionist pointed out to Dr. Garrity that Mary was reappointing many patients for the completion of their oral prophylaxis (tooth cleaning) and many of them were needing three or four extra appointments. Dr. Garrity was enraged with Mary's "slow work" and said that all his patients had grown accustomed to having their teeth cleaned in one appointment. Mary replied that she found advanced cases of periodontal disease in most of his patients. It concerned her that patient records showed no acknowledgment of these conditions which had obviously existed for years. The previous hygienist had evidently only cleaned above the gum line and had left heavy scales of tartar on the teeth. Mary felt that many of these patients should be referred to a periodontist for special treatment but Dr. Garrity refused to entertain this idea. He remarked, "Mary, I know that you are young and idealistic, but the fact is that patients come to the dentist for fillings and that's about it. People can't afford periodontal surgery anyway so the best we can do is keep filling their teeth until the periodontal disease gets so bad that they need dentures."

Mary felt defeated. She spent the next several months practicing dental hygiene as Dr. Garrity expected her to. She finished in one hour, knowing that she was leaving many areas of gum disease untouched. She no longer discussed dental disease prevention with her patients and discovered that it made her job much easier. The patients were happier because the cleaning only took one hour and they did not suffer as much discomfort during the procedure. Dr. Garrity was extremely pleased with the way things were running in his office and offered Mary a small raise in salary. Two weeks later Mary submitted a one week notice of resignation and found a job in another office.

Source: Written by Karen A. Brown, Albers School of Business, Seattle University.

INTRODUCTION

These incidents seem to have little in common. On closer inspection, however, they all deal with the issue of individual and organizational goals. As individuals, all of us have goals that we are trying to achieve. For you, it may be obtaining a college degree and finding a good job. Or, becoming a better skier or tennis player. Even though we may not recognize it explicitly, our individual behavior is directed toward achieving a wide variety of explicit and implicit goals. Humans attempt to be purposive. The same is true for organizations. They have goals that help direct their activities and provide a basis for measuring performance. Profitability for the business firm; successful patient care for the hospital; rehabilitation of inmates for the custodial institution; achieving national recognition for a university; nuclear deterrence for the military; all are examples of organizational goals.

The incidents illustrate individual and organizational goals, but, even more dramatically, they suggest that the determination and integration of diverse goals is often difficult. There are problems in establishing overall goals which guide organizational activities. The National Tuberculosis and Respiratory Disease Association had an overriding goal but when TB was conquered there was a goal crisis. In the church incident, two goals conflicted: Was it more important to have the most professional sounding choir or to have a "good" choir with satisfied members and friendly relationships?

The incidents also illustrate the potential conflict between the personal goals of individuals and those of the organization. Bob Albright had the goal of graduation and desperately needed the class. However, Professor Garcia saw the need to maintain the limits so that the appropriate climate for interpersonal interactions could be achieved. As head flight attendant, Sally Toski saw the organizational goal of trying to screen out ineffective flight attendants but could not bring herself around to giving a negative report. Dental hygienist Mary Washington tried to adhere to her professional goals of excellent dental care, but these ran counter to Dr. Garrity's more pragmatic views.

As individuals, we are continually faced with the issue of which goals we really want and how much effort we are willing to put into achieving them. We may desire higher grades, but we also want to spend more time sailing, skiing, and golfing or working part-time to buy a car. Goal conflicts arise between individuals when achieving one goal means that others must sacrifice theirs. In this chapter we will look more closely at individual and organizational goals under the following topics:

What are Goals?
The Importance of Values
All Organizations Have Goals
Goals of the Individual Participant
Commitment to the Organization
Relationship Between Goals and Performance
Goal Conflicts
So What? Implications for You

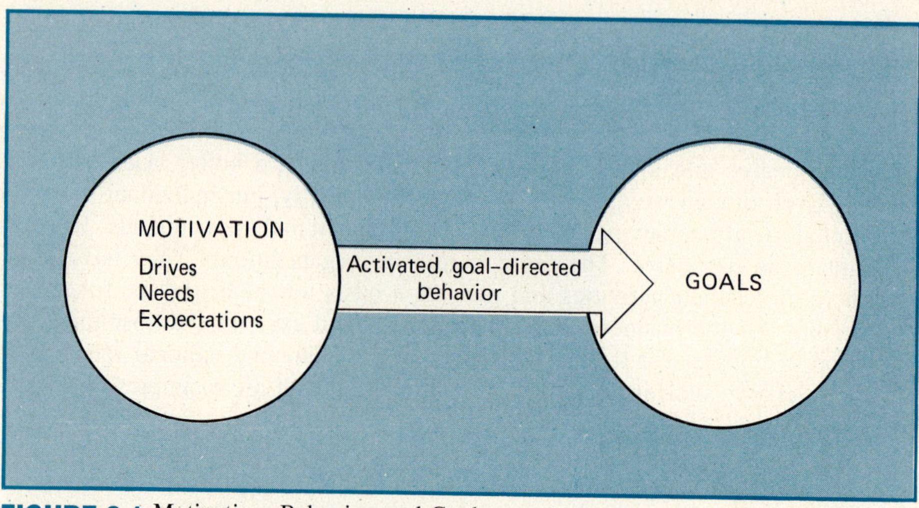

FIGURE 3.1 Motivation, Behavior, and Goals

WHAT ARE GOALS?

Goals are *representations of future conditions that individuals, groups, or organizations desire and strive to achieve.* Simply stated, they are desired results toward which behavior is directed. In this sense, goals include missions, purposes, objectives, targets, quotas, and deadlines. Individuals entertain personal goals and they try to act or behave in ways necessary to achieve them. Collectivities, such as groups and organizations, also have a variety of goals that direct activities. It is important to recognize that *goals give direction to behavior.* We have a vast potential for behaving in different ways, but our actual behavior is determined by our intended goals. The same it true for groups and organizations. Behavior is goal directed. For example, you have the goal of completing your education. This goal affects your behavior and directs a great many of your activities. Once you have established such a goal, it constrains the ways you behave. You might like to go to Hawaii or Bermuda in the middle of winter classes, but this would not be compatible with your goal of graduating in June. Managers might like to be more responsive to society's needs, but they must make a profit to survive. Thus goals not only provide direction to behavior; they also serve as major constraints and limitations on the ways we act.

The relationship between motivation, behavior, and goals is illustrated in Figure 3.1. A *motive* is that which prompts a person to act in a certain way or at least develop a propensity for a specific behavior. This urge to act is directed at the accomplishment of goals. The process of motivation will be discussed more completely in Chapter 4, "Motivation and Performance."

Official and Operational Goals

The real importance of a goal is how it affects behavior. How much effort and commitment is the individual or organization willing to make in order to accomplish the goal? A student may have a stated goal of graduating *magna cum laude*. However, if he only works at the level of C−, just enough to survive, then the expressed goal has had little effect on behavior. Simply stating an official goal does not make it real unless actual behavior is directed toward achieving it.

This is a particularly difficult problem when analyzing organizational goals. Official goals are often stated in broad, ambiguous terms to justify the activities of the organization. For example, the official goal of a mental hospital may be to treat and cure mental illness. However, the hospital may be geared to the custodial care of patients and actually provide little in the way of treatment. In other words, its stated goals may be nonoperational. We are concerned here primarily with the operational goals of individuals and organizations: those that actually provide direction to behavior.

THE IMPORTANCE OF VALUES

Our basic values affect the goals we set and the means for their accomplishment. Value systems provide an overall frame of reference for goal setting; they are normative views held by individuals (consciously or subconsciously) of what is good or desirable. Values provide standards by which people are influenced in their choice of actions. Social values reflect a system of shared beliefs about desired goals and norms for human conduct. When we use the words "should" or "ought," we are making value statements. The Ten Commandments are value statements about desirable human behavior. The laws of a nation are value systems in elaborate codified form governing both personal and organizational behavior. The Bill of Rights is a reflection of our society's emphasis on individual freedom.

Organizations appear to hold certain values, but defining them precisely and showing how they influence goal setting and decision making is difficult. However, there are several broad generalizations that apply. Organizations depend for their very existence on some minimum level of commonality with the external society and among internal participants. Every human participant brings a certain set of values to the organization. The influx of values comes also from a wide variety of external sources: customers, competitors, suppliers, governments, and other elements of the organization's task environment. In considering issues of value, we should recognize at least five levels (Kast & Rosenzweig, 1979, p. 150):

Individual values. Those values held by individuals that affect their actions.

Group values. Those values held by small informal and formal groups that affect the behavior of individuals and also the actions of the organization.

Organizational values. Those values held by the organization as a whole: a composite of individual, group, total organizational, and cultural inputs.

Values of constituents of the environment. Values held by those in direct contact with the organization: customers, suppliers, competitors, government agencies, and the like.

Cultural values. Values held by the entire society.

Value systems provide a framework for goal setting. They provide the means for determining: (1) which goals are legitimate or illegitimate; (2) relative merit among several goals; and (3) the legitimacy or merit of potential means for achieving goals. In the incidents at the beginning of this chapter, we saw how the values of individuals strongly influenced their goals and their behavior. For example, dental hygienist Mary Washington had adopted certain professional values during her education that ran counter to Dr. Garrity's views. The Community Church was suffering a major value conflict between technical excellence and congenial social climate.

ALL ORGANIZATIONS HAVE GOALS

Organizations are goal-seeking systems. They are created to serve purposes that individuals and informal groups cannot accomplish. Organizational goals pertain to the purposes and desired conditions which the organization seeks to achieve. Survival, growth, profitability, and stability are examples of such goals. Yet, even though it is useful to talk about organizational goals, we should recognize that the idea of such goals is a convenient abstraction that to some extent personifies the organization: attributing individual human qualities to a social system. In fact, individuals have goals but collectivities of people do not. That is to say, the actual goals of any organization are a reflection or composite of all the individuals who can influence the activities of the organization. "The important point is that the goal of any organization is an abstraction distilled from the desires of members and pressures from the environment and internal system" (Hall, 1977, p. 70). In this view, an organization is a coalition of many individual participants, each of whom has individual goals that they are attempting to satisfy through collective activities. Stockholders, executives, employees, customers, suppliers, and many others have goals that they try to impose on the business organization. These organizational participants have different and frequently conflicting goals. The actual operational goals of the organization result from a continuous bargaining/learning process. Therefore, organizations have multiple goals. These goals are frequently not stated officially and are often in conflict. There may be inconsistencies and ambiguities. The goal-set of the organization is continually changing as a result of this process.

With this view in mind, we can consider goals from three primary perspectives: (1) the environmental level—the constraints imposed on the organization by society; (2) the organizational level—the goals of the organization as a system; and (3) the individual level—the goals of the organizational participants.

If the organization is to survive, it must perform a function for the broader society. It needs inputs of resources and people, and the society must be willing to accept and utilize the outputs. For example, the business organization receives inputs from the society in the form of people, materials, money, and information; it transforms these into outputs of products, services, and rewards to the organizational members sufficiently large to maintain their participation. For the business organization, the market provides a mechanism for recycling of resources between the firms and its environment. Organizations as a subsystem of their environment must accomplish certain goals and operate under constraints that are determined by the broader society. For example, the automotive company must compete with domestic and foreign car producers in attracting customers. However, it must also operate under governmental constraints concerning safety, pollution, and fuel economy. These environmental forces have a significant impact on the operating goals of the organization.

Organizational goals express the purposes and desired conditions that the organization seeks as a distinct entity. Wide variations in activities make it difficult to delineate any goal-set that would be appropriate for all organizations. In business organizations there is a trend toward more explicit definitions of the multiple goals necessary for effective and efficient long-term operations. Peter Drucker was among the first to emphasize the importance of "managing by objectives." He suggested that "objectives are needed in every area where performance and results directly and vitally affect the survival and prosperity of the business" (Drucker, 1954, p. 63). He advocated that objectives be set in eight areas: (1) market standing; (2) innovation; (3) productivity; (4) physical and financial resources; (5) profitability, (6) manager performance and development; (7) worker performance and attitude; and (8) public responsibility.

While this listing of objectives is appropriate for most business organizations, it is not readily transferable to all organizational types. Gross provides a more generalized model (suitable for all organizations) shown in Figure 3.2.

The Function of Goals

The goal-setting process and its value to the organization is becoming increasingly recognized in both the private and public sectors. The establishment of goals in businesses, with their profit-incentive, is relatively less complex than in universities, hospitals, and other public-service organizations. However, even in public organizations there is a growing awareness that clearly defined and integrated goals are vital to the effective and efficient management of operations. Operational goals in the organization may function to:

1. *Legitimize activities* of the organization in the society.
2. *Guide activities* by focusing attention and behavior in purposeful directions.
3. *Develop commitment* of various individuals and groups to organizationally desired activities.
4. *Serve as standards* to assess the performance of the organization.
5. *Reduce uncertainties* in the decision-making processes.
6. *Evaluate change* and serve as a basis for organizational learning and adaptation.
7. *Provide a basis for structural design* by setting the initial constraints for determining which structures are appropriate to which tasks.
8. *Set the framework for the planning and control system* of which goal-making is the foundation. (Albanese, 1978, p. 48; Porter, Lawler, & Hackman, 1975, pp. 78–79; Hrebiniak, 1978, p. 53.)

Satisfaction of interests Organizations exist to satisfy the interest (or needs, desires, or wants) of various people, both members and outsiders. These interests are multiple, hard to identify, and overlapping. The satisfaction (or dissatisfaction) of these interests may vary by its intensity and by the location and number of people involved. This category of purposes is close to what is often referred to as *welfare, utility, benefit,* or *payoff.*

Output of services or goods The output of an organization is composed of those products which it makes available for use by clients. These products may consist of services (tangible or nontangible) or goods. The quality and quantity of any product may sometimes be expressed in monetary as well as physical units. From the viewpoint of the organization as a whole, the output of any unit or individual is an intermediate or partial product rather than an end product.

Efficiency or profitability When available inputs are perceived as scarce, attention is directed toward making efficient use of inputs relative to output. Since there are many ways of calculating input and output and of relating the two, there are many varieties of input-output objectives. Some of them are referred to as "efficiency" or "productivity." "Profitability" is applicable whenever output as well as input may be expressed in monetary terms.

Investment in organizational viability In a minimal sense viability means the survival of an organization without which no other purposes are feasible. In a fuller sense it refers to an organization's growth. In either sense viability requires the diversion of inputs from the production of output and their investment in physical, human and organizational assets.

Mobilization of resources In order to produce services or goods and to invest in viability, an organization must mobilize resources that may be used as inputs. Because of the difficulties of obtaining scarce resources from the environment, "mobilization logic" may differ from "use logic."

Observance of codes Codes include both the formal and informal rules developed by the organization and its various units and the prescribed behaviors imposed upon the organization by law, morality and professional ethics. These codes may be expressed in terms of what is expected or what is prohibited. In either case, code observance purposes are usually expressed in terms of tolerated margins of deviation.

Rationality Rationality here refers to action patterns regarded as satisfactory in terms of desirability, feasibility, and consistency. *Technical* rationality involves use of the best methods developed by science and technology. *Administrative* rationality involves the use of the best methods of governing organizations.

FIGURE 3.2 Major Categories of Organizational Goals. **Source:** Bertram M. Gross, *Organizations and Their Managing,* © 1968 by The Free Press, a division of Macmillan Publishing Co., Inc.

Goal-Setting Processes

The goal-setting process is frequently a combination of rational, deterministic methods and adaptive, bargaining approaches. Although all organizations can point to formally expressed or informally determined goals, the goal-setting process is actually a complex interplay of internal and external forces and constraints. "In practice, goals are often set in a complicated power play involving various individuals and groups within and without the organization, and by reference to values which govern behavior in general and the specific behavior of the relevant individuals and groups in a particular society" (Etzioni, 1964, pp. 7–8).

Organizations are learning, adapting systems with multiple goals. This view stands in contrast to that of the organization as a mechanistic system contrived to maximize a single goal. Goal-setting is primarily a political process. Goals are formulated as a result of bargaining among the various interest groups. Thus, stockholders require profits, employees want wages and favorable working environments, managers desire power and prestige, and customers demand quality products. The membership of participating groups and the balance of power change over time; therefore, the goals of the organization are continually shifting to reflect these changes. Because the demands of the various participating groups are frequently in conflict, it is rarely possible to maximize the goals of any one individual or group. Rather, the organization seeks to satisfy the goals of all parties in order to maintain their participation.

Goals are also continually being modified because of changing aspirations. The business that has achieved its sales quota within a given year will usually raise its goals. Lack of success will cause the organization to seek alternative means, or, if this is unsuccessful, to adjust the goal downward.

In most organizations there is a hierarchy of goals ranging from broad statements of mission down to more specific operational objectives. A statement of mission is usually of a general nature and its degree of achievement is difficult to measure. For example, most universities define their mission as the transmission of knowledge (teaching), the creation of knowledge (research), and the application of knowledge (service to the community). To fulfill this mission it is necessary at some point to establish operational goals in each of these areas.

In analyzing goals it is necessary to decide how they are to be accomplished—the *means* of attainment. In the organization, the relationship between ends and means is hierarchical. Goals established at one level require certain means for their accomplishment. These means then become the goals for the next level, and more specific operational objectives are developed as we move down the hierarchy. A fire department has the primary goal of reducing fire losses. The means for attaining this end are preventing and extinguishing fires. These means then become the goals of the next level in the organization and lead to the creation of two functions—fire prevention and fire fighting.

The hierarchy of goals has important implications for organization structure. Generally, the division of labor and functional specialization within the organization are based on the ends-means chain. The business organization may have sales, finance, production, and research departments, each of which has specific goals related to its functional area. This development of more specialized goals for different units frequently leads to interdepartmental goal conflicts. For example, the sales department's goal may be increased sales, the production department's efficient production, the finance department's efficient capital utilization, and the research department's goal the development of new products. These goals may not be totally compatible; maximizing the performance of one department may lead to sacrificing the goals of another. The sales department's goal of increased sales might lead to a wider and more varied product line. This could run counter to the production department's goal of efficient output through standardization and high-volume runs. The finance department's goal of efficient use of funds might be in conflict with the research goal of product improvements that promise a long-term and uncertain payoff. This is another reason why the goal structure of the organization is never perfectly rational. The actual goals are the result of the power interplay and negotiations among different departments and individuals.

GOALS OF THE INDIVIDUAL PARTICIPANT

We have suggested that the environment provides certain constraints and determinants of organizational goals and that systems goals are developed by the collectivity of people comprising the organization. We turn now to the third level of analysis, the goals of individual participants.

Individual behavior is goal directed. This, however, should not be interpreted to mean that as individuals we always establish clearly defined and well-articulated goals to guide our behavior. It clearly depends on the situation. Where the situation is relatively certain and we have a well-defined task, it is likely that we will engage in a rational, analytic process that specifies definite and measurable goals. For example, you may have established certain goals for your course grades this term and planned your behavior accordingly. However, when faced with an unpredictable environment—such as what the job market will be at your time of graduation—or a dilemma of conflicting personal values—such as a change in career direction—we tend to have fairly general and ill-defined goals.

In situations of the latter type, we are actually involved in *domain and direction* planning rather than goal-directed planning.

> Most people feel they *should* choose their goals first and then plan their actions in light of these goals. The norm is that one should act and plan in light of predetermined, and preferably quite specific, goals. For many Americans the rational norm is so strong that we are puzzled and upset when this expectation is violated. This article argues that the rational norm holds for only some planning situations. Indeed, in many situations, we may discover our goals only by acting (McCaskey, 1977, p. 456).

Faced with external or internal uncertainty, we develop broad images about our future and establish general domains within which we operate. As McCaskey puts it, "A person's choice of a domain marks his or her boundaries for action and commitment" (p. 457).

This statement is applicable to much of our behavior. For an example close at hand: the present authors did not specifically establish a goal of writing a textbook in organizational behavior until long after they had developed a general interest in the domain and some commitment to the field. Teaching classes, testing ideas with students and colleagues, and much else *preceded* the goal of writing this book. In effect, the plunge into the domain was taken and the goal, rather than directing activities, emerged out of them. Think carefully a moment about your own life and you will probably recognize a similar series of circumstances.

We have suggested that organizations are established to accomplish purposes that cannot be accomplished by individual actions. It is tempting to assume that organizational goals and the goals of individual participants are complementary. This, in effect, was the assumption of classical economic theory and most traditional management theories. Employees were compensated through monetary and other inducements for their participation in meeting organizational goals, thus assuring that they adhere to the organization's goals. This simple assumption of compatibility failed to take into account many built-in bases for conflict between organization and individual goals. First, people are much more complex than the rational-economic assumptions. We have many needs and aspirations that are not easily met in purely economic terms. Second, the organization itself has a complex, multiple-goal set.

The early investigators of human relations in organizations saw the need for greater emphasis on human satisfaction as well as technical efficiency. "An industrial organization may be regarded as performing two major functions, that of producing a product and that of creating and distributing satisfactions among the individual members of the organization" (Roethlisberger & Dickson, 1939, p. 552). Although they saw the need for creating greater human satisfaction, it was frequently viewed as a *means* for obtaining better organizational efficiency rather than as an end in itself. Increased satisfaction would lead to organizational goal accomplishment.

There is a trend toward thinking of *participant satisfaction* as a primary goal.

> We are not merely interested in the economic success or technological efficiency aspects of a system, but also and more importantly in its social efficiency aspects. . . . In general, social efficiency entails personal goal attainment on the part of the members at all levels in an organization, and this includes involvement, satisfaction, participation, and other variables associated with intrinsic motives and psychological rewards (Georgopoulos, 1973, p. 104).

We raise an even more critical issue when we question whether or not organizational goals and human needs are compatible. Many practices that are developed to increase organizational efficiency may create human dissatisfactions. A high degree of task specialization on the assembly line may lead to technical efficiency but may also create employee apathy and boredom. A rigid authority structure may seem desirable from the managers' standpoint, but others may resist effectively.

However, we should not over-emphasize the possible conflict between organizational goals and human satisfaction.

> Within limits, happiness heightens efficiency in organizations and, conversely, without efficient organizations much of our happiness is unthinkable. Without well-run organizations our standard of living, our level of

> culture, and our democratic life could not be maintained. Thus, to a degree, *organizational rationality and human happiness go hand in hand.* But a point is reached in every organization where happiness and efficiency cease to support each other. Not all work can be well-paid or gratifying, and not all regulations and orders can be made acceptable. Here we face a true dilemma (Etzioni, 1964, p. 2).

In the following discussion we do not assume that organization and individual goals are either compatible or incompatible; they are both. Without a minimum degree of compatibility, organizations could not exist. But, total agreement is impossible and goal conflicts do exist.

Inducements/Contributions Model

The inducements/contributions model provides a basis for understanding the relationship between personal and organizational goals (Barnard, 1938). The basic aspects of this model are:

1. An organization is a system of interrelated social behaviors of a number of persons whom we shall call the *participants* in the organization.
2. Each participant and each group of participants receives *inducements from* the organization in return for which he makes *contributions to* the organization.
3. Each participant will continue to participate in an organization only as long as the inducements offered him are as great or greater (measured in terms of *his* values and in terms of the alternatives open to him) than the contributions he is asked to make.
4. The contributions provided by the various groups of participants are the source from which the organization manufactures the inducements offered to participants.
5. Hence, an organization is "solvent"—and will continue in existence—only as long as the contributions are sufficient to provide inducements in large enough measure to draw forth these contributions (March & Simon, 1958, p. 84).

Individuals will continue to participate in the attainment of organizational goals only as long as the organization provides inducements that meet their personal goals. This inducement may be primary if the goals of the organization have direct personal value for the individual—such as church membership or participation in a voluntary charitable organization—or secondary if the organization offers personal rewards—money, status, position—to individuals in return for their contributions. The latter case is probably true for most employees in business organizations.

In this model, once the individual has made the decision to participate, she accepts an organizational role. The role prescriptions require that her actions be guided primarily by organizational goals that become internalized: automatically evoked and applied during performance of the role.

> By whatever means the individual was originally motivated to adopt the role in the first place, the goals and constraints appropriate to the role become a part of the decision-making program, stored in his memory, that defines his role behavior (Simon, 1964, p. 13).

COMMITMENT TO THE ORGANIZATION

The inducements-contributions model suggests a reciprocal relationship between the individual and the organization. It is apparent that individuals who are committed to organizational goals are more likely to be high performers and more likely to have a higher level of satisfaction. Commitment strengthens the ties between the individual and the organization and contributes greatly to performance, success, and satisfaction. Committed people are less likely to leave the organization, have lower absenteeism, and generally require less supervision and control. Through commitment there is a fusion of individual and organizational goals and the relationship is personalized. This involvement causes the individual to perceive individual and organizational success as highly compatible.

Commitment can be thought of in terms of: (1) a sense of identification with the organizational mission; (2) a feeling of involvement or psychological immersion in organizational duties; and (3) a feeling of loyalty and affection for the organization as a place to live and work (Buchanan, 1975, p. 68). The degree of an individual's commitment appears to be directly associated with the length of tenure (long-term employees tending to show higher commitment), surrounding group attitudes toward the organization, early (first year) job challenges, history of hierarchical advancement and personal achievement, task identity, and the extent to which a positive self-image is reinforced by the organization (Steers, 1977). Commitment is thus a function of the inducement/contribution model discussed above. That is, individuals who perceive a favorable balance between the inducements and their individual contributions have high commitment.

Internalization of Organizational Values and Goals

Through the socialization process and the development of the psychological contract the individual usually accepts and internalizes various organizational values and goals. The person accepts these as his or her own and begins thinking in terms of "my team" or "my school" or "my company." Internalization occurs when the individual develops a personal commitment to achieve organizational goals. It is one of the most effective means of integration because it removes conflicts between individual and organizational goals. But this is rarely if ever totally accomplished. Few participants are fully committed to all organizational goals. However, to the degree that individuals do internalize organizational values and goals and develop high commitment, it is a key factor in providing integration. It helps develop intrinsic control of individual behavior and minimizes the need for extrinsic controls. This type of involvement is more likely to be found for active members in voluntary associations such as political parties and religious organizations. It is typically found among the managerial elites in business corporations and public organizations, but less likely among lower-level participants. It is almost never found among inmates in coercive organizations such as correctional institutions.

RELATIONSHIP BETWEEN GOALS AND PERFORMANCE

A major issue for individuals and organizations is the relationship between the establishment of goals and subsequent performance. Does the fact that we have specific and obtainable goals affect our effort and performance? We had some insights into these issues in the incident concerning the National Tuberculosis and Respiratory Disease Association. The clearly defined goal of eliminating tuberculosis did seem to provide a sense of organizational direction and led to a high level of commitment, effort, and performance. It was more difficult to focus activities on the more generalized goal of fighting a vast array of respiratory diseases.

Investigations

Many early psychological investigations found that successful goal achievement tends to increase levels of aspiration (Lewin, 1944); that is, when a goal is achieved, more difficult goals are set for future performance. This tends to hold true for organizations as well as individuals (Cyert & March, 1963, pp. 34–43). For example, when the corporation has been successful in attaining sales or profit goals, it typically sets higher goals for the next year.

Recent studies have set up ways for looking more specifically at the problem. Defining *goal* as simply that which the individual is consciously trying to accomplish, Locke and his associates (1968) paved the way in a series of controlled laboratory experiments that tested the effects of goal setting on performance; subsequent research generally supported their model of conscious goals regulating actions (Latham & Yukl, 1975). Concepts deriving from these studies have been applied in a number of organizations. Based on 27 field studies of the relationship between goal setting and performance, Latham and Yukl found substantial support for the following ideas:

1. Difficult goals, when accepted by the individual, tend to lead to higher levels of performance than do easy goals.
2. Specific goals tend to lead to higher levels of performance than do generalized goals or no goals.
3. Performance feedback (knowledge of results) tends to lead to the establishment of more difficult goals *and* to higher levels of performance.
4. In contrast to performance feedback, monetary incentives are more likely to increase goal acceptance and commitment than to induce an individual to set harder goals.
5. With respect to the question of whether participative goal setting results in higher performance than assigned goals, the research results are not conclusive. There is some supportive evidence of the superiority of

HERMAN

"Your dinner's getting cold."

participative goal setting, but only under certain conditions and with certain types of employees.

There is the need for further testing of these concepts, particularly in field research. However, there is sufficient evidence to suggest that these conclusions have direct applicability for the manager, particularly in designing programs such as management-by-objectives (Latham & Locke, 1979).

Goal-Setting Process, Performance, and Satisfaction

Difficult and specific goals lead to higher performance, but only when *accepted by the individual*. This qualification is important. Unless the individual accepts and is committed to the goals, performance does not improve. In fact, the reverse may follow; difficult goals that are assigned but not accepted may actually lead to resistance, apathy, and a decline in both performance and satisfaction. A key issue for the manager, therefore, is not only the establishment of goals, but the development of a goal-setting process that will maximize acceptance and commitment.

Intuitively, we would like to believe that a participative or collaborative setting of goals leads to higher levels of acceptance, performance, and satisfaction than does the assignment of goals from above. Vroom expresses this view:

> When the entire pattern of results is considered, we find substantial basis for the belief that participation in decision making increases productivity (Vroom, 1964, p. 226).

The literature is not in total agreement on the point. While a number of studies have found a positive relationship between participation and performance (Coch & French, 1948; Likert, 1961), others have found little relationship between these variables (Ivancevich, 1976; Latham & Yukl, 1976). However, there do not appear to be any studies suggesting that participation will decrease performance; this is encouraging for our viewpoint.

There is a logical basis, if not yet a conclusive empirical one, for suggesting the importance of participation in the positive motivation of employees to meet organizational goals (Mitchell, 1973). Participation helps clarify expectations and increases the likelihood that employees will work for outcomes they value. Participation increases the effect of social influence on behavior; that is, collaboratively set goals tend to be reinforced by the social group. Participation also increases the amount of control that the individual has over his or her own behavior.

There is stronger research evidence to indicate that participation in goal setting leads to higher levels of satisfaction than does assignment of goals from above. But, the participation must be genuine to have this positive effect. Pseudo-participation ("They asked us but they really didn't want our view") has adverse consequences for both performance and satisfaction. In fact, it generally leads to worse consequences than assigned goals and autocratic decisions.

There is also sound evidence that feedback to employees on their performance tends to increase both quality of performance and level of satisfaction. Positive feedback seems to be best, but any type of feedback is better than none. People, particularly those with high-achievement motivation, want to have knowledge about how well they are performing. Without such feedback they lose interest and both performance and satisfaction suffer.

This discussion suggests some general guidelines for practicing managers: (1) difficult and specific (measurable) goals tend to improve performance; (2) participation is likely to improve acceptance of goals; and (3) feedback on performance in achieving goals is positively related to performance and satisfaction. These concepts seem simple and rather obvious. However, they are frequently violated in real-world situations.

GOAL CONFLICTS

There are many potential goal conflicts in organizations. Frequently these occur at the individual level, where it is difficult to satisfy divergent goals. For example, should you seek a position that pays the highest immediate salary or one that offers the best long-run career opportunities? As individuals, we are seeking to satisfy multiple, and often conflicting, personal goals in our organizational experiences.

In addition, there are many potential areas of conflict between the needs

BOX 3.1
INDIVIDUAL AND ORGANIZATION

"The organization is different from the sum of its members," conveys a concept important to administration. An organization or collectivity has requirements for its survival and growth that are often distinct from the requirements for its members' security and development. . . .

An administrator or manager typically faces criteria of both individual and organization; as a person, one has personal needs and attitudes that serve to guide action, and as an administrator, one has organizational role obligations that provide guides to ensure the organization's well-being. At times, these criteria are mutually supportive—achievement of one's personal objectives often contributes to organizational objectives and, over time, organizational objectives are necessary for the fulfillment of individual needs. All too often, however, these equally valid and desirable criteria conflict, giving rise to dilemmas of administration.

Source: John D. Aram, *Dilemmas of Administrative Behavior* (Englewood Cliffs, N.J.: Prentice-Hall, 1976), p. 3. © 1976. Reprinted by permission.

and goals of the organization and those of its members. This is a basic dilemma facing all members of social organizations. We cannot accomplish our goals as isolated individuals; and the requirements of organized activity demand that we subordinate some of our individual autonomy in order to cooperate in organizational endeavors.

Goal conflicts also occur within and among informal and formal groups in organizations.

> These we may term *organizational conflicts* because they are either institutionalized (a direct result of formal organization and technological processes) or emergent (emerging informally within the formal organizational context as a result of individual and social goals). Because the organization is a goal-directed system composed of independent goal-seeking subsystems, it is probably inevitable that subsystems or individuals within the organization will experience conflict. Competition for scarce resources or goals is the substance of organizational conflict (Herbert, 1976, p. 351).

In Chapter 8, "Conflict and its Management," we will look in more detail at various types of organizational conflicts. In this section, we are concerned with the existing tension between individual and organization.

A Continuing Dilemma

Many contemporary behavioral scientists see a continuing conflict between organizational role requirements and individual goals. McGregor was among the first to investigate this conflict. He said that the traditional managerial approach (Theory X) imposes external controls on the individual through close supervision, structuring of behavior, and an atmosphere of constraint. This approach creates conflict between the organization and the individual. He proposed a new managerial approach (Theory Y), which provides an opportunity for individual growth, satisfaction of higher-level needs, and integration of personal and organizational goals.

> The central principle which derives from Theory Y is that of integration: the creation of conditions such that members of the organization can achieve their own goals *best* by directing their efforts toward the success of the enterprise (McGregor, 1960, p. 49).

Argyris sees an even more fundamental conflict between individual and organizational goals (1964). He speculates that there is basic incompatibility between the structural and technological requirements of organizations in fulfilling their purposes and the needs of mature individuals. Organizational efficiency and goal accomplishment are achieved at a high human cost to the participants. He says that the psychologically mature individual in our society grows from being passive as an infant to active as an adult; from being dependent to being relatively independent; from being in a subordinate position to achieving equality of position; and is moving continually toward self-actualization. In contrast, formal organizations with their norms of rationality and emphasis on structure, formally designated roles, chain of command, task specialization, rigidly defined authority patterns, and administrative controls require the individual to work in a situation in which he is dependent, subordinate, and submissive.

According to this view, the requirements of the organization for goal achievement are in conflict with the individual's basic needs for development and self-actualization. Although Argyris does suggest introducing certain modifications into organizations to minimize the more adverse consequences he sees participants subject to, one senses that such a program can go only so far.

In a sense, it is unrealistic to expect perfect compatibility and optimal satisfaction of individual and organizational goals. The individual *must* give up some individual autonomy and self-expression to participate (and gain the advantages of membership) in the organization. This is as true of participating in the informal group or family as it is in the formal organization. Organization thus reduces personal autonomy in some spheres, but it also enhances opportunities for satisfaction in other areas. It is a trade-off that is never optimal for either the organization or the individual. For example, it could be argued that participation in an organization's retirement program reduces personal autonomy and individual discretion. However, doesn't it also increase independence and autonomy for the retiree?

Any assumption that the business or any other organization should be able to satisfy *all* the goals of its participants and still accomplish its goals is in direct conflict with the requirements of collective activity. Of course, this does not mean that managers should not strive for better goal integration. Better integration has great value to the organization and the individual in terms of effectiveness, efficiency, and participant satisfaction. And some goal integration and compatibility is necessary in every organization. Nevertheless, conflicts are inevitable and one of the major responsibilities of management is to deal with them effectively.

Much of the literature emphasizes the importance of more democratic, less authoritarian, less hierarchically structured organizations as a means for integrating individual and organization goals. They stress the need for power equalization among organizational participants and have a humanistic orientation that places high value on participant satisfactions rather than purely economic-technical yields. We generally support these views and will be looking in the chapters ahead at various approaches that can be used to achieve better integration of individual and organizational goals.

SO WHAT? IMPLICATIONS FOR YOU

As a Member in an Organization

Generalizations	Implications
1. Organized activities require that the individual accommodate to the goals of the collectivity.	1. Recognize that the organization cannot meet *all* of your individual goals. There will be conflicts and you will continually have to make adjustments.
2. Many apparent goal conflicts stem from value differences. People have different views of what is good or desirable. These value differences are always apparent in organizational life.	2. Try to understand your basic values and how they affect your goals and the means by which you accomplish them. Recognize that others may have different values that influence their goals and behavior.
3. Goals give individual behavior a direction. We all attempt to act purposively.	3. Recognize that you have a vast potential to behave in different ways, but your actual behavior is determined by your intended goals.
4. As individuals, we are continually faced with the issue of *which goals* we really want and how much effort we are willing to put into achieving them.	4. Try to think clearly about what your real goals are and to develop explicit priorities.

Generalizations	Implications
5. The inducements/contributions model suggests that people make contributions to organizations in proportion to the inducements received from the organization.	5. In your career planning it is important that you clearly assess this model. What types of inducements will the organization provide and what are the contributions required of you? Is there a positive balance sufficient to maintain your long-term satisfaction?
6. Commitment to organizational goals strengthens the ties between the individual and the organization and positively affects performance and satisfaction.	6. Assess your commitment to organizational goals. Without a relatively high level of commitment, you are not likely to be a satisfied nor a productive employee. Better to seek another organization.
7. Difficult, specific goals lead to higher performance than do easy, general goals.	7. Set challenging specific goals for yourself. Don't be satisfied with saying, "I will do the best I can."
8. Successful achievement leads to higher aspirations and more difficult goals.	8. Be realistic; set difficult but not impossible goals. When faced with a difficult task, set interim goals that can be achieved.
9. People perform better when they have feedback on the results of their labors. Individuals with a high need for achievement desire substantial feedback on performance.	9. Actively seek responses about your performance that will help you guide its direction. Take the initiative in seeking this information; don't wait to be checked up on.
10. Individuals try to satisfy multiple and often conflicting goals in their organizational lives.	10. Recognize the potential for intrapersonal goal conflicts. Be realistic in your assessment of your personal goals and try to reassess your priorities on a regular basis.

As a Current or Future Manager

Generalizations	Implications
1. The overall goals of every organization are (1) effectiveness	1. As a manager you should continually recognize these overall

Generalizations	Implications
in accomplishing objectives, (2) efficiency in the utilization of resources, and (3) satisfaction of the participants.	goals; none can be neglected if your organization is to be successful over the long run.
2. People come into the organization with established values that influence their goals and their behavior.	2. Expect diversity in the value-systems of your subordinates. They may emphasize different goals and practice different means to achieve them.
3. Organizations depend for their existence on a minimum level of value sharing among internal participants and with the external society.	3. Be aware of commonly shared values that make your organization possible. Emphasize mutually shared values and work to increase their ranges.
4. Any organization is a coalition of many participants, each of whom has individual goals that he or she is attempting to satisfy through collective activities.	4. Seek to maintain the support and contributions of various groups and individuals. In effect, attempt to satisfy a variety of goals.
5. Some of the major functions of goals in organizations are to guide and legitimize activities, to develop commitment, to serve as standards, to reduce levels of uncertainty, and to set the framework for the planning and control systems.	5. Devote substantial attention to the establishment of goals. They serve vital purposes for effective organizational functioning.
6. In the organization, the relationship between ends (goals) and means is hierarchical. Goals established at one level require certain means for their accomplishment. These means then become the subgoals: specific ends for operations at the next level. Operational objectives with greater specificity are developed as we move down the hierarchy.	6. Have a clear understanding of the hierarchy of goals. Establish general goals and missions and support them with more specific goals for lower levels of the organization.
7. Commitment to organizational	7. Work to enhance commitment

Generalizations	**Implications**
goals increase individual performance and satisfaction.	of employees to organizational goals. Selection, training, and effective socialization processes can help. Use participation to enhance commitment.
8. Internalization of goals and commitment provide intrinsic control over individual behavior and minimizes the need for extrinsic control.	8. Recognize these alternative ways of affecting the behavior of subordinates. Intrinsic control is probably more effective and flexible than rigidly designed extrinsic control systems. Recognize that both types of control may be necessary.
9. People perform better when they have difficult, specific goals rather than easy, general goals.	9. Try to develop reasonably difficult and specific goals for your subordinates. Don't settle for easy goals and generalized expression, such as "do your best."
10. Successful performance tends to raise the level of aspiration, leading to the acceptance of more difficult goals.	10. Set challenging but realistic goals. Recognize that success tends to be reinforcing. Again, emphasize feedback concerning results.
11. The evidence of the relationship between participation in goal setting and performance is not conclusive. Both assigned and consensus goals can improve performance.	11. Recognize that participation in goal setting is functional in many situations. There is no evidence that participation leads to lower performance, so why not act on probabilities?
12. Participation in goal setting and feedback on performance tend to increase participant satisfaction.	12. Strive to achieve participant satisfaction. Satisfied employees tend to have high commitment to the organization, lower absenteeism and turnover, and are less resistant to change. Besides, what's wrong with creating a more satisfying organizational climate? This may be a goal in itself.

LEARNING APPLICATION ACTIVITIES

1. Write a short vignette based on your own experience that reflects an organizational situation where there was significant conflict over goals.

2. Describe a situation in which your goals conflicted with organizational goals. List the underlying forces (such as differences in perception, values, and interests) that contributed to these goal conflicts.

3. Select a specific organization (such as a church, business, university, or hospital) and obtain information concerning its goals. Try to answer questions such as:

(a) Are its official goals written and publicized?
(b) Who developed these goals?
(c) Are they relatively fixed or do they change?
(d) To what extent are the official goals also the operational goals? (This may be difficult to determine, but you can obtain impressions from organization participants.)

4. Think about the relationship between goals and performance. Use the general results from research in this area (pp. 76–80) to evaluate your own relevant experience.

Step 1: Answer the following questions based on your experience.
(a) Do difficult goals lead to higher levels of performance than easier goals?
(b) Do specific goals lead to higher performance than general goals?
(c) How important is it for you to have feedback on your performance?

Step 2: Share your answers in groups of four to six.

Step 3: Discuss how your conclusions might be translated into effective goal setting in specific organizations.

5. The introduction to Hewlett-Packard Company's objectives say:

The achievements of an organization are the result of the combined efforts of each individual in the organization working toward common objectives. These objectives should be realistic, should be clearly understood by everyone in the organization, and should reflect the organization's basic character and personality.

The seven corporate objectives are:

First Objective: Profit.	To achieve sufficient profit to finance our company growth and to provide the resources we need to achieve our other corporate objectives.
Second Objective: Customers.	To provide products and services of the greatest possible value to our customers, thereby gaining and holding their respect and loyalty.

Third Objective: Fields of Interest.	To enter new fields only when the ideas we have, together with our technical, manufacturing, and marketing skills, assure we can make a needed, profitable contribution to the field.
Fourth Objective: Growth.	To let our growth be limited only by our profits and our ability to develop and produce technical products that satisfy real customers' needs.
Fifth Objective: Our People.	To help HP people share in the company's success, which they make possible; to provide job security based on their performance; to recognize their individual achievements; and to help them gain a sense of satisfaction and accomplishment from their work.
Sixth Objective: Management.	To foster initiative and creativity by allowing the individual great freedom of action in attaining well-defined objectives.
Seventh Objective: Citizenship.	To honor our obligations to society by being an economic, intellectual, and social asset to each nation and each community in which we operate.

Source: Hewlett-Packard Company Annual Report 1979

Step 1: Meet in groups of four to six to consider the following questions concerning Hewlett-Packard's objectives.

a. What are the importance of these goals to the organization? Do you agree that they give some indication of the company's basic character and personality?
b. What was your personal reaction to these goals? Do they seem appropriate and balanced?
c. Do you see any potential conflict among these goals?

6. Review the major functions of goals in organizations (p. 71); (a) legitimizing activities; (b) guiding activities; (c) developing commitment; (d) serving as standards; (e) reducing uncertainties; and (f) setting the framework for the planning and control system.

(a) Investigate a specific organization to see how various goals serve these functions.
(b) Share your findings in groups of four to six.

7. In groups of three to five, select either: (a) an actual organization that is familiar to at least one person in the group; or (b) a hypothetical organization (a new venture, such as a hobby shop, tavern, or restaurant) for which the group would serve as founding partners, officers, or directors. In either case, each group should have a reasonable degree of expertise with regard to the specific type of organization selected, so that the goal-setting process can be simulated realistically.

Step 1: Write a description of a successful organization. Jot down the first thoughts that come to mind concerning organizations in general and the specific one that you are using. Brainstorm ideas without evaluating them at this stage. Push yourselves to be long-range and comprehensive. From management's point of view, what would an ideal organization be like?

Step 2: Refine the ideas expressed in Step 1 by listing the important areas of concern or key dimensions (e.g., size, profitability, customer relations, employee relations) that will be important to you as managers in determining success.

Step 3: Rank the above items by priority, identifying the most important as *1,* the second most important as *2,* and so forth throughout the list.

Step 4: Take the five most important dimensions and describe how you will measure performance and/or judge results. Be as specific as possible, while recognizing that not all indicators can be quantified.

Step 5: For each of the key areas of concern that you identified in Step 4, write several specific objectives for a relatively short time period—one year or less.

Step 6: For each of the areas identified in Step 4 write several long-term goals—one year or more.

Step 7: Take a few minutes to think about how you will follow up and evaluate progress toward your goals.

Step 8: Share the results of your goal-setting efforts with another group. Note the similarities and differences across types of organizations (public-private, large-small, new-old, etc.). What conclusions emerge?

REFERENCES

Albanese, Robert. *Managing: Toward Accountability for Performance*. Rev. ed. Homewood, Ill: Richard D. Irwin, 1978.

Aram, John D. *Dilemmas of Administrative Behavior.* Englewood Cliffs, N.J.: Prentice-Hall, 1976.

Argyris, Chris. *Integrating the Individual and the Organization*. New York: Wiley, 1964.

Barnard, Chester I. *The Functions of the Executive*. Cambridge, Mass.: Harvard University Press, 1938.

Buchanan, Bruce. "To Walk an Extra Mile: The Whats, Whens, and Whys of Organizational Commitment." *Organizational Dynamics* 3/4 (Spring 1975): 67–80.

Coch, Lester, and John R. P. French, Jr. "Overcoming Resistance to Change." *Human Relations* 1 (November 1948): 512–532.

Cyert, Richard M., and James G. March. *A Behavioral Theory of the Firm*. Englewood Cliffs, N.J.: Prentice-Hall, 1963.

Drucker, Peter F. *The Practice of Management*. New York: Harper & Row, 1954.

Etzioni, Amitai. *Modern Organizations*. Englewood Cliffs, N.J.: Prentice-Hall, 1964.

Georgopoulos, Basil S. "An Open-System Theory Model for Organizational Research." In Anant R. Negandhi (Ed.), *Modern Organizational Theory.* Kent, Ohio: Kent State University Press, 1973.

Gross, Bertram M. *Organizations and Their Managing*. New York: Free Press, 1968.
Hall, Richard H. *Organizations: Structure and Process,* 2nd ed. Englewood Cliffs, N.J.: Prentice-Hall, 1977.
Herbert, Theodore T. *Dimensions of Organizational Behavior.* New York: Macmillan, New York, 1976.
Hrebiniak, Lawrence G. *Complex Organizations*. St. Paul, Minn.: West, 1978.
Ivancevich, John M. "Effects of Goal Setting on Performance and Job Satisfaction." *Journal of Applied Psychology* 61 (October 1976): 605–612.
Kast, Fremont E., and James E. Rosenzweig. *Organization and Management: A Systems and Contingency Approach,* 3rd ed. New York: McGraw-Hill, 1979.
Latham, Gary P., and Edwin A. Locke, "Goal Setting—A Motivational Technique That Works." *Organizational Dynamics* 8 (Autumn 1979): 68–80.
Latham, Gary P., and Gary A. Yukl. "Effects of Assigned and Participative Goal Setting on Performance and Job Satisfaction." *Journal of Applied Psychology* 61 (April 1976): 166–171.
———"A Review of Research on the Application of Goal Setting in Organizations." *Academy of Management Journal* 18 (December 1975): 824–845.
Lewin, K., T. T. Dembo, L. Festinger, and P. S. Sears. "Level of Aspiration." In J. M. Hunt (Ed.), *Personality and Behavior Disorders,* New York: Ronald Press, 1944, pp. 333–378.
Likert, Rensis. *New Patterns of Management*. New York: McGraw-Hill, 1961.
Locke, Edwin A. "Toward a Theory of Task Motivation and Incentives." *Organizational Behavior and Human Performance* 3 (May 1968): 157–189.
March, James G., and Herbert A. Simon. *Organizations*. New York: Wiley, 1958.
McCaskey, Michael B. "Goals and Direction in Personal Planning." *Academy of Management Review* 2 (July 1977): 454–462.
McGregor, Douglas M. *The Human Side of Enterprise*. New York: McGraw-Hill, 1960.
Mitchell, Terence R. "Motivation and Participation: An Integration." *Academy of Management Journal* 16 (December 1973): 670–679.
Porter, Lyman W., Edward E. Lawler III, and J. Richard Hackman. *Behavior in Organizations*. New York: McGraw-Hill, 1975.
Roethlisberger, F. J., and William J. Dickson. *Management and the Worker.* Cambridge, Mass.: Harvard University Press, 1939.
Simon, Herbert A. "On the Concept of Organizational Goals." *Administrative Science Quarterly* 9 (June 1964): 1–22.
Steers, Richard M. "Antecedents and Outcomes of Organizational Commitment." *Administrative Science Quarterly* 22 (March 1977): 46–56.
Vroom, Victor. *Work and Motivation*. New York: Wiley, 1964.

4
Motivation and Performance

LEARNING OBJECTIVES

After reading this chapter you should be able to:

1. Understand more about why people behave the way they do.
2. Define motivation and explain what causes it to occur.
3. Describe a process of how behavior is energized, directed, and sustained.
4. Identify factors that affect behavior, particularly performance in work organizations.
5. Outline a managerial approach for facilitating motivation and improving performance—your own and others.

A PROMOTION?

Bill Jackson is a sales representative for a major college textbook company. He grew up in the Seattle area and graduated from the University of Washington with a degree in marketing. He is an avid skier and is a member of the Seattle Tennis Club. During recent years he has become a sailing enthusiast and owns a 27-foot sloop. During the early years of his career Bill turned down opportunities to move to Texas and Los Angeles as a regional manager. Several years ago he did move to San Francisco to become regional manager. In June 1981, he was invited to New York to become editor of the management series in the college division. The move to headquarters would mean a 25-percent increase in pay and an opportunity for experience that would increase his chances of continued advancement in the corporate hierarchy. Bill thought long and hard about the move and eventually decided not to make it. In the course of his deliberations he also decided that he didn't like being regional manager, so he asked to be transferred back to Seattle to his old job as sales representative in business and economics. In 1982, Bill won a special award as the company's most outstanding sales representative.

WINNING ISN'T EVERYTHING

The women's basketball team at Northern State University had enjoyed the best season in its history. They had won 25 games and lost only two, one of which was in the regional finals where they were runners-up. Because there were no seniors on the team, there was a great deal of talk about future potential and continued success at the regional, and even national, level.

Some rumors of dissension on the team were reported in the campus newspaper, but they were overshadowed by the positive aspects of a winning season. However, shortly after the end of the season the director of athletics, John Butler, was approached by a delegation of players who presented a petition signed by nine of the twelve members of the varsity squad. The petition said in effect that the nine players would not return for the next season if Coach Adams was still there. The crux of their complaint was that the "climate" was completely negative. The coach concentrated on faults and mistakes and, according to the petitioners, "she had not uttered one word of encouragement during the entire season." The players had encouraged and praised each other, but the coach had not commended anyone as far as they could recall.

Butler met with Coach Adams to discuss the situation and ultimately renewed her contract for one year, after making several suggestions aimed at increasing her effectiveness. When the next season rolled around, none of the nine petitioners showed up. Several had transferred to other schools and others had dropped out of intercollegiate athletics to pursue other activities. In most cases, they had to give up their athletic scholarships because they had quit voluntarily.

SAVE YOUR JOB

(Miami/Associated Press/December 9, 1978) Eastern Airlines' 36,000 employees, all of whom took part in a "Save Your Job" wage deferral program, yesterday received an early

Christmas present: more than $60 million in deferred earnings and profit-sharing bonuses. And company officials, enjoying their most profitable year ever, said more money was on the way.

The payout announced Friday comes to an average of about $1,660 per employee, but the division will be based on each employee's salary and prior contributions. The proceeds came from two programs instituted by Eastern Chairman Frank Borman. The first, a wage freeze in return for a share of any future profits, came in 1976 after Eastern had endured a poor financial year in 1975.

"When Borman took over (in early 1976) the company was in bad shape," said James Ashlock. "We couldn't get any more credit or anything. Frank talked the employees into a wage freeze and they accepted it. In return, we promised profit-sharing for five years." He said the action helped bring the company from "the point of bankruptcy" to near-record profits in 1976.

In mid-1977, Borman persuaded the employees to accept a 3.5-percent wage deferral to help attain a profit target of two cents on every revenue dollar. "It was a kind of 'Save-Your-Job' self-help improvement program," Ashlock said.

Reprinted by permission.

DRYTOX CORPORATION

Liz Connell was in the midst of preparing her 1984 objectives for her branch office. She was in her second year as manager in Memphis. In her first year, the branch had done quite well, with an overall record that was 12 percent over the sales quota. This year, however, it looked as though the results might be less than projected. She reflected that her 1983 objectives may have been too ambitious. The company as a whole had prided itself on maintaining a 20-percent growth rate for the past ten years. This overall goal was translated down through the regions and branches, with individual managers expected to develop objectives and action plans that would ensure continued success. Liz was concerned about meeting her 1983 objectives and also about developing a more realistic target for 1984. She felt a great deal of pressure and sometimes wondered if, even with the challenges and the bonuses, being a branch manager was really worth it.

Liz had begun with Drytox as a customer service representative after graduating with a B.A. in marketing from the University of Illinois. While working in Chicago she obtained an M.B.A. degree through a special part-time program at Northwestern University. At that point she decided to become a sales representative and had been quite successful in this phase of the business. Although there was no explicit policy to this effect, she noticed that several sales representatives from her training class had been asked to resign after they had missed their quotas two years in a row. During one recession, the president of the company had written a letter to all employees suggesting that the 20-percent growth goal would not be taken too seriously because of unfavorable economic conditions. In spite of this "view from the top" Liz observed that there was still considerable turnover among sales representatives, in particular those who missed their quotas one time too many. She wondered if the same thing could happen to branch managers.

EMPLOYEE RECOGNITION

Payroll Department Manager, Joe Heath, was mulling over the memo from Charles Jackson, vice president for human resource development. It concerned follow-up to the workshop held four months ago, when all of the department heads had agreed to take some explicit action to provide more recognition for employees. The memo included the sentence: "At our workshop next week we will hear reports from each of you on how you carried out the Employee Recognition theme in your department." Joe was eager to report the results of payroll's program, and he wanted to tell the complete story—the minuses as well as the pluses.

His thoughts drifted back to the October 26 staff meeting, when he first mentioned that he had committed the department to develop an explicit plan for employee recognition. The response was lukewarm at best. His assistant and the three section leaders were all fairly negative. "It's hokey." "It'll take too much time." "We've tried it before and it never works." "What we really need is more money." "Some of my people need to be recognized with a swift kick in the seat of the pants." Mary, Joe's secretary, sounded the only positive note: "I think it would be nice to recognize the really hard workers once in awhile. As it is now, they don't know if anyone really cares. Several people have asked me whether extra effort and attention to quality make any difference."

The staff discussed several ideas and finally settled on naming an outstanding employee for a six-month period in each of the three sections. Joe pushed for employee involvement in developing the criteria and in the selection process. The others were skeptical, but Joe persisted and finally prevailed. After the criteria were developed and made public, the employees were asked to nominate their co-workers. The final selection of three winners was made by the section leaders from the list of nominees. Thirty-five people were nominated two or more times. Joe wrote each of them a letter of commendation, letting them know that they had been acknowledged by their colleagues.

When Joe presented certificates of merit to the winners and their sections leaders said a few nice words about them, all three of the winners had tears in their eyes. After the ceremony, Mort, the section leader who had been most skeptical of the employee recognition program, said: "You've made a believer out of me. I couldn't imagine that such a simple thing could have this much impact. And, you know, the payroll process has never been smoother."

INTRODUCTION

Bill Jackson, Coach Adams and her players, Eastern Airlines employees, Liz Connell, Joe Heath, and other individuals described in these situations behaved or acted in a variety of ways. Our reaction while reading of them depends on the degree to which we identify with their character and set of circumstances. We tend to evaluate (approve or disapprove of) the behavior of others based on what we would do in a similar situation. If we really want to understand behavior, we need to empathize; that is, we need to see and feel the situation from the other person's point of view.

Why *do* people behave the way they do? What causes some people you know to be aggressive and others to be docile? What causes some students to be serious about homework and preparation while others slide by? What causes some workers to seek more responsibility while others avoid it? A better understanding of *motivation—that elusive "something" that energizes, directs, and sustains effort*—will help us answer these questions. In turning to motivation theory and research in general, we must not lose sight of the fact that a manager's major emphasis is on improving performance; because, although motivation and performance are directly linked in many cases, in other cases they are not. Intervening variables and constraints mediate the effort-performance link and thereby affect results. We need to consider these variables and their interrelationships if we are to understand the connection between motivation *and* performance.

No one has ever touched or seen a motive; it is an elusive phenomenon for which various explanations have been given. In this chapter we will explore theories, identify common threads of understanding, and outline appropriate managerial action based on our current body of knowledge. The following topics will be covered:

Motivation and Performance Defined
Context of Behavior
Hierarchy of Needs
Motivation-Hygiene Concept
Achievement Motivation
Enriched Work
The Role of Expectations
The Process of Motivation and Performance
Contingency Views of Motivation
So What? Implications for You

MOTIVATION AND PERFORMANCE DEFINED

A *motive* either causes a person to act in a certain way or develops a propensity for specific behavior. This urge to action can be touched off by external stimuli (inducements), or it can be internally generated in individual physiological and thought processes (drives, impulses, or intentions). The concept of motive covers a range of causes that vary in terms of degree to which they are available to consciousness. For example, breathing, under normal conditions, is unconscious behavior; we do it automatically. On the other hand, deciding whether or not to run for an elective office is very conscious behavior: a deliberate action that is preceded by considerable analysis and reflection.

In a broad way, motivation can be considered in terms of *gaps* and the inherent urge for organisms to close gaps—either physiological or psychological. Organisms such as human beings exist in a state of dynamic equilibrium. They are open systems that maintain a balanced existence in their physical and mental environment. It is a dynamic, rather than a static, equilibrium because changes occur over time. Living organisms have a tendency to maintain a balance (homeostasis) by coordinated responses to internal and external conditions. This tendency to return to a balanced condition is the essence of motivation. Whenever a gap occurs the organism is motivated to close that gap by some appropriate action (behavior).

From a state of dynamic equilibrium or balance a person experiences a gap or deficiency or imbalance that leads to an urge to close the gap or restore balance. This urge (experienced as a push or pull) can vary in terms of the degree of conscious thinking and behavior that attends it. Examples of gaps are needs, wants, tensions, discomforts, expectations, or objectives. Goals are implicit in all of these conditions. A person engages in some behavior to satisfy a need, fulfill a want, reduce tension, relieve discomfort, meet an expectation, or achieve an objective. Some gaps, along with the related behavior to close them, are relatively internal and natural. Physiological and safety needs are the primary examples. Oxygen, water, and food are necessary for any person to maintain a dynamic equilibrium in the environment. Other gaps are more external and contrived; they have a primarily psychological basis. People consciously create gaps by setting goals, whether these goals be desired conditions, expected results, or specific objectives. Such goals can be short range or long range: from passing a mid-term exam to obtaining a degree in finance; from obtaining a job all the way to becoming independently wealthy. In all cases, behavior is induced to close the gaps that either occur naturally or are contrived by people as they cope with their entire life space. It is obvious that motivation, the urge to act, stems from many sources in an individual's life space—familial, social, recreational, and occupational.

Much of the research and theory building with regard to motivation has been in connection with work organizations. Why do people work at all? Why do some people work harder than others? Is work an end in itself or is it merely the means to achieve other goals through the acquisition of money? Obviously, money is the means for satisfying some basic human needs in modern society—food, shelter, and transportation. Additional amounts can be used for leisure time activities and acquiring personal property over and above survival needs. Work is also a means to achieve other goals such as status or prestige in a social system: the immediate organization, the community, or society at large. A primary concern in considering motivation is its relation to performance. In specific activities such as athletic events or academic pursuits performance is relatively

BOX 4.1
PERFORMANCE: EFFICIENCY AND EFFECTIVENESS

Every organization has work to do in the real world and some way of measuring how well that work is done. The responsibility of a manager is to see that the work gets done as efficiently and effectively as possible, whether it consists of producing goods, winning games, teaching pupils, preventing crimes, defending a frontier, making scientific discoveries, staging an entertainment, or any of the myriad other tasks that organizations undertake. The devices that measure efficiency and effectiveness are as diverse as the tasks themselves, but are inescapable from the manager's standpoint; he must ordinarily accept the conventional yardsticks, whatever they are. If the organization is a retail store, he cannot decide to disregard profitability; if it is a professional baseball team, he cannot replace the number of games won and lost with some other measure of performance more to his liking. He can, and often will, introduce additional measures of performance to move the organizational program in one direction or another, but these are not likely to have much effect unless the conventional yardsticks are satisfied at the same time.

The conventional yardsticks of performance cover both efficiency and effectiveness. An organization is efficient if, compared to similar organizations, its output is relatively high in relation to its input. It is effective if it achieves its intended goals. An organization may be highly effective without being especially efficient. Some victorious armies have been very wasteful. An organization may also be very efficient without being effective. Some declining businesses are models of operating efficiency. Efficiency and effectiveness are closely related but they are not interchangeable.

Although efficiency and effectiveness are both important, effectiveness is more important. In the numerous situations that require a choice between them, it is generally advisable to make some sacrifice of efficiency for the sake of higher effectiveness, provided that the organization's survival is not thereby jeopardized. Most good managers grasp this principle intuitively, but it is helpful, even for them, to understand the reasons for it.

Source: Theodore Caplow, *How to Run Any Organization* (Hinsdale, Ill.: Dryden Press, 1976), pp. 90–91. © 1976 by Theodore Caplow. Reprinted by permission of Holt, Rinehart & Winston, CBS College Publishing.

easy to measure and evaluate. The team with the most points wins a football game; the player with the lowest total score wins a golf tournament; and the first runner across the finish line wins the marathon. A grade of 3.7 indicates better performance on selected criteria than a grade of 2.7. Performance in other situations—the work organization, for example—may be more difficult to evaluate because the goals are not always "crisp" and measurable (Perry & Porter, 1982). This is especially true for service organizations in the public sector. Furthermore, it may be impossible at times to separate individual and group performance in an organizational context.

Most individuals, groups, and organizations have multiple goals that change over time. A general approach to evaluating performance is addressed in Box 4.1, which calls attention to the dual goals of effectiveness and efficiency. We include participant satisfaction and organization improvement in our scheme of organizational performance. More specific and different criteria for evaluating performance could be developed for any particular organization.

What causes good or bad performance? The answer to this question depends on whether the focus of attention is individual or organizational. If it is individual, we look at ability and effort. If it is organizational, the analysis is much more complex because of constraints and interdependencies that affect performance. We will look at a number of these factors and forces in subsequent sections of this chapter. At this point, it is important to recognize that in many cases effort is linked to performance and that effort stems from *motivation—that which energizes, directs, and sustains behavior.* The linkages and relationships are affected by the context of behavior in work organizations.

CONTEXT OF BEHAVIOR

The motivation to exert effort occurs in a context of past experience and a current situation. Figure 4.1 indicates the complexity of this process by showing many of the variables involved. To understand and predict behavior it is important to know something about the person as an individual, including inherent and acquired traits or characteristics. The personality of a human being is a complex combination of physical, mental, and emotional attributes. Values, attitudes, beliefs, tastes, ambitions, interests, habits, and other characteristics comprise a unique *self.* A particular set of these characteristics develops over time; the whole person is a unique composite patterned from past experience.

The various attributes that make up the whole person have direct and indirect effects on behavior. For example, habits are programmed responses that occur in certain situations. Joe always seems to speak up in meetings while Sandra says nothing unless asked a direct question. Sandra listens actively and hears what others are saying. Joe, on the other hand, tends to miss the points that others are making because he is intent on getting his ideas across at the next opportunity.

Values, attitudes, and beliefs affect behavior less directly. They provide a propensity to act in certain ways if the occasion calls for a decision or an action. For example, values about ethical and unethical behavior would affect whether you, as purchasing agent, would accept a gift from a sales representative. A free lunch or a ballpoint pen might be appropriate, whereas two tickets to the football game or a free trip to Hawaii might literally be out of bounds.

These examples suggest another aspect of the context within which moti-

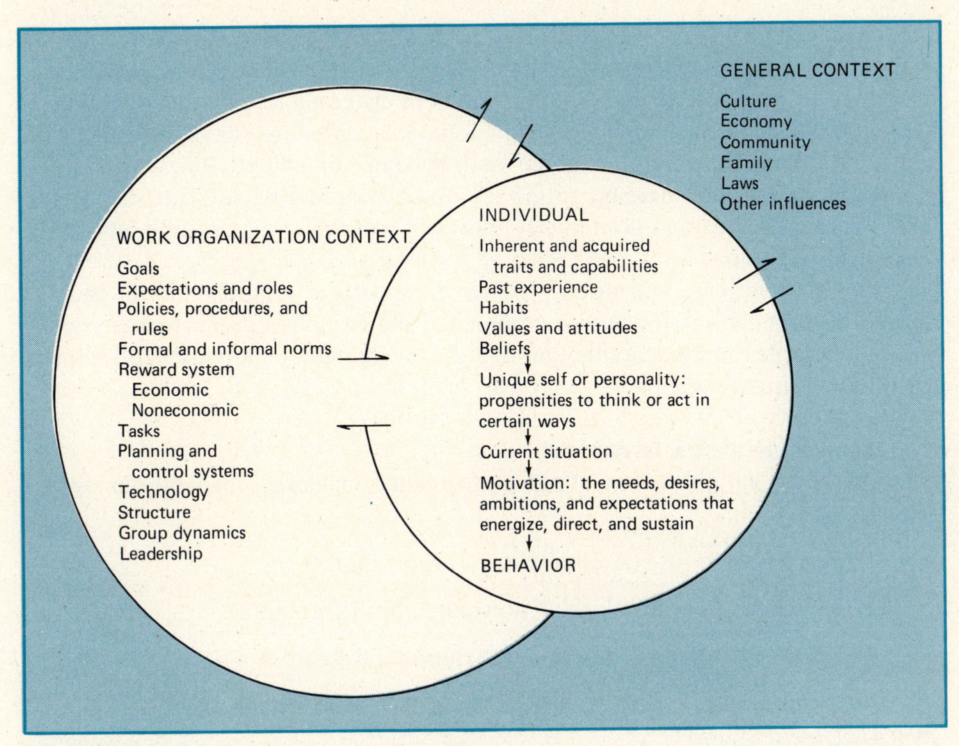

FIGURE 4.1 The Context of Individual Behavior

vation and behavior occur—the unspoken code. Personality develops within many organizational settings—family, school, church, and work. Individuals are socialized to behave in certain ways as organizational members. *Societal culture* is the broadest context within which values are developed for guiding how people should behave in various situations. *Work organizations* provide more specific guidelines in terms of policies, procedures, and rules for appropriate behavior. Individuals go through explicit orientation and training early in their association with a specific organization. Over time, they learn through experience what behavior is appropriate in that context, but the guidelines for behavior (norms) may be explicit or implicit. The official workweek may be 35 hours but it is "understood" that those that get ahead seem to average closer to 50 hours per week, and they seem to be around whenever the boss is working overtime. Liz Connell (*Drytox Corporation*) learned to pay attention to how top management acted rather than what they said. When some of her co-workers were fired for missing their quotas, she discounted the president's statement that "the 20-percent growth goal would not be taken too seriously because of unfavorable economic conditions." Thus, the unspoken goals, expectations, and role prescriptions became a more important part of the work-organization context for Liz's behavior. She thrived in Drytox's competitive environment and was motivated to expend considerable effort that led to superior performance and a promotion to branch manager. Bill Jackson was also a winner (*A Promotion?*), but he had to override company expectations by listening to what his own values dictated he should do. Whereas other regional managers may have jumped at the chance to move to the home office and become an editor, Bill weighed the intangibles against the increase in money and status and decided to stay in the field. Family, leisure, and community interests may have directed his efforts to a significant degree.

At this point, we will not try to cover all of the relationships at play in Figure 4.1. It is enough for now to appreciate the complexity of what can occur between variables and the fact that motivation is affected by individual differences in particular situations.

Basic Variables Involved

The basic variables that affect performance in work organizations are as follows:

(1) Performance = *f* (Ability, Effort, Opportunity)

(2) Ability = *f* (Technology, Knowledge, Skill, Strength)

(3) Effort = *f* (Needs, Goals, Expectations, Rewards)

(4) Opportunity = *f* (Current Situation, Past Performance)

In equation (1) the relationship is multiplicative. That is, if any of the three variables are zero, then performance is also zero. Given a reasonable opportunity, ability × effort will yield performance. The Eastern Airlines employees (*Save Your Job*) had to believe that there was an opportunity for their effort and ability to pay off in the long run. Holding opportunity and ability constant, performance then depends on effort (motivation). Effort, in turn (equation 3), is a function of several factors that may be additive: needs, goals, expectations, and rewards. Needs and goals represent gaps that occur naturally or are created by the individual. In either case, the person acts (expends effort or is motivated) to close the gap and restore equilibrium. Expectations and rewards also help us account for people's actions by focusing our attention on the consequences of behavior and the relation of subsequent effort to past consequences. For example, we may speculate on the level of effort Joe Heath (*Employee Recognition*) might expect from the three award winners during the next six months. Let us consider the elements represented by these equations and attempt to order them in a general model that will help us understand the process of motivation and performance.

HIERARCHY OF NEEDS

The number and variety of human needs underlying behavior is illustrated by Henry Murray's work (Murray, 1938, pp. 76–83). He set forth more than 40 physical (viscerogenic) and mental (psychogenic) states or conditions that induce

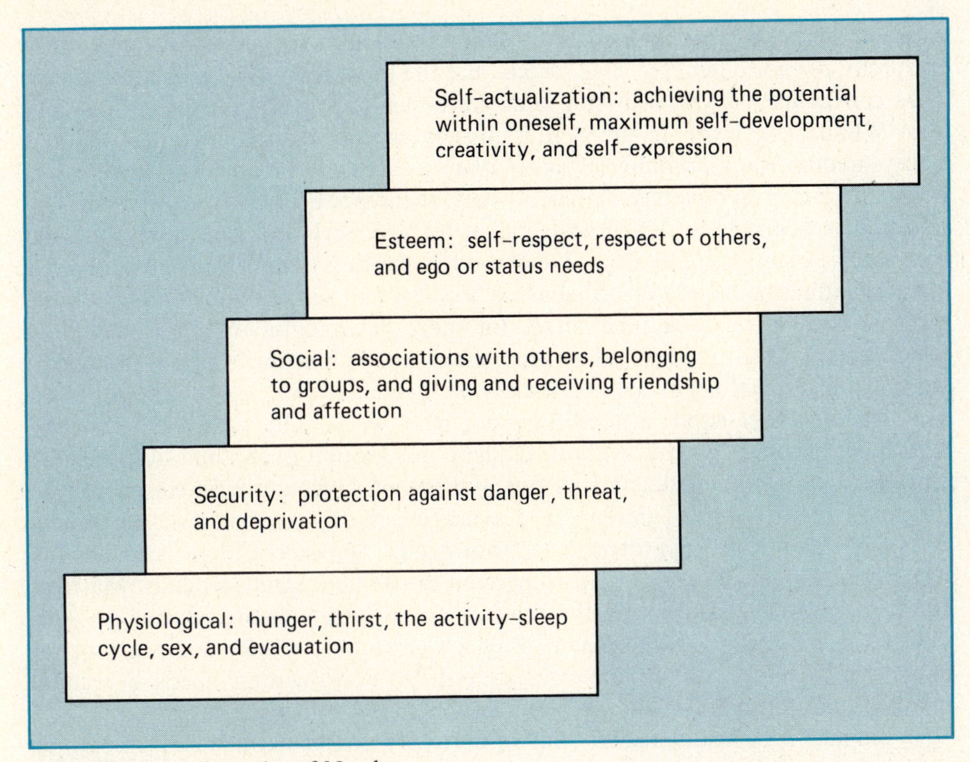

FIGURE 4.2 Hierarchy of Needs

behavior. Subcategories of physical needs are lacks (leading to intakes), distensions (leading to outputs), and harms (leading to retractions). The psychogenic needs (more than 30) stem primarily from responses to conditions external to the individual and the attempt to achieve mental or emotional satisfaction. The list includes order, achievement, recognition, deference, nurturance, exhibition, and many others. Each need (or combination of several) could serve to explain individual behavior in specific situations and at particular points in time.

The relative strength of a need determines whether or not it will be active in evoking behavior. For example, one's primary need for food may be overshadowed by a secondary need to lose weight and thereby gain self-respect and recognition. To understand and predict behavior we need to know which needs are more important within certain time frames. From a managerial perspective, trying to be cognizant of such a large number of explanatory factors is neither practical nor possible. We need a simplified, workable framework that can be applied in everyday affairs.

The need hierarchy was developed by Abraham Maslow as an alternative to viewing motivation as a series of relatively separate and distinct drives (Maslow, 1943). His concept stressed a hierarchy (Figure 4.2) with certain "higher" needs becoming activated to the extent that certain "lower" needs become satisfied. These five basic needs are related to each other and are arranged in a hierarchy of "prepotency." This means that the most prepotent goal will monopolize consciousness and will tend to evoke behavior in response to it.

While these levels in the need hierarchy can be separated for analysis and understanding, they probably all participate in actual behavior. The lower-level needs are never completely satisfied—they recur periodically—and if their satisfaction is deprived (a deficiency or gap) for any period of time, they become extremely potent as motivators. On the other hand, a completely satisfied need is not an effective motivator of behavior. Esteem and self-actualization needs are rarely satisfied; we seek indefinitely for more satisfaction of them once they become important to us. Yet they are usually not significant until physiological, security, and social needs are reasonably well satisfied (McGregor, 1960).

On the other hand, a need does not have to be fully satisfied before the next level becomes potent. A more realistic description of the hierarchy can be enunciated in terms of decreasing percentages of satisfaction as we go up the hierarchy of prepotency. Perhaps the average person is satisfied 85 percent in physiological needs, 70 percent in security needs, 50 percent in social needs, 40 percent in self-esteem needs, and 10 percent in self-actualization needs (Maslow, 1943, pp. 388–389). Moreover, the relative mix of needs change during an individual's psychological development. Physiological and security needs are dominant early in life, with social, esteem, and self-actualization needs becoming relatively more important as a person matures.

Managers typically report that opportunity for growth, achievement, or sense of accomplishment are the most important rewards for them in a work context. And they assume that for hourly employees pay and job security are the most important. However, there is evidence that hourly employees have the same reward preferences as top managers (Cooper, Morgan, Foley, & Kaplan, 1978; Rand, 1977). This suggests the pervasiveness of Maslow's hierarchy and the potency of higher order needs in a society where physiological, safety, and social needs seem to be reasonably well satisfied. These general tendencies and averages are a good first approximation in understanding and predicting human behavior. However, there are significant individual differences in motivation and performance that must be recognized in any organizational situation.

MOTIVATION-HYGIENE CONCEPT

Much research and theorizing has been focused on what stimulates people and what doesn't in work situations. A basic approach is to ask people about their work via questionnaires and/or interviews. An early study involved interviews with 200 engineers and accountants, representing a cross section of Pittsburgh industry. They were asked about events they had experienced and that had resulted in either: (1) a marked improvement; or (2) a significant reduction in job satisfaction (Herzberg, 1966).

The results of this and similar studies seem to point to two rather distinct sets of factors: one relating primarily to job satisfaction and the other relating primarily to job dissatisfaction.

> Five factors stand out as strong determiners of job satisfaction—*achievement, recognition, work itself, responsibility,* and *advancement*—the last three being of greater importance for lasting change of attitudes. These five factors appeared very infrequently when the respondents described events that paralleled job dissatisfaction feelings. . . .
>
> When the factors involved in the job dissatisfaction events were coded, an entirely different set of factors evolved. These factors were similar to the satisfiers in their unidimensional effect. This time, however, they served only to bring about job dissatisfaction and were rarely involved in events that led to positive job attitudes. Also, unlike the "satisfiers," the "dissatisfiers" consistently produced shortterm changes in job attitudes. The major dissatisfiers were *company policy and administration, supervision, salary, interpersonal relations,* and *working conditions* (Herzberg, 1966, pp. 72–74).

The environmental variables were labeled *hygiene* factors, indicating a relevance to the concept of preventive maintenance. The satisfier factors were labeled *motivators,* implying their effectiveness in evoking individual behavior toward effort, performance, and satisfaction. The motivation-hygiene concept has stimulated considerable thought (both pro and con) and research focused on work motivation. The concept is intuitively appealing and applicable. It makes an important contribution by recognizing the complexity of motivation: in particular, that there is more involved than money and other extrinsic factors (Steers & Porter, 1979, p. 395).

Relationship to Need Hierarchy

How does the motivation-hygiene concept fit with the need-hierarchy concept described previously? The hygienic factors can be related to physiological and security needs. In modern industry the environmental nature of most jobs has been basically satisfactory with regard to these lower-level needs. That is, working conditions (safety, lighting, ventilation, etc.) and salaries have generally been acceptable. Thus, in Maslow's terms these satisfied needs are not effective motivators. On the other hand, if these conditions are not reasonably satisfactory according to present norms, workers can become disenchanted and not even approach normal effort. It is unlikely, however, that concentration on improving these facets of the job environment will lead to extraordinary effort; that is, effort "above and beyond the call of duty."

Assuming reasonably good environmental conditions, how can more than normal effort be generated? Concentration on motivators involves recognition of higher-level needs such as esteem and self-actualization. Psychological growth comes from working at a task that is inherently interesting, achieving goals, and receiving recognition for such achievement. The system must provide opportunity for individuals to assume responsibility and to be innovative or creative in their work.

One popular myth is that what we are calling hygienic factors—those related to physiological and security needs—are enough to motivate "workers," while motivators, such as the promise of esteem or self-actualization, should be considered only when dealing with "managers." This dichotomy is unfortunate because it perpetuates a chasm between subsystems of organizations that really should be integrated for effective and efficient performance. All are managers; all are workers. There is really no way to draw a meaningful line of demarcation. The research findings indicate that the hygiene-motivator concept applies to people in all walks of life and at all levels in both private and public organizations (Newstrom, Reif & Monczka, 1976). Contrary to prevailing belief, the needs of the blue-collar worker of the assembly line are not significantly different from those of the white-collar worker. Both groups report that achievement and recognition are important aspects of their jobs (Herzberg, 1968, p. 66; Rand, 1977).

The relationship of motivation to individual effort is summarized in Figure 4.3. Effort is calibrated as a percentage of individual capacity. If related to physical productivity, it could be readily measurable. However, if it refers to artistic or creative output, evaluation would be much more difficult. In either case, we might consider that "normal" effort averages somewhat less than 100 percent of capacity. For the sake of illustration, let us assume (rather generously) that individuals normally operate at about 65 percent of capacity over the long run. For short periods of time, effort at 115 percent (maybe even more) is not uncommon. Sustained effort at such levels is not likely. What factors are involved in moving from 65 to 85 percent over the long run? How can we get the effort of subpar individuals (50-percenters) up to the norm?

As indicated, the hygienic and motivational factors are congruent with the need hierarchy. The two systems overlap somewhat; hygiene covers social, security, and physiological needs, while motivators reflect self-actualization, esteem, and social needs. In relating these to individual effort, we see that attention to hygienic factors leads to a long-run average of normal effort. In tapping latent human capability, the motivators become relatively more important.

The hygienic factors can lead to dissatisfaction and below average effort if they are neglected or take a turn for the worse: salaries not keeping up with inflation or actually decreasing, for example. But excellent working conditions, good interpersonal relations, adequate salary, competent supervision, and clear policies are not enough to induce the extra effort required to tap latent human capability. The motivators (linked visually to higher needs in Figure 4.3) should be brought into play in order to get beyond normal or average effort. We will consider several motivators in more detail; for example, achievement.

ACHIEVEMENT MOTIVATION

The need for achievement, while not set forth explicitly in Maslow's hierarchy, underlies esteem and self-actualization. Similarly, Herzberg's motivators emphasize the recognition of achievement as important for personal satisfaction.

Like any other physical or psychological attribute, the need for achievement varies according to the individual. Some individuals rate very high, others very low; groups, organizations, or societies could be rated according to the degree

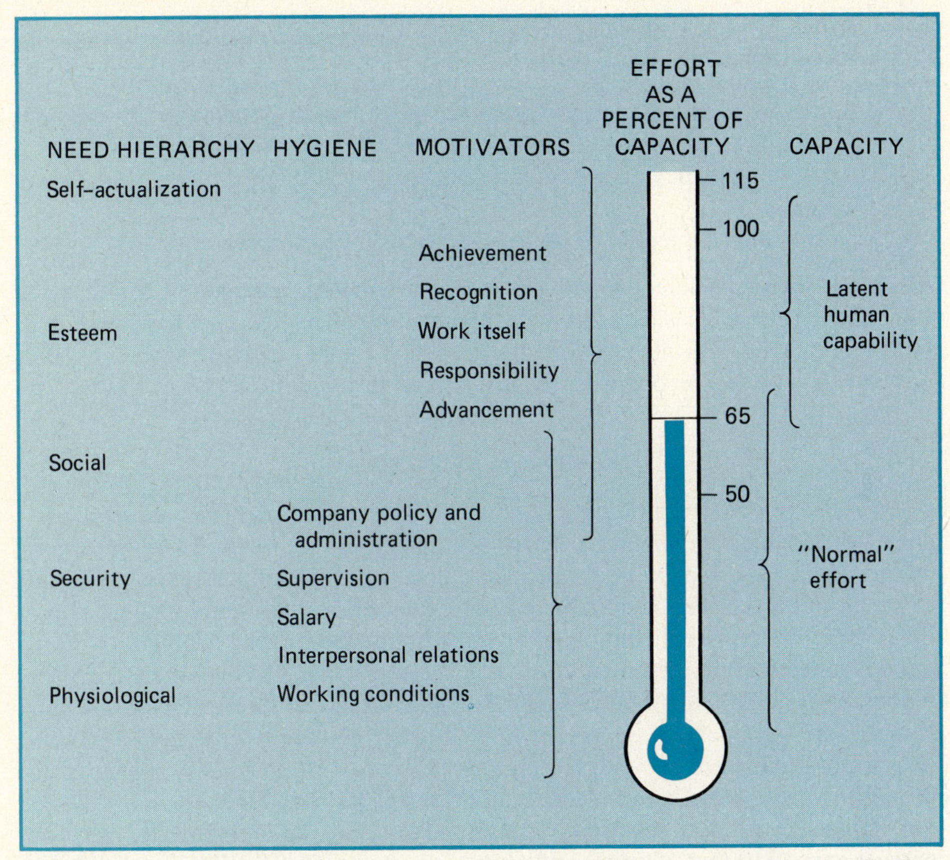

FIGURE 4.3 Relationship of Motivation to Individual Effort. **Source:** Fremont E. Kast and James Rosenzweig, *Organization and Management: A Systems and Contingency Approach,* 3d ed. (New York: McGraw-Hill, 1979), p. 251. © 1979 Reproduced with permission.

of achievement-related motivation evident in the total system. McClelland (1981) emphasized the achievement motive in the propensity for economic growth in various countries. In Western culture, the Protestant Ethic and Social Darwinism have fostered high achievement motivation. The free enterprise system has provided opportunity and a supportive environment. However, the same phenomenon is evident in other economic systems. Economic growth, corporate profits, and individual remuneration are seen as indicators of achievement and are not always sought in themselves. They merely provide an indication to the individual, organization, or society that performance has been good, recognized as such, and rewarded accordingly.

McClelland (1962) found that business managers, particularly entrepreneurs, have relatively more achievement motivation than other identifiable groups in society. He suggests that achievers:

1. Like situations in which they take personal responsibility for finding solutions to problems.
2. Have a tendency to set moderately high goals and to take calculated risks.
3. Want concrete feedback as to how well they are doing.

Individuals with high achievement motivation are inclined to take moderate risks rather than gamble on situations with high potential payoff *and* high potential failure. The achiever will be interested in a consistent string of successes and not want to spoil the record with an unsalvageable failure.

ENRICHED WORK

So far, we have concentrated on individual characteristics and the organizational context or work environment as means to understand motivation and behavior. Another major variable is the work itself. The set of job-related characteristics can be an important factor in inducing individual effort and tapping latent capabilities (see Figure 4.3). If the job is inherently interesting, the problem of motivation is much less marked than if it is not. Leisure-time activities such as sports or hobbies provide clues concerning what is involved in interesting tasks. For example, the considerable energy devoted to playing racquetball, golf, or slow-pitch softball is rewarded with a sense of personal responsibility, challenge to our abilities, and immediate feedback on how well we are doing.

If doing a task is rewarding and satisfying, we do not have to rely on coercive control (threat of firing) or elaborate systems of extrinsic rewards (praise or promise of extra pay) to induce individual effort. By including explicit goal setting and enrichment in job design, it is possible to improve performance and satisfaction (Umstot, Mitchell, & Bell, 1978). Key elements of enriched work are meaningfulness (skill variety, task significance, and task identity), autonomy/responsibility, and knowledge of results (feedback) (Hackman, Oldham, Janson, & Purdy, 1975). Not all jobs can be enriched significantly, and some people will not be as motivated by the work itself as others. In general, however, when you ask people to think about their work experience and describe a specific situation in which they felt especially good and voluntarily worked extra hard or long, they often identify something about the work itself. They describe a challenging task or an interesting, nonroutine assignment. Often, they describe a situation with more than the normal amount of personal responsibility. Thus, the work itself is an important factor in creating motivating conditions.

Figure 4.4 shows an integrated model of enriched work. Obviously, jobs vary considerably in terms of the degree to which they are or can be enriched. Long-run trends in work simplication and mechanization have led to increased overall productivity but also to a plethora of jobs that are not particularly motivating for human beings. Of course, some people may want it that way. They

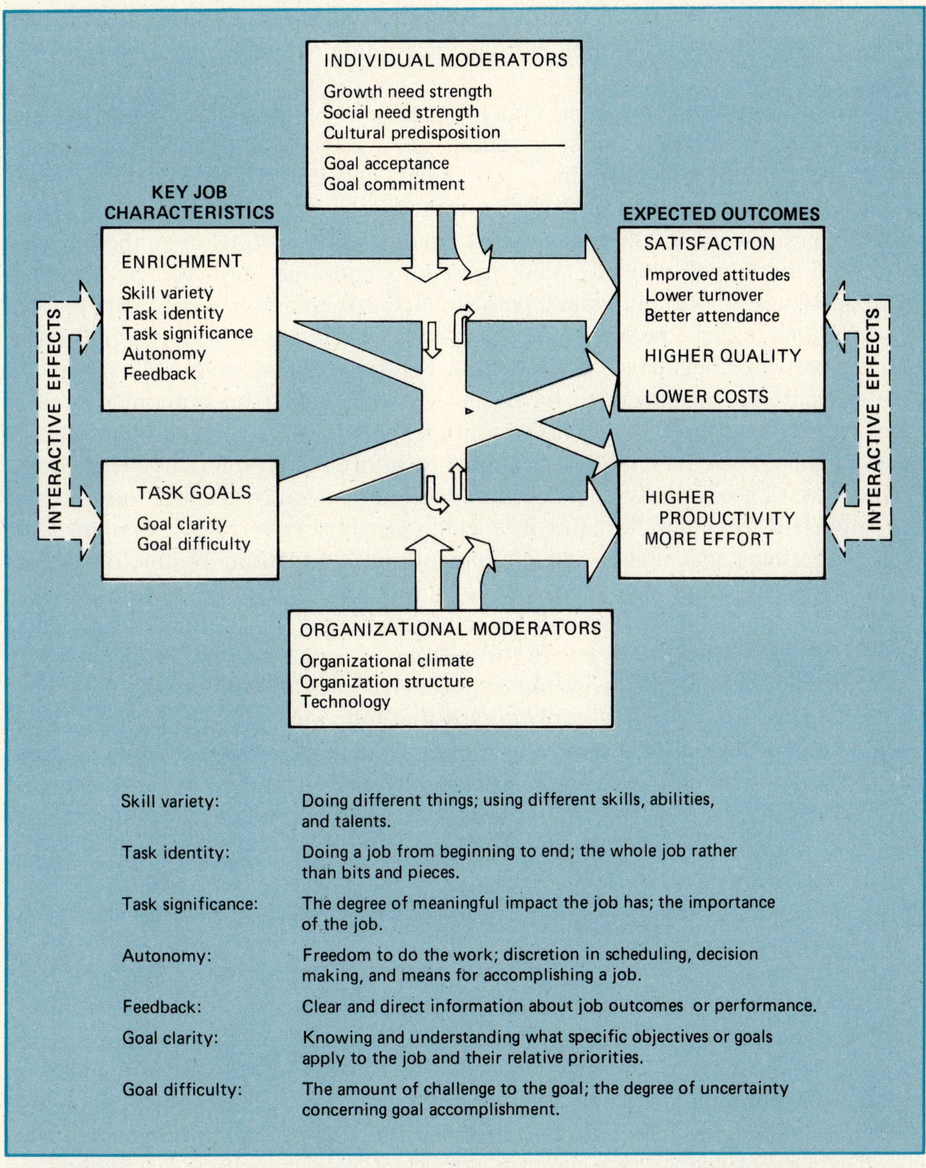

FIGURE 4.4 An Integrated Model of Enriched Work. **Source:** Denis D. Umstot, Terence R. Mitchell, and Cecil H. Bell, Jr., "Goal Setting and Job Enrichment: An Integrated Approach to Job Design, *Academy of Management Review,* October 1978, p. 877.

are interested in a job primarily as a means to earn income sufficient to pay for meaningful leisure-time activities. This is not to say that many people would not express satisfaction with very routinized jobs. For our present discussion, however, such findings would not tell us anything conclusive, because we do not know what they might say if given a meaningful choice between two alternatives: their current situation and a job enriched according to the characteristics shown in Figure 4.4.

In any case it seems important to make jobs as meaningful as possible in any given work situation. Most situations allow opportunities for increasing the variety of skills used, identifying a job as part of a composite task, and emphasizing the importance of an individual's contribution. Moreover, there is typically room to increase individual responsibility in *how* a job is done, even though *what* is to be done is well defined. Also, most jobs could be improved by means of more feedback about individual performance. A common complaint in work organizations is that "nobody ever tells you anything about how you're doing—either positive or negative." As shown in Figure 4.4 (denoted by the size of the arrows), enrichment seems to have considerable impact on outcomes such as satisfaction (manifested by improved attitudes, lower turnover, and better attendance), quality, and costs; it has less impact on effort and productivity. The reverse is true for task goals. Individual differences and organizational conditions mediate the impact of job characteristics in specific circumstances. For example, technology (perhaps machinery and equipment) may constrain productivity even though enrichment and task goals induce more effort. Individuals with high needs to achieve and self-actualize will be influenced more by enrichment and task goals than those with low needs in these areas.

Specific, difficult goals are important ingredients of highly motivating work (Locke, 1978). They provide explicit gaps that individuals strive to close. Goals should be challenging yet reasonable enough to be accepted. Individual commitment to organizationally relevant goals leads to more effort that, in turn (assuming reasonable ability), can lead to increased effectiveness, efficiency, and satisfaction.

THE ROLE OF EXPECTATIONS

Concentration on various human needs helps us understand *what* motivates people and causes expenditure of effort. The strength of needs or goals at any point in time gives us a first approximation of *where* individual effort will be focused. Another major area of concern is how much effort will be focused on satisfying a particular need or achieving a specific goal. The emphasis in this case is on explaining, not only the direction, but the *degree and persistence* of effort as well. Expectations play an important role in helping us understand differences in the amount of effort expended in any direction.

The common themes in using *expectations* to explain human behavior are: (1) conscious decisions by individuals (in a work situation or the world at large) to behave in certain ways; (2) individual values with regard to choosing desired outcomes; (3) individual expectations concerning the amount of effort required to achieve a certain outcome; and (4) individual expectations concerning the probability of being rewarded for achieving a desired outcome. These concepts have been modeled and tested by many writers-researchers (Vroom, 1964; Porter

& Lawler, 1968; Mitchell, 1974). The elements in this model—expectations, effort, performance, and satisfaction—are connected in the overall process of motivation. People are motivated to expend effort if they believe that there is a reasonable probability that their effort will accomplish a desired outcome (performance) and that this will be followed by intrinsic or extrinsic rewards leading to satisfaction. A positive experience will affect the individual's propensity to engage in similar efforts at a future time, thus renewing the motivation process.

THE PROCESS OF MOTIVATION AND PERFORMANCE

For managers, it is not enough to know what motivation is; one must know how it happens. A better understanding of the process of motivation will allow us to facilitate its occurrence and thereby improve performance. Our ultimate objective is to create conditions within which people are motivated to engage in appropriate activities that lead to organizational effectiveness and efficiency, as well as to their own satisfaction.

Organizational Context

As shown in Figure 4.5, the overall context of behavior includes the external environment plus internal factors such as organizational goals and values, technology, structure, and managerial processes. These factors, individually and collectively, affect the motivation of individuals and groups in organizations.

An organization's goals and values (explicit or implicit) affect motivation by identifying desired outcomes or results and indicating appropriate behavior that may be used in attempting to achieve them. Clear, reasonably difficult goals that are accepted by participants induce effort and channel it in appropriate directions (Locke, 1978; Latham & Locke, 1979). Values provide norms or guidelines that deem what is appropriate behavior in a specific organization. For example, employees in a gourmet restaurant might be encouraged to provide maximum personal attention in a leisurely manner, whereas speed and customer turnover might be more appropriate in a low-cost family restaurant.

The type of technology used in an organization also affects motivation. In some cases human activity is paced by the speed of machinery on an assembly line. In other cases tools, equipment, and procedures are merely adjuncts to human effort, which is the key to productivity. Structural relationships, job descriptions, and role expectations also play an important part in determining the amount and focus of human endeavor. Technology and structure are primary determinants of how the work is divided up and integrated. The resulting roles—salesperson, technician, supervisor, general manager—provide an indication of how much and what kinds of effort are required to fulfill the expectations that organization members have for various positions.

Managerial processes also affect motivation. For example, leadership style—categorized according to degree of participation in decision making—affects commitment and subsequent effort. The way in which goals are set, decisions made, or communication carried out is often as important as what the

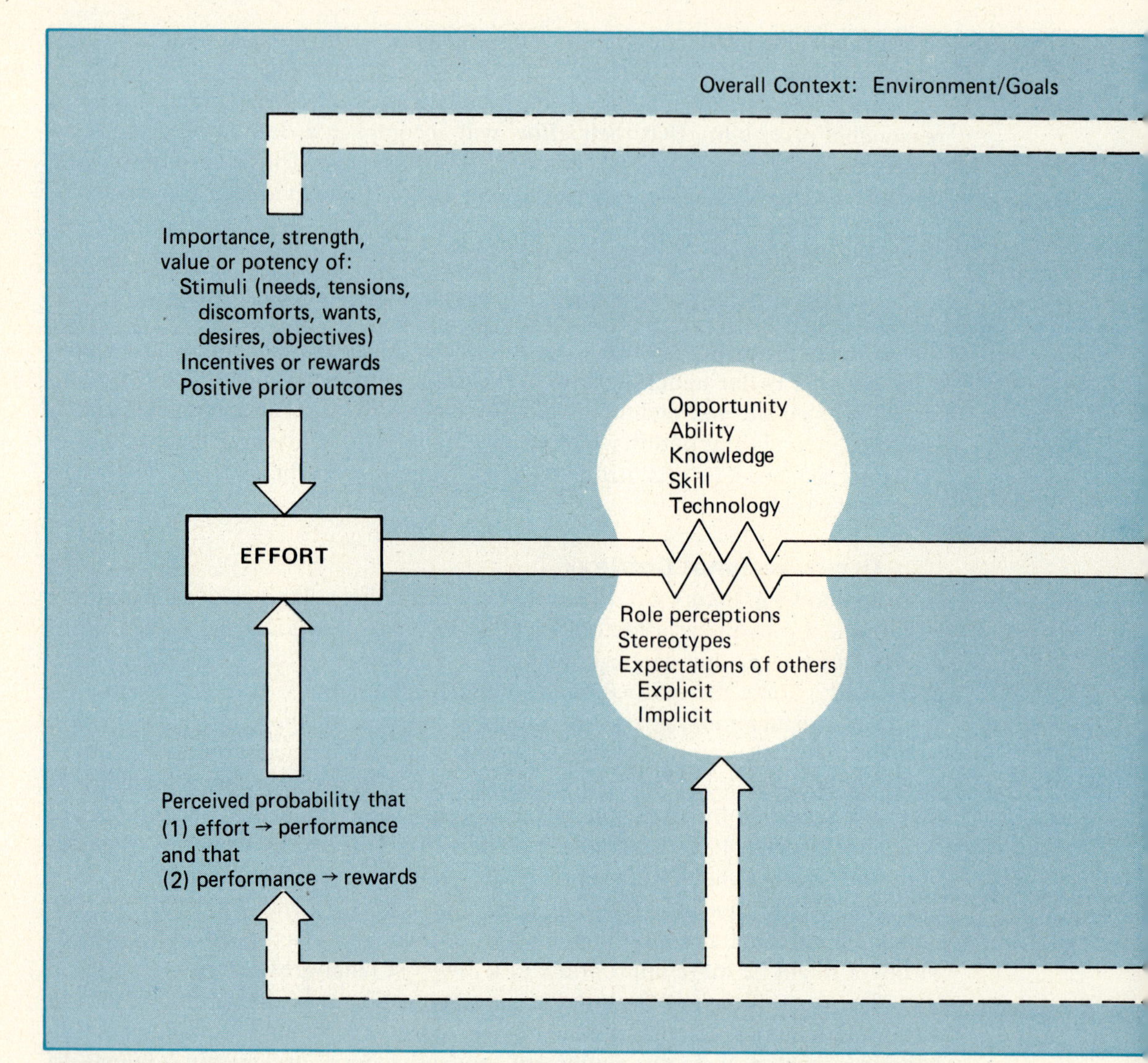

FIGURE 4.5 The Process of Motivation: Factors Affecting Individual Effort, Performance, and Satisfaction. **Source:** Fremont E. Kast and James Rosenzweig. *Organization and Management: A Systems and Contingency Approach,* 3d ed. (New York: McGraw-Hill, 1979), p. 246. © 1979. Reproduced with permission.

goals are, what choices are made, and the content of messages. Depending on the situation, extremely autocratic or laissez faire approaches can be demotivating. An appropriate managerial style is important in providing an organizational context within which individual motivation can occur and latent human capability can be tapped.

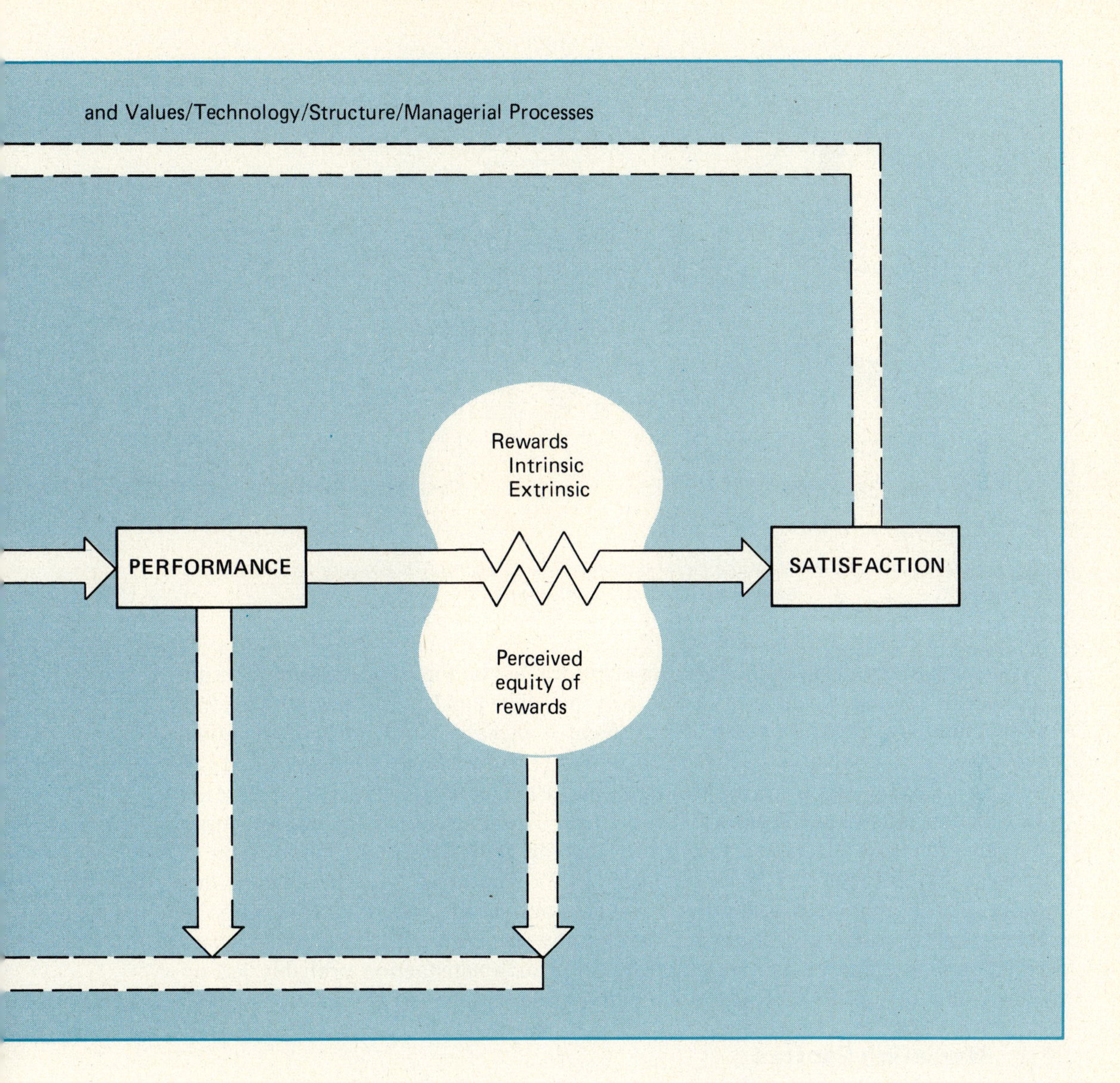

Key Variables

The key variables in the motivation process are effort, performance, and satisfaction (see Figure 4.5). In conscious, formal activities—particularly those in work organizations—*performance* is primary. It connotes a degree of excellence as measured by a standing set of expectations. This invocation of a standard

"Ladies and gentlemen, allow me to introduce Mr. Gregory. Mr. Gregory will be heading up our new incentive program."

suggests that raw effort alone is not enough; it must be focused in an appropriate manner to achieve meaningful results. On the other hand, *effort* is essential; the best intentions are useless if that ingredient is lacking. Thus, in understanding the process of motivation we need to know: (1) how effort is induced; and (2) how effort is focused toward meaningful performance. In general, the degree of satisfaction follows the level of performance. The level of satisfaction, in turn, has an effect on the amount of effort that an individual will put forth in a subsequent time period (Organ, January 1977). The three key variables in the process of motivation are thus linked over time periods. The award winners in the payroll department (*Employee Recognition* vignette) enjoyed increased satisfaction at the end of one six-month period. Such satisfaction probably led to increased effort during the next six-month period.

Mediating Factors

A number of factors affect the process of motivation in work organizations. They mediate the linkages between effort and performance and between performance and satisfaction. A basic factor is opportunity, without which there is no need for effort. Enthusiasm turns into apathy when requests for increased responsibility and challenging work are repeatedly denied. Both interest and ability can wither if opportunity to perform is not made available for long periods of time.

As shown in the model, the relationship between effort and performance is affected by an individual's abilities and role perceptions (the explicit and implicit expectations of what one is supposed to do). If a person lacks the necessary skill or knowledge to accomplish a task, extraordinary effort will not lead to better performance. People tend to choose activities and occupations wherein they have a good probability of doing well. Aptitude tests provide information that is helpful in deciding whether one has a reasonable chance of success as a surgeon, accountant, mechanic, typist, computer programmer, or what have you. Of course, within a range of capability, extra effort can and does lead to improved results. Through hard work some people are able to achieve more of their natural potential than others. Individuals are motivated to do so because of expectations that hard work will pay off.

If effort is misdirected, improved performance may not be organizationally relevant, and hence not rewarded. For example, a basketball player might: (1) concentrate on shooting rather than defense and overall team play; (2) win the high scoring honors; and (3) be on a losing team. Or, a salesperson might: (1) concentrate on easy-to-sell, low-profit items; (2) win a sales contest based on volume; and (3) unknowingly contribute to a decreased profit for the company. This suggests the need for continued attention to role expectations so that preconceived notions can be verified, modified, or dispensed with in order to focus behavior in the desired directions. Well-designed management by objectives (MBO) programs can facilitate this process by identifying key areas and prioritizing the objectives and actions plans that are most appropriate for a given time frame. Appropriate role perceptions are important in linking effort and performance in ways that are meaningful for the individual and relevant for the organization.

Intrinsic rewards (those based on the nature of the job itself) include enjoyable work, a healthy sense of challenge and responsibility, and self-esteem stemming from job performance. Extrinsic rewards (aspects external to the job) include pay, recognition and praise, and the esteem of others. The range of possible rewards has a direct effect on satisfaction, but satisfaction is also affected by the perceived equity in the reward system (Adams, 1963; Carrell & Dittrich, 1978). Individual behavior is affected by a person's perception of the performance-rewards relationship as it applies to others. We may compare ourselves with a specific person or with a general class of persons in similar roles. Apparent inequity (others getting the same reward for less output or more reward for the same output) is a source of tension. Tension-reducing behavior could include a petition for more rewards (pay or other benefits) or a reduction of output (quality and quantity) in order to restore the situation to one of perceived equity or balance.

In recent years professional athletes have provided examples of such behavior. Many established stars played out their options in order to renegotiate their contracts or change teams. They were responding to relatively long-term, no-cut contracts for a few superstars, particularly rookies who had not proven themselves over the long run. On an absolute scale $100,000 per year may seem like reasonable compensation. However, if someone else on the team is making $500,000 per year, it may be difficult to accept the differential as equitable.

While six-figure equity disputes make the headlines, the "equal pay for equal work" problem is far more widespread. Multimillion dollar retroactive

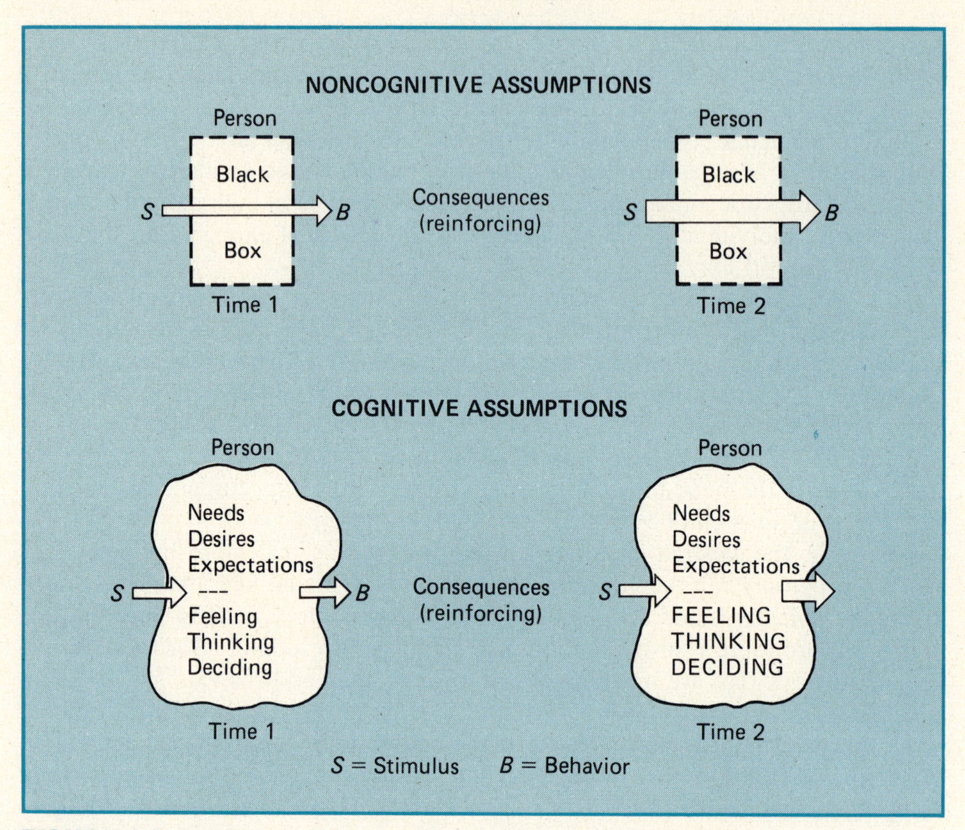

FIGURE 4.6 Cognitive and Noncognitive Assumptions about Behavior

settlements have been made by a number of organizations that apparently were systematically paying women less than men for essentially the same type of work (and performance). Inequities of a few cents per hour or a few dollars per week are enough to create tension, affect satisfaction, and modify subsequent effort.

Noncongnitive Explanations

A major distinction operative in the sciences of human behavior is that between cognitive and noncognitive explanations (see Figure 4.6 and Box 4.2). The bulk of the work in motivation research nowadays assumes that it is important to understand internal states and processes of individuals: needs, tensions, and discomforts or wants, expectations, and objectives. This, the cognitive school, puts great emphasis on understanding what people feel and how they think in order to predict how they will behave in a given situation.

The noncognitive approach eschews any attempt to understand internal conditions and processes. In effect, the individual is thought of in terms of a "black box" wherein feeling and thought processes are unknown and unknowable. Behavior occurs and is directed and sustained by virtue of the conditioning effects of reinforcement. Behavior is modified because of the consequences that follow it. That behavior which is ignored or punished tends to decrease or cease. That which is rewarded—positively reinforced—tends to increase or persist. To understand and predict behavior, it is sufficient to focus on past overt actions and their consequences as issuing from the individual's external environment.

In terms of Figure 4.5, the focus of attention would be on performance and subsequent events. In a work situation, three basic things can follow behavior or evidence of performance: (1) positive reinforcement; (2) no action; or (3) punishment. When behavior is positively reinforced with some type of reward, the primary effect is that behavior will be repeated in the future under similar conditions. For the individual, the secondary effects are increased satisfaction and a tendency to try to improve performance. If there are no perceptible consequences of behavior or performance, the primary effect is a decrease in the likelihood that it will be repeated. The secondary effects for the individual would be a decrease in satisfaction and a tendency to be unsure about appropriate future behavior and perhaps to try other alternatives.

If behavior or performance is followed by punishment, the primary effect is a pronounced decrease in the likelihood that it will be repeated. It may even stop completely. For the individual, there is reduced satisfaction and other secondary effects such as heightened tension, decreased communication, and a tendency to avoid the source of punishment or perhaps get even with it. In this account the degree of satisfaction plays a primary role in explaining subsequent behavior. Individuals learn behavior that leads to increased satisfaction. Behavior is shaped because of the reinforcing effects of positive consequences. The importance of feedback is evident because consequences must be felt or perceived in order to be effective in modifying behavior.

In a classroom situation, the behavior of both students and teachers is shaped by what seems to work. That is, actions that are positively reinforced will tend to be repeated. A particular teaching style will be developed and maintained if the appropriate amount and kind of learning takes place or if performance is rewarded by positive feedback from students. Similarly, student behavior in class and on exams will be shaped by feedback from peers and teachers. If participation is rewarded it will tend to persist and increase. If it is ignored or punished through belittlement it will tend to decrease or stop.

The same approach can be used to analyze work situations. If someone is rewarded for making suggestions about how the job might be done better, he will continue to make suggestions and try to improve organizational performance. If his proposals are ignored or punished (perhaps through ridicule from the boss or resentment from co-workers) he will *learn* to keep quiet and not make waves.

Many organizations have made conscious efforts to shape behavior by explicitly identifying goals and expectations and then positively rewarding good performance. Absenteeism has been cut dramatically by including employees with perfect attendance for one month in a lottery or allowing them to select a prize of their choice. Parsons Pine Products, Inc. of Ashland, Oregon, pays employees an extra eight hours' wages if they are neither absent nor tardy for one month. Employees also receive bonuses from refunds of state industrial

BOX 4.2
HUMAN BEHAVIOR: BEHAVIORISTIC or HUMANISTIC?

Behavioristic

We do not need to try to discover what personalities, states of mind, feelings, traits of character, plans, purposes, intentions, or other prerequisites of autonomous man really are in order to get on with a scientific analysis of behavior. . . .

By questioning the control exercised by autonomous man and demonstrating the control exercised by the environment, a science of behavior also seems to question dignity or worth. A person is responsible for his behavior, not only in the sense that he may be justly blamed or punished when he behaves badly, but also in the sense that he is to be given credit and admired for his achievements. A scientific analysis shifts the credit as well as the blame to the environment, and traditional practices can then no longer be justified. These are sweeping changes, and those who are committed to traditional theories and practices naturally resist them. . . .

What is needed is a technology of behavior, but we have been slow to develop the science from which such a technology might be drawn. One difficulty is that almost all of what is called behavioral science continues to trace behavior to states of mind, feelings, traits of character, human nature, and so on. . . .

As the interaction between organism and environment has come to be understood, however, effects once assigned to states of mind, feelings and traits are beginning to be traced to accessible conditions, and a technology of behavior may therefore become available. . . .

A scientific analysis shifts both the responsibility and the achievement to the environment. . . .

But environmental contingencies now take over functions once attributed to autonomous man, and certain questions arise. Is man then "abolished"? Certainly not as a species or as an individual achiever. It is the autonomous inner man who is abolished, and that is a step forward. But does man not then become merely a victim or passive observer of what is happening to him? He is indeed controlled by his environment, but we must remember that it is an environment largely of his own making.

Source: B. F. Skinner, *Beyond Freedom and Dignity* (New York: Knopf, 1971). ©1971 by B. F. Skinner. Reprinted by permission of Alfred A. Knopf, Inc.

insurance premiums that are based on lost-time accidents ("Using B' Mod to Boost Attendance and Timeliness," 1978). Another company reported 60-percent reductions in work-hours per aircraft subassembly after they began posting targets and weekly results (Rose, 1977). Similar results have been noted at Emery Air Freight, Michigan Bell, Connecticut General Life, General Electric, Standard Oil

(**Box 4.2**, cont.)

Humanistic

I have come to realize that the basic difference between a behavioristic and a humanistic approach to human beings is a *philosophical* choice. This certainly can be discussed, but cannot possibly be settled by evidence. If one takes Skinner as of some years ago—and I believe this is his view today—then the environment, which is part of a casual sequence, is the sole determiner of the individual's behavior. . . .

My experience in therapy and in groups makes it impossible for me to deny the reality and significance of human choice. To me it is not an illusion that man is to some degree the architect of himself. . . . The degree of self-understanding is perhaps the most important factor in predicting the individual's behavior. So for me the humanistic approach is the only possible one. . . .

Choosing the humanistic philosophy . . . means that very different topics are chosen for research and different methods for validating discoveries. It means an approach to social change based on the human desire and potentiality for change, not on conditioning. It leads to a deeply democratic political philosophy rather than management by an elite. . . .

What is really at issue is the confrontation of two paradoxes. If the extreme behaviorist position is true, then everything an individual does is essentially meaningless, since he is but an atom caught in a seamless chain of cause and effect. On the other hand, if the thorough-going humanistic position is true, then choice enters in, and this individual subjective choice has some influence on the cause-and-effect chain. . . .

We are, as a people, beginning to refuse to allow technology to dominate our lives. Our culture, increasingly based on the conquest of nature and the control of man, is in decline. Emerging through the ruins is the new person, highly aware, self-directing, and explorer of inner, perhaps more than outer, space, scornful of the conformity of institutions and the dogma of authority. He does not believe in being behaviorally shaped, or in shaping the behavior of others. He is most assuredly humanistic rather than technological.

Source: Carl R. Rogers, "In Retrospect: Forty-Six Years," *American Psychologist 29/2 [February 1974]*:115–123.

of Ohio, Weyerhaueser, B. F. Goodrich, Emerson Electronics, and for garbage collecting in Detroit (Hamner & Hamner, 1976). The target behaviors include productivity, quality of products or services, safety, absenteeism, scheduling, and supervisory competence. The vignette at the beginning of the chapter about Eastern Airlines is an example of a corporate-wide approach (profit sharing) to the rewarding of employees for good performance.

Such shaping of behavior is often referred to as a top-down managerial approach. However, we are all involved in the consequences of others' behavior; we can reward it or not, and thus affect the likelihood that it will be repeated. Subordinates could shape the managerial style of bosses by recognizing and praising good behavior (from their point of view). This possibility has been demonstrated in school settings where students, with minimal behavior modification training, were able to change the behavior of their teachers—with the teachers liking the results (Gray, 1974).

Cognitive Explanations

Cognitive explanations of the motivation process focus on the experienced gaps to which behavior is a response: gaps that are activated by individual feeling or thinking. Internal physiological and psychological conditions are understood to result in effort being expended (Murray, 1938). According to one such approach, behavior is induced because the individual wants to satisfy needs, reduce tensions, and relieve discomforts. The amount of effort expended depends on the strength or potency of particular drives at any point in time. For example, people may tend to work hard when they are in a probation period on the job or when there is a serious threat of being let go because of an economic downturn. This drive would be less potent when a person's job is reasonably secure.

Another approach to explaining how effort is induced focuses more on external, future-oriented factors and expectations. People will work hard if they perceive a reasonable probability that their effort will lead to good performance and appropriate rewards. This approach assumes that people can consciously link the key variables, effort-performance-satisfaction, and adjust their behavior in accord with anticipated outcomes. It presumes a more active role for the individual as she consciously identifies wants, desires, and objectives and then adjusts effort according to whether or not it pays off over time.

For example, Helen Chan wants to be a certified public accountant. Her career decision was partially influenced by the fact that an uncle had succeeded in this line of work; it was reinforced by her high grades in beginning accounting courses. Sam Melberg switched from accounting to systems analysis because he had a knack for programming and had read a *Business Week* article that reported higher starting salaries for computer specialists than for accounting graduates. Paul Miller worked part-time for a large supermarket chain and thought he might seek a career with that company after he finished his degree in marketing. However, the more he learned of managerial opportunities, working conditions, and the compensation system, the more he looked around for alternative jobs.

CONTINGENCY VIEWS OF MOTIVATION

Figures 4.1 (The Context of Individual Behavior) and 4.5 (The Process of Motivation) help us visualize the complexity involved in understanding and predicting human behavior in work organizations. As we have seen, the key variables in motivation are effort, performance, and satisfaction. But the process is affected by many other variables: those such as opportunity, ability, roles, rewards, and equity. Our model addresses causes of behavior—that which induces effort. It must also include the role of expectations, estimates of whether effort will lead to good performance and adequate rewards. This is particularly important in considering the degree and persistence of effort in work situations. Also important is the concept of strength or potency of various stimuli or incentives. This includes needs or urges (physiological and psychological) that occur when there is a gap between a current condition and a desired condition (goal). Effort is expended (consciously or subconsciously) to close the gap and achieve satisfaction. Positive outcomes increase the probability that a specific bit of behavior or action will be repeated the next time the same stimulus occurs.

As we have indicated in previous sections, researchers and writers have provided different explanations for what causes behavior and how effort and performance are linked. These debates in the literature are interesting and the questions deserve continuing attention. However, managers want to know the practical implications of a theory or set of theories. Fortunately, a reasonably consistent set of guidelines can be developed, regardless of which theories one favors. A fundamental concept is that managers do not motivate subordinates. Motivation is personal and internal. Therefore, the most that managers can do is create conditions under which people are motivated to behave in certain ways. A primary concern is the amount of effort people are willing to expend in pursuing personal and organizational goals. In most endeavors, particularly those in work organizations, the ultimate concern is good performance. Thus, the central question is "How is motivation related to good performance?"

The Motivation-Effort-Performance Connection

Box 4.3 provides a list of diagnostic questions for analyzing these linkages. For example, if goals aren't crisp enough to be measured, then performance is fuzzy and not a good indicator of motivation (Perry & Porter, 1982). More specifically, if performance cannot be linked to individual behavior it is not a good indicator of motivation. When other factors, such as opportunity, ability, and technology, are more important than effort in determining performance, then other measures of motivation are needed to see whether one is eliciting normal effort from people or tapping latent capability. Emphasis on short-run performance may lead to improving factors that are directly linked to output or productivity. A long-run perspective would include recognition of the role that motivation may play in the improvement process; for example, by inducing people to participate in designing ways to do the job better.

If answers to the diagnostic questions are clear-cut, we have some guidelines. If performance is a direct function of effort (motivation)—that is, if there are no confounding variables intervening to cloud the analysis—then guidelines based on principles of goal setting, operant conditioning, expectancy theory, and equity ideas can be developed and applied in specific situations. The particular technique used should be a function of the work context and the people involved. A number of principles, based on Spitzer's synthesis of the motivation literature,

BOX 4.3
QUESTIONS ABOUT MOTIVATION AND PERFORMANCE: IMPLICATIONS FOR ACTION

1. Can performance be defined in individual, behavioral terms? If not, develop a separate measure of motivation.
2. Is motivation important for performance, or are abilities and situational factors more important? If motivation is important, but not the same as performance, develop a separate measure of motivation.

If one cannot meet the requirements of questions 1 and 2, it may not be worth it to proceed further. If, however, motivation is important for performance and performance is a good reflection of motivation or a good measure of motivation exists, then proceed with the analysis.

3. Is the reward system rigid and inflexible? In other words, are people and tasks grouped into large categories for reward purposes?
4. Is it difficult to observe what people are actually doing on the job?
5. Is an individual's behavior dependent heavily on the actions of others?
6. Are there lots of changes in people, jobs, or expected behavior?
7. Are social pressures the major determinants of what people are doing on the job?

If questions 3 through 7 are answered with a no, then some system combining a needs analysis with goal setting, operant, expectancy, and equity ideas should be effective.

Source: Terence R. Mitchell, "Motivation: New Directions for Theory, Research, and Practice," *Academy of Management Review* 7/1 (January 1982):86. Reprinted by permission.

are set forth in Box 4.4. Although they seem to range into leadership style and managerial behavior in general, the suggestions are all aimed at providing a climate within which individuals become motivated, expend effort, and perform well.

Positive Reinforcement

We need to pay special attention to positive reinforcement as a means of influencing behavior, eliciting effort, improving performance, and increasing satisfaction. The application of positive reinforcement is the same regardless of whether one favors cognitive or noncognitive explanations for its effectiveness. From the specific suggestions presented in Box 4.4, we can derive the following ideas:

Rewards are more effective than punishment.

To optimize the appropriate behavior, rewards should be suited to the individual.

BOX 4.4
APPLYING PRINCIPLES OF HUMAN MOTIVATION

Use appropriate methods of reinforcement.

Make rewards contingent on performance
Recognize personal differences about what is rewarding
Provide feedback and rewards as soon as possible

Eliminate unnecessary threats and punishments.
Make sure that accomplishment is adequately recognized.
Provide people with flexibility and choice.
Provide support when it is needed.
Provide employees with responsibility along with their accountability.
Encourage employees to set their own goals.
Make sure that employees are aware of how their tasks relate to personal and organizational goals.
Clarify your expectations and make sure that employees understand them.
Provide an appropriate mix of extrinsic rewards and intrinsic satisfaction.
Design tasks and environments to be consistent with employee needs.
Individualize your supervision.
Provide immediate and relevant feedback that will help employees improve their performance in the future.
Recognize and help eliminate barriers to individual achievement.
Exhibit confidence in employees.
Increase the likelihood that employees will experience accomplishment.
Encourage individuals to participate in making decisions that affect them.
Establish a climate of trust and open communication.
Minimize the use of statutory powers.
Help individuals to see the integrity, significance, and relevance of their work in terms of organizational output.
Listen to and deal effectively with employee complaints.
Point out improvements in performance, no matter how small.
Demonstrate your own motivation through behavior and attitude.
Criticize behavior, not people.
Make sure that effort pays off in results.
Encourage employees to engage in novel and challenging activities.
Anxiety is fundamental to motivation, don't eliminate it completely.
Don't believe that "liking" is always correlated with positive performance.
Be concerned with short-term and long-term motivation.

Source: Dean R. Spitzer, "30 Ways to Motivate Employees to Perform Better." Reprinted with permission from the March 1980 issue of *Training, The Magazine of Human Resources Development*, pp. 51–56.

Feedback in form of rewards (or punishments) should be given frequently and consistently.
Both social group processes and the formal reward system can influence behavior. (Mitchell, 1976.)

The opportunity to provide positive reinforcement is available in most work organizations. The most effective reinforcers are:

Money (if it is tied to performance)
Praise or recognition
Freedom to choose one's own activity
Opportunity to see oneself becoming better, more important, or more useful
Power to influence both co-workers and management. (Hamner & Hamner, 1976, p. 9.)

The first step in adhering to such a program is to make the work itself as interesting (and intrinsically motivating) as possible. A boring job requires extrinsic inducements and rewards in order to elicit the effort required. Another step would be to develop clear, challenging goals (that are accepted) for individuals and organizational units—preferably with widespread and bottom-up participation in the process. Extensive and intensive discussions of objectives and roles should lead to mutual expectations that are well understood. If all of these elements are in place, individual and organizational performance can be measured and evaluated and the process of feedback and positive reinforcement continued. A word of praise or a bit of recognition (recall the *Employee Recognition* vignette) can be used in almost every situation, and the benefits far outweigh the costs. The overall system is likely to gain in terms of effectiveness, efficiency, and participant satisfaction.

SO WHAT? IMPLICATIONS FOR YOU

Understanding motivation—what it is and how it occurs—is an important step in explaining human behavior in organizations. The next step is applying such knowledge in organizational contexts, either as individual participants or as managers.

As a Member in an Organization

Generalizations	Implications
1. Individuals are different. Values, attitudes, and beliefs that are shaped over time result in a unique person and a propensity to behave in certain ways.	1. Know yourself. Understand what makes you tend to respond in certains ways to internal and external stimuli. Identify your own personal guidelines for behavior.
2. The general societal context	2. Be aware of the forces around

Generalizations	Implications
and specific organizational situations affect individual motivation and behavior.	you that affect your behavior. How do you cope with them, accept, adapt, or try to change them? Be realistic concerning what can be changed.
3. The urge to behave (in particular, to expend effort) is a function of gaps and the human tendency to close them and maintain a dynamic equilibrium. Gaps may be physiological, psychological, or a combination of both. They may be internal, inherent, and immediate and/or external, contrived, and future-oriented.	3. Be aware of the various kinds of gaps that effect behavior in you. What needs do you try to satisfy? What goals do you try to achieve? What conscious and unconscious behavior allows you to maintain a dynamic equilibrium in your life?
4. Habits govern a large amount of human behavior. We respond to many gaps relatively unconsciously.	4. Assess your typical responses to organizational stimuli (gaps) in order to make sure they reflect how you want to behave. Check to see that your behavior is functional. In other words, is it consistent with your own values and aspirations as well as organizational needs and expectations?
5. Natural drives, conditioned by individual experience over one's life, provide each individual with a propensity to behave in certain ways.	5. Think about Maslow's framework of a need hierarchy in terms of the needs that underlie your own urge to behave in certain ways. Weighing the potency of various needs in your life will help you understand and predict your own behavior in organizational situations.
6. Goals have a direct effect on behavior. Clear, demanding goals, once accepted, lead to improved performance.	6. Identify your personal goals as explicitly as possible. What do you want to accomplish? By setting challenging, reasonable objectives you can focus your efforts in areas that are important to you. Develop action

Generalizations	**Implications**
	plans and target dates that help you accomplish your goals.
7. Effort is essential but not sufficient to ensure good performance. Ability, in the form of knowledge, skill, and organizational technology, is also important.	7. Maximize the probability of your effort leading to good performance by finding situations where your abilities match the requirements. Increase your chances by continually upgrading your knowledge and skill, in both depth and breadth.
8. Individuals are motivated to expend effort when they think it will lead to good performance that will be appropriately rewarded.	8. Know the overall reward system and the relative weight you put on various kinds of rewards. Choose work that is rewarding in and of itself. Let others know what your reward preferences are so they can be taken into account in designing jobs and compensation systems.
9. Behavior that is rewarded tends to be repeated.	9. Modify or shape your own behavior in ways you think is appropriate. Keep explicit records or graphs that allow you to know when you have achieved personal objectives. Your own satisfaction is an important reward. If your job has some distasteful aspects, do those chores first so that the more desirable activities become rewards in and of themselves. This approach can offset the common tendency to procrastinate.
10. We are all involved in shaping the behavior of those around us, whether consciously or unconsciously.	10. To modify or shape the behavior of peers and superiors, make sure you reinforce behavior that is good from your point of view. To some degree, this will increase the likelihood that such behavior will be repeated in the future.

As a Current or Future Manager

Generalizations	Implications
1. A person cannot motivate another person. Motivation is internal; it is what energizes, directs, and sustains behavior.	1. Create conditions that allow and encourage motivation to take place in subordinates. Recognize the vital role that managers play in tapping latent human capability.
2. Positive or negative assumptions about human nature tend to be fulfilled. Optimism can lead to success; pessimism can lead to failure.	2. Be as positive as possible for as long as possible. You may experience disappointments, but remember: optimists are wrong about as often as pessimists, but they have more fun. Set a positive tone for your subordinates. It will pay off in terms of increased effectiveness, efficiency, and participant satisfaction.
3. People are different in terms of what motivates them. They have different needs, desires, and goals. And the strength of motivating forces varies over time for individuals.	3. Differentiate your approach to creating motivating conditions for individuals as much as possible. Try to understand each individual and diagnose each situation so that your approach fits the circumstances. Recognize that this makes managing more difficult than assuming that people are identical.
4. People think about and decide how to behave in organizations.	4. Make organizational and personal expectations known to subordinates. Provide information that they can use in deciding how to behave. This includes performance goals and potential rewards.
5. Difficult, specific goals, once accepted, lead to improved performance.	5. Develop challenging, realistic goals for each subordinate by means of a participative, interactive process. Be sure that specific objectives are understood and accepted.
6. Effort is essential but not suf-	6. Make sure that the subordi-

Generalizations	Implications
ficient to ensure good performance. Ability in the form of knowledge, skill, and organizational technology, is also important.	nates have the ability (knowledge, skill) to perform up to your expectations. Make sure that organizational constraints do not preclude the accomplishment of goals. Continuing gaps can create dysfunctional tension and lead to frustration. Match people and tasks in terms of your expectations and their ability. Encourage subordinates to develop their knowledge and skill.
7. Individuals are motivated to expend effort when they think it will lead to good performance that will be appropriately rewarded.	7. Involve subordinates in the goal-setting process so that they can strive for results that are both personally and organizationally relevant. Determine individual differences and reward preferences and adjust your behavior accordingly as much as possible.
8. In the long run, rewards are more effective in shaping behavior than punishment. While punishment can be effective in the short run, it has potential negative side-effects such as decreased communication, increased alienation, and behavior aimed at getting even.	8. Positively reinforce the good aspects of your subordinates' performance. Use praise and recognition to spotlight good results. Try not to harangue subordinates about substandard performance. Instead, use explicit records, such as charts and graphs (and encourage subordinates to develop their own) so that results become valid public data. In this way, negative feedback is obvious and self-induced, thus allowing you to concentrate on positive reinforcement of individual strengths.
9. The job itself is an important aspect of motivation. The nature of the job can induce effort or it can actively discourage it	9. Design jobs so that they are as enriched as possible by including characteristics such as skill variety, task identity, task sig-

Generalizations	Implications
and thus require other means of ensuring a good day's work for a day's pay.	nificance, autonomy, and feedback. Recognize that not all jobs can be enriched significantly and that some people respond to such jobs more than others. Keep in mind that needs differ in strength with different people. Match people and jobs accordingly.
10. Lack of feedback is cited by people in organizations as a pervasive and important problem.	10. Develop a managerial approach that facilitates and encourages feedback. Target key areas where results show up; develop challenging, realistic objectives that are accepted by all concerned; agree on action plans; make performance expectations explicit; engage in performance evaluation on a continuing basis (rather than once a year); and maintain a two-way communication process.
11. Latent human capability is a vast resource that can be tapped if individuals are motivated to expend effort that is focused in organizationally relevant directions.	11. Make sure that factors such as pay, working conditions, interpersonal relations, supervision, and policies and procedures are adequate enough to ensure normal effort. Devote particular attention to factors that evoke effort beyond the norm; for example, job enrichment, allocation of more responsibility, recognition for achievement, and hierarchical advancement.

LEARNING APPLICATION ACTIVITIES

1. Write a vignette based on your experience that illustrates significant changes (higher or lower) in the amount of effort you put into a particular task.

2. Using Figure 4.4 for ideas, design (enrich?!) the "job" of student in this class. Give specific examples of how each of the dimensions would be involved.

3. Observe a friend's behavior over the course of a day and speculate why he or she acts in a certain way. Ask your friend to explain (i.e., identify causes) and then compare your speculations with his or her explanations.

4. Review the hierarchy of needs shown in Figure 4.2.

Step 1: Give an example from your own experience of how each level affects your behavior.

Step 2: Share your examples in a group of four to six colleagues. Discuss the relative potency of the five levels as causes of behavior.

Step 3: In the total class, discuss the usefulness of the need hierarchy concept in explaining human behavior.

5. Review the *Drytox Corporation* vignette.

a. How would you describe the prevailing climate in the company?

b. What motivates Liz Connell?

c. If you were Liz, would you attempt to renegotiate your 1984 objectives with your boss? Why or why not?

6. *Step 1:* (a) Think of a recent situation (preferably in a work organization) when you felt really good, willing to work hard, and excited about your job. Describe the essence of that situation in several sentences.

(b) Think of a recent situation (preferably in a work organization) when you felt really bad, ready to quit, and dissatisfied with your job. Describe the essence of that situation in several sentences.

Step 2: Share your descriptions with a group of four to six colleagues.

Step 3: Develop a group summary by stating the essence of each situation in one word or a phrase. Post the results on a blackboard or on the wall (using flipchart sheets).

Step 4: Compare the results with the motivator and hygiene factors shown in Figure 4.3. Discuss the results in the total class.

7. Using the motivators (Figure 4.3) as guidelines, list some action steps you would take, as a manager, to tap the latent capability of your subordinates.

8. Assume you are a management consultant. Use the questions in Box 4.3 to analyze a work situation with which you are familiar. Recommend a plan of action for improving performance *and* satisfaction.

9. Select several of the suggestions for applying principles of motivation in Box 4.4 and describe step by step the specific actions you would take as a manager to carry them out.

REFERENCES

Adams, J. Stacy. "Toward an Understanding of Inequity." *Journal of Abnormal and Social Psychology* 67 (November 1963): 422–436.

Caplow, Theodore. *How to Run Any Organization*. Hinsdale, Ill.: Dryden Press, 1976.

Carrell, Michael R., and John E. Dittrich. "Equity Theory: The Recent Literature, Methodological Considerations, and New Directions." *Academy of Management Review* 3 (April 1978): 202–210.

Cooper, M. R., B. S. Morgan, P. M. Foley, and L. B. Kaplan. "Changing Employees Values: Deepening Discontent?" *Harvard Business Review* 57/1 (January-February 1979): 117–125.

Gray, Farnum. "Little Brother is Changing You." *Psychology Today,* March 1974, pp. 42–46.

Hackman, J. Richard, Greg Oldham, Robert Janson, and Kenneth Purdy. "A New Strategy for Job Enrichment." *California Management Review* 17/4 (Summer 1975): 57–71.

Hamner, W. Clay, and Ellen P. Hamner. "Behavior Modification on the Bottom Line." *Organizational Dynamics* 4/4 (Spring 1976): 3–21.

Herzberg, Frederick. "Motivation, Morale, and Money." *Psychology Today,* March 1968, p. 42.

———. *Work and the Nature of Man.* Cleveland: World Publishing Company, 1966.

Kast, Fremont, and James Rosenzweig. *Organization and Management: A Systems and Contingency Approach,* 3d ed. New York: McGraw-Hill, 1979.

Kennedy, Ray, and Nancy Williamson. "Money: The Monster Threatening Sports." *Sports Illustrated,* 17 July, 1978, pp. 28–88.

Kramarsky, David, "The Blue Collar View of Management." *Administrative Management* 37/3 (March 1977): 26–29, 104–105.

Latham, Gary P., and Edwin A. Locke. "Goal Setting—A Motivational Technique that Works." *Organizational Dynamics* 8/2 (Autumn 1979): 68–80.

Lawler, Edward E. "Workers Can Set Their Own Wages—Responsibility." *Psychology Today,* February 1977, pp. 109–112.

Likert, Rensis. *The Human Organization,* New York: McGraw-Hill, 1967.

Locke, Edwin A. "The Ubiquity of the Technique of Goal Setting in Theories of and Approaches to Employee Motivation." *Academy of Management Review* 3 (July 1978): 594–601.

Madsen, K. B. *Theories of Motivation.* 4th ed. Kent, Ohio: Kent State University Press, 1968.

Maslow, A. H. "A Theory of Human Motivation." *Psychological Review* 50 (July 1943): 370–396.

McClelland, David C. *The Achieving Society.* Princeton, N.J.: Van Nostrand, 1961.

———. "Business Drive and National Achievement." *Harvard Business Review* 40/4 (July-August 1962): 99–112.

McGregor, Douglas M. *The Human Side of Enterprise.* New York: McGraw-Hill, 1960.

Mitchell, Terence R. "Applied Principles in Motivation Theory." In Peter Warr (Ed.), *Personal Goals and Work Design.* London: Wiley, 1976, pp. 163–171.

———. "Expectancy Models of Job Satisfaction, Occupational Preference and Effort: A Theoretical, Methodological, and Empirical Appraisal." *Psychological Bulletin* 82 (December 1974): 1053–1077.

———. "Motivation: New Directions for Theory, Research, and Practice." *Academy of Management Review* 7/1 (January 1982): 80–88.

Murray, Henry A. *Explorations in Personality.* New York: Oxford University Press, 1938.

Newstrom, John, William E. Reif, and Robert M. Monczka. "Motivating the Public Employee: Fact Versus Fiction." *Public Personnel Management* 5 (January-February 1976): 67–72.

Organ, Dennis W. "A Reappraisal and Reinterpretation of the Satisfaction-Causes Performance Hypothesis." *Academy of Management Review* 2 (January 1977): 46–53.

———. "Inferences About Trends in Labor Force Satisfaction: A Causal-Correlational Analysis." *Academy of Management Journal* 20 (December 1977): 510–519.

Perry, James L., and Lyman W. Porter. "Factors Affecting the Context for Motivation in Public Organizations." *Academy of Management Review* 7/1 (January 1982): 89–98.

Porter, Lyman, and Edward E. Lawler III. *Managerial Attitudes and Performance.* Homewood, Ill.: Irwin and the Dorsey Press, 1968.

Rand, Thomas M. "Diagnosing the Value Orientations of Employees." *Personnel Journal* 56 (September 1977): 451–453.

Rogers, Carl R. "In Retrospect: Forty-Six Years. "*American Psychologist* 29/2 (February 1974): 115–123.

Rogers, Carl R., and B. F. Skinner. "Some Issues Concerning the Control of Human Behavior: A Symposium." *Science* 124 (30 November 1956) 1057–1066.

Rose, Harvey N. "Managerial Graffiti." *Journal of Systems Management,* April 1977, pp. 20–22.

Skinner, B. F. *Beyond Freedom and Dignity,* New York: Knopf, 1971.

Solomon, Steven. "How a Whole Company Earned Itself a Roman Holiday." *Fortune,* January 15, 1979, pp. 80–83.

Spitzer, Dean R. "30 Ways to Motivate Employees to Perform Better." *Training/HRD,* March 1980, pp. 51–56.

Steers, Richard M., and Lyman W. Porter. *Motivation and Work Behavior,* 2d ed. New York: McGraw-Hill, 1979.

Umstot, Denis D., Terence R. Mitchell, and Cecil H. Bell, Jr. "Goal Setting and Job Enrichment: An Integrated Approach to Job Design." *Academy of Management Review* 3 (October 1978): 867–879.

"Using B' Mod to Boost Attendance and Timeliness." *Training,* September 1978, pp. 6–8.

Vroom, V. H. *Work and Motivation*. New York: Wiley, 1964.

PART THREE

INTERPERSONAL, INTRAGROUP, AND INTERGROUP RELATIONSHIPS

Part Three builds on the study of individual behavior to consider interpersonal, intragroup, and intergroup relationships. Organizations are social as well as technical systems, and it is important to understand such fundamental social processes as communication, leadership, group dynamics, and conflict. Knowledge of these social relationships is vital to understanding human behavior in organizations. Effective management of these processes is a challenging and rewarding function.

Chapter 5 discusses communication and describes its central role for human behavior in organizations. It presents a general model of communication, then compares and contrasts the process at three levels: intrapersonal, interpersonal, and organizational. It identifies several chronic communication problems in organizations and presents personal and organizational strategies for improving communication skills and outcomes.

Chapter 6 covers influence systems and leadership. It compares and contrasts various interpersonal ways of influencing behavior in organizations. The attributes and behaviors of effective leaders and their effect on organizational performance are considered. Contingency views and the desirability of flexible leadership styles are emphasized, with guidelines for leadership behavior in specific situations provided.

Chapter 7 considers in detail the effect of group processes on individual behavior and organizational activities. It considers a number of factors that affect group dynamics and organizational outcomes. Various types of groups are discussed. Groups are extremely important in the study of organizational behavior because of their potential impact on individual satisfaction and on organizational performance. Suggestions for how groups can learn to be more effective are included.

Chapter 8 focuses on one of the more difficult problems in organizations—conflict and its management. The functional and dysfunctional aspects of conflict and cooperation are considered. The causes of conflict are considered, including contextual factors and intrapersonal, interpersonal, intragroup, and intergroup processes. Various approaches to managing conflict more effectively are presented.

5
Communication

LEARNING OBJECTIVES

After reading this chapter you should be able to:

1. Define communication and describe its relationship to human behavior in organizations.
2. Explain a general model of the communication process.
3. Identify and give examples of various purposes of communication.
4. Compare and contrast communication processes at three levels: intrapersonal, interpersonal, and organizational.
5. Identify and give examples of several chronic communication problems in organizations.
6. Outline several personal and organizational strategies for improving communication skills and outcomes.

TALKING TO HIMSELF

"I need to make a decision soon," thought Jeff, "in order to get the family settled before school starts." The job offer had come up unexpectedly about three weeks ago and he had told Joe Kemper, president of Sunrise Construction, Inc. that he would let him know in a month. As manager of the Bend, Oregon Branch of the First National Bank of Portland, Jeff had helped Sunrise with the financial aspects of its condominium construction projects. It was a successful company in a growth industry. However, Jeff was well aware of similar companies that had prospered for a short period of time and then gone bankrupt. The new job (as a vice-president) meant a significant increase in pay and stock options that might be quite valuable in the future. On the other hand, he was leery of the fast pace of the construction business and was concerned about fitting into the life style of Joe Kemper and the other officers of Sunrise. Also, the new job would require that he move to Portland.

Jeff Hughes had been with First National for ten years after graduating from Portland State University with a degree in finance. He had made normal progress as far as he could tell, based on comparisons with others that had been hired about the same time. He was one of 13 branch managers reporting to the eastern Oregon district manager, a senior vice-president. His branch seemed to be doing okay, but he wasn't sure. The regional manager had not given him any indication of his promotion potential. Of course, Jeff had not asked him a direct question. He was aware that specialists with M.B.A. degrees were being hired directly into some of the top jobs in the Portland headquarters. Jeff and his family liked the situation in Bend and were involved in many civic and recreational activities. His wife was active in PTA; the kids participated in scouting, swim team, and little league; and Jeff was an officer in the Lions Club, played golf regularly, and was an avid skier. He knew he had to make a decision by the end of the week, but so far the situation was still unclear in his mind.

CLOSE THE DOOR?

Professor Bob Hancock was working in his office at home, editing a manuscript for publication. His wife, Anne, was also in the office typing a letter. The door was open and both the washer and dryer were running in the laundry room across the hall. The telephone rang. (It was Dick wanting to check on the starting time for tomorrow's golf game.) Bob couldn't hear very well and he thought that if the door were closed and Anne stopped typing it would improve his ability to hear what Dick had to say. Therefore, he signaled with his left arm by bending his hand and forearm forward several times briskly. To Bob this clearly meant for Anne to "please close the door." However, Anne got up and left the room. Bob rose, closed the door and proceeded to discuss the arrangements for tomorrow's golf game with Dick. He then hung up and returned to editing the manuscript. Several minutes later Anne returned and said, "What was the secret telephone call about?"

TO SPEAK OR NOT?

Lisa was writing in the diary she kept for her organization behavior class. She wasn't too keen about recording her thoughts and feelings concerning the various experiences in class, but it was a requirement and she might as well get it done. Here are her comments:

Today we had a group of seven people trying to develop a proposal to present to the top management of Acme Aircraft Corporation. Tom was in my group and, as usual, he "had all the answers," and tried to dominate the discussion. I don't like him. Last week when we were working as a pair on the field trip project, it was a disaster. He didn't like anything I suggested and made me feel stupid. I was almost in tears, but I didn't say anything at the time. I told Jan about it later and she said, "I know, I've had the same problem with him. Somebody should set him straight." I wish I could bring myself to tell him what I really think.

Well, anyway, our group didn't seem to get anywhere for thirty minutes or more. Several people argued with Tom. I had some good ideas, but I didn't say anything. After about 45 minutes Bob said, "Lisa, you haven't said much so far, what do you think?" I was confused (I had been daydreaming about my date for the weekend) and stammered something like, "We seem to be on the right track; I think we have a good plan." The group proceeded to refine the plan and pick Bob to present it.

At the time, I was mad at Bob for "picking on me." However, as I think about it now, maybe he was being helpful by trying to include several of us (who had been quiet) in the discussion. One of my goals this quarter is to say what I think in face-to-face discussions. But so far, even when I am invited to do so, I can't get the words out.

WANTED OR NOT?

During her last two quarters in the M.B.A. program at State University, Wilma interviewed with a number of large public and private organizations. One company, Advanced Electronics, was high on her list. She was invited to the company's main plant for an interview and further negotiations. A friend and former classmate, who had taken a job with Advanced the year before, urged her to consider it seriously. She was particularly interested in production supervision with a relatively new division that manufactured peripheral equipment for computer systems. Although the pay was less than she had expected and shift work was involved, Wilma felt that there was considerable opportunity for personal progress.

Her interviews with key managers seemed to go well and she assumed she would have a job offer as soon as the details were ironed out and the paper work was completed. The division manager's parting words were something like, "We hope you give our offer serious consideration and we look forward to having you as a member of our managerial team." When she returned home after this interview, she found a form letter from the personnel department of Advanced Electronics that read as follows:

ADVANCED ELECTRONICS
Committed to Excellence

Thanks for getting in touch with us. We're pleased to hear that you are interested in a career with Advanced.

Careful personal attention for each applicant takes time, so we're sending you this response to let you know that we are processing your inquiry. Depending on the volume of activity in your special field at the time, this processing may take several weeks.

If we have an opening that we feel you are qualified for, we'll notify you as quickly as possible. If you don't hear from us it means that we don't have a suitable opening now. We will keep your file for a year and would like for you to notify us of any changes in your qualifications or plans.

Again, thanks for your interest in Advanced.

Advanced is an equal opportunity employer.

Wilma was confused; she wondered which message to believe.

CITY MANAGER'S OFFICE

One of the first actions Bill Donaldson took after he became city manager of Tacoma, Washington, was to have his office door removed and stored in the basement of the County-City building. This was the ultimate in "open-door policies." Moreover, his desk was in one corner of a large L-shaped room with several low partitions. Four desks were in immediate proximity to the city manager and provided space for an administrative assistant, an urban fellow, a management intern (rotating every three months from the various city departments), and a special projects coordinator. These various "assistants" were kept well informed because of their ability to hear and observe Bill's interactions with visitors and callers. The scene was often hectic with three or more face-to-face or telephone conversations in progress simultaneously. A meeting with one or more department directors might be interrupted when the mayor or a member of the city council would "drop in" to make a suggestion or ask a question. Many people in the organization thought Donaldson's behavior was a bit bizarre and inappropriate, but others said, "He's crazy like a fox; that open door and all those people make it difficult for secret bargains to be made or nefarious schemes to be hatched."

The missing door and the open environment had differing consequences on members of the organization. Some department directors welcomed it as an indication of a "breath of fresh air." It was one sign of a managerial style that was to include more participation by middle managers and lead to delegation of decision making to the various directors. Others worried about the problem of access to the city manager when they wanted to discuss confidential matters. The topic of "the city manager's office" came up at several top management team workshops over a period of several years. The problems and opportunities that the new arrangement presented were thoroughly discussed and Donaldson decided the advantages outweighed the disadvantages.

Donaldson used the same strategy when he left Tacoma to become city manager of Cincinnati, Ohio; he removed the door to his office. After several years he moved on to become director of the Philadelphia Zoo. He heard reports of considerable confusion in Cincinnati after he left because they couldn't find the door.

NETMA

When Edward Carlson was chief executive officer of United Airlines, he described their approach to improving communication in an organization of approximately 50,000 employees.

We work pretty hard at communications, all of us. We use a word around here—it's not as popular now as it was at first—NETMA, which means "Nobody ever tells me anything." I think that to a great extent that's disappeared. For a while, though, I thought we were overcommunicating. We were spending a lot of time telling everybody too much. But people have now found the formula.

We still have the daily *Employee Newsline,* and an employee's newspaper, which once a month carries a supplement of more in-depth stories. We do a *Supervisors' Hotline,* and more and more we're doing audio-visuals for employees—we're doing television training films.

We use the *Employee Newsline* to tell our employees about immediate company and industry news, policies, plans, and objectives. It's also used to squash rumors before they spread. Employees are really interested in news that personally involves them— things like wages, personnel policies, interline travel, labor problems, daily company operations, financial news, and so on.

The *Newsline* is the fastest way to communicate with all employees at once. It enables us to speak with one corporate voice on corporate and division issues. This is really important for a company as big as United.

The *Supervisors' Hotline,* on the other hand, is a biweekly newsletter which goes to first-line supervisors. They are encouraged to discuss items contained in the *Hotline* with those who report to them, thus building person-to-person communication.

We are fortunate in having employees who have come forward and pointed out problems and suggested solutions. In my visits I constantly encourage employees to raise problems and suggestions. In turn, we are careful to respond to their ideas, because we really do care about what our employees are thinking.

As you get older, if you're in the corporate world, and if you're successful and have made a little money, and if you've received some recognition, there may be a tendency to withdraw. You begin to enjoy seeing only the people with whom you're comfortable, the ones who think the same way that you do, at the golf club and at businessmen's lunches.

You don't like bad news. And there's not the incentive to work as hard as you did before because you've got it made. Then the word gets out—"Stay away from this fellow; he's in a bad mood, and he doesn't want to hear that." And that's the beginning of what I call corporate cancer.

But if you're willing to get out and to be a part of visible management then you have to be willing to accept criticism that comes from face-to-face meetings with employees. If you have employees who are members of a union, they just might tell you, "You can't fire me, and here's what I think of your management." But if you're willing to go out and meet with them, pretty soon you learn how employees feel about their company. Then you can try to create a program where they believe in you—and in fact, in all of the officers, because nobody sings solo.

Source: " 'Visible Management' at United Airlines," *Harvard Business Review* 53/4 [July-August 1975]: 90–97. Reprinted by permission of the *Harvard Business Review.* Excerpt from " 'Visible Management' at United Airlines," an interview with Edward E. Carlson.

INTRODUCTION

Effective communication is a difficult and precarious human endeavor, as indicated in the foregoing vignettes. Bob Hancock thought his arm signal was perfectly clear. Lisa may never be assertive enough to confront people like Tom. Wilma received conflicting messages from Advanced Electronics. Bill Donaldson's missing door was interpreted several different ways.

In our attempt to communicate—verbally or nonverbally, orally or in writing—it is likely that we will be misunderstood. Likewise, when we are on the receiving end we probably will not get the message as it was intended. There is much truth in the following sign that hangs in the offices of many managers.

> I know you believe you understand what you think I said. However, I am not sure you realize that what I think you heard is not what I meant.

When you ask the members of an organization, "What are your problems?" or "What gets in the way of this organization being as effective, efficient, and as satisfying for its participants as it could be?", the answer inevitably includes some reference to communication difficulties. Thus, better communication is usually an important leverage point for improving organization performance. Understanding communication is crucial to understanding human behavior in organizations. It is an essential ingredient, without it there is no organization. That is, without communication there is no way for two or more people to be engaged in a joint endeavor. The foregoing incidents and situations illustrate the variety of communication issues that arise in human organizations. In this chapter we will focus on understanding the communication process, identifying typical communication problems, and outlining ways to improve communication. The following topics will be covered:

Communication Defined
The Communication Process
Intrapersonal Communication
Interpersonal Communication
Organizational Communication Systems
So What? Implications for You

COMMUNICATION DEFINED

Communication is the transfer of meaning or information between sender and receiver. This relatively simple, straightforward statement masks a complex phenomenon that has been studied from many points of view. Dance reviewed 95 definitions in an attempt to clarify the concept, and found 15 relatively distinct, recurring themes shown in Box 5.1. The scope of communication studies can vary significantly depending on: (1) the level of observation; (2) the presence or absence of an intent on the part of the sender; and (3) the evaluation of whether or not an act of communication is successful. Within this framework, the broadest view of communication would include transfer of meaning at all levels (machine, animal, and human), with or without intent on the part of a sender and whether or not the act was successful. The narrowest view of communication would involve the successful transfer of intended meaning from one human being to another.

Clearly, this latter view of communication is too restricted for our purpose of understanding human behavior in organizations. People problems often stem from unintended consequences of communication acts. Lack of understanding or misunderstanding are typical organizational problems. Think of the number of times you have been in trouble in an organizational context because you didn't get the message—instructions were unclear, a memo was misinterpreted, or both. In modern organizations machine-machine and human-machine communication is becoming increasingly important. The problems and opportunities stemming from improved communications or information-processing technology will be covered in Chapter 9. In this chapter we will focus on the human level—communication between people in an organizational context. We will also consider intrapersonal (thought processes within a person) communication briefly, in terms of its role in shaping individual personalities.

The phrase "transfer of meaning" implies some information content in messages. It includes facts, data, and knowledge. A fact is something that has happened in the real world and can be verified. Data are facts obtained through empirical research or observation. Knowledge represents facts or data that are gathered and stored for future reference. When information is transmitted from sender to receiver it has an increment of knowledge or at least changes the degree of uncertainty about a given situation from the receiver's point of view. It can have an impact on knowledge, values, beliefs, attitudes, opinions, or feelings.

COMMUNICATION PROCESS

A basic symbolic representation of the communication process is shown in Figure 5.1. It begins with an information source that provides the message that is to be transmitted to a destination, and continues over time in a series of interactions. Typically a message is encoded into gestures, words, or other symbols so that it can be transmitted to a receiver and then decoded at the destination. Any "noise" source interferes with the transmission of the message between sender and receiver, regardless of the size or sophistication of the system. Communication always requires three basic elements—the source, the message, and the destination. This is true regardless of the medium—verbal or nonverbal, oral or written, telephone or television.

The usefulness of diagramming the communication process is explained by Schramm as follows:

> Now it is perfectly possible by looking at those diagrams to predict how such a system will work. For one thing, such a system can be no stronger than its weakest link. In engineering terms, there may be filtering or dis-

BOX 5.1

VARIOUS VIEWS OF THE CONCEPT OF COMMUNICATION

1. Symbols/Verbal/Speech	Communication is the verbal interchange of thought or idea.
2. Understanding	Communication is the process by which we understand others and in turn endeavor to be understood by them. It is dynamic, constantly changing and shifting in response to the total situation.
3. Interaction/Relationship/Social Process	Interaction, even on the biological level, is a kind of communication; otherwise common acts could not occur.
4. Reduction of Uncertainty	Communication arises out of the need to reduce uncertainty, to act effectively, to defend or strengthen the ego.
5. Process	Communication: the transmission of information, ideas, emotions, skills, etc., by the use of symbols—words, pictures, figures, graphs, etc. It is the *act* or process of transmission that is usually called communication.
6. Transfer/Transmission/Interchange	The connecting thread appears to be the idea of something being transferred from one thing, or person, to another. We use the word ''communication'' sometimes to refer to what is so transferred, sometimes to the means by which it is transferred, sometimes to the whole process.
7. Linking/Binding	Communication is the process that links discontinuous parts of the living world to one another.
8. Commonality	It (communication) is a process that makes common to two or several what was the monopoly of one or some.

9. Channel/Carrier/Means/Route	The means of sending military messages, orders, etc. as by telephone, telegraph, radio, couriers.
10. Replicating Memories	Communication is the process of conducting the attention of another person for the purpose of replicating memories.
11. Discriminative Response/Behavior Modifying/Response Change	Communication is the discriminatory response of an organism to a stimulus. . . . So, communication between two animals is said to occur when one animal produces a chemical or physical change in the environment (signal) that influences the behavior of another.
12. Stimuli	Every communication act is viewed as a transmission of information, consisting of a discriminative stimuli, from a source to a recipient.
13. Intentional	In the main, communication has as its central interest those behavioral situations in which a source transmits a message to a receiver(s) *with the conscious intent to affect the latter's behaviors.*
14. Time/Situation	The communication process is one of transition from one structured situation-as-a-whole to another, in referred design.
15. Power	Communication is the mechanism by which power is exerted.

Source: Frank E. X. Dance, "The 'Concept' of Communication," *The Journal of Communication* 20 [June 1970]:201–210. Reprinted by permission of the International Communication Association.

tortion at any stage. In human terms, if the source does not have adequate or clear information; if the message is not encoded fully, accurately, effectively in transmittable signs; if these are not transmitted fast enough and accurately enough, despite interference and competition, to the desired receiver; if the message is not decoded in a pattern that corresponds

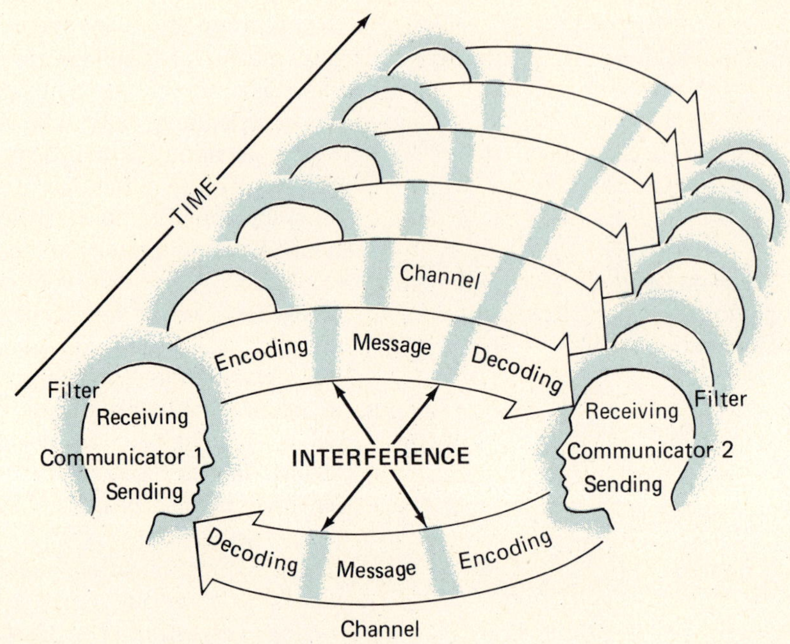

FIGURE 5.1 The Communication Process

> to the encoding; and finally, if the destination is unable to handle the decoded message so as to produce the desired response—then, obviously, the system is working at less than at top efficiency. When we realize that *all* these steps must be accomplished with relatively high efficiency if any communication is to be successful, the everyday act of explaining something to a stranger or writing a letter, seems a minor miracle (1954, pp. 4–5).

Technical problems such as static on the FM receiver in your automobile or "snow" on your television set are easy to identify. When interpersonal communication is involved, the problems of content and meaning of messages (semantics) become important.

In communication systems the goal is *understanding*—getting the sender and receiver "tuned" together for a particular message. Although repetition (redundancy) can be helpful, there is no direct correlation between the amount of communication or information transmission and the degree of understanding. Several basic problems are apparent (Guetzkow, 1965, p. 551). Some of the sender's meaning is lost in the process of encoding and transmitting a message. A memo may not reflect accurately the manager's feeling about a situation. Direct conversation with subordinates may help clarify it, but even in this case the tone of voice or the facial expression can alter the message significantly.

Another problem in achieving understanding in the communication process is that of decoding. Even if a message is encoded and transmitted accurately, it is unlikely that it will be decoded in the same way by everyone receiving it. People read, see, and hear what they want to read, see, and hear. Memos, statistics, and diagrams are interpreted in terms of value systems that are as unique to individuals as fingerprints. A person's perception of the situation depends on his or her total past experience; messages are distorted as receivers "read in" meanings not intended by the sender. A report from headquarters to several branches might be interpreted in several ways, with each receiver quite satisfied that he or she got *the* message.

Understanding is facilitated if there are means and time for feedback and verification. If the issue can be talked out, there is a chance that people can empathize and understand. However, time pressure works against this process; if the flow of information about complex issues is accelerated, the probability of complete understanding decreases. The physical distance between communicators and the nature of the media also affect the process (McCaskey, 1979).

INTRAPERSONAL COMMUNICATION

Two aspects of communication suggest beginning with intrapersonal communication processes. "The meaning of communication is more dependent on the response it elicits than on the intent of the communicator. The reactions of people—their behavior—tell us about the message they have received" (Rath & Stoyanoff, 1982, p. 171). We need to know about their values and beliefs—their conceptual system—in order to understand how they might perceive, interpret, and organize messages and information. Another reason for looking at intrapersonal communication is that we have physiological communication processes that are important for functioning in our environment. Lack of food results in hunger pangs, a message to the brain that suggests action, such as eating. Sitting on a hot stove triggers a message to the brain that leads to the action of getting off. Many neurophysiological communication processes are lightning fast, but they follow the same communication process shown in Figure 5.1. The same problems with interference are often evident. Hypothermia, for example, can create a sense of well-being that interferes with a more fundamental message that we are slowly freezing to death.

The concept of intrapersonal communication includes talking to oneself. For example, Jeff Hughes was mulling over in his mind the pros and cons of accepting the offer of a new job. He was generating ideas, asking himself questions, and trying to balance a number of factors that affected his decision-making process.

Personal Development

Intrapersonal communication serves several functions in personal development (Dance, 1967).

1. Integration of the individual in his or her environment.
2. Development of mental processes, particularly the use of symbols.
3. Regulation of behavior or socialization.

The growth and development of individuals from birth to maturity is such a natural process that we tend to take it for granted. In reality, it is quite complex and only comes to our attention when problems occur; when a person doesn't fit in, or when the ability to communicate seems to be impaired. Healthy individuals maintain a rather constant flow of communication with their environment that facilitates a dynamic equilibrium. They are at *ease* with their surroundings, including people they interact with. Increasing attention has been focused on holistic medicine and the integration of physical and mental well-being. In this context problems are described in terms of *dis-ease* or the lack of integration with the environment (Wright, 1975). In terms of intrapersonal communication, problems can be described as information overload, losing touch with reality, or mental illness. This view of mental illness resulting from information overload suggests that if individuals can remain in equilibrium with their environment, they are healthy. In a sense they are able to cope with external conditions and maintain a normal role in society. If they are unable to process information—both internal and external flows—efficiently, however, a condition of information overload occurs and there is a breakdown in the individual, particularly the intrapersonal communication system. The overload may develop because of inability to screen out irrelevant data for the individual's decision-making processes. This same concept might be applied to group and organizational health, as we will see later.

Communication is closely related to the development of mental processes. Potential stimuli cannot be acted on until they are received. Mental actions become more and more complex as the child develops the ability to speak, read, and write. The use of symbols (language, mathematics, etc.) depends on mental ability and an increasing amount of stored knowledge. A flow chart of a computer process is meaningful only if the arrows and boxes are meaningful. The capacity for mental action or the ability to process information internally has a significant effect on a person's communication skills as either a sender or receiver of messages.

A third function of human communication is regulation or control. In terms of intrapersonal communication, this takes the form of self-control via internalized rules or norms of behavior. As individuals grow and develop in the context of families, schools, work organizations, or other institutions they are socialized (see Chapter 2) to behave in certain ways, depending on particular roles and situations. This propensity to behave in certain ways has an effect on, and is affected by, communication processes.

As an individual develops into a unique self or personality, he or she also develops a self-image. This image may or may not coincide with the views of others, depending on the amount of interaction and the degree of openness in communication with them. We will look at this concept more closely in discussing

strategies for improving intrapersonal communication as a first step toward improving interpersonal and organizational communication skills.

Learning

The capability to think and behave is inherent in human beings. The extent to which this capability is developed and the specific thoughts or behaviors of individuals are the result of learning. Formal education provides a body of knowledge and specific skills to enable us to function in society. Direct experience and observation (vicarious experience) also play a large part in the growth and development of human beings over their entire life. We learn continually from the moment we are born. We are taught to distinguish shapes and recognize different colors. We learn to associate good feelings with a smile and bad feelings with a frown. We learn how to function as a member of a family, social group, athletic team, or work organization. Late in life, we learn how to not work; that is, retire.

The learning process involves communication with significant others with whom we come in contact. It also involves considerable intrapersonal communication as we receive and categorize information for storage as knowledge. We relate new ideas to old ideas with the result being reaffirmation or, perhaps, some adjustment. A major part of the learning process is internalization of the many symbols that facilitate communication in a particular culture. Some symbols, such as facial expressions, transcend cultures; they mean the same in Japan and Norway or Canada and Italy (Ekman, 1975). Other symbols such as language have to be learned in each culture in order to communicate with ease. When symbols mean essentially the same thing to sender and receiver, communication is facilitated. But the same symbol can have different meanings within a culture depending on specific circumstances. For example, a "thumb up" sign generally indicates a positive outcome or condition. During a baseball game, however, the same sign from an umpire means the runner is out, or, if aimed at the manager, it means that he or she is banished from the field.

Learning involves developing connotations of words that have special meaning for subgroups. For example, the word "sharp" can describe an intelligent person or a businessman whose practices are of questionable legality. The term "bureaucratic" can describe basic characteristics of large, complex organizations (in academic terms) or it can connote red tape, inefficiency, and ineffectiveness (in modern street language). The word "cool" can describe the temperature, a person who is emotionally distant, or someone who carries himself well—"has it together." The term "basement" means the part of a house that is partially or completely below ground level or it can mean absolutely nothing to someone who has never seen or heard of such a structure (as one of the authors found out when he made reference to his basement while lecturing in a foreign country). The term "nerd" cannot be found in the dictionary; yet, it is a meaningful adjective to young people across the country.

Learning is a never-ending process of individual growth and development.

BOX 5.2
HELP! UH, I MEAN, FIRE!

Many Police Departments conduct public-education programs to teach people what to do to avoid being mugged, thugged, raped, robbed, and assaulted on the street. Tips on what to do—avoid walking in unlighted areas at night; try to go places in the company of friends or relatives; when walking alone, use busy streets, with lots of other people around, etc.—are given, and they all seem reasonable and straightforward.

But a surprise suggestion is included in the education program: If you are being attacked and need help, and if there are other people around, don't yell *Help*, yell *Fire*. The police officers explain that their experience has shown that people who yell *Help* get less help from passers-by than people who yell *Fire*. The reason seems to be in the *meaning and implication* of the two different words, and the *responses they evoke in others*. The cry *Help* signals that someone else has a problem, and passers-by may easily decide not to get involved in someone else's problem. The cry *Fire*, on the other hand, signals that all people within earshot may have a problem, and passers-by and onlookers are more likely to come to the aid of the victim by stopping and finding out what is going on.

Both internal and external communication is essential. At any point in time the whole person is involved in communicating.

Factual knowledge, values, and beliefs comprise an individual's conceptual system or cognitive map. This system is unique for every individual and affects that individual's way of thinking and propensity to behave in certain ways. Figure 5.2 shows a model of cognitive development over time. In the beginning, human beings have a relatively closed, simple, unenriched view of the world. As they learn through education and experience, their conceptual system can grow to be open, complex, and enriched. The process can go both ways—progressing through ever widening spheres of interaction and the development of cognitive complexity. Or, a person may stop learning or even retrogress and become more closed minded (Rokeach, 1976). Obviously, communication is a crucial element of this growth process. At any point in time the person can be relatively open or relatively closed as a receiver and processor of information. A typical problem is stereotyping, where all elements of a class of objects or persons is labeled with some characteristic. The belief that all football players are dumb would lead one to ignore, or at least discount, the comments of Terry Bradshaw or Earl Campbell on the energy crisis. Because physicians tend to be held in awe, the comments of Dr. Ralph Butterfingers would be considered credible. The same tendency holds in work organizations when we have stereotypic views of blue-collar versus white-collar workers or managers versus nonmanagers.

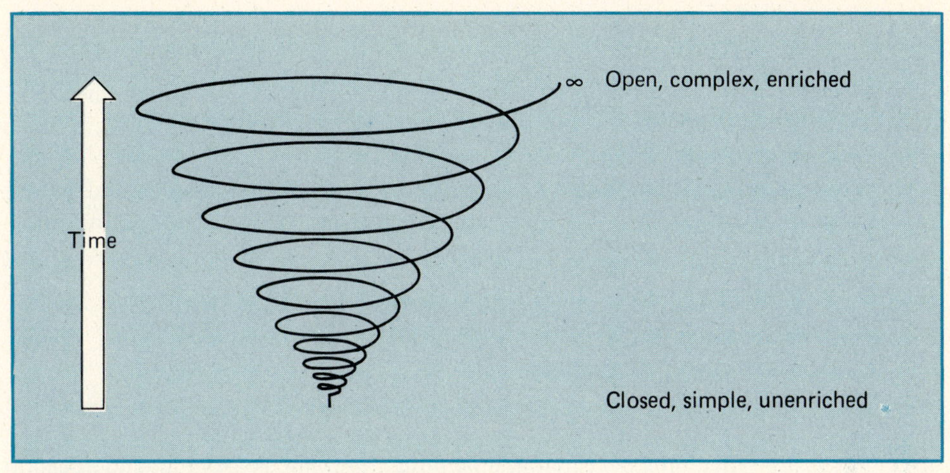

FIGURE 5.2 A Model of Cognitive Development

Perception

Perception is basic to understanding communication and behavior because it is the means by which stimuli affect an individual. A stimulus that is not perceived has no effect on behavior. Another key idea is that people behave on the basis of *what is perceived* rather that *what is*. A direct line to "truth" is often assumed, but each person really has only one point of view, based on individualistic perceptions of the real world. Some considerations can be verified in order that several or many individuals can agree on a consistent set of facts. However, in most real-life situations many conditions are not verifiable and are heavily value laden. Even when facts are established, their meaning or significance may vary considerably for different individuals. Figure 5.3 is a model of the way perceptions are formed and hence influence individual behavior. Numerous external forces such as the stress of the situation, group pressure, and reward systems are involved. Past experience has a direct influence on the interpretation of stimuli. Several basic processes (mechanisms) of perception formation can be identified—selectivity, closure, and interpretation. The concept of *selective* perception is important because voluminous information is received and processed. Individuals select information that is supportive and satisfying. They tend to ignore information that might be disturbing. For example, after purchasing a new automobile, buyers typically pay more attention to ads for the model purchased and tend to ignore ads for others. In this way, they are more likely to be satisfied with their decision.

The same stimulus can be interpreted differently by several individuals. *Interpretation* depends on past experience and the value system of each particular person. An attitudinal set, or propensity to think or act in a certain way, provides a framework for interpreting various stimuli. Not only do we perceive selectively, we interpret the situation in ways that will be supportive.

The process of *closure* in perception formation relates to the tendency of individuals to have a complete picture of any given situation. Thus, a person may perceive more than the information seems to indicate. We add to the information input whatever seems appropriate in order to close the system and make it meaningful and supportive.

While there is a tendency to perceive supportive information and ignore disturbing information, it is obvious that threatening, bad, or frightening information does come through. We cannot ignore the real world indefinitely, assuming that we are in the "normal" range in terms of sanity.

Cognition and Attribution

Individuals have cognitive systems that represent what they know about themselves and their environment. These systems are developed through cognitive processes—including perceiving, imagining, thinking, reasoning, and decision making. The more we understand about an individual's cognitive system, the better we are able to predict his or her behavior.

Cognition is a conscious, deliberate process of acquiring knowledge. Attribution is the tendency to make judgments about causal relationships. We infer from smiling faces and heads nodding up and down that the audience likes and agrees with a statement we have just made. This is a rather simple straightforward inference that seems quite plausible. However, a series of such nonverbal expressions over the period of a one-hour lecture could lead the speaker to infer that he was right on target and brilliant. Someone else might infer that this particular audience would be pleased by anything. Attribution is crucial in understanding human behavior in organizations because it is so natural and pervasive. We infer motives from the behavior of people we interact with. Moreover, we judge others in terms of their behavior; we judge ourselves in terms of our intentions.

In judging others and inferring cause-effect relationships we may attribute a certain behavior to internal or external factors. Internal causes are under the control of the individual while external causes are not. Poor performance may be attributed to lack of ability or effort. On the other hand, we might attribute it to faulty raw material or poor supervision. A person's conceptual system (values and beliefs) may lead to general tendencies to infer cause-effect relationships. For example, a person with a rather pessimistic view of human nature would infer internal causes for failure. A person with a negative view of bureaucracy may attribute lack of individual performance to the overall stifling environment in the organization. Attribution is part of a person's internal mental processes and it affects all communication.

Ideation

Another aspect of intrapersonal communication is ideation: the formation or conception of ideas by the mind. This includes initiating thoughts, mulling them over, and refining them for storing or transmitting to others. It also involves

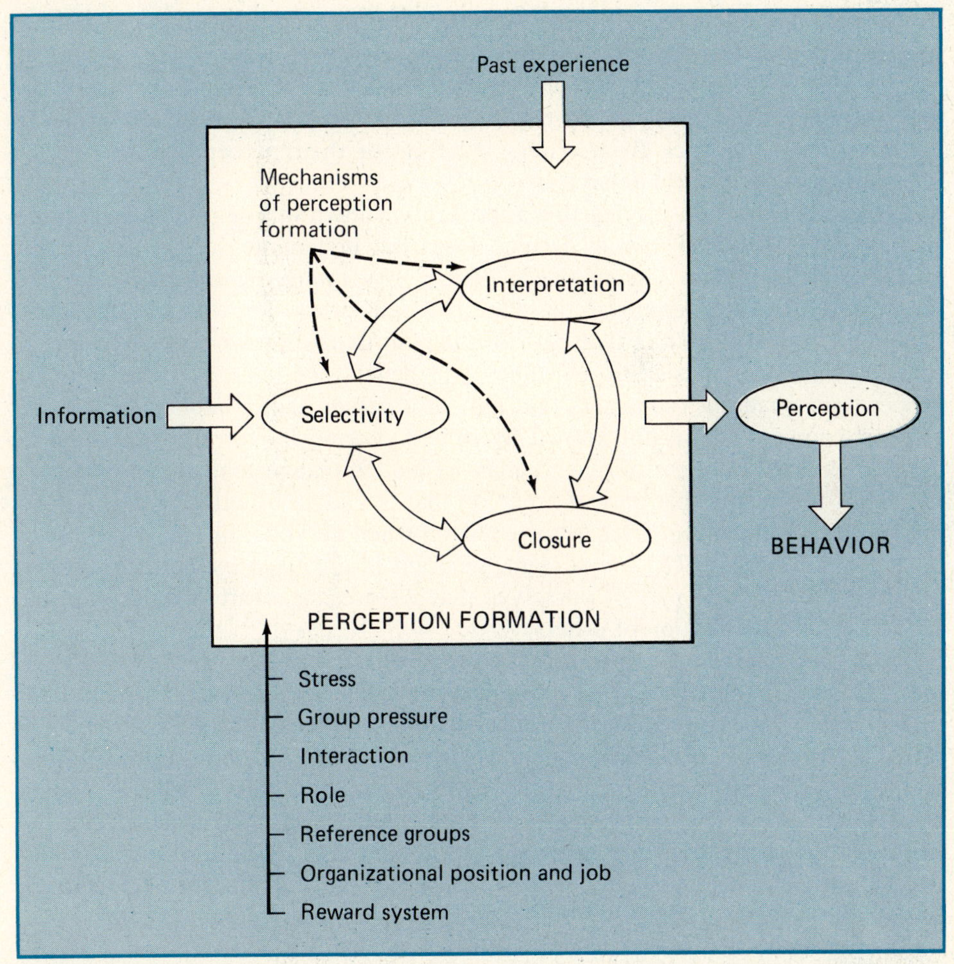

FIGURE 5.3 Perception Formation and its Effect on Behavior. **Source:** Adapted from Joseph A. Litterer, *The Analysis of Organizations,* 2d ed. (New York: Wiley, 1973), p. 103. © 1973. Used with permission.

receiving the beginnings of an idea and then processing it. This might include ultimate rejection, refinement, or elaboration.

Ideation involves talking to oneself, an obvious form of intrapersonal communication. The amount of ideation is related to the degree of cognitive complexity. That is, more ideation occurs when a person's conceptual system is open, complex, and enriched. A closed, simple, unenriched conceptual system would not be a fertile ground for ideas to be refined or elaborated. Potentially disturbing stimuli would not be perceived and might deliberately be ignored.

Improvement Strategies

It is our view that an open, complex, enriched conceptual system is important for good intrapersonal communication. Moreover, it is a key building block for good interpersonal and organizational communication processes. How does one improve in this regard? The first step is to know more about oneself: to develop an explicit picture of one's conceptual system, including values and beliefs. This might be done by thinking about them. However, it is probably helpful to get feedback from others in terms of their perceptions of you, as inferred from your overt behavior.

A means for considering this approach is shown in Figure 5.4. The model is called the *Johari Window,* derived from the first names of its originators, Joseph Luft and Harry Ingham (Luft, 1969, p. 13). Two basic dimensions are self and others. On each dimension there are two categories—known and not known. The upper left quadrant is that part of a person that is known to oneself and to others. Characteristics such as values and beliefs are *open* and evident. The upper right quadrant represents that part of a person that is *hidden*—things the person knows that are not known by others. Animosity for the boss may be hidden on purpose. Fear of heights may be hidden inadvertently. The lower left quadrant represents that part of a person that is known by others but unknown by the person, the *blind* area. An eye twitch when nervous, or a silly grin when angry are examples. The lower right quadrant is *unknown* by both the person and others. It is that part of ourselves that we are not aware of and that does not come to the attention of others.

If our goal is to increase the open area of our personality, we need to do two things. First, we need to engage in more self disclosure, thus reducing the hidden area. This can be done by expressing our opinions, attitudes, and feelings about various issues in the presence of others. In a sense, we exhibit more behavior for others to observe and reflect on. Second, we need to solicit feedback from others about their impressions of that behavior. This type of feedback, if it is accepted and internalized, can reduce the blind area. Simultaneous reduction of the hidden and blind areas results in more of our person being open to the world, particularly to those with whom we interact on a continuing basis.

It is obvious that our open window might vary in size depending on the particular group we are involved with. With our family it may be larger than with our work organization. Self disclosure and feedback is a functional process that depends on trust and a willingness to take risks. If it turns out to be a rewarding process, it will continue. If the results are threatening (i.e., the feedback is painful), the process will probably decrease or cease. Thus, it requires care and nurture to develop an open personality. Over the long run the payoffs can be beneficial in terms of healthy intrapersonal communication and providing the foundation for good interpersonal and organizational communication processes.

INTERPERSONAL COMMUNICATION

Any organization is comprised of two or more people in social relationships. A relationship, in turn, requires communication—verbal, nonverbal, or both. And, communication is behavior. Therefore, to really understand human behavior in

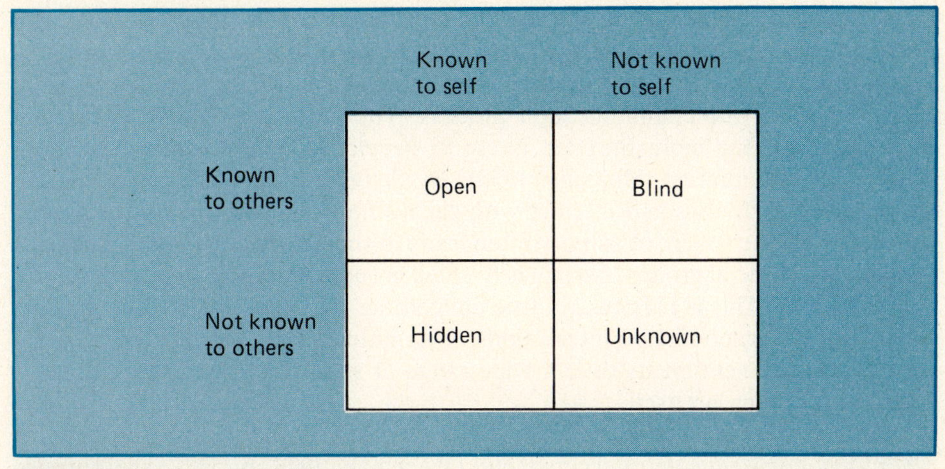

FIGURE 5.4 The Johari Window

organizations we need to know more about interpersonal communication: its goals, outcomes, problems, and strategies for improvement.

Goals

Within the context of our basic definition—"the transfer of meaning"—interpersonal communication has a more specific sense.

> *Communication* comes from the Latin *communis,* common. When we communicate we are trying to establish a "commonness" with someone. That is, we are trying to share information, an idea, or an attitude. . . . The essence of communication is getting the receiver and the sender "tuned" together for a particular message (Schramm, 1954, p. 3).

The goal is *understanding*—a condition in which the meaning of a message for John is exactly what Sally intended. Complete understanding is rare, as we shall see later when we discuss typical communication problems. However, the goal in any interpersonal communication is better understanding (or at least less misunderstanding).

A more elaborate view of the goals of interpersonal communication can be found in the work on *coorientation*—the simultaneous orientation of two persons to one another *and* to some external object such as a third person, a group, a thing, or an idea (Newcomb, 1953).

> Most basic to this kind of conceptualization is the assumption that societal phenomena are largely based on micro-social, not on individual, events. That is, a society is not composed of many persons (atoms) but of many interpersonal relationships (molecules) (Chaffee, 1973, p. 466).

Coorientation assumes some degree of understanding before two persons can communicate about any subject; that is, they have to be somewhat on the same "wavelength." The degree of understanding changes over time depending on the effectiveness of the communication process. The more two people interact in joint activities, the more they are likely to develop common sentiments about objects of joint interest (Homans, 1950). By definition, people in work organizations share activities and interact with each other. The reciprocal is also true; interaction in one sphere of activity often leads to shared activity in other spheres. Individuals in social groups, particularly small groups, are likely to evolve similar value systems. This is particularly true concerning the basic activity of a specific group. However, continued interactions of an intimate, face-to-face nature may result in shared sentiments over a wide range of subjects beyond the legitimate interests of the group itself.

Three aspects of coorientation help us understand the intentions of people when they communicate interpersonally (Wackman, 1973, p. 538). The purpose is often *actual agreement*; Grace engages Roger in a discussion about a proposed change in accounting procedures in order to get him to agree with her ideas. The degree of actual agreement may be difficult to determine, especially on complex issues. Therefore, we typically rely on *perceived agreement*—the similarity between our views on a subject and our perception of someone else's views on it. Perceived agreement tends to increase after interpersonal communication. For example, Grace is likely to *feel* that she has been successful in persuading Roger to her views; this belief may or may not be accurate. Thus, a third aspect, *accuracy*, is important. This is the similarity between our estimate of someone else's views on a subject and his or her actual views. If, after their discussion, Grace has a clearer picture of Roger's opinion of the proposed accounting procedures, then accuracy has increased. It is important to know whether the goal is agreement or accuracy, in order to determine the degree of success in interpersonal communication.

Other goals, such as entertaining and informing, are involved in interpersonal communication. Information exchange is essential in coordinating human endeavor in organizations. And entertaining can be an important function in maintaining a reasonable quality of work life. For example, *schmoozing*—small talk about nonwork issues—has an indirect effect on satisfaction and productivity (Schrank, 1978). However, in the context of work organizations the emphasis has been on persuading—changing opinions, attitudes, and behaviors. The following discussion illustrates the typical emphasis on persuasion in interpersonal communication:

BOSS (MARK): "Here is the new policy concerning early retirement."
SUBORDINATE (BILL): "It's a lousy idea. It'll never work."
MARK: "I think it's a good idea. A lot of people around here may want to take advantage of it."
BILL: "Nonsense. Nobody wants to be put out to pasture. People need to keep

active. Age has nothing to do with ability. We've got a lot of good years ahead of us."

MARK: "I don't know, some people tend to slow down a bit after they pass 60. I thought you might be interested in spending more time on your boat."

BILL: "I spend enough time on the boat already. Besides, it takes a lot of money to keep the thing running."

There is enough understanding of this issue for Mark and Bill to engage in a discussion of it. They obviously don't agree. And Mark doesn't have a very accurate perception of Bill's views on the subject. He appears to be attempting to influence or persuade Bill on two levels: (1) that early retirement is a good idea; and (2) that Bill ought to take advantage of the opportunity. If persuasion is the primary function of the communication we would tend to consider this interchange to be relatively ineffective. On the other hand, if we consider increased accuracy to be the primary function, the communication process may have been effective.

Whether one focuses on agreement ("Here's what you should think.") or accuracy ("What do you think?") can be important in building interpersonal relationships. The latter approach is a positive stroke that implies "You're important and your ideas are worth listening to." A response in kind can be a positive stroke as well, and lead to mutual respect. The degree to which a person emphasizes persuading or informing (or exchanging information) is a function of cognitive complexity, open-mindedness, and tolerance for ambiguity. Common sentiments typically underlie long-lasting relationships. However, mature relationships can accommodate differences of opinion on some issues, as long as there is a positive balance of mutual attractiveness. The role of communication in building an interpersonal relationship over time may be more a function of increased *accuracy* in perceiving each other's views, rather than toward greater agreement.

> In summary, "perfect communication" between two persons, totally free of constraints, would not necessarily improve agreement, and it might well reduce congruency (perceived agreement). If the two are motivated to coorient, it can facilitate understanding. But it should always improve accuracy, even to the absolute point where each person knows precisely what the other is thinking; this would be perfect communication in a quite literal sense. And yet they might disagree (and know they disagree), and even choose not to coorient to the same things in the same degree (McLeod & Chaffee, 1974, p. 487).

In an organizational context enough consensus (patterns of agreement-disagreement and accuracy-inaccuracy) is required to ensure continuing joint effort toward common goals. However, unanimity is obviously a utopian concept in most situations. Thus, it is important to have realistic goals when considering the functions of interpersonal communication in organizations.

Outcomes

The effectiveness of interpersonal communication is not an either/or condition; it is a matter of degree. Moreover, it should be considered in terms of various outcomes that may be explicit or implicit for the communicators. Understanding is the general outcome that underlies the degree of effectiveness for all attempts at interpersonal communication. The following equation illustrates this point:

$$\frac{\text{Receiver's message and intent}}{\text{Sender's intent and message}} = 1$$

We can illustrate this relationship for relatively simply messages, such as those conveying facts or numerical data. For example, the gas station attendant asks, "Do you know your license number?" You reply, "IPE 939." He writes down ICD 939. You say, "No, its IPE 939." He frowns slightly while correcting the information on the sales slip. Clearly the initial communication process was less than 100 percent effective in terms of the information transferred.

When we move to more complex intentions and messages the probability of 100 percent effectiveness drops dramatically. When the boss says, "Your work is generally satisfactory, but could be improved," you may be unclear about the specific message intended. You may hear the first part and ignore the second part, or vice versa. The boss may be setting you up for dismissal. Or, for a boss that is slow to praise subordinates, the message may be intended as extremely laudatory. Thus, we begin to see the problems in determining effectiveness when complex messages are involved. Assuming that there is some degree of understanding (getting the message intended) in interpersonal communication processes, we can look at another level of outcome: the degree to which purposes such as pleasure, improved relationships, attitude influence or persuasion, or action (behavior) are accomplished.

An important outcome of interpersonal communication can be pure *pleasure*. Interaction can be a goal in and of itself. It can be written (pen pals), spoken (relating a humorous anecdote), or nonverbal (a smile, a nod of approval, the caress of a loved one). Continued interaction can lead to additional outcomes, but a pleasure component may be present as well. It is a large part of casual, short-lived encounters such as seatmates on an airplane. In work organizations the discussion of nonwork issues (small talk) is probably inevitable and may be functional. It provides a change of pace where interpersonal interaction occurs for the fun of it. Indeed, humor can be a powerful tonic.

The effectiveness of interpersonal communication is often measured in terms of *improved relationships*. The focal point is typically the degree of agreement between two persons about other people or ideas. Common values and shared sentiments lead to or flow from improved interpersonal relationships. This view leads to persuasion as a focal point in discussions of interpersonal communication. However, a more mature approach to improved relationships concentrates more on understanding and accuracy than on agreement. "The major change over time in the acquaintance process is toward increased *accuracy* of perceiving the friend's position—rather than toward greater agreement or balance" (McLeod & Chaffee, 1973). This suggests that the individuals involved are tolerant enough to accept different points of view. In a sense, people agree to disagree on certain issues, but maintain a meaningful relationship and engage in joint activities.

The success or failure of interpersonal communication is often measured in terms of *attitude influence*. The goal is changing another person's opinion; the means is persuasion. A large amount of the literature on interpersonal communication deals with this subject, almost as if it were the only purpose involved. From this point of view, communication is ineffective if there is no change in attitude. We prefer a broader interpretation that rests on the assumption that the major function of interpersonal communication is information exchange. Attitudes may change in the process, but this is not the focal point. Accurate understanding of another person's point of view allows one to empathize with that person (walk in their shoes). This in turn provides a foundation for improved interpersonal relations.

The sender of a message often intends for the receiver to do something—to take some *action*. Mary says, "Please close the door." Joe closes the door. The boss says, "I want you to become a better manager." Doris says, "Yes sir," but doesn't really know what to do next. She may or may not behave the way the boss intended, thus a communication attempt may or may not be effective. In work organizations, it is obvious that understanding may be more important than agreement. For example, subordinates may engage in appropriate behavior and take the intended action steps whether they agree or not. Of course, individual and organizational well-being is enhanced when agreement is coupled with mutual understanding.

In our discussion of various communication outcomes we have indicated that the process is rarely 100 percent effective. Interpersonal problems are often caused by communication breakdowns. Let us turn now to consideration of some of the many problems in the interpersonal communication process.

Problems

When we put two individuals, Sue White and Bill Collins, into the basic model of a communication process (Figure 5.1), we can begin to see a number

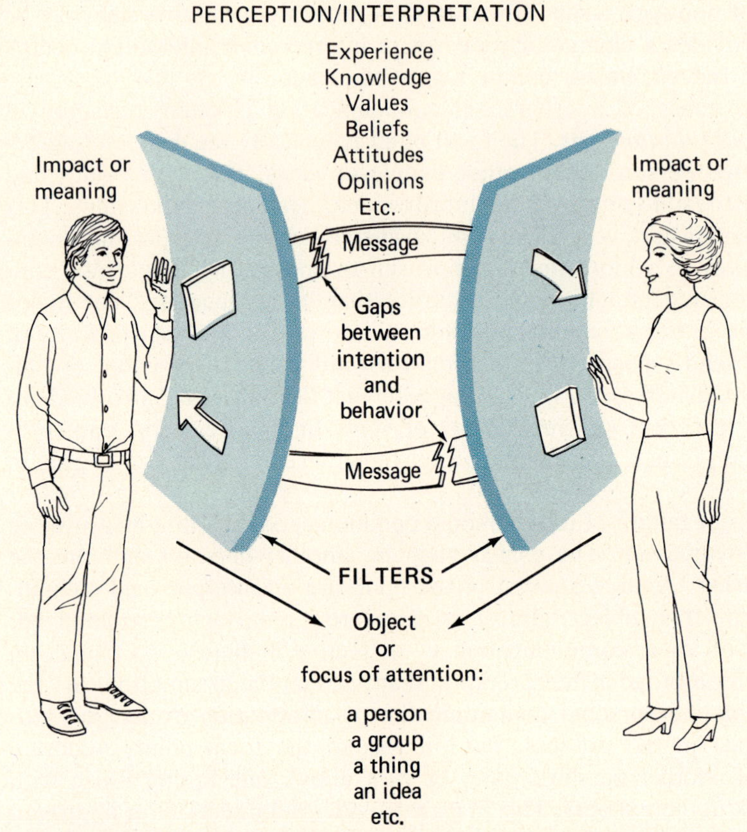

FIGURE 5.5 The Interpersonal Communication Process

of familiar sources for potential problems. As shown in Figure 5.5, Bill has in mind some intentions that are partly conscious and partly subconscious. His behavior toward Sue takes the form of verbal and nonverbal behavior. Sue senses (hears, sees, feels, etc.) that behavior through a filtering system based on her past experience. The meaning of a message is not fully accounted for in the words or actions of the sender; the meaning depends on the perception and interpretation of the receiver. Thus, two obvious problems are: (1) a gap between Bill's intentions and his behavior; and (2) misperception and misinterpretation by Sue. When she responds there may be a gap between her intentions and her behavior. And Bill may likewise misperceive and misinterpret the message. This deteriorating cycle obviously has adverse consequences for their relationship. Some means must be found to improve the communication process—to bring intentions and impact closer together.

Obvious communication problems can be recognized and dealt with. A more serious concern is the *illusion* of communication. In such cases there is an assumption that the message is clear and that it has been received. Bill says,

"Sue, if you have any questions about the new procedure just check with me." Bill thinks Sue doesn't understand the new procedure and that his offer of help is an indication of what he really thinks. Sue thinks Bill expects her to understand the new procedures and that (based on her observation of his lack of patience with others who have asked questions) she doesn't dare ask a question for fear of being seen as incompetent. Later, after several reports are fouled up, Bill says, "I thought I told you to check with me if you had any questions." And Sue replies, "I know you said it but I didn't think you meant it." The illusion of communication is especially troublesome in situations where one-way communication is prevalent. The written memo is particularly dangerous because we assume that putting it in writing will make the message abundantly clear. "How could you misunderstand; it's right there in black and white!" The illusion of communication is a more serious problem than lack of communication, because in the latter case we recognize some difficulty, attempt to determine the causes, and make changes.

Gaps between intentions and behavior may start with a lack of clarity or internal agreement on the part of the sender. If Bill is really not sure what he wants to say to Sue, it is unlikely that he will send a clear message. His conscious and subconscious intentions may conflict and result in different signals being sent verbally and nonverbally. On the other hand, he may be very sure of what he wants to say but be using a language that Sue doesn't understand. This problem is straightforward when the speaker uses Swahili and the listener doesn't know a word. It is a more subtle matter when Bill speaks accounting or computer jargon that Sue has not yet picked up.

A number of the causes of miscommunication rest with the receiver. Sue may read into a frown or a wink more meaning than Bill intended. Her values, attitudes, and beliefs are part of her filtering system: distorting messages by screening some things out, adding some things in or reading between the lines. Like many of us, Sue may tend to see and hear what she wants to see and hear and not hear or see what is unpleasant or demeaning. There is no way we can eliminate this filtering process of selective perception and interpretation. It is a fundamental part of each of us. Differences in nonverbal signals (gestures, physical proximity, timing, etc.) make communicating across cultures a complex and difficult process even when we understand the words. The nuances in the "silent" language often lead to misinterpretation (Hall, 1959).

The human tendency to be evaluative and defensive are formidable barriers to effective interpersonal communication (Rogers & Roethlisberger, 1952; Gibb, 1961). When discussing another person or an idea we tend to be judgmental; that is, we express approval or disapproval. The receiver is then put on the spot to either agree or disagree. Such behavior presumes that the goal of communication is persuasion and agreement, rather than understanding. Evaluation and defensiveness make it hard for us to express ourselves clearly or listen actively. Thus, it is difficult to transmit meaning accurately in interpersonal communication. Barbara says, "This new reporting format is lousy; it won't work." Walt (who designed the new format) responds, "I spent a lot of time on it. You are against anything different. Everyone else likes it.'' Instead of trying to understand the purpose of the new format and determine whether or not the proposed design meets the needs, Barbara and Walt are focusing on likes and dislikes aimed at each other as well as the report format itself.

Reflect on your own past experience and note how much evaluative and defensive behavior you engage in. Observe others in conversation. Note how difficult it is to refrain from such behavior. An underlying or causal factor is the level of trust between people. The lower the level of trust, the more likely that communication will be heavily laden with evaluative and defensive comments in order to protect our self-image. The higher the trust level, the more open the communication process and the less need there is for barriers and facades.

Another barrier that keeps people from operating on the same wavelength is a difference in status. Misunderstandings often occur when a person of lower status is reluctant to attempt to clarify a message from a superior. The status difference may be based on hierarchical position or technical expertise. In either case, it can be a barrier to accurate transmission of messages and mutual understanding.

Improvement Strategies

Given the uniqueness of each human being and the fact that the meaning of messages is in the mind of the receiver, perfect communication is impossible. Thus, the goal for improvement is to reduce uncertainty and misunderstanding to the point where there is enough mutual understanding to satisfy the needs of the situation. The receiver gets the sender's intent well enough to respond appropriately.

A first step in improving interpersonal communication was covered in the section on intrapersonal communication; that is, the striving to become more open through giving and receiving feedback. In terms of the Johari Window, large hidden or blind areas hinder effective interpersonal communication. Knowing something of your own filters as well as those of others can be helpful in communicating accurately.

A supportive climate is both a goal and a condition of effective interpersonal communication. Different conditions, mind sets, or values are nourished by different climates, as the following list illustrates (Gibb, 1961, p. 143):

Defensive Climate	*Supportive Climate*
1. Evaluation	1. Description
2. Control	2. Problem orientation
3. Strategy	3. Spontaneity
4. Neutrality	4. Empathy
5. Superiority	5. Equality
6. Certainty	6. Provisionalism

The conditions listed for a supportive climate reflect open-mindedness, tolerance for ambiguity, joint effort, exploration of ideas, and mutual understanding. Such a climate builds on itself and increases the likelihood of improved interpersonal relationships. A defensive climate, on the other hand, reflects the opposite of such conditions and is likely to lead to deteriorating relationships.

A supportive climate also connotes and encourages two-way communication. This is an important concept in improving interpersonal communication. We have noted how one-way communication often leads to misunderstanding. It is interesting that we often engage in a two-way process when transmitting information such as a telephone number. The operator says "415–778–5226." You repeat the number and ask, "Is that right?" The operator says, "Yes," and we feel confident that we have the correct information. When transmitting more complex information we do not use this two-way process nearly as effectively. We assume we get the message. Research has shown that two-way communication increases accuracy of transmission and confidence of the receivers. It also increases the amount of time it takes to transmit a message (Tesch, Lansky, & Lundgren, 1972).

Using a two-way process is a simple idea, yet it is difficult to put into practice. Many conversations consist of a series of one-way statements—people talking past each other. You have probably tried the experiment where, in a group setting, a person cannot speak until he or she has summarized what the previous speaker has said to that person's satisfaction. Conversation often grinds to a halt because people are unable to concentrate enough to repeat the speaker's intended message.

Box 5.3 provides guidelines for receiving and feedback skills, each of them important in improving interpersonal communication. When presenting an idea or an opinion it is incumbent on the communicator to be clear, concise, and complete. One should strive to make verbal and nonverbal signals congruent. One should describe feelings accurately so that the receiver does not have to guess whether you are happy, sad, or angry.

An important skill is the ability to describe people, things, or ideas without evaluating them. For example, if Sally can say, "Ralph, I feel frustrated because you have interrupted me three times in the last ten minutes," rather than, "Ralph, you are rude and insensitive," her message will be clearer. In the latter case Ralph is likely to be uncertain about what Sally means, become defensive, and counterattack with some derogatory comment about her as a person. In the former case he knows how she feels and why. It is up to him to decide what to do about it. He may change his behavior and their relationship may improve. On the other hand, he may not change and then Sally has to decide what to do next.

Receiving skills are also important in improving interpersonal communication. Listening is a lost art. Unfortunately, a typical remedy for *lack of communication* is *more words* in a one-way stream. We do not pay sufficient attention to increasing understanding via a two-way process. Active listening requires effort. In an audience or even in a one-to-one conversation we tend to listen passively and maybe even lapse into daydreaming. Active listening is a skill that can be learned. People can be trained to read other people quite accurately by combining verbal and nonverbal signals, including posture, tone of voice, gestures, and eye movements (Goleman, 1979).

BOX 5.3
A SUMMARY OF GUIDELINES FOR CLEAR INTERPERSONAL COMMUNICATION

The communicator seeking to improve his communication clarity should:

1. Have a clear picture of what he wants the other person to understand.
2. Analyze the nature and magnitude of his attitudes toward both the topic and the person with whom he is communicating.
3. Assess his own communication skills and those of the person listening.
4. Seek to identify himself with the psychological frame of reference of the person receiving his ideas.
5. Develop a realistic expectation for the degree of clarity obtainable in a given context.
6. Make the message relevant to the person listening by using that person's language and terms.
7. State his ideas in the simplest possible terms.
8. Define before developing and explain before amplifying.
9. Develop one idea at a time, take one step at a time.
10. Use appropriate repetition.
11. Compare and contrast ideas by associating the unknown with the known.
12. Determine which ideas need special emphasis.
13. Use as many channels as necessary for clarity.
14. Watch for and elicit corrective feedback in a variety of channels.
15. Eliminate or reduce noise if it is interfering.
16. Pace his communication according to the information-processing capacities of the channel and the person listening.

Source: Myron R. Chartier, "Clarity of Expression in Interpersonal Communication." Reprinted from J. William Pfeiffer and John E. Jones (Eds.), *The 1976 Annual Handbook for Group Facilitators* [La Jolla, Calif.: University Associates, 1976], p. 155. Used with permission.

Two simple skills that can be learned rather easily are checking perception and checking for meaning. In both cases, active listening requires paying attention to verbal and nonverbal signals (both the words and the music). Rather than guessing or assuming intentions or feelings, checking can prevent misunderstanding. Al says, "you're fired," while grinning directly at you. You might want to check for meaning by asking, "you're kidding, aren't you?" In our previous example with Bill and Sue we noted gaps between intentions and behavior as well as misperceptions and misinterpretations. In each of these cases, checking for meaning could improve the communication process and prevent a deterioration in their interpersonal relationship. For example, Sue might have said, "Do

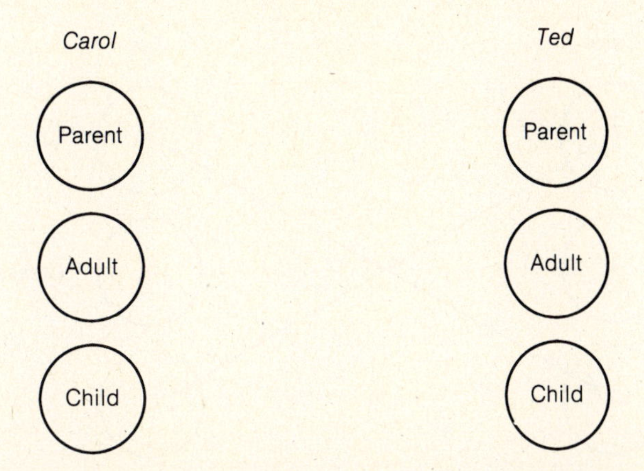

you really want me to check with you or do you expect me to know the new procedure?'' Paraphrasing the sender is a simple step, so simple that it seems silly and unnecessary. However, it can save a lot of trouble stemming from the illusion of a communication and its consequences. ''Do I understand you to mean . . . ?'' ''No, what I really meant was. . . .'' This type of exchange is effective in improving accuracy and enhancing mutual understanding. It is a simple process, but underutilized.

Transactional Analysis

Transactional analysis (TA) is a means of diagnosing interpersonal communication problems (Harris, 1969; James, 1975). It is based on the concept that each of us has three ego states or ''selves within,'' labeled Parent, Adult, and Child. Interaction between individuals can be diagnosed in terms of these three selves. That is, as shown above, Carol and Ted each have Parent, Adult, and Child components that can interact. Each of these ego states are present at all times in mature adults and take relative prominence based on our propensity to behave in certain ways and in the specific situation. The *Parent* within us sets limits, gives advice, disciplines, guides, protects, makes rules, teaches, nurtures, judges, and criticizes (Anderson, 1973). The *Adult* functions include sensing problems, gathering information, diagnosing situations, generating alternatives, evaluating alternatives, and making choices. To the *Child* belongs capacities for being natural, loving, spontaneous, creative, carefree, fun-loving, exciting, adventurous, curious, trusting, or joyful. They may lead to behavior such as anger, rebellion, fright, or obedience (conformance).

> You are all three persons. All three are important. No ego state is better than any other. The situation and the Adult determine what is appropriate. It is desirable to have your Adult functioning all the time to be aware of the Parent, the Child, and the situation so that the Adult can help with the decisions. The Adult can turn off the Child or the Parent or both. You do have some control over your emotions. This is not the same as suppression or repression. It involves the changing of ego states (Anderson, 1973, p. 147).

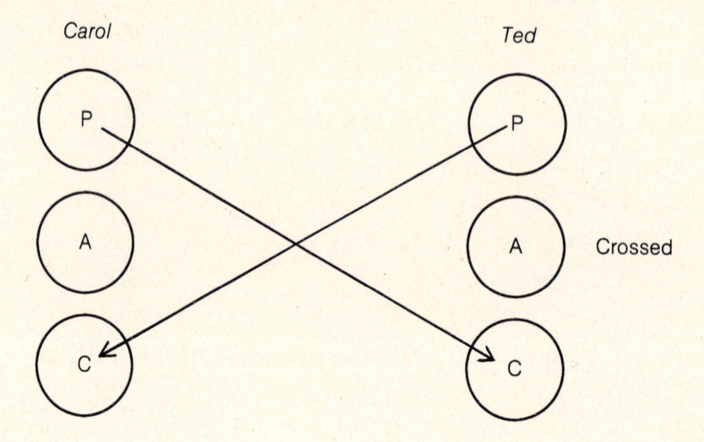

Awareness of these selves within can help us understand communication problems and get on track in overcoming them. Interpersonal communication can be analyzed in terms of transactions between ego states—P⇄C, A⇄A, and so on. Crossed and ulterior transactions are typical communication problems. For instance, Carol speaks to Ted from a Parent point of view, as shown above, when she admonishes him for having such a sloppy desk when he can't find the report she needs. Instead of saying, "Yes, you're right I really should straighten out this mess" (obedience, a parallel P⇄C transaction), he responds by saying, "The reason your desk is clean is that you never do anything" (a critical, judgmental parent).

Ulterior transactions involve two simultaneous messages, one overt and the other covert, as demonstrated in the drawing on page 163. For example, Carol says, "Do you think we can get this report to the main office by four o'clock?" What she really means (perhaps reflected in her posture, tone of voice, etc.) is, "Stop fooling around and get to work!" Ted gets the ulterior message and responds, "I have too much work to do; I can't do everything" (rebellion).

Shifting to the Adult mode can be helpful in many transactions. It can forestall a deteriorating situation that starts with a Parent-to-Child message or vice versa. It shifts the interpersonal relationship from blaming to joint problem solving. This shift is shown in the drawing on page 164. For example, Carol says, "This advertising copy is really lousy. The customer doesn't like it." A typical response from Ted might include: (1) the customer doesn't know what's good; (2) the instructions weren't clear; or (3) the people they send us from personnel aren't as good as they used to be. A better response might be, "Well, we'd better take another crack at it. What is it the customer doesn't like? Do you have any specific suggestions for improving it?" If Carol responds in the Adult mode the transaction can become increasingly positive and rewarding for both parties.

Transactional analysis is appealing as a diagnostic tool because of its simplicity and the use of familiar terminology. It is easy to recognize the "games

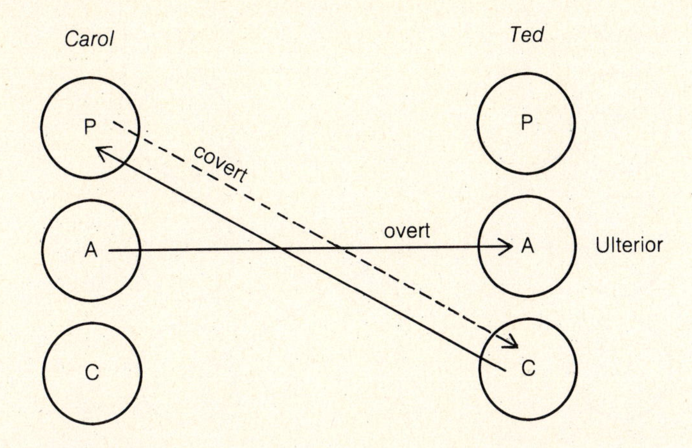

people play'' in interpersonal communication that hamper the development of good relationships (Berne, 1964). Once a person understands the role of the selves within—how they affect our behavior—change is possible. Again, all three ego states are useful and appropriate at times. The goal is to have the Adult relatively more in control in order to determine when a Child-like response is appropriate for creativity or when a Parent-like response is needed to restore order out of confusion. For transactional analysis to be useful, both parties involved must understand the concepts and be able to use them to enhance the probability of mutual understanding.

ORGANIZATIONAL COMMUNICATION SYSTEMS

We have seen how difficult it is to transfer meaning accurately from one person to another. When we add people to the communication system, the network of pairs and groups becomes increasingly complex. On the technical level, we have to develop a capacity for transmitting all of the potential messages. Our telephone system is a good example. In the old days, the village operator could connect the sender and receiver manually; modern systems require electronic switching devices to handle the traffic. Within organizations, the same technical requirements exist and have been met with sophisticated communication equipment—typewriters that remember, copiers that collate and staple, and computers that store and process vast amounts of information.

On the semantic level, progress has not been as dramatic. The more people involved, the more difficult it is to ensure that everyone gets the message. Communication networks take many forms such as person-to-group, group-to-group, or mass communication (one-to-many or group-to-many). Our concern here is with organizational communication systems. Therefore, we will not be concerned with mass communications (in the technical sense) even though some organizations are larger than many communities.

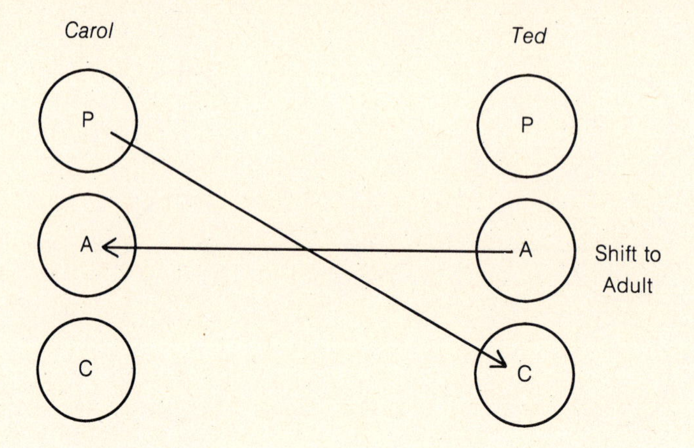

Types of Messages

Organizational communication systems include messages between members of the organization (internal communications) and messages between members and persons outside of the organization (external communications). Any person may either be a sender or a receiver of a communication—a message containing information. Considering the two dimensions—members-nonmembers and senders-receivers—it is possible to construct a matrix that illustrates types of messages in organizational communication systems (see Figure 5.6).

Quadrant 1 consists of communication between organization members. It includes messages that are generated, transmitted, and received internally. Examples are goals, action plans, scheduling and coordination, feedback for control, and schmoozing (informal interactions). A variety of oral and written means are used to transmit messages internally. For example, the weekly production schedule is often displayed in chart form and then serves as the focal point for a staff meeting in order to coordinate the efforts of several interdependent work groups.

Quadrant 2 consists of communication from organization members to people in the environment. It includes messages that are generated internally, transmitted across organization boundaries, and received by persons outside the organization. Examples are public relations, advertising, bills to customers, orders to suppliers, and responses to questions from customers, suppliers, government agencies, or other contacts. The primary purposes of member-to-nonmember messages is to influence the thoughts and actions of people and organizations in the environment that are directly relevant to the well-being of the focal organization.

Quadrant 3 consists of communication from people in the environment to members of the organization. It includes messages that are generated externally, transmitted across organization boundaries, and received by persons inside the organization. Examples are inquiries, customer complaints, advertising and invoices from suppliers, and a variety of messages from government agencies such as the Internal Revenue Service, the Federal Trade Commission, or the National Labor Relations Board. The primary purposes of nonmembers to member mes-

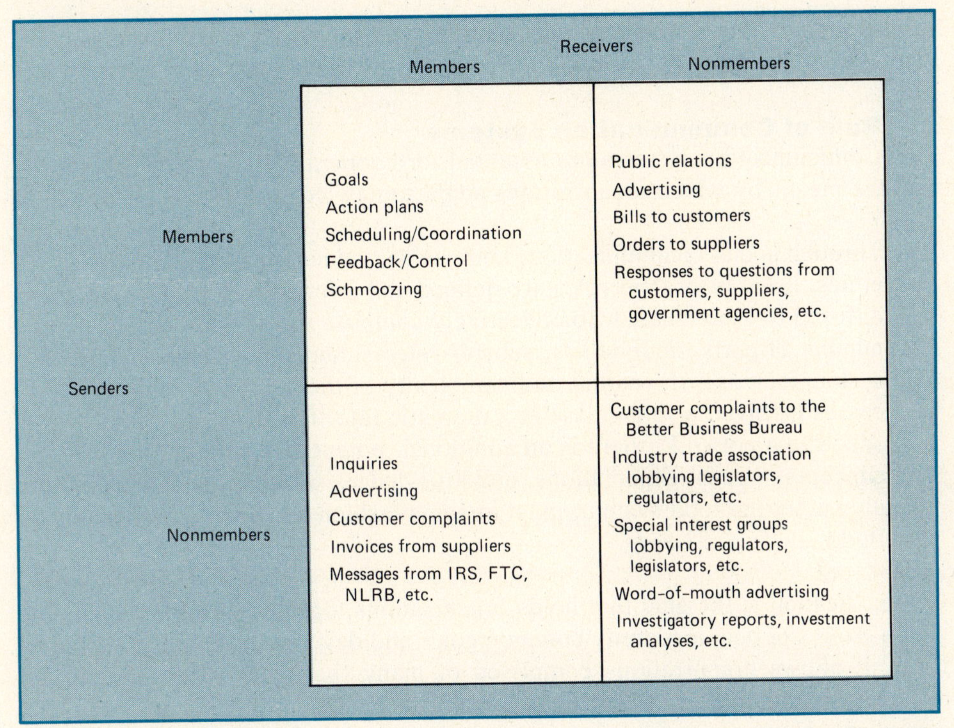

FIGURE 5.6 Examples of Types of Messages in Organizational Communication Systems

sages is to influence the thoughts and actions of people in the organization and, perhaps, the organization as a whole.

Quadrant 4 consists of communication between people in the environment of the focal organization. This is not organizational communication. However, messages that are generated, transmitted, and received externally may be relevant to organization members. Examples are customer complaints to the Better Business Bureau, industry trade association lobbying legislators or regulatory agencies, special interest groups lobbying legislators or regulatory agencies, word-of-mouth advertising, investigatory reports concerning products or practices, and investment analyses. The purposes of nonmember to nonmember messages may be directly related to the organization or indirectly related when the primary focus is an entire industry or society in general.

Organizations often develop special roles to handle the various types of communication. Production schedulers or internal auditors deal primarily with intraorganizational messages. Public information officers or purchasing agents deal primarily with messages to external people. Receptionists or complaint handlers deal primarily with messages from external people. Of course, almost everyone in an organization is involved in or affected to some degree by the various communication endeavors identified in all four of the quadrants in Figure 5.6.

Role of Communication Systems

Communication systems are essential for cooperative effort, and they provide the means by which organizations adapt to new conditions.

> Through social communication, knowledge, values, norms, standards, ethics, laws, rules, and roles are defined and information about them diffused to individuals who collectively compose the system. . . . As the number of parts—individuals, subsubsystems, and subsystems—within a system increase, the nature and complexity of the communication processes involved also increase at a dramatic rate. For each individual added to a network, there is an additional, potentially different set of concepts, values, expectations, and knowledges which the subsystem, and ultimately the total system, must in some fashion accommodate (Ruben & Budd, 1975, p. 93).

Communication is the glue that holds organizations together. It is the means by which groups of people identify common goals and develop the means to achieve them. It allows organizations comprised of many thousands of individuals to achieve a common purpose. It does not presume unanimity; that is, complete agreement. However, it does require enough mutual understanding to allow coordinated effort. Thus many communication attempts in organizations are designed to inform participants about objectives and action plans as well as to persuade them with regard to the merits of both. At the very least, it is important that messages be understood, so that intentions and actions are synchronized.

Managerial Communication

The ultimate purpose for an organization communication system is to facilitate planning, implementing, and controlling activities. Communication provides the information necessary for participants to make appropriate decisions. Given the complexity of communication processes, however, these goals are difficult to achieve. There are several media, multiple channels, and many sources of interference.

A number of system-wide symbols send subtle messages that affect human behavior in organizational contexts. The location of offices often parallels the organizational hierarchy, with the executive suite on the top floor and shipping-receiving or janitorial services in the basement. On a particular floor, the size and location of the office as well as the thickness of the carpet and the elegance of the furniture connote status in the organization and provide subtle signals for behavior. The amount of casual conversation and horseplay varies indirectly with the amount of status indicated by physical facilities. In some organizations, uniforms provide an indication of status and affect the communication process. People with gold stars, round collars, or starched white coats are listened to more readily than people with overalls, safety shoes, or baseball caps. Other subtle differences such as pantsuits or dresses, metal or wood furniture, and potted plants or artificial flowers help create an overall atmosphere that affects communication processes and human behavior.

Within this context, a communication system ranges from formal to informal and includes a wide range of written, spoken, and nonverbal messages. The most formal messages are presented on standard forms such as those prepared for federal, state, and local regulatory agencies—the Internal Revenue Service, for instance. More flexibility is apparent in internal documents, such as plans or budgets. These vary between organizations but are usually standard across divisions or departments within one organization. Results are reported in a variety of ways—from slick multicolored annual reports to a one-page weekly summary of income and expenses for Joe's Popcorn Wagon.

The minutes and reports of scheduled meetings provide relatively formal records that can be disseminated widely. Less formal aspects of meetings include the discussions and nonverbal messages that are transmitted among the participants. Many small group and one-to-one discussions are scheduled but not recorded formally. Of course, the people involved may make notes that are relevant input for subsequent decision making. Unscheduled, casual, or impromptu meetings occur continually in organizations. A large share of organizational communication occurs in such settings, much of it directly related to the work and some of it peripheral or nonwork related. No formal record is kept and in many cases (gossip, rumors, etc.) an attempt is made to keep the conversation secret. On the continuum of formality-informality there is no presumption of good or bad. All modes are useful and appropriate, depending on the purpose and context.

One study (observations of 3,000 clerks, secretaries, technicians, professionals, and supervisors at Bell Telephone Laboratories) indicated that people at work spend about 70 percent of their time in some form of communication (Chapanis, 1971, p. 952).

Talking face-to-face	35%
Writing	16%
Reading	13%
Telephoning	6%

Of course, the amount of time spent communicating varies by type of organization (factory, bank, or hospital), function performed (producing, selling, or researching), and subsystem/level (operating/lower, coordinating/middle, or strategic/upper).

Based on observations and activity analysis of top managers (chief executive officers), Mintzberg found a tendency to use informal, verbal means rather than formal, written means.

> The manager demonstrates a strong preference for the verbal media of communication. He seems to dislike using the mail, and consequently it is used primarily for formal correspondence and for lengthy documents. The

> informal means of communication—the telephone call and the unscheduled meeting—are used to transmit pressing information and to deliver informal requests. Scheduled meetings are used for formal delivery of information and requests, and for time-consuming events that involve a number of people, notably events concerned with ceremony, strategy-making, and negotiation. . . . The manager's productive output can be measured primarily in terms of verbally transmitted information (Mintzberg, 1973, p. 44).

It is evident in modern, large-scale organizations that communication systems are becoming increasingly sophisticated. Computer technology, for example, allows high-speed manipulation of vast amounts of data, real-time access to stored information, and input-output of information in formats that are meaningful for managerial decision making. However, when elaborate, sophisticated communication systems are in place, they can constrain the communication process. Putting information in a required format may cause some of the meaning to be lost or changed. Some of the essence of a situation, as described in writing or verbally, may be altered in an attempt to gain comparability and/or efficiency. Increased capacity to collect, process, and disseminate information throughout the organization may or may not be advantageous. It can provide important information that has heretofore been unavailable, at least on a timely basis. However, it can also provide more information than can be absorbed by the human mind. In such cases it may cloud the issue by making it more difficult to identify the relevant information. The merits of elaborate, sophisticated communication systems in organizations should be judged on the basis of whether or not they provide timely, accurate information that is relevant for managerial decison making and that facilitates mutual understanding. And, of course, the benefits should outweigh the cost.

Problems

Why is it important for organizational communication systems to work reasonably well? It is because people behave on the basis of what they believe, rather than what is. Thus, if messages are not clear, if distortion occurs, and if misinterpretation abounds, then mutual understanding and coordination is impossible. It is our experience that when you ask participants to identify organizational problems, *lack of communication* is almost always cited as a major concern. This seems to be a worldwide condition (Blake & Mouton, 1968, p. 4). An obvious reason for such results is that communication is absolutely essential for organizations to function and there are so many opportunities to go wrong. The vignettes at the beginning of this chapter illustrate some of these problems.

Figure 5.1 indicates how, in general, interference can hamper the communication process. Figure 5.3 illustrates specific problems in interpersonal communication. If we multiply the opportunities for things to go awry by the number of interactions in human organizations, we see the magnitude of the problem. With the best of intentions on the part of all individuals involved, problems will occur. Behavior doesn't match intention, messages are interpreted in terms of personal values and beliefs, and inappropriate action is taken based on invalid assumptions.

Managers often assume that subordinates are getting all of the information they need when, in fact, the subordinates say, "The boss doesn't tell us anything." The same managers complain that they don't get enough information from higher echelons or from peers in other units. This seems to be a pervasive phenomenon that is not restricted to any particular level.

Communication between individuals or between units is sometimes literally interrupted. Conflict can develop to the point where all interaction ceases. One of our students reported that her colleague at work had literally not spoken to their boss, a department manager, for more than a year. Their communication was carried on through third parties and memos. Such a situation makes it difficult for the overall communication system to function and obviously has an impact on the organization's effectiveness, efficiency, and participant satisfaction.

There appears to be systematic distortion of information in organizations, sometimes deliberate and sometimes subconscious. For example, for middle managers, upward communication may be affected by the desire for advancement. They may refrain from reporting anything that might reflect negatively on their performance. In addition, "information will be tailored to the needs of the person or group to whom it is being sent. If the recipient is a superior there will be a tendency to make the information consistent with the transmitter's perception of what the recipient wants to hear" (Ference, 1970, pp. B85–B86). This gatekeeping or mindguarding can be particularly harmful if it promotes a false sense of security and forestalls recognition of potential disaster (Janis, 1972).

The grapevine can be a system-wide communication problem. If the rumor mill consistently distorts messages, accuracy suffers and mutual understanding is impossible. The longer the communication channel (i.e., the more people in the chain of receivers and senders), the more likely that the message will be garbled. Grapevine gossip seems to travel faster than official messages. Therefore, it seems inevitable that the meaning of a new policy or procedure sent from headquarters will be established in the minds of employees before the supervisor has a chance to explain it. Informal communication processes are necessary and desirable for organizations to function. However, distortions that occur via gossip and rumor can be dysfunctional in terms of morale and performance.

Strategies for Improvement

Because communication systems are so complex, we cannot consider all the technical and semantic aspects in this section. However, we can note several ideas that any manager can consider in an organizational context.

In designing formal information systems, it is important to identify the relevant information for decison making and develop some means of having it available on a timely basis. This means making sure that appropriate data are collected, processed, and made available when needed. It also means ignoring inappropriate data that may cause confusion and misdirect a manager's attention and energy.

Because of the potential distortion that may occur in any one communication channel it may be useful to develop multiple channels; that is, several sources of information. This could offset the tendency to receive only information that reflects favorably on subordinates or that indicates all is well in terms of organizational goals. It may be useful to designate a devil's advocate or a hostile witness in order to ensure alternative points of view and a mixture of positive and negative signals.

A critical design feature is the inclusion of a two-way communication process: a built-in means to receive feedback in order to ensure that messages are understood as intended. This has to be more than a perfunctory open-door policy or even a request to "check with me if you have questions." The human tendency is to not ask questions because it may reflect negatively on both the sender and the receiver. Moreover, the open door may be guarded by an invisible shield (past experiences in the office having been negative) or a secretary/assistant that acts as a gatekeeper. Concerted effort must be used to solicit feedback and to make checking for meaning a norm in the organization. Facilitating a two-way process may require getting out in the field, going to the shop floor, or walking through the office routinely in order to solicit feedback explicitly and get a sense of the situation.

Another important guideline is to use the informal system creatively. The grapevine is inevitable and a first step toward improvement is being aware of it. Rumors and gossip can be nipped in the bud if the complete story is presented in the beginning. If it is sketchy or incomplete, the human tendency is to round it out with details that probably distort the picture. Messages should be clear, concise, and complete. Encouraging people to check for meaning rather than make assumptions will also decrease the chance for distortion via the grapevine. Lastly, it may be advantageous at times to use the grapevine as one of the multiple channels for getting the message across to all interested parties in the shortest possible time. Keeping the grapevine full of relevant messages will tend to preclude its use for dysfunctional gossip and rumors.

SO WHAT? IMPLICATIONS FOR YOU

Understanding communication—intrapersonal, interpersonal, and organizational—is an important step in understanding human behavior in organizations. The next step is applying such knowledge in organizational contexts, either as individual participants or managers.

As a Member in an Organization

Generalizations	Implications
1. Human communication is a complex and difficult endeavor. The results are usually imperfect. That is, $\frac{\text{Message Received}}{\text{Message Sent}} \neq 1$	1. Recognize the complexity and difficulty and be alert to the probability of misunderstanding others or being misunderstood yourself.

Generalizations	Implications
2. A person's total past experience affects the sending and receiving of messages.	2. Be aware of how your values, beliefs, opinions, and attitudes affect the way you communicate—particularly the way you perceive and interpret messages.
3. There is often a gap between intention and behavior. People don't say what they mean. They often send mixed (e.g., verbal $\neq$ nonverbal) signals.	3. Have a good idea of what you want to communicate. Be clear, concise, and complete. Be consistent with verbal and nonverbal signals. Encourage receivers to seek clarification.
4. People see and hear what they want to see and hear. They ignore signals or embellish messages to fit their own needs.	4. Read carefully and listen actively. Be alert for intention-behavior gaps of others. Be aware of your own tendency to filter messages. Ask others for their perception of your filters and how they affect your communication.
5. The illusion of communication is a major interpersonal and organizational problem. Acting on the basis of assumptions often leads to dysfunctional consequences.	5. Check for meaning. Ask for clarification by restating ideas or instructions to see if you got the message.
6. Time pressure increases the tendency to use one-way communication.	6. Use a two-way communication process whenever possible. Invite feedback to see if the appropriate message has been received.
7. The pervasive human tendency to be evaluative fosters defensive reactions and often hampers communication.	7. Try to be less evaluative (more descriptive) of behavior, things, ideas, and feelings. Be as objective as possible. Avoid blaming; try problem solving whenever possible.
8. People often mask their feelings and real concerns with questions that seem to demand agreement from the receiver. Disagreement leads to defen-	8. Respond to invitations to be evaluative by exploring the feelings behind such questions. Listen actively for clues and try to empathize. Try to think *with*

Generalizations	Implications
siveness (withdrawal, protectionism, and blaming) by everyone involved.	people rather than *for* or *about* them.

As a Current or Future Manager

Generalizations	Implications
1. Managing includes coordinating the actions of people in organizations. It is impossible to coordinate human endeavor without communication.	1. Recognize the primary role of communication in managing. Pay particular attention to the need to communicate well in order to lead others.
2. Good communication skills are the same for every individual, including managers. The necessary skills can be learned.	2. Be aware of the implications cited for any member of an organization. Study and practice in order to become a more skillful communicator.
3. Managers have primary responsibility for ensuring mutual understanding in their work groups—particularly between themselves and their subordinates.	3. Be a role model by demonstrating good communication skills. Encourage a two-way process. Invite feedback and clarification. Check for meaning.
4. Managers can affect overall organizational communication systems. They can help design better communication processes.	4. Use your influence to improve the communication system in your organization. Emphasize the need for accuracy and mutual understanding.
5. Technology such as computers can have both positive and negative effects on communication in organizations.	5. Adapt communication technology to managerial needs. Concentrate on providing relevant information to decision makers on a timely basis. Guard against too much data (information overload) even if it is technologically feasible.
6. Multiple channels are available in organizations to transmit messages that are written, verbal, or nonverbal.	6. Use several channels and means to help get the message across. Back up written messages with oral elaboration. Back up oral messages with written confirmation.

Generalizations	Implications
7. The grapevine is an inevitable informal communication system in organizations. It can be a problem or an opportunity.	7. Recognize informal communication processes and probable distortion. Provide enough accurate information so that there is less chance for rumors to fill in the gaps. Encourage people to check for meaning rather than making assumptions when they are unsure.
8. Messages flowing upward in organizations tend to reflect favorably on the sender.	8. Recognize this tendency and use a variety of sources of information in order to get different points of view on important matters. Use objective data to measure results whenever possible.
9. Messages flowing upward in organizations tend to reflect subordinates' perceptions of what the boss wants to hear.	9. Recognize the tendency for people to tell you what you want to hear. Encourage complete reports—both the bad and the good. Positively reinforce those who give candid appraisals.
10. The *illusion* of communication is a major organizational problem that often leads to misdirected effort, wrong outcomes, and human frustration.	10. Strive for accurate message transmission and mutual understanding. Make two-way communication processes and checking for meaning an organizational way of life.

LEARNING APPLICATION ACTIVITIES

1. Write a vignette based on your own experience (work, school, family, etc.) that illustrates a communication problem (or problems).

2. *Step 1:* Draw a Johari Window (Figure 5.4) with the Open, Hidden, and Blind areas in proportion to fit your perception of yourself.

Step 2: Explain the concept to one or two good friends and have them draw their perceptions of your window. Compare notes and discuss.

Step 3: List several action steps you might take to change your window, assuming you want to.

3. Note several examples from your recent experience of messages being distorted by your filtering processes; that is, leaving out unpleasant aspects, adding in unwarranted meaning, misinterpreting nonverbal signals, and so forth. Share your examples with several colleagues and discuss ways that the distortion of messages might be reduced.

4. Over a period of at least one day, pay special attention to whether verbal and nonverbal messages of people you come in contact with are congruent. Note whether or not their facial expressions, tone of voice, and body language fit the spoken words. If the messages are incongruent, note which medium—verbal or nonverbal—you gave most credence to. Do you believe what you hear or what you see?

5. *Step 1:* Form a trio with two colleagues. Express your views on some controversial topic with one person actively listening and the other observing. Practice transmission and reception skills, expressing your ideas clearly and checking for meaning.

Step 2: After 10 minutes have the observer report on behavior that helped and hindered the communication process.

Step 3: Rotate roles and repeat the process so that each person gets to play each role.

Step 4: Summarize your thoughts and feelings about the difficulties of being a good communicator.

6. Using the Transactional Analysis framework of Parent, Child, and Adult ego states, analyze a recent conversation between you and someone else that did not go well. Speculate on how the communication process might have been improved by using TA techniques.

7. *Step 1:* Assemble a group of seven to ten people. Give someone a drawing of an object (or an object in a paper bag) that is abstract enough so that its name does not describe its shape. (An example would be a small sculpture or a machine part.) Have the person look at the paper (or feel the object in the bag) for a minute or two. Then have him or her describe it to another person.

Step 2: The second person should then describe the object verbally to a third person, and so on. Make sure the conversations between pairs cannot be overheard by others in the group.

Step 3: Compare the result with the original. Discuss the process and how it might be improved.

8. Reread the vignette *To Speak or Not?* In a group of four to six people, obtain three volunteers to play the roles of Bob, Lisa, and Tom. Have them reread the vignette and assume that Lisa and Tom have asked Bob to help them become more effective group members. Bob agrees to meet with them.

a. Carry out the meeting with people playing the roles described in the vignette.
b. The three or so people not playing roles should act as silent observers and then report their impressions.
c. Ask Tom, Lisa, and Bob to report their thoughts and feelings.
d. Discuss the results and note any implications for future behavior.

REFERENCES

Anderson, John P. "A Transactional Analysis Primer." In J. William Pfeiffer and John E. Jones (Eds.), *The 1973 Annual Handbook For Group Facilitators*. La Jolla, Calif.: University Associates, 1973, pp. 145–157.

Archer, Dane, and Robin M. Akert. "How Well Do You Read Body Language?" *Psychology Today,* October 1977, pp. 68–72, 119–123.

Berne, Eric. *Games People Play*. New York: Grove Press, 1964.

Blake, Robert R., and Jane S. Mouton. *Corporate Excellence Through Grid Organization Development*. Houston: Gulf, 1968.

———. *The New Managerial Grid*. Houston: Gulf, 1978.

Boulding, Kenneth E. *The Image*. Ann Arbor, Mich.: University of Michigan Press, 1956.

Caplow, Theodore. *How to Run Any Organization*. Hinsdale, Ill.: Dryden Press, 1976.

Chaffee, Steven H. "Applying the Interpersonal Perception Model to the Real World." *American Behavioral Scientist* 16 (March-April 1973): 465–468.

Chapanis, Alphonse. "Prelude to 2001: Explorations in Human Communication." *American Psychologist* 26 (November 1971): 949–961.

Chartier, Myron R. "Clarity of Expression in Interpersonal Communication." In J. William Pfeiffer and John E. Jones (Eds.), *The 1976 Annual Handbook For Group Facilitators*. La Jolla, Calif.: University Associates, 1976, pp. 149–156.

Clark, Herbert H. "The Power of Positive Speaking: It Takes Longer To Understand No." *Psychology Today,* September 1974, pp. 102, 108–111.

Dance, Frank E. X. "Toward a Theory of Human Communication." In Frank E. X. Dance (Ed.), *Human Communication Theory*. New York: Holt, Rinehart and Winston, 1967, pp. 288–309.

———. "The 'Concept' of Communication." *The Journal of Communication* 20 (June 1970): 201–210.

Eilon, Samuel. "Taxonomy of Communications." *Administrative Science Quarterly* 13 (September 1968): 266–288.

Ekman, Paul. "The Universal Smile: Face Muscles Talk Every Language." *Psychology Today,* September 1975, pp. 35–39.

English, Fanita. "TA: A Populist Movement." *Psychology Today,* April 1973, pp. 45–50, 98.

Fabun, Don. *Communications*. Beverly Hills, Calif.: Glencoe Press, 1968.

Ference, Thomas P. "Organizational Communications Systems and the Decision Process." *Management Science* 17/2 (October 1970):B83–B96.

Gibb, Jack R. "Defensive Communication." *Journal of Communication* 11 (September 1961):141–148.

Goleman, Daniel. "People Who Read People." *Psychology Today,* July 1979, pp. 66–78.

Guetzkow, Harold. "Communications in Organizations." In James G. March (Ed.), *Handbook of Organizations*. Chicago: Rand McNally, 1965, pp. 534–573.

Hall, Edward T. *The Silent Language*. Greenwich, Conn.: Fawcett, 1959.

Hall, Edward T., and Kenneth Friedman (interviewer). "Learning the Arabs' Silent Language." *Psychology Today,* August 1979, pp. 45–54.

Hare, Van-Court, Jr. "Communication and Information Systems." In Joseph W. McGuire (Ed.), *Contemporary Management*. Englewood Cliffs, N.J.: Prentice-Hall, 1974, pp. 192–223.

Harris, Thomas A. *I'm OK—You're OK*. New York: Harper & Row, 1969.

Hayakawa, S. I. *Language in Thought and Action*. New York: Harcourt, Brace & World, 1949.

Hebb, D. O., W. E. Lambert, and G. Richard Tucker. "A DMZ in the Language War." *Psychology Today*. April 1973, pp. 54–62.

Homans, George C. *The Human Group*. New York: Harcourt, Brace & World, 1950.

Huseman, Richard C., Cal M. Logue, and Dwight L. Freshley. *Interpersonal and Organizational Communication*. Boston: Holbrook Press, 1969.

James, Muriel. *The OK Boss*. Reading, Mass.: Addison-Wesley, 1975.

———. "Transactional Analysis: The OK Boss in All of Us." *Psychology Today*, February 1976, pp. 31–36, 80.

Janis, Irving L. *Victims of Groupthink*. Boston: Houghton Mifflin Company, 1972.

Katz, Daniel, and Robert L. Kahn. *The Social Psychology of Organizations*, 2nd ed. New York: Wiley, 1978.

LaRusso, Dominic A. *Concepts and Skills of Oral Communication*, 2nd ed. Dubuque, Iowa: Brown, 1973.

———. *The Shadows of Communication*. Dubuque, Iowa: Kendall/Hunt, 1977.

Litterer, Joseph A. *The Analysis of Organizations*, 2nd ed. New York: Wiley, 1973.

Luft, Joseph. *Of Human Interaction*. Palo Alto, Calif: National Press Books, 1969.

McCaskey, Michael B. "The Hidden Messages Managers Send." *Harvard Business Review* 57/6 (November-December 1979): 135–148.

McLeod, Jack M., and Steven H. Chafee. "Interpersonal Approaches to Communication Research." *American Behavioral Scientist* 16 (March-April 1973): 469–499.

Mintzberg, Henry. *The Nature of Managerial Work*. New York: Harper & Row, 1973.

Mitchell, Terence R. *People in Organizations: Understanding Their Behavior*. New York: McGraw-Hill, 1978.

Morris, John O. *Make Yourself Clear!* New York: McGraw-Hill, 1972.

Newcomb, Theodore M. "An Approach to the Study of Communicative Acts." *Psychological Review* 60 (November 1953): 393–404.

Parkinson, C. Northcote, and Nigel Rowe. *Communicate*. Englewood Cliffs, N.J.: Prentice-Hall, 1977.

Parlee, Mary Brown. "Conversational Politics." *Psychology Today*, May 1979, pp. 48–56.

Porter, Lyman W., and Karlene H. Roberts. "Communication in Organizations." In Marvin D. Dunnette (Ed.), *Handbook of Industrial and Organizational Psychology*. Chicago: Rand McNally, 1976, pp. 1553–1590.

Rath, Gustave J., and Karen S. Stoyanoff. "Understanding and Improving Communication Effectiveness." In J. William Pfeiffer and John E. Jones (Eds.), *The 1982 Annual Handbook for Facilitators, Trainers, and Consultants*. La Jolla, Calif.: University Associates, 1982, pp. 166–173.

Roberts, Karlene H., Charles A. O'Reilly III, Gene E. Bretton, and Lyman W. Porter. "Organizational Theory and Organizational Communication: A Communication Failure?" *Human Relations* 27 (May 1974): 501–24.

Rogers, Carl R., and Richard E. Farson. "Active Listening." In Richard C. Huseman, Cal M. Logue, and Dwight L. Freshley (Eds.), *Readings in Interpersonal and Organizational Communication*. Boston: Holbrook Press, 1969, pp. 480–496.

Rogers, Carl R., and F. J. Roethlisberger. "Barriers and Gateways to Communication." *Harvard Business Review* 30/4 (July-August 1952): 46–52.

Rokeach, Milton. *The Open and Closed Mind*. New York: Basic Books, 1960.

Rosenthal, Robert, Dane Archer, M. Robin DiMatteo, Judith Hall Koivumaki, and Peter L. Rogers. "Body Talk and Tone of Voice: The Language Without Words." *Psychology Today*, September 1974, pp. 64–68.

Rosnow, Ralph L., and Allan J. Kimmel. "Lives of a Rumor." *Psychology Today*, June 1979, pp. 88–92.

Ruben, Brent D., and Richard W. Budd. *Human Communication Handbook*. Rochelle Park, N.J.: Hayden, 1975.

Schramm, Wilbur. *The Process and Effects of Mass Communication*. Urbana, Ill: University of Illinois Press, 1954.

Schrank, Robert. *Ten Thousand Working Days*. Cambridge, Mass.: MIT Press, 1978.

Shannon, Claude, and Warren Weaver. *The Mathematical Theory of Communication*. Urbana, Ill.: University of Illinois Press, 1949.

Steele, Fritz. *The Open Organization*. Reading, Mass.: Addison-Wesley, 1975.

Tesch, Frederick E., Leonard M. Lansky, and David C. Lundgren. "The One-Way/Two-Way Communication Exercise: Some Ghosts Laid to Rest." *The Journal of Applied Behavioral Science* 8 (November-December 1972): 664–673.

Thayer, Lee. "Communication and Organization Theory." In Frank E. X. Dance (Ed.), *Human Communication Theory*. New York: Holt, Rinehart and Winston, 1967, pp. 70–115.

Tubbs, Stewart L., and Sylvia Moss. *Human Communication*. New York: Random House, 1974.

" 'Visible Management' at United Airlines." An interview with Edward E. Carlson. *Harvard Business Review* 53/4 (July-August 1975): 90–97.

Wackman, Daniel B. "Interpersonal Communication and Coorientation." *American Behavioral Scientist* 16 (March-April 1973): 537–550.

Wiener, Norbert. *The Human Use of Human Beings*. Boston: Houghton Mifflin, 1954.

Wilensky, Harold L. *Organizational Intelligence*. New York: Basic Books, 1967.

Wright, H. Beric. *Executive Ease and Dis-ease*. New York: Wiley, 1975.

Zalkind, Sheldon S., and Timothy W. Costello. "Perception: Some Recent Research and Implications for Administration." *Administrative Science Quarterly* 7 (September 1962): 218–235.

6
Influence and Leadership

LEARNING OBJECTIVES

After reading this chapter you should be able to:

1. Understand the role of leadership in organizational endeavor.
2. Compare and contrast various interpersonal ways of influencing behavior in organizations.
3. Discuss the attributes and behaviors of effective leaders.
4. Describe a contingency view of leadership and illustrate it with guidelines for leader behavior in specific situations.
5. Outline an approach to facilitating effective leadership—your own and others.

MOTHER KNOWS BEST

Bobby, age 11, was trying to explain to his friend, Kirk, why he couldn't go to the circus. Kirk had heard that kids could earn a free pass by hauling water for the elephants, and he wanted Bobby to go with him. They would have to take a bus across town and probably be gone all day. "Did you talk to your dad?" asked Kirk. "Yeah," replied Bobby, "and he told me to talk to Mom. He always says that whenever it's anything important." "Is your mom the boss?" asked Kirk. "Well, I don't know," said Bobby, "but we always have to ask her when we want to do anything. She's pretty smart, and my dad's gone a lot on trips. But even when he's here he always asks her what to do. Like when we were trying to buy a new house, he kept saying, 'It's up to you.' And when my sister was sick and had her appendix out, he kept saying, 'What do you think we ought to do?' He's some sort of boss where he works, but I think my mom is the boss around here."

WHO TO BLAME?

The class was debriefing an exercise in which several teams were competing. They were playing the role of consultants and making proposals to the management of Apex Company for a long-term contract to provide market-research services. Five member teams had been selected randomly and assigned a task of preparing and presenting a proposal to the top management of Apex. The blue team was one of the losers, and they were trying to explain why they hadn't done better. Some blamed Dan Olson, their presenter, for not explaining their ideas very well. Dan countered by saying, "I didn't really want to make the presentation, I lost when we drew the straws." Others said it wasn't Dan's fault because the Apex managers were biased in favor of the red team. Somebody said, "We had good ideas, but maybe they weren't organized very well." Finally, Marilyn turned to Professor Clark and said, "The real problem was lack of leadership. You should have appointed someone to be the leader, and then we wouldn't have wasted so much time."

MAYOR BARNOWSKI

In November Mary Barnowski had been elected mayor of Plainburg, Illinois. She had run on a reform platform that included promises for significant changes in city government. The former mayor had been in office for over 20 years and had been accused of cronyism, graft, and mismanagement. Mary appointed several new department heads during her first several months in office. However, it was becoming apparent that such changes had little effect because, other than department heads, most city employees were protected by civil service rules and could not be removed unless there was good cause. Consequently, many of her proposed changes seemed to get lost in the shuffle. Worse, it was becoming increasingly apparent that the city council was stacked 5 to 4 against her on most issues. After six months, Mary was wondering just how much power she really had in running the city government. She enjoyed the ceremony of the position, but she was finding it increasingly frustrating to try to carry out the reforms that she had promised during the election campaign.

GOOD OL' CHARLIE

Charlie Slade had worked on the maintenance crew at the brewery for about eight years. After graduating from high school, he had joined the Marines for a four-year hitch, including two years in Vietnam. He attended a community college for two years, specializing in sheet metal work and air conditioning systems. His uncle, a regional sales manager for the brewery, arranged a part-time job while Charlie attended school. After two years he went to work full time, moving from janitorial services over to the maintenance crew. Charlie was a quick learner and picked up a variety of technical skills in addition to his specialized training. He fit in well and became friends with the other six guys on the crew. He joined the department bowling team and also played on the brewery's slow pitch softball team in the city league.

Several months ago Tom, the maintenance foreman, suffered a slight stroke and decided to take early retirement. The plant manager asked Charlie if he would take over as foreman and told him that he had been highly recommended by Tom. Charlie had been uncertain, because several members of the crew had more seniority on the job. The management position carried a significant increase in pay, but salaried managers were not eligible for overtime. He knew that Tom had often been called back to the plant in the middle of the night to supervise emergency repairs. Several of his closest friends on the crew urged him to take the job, but he wasn't sure if their views reflected the total crew. He was particularly concerned about Al, who had filled in for Tom on various occasions. When he decided to accept the position, the plant manager welcomed him to management and advised him that it would be important for him to assert his authority so that his former peers would understand his new role.

Charlie tended to pattern his behavior after Tom who in his eyes had been an effective supervisor. Tom scheduled the work but expected the guys to know what to do and how to do it. He was firm but fair in pointing out problems. The guys had confidence in his technical skill and respected him as a manager.

The first few months seemed uneventful except that Charlie did notice a significant amount of horsing around on the job. When he tried to focus the crew's attention on the work, he sensed a certain coolness in their attitude toward him. An even more perplexing problem began to surface after about six months. He sensed resentment whenever he tried to help one of the crew members with a particularly difficult assignment. He began to wonder whether becoming a manager was such a good deal after all.

COMPUTER TASK FORCE

Sentry Life Insurance Company was scheduled to receive its new computer in mid-July. In January, the president appointed a task force to design the new system and coordinate the transition from current data-processing methods. The new system would take advantage of the significantly increased capacity for developing information useful in managerial decision making. Fred Williams, vice president and comptroller, was designated chairman of the task force. Ann Framholz represented the systems design staff and five other members represented the various functional departments in the company.

After several meetings, it became clear that the success of the task force depended heavily on Ann's technical expertise and her keen awareness of the needs of the various functional managers. It also became obvious that Fred tended to slow the progress of the group because he couldn't think much beyond the existing system and the need to generate formal reports to the company's various regulatory agencies. The task force made progress in spite of Fred, and he began to defer more and more to Ann's judgment concerning key design issues. Although Fred called the meetings and wrote the minutes, it was Ann who really ran the show. She delegated the work to the various members and coordinated their efforts. She wrote their final report and developed a summary presentation for top management.

After Fred made the presentation to the executive committee, the president commented, "Fred, this is an outstanding report. You are to be commended for a thorough and innovative proposal. I am proud of you."

WE'LL MISS YA, FRANK

Frank Tomita was retiring as senior vice president of Citizens Bank. The banquet was primarily a "roast," with the various speakers dredging up embarrassing incidents from his past: including the time his branch somehow translated a $50 deposit into a $5 million credit for a customer's account. Sprinkled among the barbs were a number of positive comments that warmed Frank's heart. He was credited with major responsibility for innovative moves that had kept the bank in the forefront of the industry. He was seen as tough and aggressive, but sensitive to those around him. One person said he was a great coach and teacher: "You always knew where you stood with Frank—whether you were doing a good job or not." Others cited the high standards he set for subordinates. "He expected a lot, and left you room to maneuver, but he was always available if you needed help." "He wasn't afraid to try new ideas that would help us do the job better." "We always seemed to take some time as a group to look at how things were going and discuss ways to improve our teamwork." "He always had a good sense of the overall situation, and we knew where we fit in the picture." Finally, Joe Malone, who was being promoted to Frank's job, summed up with these words: "Those of us who have worked under you for many years often thought we 'did it ourselves,' but on closer analysis maybe that's the essence of good leadership. You provided an ideal climate within which we could grow and develop (with a little prodding here and a little support there). Maybe no one is indispensable, but you made a difference. We'll miss ya, Frank."

INTRODUCTION

Bobby's mother, Dan Olson, Mary Barnowski, Charlie Slade, Ann Framholz, and Frank Tomita played key roles in the situations described above. They were involved in interpersonal relationships in ways that classify them as leaders. One of them had been elected, a few were appointed, and the others emerged naturally in response to the needs of their particular situations. The notion of a leader involves the complementary notion of an organized body of people. Leadership, then, can be seen, not only as an attribute of an individual, but also as a relationship among people in social or organizational groups.

In their own ways, each influenced, or attempted to influence, the behavior of others. They were, in turn, influenced by them. The degree to which a leader's directives are followed is one measure of leadership effectiveness. As we shall see, a more sophisticated measure of leadership effectiveneses will include the performance of the work group or organization in terms of its own stated objectives. Leading, in the fullest sense, implies tapping latent human capability: establishing a climate within which people are motivated to utilize their full potential.

Leadership has been one of the most extensively researched subjects in behavioral science during the twentieth century. It may well be the most written about and discussed aspect of organization and management. In this chapter, the subject of leadership will be considered under the following topics:

Influence Systems
The Role of Leadership
Power
Authority
Attributes of Leaders
Effective Leader Behavior
Contingency Views and Flexibility
Facilitating Effective Leadership
So What? Implications for You

INFLUENCE SYSTEMS

Leading, a central function of managing in any organization, involves influencing the behavior of other people. Influence flows in many directions: up and down the hierarchy and laterally in peer relationships. Influence denotes any "changes in behavior of a person or group due to anticipation of the responses of others" (Gould & Kolb, 1964, p. 332). An influence system involves people taking the roles of influencer and influencee. Behavioral changes can be caused by ideas or some other, inanimate factor. For example, a change in the weather may influence someone to abandon picnic or golf plans. Typically, however, influence systems refer to situations wherein behavioral changes occur as a result of relationships among people. These relationships may involve interaction which is direct (face-to-face) or indirect (through communication media). Influence is also the maintenance of behavior as it is, but other than what it would be without the intervention of the influence (Goldhammer & Shils, 1939, p. 171).

The term *influence* is often used in conjunction with other terms such as *power* and *authority*. In some cases, they are considered as mutually exclusive concepts, with influence covering those ways of influencing behavior that cannot be termed power or authority. Our approach is to consider influence as an all-inclusive concept that covers any and all modes by which behavioral change is induced in individuals or groups. This position can be summarized as follows:

> Influence includes virtually any interpersonal transaction which has psychological or behavioral effects. Control includes those influence attempts which are successful, that is, which have the effects intended by the influencing agent. Power is the potential for influence characteristically backed by the means to coerce compliance. Finally, authority is legitimate power; it is power which accrues to a person by virtue of his role, his position in an organized social structure (Katz & Kahn, 1966, p. 220).

We shall return to a more detailed discussion of power and authority in subsequent sections.

Ways to Influence Behavior

A spectrum of ways to influence behavior is indicated in Figure 6.1. Several distinct means are identified—emulation, suggestion, persuasion, and coercion—ranging from indirect, subtle approaches to very evident, direct methods.

Emulation requires no direct contact between individuals; yet it is a powerful influence on behavior. Public figures (famous athletes or entertainers, for example) are usually aware of the degree to which people imitate their behavior. Some professional athletes have refused lucrative contracts to endorse cigarettes because it would conflict with the image they wish to portray to teenagers. Books (particularly biographies), movies, and television provide wide exposure for ideas and life styles. People often consciously select certain behavior patterns and strive to adopt them.

Emulation can take much subtler forms than this, however. In organizations, participants are aware of the behavioral patterns of their co-workers and of the executives. Certain individuals become models, and their behavior patterns are adopted by others who hope to attain similar success. To a certain extent, these others *play* roles in their organizations. Many behavior patterns in organizations are perpetuated primarily on the basis of such emulation: without the need for either written role descriptions or direct interaction in the form of suggestion or persuasion. For example, Charlie Slade (*Good Ol' Charlie*) patterned his behavior after Tom, whom he saw as an effective supervisor.

Suggestion involves direct and conscious interaction between individuals, or between an individual and a group. It is an explicit attempt to influence

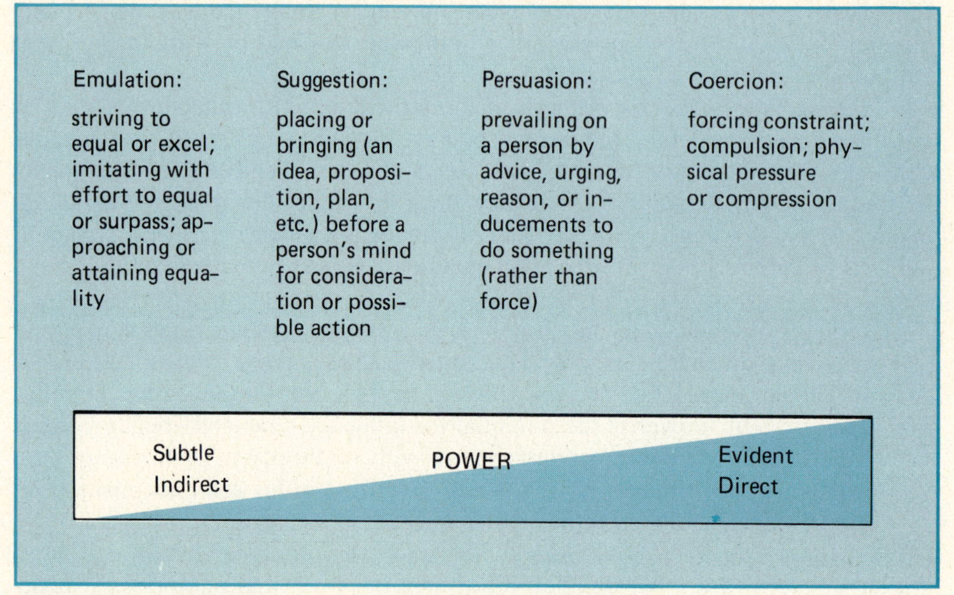

FIGURE 6.1 Spectrum of Means for Influencing Behavior

behavior by presenting an idea or advocating a particular course of action. Typically, this mode is used when several alternative behaviors are acceptable and the influencer is gently advocating a preferred pattern.

If this tolerance for different behavior in a particular role were not present, the influencer would be using some other mode, such as persuasion or even coercion. *Persuasion* implies urging and the use of some inducement in order to evoke the desired response. It involves more pressure than a mere suggestion but falls short of the type of force implied by the term coercion. Behavior modification can be viewed as a form of indirect persuasion. Positive reinforcement for a given mode of behavior tends to induce the influencee to continue in that mode. Reward systems that emphasize recognition and praise have proved successful in modifying individual behavior—reducing absenteeism, for example—in a number of organizational settings (Goodall, 1972, p. 53).

Coercion can involve forcible constraint, including physical pressure. "We will have to do some arm-twisting" is a typical phrase that figuratively describes a method of persuasion based on physical pressure. Literally, a hammerlock could coerce an indivdual into a particular bit of behavior ("say uncle," for example). A person wielding a gun, knife, or other similar weapon can forcibly evoke specific behavior from another individual or a group—the typical skyjacking episode.

Many forms of coercion other than physical force are possible. In organizations, salaries or promotions can be used to constrain or influence behavior.

In many cases, the threat of dismissal (explicit or implied) is also a powerful influencer.

Interaction-Influence Systems

The process of influencing behavior is not necessarily attached to an organizational hierarchy. Any interaction between individuals results in a transaction that has psychological and behavioral effects—in a word, influence. Taken together, these numerous relationships in groups or organizations can be termed an *interaction-influence system*.

Power and authority are key aspects of influence systems. *Power,* the ability to influence behavior, underlies the entire spectrum of means shown in Figure 6.1 The more power an individual has in a given situation, the more effective his or her influence attempts will be. *Authority,* insofar as it is institutionalized power, the recognized right to influence behavior, also underlies the spectrum of means. Typically, positions high in the hierarchy will have more influence than those at lower levels. However, this is not necessarily the case; it depends on the issues involved and the participants in the interaction-influence system. Ann Framholz's experience in the vignette about the computer task force illustrates this point.

The old adage, "Knowledge is power," has particular bearing here. Quite often the flow of influence is lateral or upward as hierarchical relationships are transcended because an individual has specific knowledge concerning a particular question. A corporate president is likely to be influenced by the advice of tax and legal advisors who point out pitfalls in a proposal. If the chief test pilot says the airplane is not ready, the first flight will be postponed, even though several hundred dignitaries and high-level corporate officials have gathered for the occasion.

In these examples, it is clear that a person in a formal position may be quite dependent on others at the same level or below. A manager needs various kinds of support in order to function in the job. This dependence increases the power of others in the organization relative to the manager (and increases their ability to influence his or her behavior). The term *functional authority* refers to the degree of dependence in the organization on a particular activity or function that the exerciser of such authority represents. Individuals in staff positions theoretically have little formal authority in organizations. However, they influence behavior effectively because of the dependence of other organizational members on them for information concerning procedures or techniques.

Location can have bearing on the ability to influence behavior. An "assistant to," although low on the status ladder, may have considerable power by virtue of his or her close proximity to a high-level executive. With little formal authority, people in such positions find others in the organization dependent on them for information about how the boss is likely to react to various proposals. Also, they are in a position to screen and filter messages in both directions: to the boss from other members of the organization and vice versa.

Many organizational relationships involve peer groups, exclusively. In such

BOX 6.1

LEADERSHIP: A BELEAGUERED SPECIES?

The most serious threat to our institutions and the cause of our diminishing sense of able leadership is the steady erosion of institutional autonomy. This erosion results from forces in both the external and the internal environment.

Time was when the leader could decide—period. A Henry Ford, an Andrew Carnegie, a Nicholas Murray Butler could issue a ukase—and all would automatically obey. Their successors' hands are now tied in innumerable ways—by governmental requirements, by various agencies, by union rules, by the moral and sometimes legal pressures of organized consumers and environmentalists. . . .

Precisely at the time when the credibility of our leaders is at an all-time low, and when the surviving leaders feel most inhibited in realizing the potentiality of power, we most need individuals who can lead. We need people who can shape the future, not just barely manage to get through the day.

There is no simple solution. But there are things we must recognize:

1. Leaders must develop the vision and strength to call the shots.
2. The leader must be a "conceptualist" (not just someone to tinker with the "nuts and bolts").
3. He must have a sense of continuity and significance in order, to paraphrase the words of Shelley, to see the present in the past and the future in the present.
4. Leaders must get their heads above the grass and risk the possibility, familiar to any rooster, of getting hit by a rock.
5. The leader must get at the truth and learn how to filter the unwieldy flow of information into coherent patterns.
6. The leader must be a social architect who studies and shapes what is called the "culture of work"—those intangibles that are so hard to discern but are so terribly important in governing the way people act, the values and norms that are subtly transmitted to individuals and groups and that tend to create binding and bonding.
7. To lead others, the leader must first know himself. . . .

More important than the right metaphor in the years ahead is the capacity to be open to the unprecedented, not to get ready for something but for anything. We must learn . . . the value of examining—of focusing attention on the conditions of life, the particular circumstances that emerge unexpectedly—and develop an alertness in adapting to them.

Source: Adapted, by permission of the publisher, from Warren Bennis, "Leadership: A Beleaguered Species?" *Organizational Dynamics,* Summer 1976, pp. 3–16.

cases, the interaction-influence system is not related to the hierarchy. This means that attempts to exercise influence must rest upon power coming from a source other than formal authority. The potential effectiveness of persuasion and suggestion depends on knowledge, prior commitments, concern for ongoing social relationships, and other similar factors.

Focus on Formal Leaders

In spite of our recognition that influence flows in all directions in social systems, our task of understanding human behavior in organizations requires us to single out the special role of the formal leader. "Given the desire for control and a feeling of personal effectiveness, organizational outcomes are . . . likely to be attributed to individual actions, regardless of their actual causes" (Pfeffer, 1977, p. 109). Indeed, we are quick to praise or blame formal leaders for the success or failure of group endeavors. A coach can be a hero or a scoundrel depending on a rather slight difference in the number of games won or lost. Much the same is true for presidents, prime ministers, and generals, although with them we are perhaps more willing to concede that a complex interplay of external and internal forces will affect ultimate performance. Our emphasis in this chapter will be on leaders as *focal persons,* predicated on the understanding that a number of factors normally come into play to limit the power and authority of formal leaders in organizational contexts.

THE ROLE OF LEADERSHIP

Leadership can be viewed: (1) as a status group (a network of elite positions); (2) as a focal person; and (3) as a function. Directors, executives, administrators, managers, bosses, and chiefs would be included in the category called leaders. Elite status can come from heredity (as in divine right of kings), election, or appointment. Identifying characteristics of those in the group has traditionally been important in studying the phenomenon of leadership.

Attention has been devoted to how leadership is embodied, with a special emphasis on technical and interpersonal expertise and that difficult-to-analyze phenomenon, charisma. This approach to understanding leadership focuses on the personality of leaders (what they are) and the behavior of leaders (what they do). Individuals who participate in unstructured, leaderless groups tend to attribute leadership to those members who define the situation in meaningful ways. Leaders emerge because "they can frame and change situations, and in so doing enact a system of shared meaning that provides a basis of organized action" (Smircich and Morgan, 1982, p. 258). Although it is recognized that leader-follower relations are reciprocal and develop via transactions over time, the emphasis is clearly on leader attributes and actions.

The leadership function involves facilitating the achievement of group goals. In modern organizations, these functions can be (and often are) performed by several or many participants. But, given our societal propensity to focus on formal leaders, it is important to understand the expectations we have of those occupying these positions. The leadership function has been defined in many ways: from something as simple as "that which leaders do" on up. Citing nearly a dozen different definitions, Fiedler (1967) concludes that a leader is "the individual in the group given the task of directing and coordinating task-relevant group activities or who, in the absence of a designated leader, carries the primary responsibility for performing these functions in the group" (p. 8). Emphasis on coordinating task-oriented group activities seems to indicate that leading is synonymous with managing. Typically, however, management is considered to be a more broadly based function, entailing activities other than leading.

> Leadership is part of management, but not all of it. Managers are required to plan and organize, for example, but all we ask of leaders is that they influence others to follow. . . . Leadership is the ability to persuade others to seek defined objectives enthusiastically. It is the human factor that binds a group together and motivates it toward goals. . . . It is the ultimate act that brings to success all the potential that is in an organization and its people (Davis, 1977, p. 197).

The above distinction stresses the role of leadership in eliciting behavioral responses that are more than routine. The essence of leadership, as stated here, is suggestive of what in earlier chapters we referred to as the tapping of latent human capability in achieving group objectives. And it relates to our concept of an interaction-influence system by stressing the role of persuasion.

One way to define leadership is in terms of the *differential exertion of influence*. This approach recognizes that in social groups there are bilateral processes of interpersonal influence. Those with a positive balance—a net outflow of influence—would be designated as leaders; those with a minus balance would be followers. Obviously, the process of identifying leaders would have to be repeated for each group because the balance in any one group would shift according to the situation. For example, the physically underdeveloped student may have been overlooked at the senior picnic, where the emphasis was on appearance, physical skill, or strength. On the way home, however, that same student's first-aid training may thrust him or her into the leadership role in the aftermath of an automobile accident.

Differential influence is apparent in informal social relationships and in formal organizations. Typically, designated position holders have a positive balance—an outflow of influence—in the influence system. However, this may not always be the case. The positional authority of an official leader may not be enough to persuade subordinates to engage in appropriate activities. Influence attempts fail and leadership is ineffective. For example, Mayor Barnowski (in the vignette by that name) seemed to be having difficulty making changes in a local government bureaucracy.

Tannenbaum and Massarik (1957, p. 3) summarize the relationship between leadership and influence systems by stating that leadership is *"interpersonal influence, exercised in situations and directed, through the communication pro-*

cess, toward the attainment of a specified goal or goals. Leadership always involves attempts on the part of the *leader* (influencer) to affect (influence) the behavior of a *follower* (influencee) or followers in a situation."

Transactions/Exchange

Several factors make social exchange a key concept in understanding leadership. First, to have leaders we must also have followers, thus two or more people are involved in interactive relationships. Second, leaders and followers exchange influence. "Influence over others is purchased at the price of allowing one's self to be influenced by others" (Homans, 1961, p. 286).

Influence attempts, such as suggesting, persuading, or coercing, are actions. They evoke reactions that vary in terms of degree of compliance. Reactions, particuarly counteractions, are also attempts to influence others. These transactions occur in context where some people are more powerful than others, where some people are more dependent than others. Superiors tend to be more powerful; subordinates tend to be more dependent. "Some 70% of the work force in the private sector has no contractual protection from arbitrary or unjust discharge" (Summers, 1980, p. 132). However, there is increasing pressure for formal processes, such as arbitration, that will ensure justice and affect the balance of power. Even without these formal checks to power, it is not a unilateral process. Followers depend on leaders for ideas, directions, and support. Leaders depend on followers for meaningful contributions toward organizational performance.

Transactions are more meaningful when there is the potential for both parties to receive net benefits. Subordinates may comply with what they consider to be questionable directives because attempting to change them would be more trouble than it is worth. Bosses may tolerate what they consider to be questionable behavior in their subordinates because they are dependent on continuing contributions of effort or expertise. Such transactions take place over time and create an organizational context for interaction and influence. As long as the system remains in balance (rewards = contributions), social exchange endures. However, there are dysfunctional extremes. Participants can leave the system collectively (as in a wildcat strike) or individually: the ultimate being, "You can't fire me, I've already quit."

The transactional analysis approach to analyzing interpersonal communication, as presented in the last chapter, can be useful in understanding social exchange, particularly superior-subordinate relationships. Socialization processes in our culture tend to foster parent-child relationships in work organizations. It is assumed that bosses have the ability and right to influence the behavior of subordinates, who are dependent on them. Such a relationship works, but it is not necessarily the most effective over the long run. A more functional approach would be an adult-adult relationship (James, 1975). Parent or child roles are not eliminated (they can be helpful in controlling activities or fostering creativity), but they are subject to the guiding hand of the adult model. Joint problem solving rather than blaming; persuading rather than coercing; setting mutual expectations rather than directing; emphasizing organizational *and* individual goals rather than excluding one or the other: all are important aspects of adult-adult relationships and contribute to mature, enduring social exchange between leaders and followers.

Relationships over Time

Social exchange, including leader-follower transactions, occurs over time. It is a dynamic relationship that is affected by current events and long-term trends in positional power and interpersonal relationships. Figure 6.2 shows the focus of social exchange between leaders and followers as a cross-hatched area. The reciprocal arrows indicate a two-way process and the areas of the circles outside of the specific situation indicate that both leaders and followers can have other roles in addition to those of superior and subordinate in a particular context. The boundaries are permeable; that is, both external and all internal factors affect the social exchange between leaders and followers.

The way in which various individual characteristics and situational forces are depicted in the diagram makes it evident that a dynamic relationship exists between leaders and followers. Situations may be redefined by members of either group: expectations changing; individuals becoming more or less competent. Thus, over time, a leader may gain or lose legitimacy in the eyes of followers, based on the degree of congruence between positional and personal power. If a leader's motives and actions appear relevant and contribute to achieving positive results in the group's primary task, credits are built up, thus allowing the leader to be more influential in the future. These *idiosyncrasy credits* provide latitude for the leader's subsequent behavior, particularly increased tolerance for suggestions and innovations (Hollander, 1978, p. 44).

The social exchange over time between leaders and followers can be viewed in terms of behavior modification. Behavior that is reinforced is likely to continue. If it is punished or ignored, it is likely to decrease or cease. "This behavioral model emphasizes that the influence process is best understood as a set of behavioral contingencies evolving over time between a leader and subordinate. . . . The independent behaviors of the leader and the subordinate toward the task or with other organizational members can produce modified behavioral consequences for either the leader or the subordinate which, in turn, can affect their relationship" (Luthans & Davis, 1979, p. 240). The relationship is strengthened when the parties involved in social exchange are aware of, and think about, causes and effects.

Thinking about causes and effects is called *attribution*. It is a complex mental process that is affected by a number of individual and organizational factors (Green & Mitchell, 1979). However, several basic aspects of this process are evident in the behavioral exchange between leaders and followers. For example, a leader may attribute good performance to a subordinate's personal skill or effort and respond with strong positive reinforcement. On the other hand, if the good performance is attributed to external factors (luck or excellent coaching), the reinforcement, if any, is likely to be weaker. Similarly, reactions to poor performance are mediated by attributing the cause to varying mixes of internal

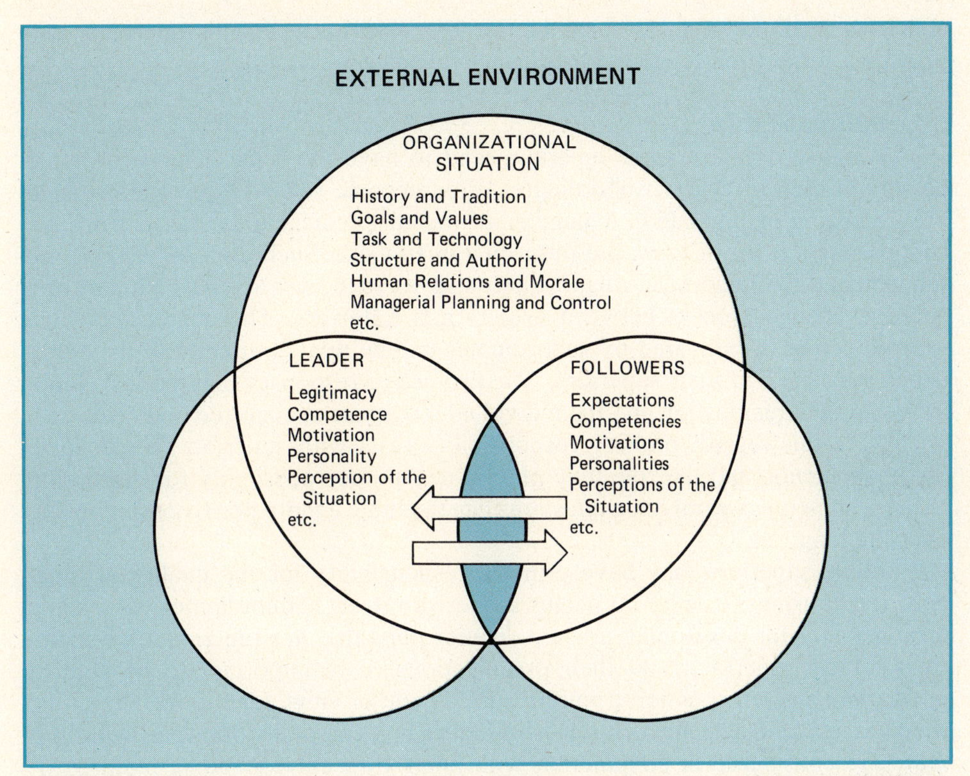

FIGURE 6.2 The Locus of Leadership. **Source:** Adapted from Edwin P. Hollander, *Leadership Dynamics,* p. 8. © 1978 by The Free Press, a division of Macmillan Publishing Co., Inc.

(lack of skill, effort, etc.) and external (bad luck, faulty procedures, etc.) factors. Extenuating circumstances, such as lack of support from data processing, may explain why a vital report is late.

Attributions are also made on the other side of the behavioral exchange. Subordinates may accept or resent criticism depending on their attribution (internal or external) of the cause of poor performance. The most typical undermining of relationships occurs when the leader blames the subordinate for failure because of lack of effort, while the subordinate sees the cause as clearly external—poor materials, ambiguous directions, or inadequate leadership. Reducing the discrepancy between the respective attributions of leader and follower is an important step in developing and maintaining a good working relationship.

Even though we know on some level that results are likely to have multiple causes, people do have a tendency to look for simple explanations. Like the members of the blue team listing extenuating circumstances for their failure in the *Who To Blame?* vignette, we can be quick to blame others and excuse ourselves. It is important for managers to concede the probability of multiple causes operating in complex organizational situations. A sign of maturity is the ability to attribute at least some of the blame to oneself. This approach will provide a foundation for functional leader-follower relationships.

Followership

Because organizational superiors tend to have the scale of power shifted heavily in their direction, subordinates often become self-protective in order to prevent being manipulated. A number of mental predicaments, taken from the subordinate's point of view, are described in Box 6.2. Such areas of tension are fundamental to hierarchical relationships and, as such, will always be a part of a social exchange process between leaders and followers. The degree to which self-protection is cultivated by subordinates will be related directly to the confidence they have in their superiors. The protective responses may be less debilitating to the organization and the individual if they are recognized and dealt with openly. In this regard, primary responsibility rests with superiors to recognize the phenomenon and the role they play in it. An open possibility for discussion of these sometimes paralyzing questions can facilitate a more positive relationship over the long run.

While superiors may have primary responsibility for the quality of long-term relationships, it is by no means a one-way street. Subordinates have some responsibility for developing upward relationships that are functional for themselves, their superiors, and their organizations. It is important to be able to understand a given situation from the boss's point of view. Identifying strengths, weaknesses, and typical work styles in higher-ups can be helpful, particularly if these are considered in conjunction with one's own corresponding features. It may be important to recognize complementary, rather than similar, skills, and compatible, rather than identical, work styles. A key element in managing upward relationships is the identification of mutual expectations. Open communication and checking for meaning are important elements in avoiding misinterpretation and providing the boss with relevant information (both good news and bad). Other basic ingredients are honesty and dependability, the lack of which can be crippling to an otherwise good relationship. Because every manager is both a superior and a subordinate, both sides of the relationship should be considered. However, education and training places primary emphasis on the attitudes and skills necessary for supervision and leadership. *Managing* the boss may be viewed by some as too proactive—involving politicking and apple polishing—but "such managers fail to realize the importance of this activity and how it can simplify their jobs by eliminating potentially severe problems. Effective managers recognize that this part of their work is legitimate. Seeing themselves as ultimately responsible for what they achieve in an organization, they know they need to establish and manage relationships with everyone on whom they are dependent, and that includes the boss" (Gabarro & Kotter, 1980, p. 100).

Self-Management

Self-management (or self-control) has been termed a "substitute for leadership" (Manz & Sims, 1980). The more people manage their own behavior while

BOX 6.2
DILEMMAS THAT SUBORDINATES MUST RESOLVE IN DEALING WITH SUPERIORS

Alliance vs. Competition: to view the superior as a trustworthy ally or as a competitor to be on guard against.

Clarifying Expectations vs. Second-Guessing: to seek explanations of what the superior wants or to stay uncertain about the superior's expectations and to risk misinterpretation.

Initiative vs. Dependence: to suggest and promote ways to achieve the organization's goals and enhance one's own development or to wait for the superior to take charge and modify personal aspirations.

Competence vs. Inferiority: to feel capable in one's work given one's experience and training or to feel inept and out of step with one's colleagues.

Differentiation vs. Identification: to come across as being very different from the superior in terms of skills, aspirations, values, and professional concerns or to identify with the superior as someone to emulate.

Relating Personally vs. Relating Impersonally: to view the superior as a fellow human facing similar problems in managing family and career and in developing friendships or to view the superior's world as different and distant and thus to relate to him or her on a utilitarian basis only.

Mutual Concern vs. Self-Interest: to keep the superior's welfare and development seriously in mind or to be totally preoccupied with one's own success.

Integrity vs. Denial: to accept the relationship with its limitations or to reject or misrepresent it.

Source: Reprinted by permission of the Harvard Business Review. Excerpt from "The Subordinate's Predicaments," by Eric H. Neilsen and Jan Gypen [September-October 1979].

achieving results that are in line with organizational goals, the less need there is for overt leadership. Some college and professional football coaches say that they don't coach place kickers because they are afraid of messing up a natural talent. Some managers have a tendency to overmanage. They lead other people with a highly directive style, when performance might improve if they would just get out of the way—not obstruct the process. Of course, the degree to which followers or subordinates can be counted on to manage themselves varies with the individual and the situation. A structured task—perhaps an assembly line with automated processes—allows little discretion for the worker. Nor does it require much in the way of leadership from supervisors. The system tends to manage itself. On the other hand, unstructured tasks—public relations or systems design, for example—allow considerable leeway for the individual. Managers can vary the amount and the kind of leadership behavior they adopt, according to the circumstances.

In many situations, self-management is essential because the individual functions independently over long periods of time. Traveling salespeople, research scientists, professors, and writers are examples. Managers that are ultimately responsible for the contributions of such workers tend to focus on results rather than methods. The same general approach might be effective for most jobs; that is, putting more reliance on subordinates to control their own actions and behave in responsible ways.

Leadership, followership, and self-management affect each other. Followers that practice good self-management require less overt leadership. But when close supervision is required, managers need the ability to influence subordinates. They must use power and authority to enhance their effectiveness as leaders.

POWER

Power is a fundamental concept in social science in the same sense that energy is fundamental in physics; it is the ability to produce intended effects (Russell, 1938, p. 35). This is a broad connotation that relates not to methods used, but only to the results. In its most general sense, power denotes (1) the ability (exercised or not) to produce a certain occurrence or (2) the influence exerted by a person or group, through whatever means, over the conduct of others in intended ways (Gould & Kolb, 1964, p. 524). This relates to the spectrum of means schematized in Figure 6.1: the suggestion being that power is involved along the entire spectrum as long as there is an ability to produce a certain occurence (Salancik & Pfeffer, 1977).

While power underlies the whole repertoire of ways in which people can influence behavior, its everyday connotation leans toward the persuasive-coercive end of the spectrum. The commonly held notion of power implies the force, if proved necessary, to control or command others. Unfortunately, this has taken on a negative cast, having been linked in people's minds with dictators and despots. Lord Acton's comment, in 1887, that "power tends to corrupt, absolute power corrupts absolutely" has been repeated often and accepted by many. But, in reality, power is neutral and lends itself to constructive ends and means as readily as to destructive ones. Good managers welcome power, otherwise they would not aspire to be leaders. But they use it wisely:

> The top manager of a company must possess a high need for power, that is, a concern for influencing people. However, this need must be disciplined and controlled so that it is directed toward the benefit of the institution as a whole and not toward the manager's personal aggrandizement (McClelland & Burnham, 1976, p. 101).

Good managers want power in order to be able to influence organizational performance, but they recognize the dysfunctional consequences of dictatorial methods. They recognize the benign uses of the collective power: that ability to affect something that stems from participation. Involvement and commitment increase the probability that subordinates will implement plans enthusiastically and accomplish goals. Effective leaders make followers feel strong and capable; they facilitate teamwork on interdependent activities; and they reward accomplishment. Good managers use their power to achieve superior results *and* to maintain high morale.

Social Power

Social power relates primarily to prestige and esteem or love and acceptance. When organizational participants are encouraged to improve their performance, the appeal is based on what the *good* employee *ought* to do. The behavior of an individual can be influenced through the medium of a small group. A boss may suggest that other participants in a work group apply pressure on a particular member to effect the desired result. The social power—in the form of love and acceptance—that peers exercise over one another is an important and integral part of the influence system in groups and organizations.

In bureaucratic organizations, the interaction-influence patterns tend to be hierarchical, with the direction of flow primarily from superior to subordinate. Power is narrowly held, centralized, and relies heavily on material incentives or sanctions. In other organizations, the interaction-influence patterns are more varied, manifesting bottom-up, horizontal, and diagonal, as well as top-down relationships. Power is widely held, decentralized, and relies more on social factors such as the esteem of others.

These comments are directed toward what is predominant or highly probable in various types of organizations. The uses of power to back up influence attempts can take many forms in a given organization, depending on the situation, yet participants come to expect certain kinds of influence attempts as normal. In general, the trend in organizations has been away from reliance on physical or monetary power bases. Social power tends to be involved in an increasing proportion of the influence attempts in organizations. It is important to remember that power exists only to the extent to which it is effective in controlling behavior; conversely, without power, influence attempts fail.

Power Equalization

"The general trend of twentieth-century society, particularly in the U.S., is toward a wider distribution of power, a broadening of participation by individuals in controlling their own lives and work" (Ways, 1970, p. 174). The nature and extent of these changes concern managers worldwide (Oates, 1977). There is a trend toward an industrial humanism where the primary concern is the individual rather than the work itself or the organization per se. Its tenets are the importance of self-actualization and the theory that individuals cannot grow and develop in an atmosphere of overwhelming positional power (authority), the form that underlies predominatly downward attempts to influence behavior. There has been a plea for more balance in the distribution of power so that influence can flow in many directions in organizations.

The balance of power between the individual and the organization, the latter represented by a superior, rests decidedly in favor of the organization. It can apply sanctions without regarding too seriously the repercussions that might stem from one individual. Collectively, however, individuals can wield considerable power, including the ultimate withdrawal of contributions in the form of a strike. This alternative is often unpalatable to the organization, and hence the power balance shifts in favor of the subordinates (as evidenced by the success of strikes by employees in critical fields such as health care or emergency municipal services).

AUTHORITY

Authority is institutionalized power, an important concept in the study of formal organizations. It is based on legal foundations (legislation, articles of incorporation, partnership agreements, bylaws) that define an organization's mission and empower its members to carry out its activities.

Without formal authority, groups typically develop power relationships and allocate status based on characteristics such as physical prowess, technical know-how, or wisdom. Identification with tradition or possession of a charismatic manner may also be decisive in establishing power bases within groups. If the organization is a legal entity, relationships are structured and positions established formally. The actual, day-to-day system may not coincide with this official version, but it may be no less efficient for that fact in achieving the objectives of the formal organization.

Need for Authority

Natural social groups develop in the form of families, clans, tribes, states, and nations. Within these groups superior-subordinate relationships develop in the form of status and role systems. Based on any of a number of characteristics, power structures evolve naturally, and they in turn are perpetuated via tradition (Jay, 1971).

It is hard to imagine that the human community could proceed in its endeavors without that institutionalized power structure which we call authority. Anarchy is inconceivable to most of us; but so is the other extreme, authoritarianism. As with so many conceptual extremes, we are interested in a workable compromise. We need enough authority to ensure cooperative action and progress toward group goals. However, we also want to encourage individuality, creativity, and innovation. Authoritarianism results from a preoccupation with hierarchical relationships so pronounced that superiors eschew consultation with subordinates. The other side of authoritarianism shows subordinates disposed toward zealous obedience to hierarchical superiors.

Given the inevitability of informal and formal organizations, there is a need for some means to ensure that efforts are directed toward appropriate objectives. "Every organization faces the task of somehow reducing the variability, instability, and unpredictability of individual human acts" (Katz & Kahn, 1978, p.

296). Authority, coupled with status and role systems, supplies this necessary element. The combination results in roles reasonably well defined so that behavior is not entirely spontaneous and unrehearsed. In many cases, behavior of organizational members is identical: starting at eight and quitting at five, for example. Members may wear certain styles of attire (even uniforms) that distinguish them from other organizations, or they may develop special behavior patterns that are essential to the work of the organization.

Traditional Authority

The charisma of leaders often evolves into traditional authority as informal status and role systems become stabilized over time. Traditional authority is exemplified by the phrase, "It has always been this way." Policies, procedures, and rules are developed by those traditionally in command. Over a period of time the system evolves to the point were directives are carried out by subordinates without question. Changes or adjustments in the system result when traditional leaders deem it necessary or desirable. The traditions in the system may be handed down explicitly in written form or implicitly in a manner similar to the transmission of folklore.

Common law has become codified into an elaborate body of official criteria for administering justice in society. Legal authority in organizations is also established by means of specific legislation. Governmental agencies are designated responsibility for a sphere of activity and are accorded commensurate authority in order to carry out their specific tasks. This framework provides the means to structure a hierarchy through which authority is delegated to positions in the system.

Most large-scale business organizations are legal entities called corporations, which derive their authority from the various states. Their charters designate what they can and cannot do, depending on the particular sphere of activity engaged in. Insurance companies have special rules and regulations, as do airlines or drug manufacturers. The authority system in a corporation is based on institutional rights granted to it by the state. This authority is delegated throughout the system on the basis of typical hierarchical patterns. Organizational participants recognize the legitimate authority based on ownership. It may be used by an owner-manager or delegated to a group of professional managers, as is the case in many large-scale, complex organizations of today.

While management has the responsibility to achieve organizational goals, an increasing number of external constraints limits traditional authority. Union contracts, regulatory boards or commissions, and new laws circumscribe managerial decision making in matters such as hiring, firing, pricing, safety, and environmental protection (Bennis, 1976).

The internal system of authority does not always work as smoothly as it would appear. Viewing the flow of authority from the top down stresses the concept that subordinate behavior can be made to conform to the expectations of the superior. However, there has always been the notion that effective authority depends on the consent of the governed.

Acceptance Theory of Authority

The institutionalized right to influence behavior may or may not be effective, depending on the consent of organizational participants. The crux of the authority relationship is that a subordinate holds in abeyance his or her own critical faculties for choosing between alternatives and uses the receipt of a command as the basis for choice (Simon, 1976, p. 126). This line of reasoning leads to a zone of acceptance from the point of view of the subordinates (see Figure 6.3). They have a certain range of tolerance within which they will accept directives without analyzing the merits of the behavior as related to the problem at hand.

The concept of a zone of acceptance is important in understanding effective authority. Unless a directive falls within this range, it will not be effective, and the influence attempt fails. In such cases, repeated attempts to influence behavior can be made with the same means, or a different approach can be used. Both Mayor Barnowski and Charlie Slade (of the chapter vignettes) were wondering what to do next in their roles as leaders. If all else fails, the various sanctions underlying the authority system can be imposed, including dismissal. But if the objective is to coordinate group effort and the result is a loss of organizational participants, the overall system has failed. Formal authority is limited by the zone of acceptance.

Individuals typically undergo a socialization process from infancy to adulthood that stresses the acceptance of authority. In modern, large-scale organizations, however, a countertrend can be detected that has narrowed the zone of acceptance for participants over the years. Employees are likely to exercise their own judgment more often and accept uncritically the directives of others in fewer situations. The educational process has fostered a long-run trend in this direction. As employees at all levels become better educated, they are less likely to defer evaluation and decision making to superiors over wide ranges of activities. More and more people want to know why a particular course of action is the desired one. This is occurring in all types of organizations—families, clubs, schools, hospitals, government agencies, and businesses.

A great deal has been written about the apparent conflict in the nature of authority. Specifically: Does authority flow downward in organizations based on an institutionalized right to employ power?; Or does authority stem from the bottom up, based on the zone of acceptance that participants maintain with respect to the directives of superiors?

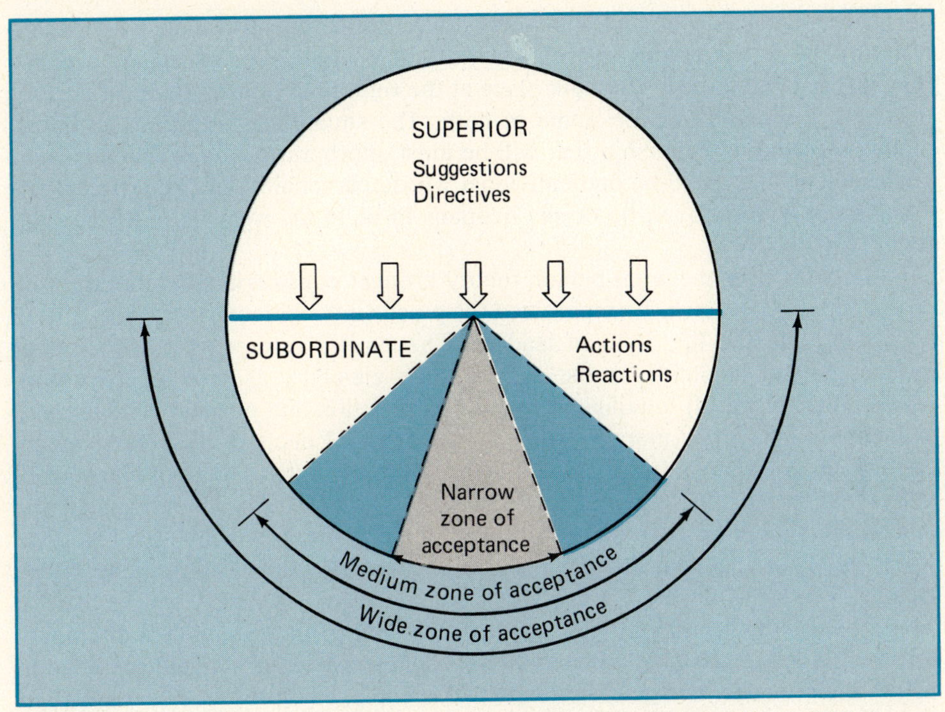

FIGURE 6.3 Zones of Acceptance: Ranges Within Which Subordinate Will Accept Directives Without Analysis

A synthesis is possible if we recognize that the rational/legal authority framework is accepted as legitimate by most participants. And when it is coupled with traditional and charismatic sources of authority, the zone of acceptance is widened significantly. The zone of acceptance relates to specific influence attempts by particular people. An appeal based on utilitarian aspects may envoke no response; the same appeal based on peer-group power may elicit the desired behavior. When positional and personal authority reinforce each other, we have added evidence of the synthesis of the acceptance theory with the right-to-command theory.

Formal authority does give positional power, a basis for influencing organizational behavior. However, it is not always enough to ensure effective cooperation. When greater reliance must be placed on other means of influencing behavior, the art of leadership becomes a vital factor.

ATTRIBUTES OF LEADERS

For centuries, philosophers have argued the pros and cons of the *great-person* theory. Was history made by people—the likes of Catherine the Great, Napoleon, Lenin, Churchill—or were such people made by history? Is there something about the personality of such individuals that enables them to have a significant effect on the course of human events? Or do such people become leaders because they just happen to be in the right place at the right time? Based on most current research, we would answer: some of both. The situation is important in determining the kind of leadership that will be most appropriate. Given the particular environment, there will be one individual whose personality and behavior fit the situation best. Moreover, he or she happens to be in the right place at the right time.

Debates over the great-person theory brought considerable attention to the so-called *trait approach*. It emphasized the personality characteristics, the system of values, and the life style of leaders. The typical research on historical or modern leaders included in the picture such elements as size, energy (both nervous and physical), intelligence, sense of direction and purpose, enthusiasm, friendliness, integrity, morality, technical expertise, decisiveness, persistence, endurance, good looks (physical and sartorial), and courage. One obvious problem is that there is little agreement with regard to which traits should be included and which should be excluded. Moreover, there is disagreement with regard to which of those included are the more important (Stogdill, 1948; Goode, 1951; Bennis, 1959).

There have been many attempts to distill out of these long lists of characteristics some key attributes such as intelligence, social maturity, cultural breadth, achievement needs, and genuine respect for people. The presence of these characteristics does not ensure leadership success, nor does their absence preclude it. However, an individual possessing these basic attributes may have a higher probability of becoming a successful leader (regardless of the followers and the situation) than someone without them. Another set of summary traits is shown in Box 6.3.

The danger of the trait approach is illustrated by Solomon (1950), who suggests that these qualities are obviously desirable in a leader but that none of them seems to be essential.

> The world has seen numerous great leaders who could hardly lay claim to any kind of formal education. History is replete with nontrained, nonacademic Fords, Edisons, and Carnegies who couldn't even claim a grammar school education yet managed to become leaders whose influence was felt around the globe. As for appearance of robust health, need we mention more than the delicate Gandhi, or George Washington Carver, the frail, shriveled, insignificant little Negro who was one of America's greatest scientists? And so many more like them? As for high ideals, fine character, etc., where would Hitler, Capone, or Attila the Hun rate here? (p. 15)

These latter cases may be examples of situations in which a particular personality defect seemed to be called for in the environmental context. A sick society may choose a sick leader (Brown, 1954, p. 222).

BOX 6.3
WHAT MAKES A SUPERLEADER?

(Associated Press, LOS ANGELES) Why do people work hard for one boss and loaf under another?

Dr. Warren Bennis, professor of management at the School of Business Administration at the University of Southern California, says it is a matter of whether the boss can imbue his office with the energy of a mission.

"People would rather dedicate their lives to a cause they believe in than lead lives of pampered idleness," Bennis says. "The leader of a cult, a traditional religion, an army or a dynamic corporation can tap this desire."

Bennis, a management expert, set out four years ago to determine what makes a "superleader." To do so, he interviewed 90 of them, including chief executives of some of the nation's biggest corporations, university presidents, public officials, newspaper publishers and the coaches of consistently winning athletic teams.

On average, the "superleaders" were 56-year-old males who had graduated from college and were making about $300,000 a year. Most of them, he also found, were enthusiastically married to their first wife.

Statistics aside, Bennis identified five traits his superleaders had in common:

- *Vision:* the capacity to create a compelling picture of the desired state of affairs that inspires people to perform.
- *Communication:* the ability to portray the vision clearly and in a way that enlists the support of their constituencies.
- *Persistence:* the ability to stay on course regardless of the obstacles encountered.
- *Empowerment:* the ability to create a structure that harnesses the energies of others to achieve the desired result.
- *Organizational ability:* the capacity to monitor the activities of the group, learn from the mistakes and use the resulting knowledge to improve the performance of the organization. . . .

Bennis also noticed that a lot of the leaders he studied did not seem so super outside their area of expertise.

"Socially, a lot of these people are absolute misfits. Very few of them seem to be capable of small talk," he says. "For them, nothing is done without a purpose, and when they're not on that purpose, they're boring. It's as if there's a range of intensity and outside of their range they tune out."

Thus, he says, superleaders are happiest on the job.

"They are very happy, on the whole. But if they can't play in their playground, they can be very depressed," he says. "They're ecstatic when they're acting within their own context, but outside of it they're not."

Source: Stephen Fox, Associated Press, Los Angeles, November 21, 1982.

EFFECTIVE LEADER BEHAVIOR

The trait approach refers to what a leader is. Another approach to understanding leadership success concentrates on what the leader does—the mode of behavior or performance style. Terms such as autocratic, democratic, bureaucratic, and laissez-faire have been used to describe the general approach adopted by leaders. To research the effectiveness of various styles, it is necessary to hold other elements constant. Any findings have to be interpreted in the light of a similar environmental situation used in an experiment or observed in real organizations. One study concentrated on the impact of three basic leadership styles in task-oriented groups (White & Lippitt, 1953). Three relatively distinct styles are described in Box 6.4.

In the White-Lippitt experiments, the leaders "assumed the designated roles for a given period," with all other aspects of the groups held as constant as possible. The difference in leadership styles made manifest prompts certain conclusions with regard to their effect on individual participants and group behavior.

Although the quantity of work was slightly greater in authoritarian groups, the quality of work in democratic groups was consistently better. When the leader left the room, the autocratic groups collapsed completely, whereas the performance in democratic groups decreased only slightly. With the laissez-faire approach, the findings indicated that complete permissiveness is generally ineffective in terms of group performance. It did not seem to produce any other benefits, such as improved morale or satisfaction of individual group members. These dimensions were improved, along with performance, in democratic groups. While the quantity of output in authoritarian work groups was slightly better than under a democratic approach, there were serious negative side effects that cast doubt on the long-run usefulness of an autocratic style. It would seem that on balance, a democratic-participative approach was the most effective and efficient. These findings have been corroborated by similar experiments and in actual industrial situations.

In stable/mechanistic organizations, leadership style based on a depersonalized bureaucracy may be appropriate. The system of rules and regulations is designed to cover all exigencies. Hence the role of the leader is one of monitoring routine activity within the guidelines established by the system itself. A bureaucratic style that stresses administrative tidiness, regularity, and accuracy is evident in many of today's large-scale organizations. In adaptive/organic organizations, however, a more flexible style is called for in order to cope with diverse human resources that are engaged in complex activities.

Specific Behaviors

A major task in leadership research has been to identify those specific behaviors that account for leadership effectiveness. Reviewing the research and commentary on leadership behavior, Bowers and Seashore (1966, p. 247) concluded that, in spite of the variety of terms used, there is a great deal of common conceptual content. They distilled the following four dimensions of effectiveness:

BOX 6.4

THREE BASIC LEADERSHIP STYLES

Authoritarian	Democratic	Laissez-Faire
1. All determination of policy by the leader	1. All policies a matter of group discussion and decision, encouraged and assisted by the leader	1. Complete freedom for group or individual decision, with a minimum of leader participation
2. Techniques and activity steps dictated by the authority, one at a time so that future steps were always uncertain to a large degree	2. Activity perspective gained during dicussion period. General steps to group goal sketched, and when technical advice was needed, the leader suggested two or more alternative procedures from which choice could be made	2. Various materials supplied by the leader, who made it clear that information would be supplied when requested and took no other part in work discussion
3. The leader usually dictated the particular work task and work companion of each member	3. The members were free to work with whomever they chose, and the division of tasks was left up to the group	3. Complete nonparticipation of the leader
4. The dominator tended to be "personal" in the praise and criticism of the work of each member; remained aloof from active group participation except when demonstrating	4. The leader was "objective" or "fact-minded" in praise and criticism and tried to be a regular group member in spirit without doing too much of the work	4. Infrequent spontaneous comments on member activities unless questioned and no attempt to appraise or regulate the course of events

Source: After Table, pp. 26–27, in *Autocracy and Democracy* by Ralph K. White and Ronald Lippitt. © 1960 by Ralph K. White and Ronald Lippitt. By permission of Harper & Row, Publishers, Inc.

1. *Support:* Behavior that enhances someone else's feeling of personal worth and importance.
2. *Interaction facilitation:* Behavior that encourages members of the group to develop close, mutually satisfying relationships.

3. *Goal emphasis:* Behavior that stimulates an enthusiasm for meeting the group's goal or achieving excellent performance.
4. *Work facilitation:* Behavior that helps achieve goal attainment by such activities as scheduling, coordinating, planning, and by providing resources such as tools, materials, and technical knowledge.

Support and interaction facilitation are obviously *people* concerns. Emphasizing these dimensions involves a recognition of the value of the individual and the place of individual concerns in maintaining and improving interpersonal relationships and group processes, such as teamwork. Goal emphasis and work facilitation relate to *task* concerns and to the path-goal theory of leadership (House Mitchell, 1974). Good leaders are typically seen by subordinates as helpful in both setting goals and in structuring or designing means of achieving them. This approach builds on the concept of achievement motivation; if goals are achieved and performance is rewarded appropriately, there is an increase in satisfaction. Performance leads to satisfaction and increased motivation in the future.

These four dimensions of behavior are an elaboration of several two-factor models that call attention to people versus production, relationship orientation versus task orientation, or group maintenance versus goal achievement. Of primary concern is the question of whether behavior on these dimensions is mutually exclusive. Does emphasis on task preclude emphasis on people and vice versa? In describing leadership behavior in existing organizations, we can find examples of varying degrees of emphasis on these behaviors. Some managers are relatively task oriented; others focus on relationships. Which is best? We will explore this question in subsequent sections; however, a general guideline is that all four factors in the above model are important and should be emphasized as much as possible, depending on the constraints of the situation (Hollander, 1978, p. 115). It is unrealistic, however, to expect simultaneous attention to all of the dimensions of effective leader behavior. Some tradeoffs are necessary and bound to occur. Goal emphasis may be paramount in initiating a program of management by objectives. Interaction facilitation may actually need to be decreased in an organization that seems to spend nearly all of its time in meetings (leaving little time to work on the task). An appropriate balance should be maintained according to the particular situation.

Organizational Context

The external environment of the organization is part of the context within which leadership takes place (see Figure 6.2). Prevailing cultural norms and industry practices provide general guidelines for behavior. Books, periodicals, movies, and television provide explicit role models for leaders in a variety of organizations—business, governmental, military, religious, and educational. These general influences are coupled with specific organizational conditions to provide an overall context for leader behavior.

Box 6.5 describes this context in terms of the rhetoric versus the reality of managerial work. In coping with what Sayles (1979) calls the "peripatetic flurry" of reality, one finds that leadership skills are important because the core activities in organizations involve people in need of direction. According to Sayles (pp. 16–18):

1. Management is a contingency activity; managers act when routines break down, when unanticipated snags appear.
2. People in organizations . . . require human contact to clarify and legitimate feelings and decisions.
3. Most managerial choices arise out of interpersonal processes—advice solicitation, negotiation, persuasion, sounding out, and consensus building.

A basic approach to understanding the internal organizational context is to consider forces in (1) the leader, (2) the followers, and (3) the situation. An example of this approach would be to analyze each element in order to determine the degree of participation that might be appropriate in decision making (Tannenbaum & Schmidt, 1973, pp. 178–179):

Leader:
Own value system
Confidence in his or her subordinates
Own leadership inclinations
Feelings of security in an uncertain situation

Follower(s):
Independence-dependence needs
Willingness to assume responsibility for decision making
Tolerance for ambiguity
Degree of interest in participating
Degree of identification with organization goals
Knowledge and experience (or growth potential)
Expectations concerning participation

Situation:
Values and traditions in the organization
Group effectiveness
Nature of the problem
Pressure of time

Consideration of these factors and forces can also be related to the degree of emphasis on the various behaviors in the four-factor model described previously. For example, the amount of support provided to subordinates might vary with our perception of individual needs in this regard. More emphasis on work facilitation might be provided if subordinate knowledge and experience are minimal.

BOX 6.5
THE RHETORIC AND REALITY OF MANAGERIAL WORK

In setting the stage for his discussion of *leadership,* Leonard Sayles describes the rhetoric and reality of managerial work as follows:

Rhetoric	Reality
Thoughtful decision making.	Most of the workday is devoted to interaction with other people; getting and exchanging information, persuading and negotiating.
Clearly scheduled and logically planned workday.	Impromptu, sporadic, and unplanned contacts; jumping from issue to issue and among different people.
Efforts devoted to "leading" subordinates, who defer to higher status.	Most of the time with outsiders; even subordinates challenge frequently the manager's authority.
Decisions made by rational judgment of individual in correct position to evaluate all the factors.	Decisions are the product of a complex brokerage and negotiation process, extending over time and involving large numbers of interested parties.
Objectives and goals clear and consistent.	Multiplicity of goals identified with different groups and interests that are conflicting and even

Similarly, interaction facilitation and goal emphasis could be emphasized or not, depending on our own inclinations and our assessment of a group's effectiveness and the specific nature of a given problem.

It is important to recognize that organizational contexts are not static. Forces operating in and on the leader, the followers, and the situation as a whole change continually. Each situation requiring active leadership should be diagnosed according to the specific factors that could affect the ability of the leader to influence the behavior of others. This suggests the need for some flexibility if the leader's behavior is to be effective in a variety of contexts. "The most effective leaders appear to exhibit a degree of versatility and flexibility that enables them to adapt their behavior to the changing and contradictory demands made on them" (Stogdill, Autumn, 1974, p. 14).

Organizational Performance

Organizational theory and management practice relate to task-oriented groups. Therefore, productivity is an important measure of managerial perfor-

Rhetoric	Reality
	contradictory; often-changing priorities.
Results proportionate to individual effort and capability; steady progress, decisive accomplishment.	Results are the product of many uncontrollable forces which are slow to emerge and difficult to predict; incremental steps—two back, three forward.
Authority equal to responsibilities.	Significant deficiencies in the power to command resources and permissions necessary to fulfill assigned objectives.
Clear goals established and subdivided into milestones and benchmarks.	While managers need to break down larger activities into explicit goals and subgoals, in fact, most of the managers' tasks have no beginning or end; problems flow through, and there is often little possibility of neatly completing activities or solving organizational problems "once and for all."

Source: Leonard R. Sayles, *Leadership: What Effective Managers* Really *Do . . . and* How *They Do It,* McGraw-Hill Book Company, New York, 1979, p. 12. Used with permission.

mance, which depends in turn on leadership effectiveness. However, attributing organizational outcomes to specific leader behaviors is probably an oversimplification.

In discussing this issue, Pfeffer (1977, p. 106) suggests three reasons why the observed effects of leaders on organizational outcomes should be evaluated. "First, those obtaining leadership positions are selected, and perhaps only certain, limited styles of behavior may be chosen. Second, once in the leadership position, the discretion and behavior of the leader are constrained. And third, leaders can typically affect only a few of the variables that may impact organizational performance." The vignette describing Mayor Barnowski's frustrations after six months in office illustrates the impact problem. In spite of these inherent problems, there have been numerous attempts to establish a relationship between specific leadership behavior and group performance. At best, the results are mixed (Stogdill, 1974, pp. 418–420). "Whether or not leader behavior actually influences performance or effectiveness, it is important because people believe it does" (Pfeffer, 1977, p. 110). Moreover, formal leaders often encourage the attribution of organizational success to their personal effectiveness.

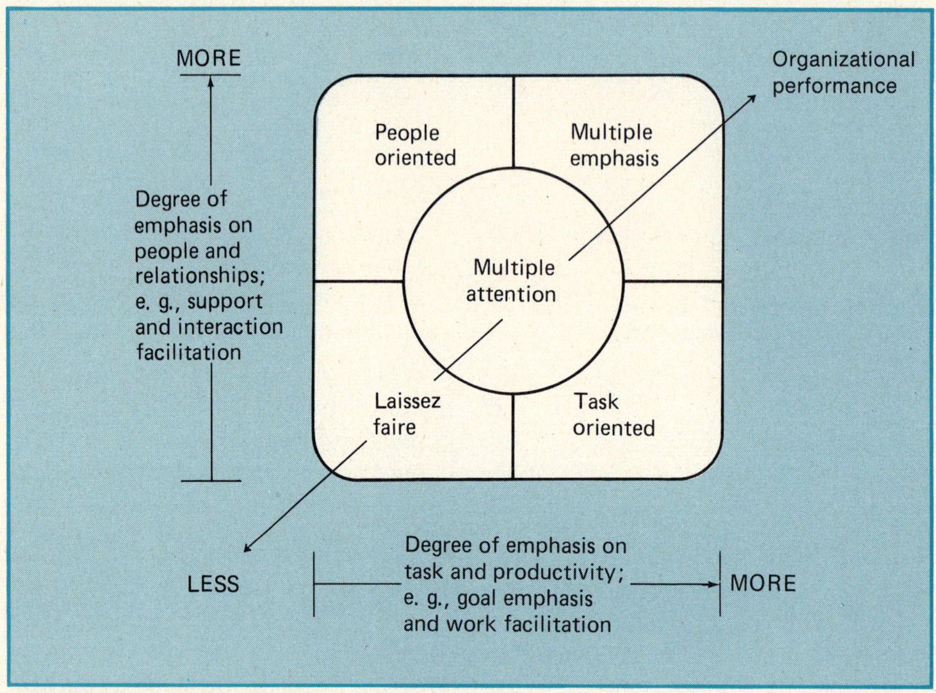

FIGURE 6.4 Leader Behavior and Organizational Performance: The Need for Balanced Emphasis on *Both* Work Results and Human Resource Development

While the impact of the formal leaders is often constrained by situational factors beyond their control, they can have some influence (positive or negative) on performance in almost all cases. Therefore, it is important to understand as much as possible about effective leader behavior, if only in terms of probabilities of success for various styles. Research results concerning the effect of specific behaviors on performance suggest the need for a balanced approach (see Figure 6.4). A commitment to multiple long-run performance criteria (effectiveness, efficiency, and participant satisfaction) will favor an emphasis on supporting subordinates, encouraging interaction among group members, setting challenging and realistic goals, and facilitating the work of the organization.

Long-run organizational performance is enhanced if attention is paid to *both* work results and the development of human resources. An exclusive attention to one of these, or a laissez faire lack of attention to either, is rare. It is more common for managers to give some attention to both concerns (the area of the circle in Figure 6.4). However, their approach often involves compromising some aspects of task accomplishment or group maintenance in order to achieve satisfactory performance. The ultimate goal is superior organizational performance via emphasis on tasks and productivity (results) as well as people and relationships (team building) (Blake & Mouton, 1978).

Effective leaders are able to do both. Their work groups perform well and they are regarded highly by their subordinates in terms of managerial competence and interpersonal skills. Frank Tomita *(We'll Miss Ya Frank* vignette) was, in the eyes of his subordinates, able to emphasize results *and* human resource development.

CONTINGENCY VIEWS AND FLEXIBILITY

Our discussion of traits, styles, and behavior inevitably brings us to the conclusion that there is no simple, cookbook technique that guarantees success. It all depends on the leader, the followers, and the situation: this last defined by the nature of the task, the authority relationships, and the group dynamics. Such factors are part of the organizational context or psychosocial system within which a leader must function. A contingency view in diagnosing situations, coupled with flexibility in behavior, will improve the probability that a leader's influence attempts will be successful.

Blake and Mouton (1982) argue that a contingency view (situationalism) is appropriate for deciding how to achieve the organizational conditions shown in Figure 6.5, but that all leaders should strive to achieve these conditions at all times. "From an everyday perspective, it might be thought that a kernel of truth is embedded within situationalism. This relates to the observation that no two situations are alike, and, therefore, it follows that each must be managed differently. Unfortunately, this idea precludes management by principles. A sound resolution must retain management by principles across situations while applying them in ways appropriate to circumstances. This leads to the distinction between principles themselves and the tactics of their application" (p. 286). Organizational science provides us with basic principles to guide managerial intentions. Effective leaders are artists; they have the knack of knowing when and how to act in a variety of situations.

Figure 6.6 shows a continuum of leadership behavior, with the basic variable being the degree of authority used by a manager vis à vis the amount of freedom left for subordinates in making decisions. Different styles can be identified across the continuum from boss-centered leadership to subordinate-centered leadership. We should not infer from these schemata that a manager of a certain persuasion always makes a decision and announces it unprepared, or that another always defines limits and then asks the group to take a vote. Different styles will be appropriate in different situations. In a military combat situation, subordinates must rely on the decision making of their group leader. The crew of a ship hit by a torpedo would not be inclined to discuss the alternatives and then vote. If the captain announces, "abandon ship," the order would be carried out immediately. On the other hand, in situations where time permits, it may be useful to include subordinates in the decision-making process. This does not necessarily mean that a vote will be taken and that the majority rules. A manager may say something to the effect that he is interested in the various points of view and that an exhaustive study of the question should be made. However, the manager may state emphatically in the beginning that he will make the decision at the end of

Principles	Key Words
1. Fulfillment through participation is the motivation that gives character to human activity and supports productivity.	Participation
2. Open communication is essential for the exercise of self and shared responsibility.	Candor
3. Accepting others as capable of reaching standards of excellence promotes trust and respect.	Trust and respect
4. Shared participation in problem solving and decision making stimulates active involvement and commmitment, productivity and creative thinking.	Involvement and commitment
5. Conflicts are solved by direct confrontation of their causes, with understanding and agreement as the basis of cooperative effort.	Conflict resolution
6. Mutual agreement is the strongest basis for supervision.	Consensus
7. Effective interaction between boss and subordinate enhances synergy.	Synergy
8. Management is by objectives.	Goals and objectives
9. Organization members who cooperate are interdependent in giving mutual support.	Mutual support
10. Learning from experience is through critique and feedback.	Change and development

FIGURE 6.5 Emerging Behavioral Science Principles Significant for the Effective Exercise of Leadership. **Source:** Robert R. Blake and Jane Srygley Mouton, "Theory and Research for Developing a Science of Leadership," *The Journal of Applied Behavioral Science* 18/3 [1982]: 285.

the discussion. In other cases, the authority to make decisions may be decentralized completely with only broad guidelines established by the manager.

Diagnosing Situations

Box 6.6 develops prescriptions for a leader's behavior based on the answers to a series of questions related to problem attributes. By asking each of these questions in sequence, one can classify problems into types. Each type can be identified with an appropriate leadership style or behavior, ranging from completely autocratic to highly participative. Participative approaches range from one-on-one consultation to consultation in a group meeting and finally to delegation to a group. This type of analysis leads to a matching of leadership behavior with specific problematic situations.

In current management literature it is easy to identify a preference for a participative leadership style. Such an approach may or may not be possible; it may not even be appropriate. Based on research involving a number of practicing

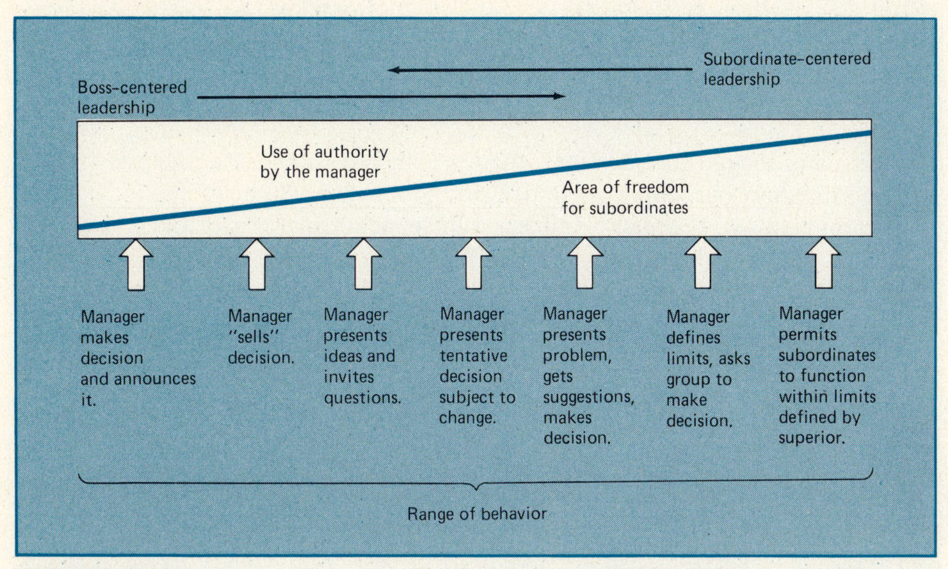

FIGURE 6.6 Continuum of Leadership Behavior. **Source:** Reprinted by permission of the *Harvard Business Review.* Excerpt from "How to Choose a Leadership Pattern," by Robert Tannenbaum and Warren H. Schmidt (March-April 1958): 96. © 1958 by the President and Fellows of Harvard College; all rights reserved.

managers responding to case situations, Vroom and Yetton (1973) observed that managers typically have to resort to a variety of styles, depending on the situation. However, they concluded that most managers would be more effective if they were both more autocratic and more participative (p. 153). They found that managers tended to shy away from an autocratic approach, even when it was most appropriate according to the model, and they tended to be less participative than called for by the model in other situations. This suggests that to be more effective, managers need increased flexibility. A leader must be a good diagnostician and match the situation with an appropriate style: sometimes relatively autocratic and sometimes quite participative.

On balance, it is important for leaders to recognize the complexity of human motivation, social exchange, group dynamics, and organizational contexts. The best leaders seem to have a tolerance for ambiguity and conceptual ability to cope with multidimensional situations. They emphasize support and interaction facilitation as well as goal emphasis and work facilitation; and they are both autocratic and participative, depending on the situation.

FACILITATING EFFECTIVE LEADERSHIP

Leadership is the part of management relying most heavily on interpersonal relationships and focused on bringing out hidden stores of talent. Leadership

BOX 6.6
DECIDING HOW TO DECIDE

A series of diagnostic questions about problem attributes can help leaders determine how participative the decision process should be. Need for quality, probability of acceptance, time available, goal congruence, and potential conflict among subordinates are key factors in deciding whether an autocratic, consultative, or group decision-making process is most appropriate.

Problem Attributes	**Diagnostic Questions**
The importance of the quality of the decision.	Is there a quality requirement such that one solution is likely to be more rational than another?
The extent to which the leader possesses sufficient information/expertise to make a high-quality decision.	Do I have sufficient information to make a high-quality decision?
The extent to which the problem is structured.	Is the problem structured?
The extent to which acceptance or commitment on the part of subordinates is critical to the effective implementation of the decision.	Is acceptance of decision by subordinates critical to effective implementation?
The prior probability that the leader's autocratic decision will receive acceptance by subordinates.	If you were to make the decision by yourself, is it reasonably certain that it would be accepted by your subordinates?
The extent to which subordinates are motivated to attain the organizational goals as represented in the objectives explicit in the statement of the problem.	Do subordinates share the organizational goals to be obtained in solving this problem?
The extent to which subordinates are likely to be in conflict over preferred solutions.	Is conflict among subordinates likely in preferred solutions?

Source: Reprinted, by permission of the publisher, from "A New Look at Managerial Decision Making," by Victor H. Vroom, *Organizational Dynamics*, Spring 1973, p. 69.

functions are important in group activities and are not necessarily the responsibility of one person. But, however unilateral or participative the decision-making process, formal leadership roles are crucial in organizations. That is why it is necessary to develop an organizational program for facilitating better leadership throughout the hierarchy and to cultivate in leaders and leadership candidates skills for self-assessment.

Our initial concern in facilitating effective leadership is with the question of whether leaders are born or made. If we believe that values, attitudes, knowledge, skills, and behaviors are relatively fixed by early adulthood, then our strategy will be one of selecting those with the right propensities and matching them with appropriate situations. On the other hand, if we believe that values and attitudes can change, and that knowledge, skills, and behavior can be improved, our emphasis will be on experience, coaching, and training. Even with the latter approach, selection and matching are still important in improving the probability of success.

Assuming that we have selected people with reasonable potential, what can we do to increase the probability that their potential will be realized? One important method is exposure to good examples of leadership attitudes and behavior that can become models early in organizational experience. Another is promotion of the feeling that one is looked upon as a valuable resource. This is likely to have an impact on a candidate's values and lead her to develop appropriate attitudes and skills. Early opportunities to practice leadership skills are also important. Experience as a follower for thirty years is not the best preparation for leadership responsibility. Rotation through a number of jobs and relationships in an organization also helps prepare people for leadership roles. It allows one to experience a variety of superior-subordinate relationships and to assess personal effectiveness in different situations. Explicit coaching can also be helpful in the development process. Formal training programs can be useful in increasing knowledge, developing skills, and changing attitudes.

An approach that has been receiving increasing attention in organizations is the assessment center (Byham, 1971). The center is not necessarily a physical entity. It is a centralized process of measuring managerial potential in an organized and detailed manner. Basically, employees go through a series of exercises or simulations as a group. Their behavior in these exercises is observed by trained assessors: typically, higher-level line managers. The assessors are there to observe behavior in situations designed to be organizationally realistic. The candidates may discuss cases or critical incidents from their work history in order to demonstrate their analytical and communication skills. They may engage in simulation exercises that call for a variety of skills connected with overall leadership ability. They may, for instance, be asked to respond meaningfully to an in-basket of memos, letters, reports, and the like within a certain time limit. All the exercises are designed to provide insight into a candidate's behavior and potential over a concentrated period (generally one or two days). They have the dual benefit of helping to identify potential leaders and of providing feedback about strengths and weaknesses that can guide future training and development endeavors.

To encourage necessary flexibility among potential leaders, managers might be encouraged to consider systematically the leader (themselves), the followers, and the situation. The first step is self-assessment; this requires feedback from a variety of sources—diagnostic instruments, superiors, peers, and subordinates. If the feedback shows a gap between current behavior and desired behavior, there are two options: (1) to maintain it; (2) to change it. A decision to take the second option is not enough, however. Leadership style should be relatively natural and comfortable. New behavior can be learned if it is practiced, but, if a desired style is used ineptly or insincerely, the results might be disastrous. Once a general personal style is determined, one should ascertain where that style is most appropriate and where it would need modification in order to be more effective. This includes assessment of potential followers in terms of their abilities, attitudes, and expectations. It is equally important to perceive situations accurately in order that an appropriate leadership style (on the scale from autocratic to collaborative, for example) might be used.

If we believe that growth and development are limited by character and that flexibility in an individual is difficult to achieve, we can then attempt to match leaders and situations. We can use assessment techniques to determine whether an individual is task-oriented or relationship-oriented, and we can diagnose situations in terms of positional power, task structure, and leader-member relations (Fiedler, Chemers, & Mahar, 1976). Individuals could be reassigned to fit the proper niche or changes could be made in the organization; that is, the situation could be changed to fit a given leader's style. A line manager could be shifted to a staff position and vice versa. A functional organization could be redesigned to emphasize projects that take advantage of the entrepreneurial skills and charisma of key managers (see Chapter 10). An important part of leadership training is to help managers understand the range of organizational situations outside of which their style is likely to be inappropriate.

If we believe that leaders can adjust behavior according to the situation, we need at least minimal guidelines so that situations and behavior are matched. Assessing the appropriate degree of participation in decision making is an example of this approach (see Box 6.6). For optimum succcess it is important that the leader and the followers be aware of the diagnostic framework so that mutual expectations follow generally the same timetable and there are few surprises. This latter point is essential. By and large followers can adjust to a variety of leadership styles. Their major complaint concerns inconsistencies and surprises: an autocratic approach when people expected to participate or an invitation to participate when it is deemed unnecessary and burdensome.

The matching approach, coupled with training, provides the means by which to develop leadership talent while using available skills more effectively. Concerted attention in both directions will result in long-run benefits for the system as a whole.

SO WHAT? IMPLICATIONS FOR YOU

Understanding leadership—what it is and how effective leaders behave—is an important step in understanding human behavior in organizations. The next step is applying such knowledge in organizational contexts, either as individual participants or managers.

As a Member in an Organization

Generalizations	Implications
1. Individual behavior is influenced in many ways including emulation, suggestion, persuasion, and coercion.	1. Be aware of the ways your behavior is influenced by others. Be aware of the ways you influence the behavior of others.
2. Key figures (top managers) are often role models that unconsciously influence people who emulate them.	2. Check to see if you are emulating any particular model. Are you restraining your own natural tendencies? Is your model effective in terms of both organizational performance and subordinate confidence?
3. Knowledge is power; it enables a person to influence others.	3. Develop both technical and managerial expertise (including leadership skills).
4. Followers' zones of acceptance affect the ability of leaders to influence behavior (power).	4. Know your zone of acceptance with regard to the influence attempts of others—bosses and peers. Establish mutual expectations whenever possible.
5. Leaders have different personalities, competencies, and managerial styles.	5. Learn to identify leader differences (not necessarily right or wrong) and adapt your behavior somewhat, without sacrificing your personal integrity.
6. Leadership functions can be performed by all group members from time to time, depending on the specific situation.	6. Be alert for opportunities to lead (influence) a group by clarifying objectives, facilitating good interpersonal relationships, providing needed expertise, reinforcing appropriate behavior, summarizing progress, and identifying accomplishments.

Generalizations	Implications
7. A person with reasonable intelligence, social maturity and breadth, achievement needs, and genuine respect for people has a higher *probability* of becoming a successful leader (regardless of the followers and the situation) than someone without such attributes.	7. Make an assessment of yourself as to these basic attributes. Develop them as much as possible. Recognize that without them, achieving a leadership position (and being successful) may be more difficult. But, recognize also that other factors—charisma, expert or coercive power, legitimate authority—may determine who becomes a leader in specific situations.
8. Leadership skills can be developed and improved. Effective leader behavior can be learned.	8. Assess your strengths and weaknesses in terms of effective leader behavior. Take advantage of opportunities to practice (committee assignments, filling in for the boss temporarily, etc.). Solicit feedback from others concerning your performance and use it to guide your development.
9. Leaders are dependent on followers (their knowledge, skill, effort, etc.) for the individual and collective support that is necessary to accomplish group goals.	9. Know when you (either individually or as part of a group) have the power to influence the decisions and behavior of superiors. Use your power wisely on important matters; don't waste it on trivial issues.
10. Follower behavior and organizational consequences (results, reactions of others, etc.) affect leader behavior in future transactions.	10. Recognize that your response to influence attempts can affect your boss's subsequent behavior. Be alert to opportunities for positively reinforcing good behavior so that it will tend to be repeated.
11. Subordinates experience many quandaries about dependence, inferiority, and competition with the boss versus initiative,	11. Accept these apparent conflicts of interest as normal in your role as a subordinate. If possible, discuss them with

Generalizations	Implications
competence, and collaboration with the boss.	your boss(es) and try to develop clear expectations that can help minimize behavior proving detrimental to a mutually beneficial relationship.
12. Subordinates can help develop a good leader-follower relationship. They can "manage the boss" to some degree.	12. Assess your degree of "fit" with the boss' style. Accommodate where possible, without sacrificing your integrity. Use complementary skills to good advantage.

As a Current or Future Manager

Generalizations	Implications
1. Role models influence the behavior of others, particularly subordinates, via emulation.	1. Recognize that what you do may be more important than what you say in a leadership role. Make a conscious attempt to use effective leadership behavior at all times.
2. Less coercive means of influencing behavior (persuasion and suggestion) tend to be more effective over the long run. They foster good relationships and development of subordinates. Coercion can work in the short run, but it can have negative side effects and lead to deteriorating relationships.	2. Emphasize suggestion and persuasion as much as possible. Use coercive means (e.g., threats of sanctions) only when necessary to ensure cooperation and compliance that is essential for group progress.
3. Power, the ability to influence behavior, is essential for effective leadership. Sources of power include charisma, official position, technical expertise, and managerial competence.	3. Welcome power and use it wisely toward achieving positive organizational results, rather than toward self-aggrandizement. To achieve and maintain the ability to influence the course of events, cultivate multiple sources of power.
4. Communication skills, particularly persuasion, are essential	4. Develop your communication skills through study and prac-

Generalizations	Implications
for effective leadership. Influence attempts are carried out via interpersonal or person-to-group communication processes.	tice. Quiet competence may go unnoticed. Therefore, be alert for opportunities to demonstrate your persuasive abilities.
5. Leaders are dependent on followers for support; that is, the expertise and effort needed to accomplish group goals. Trends toward power equalization and narrower zones of acceptance limit the ability of formal leaders to influence the behavior of followers.	5. Recognize the limits of your formal authority and your dependence on subordinates (and peers) for support. Build positive relationships that are mutually beneficial. Emphasize persuasion in your influence attempts.
6. Leadership is a process of social exchange between leaders and followers. It involves transactions over time and bilateral influence.	6. Recognize that leading is not a static, one-way phenomenon. Be aware that you are both influencer and influencee, and that the process involves a series of transactions over time. Develop relationships that include mutual benefits for you and your subordinates.
7. External environmental (culture, laws, etc.) and internal contextual (tradition, policies, etc.) forces affect leader-follower relationships, often constraining leader behavior.	7. Be aware of external and internal forces that constrain your behavior, particularly your interactions with subordinates. You will be more effective if your influence attempts are seen as legitimate by people who are affected.
8. Managers tend to look for simple cause-effect links when evaluating subordinate behavior; for example, they attribute poor performance to lack of skill or effort.	8. Recognize that results often depend on more than a subordinate's skill or effort—including contextual constraints and your own leadership behavior. Work toward congruence in the attributions you and your subordinates make regarding individual and work group performance.

	Generalizations		Implications
9.	Retaining a leadership role is often more difficult than attaining it, particularly if it is an appointed position. Situations, including followers, change over time and may require different skills and behavior.	9.	Be sensitive to the limits of positional authority. Try to develop a sense of personal authority that transcends particular roles or positions. Recognize changing situations that call for adjustments in leader-follower relationships.
10.	Subordinates experience many quandaries about dependence, inferiority, and competition with the boss versus initiative, competence, and collaboration with the boss.	10.	Recognize these apparent conflicts of interest as normal for subordinates. Indicate your recognition by discussing the potential for dilemma openly. Develop clear expectations that can help minimize behavior that is detrimental to a mutually beneficial relationship.
11.	Likeability is a basic leader asset, but over time other factors such as general competence and the ability to get results become at least as important in the eyes of the followers.	11.	Earn the respect of your subordinates and instill confidence in your ability by obtaining needed resources and focusing on the attainment of group goals. Highlight individual and organizational accomplishments.
12.	Organizational performance involves both task accomplishment and team building.	12.	Show explicit concern for tasks and productivity as well as people and relationships. Be supportive and facilitate interactions; emphasize goals and help group members attain them.
13.	The appropriateness of any leadership style depends on the circumstances: the nature of the task and the personalities and expectations of the people involved.	13.	Be as flexible as possible. Adjust your behavior to fit the situation, including your followers. However, stay within a range of behavior that is reasonably comfortable for you. A facade that is incongruous with your basic personality could have negative consequences.

Generalizations	Implications
14. Autocratic, consultative, and group consensus are all appropriate means of making decisions, as long as quality and acceptance are taken into account. Time available is always a constraint and the growth and development of subordinates can be a consideration.	14. Diagnose situations or problem types in terms of quality requirements, information available to you, probability of acceptance by subordinates, shared goals, potential conflict over possible solutions, and time available. Base the degree of subordinate participation on relevant criteria that are understood by everyone involved.
15. Leadership skills can be improved. Effective leadership behavior can be learned. Leaders can be matched with situations in order to improve the overall system.	15. Assess your strengths and weaknesses in terms of effective leader behavior. Concentrate on improving knowledge and skill in areas where you sense a need to change. Solicit feedback from others (bosses, peers, and subordinates) concerning your performance and use it to guide your development. Seek leadership positions that fit your attitudes and skills.
16. Effective leadership involves developing subordinates to assume leadership roles and be successful.	16. Provide subordinates with opportunities to practice leadership skills. Delegate when possible. Facilitate participation and involvement in leadership functions in group processes. Give feedback on a continuing basis (particularly positive reinforcement for effective behavior) and in formal coaching/counseling sessions.
17. The effectiveness of leaders depends partly on the support and encouragement given them by their bosses.	17. Analyze your own personality and leadership style. Exercise some judgment concerning whom you will work for in order to enhance your development.

LEARNING APPLICATION ACTIVITIES

1. Write a vignette based on your own experience that illustrates leadership issues: effective or ineffective attempts of someone to influence the behavior of others.

2. Pretend you are Charlie Slade (*Good Ol' Charlie* vignette).

a. Describe the problem as you see it.

b. List at least three alternative courses of action for you.

c. What are the pros and cons of each alternative?

d. Which alternative would you choose? Why?

e. What do you think will happen when you take the action you have chosen?

3. *Step 1.* Complete the following sentences:

a. I do my best work for bosses (leaders) who . . . .

b. I do my worst work for bosses (leaders) who . . . .

Step 2. Share the completed sentences with four to six colleagues.

Step 3. Develop two lists of descriptors; one for *best bosses* and one for *worst bosses*.

Step 4. Compare your lists with suggestions for effective leader attributes and behavior set forth in the chapter.

4. Identify several leaders in organizations of which you are a member. Check them against Figure 6.4 and the four-factor model on page 203. How do they compare? How close do they come to multiple emphasis of the factors involved in effective leadership?

5. Illustrate the concept *zone of acceptance* with examples from family, school, and work situations. Note whether the zone is narrowing or widening in the situations you have identified.

6. Read the following position-description pairs and try to visualize the situational differences from the leader's perspective.

The Secretary of the Army	....	An infantry platoon leader
The director of an outpatient pediatrics clinic	....	A chief surgeon in an operating room
The V.P. of advertising for a large resort complex	....	The captain of a cruise ship
The mother superior in a convent	....	The "head" of a commune
The sports editor of a large metropolitan newspaper	....	The vice principal of a high school
The chairperson of the history department	....	The chief of the campus police
A production manager	....	A director of personnel
The coordinator of a regional planning task force	....	A supervisor on an assembly line

7. *Step 1.* List as many forces or factors as you can think of that might affect leadership styles.

Step 2. Form a group of four to six people and develop a composite list using the following subheadings in your analysis:

Forces or factors in the leader.

Forces or factors in the follower(s).

Forces or factors in the situation.

Step 3. In the total class discuss how situational analysis can help in determining appropriate leader behavior.

8. Outline some steps you will take to become:

a. A more effective follower.

b. A more effective leader.

REFERENCES

Bennis, Warren. "Leadership: A Beleaguered Species?" *Organizational Dynamics* 51 (Summer 1976):3–16.

———. "Leadership Theory and Administrative Behavior." *Administrative Science Quarterly* 413 (December 1959): 259–301.

Blake, Robert R., and Jane Srygley Mouton. *The New Managerial Grid*. Houston: Gulf, 1978.

———. "Theory and Research for Developing a Science of Leadership." *The Journal of Applied Behavioral Science* 18/3 (1982): 275–291.

Bowers, David G., and Stanley E. Seashore. "Predicting Organizational Effectiveness with a Four-Factor Theory of Leadership." *Administrative Science Quarterly* 11/2 (September 1966): 238–263.

Brown, J.A.C. *The Social Psychology of Industry*. Baltimore: Penguin, 1954.

Byham, William C. "The Assessment Center as an Aid in Management." *Training and Development Journal* 2/12 (December 1971): 10–22.

Davis, Keith. *Human Behavior at Work,* 5th ed. New York: McGraw-Hill, 1977.

Fiedler, Fred. *A Theory of Leadership Effectiveness*. New York: McGraw-Hill, 1967.

Fiedler, Fred E., Martin M. Chemers, and Linda Mahar. *Improving Leadership Effectiveness: The Leader Match Concept*. New York: Wiley, 1976.

Gabarro, John J., and John P. Kotter. "Managing Your Boss." *Harvard Business Review* 58/1 (January-February 1980): 92–100.

Goldhammer, Herbert, and Edward A. Shils. "Types of Power and Status." *American Journal of Sociology* 45/2 (September 1939): 171–182.

Goodall, Kenneth. "Shapers at Work." *Psychology Today,* November 1972, pp. 53–62 and 132–138.

Goode, Cecil E. "Significant Research on Leadership." *Personnel* 28/2 (March 1951): 342–350.

Gould, Julius, and William L. Kolb, eds. *A Dictionary of the Social Sciences*. New York: Free Press, 1964.

Green, Stephen G., and Terence R. Mitchell. "Attributional Processes of Leaders in Leader-Member Interactions." *Organizational Behavior and Human Performance* 23 (June 1979): 429–458.

Hollander, Edwin P. *Leadership Dynamics*. New York: Free Press, 1978.

Homans, George C. *Social Behavior: Its Elementary Forms*. New York: Harcourt Brace Jovanovich, 1961.

House, Robert J., and Terence R. Mitchell. "Path-Goal Theory of Leadership." *Journal of Contemporary Business* 3/4 (Autumn 1974): 81–97.

James, Muriel. *The OK Boss*. Reading, Mass.: Addison-Wesley, 1975.
Jay, Anthony. *Corporation Man*. New York: Random House, 1971.
Katz, Daniel, and Robert L. Kahn. *The Social Psychology of Organizations*. New York: Wiley, 1966.
———. *The Social Psychology of Organizations*, 2nd ed. New York: Wiley, 1978.
Luthans, Fred, and Tim R. V. Davis. "Leadership Reexamined: A Behavioral Approach." *Academy of Management Review* 4 (April 1979): 237–248.
Manz, Charles C., and Henry P. Sims, Jr. "Self-Management as a Substitute for Leadership: A Social Learning Theory Perspective." *Academy of Management Review* 5/3 (July 1980): 361–367.
McClelland, David C., and David H. Burnham. "Power is the Great Motivator." *Harvard Business Review* 54/2 (March-April 1976): 100–110.
Neilsen, Eric H., and Jan Gypen. "The Subordinate's Predicaments." *Harvard Business Review* 57/5 (September-October 1979): 133–143.
Oates, David. "How Far Will Worker Power Go?" *International Management*, February 1977, pp. 10–13.
Pfeffer, Jeffrey. "The Ambiguity of Leadership." *Academy of Management Review* 2/1 (January 1977): 104–112.
Russell, Bertrand. *Power*. New York: Norton, 1938.
Salancik, Gerald R., and Jeffrey Pfeffer. "Who Gets Power—and How They Hold on to It." *Organizational Dynamics* 5/3 (Winter 1977): 3–21.
Sayles, Leonard R. *Leadership: What Effective Managers Really Do . . . and How They Do It*. New York: McGraw-Hill, 1979.
Simon, Herbert A. *Administrative Behavior*, 3d ed. New York: Free Press, 1976.
Smircich, Linda, and Gareth Morgan. "Leadership: The Management of Meaning." *The Journal of Applied Behavioral Science* 18/3 (1982): 257–273.
Solomon, Ben. *Leadership of Youth*. New York: Youth Services, 1950.
Stogdill, Ralph M. "Personal Factors Associated with Leadership: A Survey of the Literature." *The Journal of Psychology* 72/1 (January 1948): 35–71.
———. *Handbook of Leadership*. New York: Free Press, 1974.
———. "Historical Trends in Leadership Theory and Research." *Journal of Contemporary Business* 3/4 (Autumn 1974): 1–17.
Summers, Clyde W. "Protecting *All* Employees Against Unjust Dismissal." *Harvard Business Review* 58/1 (January-February 1980): 132–139.
Tannenbaum, Robert, and Fred Massarik. "Leadership: A Frame of Reference." *Management Science* 4/1 (October 1975): 1–19.
Tannenbaum, Robert, and Warren H. Schmidt. "How to Choose a Leadership Pattern." *Harvard Business Review* 36/2 (March-April 1958): 95–101.
———. "How to Choose a Leadership Pattern." *Harvard Business Review* 51/3 (May-June 1973): 162–180.
Vroom, Victor H. "A New Look at Managerial Decision Making." *Organizational Dynamics* 1/4 (Spring 1973): 66–80.
Vroom, Victor H., and Philip W. Yetton. *Leadership and Decision-making*. Pittsburgh: University of Pittsburgh Press, 1973.
Ways, Max. "More Power to Everybody." *Fortune*, May 1970, pp. 173–175, 290–299.
White, Ralph, and Ronald Lippitt. *Autocracy and Democracy*. New York: Harper & Row, 1960.
———. "Leader Behavior and Member Reaction in Three 'Social Climates.' " In Dorwin Cartwright and Alvin Zander (Eds.), *Group Dynamics: Research and Theory*. New York: Harper & Row, 1953, pp. 385–411.

7
Group Dynamics

LEARNING OBJECTIVES

After reading this chapter you should be able to:

1. Define "group" and describe several types of groups.
2. Describe and explain a number of dimensions and levels of group behavior that affect group performance.
3. Identify and discuss a number of variables in a group's environment that can affect that group's performance.
4. Identify dysfunctional and functional group behaviors in a meeting or in a group exercise.
5. Explain how group phenomena affect organizational outcomes.
6. Understand how groups can learn to be more effective.

THE MEETING

Simon Jennings was both bored and irritated. For more than a year now, since his promotion to department head, he had been coming to weekly department head meetings and he didn't like them very much. The boss, George Olson, usually presented a long agenda. Most items were informational, although the boss sometimes asked the group's opinion on a few matters. The meetings bored Simon because he knew something about most of the items already, and besides, they didn't seem all that important. What really irritated Simon was that the big problems facing the whole group, such as a lack of long-range objectives, were never raised in these meetings. He was worried about what he sensed was a drifting posture on the part of the organization rather than a positive proactive response to opportunities.

Simon didn't say anything, however. "If I criticize the way the meetings are being run, George will read it as disloyalty," he thought. "Furthermore, the other department heads probably wouldn't support me openly—although I know darn well they feel the same way—and they'd leave me out on a limb."

The next meeting was the same. And the next. And the next. . . .

MARGE

Marge Goldman was feeling upset and left out. She was attending a meeting of seven den leaders and officers of Cub Scout Pack 419. She and other parents who were officers of the pack were planning the Cub Scout events for late spring and early summer, and the meeting, from her standpoint, was not going well. One of the parents, Al Whitehead, was talking a large percentage of the time, and when he talked he usually looked at Fred Schrieber or the Cubmaster, Don Nordlund. In addition, Al was sitting with his back partly turned toward Marge. Twice she tried to interject an idea and was cut off by a rapid interchange between Al and Fred. Finally, she blurted out, "I disagree with what's being decided tonight; I don't think we're being realistic at all. You're asking a few parents to take on entirely too much." There was a momentary silence, and Marge thought people looked flustered. She felt embarrassed by her own outburst, but she was still angry and ready to fight.

THE ENGINEERS

On Friday, Art, Joe, and Erik took their usual coffee break in a corner of the headquarters building cafeteria. They had been working hard on some critical engineering aspects of a major freeway project that was now six months behind schedule. Their boss, Ed, had been putting on pressure, and they were getting a bit edgy, although relationships were still pretty good.

Joe was clearly irritated: "The boss has given half of the draftsmen to Jim to work on the bridge approaches; Jim should have contracted out that work three months ago, and now it's coming out of my hide. I think Ed gives in to him more than he should." "Yeah," agreed Erik. "I don't think Jim should think he's anything so special around here just because he has an advanced degree. Besides, I can't find him half the time when we need to coordinate things. He's either out in the field or someplace else—maybe he's goofing off. . . . ." The conversation continued this way for a few minutes, and finally Art said, "I'd better get back to work . . . I'll see you guys tonight; be sure to be on time."

On Monday, at the regular project meeting, Jim was puzzled and irritated, and wondered if people had been talking about him. When he came into the meeting, it seemed as if talking stopped, and everyone seemed less friendly than usual. In addition, two people who usually greeted him in a friendly way merely continued their conversation.

Jim wasn't much involved socially with this group. Four or five of them seemed to get together on weekends a good deal, but Jim wasn't sure exactly who was included. The thought went through his head: "I wonder if these guys have been out socializing and criticizing me and the bridge project. . . ."

The meeting began and proceeded without many particular signs of disagreement, and Jim mused, "Maybe I'm getting a little paranoid. On the other hand, I'd better keep my guard up."

THE WORKSHOP

The room for the two-day workshop sponsored by the college was fairly standard, but narrower than most. Tables and chairs had been placed in straight rows in front of the lectern and visual aid materials. When the workshop started, Gordon Alberts, professor of management at the college, considered the possibility of trying to change the room arrangement at the first break, but when time for the break came, people seemed to be settled in and discussion was going fairly well. So he dismissed the idea.

As participants were leaving at the end of the second day, Mary Wilson, who had been sitting toward the far end of the front row, said, "It was a very good workshop, but I couldn't hear people in the back of the room, let alone see them very well. I would have liked to have gotten better acquainted with people, too."

ONE-ON-ONE

Department manager Joan Carlson felt that meetings with her boss, Fran Akers, were usually somewhat strained. There was nothing particularly wrong, yet she never really felt comfortable when the two met for their meetings every other week to review progress on various programs. Things were especially tense when Joan needed to request funds for some project, or when she mentioned a policy problem. It seemed to her that Fran was frequently negative or defensive or expected Joan to present arguments in perfect form. On some occasions, Joan would try to find some convenient reason for including another department manager or her assistant, Bill Ostrander. These three-person meetings were usually more comfortable, and Joan believed that more was accomplished.

THE JOGGERS

Hank had been feeling somewhat out of shape for several months so he decided to take up jogging. He went out and bought new Adidas running shoes, a sweat suit, and several pairs of heavy socks.

The first day out he ran one block, was

winded, and quit. The next day was a little better, and before long he was running a mile. The mile soon became three miles.

Hank began to notice other regulars who seemed to be running about the same time. He said "hi" to a person who turned out to be Lee, and soon they were running together and talking as they ran. One day, Lee brought along Elaine and before long they were joined by Fred. And then Al.

In due course the five people were meeting regularly at 6:30 A.M. Mondays, Wednesdays, and Fridays. From time to time they noticed there were other runners, but the five did not seem to want to include any more people. They had become a closed, cohesive group.

Hank looked forward to these jogging sessions, which were really one of the highlights of his current life. It occurred to him after about a year of their jogging together that the morning run was the only contact the group had. He occasionally thought it would be interesting to socialize at a party or dinner, or something, but, on the other hand, he didn't want to disturb things.

INTRODUCTION

Each of the situations described above involves a group, although the den leader, workshop, and jogging groups are probably less permanent than the other three. Two of the groups, the joggers and the three engineers, are spontaneous, unplanned groups in the sense that they exist outside of any formal, planned, organizational relationships. Some of these groups have a problem with one or more of the dimensions discussed in this chapter; that is, a problem in the sense that the group is less effective than it otherwise might be in terms of either performance or member satisfaction.

Groups are extremely important to study in organizational behavior because of their powerful impact on individual satisfactions and on organizational performance. Almost everyone belongs to one or more groups and usually several, whether centrally or casually. For most people, group relationships are indispensable for the expression or fulfillment of a number of needs. The need for affiliation, for affection and warmth, and for self-esteem and the esteem of others are among the needs that can to some extent be met through group membership.

At another level, shared sentiments and norms among group members are powerful determinants of both individual and group performance. This holds true for task performance all the way from manual labor to making policy decisions. In many ways, groups are the basic building blocks of organizations (see Box 7.1). Among other functions they perform, they serve as mechanisms for communication, coordination, and control, as well as for meeting emotional needs.

In this chapter we shall define what we mean by a group, examine different types of groups, and look at a number of phenomena in the dynamics of group behavior that affect individual behavior and various organizational outcomes. The topics of the chapter are shown below:

Group Defined
Formal and Informal Groups
Temporary and Permanent Groups
Cliques, Cabals, and Coalitions
Primary and Secondary Groups
Dimensions of Group Life
Four Levels of Group Work
Groups Can Learn to Work More Effectively
So What? Implications For You

GROUP DEFINED

A group is *a number of persons who, for at least a brief period of time, have some psychological and/or task interdependency, which includes interaction with each other in a face-to-face situation.* This definition assumes that the interdependency and interaction centers around some common goal(s) or needs.

The people in a small accounting department constitute a group, a committee to plan an office party is a group, a small task force appointed by a president

BOX 7.1
GROUPS AS BUILDING BLOCKS

Management should consider building organizations using a material now understood very well and with properties that look very promising, the small group. Until recently, at least, the human group has primarily been used for patching and mending organizations that were originally built of other materials.

Source: Harold J. Leavitt, "Suppose We Took Groups Seriously," in Eugene L. Cass and Frederick G. Zimmer, eds., *Man and Work in Society,* Van Nostrand Reinhold Company, New York, 1975, p. 77.

of the United States to study energy reserves is a group, and an immediate family consisting of mother, father, and children is a group. Lawyers of the State of New York are not a group in the sense of the above definition; nor are boat owners on the Great Lakes. Students and an instructor in a large lecture hall, viewed as a totality, are probably not a group; students and an instructor in a discussion seminar are.

There are a number of classification schemes in the contemporary literature used to describe types of groups. Among these, two dichotomies seem to have particular relevance to organizational life: formal versus informal; and primary versus secondary. Other categories, such as *cliques, cabals, coalitions,* and other dichotomies, such as temporary versus permanent, also prove useful in thinking about groups.

FORMAL AND INFORMAL GROUPS

Groups in organizations can be classified as formal or informal. A *formal group* exists with the approval of the hierarchy (bosses) and has specific functions to perform. Formal groups would ordinarily consist of the individuals who report to a common superior, task forces formed on an ad hoc basis to work on a particular problem, and committees or boards that meet periodically to carry out prescribed activities. Looking at Figure 7.1, we see that any one of the triangles shown is likely to be a formal group meeting our preliminary definition of groups in general. Similarly, a task force of persons appointed from several of the triangles to investigate the feasibility of purchasing another company is a formal group, as is the standing finance committee.

It should be noted that we have put a question mark in the triangle headed by executive *C* because that executive *never* meets with his or her subordinates as a group in a face-to-face situation. Absurd? Yes, but it sometimes happens. We can assume that such a nongroup has both task and psychological interdependency, however, and that considerable subgroup activity occurs.

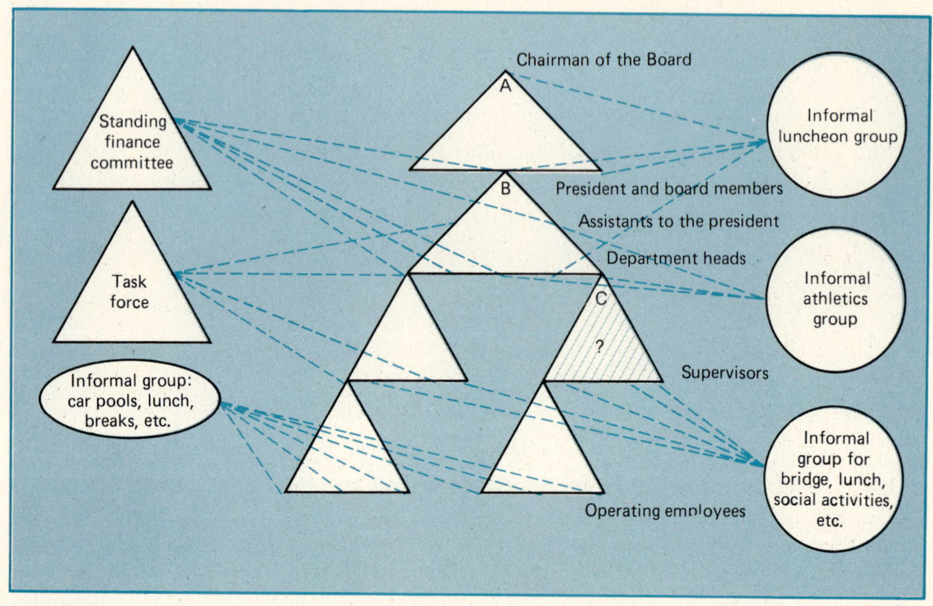

FIGURE 7.1 Formal and Informal Groups in a Hypothetical Organization

By *informal groups,* we mean those groups that arise spontaneously because of proximity or similarity of work, mutual attraction, mutual need fulfillment, or a combination of such reasons. These groups are typically not sanctioned in the sense that there has been any official approval for their existence; they simply come into being. For example, the chairman of the board, the president, and the treasurer-controller frequently have lunch together at a club (see Figure 7.1). Another group of executives might play racquetball together twice a week. Supervisors who seek each other out for advice about operating matters or to commiserate about what they see as bad company policies, play bridge together during the noon hours, make a point to eat lunch together in the company cafeteria, and interact socially away from the plant comprise an informal group (*The Engineers* vignette offered a prime example of the type). At the operating employee level, an informal group might consist of seven people who work on the first floor in the building, lives in the same end of the city, and have formed two car pools. As a result of this connection, they frequently take breaks together and four or five will usually congregate to eat lunch together.

In an earlier chapter, we made reference to *schmoozing*, a Yiddish term for "socializing." This, and all it implies, may be seen as the central purpose of the informal group. As one author describes it, the schmooze factor is part of the glue that holds organizations together (Schrank, 1978). Some jobs permit much more schmoozing than others, but inevitably people find a way to socialize at work.

BOX 7.2
FRIENDSHIPS ON THE JOB

Peers of different age, sex, and profession are discovered on the job. On the basis of joint commitment to mobility, to office politics, or to making technical and bureaucratic work seem more pleasant, people attach themselves at various levels of intimacy. From these office and occupational friendships, new networks emerge that may be combined with primary friendships from childhood and school. The office or network friendship may remain relatively superficial, or it may become the basis of deeply intimate friendship, depending upon the participants' mutual attraction, their willingness to surrender part of their private reserves to each other, and their willingness and ability to be tolerant of each other's private idiosyncrasies.

Whether they are deep friendships or merely friendships of convenience, such networks are based upon minimal standards of reciprocity, on the exchange of favors, information, the hiring of protégés, preference of all kinds in business and professional transactions. Network loyalties may also include overlooking or not reporting a network member's faults and defalcations, and may also include active collusion in the pursuit of the individual or collective interests of network or clique members, even at the expense of the organizations that employ the network members, or at the expense of the public interest as embodied in the law.

Source: Joseph Bensman and Robert Lilienfield, "Friendship and Alienation," *Psychology Today* 13[October 1979]:60,63. Reprinted from *Psychology Today Magazine*. © 1979. Ziff-Davis Publishing Co.

TEMPORARY AND PERMANENT GROUPS

The task force shown in Figure 7.1 would be considered a temporary group in the sense that it would be disbanded when its work was done. The other groups in the figure can be considered permanent because they tend to be ongoing over relatively long periods of time. The degree of group permanency as perceived by organizational members may have both positive and negative consequences. On the positive side, the perception of permanency may provide a satisfying kind of security for group members; on the negative side, it may make it difficult to effect changes necessary for organizational vitality. People can become entrenched, making the introduction of new ideas and new people difficult.

CLIQUES, CABALS, AND COALITIONS

Informal groups composed of people who regard things similarly and who interact with one another frequently are often called *cliques*. This type of group usually revolves around multiple interests and is likely to grow out of a measure of mutual affection and a sharing of attitudes and goals. Their organizational relevance, in addition to providing an avenue for schmoozing and other need satisfactions, is that they tend to have a significant impact on events in the formal organization. Decisions may be made in cliques, or the information transmitted and discussed in cliques may have a major effect on decisions made in more formal settings. One of the authors recalls riding in a car pool to and from work and the conversations that frequently focused on company matters. These conversations had a great impact on company decision making in ways that would not have occurred in the absence of such clique behavior. (We are not recommending this behavior; we are simply saying that it occurs.)

The term *cabal* implies a conspiratorial clique, and these, too, exist from time to time. Bennis (1976) refers to the "young Turks," who are usually fighting the cliques in power, as cabals:

> They (the cliques) have the dough, the resources; they're the establishment. The cabals are usually the younger people who are fighting the cliques. There's a high price to pay in this situation, because it really means revolution. It means that the cabals ultimately take over. Good cliques know how to co-opt cabals. They absorb protest and establish a new equilibrium through a very interesting and important way of politics, which is to co-opt. And when they don't co-opt, they get into very deep trouble (p. 89).

The concept of the *coalition* is not dissimilar from the concepts of cliques and cabals. A coalition might be defined as a "subset of persons within a larger group who agree to cooperate so that they can obtain a common reward" (Zander, 1979, p. 438). A coalition might not be a clique in the sense that there is personal liking; it may have come into existence in a more calculated way, around some issue or challenge. Frequently, coalitions are comprised of more than one subset of persons within a group or within the larger organization.

Cliques, cabals, and coalitions are real and probably universal phenomena of organizational life. In particular, the frequent existence of cabals constitutes a major challenge to managerial ingenuity.

PRIMARY AND SECONDARY GROUPS

A distinction can be made between the more intense, close, and durable affiliations in some groups, called *primary groups,* and the less meaningful and more transient affiliations in other groups, called *secondary groups*. The family and the small friendship clique are primary groups. Many other groups, such as an ad hoc committee, students taking a particular course together, or five community leaders coming together to work on an energy supply problem, are secondary groups.

BOX 7.3
THE PRIMARY GROUP

By primary groups I mean those characterized by intimate face-to-face association and cooperation. They are primary in several senses, but chiefly in that they are fundamental in forming the social nature and ideals of the individual. The result of intimate association, psychologically, is a certain fusion of individualities in a common whole, so that one's very self, for many purposes at least, is the common life and purpose of the group. Perhaps the simplest way of describing this wholeness is by saying that it is a "we"; it involves the sort of sympathy and mutual identification for which "we" is the natural expression. One lives in the feeling of the whole and finds the chief aims of his will in that feeling.

It is not to be supposed that the unity of the primary group is one of mere harmony and love. It is always a differentiated and usually a competitive unity, admitting of self-assertion and various appropriative passions; but these passions are socialized by sympathy, and come, or tend to come, under the discipline of a common spirit. . . .

The most important spheres of this intimate association and cooperation—though by no means the only ones—are the family, the play-group of children, and the neighborhood or community group of elders.

Source: Charles H. Cooley, *Social Organization*. New York: Scribner. © 1909, 1937 Charles Scribner's Sons.

The formal face-to-face work group is essentially a secondary group, but it may or may not have some of the characteristics frequently seen in family or friendship groups. The family group typically differs from groups in work organizations along a number of dimensions, including norms about emotions, expressed interest in the person, standards or rules, and how status comes about (Black 1961; Parsons et al. 1953; Resnick, 1979). As shown in Figure 7.2, work groups tend to have features that differ from family groups: considerably less emotionality, higher task orientation in contrast to interest in the individual per se, more reliance on rules, and status based on achievement in contrast to status based on age and sex.

A major issue for organizations is how much emotionality, how much task orientation, how much attention to individual needs, and how much role and status based on dimensions other than achievement should there be for optimum effectiveness and member satisfaction? In other words, how much should the organization develop or suppress the characteristics of the primary group—of the family group in particular?

Many organizations have suppressed individualism and emotionality in for-

Dimension	Primary Group (family)	Group in the Secondary System (work)
Emotions	Encouragement of emotionality	Discouragement of emotionality
Scope of interest in the person	Wide range of interest in and knowledge about the person; persons are valued as ends in themselves.	Relationships tend to have a much higher task orientation; persons are means to an end
Rules and standards	Considerable attention can be paid to individual needs (emphasis on the obligations of friendship or family membership)	Rules and standards tend to apply uniformly to many people (emphasis on the obligations of institutional membership)
Status and role	Persons have a certain status by virtue of being born into a family; differentiated roles emerge based on age and sex (ascribed status and role)	Status and role are derived largely from achievement

FIGURE 7.2 Differences between Primary and Secondary Groups. **Source:** Adapted from Herman Resnick, "A Social System View of Strain," *Administration in Mental Health* 7/1 (Fall 1979): 56. By Permission of Human Sciences Press, New York. © 1979.

mal groups to the point that effective problem solving and member satisfaction have been impaired. Conversely, those organizations that have enhanced these dimensions have improved decison making and satisfactions and have probably contributed to social stability by partially compensating for the decline in family ties of urban, mobile societies. The frequent successes of genuinely participative approaches in such programs as *flextime* are indicative that organizations can readily provide for more attention to individual needs than is customary. (Under flextime, employees can be flexible about arriving at work and leaving within some broad guidelines.) On the other hand, we see the primary group tendency to differentiate status and roles based on birth, age, and sex to be dysfunctional in contemporary formal organizations. It is clear that women have been discriminated against relative to job assignments and salary levels in many organizations. The women's rights movement could be interpreted as a challenge to the carry-over of family role and status differentiation into the organization.

In some societies substantial effort is devoted to maintaining characteristics of the family group within larger organizations. For example, in Japan large enterprises take on many of the functions of the extended family group. As mentioned in Chapter 2, there is generally a life-long commitment between the organization and the individual. The *Nenko* system of permanent employment provides employees with job security and promotes strong company loyalty, social ties, and group cohesiveness (Oh, 1976). It should be noted, however, that this concept applies disproportionately to women and men. Women are rarely found occupying managerial or professional jobs in major Japanese firms, and they are typically considered temporary employees and subject to layoff in business downturns (Ouchi, 1981, p. 24).

The concept of *wa,* the spirit of harmony, is a fundamental principle of Japanese thought. This spirit emphasizes a high degree of collaborative rather than competitive behavior among members of the organization. It is reflected in the system of decision making that emphasizes group consensus building and harmony, the *ringi* process. "The *ringi* system allows everyone who is likely to be involved in implementation to participate in the making of the decision. This feeling of participation is very important for the spirit of *wa*" (Bowen, 1977, p. 131).

This spirit of harmony and the model of the extended family provide for group cohesiveness and social support, but it also suppresses individualistic behavior. After observing the highly aggressive and competitive behavior of several American students, one of our Japanese students suggested that in Japan there is an old saying, "The nail that stands out above the rest has to be hammered down."

OTHER DIMENSIONS OF GROUP LIFE

There are a number of other dimensions of group life that are important. These dimensions have an impact on group and organizational effectiveness, efficiency, and development as well as on member satisfactions.

Size

One of the most obvious dimensions of importance is size. We are all aware that the dynamics of two-person behavior seem to be different from the dynamics of three or four people interacting, and that groups can become so large as to become unwieldy.

A two-person group (dyad) differs from a three-person group (triad) in that in the triad each person can act as an intermediary between the other two. Further, any one-to-one interaction is more complicated by a third person being present, and there is no longer any undiluted reciprocity between the two (Simmel, 1955).

In an organizational context, individuals in a dyad are less likely to criticize the performance of the other person, but such confrontation is more likely to occur in a triad. The reason may be that in a triad the person doing the confronting has the possibility of support from the third person and, similarly, the person being confronted has the possibility of support. Indeed, the third person can do both—support one party on one aspect, and support the second party on other dimensions of the question—which is perhaps the essence of the intermediary role. (All is not always well in groups of three, however, as we shall see later.)

Experimental evidence suggests that two-person groups are indeed different from larger groups with regard to confrontation. Experimenters have found that, in contrast to groups of different number, two-person groups showed a high degree of tension and yet showed low rates of active disagreement and antagonism. The experimenters interpreted these results as follows:

> In a group of two it is impossible to form a majority except by unanimity. Either person in the dyad possesses power to influence the decision by withdrawal or veto. Neither person is able to influence the other by bringing a majority to bear against him. In this sense there is no public opinion or group sanction to which either can appeal. Similarly, there is no good officer, mediator, or arbitrator for the differences. Consequently, each person is under pressure to behave in such a way that the other will not withdraw and will continue to cooperate even though he may have to yield a point at a given time. Essentially, this is the problem of allowing the co-participant to "save face" when he does yield a point. The dominant person is thus under pressure to avoid the implication of superiority, and to persuade the other by gentle and self-effacing means (Hare, Borgatta, & Bales, 1955, pp. 402–403).

Groups of three seem to have an aspect that is particularly interesting. Although the coalitions can shift, such groups frequently segregate into a pair and a relative isolate. This conclusion emerged from experimental research in which the interaction of three-person groups in a series of problem-solving sessions was observed (Mills, 1953, pp. 351–357).

Group size is also associated with other consequences. Tension release for each individual, such as joking, laughing, increases markedly as the size of the group varies from two to seven. Showing solidarity, such as raising others' status and giving help, increases slightly. Giving opinions and asking for opinions decreases per person. These trends are seen as stemming from two major factors: (1) the reduction of available talking time for members as the size of the group increases; and (2) the desire "to maintain a more or less adequate relationship with each other" while having less time to do so (Hare, Borgatta, & Bales, 1955, pp. 401–402).

The number of relationships that are potentially impacting on individuals at any one time in a group is $n\ (n-1) \div 2$ with n representing the number of persons in the group. Thus, a two-person group has one possible pair relationship, a three-person group has three possible pair relationships, a four-person group has six, a six-person group has fifteen, and a seven-person group has twenty-one possible pair relationships.

We sometimes remind large groups of this phenomenon in an attempt to help avoid premature discouragement about slow progress in improving group processes. For example, in one city government situation, the regular meeting of department heads involves the city manager, three assistants, and fourteen department heads—153 potential two-person relationships! And this does not account for cliques, task forces, or overlapping group memberships, which we know to be in existence.

The dimension of odd- versus even-number groups also appears to have some consequences. Research results indicate that there is more disagreement in groups of four, six, or eight than in groups of three, five, or seven members. The higher disagreement in even-number groups seems to be associated with the formation of subgroups of equal size (Berelson & Steiner, 1964, p. 360). One interpretation could be that there is a power standoff in even-number groups. Another, perhaps more plausible interpretation, based on our knowledge of two- versus three-person groups, is that it is easier for a mediator to emerge in odd-number groups. (One can speculate that juries in the United States with their twelve members have inherent difficulty in contrast to such bodies as the Supreme Court with its nine members.)

Group size of four to six seems to be the most satisfying to participants. Inferences drawn from research results include the following:

> Maximal group satisfaction is achieved when the group is large enough so that the members feel able to express positive and negative feelings freely, and to make aggressive efforts toward problem solving even at the risk of antagonizing each other, yet small enough so that some regard will be shown for the feelings and needs of others; large enough so that the loss of a member could be tolerated, but small enough so that such a loss could not be altogether ignored (Slater, 1958, p. 138).

Satisfaction is one desirable outcome; the quality of decision making, of course, is another. A review of the research on effectiveness in decision making concluded as follows:

> If the quality of the group's solution is of considerable importance, it is useful to include a larger number of members, e.g., seven to twelve so that many inputs are available to the group in making its decision (Cummings, Huber, & Arendt, 1974, p. 473).

Some additional implications about group size come out of the research. The larger an informal group, from about seven persons up to as many as fifteen or twenty, the greater are the demands made on the leader and the more he or she is differentiated from other members. The larger the group, the more the members tolerate direction by a leader and the more the proceedings are centralized. The larger the group, the greater the tendency toward domination by the more active members and the more restricted (voluntarily or otherwise) the participation of rank-and-file under these conditions, discussions become less exploratory, group atmosphere becomes less intimate, and there is less satisfaction. Finally, the larger the group, the more there is a tendency to form subgroups and to formalize rules and procedures (Berelson & Steiner, 1964, p. 358).

Physical Settings

Physical settings have a powerful effect on group behavior. For example, persons in a high centrality seating arrangement (Person a, Figure 7.3) tend to

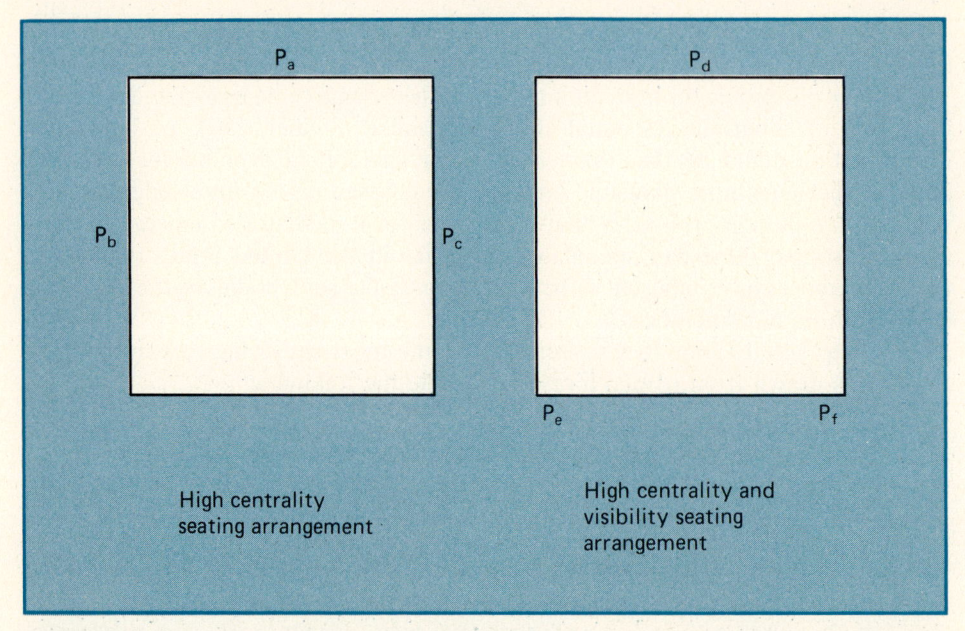

FIGURE 7.3 Seating Arrangements. **Source:** Based on R. L. Michelini, R. Passalacqua, and J. Cusimano, "Effects of Seating Arrangement on Group Participation," *The Journal of Social Psychology* 99 (August 1976): 180.

initiate more communications than others, and persons in a high centrality and visibility location (Person d) tend to receive communications with the most frequency (Michelini, Passalacqua, & Cusimano, 1976, pp. 179–186). One implication of this is that the seating arrangement will partially determine who is dominant in a group. Another example: People who sit at the ends of the table in meetings tend to participate more and are seen as wielding more influence than persons sitting at side positions (Stogdill, 1974, pp. 248–49). As still another example, the sharing of technical information between colleagues in laboratories has been found to be a function of the distance between the persons' desks (Steele, 1973, p. 65). It is easy to speculate on the consequences of having two people, whose areas of specialty have the potential for complementing each other, located at opposite ends of a long, crowded room. Obviously, talent is being wasted. Organizational effectiveness, then, may be influenced by where people are physically located in a group.

Experiments have found that the most preferred seating arrangement for a conversation is across a corner, the next most preferred arrangement is across a table, and the least preferred is a side-by-side arrangement (Steele, 1973, p. 34). Given this, how does one explain the long, rectangular meeting table we frequently see in conference rooms that emphasizes side-by-side seating and makes it difficult for several people on a given side to see each other? Undoubtedly, such tables and meeting rooms are functional for maintaining formality and

BOX 7.4
WHAT YOUR OFFICE SAYS ABOUT YOU

On the subject of how to arrange your movables, for a long time about the only explicit advice available came in those cheery little guidebooks on power, how to get it, how to flaunt it. Place your desk so that the visitor has to walk as far as possible to reach it, even complicating his passage with strategically situated pieces of executive furniture. Use your mahogany lifeboat as a barrier, forcing the quaking supplicant to sit directly opposite you, preferably in an uncomfortable chair.

That was the old cliche. Gradually, however, as the corporate world increasingly held up openness as a value, power-office arrangements came to be viewed as a hindrance to the one managerial task that everyone agreed on: communicating with others. Some dirty minds even began to suggest that having your desk perched atop a raised platform reflected "power needs" or, worse yet, insecurity.

Hence, the new cliche—the managerial office as conversation pit. Replace that hopelessly squarish desk with a round table, which visitors can draw their chairs up to. There's no hierarchy here—though, as Bosti President Michael Brill points out, most managers immediately reestablish one by having a slightly different chair for themselves or by staking out the choice spot, back to the window or to the nearest wall. Have to be within arm's length of the old credenza, you know—the phone and all that.

While few managers have completely given up desks in the interest of achieving living-room ambience, the vast majority of offices of any size now make at least a nod toward parlor informality. Indeed, the office layout most frequently sought by senior executives today consists of a space divided into three areas: work-surface area (where the desk is, usually), the informal conversational area (the couch and visitors' chairs), and the conference area (a long table with a place for Papa Bear at the head). Might not two areas to gather in be redundant? No, say the experts, you need the more hierarchical ordering of the conference table for when the factory hands come to visit; they'd be horribly ill at ease if invited to sit down with the senior V.P. on his crewelwork divan.

Source: Walter Kiechel III, "What Your Office Says About You," *Fortune*, 31 May 1982, pp. 161–62.

control and one-on-one contact with a chairperson, but these arrangements are highly dysfunctional if one wants to increase participation and ease in communications. Why not elliptical, hexagonal, or round tables? (Maybe King Arthur was showing considerable insight when he developed his round table for seating the key members of his court.)

Summary Comment on Size and Physical Arrangements

Effectiveness, efficiency, and participant satisfaction in group problem solving, then, is affected by group size and physical arrangements. Benefits seem to increase with group size up to about five to seven members. With more people, the process often becomes unwieldy, making it more difficult to tap available resources and maintain input that is balanced according to degree of expertise. Larger numbers make it more likely that a few individuals will dominate the proceedings and others will feel left out. Thus, participant satisfaction begins to decrease when groups become too large. Obviously, size can vary somewhat according to the specific problem, the kinds of people involved, the information-sharing component of the process, and other factors. However, we can't be too far wrong if we design problem-solving groups in the 5 to 7 range. If larger groups are necessary for political (representational) purposes, an appropriate strategy would be emphasis on subgroups or task forces for effective problem solving, at least through which to generate tentative solutions that are then ratified by the total group.

The physical setting for group problem solving can also be an important factor in effectiveness, efficiency, and participant satisfaction. Recall your experience at a tavern or restaurant with a group of ten people. Have you ever been on the corner of a rectangular seating arrangement and felt left out? Have you noticed how difficult it is to communicate with people on your side of a long table? It is usually easier to communicate with someone across from you than next to you. This suggests that, for optimal communication processes, the seating configuration should be as nearly round as possible. This seems like a minor point, but there is evidence to support its importance in effective group processes (Cummings, Huber, & Arendt, 1974).

Cohesiveness

Another important group dimension is cohesiveness, a phenomenon that is related to the concepts of norms and conformity. Cohesiveness means the degree of attraction the members have for each other and *their* group.

Members of a highly cohesive group tend to conform to the production standards set by the group, whether high or low, but groups lacking in cohesiveness have high variability in productivity among group members. High cohesiveness is accompanied by lower anxiety, as measured by feelings of nervousness or of being somehow under pressure to achieve higher productivity. The degree of cohesiveness is associated with (1) the extent to which members are accorded prestige for their own jobs by other group members, (2) the range of opportunities for interaction within the group, and (3) the duration of the shared membership on the job (Seashore, 1954, pp. 98–99). Furthermore, interpersonal warmth and, therefore, probably cohesiveness, increases as groups are more successful (Blanchard, Adelman, & Cook, 1975, pp. 1020–1030).

If we look at the phenomenon of attraction to the group per se, a number of other consequences emerge, most of which appear obvious. Those for whom the group has strong attraction are more likely to take on responsibilities for the group (e.g., to volunteer to do a particular task), to attend and to participate in meetings, to try to influence others, to be willing to listen to others, and to accept the opinions of other group members. In addition, the greater the attraction to the group, the higher the value members will place on their group's goals and the more they will adhere to its standards (Cartwright & Zander, 1960. pp. 88–89).

To summarize, a group's cohesiveness is profoundly related to its effectiveness in working toward *group goals* and, most likely, to the depth and quality of member satisfactions. This, coupled with the fact that the experience of group success engenders interpersonal warmth (and probably cohesiveness in the group), gives us the outline of our task. The management challenge is to try to create a climate in which goals sought by groups are congruent with organizational goals, and in which groups can experience group success.

Norms

We have alluded to *norms* on several occasions. A norm can be defined as "an idea in the minds of the members of the group, an idea that can be put in the form of a statement specifying what the members . . . should do, ought to do, are expected to do, under given circumstances" (Homans, 1950, p. 123). For example, one of the authors attended a meeting of police officers, only to sit in a chair that was immediately and vehemently identified as "the major's chair." (The author moved.) This rule was not written, was probably rarely talked about; but, to those abiding to it, it identified and proscribed a high centrality, high visibility position. Thus, a norm is an idea—frequently implicit rather than explicit—that is held in common by group members.

Group norms or standards have a powerful effect on productivity. The greater the group cohesiveness, the greater the effect of group norms and the less variability in output among group members. In short, cohesive groups in large measure control output, whether high or low.

In the productivity studies at the Hawthorne Works of Western Electric in the 1930s, it was found that workers had an output norm considerably below the official standards set by management and which produced earnings below what the workers could have earned under the group incentive system. This group norm was enforced by pressure from the group (Roethlisberger & Dickson, 1956, Chapter 18). Among the male workers, one of the devices used to control behavior was a game called "binging" in which one worker would strike another on the upper arm, thus interfering with the struck person's ability to concentrate on what he was doing at the time. The person who was binged now had the privilege of retaliating by "binging" with one blow. The following actual dialogue between two workers illustrates how this game was used to control production. The workers' names were originally coded "6" and "8," but we will call them Bill and Irving (Roethlisberger & Dickson, 1956, pp. 422–423).

IRVING: (To Bill) "Why don't you quit work? Let's see, this is your thirty-fifth row today. What are you going to do with them all?"

BILL: "What do you care? It's to your advantage if I work, isn't it?"

IRVING: "Yeah, but the way you're working you'll get stuck with them."

BILL: "Don't worry about that. I'll take care of it. You're getting paid by the sets I turn out. That's all you should worry about."

IRVING: "If you don't quit work I'll bing you." Irving struck Bill and finally chased him around the room.

OBSERVER: (A few minutes later) "What's the matter, Bill, won't he let you work?"

BILL: "No. I'm all through though. I've got enough done." He then went over and helped another wireman.

Some of the forces that gave rise to the group output norm in the bank wiring observation room can be seen in interviews with other workers. Some were afraid that high productivity would result in layoffs; others feared that quotas would be raised, as shown in the following verbatim accounts from interviews. We will call these workers Nate, Dennis, and Ernesto.

NATE: "No one can turn out the bogey consistently. Well, occasionally some of them do. Now since the layoff started there's been a few fellows down there who have been turning out around 7300 a day. They've been working like hell. I think it is foolishness to do it because I don't think it will do them any good, and it is likely to do the rest of us a lot of harm."

INTERVIEWER: "Just how do you figure that?"

DENNIS: "Well, you see if they start turning out around 7300 a day over a period of weeks and if three of them do it, then they lay one of the men off, because three men working at that speed can do as much as four men working at the present rate" (Roethlisberger & Dickson, 1956, p. 417).

INTERVIEWER: "You say there is no incentive to turn out more work? If all of you did more work, wouldn't you make more money?"

ERNESTO: "No, we wouldn't. They told us that down there one time. You know, the supervisors came around and told us that very thing, that if we would turn out more work we would make more money, but we can't see it that way. Probably what would happen is that our bogey would be raised, and then we would just be turning out more work for the same money. I can't see that" (Roethlisberger & Dickson, 1956, p. 418).

Thus, in this instance, fears about being laid off or simply fears about doing extra work for no additional reward were forces underlying the group norm that tended to keep production around 6,600 units on the average.

In the above illustration of "binging," conflict is an outcome associated with whether group members adhered to or violated group norms. However, cooperation or conflict—particularly between groups—frequently is a norm in itself. In a glass factory, for example, approximately 40 men on each of the two shifts in the blowing department were divided into two fairly distinct factions. One faction, the "old-timers" were men in their fifties and early sixties who had

BOX 7.5
WORK BANKING

A few weeks later on a summer night, the Greek came by and said, "Let's take a walk." We walked to the back end of the plant, out onto the loading platform. There I could not believe my eyes. I saw two guys burying a thirty-foot propeller shaft in the backyard. I burst out with, "What the hell are you guys doing?" They said, "Hey fellows, you watch us be heroes at the end of the month when the boss gives us that we-need-to-break-quota bullshit." I admit that this was an extreme case, but if you can get a group of workers to tell work-banking stories, you will hear some fantastic tales.

Source: Robert Schrank, *Ten Thousand Working Days,* Cambridge, Mass; MIT Press, p. 82.

come up through the ranks slowly. The other faction, the "young men," ranged from their early twenties to early forties and had made their progress with the company in recent years. The old-timers viewed the young men as "not real glassworkers," in the sense that the quality of their work was inferior (in reality, it was satisfactory by management standards) and that they could not do all of the operations in the shop. When the young men got into difficulties, the old-timers did not help, but displayed some delight in the young persons' predicaments; when asked for advice, they were "too busy" or gave misleading information. The young men responded by being critical of the skills and personalities of the old-timers. Thus, the norms of these two informal groups clearly included the withholding of cooperation and support, which in turn had the effect of retarding production and employee development (Whyte, 1961, pp. 162–163).

There can be group norms about virtually any dimension of group life. Norms can include such matters as expectations about starting time, what subjects can be brought up, how much support is expressed, and who can speak the most frequently. As an illustration about starting time, in our work with one Native American Indian tribe, whose central occupation was fishing, we found that tribal council meetings never started earlier than one hour late, and often two or more. In another tribe, which had had a decade or so experience in running small business enterprises, council members were consistently on time. Obviously, group norms are influenced by the broader culture in which the group is immersed. Thus, research and experience clearly suggest that group norms have a powerful controlling effect on productivity and on group behavior in general.

Conformity

There is some evidence that a significant percentage of persons will yield to group pressures even when the group position is contrary to fact. In a series of experiments, for example, eight persons were instructed to do a series of matchings of a given line with three unequal lines, and to announce their judgments publicly. In the middle of this "test," one person (called the *critical subject*) suddenly found himself contradicted by the entire group, and he was contradicted again and again during the experiment. (The other seven members of the experiment had previously met with the experimenter and had been instructed to make large errors, unanimously, at certain points in the experiment.) The results were as follows:

1. One third of all of the estimates by the critical subject (there was a total of 50) had errors identical to, or in the direction of, the erroneous majority. (There were practically no errors in the control groups in which members wrote down their estimates in contrast to reporting orally.)
2. About two thirds of the critical subjects in the series had correct estimates in spite of pressures from the majority.

Among the subjects who yielded were some who experienced "distortion in perception" and were not aware that their estimates were changed or modified. Most of those who yielded experienced *distortion of judgment* in the sense that they came to believe their estimates were inaccurate; these subjects tended to have considerable doubt and lack of self-confidence. Another group of yielders were those who experienced neither a distortion in perception nor a distortion in judgment. These subjects simply had an overpowering need not to appear different or inferior but knew what they were doing (Asch, 1960, pp. 190–94). One implication is that there can be a significant proportion of group members predisposed toward norms of conformity.

Groupthink can be the consequence if, for whatever reason, norms of high conformity develop in a group. Janis (1972) uses the term purposely to connote the detrimental aspects of group pressure as described by George Orwell in *1984* (Orwell, 1949). Janis has written about this phenomenon in foreign-policy decisions and about the fiascoes that resulted, including the inclination of a group of top officials of the Kennedy administration to support an invasion of the Bay of Pigs by Cuban exiles. High-level members of the administration were so anxious to avoid being perceived as dissidents that they suppressed their grave misgivings about the operation.

A clear implication of the groupthink phenomenon is that groups need to find ways to surface concerns and alternative views if they are to make the best decisions. Indeed, Janis found this to be the case in such incidents as the Cuban missile crisis, when the top leaders in the United States government effectively responded to a crisis occurring when the Soviet government shipped missiles into Cuba. Having learned from the Bay of Pigs fiasco, President Kennedy and his advisors altered group processes in several ways. Every person was expected to participate as a "skeptical generalist" and not promote the intentions of a particular agency. There was a free-wheeling discussion, outsiders were brought in to present alternate views and were encouraged to participate in the discussions, and subgroups were frequently used to enhance the openness of discussion to bring back optional views.

BOX 7.6
GROUPTHINK

Groupthink refers to a deterioration of mental efficiency, reality testing, and moral judgment that results from in-group pressures.

The tentative inferences I have extracted can be summarized in terms of three specific ways that groupthink tendencies might be counteracted:

1. The leader of a policy-forming group might assign the role of critical evaluator to each member, encouraging everyone to give high priority to airing his objections and doubts openly. This practice may need to be reinforced by the leader's acceptance of criticism of his own judgments in order to discourage the members from soft-pedaling their disagreements.
2. The key leaders in an organization's hierarchy, when assigning a policy-planning mission to any group within their organization, might adopt an impartial stance instead of stating preferences and expectations at the outset. This practice requires each leader to limit his briefings to unbiased statements about the scope of the problem and the limitations of available resources, without advocating any specific proposal he would like to see adopted, so as to allow the conferees to develop an atmosphere of open inquiry and explore impartially a wide range of policy alternatives.
3. The organization might routinely follow the administrative practice of setting up several independent policy-planning and evaluation groups to work on the same policy question, each carrying out its deliberations under a different leader. This would prevent the appraisal of policy alternatives from remaining in the hands of one insulated group, a prime condition that fosters miscalculations based on concurrence-seeking tendencies.

Source: Irving L. Janis, *Groupthink: Psychological Studies of Policy Decisions and Fiascoes,* 2d ed. Boston: Houghton-Mifflin, 1972, pp. 9, 172.

Status and Equity

Although status has organization-wide implications, the concept has direct relevance to behavior in groups. We will look at status, status incongruence, and status anxiety, all of which can be group phenomena. Status, like groups, has both formal and informal aspects. *Formal status* is the rank held by a person in the authority structure or in the hierarchy of rights and privileges assigned in the organization. *Informal status* is the prestige ranking given to a person in a group or organization. Informal status can be influenced by such dimensions as family, social, and economic background, age, seniority, education, and the degree to which one typifies the various norms of the group. These two kinds of status, formal and informal, are likely to be correlated (although not necessarily so) and tend to overlap and interact with each other.

Some of the ingredients that seem to influence perceptions of one's formal status are assigned role, job title, amount of pay, type of payment (i.e., whether one's wages are quoted in terms of a monthly salary or in terms of an hourly wage), dress, working hours, physical trappings of one's work station, and circle of acquaintances. These are "formal" matters in the sense that they are visible and obvious and tend to be under management control. As the researchers emphasized in the Hawthorne studies:

> A person who by his rank and service has achieved a certain social status regards anything, whether real or imaginary, tending to alter this status as unfair or unjust.
>
> It is not possible to treat . . . material goods, physical events, wages, and hours of work as things in themselves, subject to their own laws. Instead, they must be interpreted as carriers of social value. For the employee in industry, the whole worker's environment must be looked upon as being permeated with social significance (Roethlisberger & Dickson, 1956, pp. 365, 374).

Thus, a wide variety of conditions in the work setting affects the status attributed to a person as well as the feelings one has about being fairly or unfairly

BOX 7.7

AIRPLANE CRASHES AND GROUP DYNAMICS

In Portland, Ore., in December, 1978, . . . a McDonnell Douglas DC8 flight from New York and Denver crashed several miles short of the runway because it ran out of fuel.

Ten of the 189 on board were killed, so the accident received only brief national attention, but among pilots it is much discussed. The plane ran out of fuel while crew members were preoccupied with a landing-gear problem that had forced them to circle Portland.

Excerpts from the safety board's report tell of a copilot and flight engineer who knew the fuel situation was becoming critical but didn't do enough to warn the captain.

There is no question: a study of a transcript of the cockpit conversation confirms that warnings were made but were subtle, gentle and deferential to the senior captain. They went unheard or unrespected.

Source: Douglas B. Feaver, "Pilots Learn to Handle Crises—and Themselves," *Washington Post,* 12 September 1982, p. A6. © The Washington Post.

treated. The feeling usually accompanying a perception of unfair treatment is anger, with the person likely trying to alter the situation (Homans, 1950, pp. 232–264). This could include either direct or indirect aggressive acts in the group situation.

Status incongruence is present when the various indicators of formal status seem to be out of line with one another. The internal tension caused by status incongruence is *status anxiety*. An example of status incongruence might be when a person's pay and work trappings, such as the size and location of her desk, are perceived by that person/or others to be significantly below or above the level of responsibility of the job. If significantly below, one can hypothesize that the person will feel unfairly treated and try to do something about it. This has been confirmed by a considerable amount of research on the relationship between perceived equity of wages and job performance. For example, underpaid subjects tend to reduce the quantity or quality of their work (Evan & Simmons, 1969, pp. 224–237).

If the pay and work trappings are significantly above those perceived to be in line with the job responsibilities, other people will tend to react adversely in one way or another. For example, if one's pay is perceived as too high relative to others', or if one is perceived as not working as hard as others and drawing the same pay, the group may try to unload undesirable chores on that person (frequently called *sandbagging*). This is an indirect, but aggressive act. On the other hand, a person who feels overpaid will try to reduce status anxiety by increasing the quality of work (Adams & Jacobsen, 1964, pp. 19–25).

Problems can also occur if a group member has a higher prestige ranking than the formally appointed leader. A number of tensions can occur, including anxiety on the part of the formal leader. The latter may try to reduce anxiety in any number of ways: from expending extra effort to displaying aggression toward, or soliciting support from, the higher-status person. For example, a young research scientist, newly appointed as director of a laboratory, might make an extra effort to seek the opinion of an internationally known scientist in the group before making crucial decisions.

Sex

The forces in society that shape personality appear to have affected women and men differently with regard to how they behave in groups. A number of studies indicate that while both women and men have a wide repertoire of behaviors available, women tend to select more of a social-affective emphasis in mixed-sex task groups and in family interaction, while men tend to select more of a task emphasis (Aries, 1976, p. 67).

One example of this research, an experiment involving two all-male groups, two all-female groups, and two mixed groups, each having five to seven members, tended to confirm the above conclusions and found some additional information. The males in all-male groups talked very little about themselves, their relationships with significant other persons, or their feelings. Females in all-female groups shared a great deal about themselves, their feelings, and their relationships with family, friends, and lovers. Themes of competition, practical joking, superiority, and aggressiveness were evident in the all-male groups, while themes of intimacy and interpersonal relations emerged for the women. While the women gained a sense of closeness through self-revelation, the men acknowledged warmth and friendship through joking and laughter.

In the mixed groups, males talked much more about themselves and their feelings. They also addressed individuals in the group more frequently. The presence of women seemed to change the all-male style of interaction to one that was more personal and revealing and less competitive. Females in the mixed groups talked less about home and family, perhaps, as the researcher surmised, because of a reflection of "the female desire to present themselves as more competent and independent when males are present." However, the women spoke less in the mixed groups, initiating only about one third of the interaction. As to the latter result, one of the concerns expressed by the researcher was that "very capable women might follow the lead of less capable men, and may not be able to work to the level of competence to which they are capable" (Aries, 1976, p. 7).

FOUR LEVELS OF GROUP WORK

As shown in Figure 7.4, organized effort on the part of a group can be categorized into one of four levels of group work. These levels are (1) the problem or product level (the physical mental work), (2) the method or procedures level, (3) the group process level, and (4) the interpersonal or affect level. We say *levels* because as group effort moves from the first to the fourth category the problems being worked on move from the relatively impersonal level of the task to the more personal level of one's feelings about the behavior of others in the group.

Problem or Product Level

At the problem or product level, the group is working on a particular task or tasks, such as making a product, providing a service, or solving a problem. This is the level that reflects what the group is mainly "in business for." An example would be a group consisting of the maintenance supervisors and engi-

I. Problem or product level (the physical or mental work)

II. Method or procedures level (the "technology" of the group meeting, including methods of decision making, agenda building, and communications, and the physical arrangements)

III. Group process level ("task", "maintenance", and "blocking" behaviors)

IV. Interpersonal relations or affect level (feelings or liking, anger, apathy, etc.)

FIGURE 7.4 Levels of Group Work

neers in a chemical manufacturing plant meeting to try to reduce maintenance costs.

Method or Procedures Level

At the method or procedures level one finds the technology of the group's activities. These include the following: (1) its modes of decision making (whether by one person, minority control, majority vote, or consensus); (2) how the agenda is decided (e.g., the degree to which group members can influence the agenda and the mechanisms that are used to influence the agenda); (3) its means of communication (e.g., whether group members use additional devices to supplement face-to-face communications such as memoranda, blackboards, or flip charts); and (4) the physical arrangements (e.g., lighting, noise level, and the design of tables and chairs).

Group Process Level

At the group process level are those group member behaviors that have been labeled "task," "building and maintenance," and "blocking" behaviors, and that serve to facilitate or hinder group progress. These behaviors were described in an article that has been reproduced and used so extensively that it warrants the level "classic" in group dynamics literature (Benne & Sheats, 1948, pp. 41–49). Over the years, many trainers in group dynamics workshops have used and confirmed these categories of behaviors, or "roles" or "functions," as they were originally called.

Important leadership functions cannot be isolated from membership functions, and there is ideally a sharing of responsibility in carrying them out. In short, a number of important functions need to be performed in order for a group to be optimally effective, and these are not just the province of the formal leader. Different people can perform these functions at various times, and everyone in a group might display some of these behaviors when timely.

Group task behaviors are the communicating and problem-solving activities pertaining to the substantive tasks of the group. Group building and maintenance behaviors have the purpose of ensuring full participation of group members and of maintaining the group as a group. These behaviors tend to pertain to the emotional aspects of the group. Dysfunctional individual behaviors serve to meet individual needs but tend to be detrimental to effective group functioning. Looking at Figure 7.5, then, we see that the first two columns, are behaviors that generally enhance group effectiveness, while the behaviors described in the third column are hindering behaviors.

While Figure 7.5 is generally self-explanatory, we will comment on a few of the behaviors. Paraphrasing, from the "group task behaviors" column, is so vital to effective communications that in our consulting practices we frequently involve a group in practicing this skill before tackling a substantive issue. Being able to provide information, such as one's feelings about being embarassed about some failure of the group, can be helpful in the group's facing up to its tasks more effectively (Zander, 1977, p. 70). Signals of encouragement, from the "group

EFFECTIVE BEHAVIOR		INEFFECTIVE BEHAVIOR
Task Behaviors	**Maintenance Behaviors**	
1. Initiating-Contributing: Proposing tasks, goals or actions; defining a problem in a new way; suggesting a procedure or a way of organizing.	1. Encouraging: Being friendly, warm and responsive to others; indicating by facial expression or remark the acceptance of others' contributions.	1. Attacking (Aggressive Behavior): Deflating others' status; attacking the group or its values; joking in a barbed or semi-concealed way; trying to take credit for another's contribution.
2. Information and/or Opinion Seeking: Asking for relevant facts; asking for clarification of the values underlying the task or suggestions being made.	2. Harmonizing: Attempting to reconcile disagreements; reducing tension; getting people to explore differences.	2. Blocking: Disagreeing and opposing beyond "reason"; resisting stubbornly the group's wish for personally oriented reasons; using hidden agenda to thwart the movement of a group.
3. Information and/or Opinion Giving: Offering facts; expressing feelings; giving opinions.	3. Gate Keeping: Helping to keep communication channels open; facilitating the participation of others; suggesting limits or length of presentations to give everyone a chance to communicate.	3. Dominating: Asserting authority or superiority to manipulate the group or certain of its members; interrupting contributions of others; controlling by means of flattery or other forms of patronizing behavior.
4. Paraphrasing: Checking on meaning, "Is this what you mean?" "If I hear you correctly, you are saying . . ." or "Let me see if I understand . . ."	4. Consensus Testing: Asking to see if a group is nearing a decision; sending up a trial balloon to test a possible conclusion.	4. Playboy/Playgirl Behavior: Making a display in "playboy/playgirl" fashion of one's lack of involvement; "abandoning" the group while remaining physically with it, perhaps through cynicism or nonchalance.

FIGURE 7.5 Effective and Ineffective Behavior in Groups. **Source:** Paraphrased and adapted from Kenneth D. Benne and Paul Sheats," Functional Roles of Group Members," *Journal of Social Issues* 4 (Spring 1948): 41–49.

maintenance behaviors'' column, are extremely important for people to participate freely. We can demonstrate this by exaggerating the opposite phenomenon: By sitting in stony silence we can literally freeze the effectiveness of a person who is trying to make a contribution. The *gate keeping* function is important, and might be as simple as ''Sally, I'd like to hear your opinion on this matter; you've had some experience with this kind of problem.'' *Consensus testing* can be important; sometimes groups have reached a consensus long before anyone bothers to check.

As suggested by the last column in Figure 7.5, hidden agendas can block group progress. As groups develop more skill and trust, they learn to ''ante up'' any private agendas so that the group will understand where they are ''coming

5. Clarifying and/or Elaborating: Interpreting ideas or suggestions; defining terms; clarifying issues before the group; providing examples.	5. Compromising: When his/her own idea or status is involved in a conflict offering a compromise that yields status; admitting error; modifying in interest of group cohesion or growth.	5. Recognition-Seeking: Calling attention to oneself through boasting or reporting on one's achievements.
6. Summarizing and Coordinating: Pulling together related ideas; re-stating suggestions; offering a decision or conclusion for group to consider.	6. Standard Setting: Suggesting standards for the group to achieve in terms of how well the group works together.	6. Self-Confessing: Using the group to express nonrelated personal feelings, insights, ideologies.
7. Reality Testing and/or Standard Setting: Making a critical analysis of an idea; testing an idea against some data trying to see if the idea would work; suggesting standards for the group to achieve in terms of the task.	7. Process Observing: Making observations of group processes and supplying this information for group evaluation of its own functioning.	7. Sympathy-Seeking: Attempting to arouse sympathy through expressions of insecurity or self-depreciation.
8. Recording: Providing the "group memory" by writing down key points, suggestions and/or decisions.	8. Following: Going along with the movement of the group; serving as an audience in group discussion.	8. Special-Interest Pleading: Speaking for the "small businessman", the "housewife", "labor", etc; frequently hiding one's own biases behind a convenient stereotype.

from.'' For example, if a group member has an appointment to play golf two hours hence, it can be helpful to the group to have that information at the beginning of the meeting. In this way, agenda items of particular interest to the member who needs to leave early can be dealt with initially, in contrast to the person's trying to manipulate the group into hurrying through the various items. As to *playboy* and *playgirl* behavior, humor and fun can be tension-releasing for a group and can provide some of the reward for meeting together. However, too much playful behavior will obviously serve to block progress on tasks.

Norms are obviously important in the expression of various behaviors. Norms that support the functional behaviors in the first two columns of Figure 7.5 will contribute to group effectiveness. Norms that permit, unchecked, the behaviors listed in the third column will detract from group effectiveness.

Interpersonal Relations Level

Returning to the four-tiered scheme of Figure 7.4, we can understand the feelings that group members have about each other's behaviors, and the kinds of steps that they, and the group as a whole, take in dealing with these feelings, as belonging to the final level—that of interpersonal relations. For example, feelings of liking, affection, annoyance, anger, apathy, or hurt, stemming from such issues as control and submission, inclusion and exclusion, or closeness and distance, are all major aspects of the interpersonal-relations level of group work, as are the ways people have of addressing those feelings (Schutz, 1958).

Here's an example of an inclusion-exclusion problem. Someone on a five-person task force says, "Let's visit the Chicago plant to see how they arranged their warehouses." Everyone agrees. The following week, three of the people go to visit the plant without mentioning it to the other two until the next meeting of the task force. The explanation is, "You two were so busy with labor negotiations that we didn't want to bother you." You can imagine the anger or the hurt feelings that might be generated by the perceived slight.

These interpersonal issues deserve mention here because groups typically have difficulty with them. The control-submission issue, for example, usually appears in the form of an implicit leadership struggle, usually early in a group's life. Inclusion-exclusion is frequently an issue in the sense that people either tend to feel "in," with an accompanying sense of satisfaction, or they tend to feel "out," with corresponding feelings of dissatisfaction, hurt, apathy, or anger. The closeness-distance issue centers around such personal questions as: "How close do I want to get to these people?"; "What are the risks and what is the price of feeling close to various individuals in this group or of letting them be friendly

with me?"; "How do I handle my feelings of liking and disliking of various individuals in the group?"

GROUPS CAN LEARN TO WORK MORE EFFECTIVELY

It is our conclusion that the most effective groups have learned to work at all four levels. By an effective group we mean a group that comes out with an excellent product and one in which people have strong feelings of personal satisfaction about the way the group has worked and the way they have contributed to group success.

Probably the safest levels, and the ones at which success in developing group skills can occur most quickly, are the methods/procedures level and the group process level. At the methods level, for example, a group can easily learn how to arrange meeting rooms and how to do a better job of establishing the agenda. At the group process level, groups can readily learn to listen more effectively to each other through paraphrasing, although mastery of the technique takes practice and perseverance.

The interpersonal relations level, while it holds great promise for increasing group effectiveness, satisfaction, and personal growth, is probably the most difficult of the levels to manage. For example, if one member should get angry at another, many groups do not have the skills to manage the situation: either to the satisfaction of the people directly involved, or to the satisfaction of the total group. Effective work at this level requires not only a basic concern for other group members and a strong commitment to constructive resolution of difficulties but also experience and training in understanding and dealing with feelings.

While work at the interpersonal level can pose risks that must be met with great skill (perhaps more so than at any other level), it can also turn out to be the most rewarding personally to group members. We should note, however, that interpersonal problem solving can be seductive to a group; that is, it can become so rewarding and so engrossing an activity that a group can fail to come to grips adequately with the overall mission or task to be performed.

The method or procedures level lends itself to substantial premeeting planning and arranging, such as that relating to the way chairs and tables are arranged and to the availability of blackboards and flip charts. This is not a constant preoccupation, but effective groups will, as a group, reexamine their approach from time to time. Effective work at the group process level is essentially an ongoing matter, and highly competent groups will examine the quality of their work at this level when difficulties arise. Work at the interpersonal relations level can be ongoing in the sense that group members can learn to give off signals quickly so that others will have a fairly continuous reading on their emotional state. When serious problems arise, however, work at this level is more of an ad hoc matter.

Quick spot checking when difficulties first appear, or even before they appear, can prevent difficulties from getting worse. For example, in a planning session, whoever has the floor and is making a presentation might check early to see whether people are following the trend of thought. If one or more group members are not, explanation or elaboration can bring people aboard so that they do not feel left out or so they do not withdraw psychologically from the task.

In the vignettes at the beginning of the chapter there are a number of instances in which groups did *not* work effectively across levels. For instance, in *The Meeting,* Simon Jennings did not mention his dissatisfaction with how the agenda was established (method or procedure level) nor his feelings about the lack of group support to bring up anything controversial (group process and interpersonal levels). Similarly, in *Marge,* Marge Goldman did not (or could not) talk about her feelings concerning lack of inclusion (interpersonal relations level) and her perceptions about the lack of group building and maintenance behaviors (group process level). In the vignette of *The Engineers,* group members did not share their concerns with Jim about his having so many of the draftsmen and his not being available. Instead, they gave off nonverbal signals of disapproval, which simply made Jim trust them less. In *The Workshop,* participant satisfaction would have been higher had the professor arranged the room differently. In the *One-on-One* vignette, more frequent use of slightly larger groups would probably have improved both the quality of some of the meetings and member satisfaction. In *The Joggers,* there seemed to be an implicit norm that there was to be no socializing beyond the jogging, but no one checked it. In each of the vignettes, more understanding of, and skill in, the various levels of group work—plus a measure of more assertiveness—might have improved either group performance or member satisfactions or both. Individuals and groups can learn to work more effectively at the four levels.

SO WHAT? IMPLICATIONS FOR YOU

Some of what we have said about group dimensions and dynamics has direct behavioral implications for supervisors, managers, and leaders in most types of organizations. Other aspects have implications for anyone who wishes to make the group in which he/she participates more effective. Some of this knowledge can be used in a manipulative way; that is, covertly, without being candid about what one is doing and why. Our strong preference is for leaders and group members to be open about their desire to improve group performance and to be candid about the dimensions they see as dysfunctional to performance and to member satisfaction.

As a Member of an Organization

Generalizations	Implications
1. Formal and informal groups are the fundamental building blocks of more complex organizations.	1. Be observant and identify the formal and informal group behaviors that influence organizational activities.
2. Group attitudes, norms, and be-	2. Recognize the importance of

Generalizations	Implications
haviors have a strong effect on the individuals within the group.	these forces and how they affect your own behavior.
3. Groups are frequently reluctant to accept new members and view them as outsiders who should win their way into the group.	3. Recognize that this is a natural process and be patient about winning acceptance.
4. People frequently yield to group pressures, even when the majority is in error.	4. Lend your support to the development of a group culture that permits exploring different viewpoints.
5. Because of cultural norms, some women may tend to defer to men in group situations.	5. Yield to superior judgments, but not on the basis of sex; encourage those who seem to be too deferential to assert their information and opinions.
6. Physical settings are important to group effectivenes.	6. Be conscious of such matters as room and seating arrangements, noise levels, etc. in preparing for meetings. Take the initiative to create optimal conditions.
7. Effective group work requires a sharing of group "task" and "maintenance" behaviors; the leader/follower dichotomy is a fallacy.	7. Assume responsibility for your own behavior in terms of contributing to group effectiveness.

As a Current or Future Manager

Generalizations	Implications
1. Groups are a fundamental part of every organization.	1. As a manager you should recognize the importance of groups and try to understand the nature of the groups within your organization.
2. Group activities can be oriented toward organizational goals or away from them.	2. Use a leadership style that permits joint exploration of goals and objectives. Design the rewards so that groups are oriented toward organizational goals.
3. The effectiveness of a task	3. Give careful thought to the se-

Generalizations	Implications
force or a committee is a function both of who is assigned to the group and of member skills.	lection of members for a task force or committee, in terms of such dimensions as knowledge, acceptability to others, and group skills.
4. *Schmoozing* or socializing with organizational groups is universal and provides important human satisfactions.	4. Accept the schmooze factor and use it to improve group performance.
5. Almost any item or event—titles, location of desks, responsibilities, and pay increases, has potential meaning to people in terms of status or "fairness" and "unfairness."	5. Take into account the probable impact of changes on people's sense of status and sense of justice.
6. Physical settings are important to group effectiveness.	6. Take the initiative in designing the room and seating arrangements and in securing appropriate facilities and equipment. In designing plant and office layouts, enhance desired interdependency by location of equipment and people.
7. Dyads do not have a built-in mediator; threesomes sometimes divide into two persons against an isolate. Groups of four to seven seem to be optimal for many tasks.	7. Exercise judgment about the size of groups; adjust the size of the group to the nature of the task. Use of subgroups can be helpful.
8. Group cohesiveness may tend to extend the life of a committee or task force beyond what was required by the original assignment.	8. Review group mission and length of term at intervals and take appropriate actions.
9. Many organizations suppress emotionality to the detriment of problem solving and member satisfaction.	9. Do not make the expression of feelings off limits; this results in feelings being suppressed and affecting behavior in other ways. Listen to and observe the affective (feeling) content of what people are saying and doing.

Generalizations	Implications
10. The effectiveness of groups depends upon their ability to work effectively at the product, procedures, group process, and interpersonal relations levels.	10. Work with your own subordinate team at all four levels. Help create acceptance of the concept that groups can work more effectively at all levels.
11. Training in group skills can be an important supplement to organizational life.	11. Make resources available for training in group skills.

LEARNING APPLICATION ACTIVITIES

1. Write a vignette from your experience that illustrates functional and/or dysfunctional behaviors in a group meeting.

2. Analyze *The Meeting* vignette and note some actions Simon Jennings might take to improve department head meetings.

3. Observe the "technology" of several meetings you attend during one week. Describe the techniques and indicate how they seem to affect interaction. Discuss your findings with a group of four to six colleagues.

4. At your next group meeting pay particular attention to the effects of the physical settings on group processes. Make a list of physical characteristics and their effects. If possible, share your list with other members of the group.

5. Spend a day concentrating on doing a particularly good job of paraphrasing (checking on meaning) in your interpersonal and group interactions. In private, jot down your recollections of how things went and the extent to which you were helpful and/or the interaction was effective. Discuss in a subgroup of your class, but keep names of individuals confidential.

6. Identify the norms you think are operating in two or three groups in which you are a member. Make inferences as to how these norms are contributing to, or interfering with, group effectiveness. Revise or verify your inferences by discussing with another group member. While taking caution to avoid being critical of any individual, report your analysis to your class (or a subgroup of the class). You may want to disguise the name or nature of the group.

7. After a group task of some kind, have each person identify the extent to which the effective group behaviors as described by Benne and Sheats (Figure 7.5) were present. Share, in turn, and discuss the implications.

REFERENCES

Adams, J. Stacy, and Patricia R. Jacobsen. "Effects of Wage Inequities on Work Quality." *Journal of Abnormal and Social Psychology* 69 (1964): 19–25.

Aries, Elizabeth. "Interaction Patterns and Themes of Male, Female, and Mixed Groups." *Small Group Behavior* (February 1976): 7.

Asch, S. E "Effects of Group Pressure Upon the Modification and Distortion of Judgments." In Darwin Cartwright and Alvin Zander (Eds.), *Group Dynamics: Research and Theory,* 2nd ed. New York: Harper & Row, 1960, pp. 188–200.

Benne, Kenneth D., and Paul Sheats. "Functional Roles of Group Members." *The Journal of Social Issues* 4 (Spring 1948): 41–49.

Bennis, Warren. *The Unconscious Conspiracy: Why Leaders Can't Lead.* New York: Amacom, 1976.

Berelson, Bernard, and Gary A. Steiner. *Human Behavior: An Inventory of Scientific Findings.* New York: Harcourt Brace Jovanovich, 1964.

Bensman, Joseph, and Robert Lilienfeld. "Friendship and Alienation." *Psychology Today* 13 (October 1979): 60–63.

Black, Max, ed., *The Social Theories of Talcott Parsons.* Englewood Cliffs, N.J.: Prentice-Hall, 1961.

Blanchard, Fletcher A., Leonard Adelman, and Stuart W. Cook. "Effect of Group Success and Failure upon Interpersonal Attraction in Cooperating Interracial Groups." *Journal of Personality and Social Psychology* 31 (June 1975): 1020–1030.

Bowen, William. "Japanese Managers Tell How Their System Works." *Fortune* 46 (November 1977): 126–138.

Cartwright, Dorwin, and Alvin Zander, eds. *Group Dynamics: Research and Theory,* 2nd ed., New York: Harper & Row, 1960.

Cooley, Charles H., *Social Organization,* New York: Scribner, 1909.

Cummings, L. L., G. P. Huber, and E. Arendt. "Effects of Size and Spatial Arrangements on Group Decision Making." *Academy of Management Journal* 17 (September 1974): 460–475.

Evan, William M., and Roberta G. Simmons. "Organizational Effects of Inequitable Rewards." *Administrative Science Quarterly* 14 (June 1969): 224–237.

Feaver, Douglas B. "Pilots Learn to Handle Crises—and Themselves." *Washington Post,* 12 September 1982, p. A6.

Kiechel, Walter III. "What Your Office Says about You." *Fortune,* 31 May 1982, pp. 161–162.

Hare, A. Paul, Edgar F. Borgatta, and Robert F. Bales. *Small Groups: Studies in Social Interaction.* New York: Knopf, 1955.

Homans, George C. *The Human Group.* New York: Harcourt Brace Jovanovich, 1950.

Janis, Irving L. *Groupthink: Psychological Studies of Policy Decisions and Figures,* 2nd ed. Boston: Houghton-Mifflin, 1972.

Leavitt, Harold J. "Suppose We Took Groups Seriously." In Eugene L. Cass and Frederick G. Zimmer (Eds.), *Man and Work in Society.* New York: Van Nostrand Reinhold, 1975, pp. 67–77.

Michelini, R. L., R. Passalacqua, and J. Cusimano. "Effects of Seating Arrangements on Group Participation." *The Journal of Social Psychology,* August 1976, pp. 179–186.

Mills, Theodore M. "Power Relations in Three-Person Groups." *American Sociological Review* 18 (August 1953): 351–357.

Oh, Tai K. "Japanese Management—A Critical Review." *Academy of Management Review* 1 (January 1976): 14–25.

Orwell, George. *1984.* New York: Harcourt Brace Jovanovich, 1949.

Ouichi, William G. *Theory Z.* Reading, Mass.: Addison-Wesley, 1981.

Parsons, Talcott, Robert F. Bales, and Edward A. Shils. *Working Papers in the Theory of Action.* New York: Free Press, 1953.

Resnick, Herman. "A Social System View of Strain." *Administration in Mental Health* 7/1 (Fall 1979): 56.

Roethlisberger, F. J., and William J. Dickson. *Management and the Worker.* 1939. Reprint. Cambridge, Mass.: Harvard University Press, 1956.

Schrank, Robert. *Ten Thousand Working Days.* Cambridge, Mass.: MIT Press, 1978.

Schutz, W. C. *FIRO: A Three-Dimensional Theory of Interpersonal Balance.* New York: Holt, Rinehart and Winston, 1958.

Seashore, Stanley E. *Group Cohesiveness in the Industrial Work Group.* Ann Arbor, Mich: Survey Research Center, Institute for Social Research, University of Michigan, 1954.

Simmel, Georg. "The Significance of Numbers for Social Life." In A. Hare, Edward F. Borgatta, and Robert F. Bales (Eds.), *Small Groups: Studies in Social Interaction*, New York: Knopf, 1955, pp. 9–15.

Slater, Philip E. "Contrasting Correlates of Group Size." *Sociometry* 21 (June 1958): 129–138.

Steele, Fred I. *Physical Settings and Organization Development*. Reading, Mass: Addison-Wesley Publishing Company, 1973.

Stogdill, Ralph M. *Handbook of Leadership: A Survey of Theory and Research*. New York: Free Press, 1974.

Whyte, William Foote. *Men At Work*. Homewood, Ill.: Dorsey Press/Irwin, 1961.

Zander, Alvin. *Groups at Work*. Jossey-Bass, 1977.

8
Conflict and Its Management

LEARNING OBJECTIVES

After reading this chapter you should be able to:

1. Define conflict and differentiate it from competition and cooperation.
2. Describe functional and dysfunctional aspects of conflict.
3. Identify several psychosocial roots of conflict in organizations (including sources in intrapersonal, interpersonal, intergroup processes).
4. Identify several roots of conflict in organizations that have to do with the environment in which people work.
5. Describe and explain what happens to groups during and after conflict situations.
6. Explain several approaches to conflict management and describe their advantages and disadvantages.

DISCONNECTED

Jack Adams was really mad. Ten of his 26 employees in the central stores department at County Hospital had gone to the director of personnel with a petition that he be fired. He didn't know the specifics of their complaints, but he had been asked to meet with the director of personnel, Barbara Huff, and the hospital administrator, Roy Gillespie. He wondered whether he should contact a lawyer, just in case.

He was aware of some problems in his unit, but thought he had taken the necessary steps to correct the obvious ones. Roy had told him to "shape up" the organization when he had been hired nine months ago.

For example, a problem of coordination had been evident between the office staff and the warehouse workers. The requisition form wasn't as clear as it might be and this resulted in some mistakes in filling orders. In the past, when something was unclear a warehouse worker would go into the office and ask the person who typed up the form to clarify it. This seemed to work reasonably well but, of course, it took time. Two months ago, a new clerk in the office complained to Jack that the order pickers were harassing her. "They are always asking questions. They don't seem to know anything," she said. Jack's response was to have his secretary type up a notice to be posted in the warehouse. It read:

> Effective immediately warehouse personnel will not be permitted in the office area. Any questions concerning orders will be directed to the warehouse supervisor, Andy Smith.

The warehouse workers read the note in disbelief. One of them asked Andy, "Does that mean what it says?" Andy shrugged and said, "I guess so."

Subsequently, "customer" complaints (from the medical, nursing, and the hospital administrative staff) began to increase dramatically. At first the calls came to the office and were then referred to the warehouse with a typical comment to the effect that, "It looks okay here; something must have happened to your order after it left the office.

Later the calls began coming directly to the warehouse. Orders were being filled incorrectly, some were inordinately late, and the situation was becoming generally more confusing by the day. Meanwhile, the response of the warehouse workers was, "We followed the directions on the form and assumed they were correct." The questionable ones were collected for Andy to look at, but he sometimes didn't get around to it for several days or a week.

The office continued to order standard items in bulk shipments (perhaps a year's supply at a time), even though there was no space available in the warehouse. This meant that some items would be left on the loading dock or in the receiving area and that items were being constantly rearranged on the shelves.

The warehouse workers blamed the office staff and described Jack as incompetent. The office staff blamed the warehouse workers, but they didn't have much respect for Jack either.

I QUIT

On Tuesday morning, Jane Merrill, a Ph.D. in metallurgy and a highly competent researcher with a large aerospace contractor in California, was shocked to see the following message written across one of her technical reports;

> This is ridiculous. Your hypothesis is not plausible, and your conclusions are equally implausible. Start over.
>
> (Signed) A.M.

A.M. was Dr. Andrew Mackenzie, vice president of research, and Dr. Merrill's boss.

During lunch with a colleague that day, Jane was quite agitated and stated that she was "sick and tired of Andy's high-handed methods," and that she wasn't going to take it any longer. The colleague agreed that Mackenzie was "an abrupt, cold fish," and tried to reassure her that he treated everyone that way. Over the next several days, Jane indicated to several of her colleagues and friends in the company that she was extremely unhappy with Dr. Mackenzie.

Late on a Friday afternoon, three weeks later, Jane wrote out her resignation, giving two weeks notice and stating that she was going to work for a competitor. She then walked into Dr. Mackenzie's office, handed the resignation to him without comment, and walked back to her office. Shortly thereafter, she left for Las Vegas for the weekend.

On Monday morning, about five minutes after Dr. Merrill had arrived at her office, the telephone rang. It was James Bronsen, personnel director. "Jane," he said, "I'm sorry to hear about this unfortunate business, but Andy thinks you might as well leave today. The company will pay you for two weeks, of course. You can pick up your check from me as soon as you've cleared out your desk. All you have to do after that is go to security for a few minutes. I'll expect you in 30 minutes." Bronsen sat and stared at the wall and pondered the matter. Mackenzie had ordered him to "get that woman out of here fast," and he had acquiesced. He realized that Merrill's going to a competitor created a risk of losing ideas, and he mused to himself, "I wonder if it isn't Mackenzie who should be going."

CONFLICT DEFUSED

The meeting of the personnel committee had been going all right, but when the group came to the item pertaining to time off without pay, people became somewhat tense. Henry seemed committed to the notion that time off without pay should not be allowed to extend weekends or vacations, and said, "We need people to run the plant. A lot of us would rather be reclining on some beach anytime we want to rather than working our tails off. I don't think we should give any time off without pay unless it's for an emergency." Gordon seemed upset with this comment and tried objecting, but Henry cut him off and continued.

After a few moments Karen said, "While I generally agree with you, Henry, I think we ought to list several options and analyze each one to make sure we settle on the best course of action. I'd like to hear more about what Gordon has in mind. And we haven't heard from Jim on this one." "Yeah, you're right," Henry said. "As long as everybody agrees with *my* solution." He grinned, and everybody laughed.

ANNUAL NEGOTIATIONS

The annual contract negotiations between Local 970 and the company had not been going well. Charlie, labor relations director for the company had said to his colleagues on the negotiating team after the previous session, "Al's got a burr under his saddle about something. We may have tough going this year. I wonder if we shouldn't have spent more time trying to solve some of those grievances over the last few months rather than pushing them to arbitration."

Today, after about an hour during which

Charlie had been explaining the company position on several issues, Al, the representative of the International who was serving as chief negotiator for the local, interrupted and said: "Gents, that's it. I think it's time we got a strike vote from our members. I don't see anybody in the union buying what the company proposes. Fifty-cents-per-hour increase is ludicrous. As a matter of fact, it's downright insulting. And on top of that, you want to make us do maintenance work, which we've never done in the past. We're going to adjourn this meeting right here and now. When we come back Thursday, I think you'll be more prepared to listen to us."

THAT'S MY TERRITORY

Carol was a new supervisor in the marketing department of Midtown Manufacturing Company. She was about thirty, new to the organization, assertive in a friendly way, and anxious to please and to be accepted. The ages of the other supervisors ranged from 24 to 63.

Bill was 29 and had started with the company right out of college about seven years ago. He had worked hard, considered himself a "comer," and was proud of the contacts he had cultivated through attending trade association meetings. Most of those were meetings that Midtown representatives had not attended before Bill had arrived. Although it was not always easy to prove that attendance at these particular meetings would bring in this or that order, some business could be directly attributed to Bill's efforts at the meetings.

It was customary to pour a cup of tea or coffee at the beginning of the weekly marketing supervisor's meeting, and there was usually considerable friendly banter as a result. This meeting was no exception. People were sort of jostling their way up to get a cup of coffee or tea, when Carol said to Bill, "I see you're getting ready to go to the hospital purchasing association meeting in Atlanta—I think I'll go to that meeting next year." Bill was startled, not knowing if she was kidding or serious, and said, "I don't think you'd like Atlanta that time of year." Someone walked between them at this point, and the meeting started before any further conversation could take place.

Bill was very uneasy during the meeting. "I wonder," he thought, "if this eager beaver isn't trying to horn in on my territory. I'd better keep an eye on her."

A week later, during an informal discussion in the hall between Bill, another supervisor, and the marketing department manager, the manager said, "I wonder how you folks see Carol getting along. I'm wondering if I shouldn't be giving her some additional assignments." Bill shook his head and said, "Well, I'd go a little slow until she learns more about how we do things here."

GET THINGS IN ON TIME, YOU DUMMY

On more than one occasion, the president of Cambridge division had complained to headquarters officers about the unnecessary "red tape" created by the corporate accounting office. The divisional controller, Maria Perez, and her staff were also frequently irritated by what they considered arbitrary headquarters accounting vetos over divisional recommendations regarding the hiring and transfer of employees, and with respect to people nominated by the division to attend management development programs.

One day, Maria Perez received the following memorandum from James Davidson, assistant corporate controller:

> Subject: Deadline for Submitting Pay Increase Recommendations.
> For the past several review periods, applications for pay increases for salaried employees of the Cambridge division have been sent to the corporate offices later than the published deadline date. The deadline for the spring review was April 1; however, Cambridge division requests were not submitted until April 4. These requests are being processed late *for the last time*. Beginning with the fall review period, the corporate accounting office will adhere to all stated deadlines.

Copies of this memorandum had gone to the president of the Cambridge division and the corporate vice president for finance.

Maria and her staff were very angry. They were proud of their efficiency. One of the norms in the organization was promptness; the executives frequently praised people for thorough and prompt reports. This time they had, indeed, been late during the most recent review period by one day (the dates in question involved a two-day weekend); the delay was due to the illness of a staff member. Furthermore, they knew of only one other instance of lateness, and that was when the corporate accounting office receptionist, by mistake, had returned Cambridge division recommendations without them being seen.

Maria Perez dictated the following memorandum to James Davidson:

> Your memorandum pertaining to pay increase recommendations is unacceptable as to its allegations and its tone. There is a great deal of anger about this matter among staff members here. I believe an apology is in order. Beyond that your memorandum can neither be construed in the interests of the employees nor in the interests of the corporation in general.

Copies were sent to the president of the division and the vice president for finance.

After another exchange of memoranda, James Davidson's secretary called to arrange a meeting at headquarters. Maria Perez, her anger reappearing, countered with the suggestion that the meeting be held at the Cambridge division. Through the secretarial staff she was informed that James Davidson "always had his meetings in his office." After some stewing about it, Maria decided to agree to that location. When Maria arrived on the appropriate day and hour at Davidson's office, she was ushered into an adjacent conference room where Davidson soon appeared.

INTRODUCTION

The above vignettes describe situations of conflict in organizations. Some have to do with conflict between two people (interpersonal) or within a group (intragroup), and some involve conflict between two or more units (intergroup). All tend to have ramifications beyond the immediate incident. One vignette, *Get Things in On Time, You Dummy,* involves conflict between divisional and corporate accounting offices and might be considered organizational conflict. *Annual Negotiations* involves two organizations, a company and a union, and is interorganizational conflict. One potential conflict situation, *Conflict Defused,* was managed well by some helpful group behaviors.

The study of conflict is important because conflict can either be a vitalizing force in groups and organizations or it can be debilitating and destructive. The issue is not how conflict can be avoided or done away with but how it is to be managed. And, to effectively manage conflict, we need to understand it. In this chapter we will look at the dynamics involved in the emergence of conflict, some of the consequences, positive and negative, of conflict, and some strategies for its management. The following topics will be considered:

Conflict as a Concept
Functional and Dysfunctional Aspects of Conflict and Cooperation
What Happens to Groups in Competition and Conflict
Roots of Conflict
Approaches to Conflict Management
So What? Implications for You

CONFLICT AS A CONCEPT

People differ in the scope and complexity of the meanings they attach to the words *conflict, cooperation,* and *competition,* so we want to develop some definitions for the purposes of this chapter. Dictionaries tend to define conflict with such words as "opposition," "controversy," "clash," "battle," "collision," "sharp disagreement," while cooperation is usually defined in terms of "working together toward a common purpose," "joint action," or "association for mutual benefit." Competition is defined with words like "struggle," "rivalry," and "contest," sometimes with the qualification that it does not necessarily involve destruction of one of the parties. While such meanings are adequate for common usage, it is important that we have a deeper understanding of these terms if we are to do sophisticated analyses of human behavior in organizations.

Conflict and Cooperation Defined

Conflict consists of interactive, opposing behaviors between two or more people, groups, or larger social systems having incompatible goals. It is usually experienced as troublesome, if not disruptive. The opposing behaviors may stem from a perceived loss or potential loss of something one or more of the parties has or wants. Conflict behaviors may range from intellectual jousting or malicious gossip all the way to the use of physical force to cause destruction of property or physical injury. The opposing behaviors may be overt and direct, in the sense of being obvious to all the parties involved, or they may occur sub rosa: undisclosed to the party or the parties targeted but no less negative in their consequences for being indirect. The opposing behaviors are interactive in the sense that "it takes two people to make a fight," but also in the sense that there is usually more than one cycle of behavior and counterbehavior.

Conflict behavior may be verbal or nonverbal. One can express opposition by words, by a shake of the head, by an obscene gesture, by writing a scathing memo, or by scratching the paint of a new car with a nail as it moves down the assembly line. Furthermore, conflict behavior may be active or passive. One can sometimes counter the behavior of another by tactics such as "dragging one's feet" or withholding information. It is implicit in what has been said that perceptions of a loss or of a potential loss, whether accurate or inaccurate, can create conflict.

Conflict can also be manifest or latent. The examples immediately preceding are of manifest conflict. There are at least two kinds of latent conflict: one referring to the *potential* conflict in a given situation, something between people that may or may not flare up; the second to *intrapersonal* conflict. The latter refers to interactive, opposing needs or wants within an individual. Such conflict can be latent, in the sense of there not being any effect on other people; on the other hand, intrapersonal conflict frequently gets expressed in words or other behaviors that do affect others, and to that extent becomes manifest. For example, a golfer who is angry at herself for missing an easy putt may look and act irritated for awhile, resulting in a companion's wondering if the irritation is aimed at him. Role conflict, a kind of intrapersonal conflict that we will discuss later, tends to spill over into group and organizational relationships. Largely, however, we will be dealing with manifest conflict in this chapter.

A distinction can also be made between perceived conflict and felt conflict (Filley, 1975, pp. 12–15). In the first place, perceptions, whether accurate or inaccurate, of a loss or of a potential loss, can create conflict. People tend to act on what they perceive, not on objective reality. Secondly, people have feelings about perceived losses or the threat of a loss of something they value, and these feelings give rise to overt behavior. To illustrate: in the *That's My Territory* vignette, Bill perceived Carol's comment as having the potential of taking away part of his territory, and he became uneasy, reflecting his fear and annoyance. Such feelings can arise from a situation without there being much cognitive or intellectual processing within the individual. Probably all conflict situations have perceptual aspects and feeling aspects, with perceptions affecting feelings and vice versa.

Cooperation consists of mutually reinforcing or supportive behaviors between two or more people, groups, or larger systems. The behaviors may stem from a perception that collaboration will help obtain mutual goals or just from a predisposition to behave this way. Since each of the parties involved is obtaining something desirable, or expects to, there is usually little reason for the behaviors to be sub rosa.

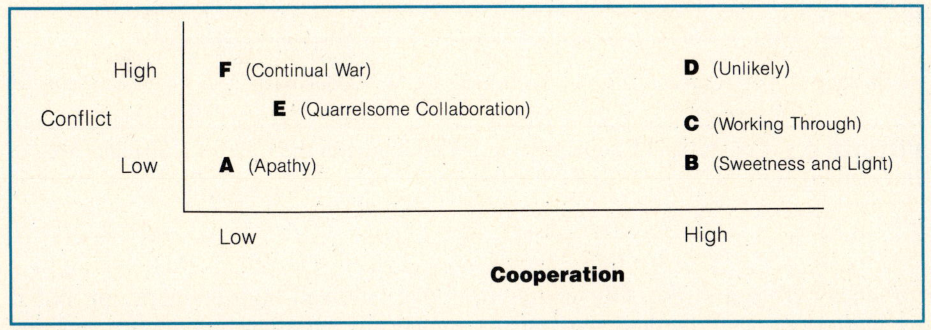

FIGURE 8.1 Different Mixes of Conflict and Cooperation in Group or Organizational Life

Cooperative behavior, like conflict behavior, may be verbal or nonverbal or both. It is usually active, although there are obviously degrees of cooperation. One person may be enthusiastic about a project, while another person is positively inclined but gives higher priority to other matters.

Are Cooperation and Conflict Separate Dimensions?

In terms of group or intergroup behaviors in the aggregate, it can be helpful to think of cooperation and conflict as separate dimensions and not on the same continuum. Both kinds of behaviors can exist simultaneously and the absence of one does not guarantee the existence of the other. For example, a group may have an absence of conflict, but the group may be so apathetic or tranquil that there is also little cooperation (see Figure 8.1, area A, Apathy). As another example, there may be a great deal of cooperation within a group on some aspects of work or group life, but also of collusion (cooperation) that discourages the conflict or competition of ideas (area B, Sweetness and Light). Or, a group may cooperate on many things while at the same time maintaining a climate that encourages the expression of different points of view. Differences and disagreements are routinely worked through so that there is consensus on most matters, and conflict does not become seriously disruptive to productive effort (area C, Working Through). Or, a group may be so burdened with unmanaged conflict that they can't cooperate on anything (area F, Continual War). Area D (High Conflict and High Cooperation) we call unlikely; it may not be a realistic category because frequent or very intense conflict is likely to reduce cooperation to nearly zero. However, we can visualize fairly high conflict on a number of issues, but with some cooperation on a few matters (area E, Quarrelsome Collaboration). An example would be a union cooperating with management in shutting down furnaces in a steel mill prior to an employee strike.

For a narrower or more specific area of interaction, it is useful to view conflict and cooperation as parts of a continuum rather than as radically separate (see Figure 8.2). For instance, there are a number of different scenes, or illustrations, that could have been derived from our episode of shutting down the

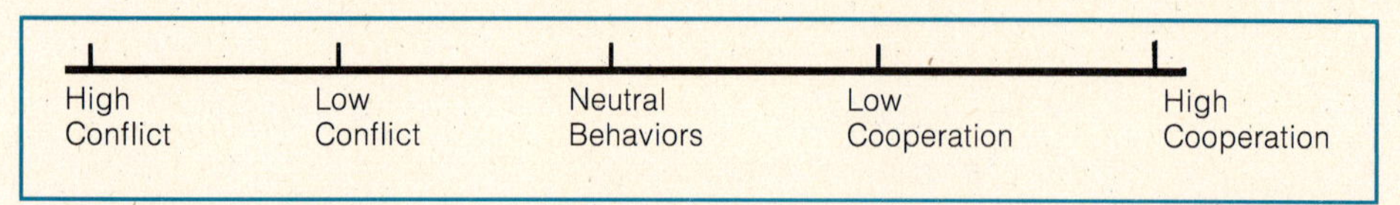

FIGURE 8.2 Conflict and Cooperation as a Continuum in the Case of a Specific Area of Interaction

furnaces before a strike. Our example, above, showed high cooperation; but if we were to present detailed accounts of the various meetings and other occasions for interaction, we might build a significant impression of conflict behaviors within the broader context of cooperating about the furnaces. Thus, in analyzing a situation, it is important to realize whether one is observing behaviors in the aggregate or more narrowly.

Are Competition and Conflict the Same?

Is competition the same as conflict? Although we see the terms as overlapping, conflict connotes both opposing interests or goals and opposing or incompatible behavior (Brown, 1983, pp. 4–9). Competition, on the other hand, may involve considerable commonality of interests or goals, and only a limited amount of opposing behaviors.

An example of conflict would be two executives locked into a kind of combat in which each is intent on the other person being fired. Both their interests and their behaviors are incompatible. An example of competition would be two supervisors working hard to be promoted when the department head retires. In this case, neither will lose the current level of responsibility and reward, and the "loser" may have other desired options open, including promotion into some other unit. Such competition might be relatively friendly. However, if such a situation included a great deal of antagonism, and behaviors were designed to thwart the other person, the situation might more aptly be labeled conflict.

Competition usually has the connotation that there are some basic ground rules and that the parties have willingly entered the contest. Rules govern how far the contest can escalate, and the parties know how much they can win or lose. Conflict, however, frequently has the connotation that there are few or no rules, and one or more of the parties may have been drawn or forced into the contest. The parties have no way of knowing how far the situation can escalate, and the outcomes have potential for being dysfunctional for at least one of the parties and perhaps for the broader system. Competition usually implies that there has been planning by higher authority; for example, top management making policies about promotion, or a sports association developing contest rules and schedules. Conflict, on the other hand, is more spontaneous or emergent and is outside of planned boundaries. (Some of these differences and similarities are summarized in Figure 8.3.)

However, the terms are not mutually exclusive, and any discussion of one

CONFLICT	COMPETITION
Differences	
Incompatibility of goals between the parties.	Considerable compatibility of goals between the parties.
Opposing behaviors.	Some opposing behaviors, some cooperative behaviors.
Few or no rules for the particular situation including limits on escalation.	Basic ground rules have been planned for this particular type of contest, including limits on escalation.
One or both parties may be drawn or forced into the contest.	Parties usually enter the contest willingly.
High probability, at least potentially, of dysfunctional consequences ordinarily assumed for at least one of the parties and the broader system.	Ordinarily, mostly functional outcomes assumed for both parties and the broader system.
Similarities	
Both can result in distortions of perceptions and "we-they" feelings and attitudes.	
Both can have functional and dysfunctional consequences	

FIGURE 8.3 Conflict and Competition: Similarities and Differences

may have applicability to the other. Because both conflict and competition involve opposing behaviors that stem from one or both parties being perceived as trying to take away something of value from the other, the dynamics of conflict and competition are likely to have common elements. Later on in the chapter we will discuss how both circumstances tend to produce distortions in perceptions and *we-they* attitudes and feelings.

FUNCTIONAL AND DYSFUNCTIONAL ASPECTS OF CONFLICT AND COOPERATION

It is implicit in our discussion up to this point that both conflict and cooperation can be functional or dysfunctional. By functionality, we mean the extent to which the behavior serves some specified, desired purpose. But we need to assess *what* the purpose is and *whose* purpose it is.

In an organizational context, there are at least three parties to any situation of conflict or cooperation: there are two immediate parties minimum, with any number of people in the broader system affected directly or indirectly. *Conflict Defused,* the vignette in which expression of opposing ideas was encouraged, showed a situation where the particular mix of conflictive and cooperative behaviors was probably functional for everyone, including the organization. The behavior described would probably result in rewards for all parties concerned.

In the case of two executives trying to undo each other, conflict is likely to be highly dysfunctional for at least one of the parties. In the vignette *I Quit,* the conflict was probably dysfunctional for both Jane Merrill and the organization because of the likely effect on other employees. In other such conflicts the effect is likely to be dysfunctional for both executives plus the organization because of side conflicts that are generated in a turbulent atmosphere. On the other hand, the executive who wins may be so clearly in the right, in terms of what is functional for the organization over the long run, that the only loser is the executive forced out. Obviously, there are degrees of functionality, with some conflict producing short-term adverse effects and some producing negative consequences that can last for years.

The Issue: Managing Conflict

The functionality or dysfunctionality of conflict is largely a consequence of how it is managed. If conflict is suppressed and then comes to the surface in an explosive revolution, it has been managed poorly. Or, if it has been suppressed, with apathy and impaired performance of organizational members the result, it has been poorly managed. If people do not use good interpersonal relations skills in dealing with each other and this results in time-consuming and painful conflicts, then they are managing both their interpersonal behaviors and the emerging conflicts poorly. Conflict is inevitable in human relations: there will always be mistakes; there will always be opposing ideas about how to do things, opposing claims on resources, and different assumptions about motives. There will always be competition to obtain a promotion, to see if *we* can do a better job than *they,* and for budgetary allocations. The issue is how well conflict is managed, not how it can be eliminated.

Functional Aspects of Conflict and Competition

If managed effectively, conflict and competition can serve a number of useful purposes. Conflict and competition are the vehicles for surfacing and resolving disagreements and different points of view. Conflict can help redefine a group's or organization's mission, can help review group norms, and can help test the limits and boundaries of policy or rule (Coser, 1956, pp. 154–157). Some level of conflict can also provide an energizing and vitalizing dimension to organizational life. The excitement of conflict, however, can escalate the situation to the point where the dysfunctional consequences may be outweighing the functional benefits.

Confirmation of both the positive and negative aspects of conflict comes from a survey of practicing managers who reported that they spend about 20 percent of their time dealing with conflict situations (Schmidt, 1974, p. 5).

Some of the positive aspects included:

1. Better ideas were produced.
2. People were forced to search for new approaches.
3. Long-standing problems surfaced and were dealt with.

4. People were forced to clarify their views.
5. The tension stimulated interest and creativity.
6. People had a chance to test their capacities.

Dysfunctional Aspects of Conflict

It is of course obvious that extreme conflict in organizations can have many dysfunctional consequences. We are all aware of the rare but tragic incidents of people having physically harmed or killed each other, of property being destroyed, of feuds going on for a lifetime. Less dramatic, but more prevalent, are the day-to-day consequences of unnecessary conflict in organizations: people being too upset to work; communications between people or groups being withheld or distorted; people resigning or being discharged needlessly; promotions being impeded.

Less obvious are the mental health and stress aspects produced by chronic conflict situations. While stress is inherent in living, excessive stress is harmful (Selye, 1974, p. 19). A great deal of emotional and physical stress can be produced by conflict situations, particularly if the conflict persists over a period of time. Consider the subordinate who has had a loud, name-calling argument with the boss. If the subordinate wants to keep his or her job, receive significant pay increases and other rewards in this setting, the immediate incident is likely to create a great deal of stress as well as impaired work performance, both of which are likely to persist unless the two people find a way to resolve their differences. One dimension of impaired performance might be the inordinate time used in talking about the conflict with others in the organization. (Some of this was going on in the vignette, *I Quit*.) If the conflict persists over a period of time, we might expect any one or more of a range of stress-induced illnesses as well as defensive behaviors to occur. The boss, of course, is also likely to be under considerable stress.

In the survey cited above, executives reported some of the negative outcomes of conflict occurring in their organizations (Schmidt, 1974, p.5):

1. Some people felt defeated and demeaned.
2. Distance between people was increased.
3. A climate of distrust and suspicion developed.
4. People and departments that needed to cooperate looked only after their narrow interests.
5. Resistance—active or passive—developed where teamwork was needed.
6. Some people left because of the turmoil. Clearly, there are widespread dysfunctional aspects of excessive conflict in organizational settings. We will say more about these consequences later in the chapter, when we discuss the roots and the ramifications of conflict.

Dysfunctional Aspects of Cooperation

Cooperation, by definition, has largely positive consequences—at least for the parties involved. Some forms can have negative consequences, however. If

BOX 8.1
THE FUNCTIONS OF CONFLICT

In loosely structured groups and open societies, conflict, which aims at a resolution of tension between antagonists, is likely to have stabilizing and integrative functions for the relationship. By permitting immediate and direct expression of rival claims, such social systems are able to readjust their structures by eliminating the sources of dissatisfaction. The multiple conflicts which they experience may serve to eliminate the causes for dissociation and to re-establish unity. These systems avail themselves, through the toleration and institutionalization of conflict, of an important stabilizing mechanism.

In addition, conflict within a group frequently helps to revitalize existent norms; or it contributes to the emergences of new norms. In this sense, social conflict is a mechanism for adjustment of norms adequate to new conditions. A flexible society benefits from conflict because such behavior, by helping to create and modify norms, assures its continuance under changed conditions. Such a mechanism for readjustment of norms is hardly available to rigid systems: by suppressing conflict, the latter smothers a useful warning signal, thereby maximizing the danger of catastrophic breakdown.

Source: The Functions of Social Conflict, by Lewis A. Coser. © 1956 by The Free Press, a Corporation.

people cooperate (explicitly or implicitly) to suppress different points of view or to suppress feelings, the results can be highly dysfunctional in terms of outcomes. In Chapter 7 we discussed how top officials in the Kennedy administration cooperated in not surfacing disagreement relative to the plan to support the invasion of Cuba by Cuban exiles. This was not just tacit agreement; there is a reported instance of the president's brother, Robert Kennedy, at a party, approaching a member of the policy-making group who had expressed some doubts about the operation, and saying: "The President has made his mind up. Don't push it any further. Now is the time for everyone to help him all they can." (Janis, 1972, p.42). The result was that the group went ahead with the decision without voicing their serious misgivings. What needed to be surfaced was both the substantive content of the problem and the norm that made dissenting taboo. The norm would have had to be examined before attended to. This is precisely what happened later when the same administration was faced with the crisis created when the U.S.S.R. began to move missiles into Cuba. The group surfaced the dysfunctional norm, corrected their processes, and the outcome was positive.

WHAT HAPPENS TO GROUPS IN COMPETITION AND CONFLICT

What happens to competing groups and to the "winners" and "losers"? The dynamics are revelant to competition and conflict both between individuals and between groups.

What Happens During Competition/Conflict

The results of many experiments and observations involving competition between groups are clear as to what happens in typical circumstances. The results of studies of competition between boys' groups (Sherif, 1966; Sherif et al., 1961) have been confirmed numerous times: with for example, managers contending with labor-management conflict in workshop settings (Blake, Shepard, & Mouton, 1964, pp. 19–41) and in experiments involving competition among young women (Sherif, 1966, p. 96).

In general, the following developments can be expected in groups competing for goals that only one group can attain, such as winning a contest or attaining a particularly attractive reward of some kind.

1. *A we-versus-they constellation of attitudes and feelings forms.* Both groups take pride in the groups accomplishments and make favorable evaluations of "our" group in contrast to favorable or less negative evaluations of characteristics of the group.
2. *Each group has distorted perceptions and judgments about the other group.* Favorable information about the other group is either ignored or interpreted in favor of one's own group. The performance of one's own group is overestimated; the performance of the other group is underestimated.
3. *Each group sees the other as the "enemy."* In addition to making disparaging remarks within one's own group about the enemy group, contact with the other group is frowned on and generally avoided. A great deal of energy is used to outwit the enemy.
4. *Group solidarity, cooperation, and morale increase if the odds are not overwhelming.* Groups in competition or conflict become more cohesive and mutual help increases. Morale goes up. However, if one of the groups in competition has grossly inadequate information or resources, members of the group may become discouraged and may refuse to compete. There is likely to be considerable friction within such a group, and members may have considerable difficulty in dividing up the work. Further, for cohesion and solidarity to increase, the external threat or challenge needs to be felt by all the members, and the group must provide emotional support for its members (Sherif, 1966, p. 197).
5. *Negative perceptions and feelings carry over into noncompetitive situations.* When one group is forced by circumstances into association with members of the group in a noncompetitive setting, mistrust and suspicion

are carried over into that new situation. The new situation may become an occasion to attack or berate the other group.

6. *Information is used to erode the position of the other group.* When negotiators or intermediaries are used to communicate between two groups in conflict, information supplied by group members to their representatives is aimed at improving the relative position of one's group rather than at clarifying matters or enhancing communications (Blake, Shepard, & Mouton, 1964, p. 24).
7. *Representatives may become either "heroes" or "traitors."* A representative who is negotiating with the other group and who acquiesces too readily to the position of the other group is branded a traitor. This can mean loss of face or status, being shunned by other members of the group, or even expulsion of the erstwhile representative from the group. Thus, it is much more comfortable to come back with a standoff than to return having lost ground or capitulated to the enemy. A representative who comes back to his or her group with an advantage gained over the other group is a hero. This can mean accolades, warmth, and increased prestige (Blake, Shepard, & Mouton, 1964, p. 28).

What Happens After the Competition/Conflict

In addition to the things that occur while two groups are in conflict, certain consequences regularly occur once the immediate contest is over. The following things happen to the winning group:

1. *The winners celebrate their success.* The winning group tends to be joyful, self-congratulatory, and revel in the glow of victory.
2. *The role of the leader(s) is enhanced.* Leaders are congratulated, their status is enhanced, and group members are even more willing to follow their lead in the future.
3. *The winning group becomes complacent.* Characteristically, the winners bask in their success and do not critique their performance. They do not examine in what respects their performance might improve for future situations. They become "fat and happy" (Blake, Shepard, & Mouton, 1964, p. 29).
4. *The winning group has little empathy for the losers.* The winners typically cannot understand why the defeated group is so defensive and sullen. Further, they cannot understand why the other group takes the matter so seriously (Blake, Shepard, & Mouton, 1964, p. 30).

The following things happen to the losing group:

1. *Gloom settles over the losing group.* The members of the losing group tend to be gloomy, morose, and subdued.
2. *The judges are seen as unfair.* The judges who hand down the decision are frequently perceived by the losing group as biased, unfair, and incompetent, and having no grasp of the problem. They are wrong, not

the group. The winners are now more convinced than ever of their position and the losers grudgingly comply with the decision although they have little commitment to it (Blake, Shepard, & Mouton, 1964, p. 52–54). The same dynamics can occur without a formal judge. For example, in the case of a product that fails to gain market acceptance, wholesalers may be blamed for not doing their job, when in fact, they are doing their jobs properly, or customers may be blamed as being unsophisticated or stupid.

3. *The leader(s) lose in status and influence.* The influence and status of the leader(s) decline dramatically (Blake and Mouton, 1961, pp. 429–430). Feelings may sometimes run so high that the leader or negotiator is deposed or resigns.
4. *Some critique of what happened may occur.* There is some attempt to assess the reasons for defeat, but considerable blaming of the circumstances, of the judges, or of each other can occur.
5. *Recriminations may occur within the losing group.* In the losing group, mutual blaming for the defeat frequently occurs. One person blames another, and other group members support the criticism or defend the person attacked. Recriminations may proliferate for a while, with some disorganization and splintering occurring. Sometimes the splintering leads to group dissolution (Sherif, 1964; Sherif et al., 1961, pp. 106–107).
6. *The losing group has little empathy for the winning group.* They see the celebration of the other group as excessive, and they resent their self-congratulatory behavior.

Thus, a whole syndrome of behaviors results from groups in competition or conflict. Clearly, some of the behaviors are mutually reinforcing and will intensify the conflict if left unchecked. For example, distrust of the other group is likely to produce defensive behavior when the groups are together, even if unwarranted by the specifics of the situation. And deliberate distortion of communications in order to gain an advantage over the other group leads to comparable behavior in return.

Some of these same dynamics occur in situations of interpersonal conflict. There is a breakdown in communications, perceptions are distorted, and ulterior motives are attributed to the other party (Rogers, 1965, p. 13).

What Happens to a Chronically Defeated Group/Person

Some of the consequences of losing listed above come to plague a chronically defeated group. These groups tend to divide into mutually disparaging cliques and isolated persons. There is a good deal of rumor of a gloomy nature, and some of the "good" people leave, with those remaining feeling more insecure than ever. The group becomes rigid in the sense that few risks are taken, innovation is squelched, and what gets done is only what members are certain is wanted by superiors. The sense of defeat leads to inaction or inappropriate behaviors, which in turn lead to a confirmation of the group's low opinion of itself. Reversing this downward cycle usually requires an intervention from outside of the group (Shepard, 1964, pp. 134–135).

Somewhat the same condition is likely to occur in the chronically defeated person: gloom, rigidity, and unwillingness to take risks. These characteristics, in turn, are likely to produce further defeat, reinforcing the person's already low self-esteem. Reversing this cycle often requires counseling or a major change in role or surrounding circumstances.

Summary of Potential Outcomes of Conflict

Figure 8.4 summarizes the potentially functional and dysfunctional outcomes of interpersonal and intergroup conflict. Some of the negative outcomes shown in the second column are obviously a result of prolonged conflict or conflict that has not been managed well. Once again, then, the issue is how well and in how timely a manner conflict is managed: not whether it is inherently good or bad.

As the figure indicates, a number of outcomes are common to both between-individual and between-group situations. The figure also suggests that there seem to be few if any outcomes from interpersonal conflict that do not also occur from intergroup conflict. However, it may be that in intergroup conflict, because of mutual emotional support within each group, there is less stress than in the case of a conflict between two people. Having said that, we should recognize that most if not all interpersonal conflict carries over to other persons. Almost inevitably, the two parties in the conflict situation enlist support from others in one way or another.

ROOTS OF CONFLICT

It is important for us to examine the roots of conflict if we are to gain insight into its management. The roots of conflict can be seen in both the *contextual aspects* of the conflict—the surrounding circumstances and the way events are structured or controlled—and in the *psychosocial processes* of the conflict—the interpersonal, intragroup, and intergroup dynamics involved.

Contextual Factors

A wide range of organizational conditions that are external to individuals and to groups, and over which individuals and groups have little or no control, tend to precipitate or shape conflict. Included in these contextual conditions are such matters as conflict over goals, limitations on resources, ways in which jobs and work flow are structured, specialization and departmentalization, territory and space, status and equity, and reward systems.

Conflict over Goals and Values. Overall organizational goals set by management and with which one or more subordinate units disagree can set off a good deal of conflict in the organization. While this conflict may be a consequence of

POTENTIALLY FUNCTIONAL OUTCOMES	POTENTIALLY DYSFUNCTIONAL OUTCOMES
Interpersonal and Intergroup Conflict	
Surfacing of issues leading to problem solving	Distorted perceptions
Revitalizing or modification of norms can help set limits or boundaries	Distorted communications
Stimulation of interests, excitement	Decreased contact
	Favorable information about the other is suppressed
	Attempts to outwit the other
	Mistrust carries over to other settings
	Emotional upset
	Excessive stress
	Physical ailments
Intergroup Conflict	
Redefinition of mission	Representatives become heroes or traitors depending on gains or losses.
Increased group cohesiveness and morale, if odds are not overwhelming	Group splintering and devisiveness, if odds overwhelming
Status and influence of winners is enhanced, at least in the short range	Status and influence of losing leader declines
	Recriminations and scapegoating occur in losing group
	Both winning and losing groups have little empathy for the other
	A defeatist psychology takes over in the chronically-losing group
	Some of the more valued members of the losing group leave

FIGURE 8.4 Potential Outcomes of Interpersonal and Intergroup Conflict

the process that is used—for example, an autocratic decision—there may be honest disagreement over goals. To illustrate: people in the manufacturing department of a wood products company may be in strong disagreement with a decision to extend company operations into the manufacture of prefabricated cabins and homes. Or, a conflict over goals might ultimately be a conflict over values. The top management of a chemical company might decide to manufacture and market a particular compound that a number of chemists and technicians in the company believe might be damaging to the local environment and therefore ethically wrong to produce.

BOX 8.2

TWO-PERSON DISPUTES

When persons are in serious discord, whether we are speaking of a discordant marital relationship, friction between an employer and an employee, a formal and icy dispute between two diplomats, or tension growing out of some other base, we tend to find certain, very common elements.

1. In such a dispute there is no doubt at all but that I am right and you are wrong. I am on the side of the angels, and you belong with the forces of darkness.
2. There is a breakdown of communication. You do not hear what I say in any understanding way; and I am unwilling and unable to hear what you are really saying. . . .
3. There are distortions in perception. The evidence which is taken in by my senses—your words, your actions, your responses to my words and actions—is trimmed and shaped by my needs to fit the views of you which I already hold. Evidence which is clearly and openly contradictory to my rigidly held views is conveniently ignored or made acceptable by being grossly distorted. Thus, a real gesture toward reconciliation on your part can be perceived by me as only another deceitful trick.
4. Implicit in all this is the element of distrust. While whatever *I* do is obviously done with honorable intent, whatever *you* do is equally obviously done with an underlying evil intent, no matter how sweetly reasonable it may appear on the surface. Hence, from the perspective of each opponent, the whole relationship is shot through with suspicion and mistrust.

I believe I am correct in saying that in any serious two-person dispute, these four elements are invariably present and often make the situation appear hopeless. Yet there are knowledge and skill available which can be applied to such a situation.

If there is to be progress in reducing this kind of tension, we have learned that the first necessity is a facilitative listener—a person who will listen empathically and will understand the attitudes of each disputant.

Source: Reproduced by special permission of *The Journal of Applied Behavioral Science,* "Dealing With Psychological Tension," by Carl R. Rogers, Volume 1, Number 1, p. 13. © 1965, NTL Institute.)

Such conflicts could emerge between individuals, between groups, and between levels of management, and might persist over long periods of time. Some of the conflict might appear in the form of passive resistance or a great deal of behind-the-scenes criticizing.

Scarce Resource. If two people or two groups want the same one thing, whether it is a promotion to a particular position or a higher percentage of next year's budget, the potential for conflict has emerged. In an organization whose profits or sources of revenue are dwindling, the potential for conflict is highly intensified. Conflict might emerge over many areas of organizational life, including budgets, promotions, salaries, work force reductions and the like. As an example, in a company that has recently experienced a large loss, the marketing vice president might order her subordinate managers to cut their staffs so that there would be a "30-percent overall reduction in employees across the marketing department." The likelihood of considerable conflict arising out of this situation is high. A school system faced with declining enrollments is likely to experience increased levels of conflict concerning which schools to close, who is to be laid off, and which programs to cut.

Role Conflict. Conflict associated with roles is a significant source of conflict. A *role* is "a set of activities or expected behaviors" associated with a particular job or position ("office") in an organization (Katz & Kahn, 1978, p. 187). *Role conflict* occurs when two or more other persons expect the person in a particular role to carry out behaviors which turn out to be mutually incompatible. An administrative assistant who has only two hours left in which to finish a complex report for the company president, and who is now summoned to an urgent meeting by a vice president, is caught in a role conflict. The conflict would be felt internally, perhaps with high anxiety, perhaps with frustration or anger, and may or may not be voiced to the superior.

Role conflict frequently occurs in matrix organizational forms in which subordinates may report to both a superior who heads up a particular project and to a manager in charge of a particular function, say engineering or finance. Because of the dual command structure, matrix forms of organization can lead to dysfunctional power struggles if conflict is not properly managed (Davis & Lawrence, 1978, p. 134). Role expectations may also include expectations from one's constituents. In the *Annual Negotiations* vignette, Charlie and Al were representing different groups, one the company and one the union. Both constituent groups may have expected Charlie and Al to drive the hardest bargain possible. We can assume Al was acting under either a mandate from the union members, or at least had their support, in making the threats he made. Charlie was undoubtedly under instructions to keep wage costs within some reasonable bounds and to preserve management's right to manage. In short, role expectations had predisposed the annual negotiations to be a conflict situation.

Wearing two or more hats—that is, fulfilling two or more offices simultaneously—also frequently leads to internal conflict as well as to conflict with others. This kind of interrole conflict can be experienced by academicians who take on administrative responsibilities while retaining major teaching and research responsibilities. Higher administrators and faculty colleagues almost inevitably place incompatible demands on the person in the dual role.

The uncertainty of a job incumbent as to what he or she is supposed to do is called *role ambiguity*. While most people do not want to be supervised closely, at some point role ambiguity begins to create considerable stress and to lower performance (Katz & Kahn, 1978, p. 206). In addition to conflict within the person, the consequence is likely to be conflict with others over who is supposed to do what. Such conflict may be intensified by the feelings of stress and the lowering of job satisfaction that accompany the role ambiguity.

Conflict can also arise because job incumbents are overqualified, or because jobs are too specialized. Considerable research indicates that many people want more autonomy and challenge in their jobs. If people feel unduly constrained in what they are doing, or if the tasks and expectations of others about their tasks are insufficiently challenging, the dissatisfaction may be acted out in various forms of conflict. The converse of being insufficiently challenged is also true; if people are in over their heads in terms of job complexity or work load, conflict may also emerge. Such persons may direct hostility or aggression toward the persons who have higher expectations about the incumbent's performance than are being met. Inner conflict for the role incumbent is also likely, and the person may deflect hostility toward bystanders, such as the family.

Work Flow. The way that the tasks of one person relate to the tasks of others and to physical materials or equipment is a frequent source of conflict. For example, if you are supposed to put the finishing touches on 20 widgets per hour, and the person next to you who is supposed to forward the almost-completed widgets sends only 12 per hour, you are likely to be somewhat agitated, particularly if your wages depend on 20 per hour. You are equally likely to be upset if it's a machine or assembly line impeding your performance. In the vignette *Disconnected,* there were severe work and communication-flow problems that were creating and intensifying conflict between people in the warehouse and the office.

One of the most vivid reports of conflict stemming from work flows comes from the restaurant industry. For decades, a chronic complaint of both the cooks and the waiters and waitresses in the industry was the friction and conflict that surrounded placing the order at the kitchen and picking up the prepared food. Waiters and waitresses would call out several orders with almost incomprehensible speed, and would yell at, and otherwise harass, the kitchen personnel if orders were wrong or late. The cooks and other kitchen help—fatigued, nervous, irritated, and frustrated—responded by yelling back, none of which helped the customer much.

The solution to the problem involved the use of a spindle placed on a high counter separating the waiters and waitresses from the kitchen employees. The customer's order was placed on the spindle, and the cooks read the order rather than trying to respond to oral instructions. Customer orders were then prepared in the sequence in which they were placed on the spindle (Porter, 1962, pp. 58–66).

Specialization and Departmentalization. Illustrations of conflict that stems from division of labor and specialization are not hard to find. Organizations are typically divided into separate departments that have specialized functions and specific departmental goals. Yet, they must also coordinate their actions with other departments. This is frequently a source of conflict. A production supervisor who has ordered parts and supplies from the stockroom and who cannot meet output goals because of apparent tardiness on the part of the stockroom employees is likely to be upset. Finding out that the delays are caused by what he perceives as unnecessary steps in paperwork procedures between the purchasing and receiving departments would probably not help much. Anger, harsh words, or trying to beat the system may result. One way to beat the system would be to have one's own little storeroom to stock up on parts that are chronically slow in arriving, or to "borrow" parts from a neighboring unit when people have left at the end of the shift. The latter, of course, widens the conflict to include other production units and people on different shifts.

Particular kinds of specialization seem to be focal points of conflict. The vice principal of a high school who is assigned to be the school's chief disciplinarian may be perceived by students as stern and unyielding. Members of an internal auditing group in a large federal agency are likely to be viewed with suspicions and annoyance. Firefighters may not wish to take on police responsibilities because of the hostility directed toward the police. Such occupations may be focal points of conflict, not because of the innate characteristics of the incumbents, but because of the specialized tasks assigned to them.

Territory and Personal Space. Although there is not a great deal of research on the consequences of *territorial* invasions within the organization, we can make inferences from related research and experience. People can become attached to corners, chairs, rooms, parking spaces, the area occupied by departments or units, and think of such areas as "mine" or "ours." Some territories are more symbolic, and consist of which kind of customers are to be called on, which strata of business community one can be friendly with, and the like. Thus, territorial claims and expectations can occur even though there may have been no formal assignment of such territory. In an example given in the previous chapter, if the consultant, when working with a police department, had remained in "the major's chair," conflict would surely have ensued. The act of another student sitting in "your" seat in class may be resented even if there is no formal seating arrangement. In the *That's My Territory* vignette, Bill thought Carol might be cutting into his territory (the hospital purchasing association meeting), so he reacted defensively.

Where people meet can also have high symbolic value. If Elaine always meets Ruth in Ruth's office, it may be that Ruth has the power to summon Elaine, or is influential enough to be perceived as having higher status, and therefore Elaine complies when Ruth "suggests" a meeting in her office. If one party

BOX 8.3
TERRITORIAL MOTIVATION

It was Darling's conclusion that motivation for territory is psychological, not physiological, that it arises from two needs in the animal for security and stimulation, and that it is satisfied by the territorial heartland the territorial periphery. I added to that my own speculation that identity is another animal need which territory satisfies, identification with a unique fragment of something larger and more permanent than the animal itself, a place, whether social or geographical, his and his alone. But we were speaking exclusively of animals other than man. Now let me extend the thought.

I suggest that there are three beginnings—three faces of Janus—psychologically motivating the behavior of all higher animals including man. They are these same needs for identity, for stimulation, and for security. How low and how ancient they may be evidenced in the evolutionary scale we have no means as yet to guess. For all we know, they may be the primordial psychological necessities of life itself. Let us restrain ourselves now to the suggestion that they are the inward, frequently conflicting impulses lending both unity to the behavior of higher beings and continuity to the higher evolutionary processes. They provide the final refutation of human uniqueness.

Source: Robert Ardrey, *The Territorial Imperative*. © 1966 by Robert Ardrey. New York: Atheneum Publishers, 1966.

suggests meeting the other on neutral ground (probably not using these words), it is probably a signal that the requesting party wants to meet as an equal. Or if one party refuses to meet on the other person's turf, this is probably signaling that she is ready to challenge the status differential. In the vignette *Get Things in on Time, You Dummy,* Maria started to do battle over whether she or James had more authority, but then Maria decided not to create an impasse over where the meeting was to occur. The conflict was broader than that, however. Implicit in this conflict was how much control the headquarters was to have over a division, and what style of interaction was to occur.

The act of a stranger walking into a work place can create resentment or hostility and performance can be affected. People usually do not like to have "their" work place, "their" department entered by strangers whose motives or mission may be suspect. Visits by top or middle-management executives may be viewed with alarm if the purpose is not clear. Even well-intentioned, friendly, walk-throughs involving chats with production employees may be perceived by supervisors as a threat to their authority or influence. A new employee is also usually looked on with distrust. Assigning a new employee to a work place

without some sort of ritual and introduction is likely to be perceived as an invasion of either physical or psychological territory.

There is considerable research to suggest that space and territorial intrusions do lead to conflict in the organization. For example, experiments over a two-year period in a study hall of a college library found that when people perceived their space to be invaded, they reacted defensively. The seating norms in this particular study hall required that, unless the room was already crowded, a new person coming into the room would sit at a considerable distance from those already there. The experimenter set out to violate these norms. Sometimes the experimenter would sit across from the "victim," sometimes next to the person; in all, five different seating configurations were tried. Typically, defensive behavior of some sort occurred; there were either defensive gestures, changes in posture, a moving away, or sudden departures (Sommer, 1969, pp. 26–27).

People also have different comfort zones in terms of proximity to others. This personal space has been likened to a bubble surrounding a person, a kind of portable territory that the person carries. This space appears to vary depending on the culture. The French, for example, tend to be more comfortable in closer proximity to others than are the English (Sommer, 1969, pp. 26–27).

Status and Equity

In the chapter on group dynamics we discussed how reductions in a person's status tends to be perceived by that person as unjust or unfair. In turn, perceptions of injustice lead to anger. Similarly, when rewards are out of line with the person's investments in the job (see Chapter 13, under "Personnel Policies and Practices"), the consequent perceptions of inequity result in anger and in attempts to bring things back into line. Alterations in status and perceptions of inequity, then, can lead to conflict and aggression within an organization.

Reward and Punishment Systems

The inequitable allocation of rewards can lead to a conflict. To carry this a bit further, the whole system of rewards and punishments in an organization can create unnecessary and dysfunctional conflict. For example, merit systems that give all or most of the monies allocated for pay increases to a few exceptional people or groups may create conflict, particularly if the cost of living is shrinking purchasing power. If jobs are interdependent, and the success of those who receive most or all of the money in the form of merit increases is partly dependent on the cooperation of others, conflict, perhaps sub rosa, is likely to result. In short, if "winning" is rewarded and cooperation is ignored, various spinoffs of the competition are likely to be dysfunctional. Conversely, if low performers receive as many rewards as high performers, conflict is likely to result. High performers will chafe under this perceived inequity and attempt to remedy the situation through direct means (such as complaining or working less) or indirect means (such as working more slowly).

Further, if there is a rampant win-lose, competitive atmosphere in the organization, accompanied by losers being punished by the withholding of rewards or being insulted or berated in front of others, dysfunctional conflict will surely ensue. People who feel unfairly put down will react defensively in some way, either directly or behind the scenes in dysfunctional ways, such as reducing communication with those in power and with those currently in favor.

Functional departmentalization, typical in most organizations, has intrinsic problems relative to rewards. If the sales department is rewarded on the number of orders that sales representatives obtain, with insufficient regard for profit margins or production schedules, conflict is likely to ensue between sales and finance and between sales and manufacturing. Overall expectations and rewards should reinforce balance and cooperation rather than divisiveness.

Psychosocial Processes

So far we have been talking about contextual factors that tend to predispose situations for conflict. We will turn shortly to the intrapersonal, interpersonal, intragroup, and intergroup processes that tend to precipitate conflict: but, first, a definition of terms.

People bring to situations certain predispositions and physical and emotional states. These are termed *intrapersonal processes*. Two people interacting create phenomena, such as a particular mode of listening to each other, that fall in the category of *interpersonal processes*. A group at work creates communications of a different order. Group membership and decision-making complexities beyond those in a two-person situation are known as *intragroup processes*. Two groups interacting create additional dynamics, such as those controlling the extent to which goals are communicated and shared between groups, or those determining the physical location where communciation can best take place across the group boundaries. These last are called *intergroup processes*. The way these processes are managed has a major influence on the extent of dysfunction conflict in an organization.

Inordinate Personal Needs. Unusual needs on the part of one or more persons can contribute to conflict. For example, if one person is particularly greedy, or has extremely high dependency needs, behavior stemming from such needs can provoke hostility or resentment on the part of others.

Fatigue, Excessive Stress, and Illness. Fatigue can contribute to conflict. For many, being tired seems to increase irritability, make tact a chore, and create a disposition toward more aggressive behavior. For example, a fatigued and harassed supervisor, who is ordinarily patient and a good listener, may order a subordinate to "get back on the job until you finish" when the latter has stopped work to ask a question. Inordinate stress is also likely to produce conflict. It is frequently related to time pressures but can also be associated with many personal or organizational problems and crises. Illness can contribute to irritability or inadequate performance, either of which can produce conflict; and excessive stress and fatigue can, of course, precipitate illness.

Disparate and Distorted Perceptions. Differing perceptions about the same thing can lead to conflict. One party's perceptions may be inaccurate; or the perceptions of both parties may be inaccurate. Simply having only a portion of the available facts may distort one's perceptions. Whatever their origin, differing perceptions of the same phenomena can lead to conflict between individuals or groups. As we have indicated earlier, conflict, in turn, results in further distortions in perceptions.

Attitudes, beliefs, or predispositions can distort one's perceptions, and thus lead to conflict. For example, being personally disposed to compete tends to result in perceiving others as wanting to compete (Zander, 1979, p. 440). Errors in one's *perceptions of the intentions* of another party can also lead to conflict or make issues more difficult to resolve. There is some evidence that managers in conflict situations see themselves as much more cooperative than the other principal party involved, and see the other party as having much more competitive an intent (Thomas & Pondy, 1977, pp. 1093–1094).

Leadership Style. The formal leader's style within a group can have a powerful effect on the amount of conflict in that group and how that conflict is managed. For example, some managers may have a one-on-one leadership style, including a tendency to play one subordinate off against the other. Some managers have autocratic, dominating, or demeaning behaviors that tend to produce conflict, whereas the more participative and more supportive approaches usually permit problems to be handled before they become major issues. In the vignette, *I Quit,* Dr. MacKenzie's behavior was seen as autocratic and nonsupportive and culminated in Dr. Merrill resigning to go to work for a competitor. Sometimes called *jungle fighters,* managers who are ruthless and wily in dealing with subordinates, peers, and superiors tend to leave a wide swath of destructive conflict behind them (Maccoby, 1976, pp. 77–78).

A lack or weakness of skills in running meetings can also be a factor in conflict. For example, research has shown that when a leader fails to help a group separate understanding the problem from making proposals for a solution, this is likely to precipitate unnecessary conflict (Maier, 1967, p. 283).

Subordinates tend to emulate or comply with the leadership style of their superiors. Sometimes it is because the subordinate is unconsciously using the supervisor as a role model; the subordinate just assumes that this is the way to behave and, through a kind of osmosis, absorbs the behavior traits of the superior. Or, more overtly, the subordinates simply behave in a way that is consistent with the leadership philosophy expressed by the superior; they comply with the norm. The superior and other managers may give off many signals about what is a "good" way to manage people and what is a "bad" way. For example, male supervisors may pick up signals that aggressiveness is equated with masculinity and behave in unnecessarily autocratic and precipitous ways. Thus, conflict-inducing behaviors on the part of type bosses tend to be reproduced by subordinate bosses, and this style and the resulting countering behaviors may permeate the entire organization. Sometimes managers and dependent subordinates slip

BOX 8.4
THE JUNGLE FIGHTER

In advanced-technology corporations, the jungle fighter may have his triumphs. He may seem to be an effective leader, developing group cohesion by making other parts of the organization appear to be the enemy. But in the long run, he becomes a liability to the company because he foments hostility and undermines the community. Sometimes a talented and brilliant jungle fighter will be brought into a corporation in trouble and given the task of reorganizing the company and getting rid of the "deadwood." The other types—craftsmen, gamesmen, and company men—deeply dislike having to fire anyone, while the jungle fighter takes pride in being feared, but rationalizes this by claiming that such fear stimulates better work. In some companies, especially during periods of recession when they have to cut back, the jungle fighter may rise to a high level, though he is likely eventually to fail in all companies where economic success depends on teamwork.

Too suspicious and sadistic, he is unable to cooperate with strong peers in highly dependent teams. (Can you imagine Bobby Fischer on a basketball team?) The craftsmen feel that he wants to emasculate them and retaliate by withholding information or acting stupid. Those whom he has betrayed, but not destroyed, patiently wait their chance for revenge.

There are two kinds of jungle fighters—the foxes and the lions. Foxes operate by seduction, manipulation, and betrayal. The lions are also wily, but like Charles de Gaulle, they dominate through their superior ideas, courage, and strength; others follow them because they are feared and revered, and they may reward the loyalty of worshipful subordinates.

Source: Michael Maccoby, *The Gamesman,* Simon and Schuster, New York, pp. 77–78. © 1976 by Michael Maccoby. Reprinted by permission of Simon & Schuster, a Division of Gulf & Western Corporation.

into a reality-avoiding, mutually reinforcing pattern that is a *folie à deux,* a kind of shared madness (Kets de Vries, 1979, pp. 125–134).

Group Norms. Customary ways of behaving also have an effect on how much conflict there is in a group and how that conflict is managed. In some groups, a teasing, sarcastic mode of interchange is the norm. As a result, people do not know if a given interaction is showing a liking or masking hostility, and people are constantly on guard in their relationships with each other. Behind the scenes, they accommodate to the teasing and sarcasm by being overly competitive and making sure that someone does not take undue advantage. Trust levels are low and excessive conflict is the result. A norm that says it is all right to disagree can lead to the effective management of conflict. Norms that do not permit

opposing points of view or the expression of attitudes or feelings lead to their suppression, and typically to some dysfunctional form of conflict.

Interpersonal and Group Skills. Group and interpersonal skills are extremely important factors in the amount of conflict that occurs and how well it is managed (see Chapter 7). The absence of such skills tends to lead to dysfunctional conflict, and frequently to conflict that is acted out in indirect ways. A combination of high intelligence, strong drives to achieve and control, and an abrasive personality can create havoc in an organization as the person rises in the organization. Frequently, such people cause so much conflict that they are fired or shelved before they reach the top; although sometimes they get there, if at considerable cost to others around them (Levinson, 1978, pp. 86–94).

APPROACHES TO CONFLICT MANAGEMENT

What can be done to manage conflict in order to minimize negative outcomes and to maximize functional outcomes? The approaches that follow are essentially attempts to modify the variables or factors that seem to be at the roots of various conflict or potential conflict situations. Some have little or no usefulness or may inflame conflict situations, some are useful under certain conditions, others have fairly wide applicability. Some are complementary and can be used together.

Limited Approaches

We will turn first to some approaches that seem *not* to work or seem to have limited utility. All of them have in common either the suppression or avoidance of an underlying problem, or attempts to force the other party into submission.

Ineffective Confrontation. Uninhibited expressions of hostility between two persons or two groups are not likely to improve matters. Name-calling or attempts to belittle the other party tend to escalate the conflict. Thus, confrontation without rules of conduct or without skills in conflict reduction may not be an approach to conflict management at all. It may simply be part of the conflict, or, indeed, an exacerbation of it.

Domination or Suppression. Cutting off disagreement or in some way punishing people for disagreeing or for raising issues seldom works. Suppression tends to result in the conflict emerging in other ways, such as resistance to changes or perpetuation of anger or resentment (Blake & Mouton, 1964, pp. 30–31). If people are explicitly warned that lack of cooperation can result in withholding of rewards, there may be some effect on surface behavior, but the underlying causes of the conflict will remain.

Moralizing and Smoothing. Admonitions about brotherly and sisterly love and cooperation, at least from neutral parties, do not seem to have much effect (Sherif, 1966, p. 86). Lectures from superiors probably serve only to drive conflict underground. Other smoothing tactics, such as trying to talk people out of arguing or raising the matter to such a high level of abstraction that no one can disagree, also tend to leave conflicts unresolved (Blake, & Mouton, 1964, pp. 67–68).

Finding a Common Enemy. If a common enemy emerges, two groups in conflict may temporarily put aside their competing behaviors. Or, finding the common enemy may provide the impetus for the two groups to resolve their differences. This strategy, however, widens the conflict (Sherif, 1966, p. 86). The "war" now includes additional parties.

Capitulation or Appeasement. Simply giving in to the other party may temporarily minimize the conflict. However, this approach is likely to leave residual feelings of resentment toward the other person or group or a decrease in self-esteem on the part of the person or group capitulating. This is, of course, the reciprocal of the domination or suppression mode.

Withdrawing. Avoiding or withdrawing from a conflict situation may sometimes be prudent, but it can also result in problems and issues not being examined and reappearing later. Remaining strictly neutral is a form of avoidance or withdrawal (Blake & Mouton, 1964, p. 93–94).

Compromise. Compromise has the most positive features of these limited approaches. Compromise is frequently useful when the situation is highly political and there is no chance to work through issues in a face-to-face situation. However, it can also result in only superficially solving a problem, with the deeper issues remaining unresolved.

Contextual Approaches with More Utility

Some approaches to conflict management are generally more successful than those listed above. Each, however, has its limitation and may be more applicable to some situations than others. We will make a distinction between *contextual approaches,* which are aimed at altering the surrounding circumstances, and *process approaches,* which are largely aimed at the dynamics between people and groups. These categories, however, are not mutually exclusive, and in some ways the distinction is artificial (Kahn, 1974, pp. 495–498). For example, the introduction of a mediator can be considered a contextual or structural approach because it temporarily restructures the rules of the game, but it is also a process approach, since the mediator seeks to inject more listening and more understanding into the relationship between the parties.

Participative Goal Clarification. Regular, participative attention to the clarification and refinement of goals will not only help keep the organization relevant to the outside world, but will help avoid internal conflict stemming from confusion or disagreement about goals. A participative, interactive process in establishing and refining goals tends to minimize the potential for dysfunctional conflict in three ways: (1) drawing on the knowledge and insights of organizational members tends to make the goals that much more realistic and creative; (2) the participative process gives people a chance to share information and expectations so that perceptions are closer together; and (3) the process builds commitment.

Finding a Superordinate Goal. The emergence of a goal that both individuals or groups want to achieve and cannot attain separately can lead to the defusing of hostility and to cooperative behavior. Major reductions in suspicion do not occur immediately, but as two groups interact in the solution of a common problem, the "enemy" begins to look less and less like an enemy, and positive relationships begin to emerge across the groups (Sherif, 1966, pp. 89–90). An illustration of this approach can be given relative to the problem described previously of the supervisor who was plagued by slow service from the parts department. A higher manager might bring this person together with the stockroom supervisor and with people from accounting and purchasing to diagnose the problem and see what corrective action could be taken. Or, one of the supervisors might take the initiative in calling such a meeting. The superordinate goal becomes that of trying to improve the work flow to avoid frustration on the part of all concerned, thus enhancing both morale and production.

Increasing Resources. Although adding resources is frequently not an option open to managers trying to avoid or solve conflict situations, imagination and ingenuity can sometimes produce additional resources. For example, a manager with a limited budget, faced with the need to provide a significant pay increase for one deputy, but concerned about the impact of this on an equally worthy second deputy, goes to higher management to increase the total budget allocation. Successful in doing this, he avoids a potential dysfunctional conflict situation. Alternately, the manager might refrain from filling a vacancy at the clerical level in order to free up funds for pay increases for the key deputies. Unfortunately, making the pie bigger is not always possible, but it is an option that sometimes has more promise than is evident at first glance. Sometimes nonmonetary rewards—for example, time off to attend a specialized seminar—may help in a particular situation.

Role Clarification. Ongoing attention to clarifying areas of responsibility and expectation that supervisors and others have of a role incumbent will obviously tend to minimize conflict stemming from those sources. In Chapter 16, we will describe a set of techniques for role analysis that is aimed directly at such clarification.

Job Redesign. If organizational members are overqualified for their jobs, enriching jobs by increasing the autonomy and decision-making aspects may head off conflict stemming from these deficiencies. Job enrichment efforts typically aim at increasing the planning and controlling aspects of a job in contrast to the *doing* aspects (Myers, 1970, pp. 55–95).

Communication and Work Flow Rearrangements. An example given earlier of how a restructuring of work flow and physical arrangements can reduce dysfunctional conflict is the use of a spindle placed between the cooks and the waitresses and waiters in the restaurant industry. Another example: Manager A is frequently annoyed because she does not receive copies of the minutes of a particular regular meeting. Her annoyance carries over into other meetings when there are discussions bearing on the topics she has missed; conflict results. The simple procedural change of adding her to the list of those to get copies of the minutes would tend to reduce the conflict.

Group Membership. The composition of a group can reduce or minimize dysfunctional conflict. For example, in the use of task forces to work on problems affecting more than one group, careful assignment of task force members from across the groups involved can be beneficial. Selecting individuals who are not likely to polarize positions unduly through their behaviors can also be a helpful strategy. On the other hand, it is important that diverse views be surfaced.

Organizational Justice. Meticulous attention to matters of fairness and to providing avenues of appeal can do much to avoid a great deal of dysfunctional conflict. For example, careful job analyses and systematic, participative job-evaluation procedures are necessary for wage and salary schedules to be perceived as equitable. Attitudes and procedures that permit questioning and appeals when people believe inequities exist tend to prevent conflict from escalating. We will discuss this more in Chapter 13.

Arbitration and Mediation. Widespread experience in labor relations demonstrates the utility of using arbitrators and mediators in resolving conflicts. Either can be functional under certain circumstances.

The arbitrator's role is usually to hand down a decision that is final and binding on both a company and a union. In the labor relations situation, the assumption is usually made that several steps of a grievance procedure have been exhausted before a matter goes to arbitration, and that most grievances or disputes will be handled between the supervisor and the subordinate, sometimes with the help of a union representative.

Unfortunately, many grievance situations take on the characteristics of two groups in conflict (the company and the union) and a win-lose psychology prevails. Each group tries to win rather than solve a problem. Other dysfunctional consequences of arbitration can be cited. For example, the arbitrator frequently encounters hostility from the losing group, and the losing side may not be committed to carrying out the decision, or may carry out the letter of the decision but not its intended spirit.

The mediator's role is to help the parties explore possible areas for agreement and facilitate the bargaining process until agreement is reached. The mediator's help comes partly from encouraging each group in the dispute to face reality with a little less distortion. The dynamics may also include reducing the hostile interactions through the mechanism of the mediator meeting separately with the two groups. Formal mediation is usually used in labor-management disputes that have escalated to a serious impasse, such as an impending strike or lockout.

Psychosocial Approaches With More Utility

In addition to the contextual approaches above, the following three major psychosocial approaches tend to have considerable utility in conflict management. These approaches not only tend to be useful in avoiding unnecessary conflict, but help minimize the adverse impacts of conflict once it has emerged. All three approaches are based on certain attitudes and skills pertaining to human interaction. To a large extent all three approaches overlap.

Development of Interpersonal/Group Process Skills. In Chapter 7, we discussed the importance of interpersonal and group process skills. If people are highly skilled in checking for meaning, there will be less distortion in communications and perceptions, better understanding, and more effective problem solving. Just taking the time to check to see if one understands what the other person is saying is symbolic of a willingness to listen to the other person and to understand what is being communicated. Other options can also assist in managing conflict. In the *Conflict Defused* vignette, both Karen and Henry were using effective interpersonal and group skills—Henry is using humor in backing away from a strong position, and Karen in bringing Gordon and others into the discussion and in encouraging a look at alternatives. Such behavior helps groups avoid premature closure on solutions.

Feedback skills are also important to the effective management of interpersonal, intragroup, and intergroup conflict. If there is extensive use of evaluative, judgmental feedback, defensiveness and retaliation are likely to be the consequence. For example, if the boss declares you a "crummy worker," you are not likely to respond in a constructive way. On the other hand, if feedback is given in as descriptive a form as possible, in areas about which you have some control, and with the motive of wanting to help, the consequences are more likely to be constructive.

Many people possessing interpersonal and group skills within normal ranges have found group dynamics and communications workshops helpful in further developing these skills. Sometimes external coaching and counseling can assist someone whose abrasive personality is creating too much conflict, and in some instances in-depth counseling may be helpful (Levinson, 1978, p. 92).

Working Through. The mode of conflict resolution that is based on the development of skills in interpersonal and intergroup processes is *working through* or *confrontation* (Blake & Mouton, 1964, pp. 122–125). Their use of the term *confrontation* includes the sense of working through to a satisfactory solution. This approach assumes a commitment to collaborative, participative styles of interaction as well as to skill development, and frequently can result in the most effective and most satisfying solutions to conflict situations. In the working-through mode, the parties to the conflict explore the conflict in some depth, including talking about their feelings about the dilemma in which they find themselves. This mode is particularly important in matrix forms of organizations in which subordinates may report to two superiors. Under those circumstances, it is important that conflicting expectations be worked through frequently.

In a research study that investigated what factors seemed to be associated with effectiveness and ineffectiveness in both manufacturing plants and research laboratories, confrontation (i.e., working through) was found to be the mode of conflict resolution in all of the more successful organizations. In contrast, the predominant mode in the less effective organizations was *forcing*. Forcing was defined as the means by which "individuals try to win their own positions at the expense of the other parties to the conflict" (Lorsch and Morse, 1974, pp. 79–83, 105–107). In short, surfacing issues, dealing with feelings about issues, and working toward solutions satisfactory to all of the parties was consistently more successful than dominating, win-lose approaches.

Participation and Leadership Style. We have already suggested that leadership style looms large in effective conflict management, particularly with respect to process approaches. To the degree that the formal leader is participative in orientation, displays and encourages effective interpersonal and group skills, and is supportive and developmental in contrast to being punitive, conflict will tend to be managed effectively.

Skills in running meetings can be particularly important in avoiding unnecessary conflict and managing small conflicts before they become big ones. For example, a leader can facilitate a group by keeping separate the several phases of a problem-solving process and by helping the group move through them. Such a series might consist of (1) agreeing on the nature of of the problem; (2) agreeing on the goal to be achieved; (3) assessing the obstacles to reaching that goal; and (4) evaluating various solutions. Careful attention to sequencing aids greatly in helping the group avoid drifting toward win-lose positions (Maier, 1967, p. 243).

The leader also plays an important role in relating a group or unit to the external environment. When a leader is perceptive and creative in improving the context in which the group or unit is working, dysfunctional conflict is less likely. For example, finding additional resources, helping find a superordinate goal, and working with others to design more effective communications, work flow, and physical arrangements will tend to minimize and reduce conflict.

Support. Implicit in the above discussion is the importance of goodwill and mutual support for interpersonal, intragroup, and intergroup processes. It is the strong sense of support conveyed between people and within groups that tends to make the confrontation of problems in interpersonal and intergroup processes constructive. Communication given with the intent to injure or to humiliate creates or intensifies conflict.

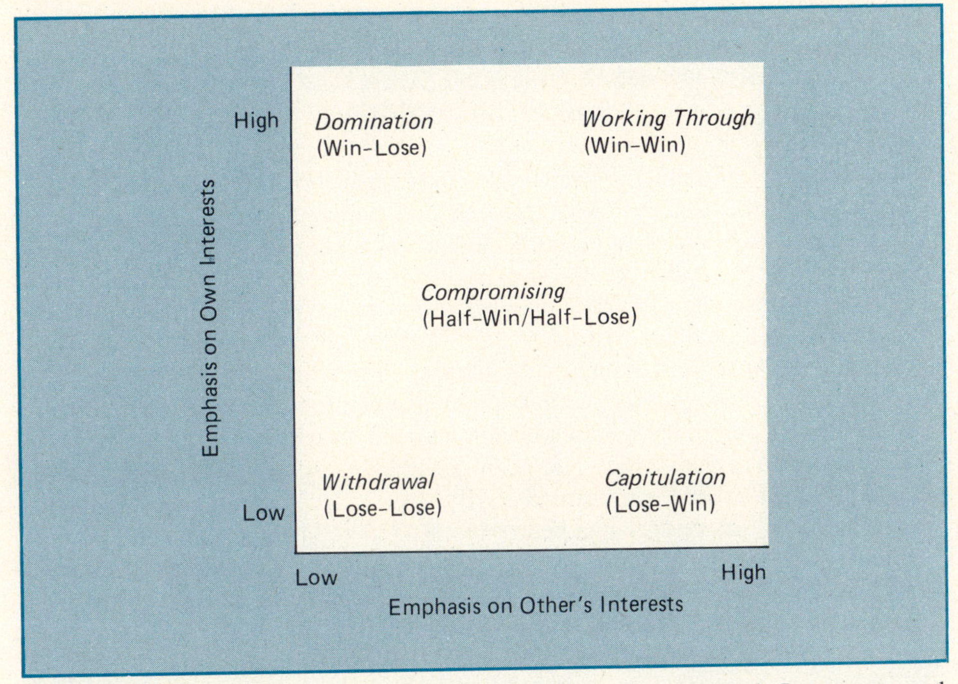

FIGURE 8.5 Five Styles of Conflict Management in Interpersonal, Intragroup, and Intergroup Relationships

A Diagram for Visualizing Modes of Conflict Management

Figure 8.5 plots a few of the process modes of conflict management on a two-dimensional chart. The conceptualization is adapted from Blake & Mouton, 1964; Thomas, 1976; Walton & McKerzie, 1965; Lorsch & Morse, 1974; Cosier & Ruble, 1981; and others. All five modes have been discussed above. The vertical axis represents the extent to which one's style of conflict resolution emphasizes one's own interests in interpersonal, intragroup, and intergroup relationships. The horizontal axis is the extent to which one's style emphasizes the other person's interests.

The domination and capitulation styles are sometimes called win-lose methods, because one person or group wins at the expense of the other. However, if two persons or groups with equal capability are determined to dominate the situation, the result can be a stalemate where, ultimately, both lose. Withdrawal, unless it is only temporary, is a lose-lose strategy, because no one's interests are advanced and no issues or challenges are pursued. Various tradeoff methods, such as compromising, voting, or using an arbitrator, are frequently used where each party gives up something substantial, or at least does not gain as much as if there were a win-win solution. These can be described as compromise, half-

BOX 8.5

CARTER'S CONFLICT MANAGEMENT SESSIONS WITH SADAT AND BEGIN

I have no way of knowing whether President Carter had any psychological advice, but the Camp David sessions had many of the qualities of an intensive group experience, such as I have described, and many of its outcomes were similar. In the first place, it was informal. There was no protocol, no standing on ceremony, no formal attire. The leaders especially, and their staff members to some extent, met simply as persons.

Secondly there were many facilitative efforts. In one tense and angry meeting near the beginning, Carter simply listened to Sadat and Begin. Then at the conclusion of the meeting he summarized, much as a facilitator might have done, the issues which had been raised by each leader. The difference was that he was able to state and clarify these issues in a calm and understanding way, where they had been expressed in highly emotional ways. On another occasion, when the hostility between Sadat and Begin ran too high, Carter acted as a facilitative intermediary, carrying messages back and forth until they were willing to meet again (Dayan, 1981).

Sources: Carl R. Rogers, "Nuclear War: A Personal Response," *APA Monitor 13*(8) (August 1982): 6–7.

lose/half-lose, or half-win/half-win outcomes. Compromise is the best solution under some circumstances. At least some of the residual consequences of a complete loss, including loss of face and hostility toward the winner, may be avoided.

In general, working through as a mode of conflict management tends to be the most functional for all parties concerned because it can produce win-win solutions. However, its success depends on skills in interpersonal, intragroup, and intergroup processes. Its success also depends on the leadership style of the superiors of those in conflict, particularly with respect to their encouragement of this mode. Its success also depends, obviously, on the willingness of the parties to work through problems, and on their commitment to this form of conflict management. We will discuss these confrontational modes of conflict management further in Chapter 16.

SO WHAT? IMPLICATIONS FOR YOU

The way conflict is managed by the people involved is significant for effective individual and organizational performance and for human satisfactions (and health) in the work place. This chapter has implications for you as a member of any group or organization and for you in a managerial/leadership role.

As a Member of the Organization

Generalizations	Implications
1. Conflict is inevitable in human relationships	1. Expect conflict. Look for its positive aspects and how to manage it.
2. Small conflicts sometimes needlessly become large ones.	2. Deal with conflict so that it is not suppressed only to emerge in other ways, and so that little conflicts do not become big ones.
3. Much conflict stems from miscommunications and distortions in perceptions between people and groups.	3. Don't be too quick to fight; empathic listening, checking on meaning, and patience can frequently help find a solution to a problem. Don't stake your career on minor differences.
4. Too much cooperation, such as adhering to "don't rock the boat" norms, can be dysfunctional for the organization.	4. Help create a climate which supports cooperation, but also a climate in which it is O.K. to talk about norms that are dysfunctional. Learn to be perceptive as to how much you can rock the boat without unwittingly damaging your career; mentors can help you with this.
5. Fatigue, stress, and illness can contribute to conflict.	5. Manage your own health and energy levels to avoid overfatigue, stress, and illness; ease up when you sense you are overdoing it; be tolerant of others whose overreactions may stem from physical conditions (e.g., you might suggest postponing a meeting if someone indicates that he or she is under excessive stress, or you might spend some time letting the person talk about the stress).
6. Conflict is frequently a consequence of complex matters in the surrounding conditions and/	6. Don't be quick to write off conflict situations as involving "personality conflicts;" solu-

Generalizations	Implications
or psychosocial processes involving more than one person.	tions may be found in changing contextual or psychosocial processes. Removing people may not remove the roots of the conflict.
7. Role conflict stemming from incompatible expectations and unclear assignments is quite common.	7. Seek clarification when you experience these situations.
8. In competitive situations, winners and losers are inevitable.	8. Learn to be a good winner by having empathy for the loser(s) and by avoiding complacency; when you lose, try to avoid blaming and see what you can learn from your loss.

As a Current or Future Manager

Generalizations	Implications
1. Competition within the organization on some dimensions can be healthy provided it does not create excessive win-lose dynamics.	1. Create reward systems so that everyone can "win" and so that it is in the interests of everyone to cooperate.
2. Persistent, unresolved conflict between two individuals is likely to have numerous dysfunctional consequences in the broader system.	2. Work with the two individuals in reducing the conflict, but also see if there are contextual or leadership aspects that can be improved.
3. Conflict can have roots in incompatible role assignments and role ambiguity.	3. Avoid making incompatible and ambiguous role assignments and help resolve them when they occur.
4. Conflict can emerge as a result of jobs being too constraining.	4. Work with subordinates to create as much autonomy and challenge as each person wants within system constraints. (Be aware that role redesign may have broader implications, including an impact on the compensation system.)

Generalizations	Implications
5. Conflict can emerge from pressures stemming from work flow.	5. Work with subordinates, and perhaps outside experts on improving work flow when frustration or conflict stemming from these areas emerges.
6. People attach personal meaning to many organizational phenomena such as territory, objects, pay, rank, or privileges; unilateral changes can lead to conflict.	6. In planning and making changes, avoid unnecessary and precipitous incursions into territorial and personal space; be aware of the status meanings of objects, space, and conditions.
7. Perceptions of inequity can lead to conflict.	7. Be cognizant of the wide range of phenomena that people see as relevant to being treated fairly or unfairly.
8. Leadership style can have a powerful effect on managing/creating conflict.	8. Decide what leadership style fits you and the situation. However, recognize that domineering, demeaning behaviors precipitate conflict, as do some tactics such as playing one subordinate off against another.
9. The leadership style of the top managers and their consequences tends to be played out down through the organization.	9. Be aware that subordinates may emulate your style, either unconsciously or consciously. They may get caught up in the webs you spin and be forced into dysfunctional conflict situations, or, your style or leadership may set an example for effective conflict management.
10. Failing to help groups separate their understanding of problems from solutions to problems can cause conflict.	10. Help your subordinates and the team in which you are the subordinate; diagnose problems before moving to solutions.
11. Competition with other units can develop the symptoms associated with we-they and winners-losers syndromes. Your	11. When cooperation is more functional than competition, develop relationships with other units that feature empha-

Generalizations	Implications
style, attitude, and communication patterns with other units will have a major effect on whether your unit cooperates effectively with other units or whether a whole syndrome of dysfunctional behaviors emerge. "Defeating" another unit may be self-defeating.	sis on common goals, sharing of information, frequent contact, and mutual problem solving.
12. Various approaches to conflict management have different utilities; some intensify the conflict. Moralizing, finding a common enemy, and ignoring conflict are usually not effective; name calling or other kinds of confrontation without skill intensifies conflict. Arbitration and mediation can be very useful where structure is important in resolving conflict. High group and interpersonal skills in working through issues, and a commitment to this mode of conflict management, has wide applicability for groups and organizations.	12. Select the conflict resolution approach which best fits the situation. Be aware of the alternatives available to you, and do not limit yourself to one approach.

LEARNING APPLICATION ACTIVITIES

1. Write a vignette from your recent experience that illustrates conflict within a group or organization.

2. Analyze the vignette *That's My Territory* in terms of the dynamics of the conflict. What were the causes of the conflict? How is it beginning to affect behavior? What might Bill do to improve the relationship with Carol? What might the marketing department manager do, if anything?

3. Analyze the vignette *Get Things in on Time, You Dummy* in terms of its dynamics and behavior of the various people. What should Maria Perez do in the meeting with James Davidson? Divide into small groups for role playing, with some individuals in each group playing the roles and others acting as observers. Discuss as a total class.

4. *Step 1:* Write a paragraph describing a situation where you felt very competitive.

Step 2: Share these experiences in groups of four to six.
(a) Why you felt very competitive
(b) What were the functional/dysfunctional consequences of this competition?
(c) What could you do differently that would reduce the dysfunctional consequences?

5. *Step 1:* Closely observe several group decision-making situations in which you are involved during a week. Focus on any conflict you observe and how it is handled by the individuals directly involved as well as by the group as a whole.
Step 2: Reflect on the norms that seem to be operating relative to conflict.
Step 3: Share your observations with a subgroup of four to six people from your class. Disguise the identity of the groups you observed and do not identify individuals.

6. In a group of four to six colleagues, discuss leadership style as it relates to managing competition and conflict in organizations. Illustrate functional and dysfunctional leader behavior with specific examples. Report your generalizations and implications to the class.

7. *Step 1:* List two or three examples of within-organization competition you have experienced and note the consequences you have perceived or felt.
Step 2: In a group of four to six colleagues, share your lists and develop some generalizations.
Step 3: Report to the class your generalizations and implications.

8. *Step 1:* (a) Make a list of how you behave when you perceive a situation to be very competitive.
(b) Make a second list of how you behave when you perceive a situation to be very cooperative.
Step 2: Meet in groups of four to six to share your list. Is there any consensus on how you behave in competitive and cooperative situations?

9. Think of a situation of intergroup conflict in which there were winners and losers. List in what ways these groups behaved similarly to the discussion of "What Happens to Groups in Competition and Conflict" and list in what ways their behavior differed. Share your observations in the total class or in subgroups.

10. *Step 1:* Describe a situation where you have faced role conflict (when two or more other persons expected you to behave differently in a role).
Step 2: What did you do and/or what could you have done to minimize this role conflict?

11. *Step 1:* Briefly describe a situation in which you or someone else successfully managed a conflict.
Step 2: Share your examples in groups of four to six. How do these examples fit into the approaches to conflict management discussed in the chapter?

REFERENCES

Ardrey, Robert. *The Territorial Imperative*. New York: Dell, 1966.

Blake, Robert R., Herbert A. Shepard, and Jane S. Mouton. *Managing Intergroup Conflict in Industry*. Houston: Gulf, 1964.

Blake, Robert R., and Jane S. Mouton. "Reactions to Intergroup Competition Under Win-Lose Conditions." *Management Science* 4 (July 1961): 420–435.

Blake, Robert R., and Jane Srygley Mouton. *The Managerial Grid*. Houston: Gulf Publishing Company, 1964.

Brown, L. David. *Managing Conflict at Organizational Interfaces*. Reading, Mass.: Addison-Wesley, 1983.

Coser, Lewis A. *The Function of Social Conflict*. New York: Free Press, 1956.

Cosier, Richard A., and Thomas L. Ruble. "Research on Conflict-Handling Behavior: An Experimental Approach." *Academy of Management Journal* 24 (December 1981): 816–831.

Davis, Stanley M., and Paul R. Lawrence. "Problems of Matrix Organizations." *Harvard Business Review* 56/3 (May-June 1978): 131–142.

Filley, Alan C. *Interpersonal Conflict Resolution*. Glenview, Ill: Scott, Foresman, 1975.

Janis, Irving L. *Victims of Groupthink*. Boston: Houghton Mifflin, 1972.

Kahn, Robert L. "Organizational Development: Some Problems and Proposals." *The Journal of Applied Behavioral Science* 10 (October-November 1974): 485–502.

Katz, Daniel, and Robert L. Kahn. *The Social Psychology of Organizations,* 2nd ed. New York: Wiley, 1978.

Kets de Vries, Manfred F. R. "Managers Can Drive Their Subordinates Mad." *Harvard Business Review* 57/4 (July-August 1979): 125–134.

Levinson, Harry. "The Abrasive Personality." *Harvard Business Review* 56/3 (May-June 1978): 87–94.

Lorsch, Jay W., and John J. Morse. *Organizations and Their Members: A Contingency Approach*. New York: Harper & Row, 1974.

Maccoby, Michael. *The Gamesman*. Bantam Books, 1976.

Maier, Norman R. L. "Assets and Liabilities in Group Problem Solving: The Need for an Integrative Function." *Psychological Review* 74 (July 1967): 239–249.

Myers, M. Scott. *Every Employee and Manager*. New York: McGraw-Hill, 1970.

Porter, Elias H. "The Parable of the Spindle." *Harvard Business Review* 40/3 (May-June 1962): 58–66.

Rogers, Carl R. "Dealing With Psychological Tensions." *Journal of Applied Behavioral Sciences* 1/1 (January-March 1965): 13.

———. "Nuclear War: A Personal Response." *APA Monitor* 13/8 (August 1982): 6–7.

Schmidt, Warren H. "Conflict." *Management Review* 64 (December 1974): 5–10.

Selye, Hans. *The Stress of Life*. Rev. New York: McGraw-Hill, 1970.

Shepard, Herbert A. "Responses to Situations of Competition and Conflict." In Robert L. Kahn and Elise Boulding (eds.), *Power and Conflict in Organizations*. New York: Basic Books, 1964, pp. 134–135.

Sherif, Muzafer. *Group Conflict and Cooperation*. London: Routledge & Kegan Paul, 1966.

Sherif, Muzafer, O. J. Harvey, B. Jack White, William R. Hood, and Carolyn W. Sherif. *Intergroup Conflict and Cooperation: The Robbers Cave Experiment*. Institute of Group Relations, University of Oklahoma, 1961.

Sommer, Robert. *Personal Space: The Behavioral Basis of Design*. Englewood Cliffs, N.J.: Prentice-Hall, 1969.

Thomas, Kenneth. "Conflict and Conflict Management." In Marvin D. Dunnette (Ed.), *Handbook of Industrial and Organizational Psychology*. Skokie, Ill.: Rand McNally, 1976, pp. 889–935.

Thomas, Kenneth, and Louis Pondy. "Toward an 'Intent' Model of Conflict Management Among Principal Parties." *Human Relations* 30 (December 1977): 1089–1102.

Walton, R. E., and McKerzie, R. B. *A Behavioral Theory of Labor Negotiations: An Analysis of a Social Interaction System*. New York: McGraw-Hill, 1965.

Zander, Alvin. "The Psychology of Group Processes." *Annual Review of Psychology* 30 (1979): 417–451.

PART FOUR

EFFECT OF ORGANIZATIONAL FACTORS ON HUMAN BEHAVIOR

Part Four looks at the organizational context of human behavior: the basic characteristics that set the stage for organizational activities and how people and groups interact. Technology, structure, decison making, planning and control, and personnel policies and practices are important determinants of, and constraints on, human behavior in organizations. They give each organization a unique culture and climate.

Chapter 9 is concerned with the impact of the technical system on the behavior of the participants. Organizational technology is the application of knowledge for the achievement of practical purposes. There are various types of technologies, and the fit between technology and organization design affects performance and satisfaction. The chapter describes the relationship between work and satisfaction in different technologies.

Chapter 10 looks at the relationship between organizational structure and behavior. Structure is concerned with the means for integrating, coordinating, and controlling cooperative activities. Structure affects the behavior of people in organizations. It influences their tasks, their relationships with other people, groups, and departments, and is a primary determinant of authority and influence.

Chapter 11 is concerned with decision-making processes. It provides a general model of individual and organizational decision-making processes and discusses their effect on human behavior. It looks specifically at group and organizational decision-making systems and recommends various techniques for improving decision making.

Chapter 12 covers two of the key functions in organizations—planning and control. It discusses a planning process model and various approaches for implementing strategies and plans. The control of human behavior is presented as an important managerial issue. Effective planning and control processes can facilitate the integration of organizational activities across levels and functions.

Chapter 13 discusses how personnel policies and practices can affect relationships between people, as well as individual and group performance. The major personnel processes are described, and detailed consideration is given to staffing, job design, work rules, performance appraisal, compensation and rewards, collective bargaining, and the determination of justice in an organizational setting.

Chapter 14 provides a summary and integration of the concepts in Part Four. It is concerned with the recognition and development of organizational cultures and climates. Organizations differ in their customs and traditions, in what is valued, in the way they operate and in the feeling they convey. These differences in culture and climate have a strong effect on the behavior of human participants in organizations. Ways of describing and measuring the characteristics that determine climate are discussed. Attention is focused on the development of organizational climates that maximize performance as well as human satisfaction.

9
Technology

LEARNING OBJECTIVES

After reading this chapter you should be able to:

1. Understand the concept of technology as the application of knowledge.
2. Appreciate the impact of technology on organizations.
3. Identify various types of technologies.
4. Recognize that the fit between technology and organization design affects performance.
5. Describe the relationship between work and satisfaction in different technologies.
6. Explain and give examples of how social and behavioral technologies are being developed and used in organizations.

THE NEW EXECUTIVE VP: D. COMPUTER

Craig Lewis, controller for Blueridge Manufacturing, dreaded the upcoming meeting with Steven Wilson, president of the company. According to his secretary, Wilson had spent most of last night pecking at his home computer terminal and would be primed with a number of difficult and embarrassing questions. Craig and the other managers were always uptight when Wilson had a long session with the computer.

Over the past six months, the introduction of the so-called "executive information system" had made significant changes in the information flow, power relationships, and general climate of the organization. Wilson now had executive terminals at his office and home hooked into the company's computer system. He had immediate access to a vast quantity of economic, financial, marketing, and personnel data. He had really caught "machine fever" and seemed to be mesmerized by the new system. He was continually analyzing information in a number of ways, challenging existing ideas and assumptions, and testing new concepts. He could tap into information from all of the divisions and functional departments in the company. After a session on the terminal, he would often call subordinates to ask them very specific questions about operations as well as to suggest "what if" type issues. He had access to so much information that the managers spent a great deal of time trying to anticipate his questions. The proliferation of questions was keeping them from getting on with their work.

It was obvious that "knowledge was power" and Wilson was using the new system as a way of extending his influence throughout the organization. Unfortunately, he had changed the long-established information/influence system and was creating havoc among his subordinates. Based on information obtained from his terminal, Wilson would call in lower-level managers to get explanations of problems and issues, by-passing the senior executives. They were often caught in the middle. Maybe the only answer would be for them all to get computer terminals. But with everyone absorbed at their terminals, who would do the managerial work of the company?

With the introduction of the executive information system, Wilson had terminated the Monday morning staff meetings with his key subordinates. Now he only called them in individually as necessary. Craig and the other managers felt that this created many problems for them. The staff meetings had provided them with information about what was happening throughout the company. It was also possible to test new ideas and address issues that were not reflected in the computer output. Craig was very concerned that many important, but less tangible areas, were being neglected, such as management education, maintaining good customer relations, and keeping tabs on newer technological and environmental developments. It almost seemed that Wilson's motto was, "If it isn't in the computer, it's not worth considering."

Craig wondered how he could help Wilson understand some of the adverse consequences of this new technology in addition to seeing the obvious benefits. It was evident that President Wilson had discovered a sophisticated new toy and was thoroughly involved. Craig felt, with a little bitterness, that D. Computer was the new executive V.P. at Blueridge Manufacturing.

THE OPERATING ROOM

Dr. Phyllis Hames had been in the operating room for nearly two hours and the heart surgery was only half done. Fortunately, the patient seemed to be doing very well and the heart-lung machine and other equipment were functioning perfectly. The anaesthetist was monitoring the equipment and watching the patient's vital signs. Dr. Hames had excellent specialists assisting her on the operation and Ms. Jones, the surgical nurse, seemed to be sharp. It was a good surgical team of highly trained specialists and she was fairly confident of the outcome.

She was thankful that the hospital had excellent diagnostic equipment and she knew the staff had really tested and observed the patient extensively before the operations. Everything possible had been done to ensure success, but, then, you never know. Experience had taught her that, even with the best of information and technology, the unexpected could arise and create serious problems. Five years ago, this type of operation would not have been possible; they hadn't developed the knowledge or the equipment. Now, it was relatively routine. Things were moving smoothly so far and, if all continued well, the patient would be up and walking within a week.

THE HANDYMAN

"What is that?" exclaimed Janet Markov as her husband George unloaded a large box from his car trunk. "It's our new Stanley automatic garage door opener." "But, it's all in pieces! Who is going to put it together?" "I am," responded George. "Look, it says right here on the box that anyone with a few simple tools can install this deluxe digital door opener in about four hours." Janet bit her tongue and walked away shaking her head. She knew that George was a great courtroom lawyer, but when it came to fixing things around the house, he was a disaster.

George excitedly opened the box to find the transmitter, receiver, chain, motor, and many other components. He assembled the tools necessary for the operation—hammer, wrenches, drill, and screwdriver. After everything was laid out on the garage floor, George surveyed the mess. "Where do I go from here?" After a moment of panic, he remembered seeing the instruction booklet in the bottom of the box. There it was, 20 pages of detailed, step-by-step instructions. George recognized that the instructions were a crucial part of the project. Containing the information and procedures required to accomplish the job, they were just as important as the components and the tools. George trusted the instructions and believed that if he followed the directions, the garage door opener would work. Fortunately, the Stanley Company had foreseen the possibility that the Georges of the world might be less than perfect in carrying out the instructions; they provided a toll-free factory service number to call in case of difficulties. Someone with the necessary technical knowledge was available to help George out.

A week later, George proudly showed Janet how the opener worked. It had taken him 16 hours and four telephone calls to the factory, but the job was done. "Really nothing to this sophisticated technology. How would you like me to build you a home computer from a kit?"

THE ASSEMBLY LINE

The alarm went off at 5:00 A.M. and Eric Sorenson rolled over to shut it off. Hell, it was another day and a Monday at that. There would be a lot of absenteeism on the assembly line—some fellows just wouldn't make it back after the weekend—and that would make the work more difficult.

The day shift started at 7:00 and Eric would have to fight the traffic to get to the plant on time. He was a spot welder on the body assembly line. The conveyor was set for 45 cars per hour and he had to perform 25 to 30 spot welds, depending on the model. Sometimes he had a devil of a time keeping up. If he got behind he had to move beyond his 15 foot work area into the next station. If things got real bad, the only way to catch up was by doing maybe 20 of the welds and let the rest slip through. No matter how bad things got or how he felt, the damned conveyor just kept going.

Not much chance to socialize on the job. His partner on the other side of the line was Jeff Washington and they got along O.K., but there was so much noise and the cars kept coming so fast that there wasn't much opportunity to talk. If they were lucky the line would break down and they could take a breather. Mondays were usually fouled up and he was counting on some breakdowns.

Eric had worked for the company for 10 years, started right out of high school. It had seemed like a good job then, better pay than anywhere else and he had plenty of money to buy a new car and run around on weekends. But after marriage and the two kids, the pay didn't seem to cover all the expenses.

He had thought about quitting many times. In fact, that's what kept him going on the line—daydreaming a lot about what he might do. He didn't dare look at the clock because it moved so slow. But, during the recession in 1983 he had been laid off for three months. Tried to find another job but nothing came up—everyone in town seemed to be out of work. So, he was relieved when he was called back to his old job.

Joe the foreman seemed O.K., maybe better than most. But, he was under a lot of pressure too and had to keep the line moving. He really wasn't the boss—the conveyor was. He couldn't stop the line except in an emergency. The guys Eric hated were those white-shirted engineers and time-study types. They were always around, seeing if they could bleed the last drop of work out of you.

Eric rolled over. Better get up and face the day. I know I can make it through this week, but how about the next 20 years? Sure, the pension will be good, but I probably won't last long enough to get the benefits.

THE ANNUAL OPERATIONS BUDGET

It was that time of year again, and Mark Cory, assistant controller for the Mercury Electronics Company, was anticipating the anguish of developing the annual operational budget. The capital budget had already been prepared and now it was time to get down to the detailed operations budgets for each of the functional areas and divisions within the company. Although Mark was an accounting major and a CPA, his educational background had not really prepared him for the difficulties involved in preparing the budget and getting it approved.

Even though the company used a participative, bottom-up approach in the budgeting process, there seemed to be substantial resistance from many managers. Some didn't like to fill out the pages of forms. Others were reluctant to sign off on the final budget, not wanting to commit to anything in writing. A few seemed to be playing a power game: Get more of the budgeted resources in order to make things easier during the year.

It didn't help much that various top executives seemed to have quite different views concerning the primary purpose and role of the operations budget. Jake Williams, the president, saw the budgeting process as the primary means for integrated planning. He wanted the budget to be based on accurate forecasts and to be as exact as possible. Budget accuracy was practically a religion with him. The vice president of marketing viewed the budget as a motivational device. He wanted to set the sales budget high enough to push people to improve; "Tough budgets, rarely achieved" was his motto. The production VP looked at the budget as a way to evaluate operating efficiency—always "Did you stay within budgeted costs?" The treasurer saw the budget as a vital part of financial planning and control. Mark's boss, the controller, saw the operations budget as the key management information and control system within the organization that served to integrate all activities. He used the budget as a basis for evaluating the performance of the various managers in the organization.

Mark agreed that the budgetary process did have a role in planning, control, motivation, and evaluation, but it was difficult for him to design a single budgetary system that met all these needs. Each year he had to fight the process through and hope to reach some degree of consensus, or at least acceptance, by all the managers involved in the process. Already he was getting a headache.

INTRODUCTION

On the surface, President Wilson, Dr. Hames, handyman Markov, welder Sorenson, and controller Cory do not seem to have much in common. They are employed by different organizations and the nature of their work is dissimilar. They may have similar human needs and motivations, but the organizational climates in which they work are very different in providing opportunities for satisfying these needs. They do have one major thing in common, however—they are all interacting with technology. To be sure, these technologies are different, but there is still a human/technological relationship.

President Steve Wilson is using an advanced technology, a computerized executive information system, to aid in the management of Blueridge Manufacturing. It is evident that this new technology offers opportunities for more effect information processing and dissemination, but it is also creating many adverse effects on the information flow, the quality of interpersonal relationships, and the general climate. This new technology significantly influences many other aspects of the company.

Dr. Hames is working in a sophisticated technological environment. The hospital facilities, operating room, diagnostic, and monitoring equipment are all part of the physical technology. However, the sophisticated knowledge that she and other specialists are using is even more important.

George Markov, in assembling the garage door opener, was very dependent on a key part of technology—the instructions. They represented the vital knowledge component.

Eric Sorenson's work life is dominated by the machine technology of the assembly line. His tasks are highly specialized and routine and he has limited opportunity to apply any expertise on his own. In effect, he has to make a personal adjustment to the technology of the assembly line.

In developing the annual operations budget, Mark Cory was dealing with a complex organizational technology. He not only was dealing with accounting techniques but was directly involved in human issues: perceptions, values and goals, motivations. Success in the budgetary processes depended upon dealing effectively with the technical and social aspects of the problem. Accounting and budgeting processes, market research techniques, and personnel selection and training procedures all represent organizational technology: the application of knowledge to achieve practical purposes.

As people in a modern industrial society we are all strongly influenced by our technologies. The automobiles we drive, the homes we live in, the schools we attend, and the organizations we work in all have human-technology interfaces. In this chapter we will look more specifically at the effect of technology on the behavior of people via the following topics:

The Concept of Technology
Technological Change
Organizations as Creators and Appliers of Technology
A Variety of Technologies

THE CONCEPT OF TECHNOLOGY

We are increasingly aware of the impact of science and technology on society and on individual lives. In the past, they have been viewed solely as the means for improving human existence: for providing the means for more effective human control over the natural, physical, and social environment. More recently, some people have come to question this view and to wonder whether all aspects of science and technology have really resulted in a better world. Conflicting values and attitudes surround, and sometimes confuse, the issue. In the authors' view, there is the need for continuing technological advancements but there is an accompanying need to strive for more effective social control in order to ensure that these changes really are improvements.

The term *technology* and *technological change* have many meanings, both broad and specific. In the narrowest view, these terms are associated with *machine technology,* the mechanization of the means for producing goods and services (substituting mechanical for human effort). This mechanistic definition emphasizes such visible manifestations of technology as nuclear reactors, assembly lines, electronic computers, transportation systems, and the vast complex of facilities and equipment necessary for developing a space shuttle system. The explicit emphasis on physical artifacts is understandable, because the machine is the most obvious physical manifestation of technology. From the anthropological approach, the history of technology is often associated with human use of primitive weapons and tools. The ability to use these instruments was a major characteristic distinguishing man from lower animals. However, it is an oversimplification to associate the advancement of technology with the history of tools and machines. Machines are merely some of the artifacts of technology.

Technology as Application of Knowledge

In the most general sense, technology refers to the application of knowledge for more effective performance of certain tasks or activities. Technology is far more than the machine and refers to the application of knowledge to attain a predetermined objective or result. Technology converts spontaneous and unreflective behavior into behavior that is deliberate and rationalized. Jacques Ellul (1964) lends a broad connotation to technology or, as he calls it, technique. ''In our technological society, *technique is the totality of methods rationally arrived at and having absolute efficiency* (for a given stage of development) in *every* field of human activity'' p. xxv). He suggests that technology has come to dominate every field and is geared to the achievement of efficiency and rationality in all human endeavors. In accord with Ellul's approach to the concept, we define technology in the following way:

> Technology is the organization and application of knowledge for the achievement of practical purposes. It includes physical manifestations such as tools and machines, but also intellectual techniques and processes used in solving problems and obtaining desired outcomes.

In this sense, computer hardware represents one aspect of technology, but software programs are equally important. The machines on the assembly line represent technology; but so do the planning, scheduling, and control procedures. Accounting and budgeting processes, market research surveys, and personnel selection and training procedures all represent technology—the application of knowledge to achieve practical purposes.

It is useful to think of *organizational technology* in a more specific sense. By organizational technology we mean the techniques used in the transformation of inputs into outputs. Organizations receive inputs, they do something to these inputs, and return outputs to the society. In accomplishing this transformation task, for example, the industrial concern utilizes both machines and other specialized technologies. The accountant may employ the computer in performing a task, but he also needs knowledge of accounting procedures. Dr. Hames needed an array of highly specialized equipment in the operating room; but, equally important, she utilized the specialized knowledge of the entire surgical team.

Concept Applicable to All Organizations

The concept of organization technology as those techniques that are used in the transformation of inputs into outputs is applicable to all organizations. It is simple to understand in a physical transformation process such as an assembly line. But it is also appropriate for other organizations, such as a hospital or university. The hospital receives human inputs (patients), utilizes technologies to help transform them in some way (physically or mentally). The university receives inputs of students, provides the appropriate climate to help transform them through some process of educational technology, and then returns them to the broader society. The view of organizational technology is illustrated in Figure 9.1.

TECHNOLOGICAL CHANGE

Science and technology have become pervasive forces in modern society and have had a profound effect on our culture. The early industrial revolution was based primarily on the replacement of human energy with mechanical energy. During the twentieth century, mass-production and assembly-line techniques have combined tools, machinery, and processes into integrated operations. Automation is an extension of the process of integrating the mechanical means of production. It also involves information feedback systems that replace human decision making

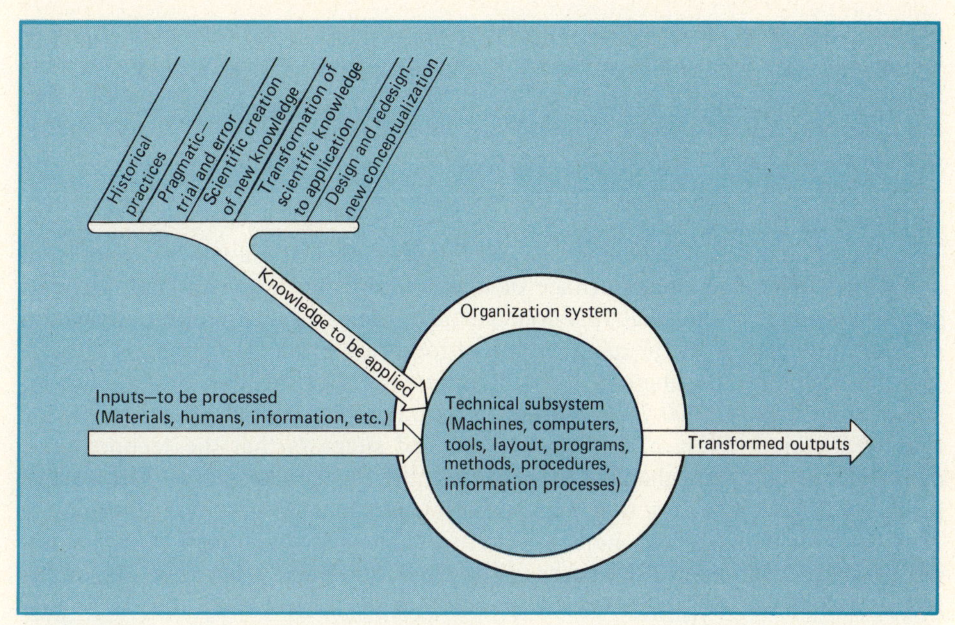

FIGURE 9.1 A View of Organizational Technology. **Source:** Fremont E. Kast and James E. Rosenzweig, *Organization and Management: A Systems and Contingency Approach,* 3d ed. (New York: McGraw-Hill, 1979), p. 178. © 1979. Reproduced with permission.

in the control phase. Computer technology has facilitated the automation of both material and information flow. Robots are being used to perform an increasing number of functions in factories and offices. Together science and technology are providing a new shape to the world. They have brought about a widening discontinuity with the past. "Science and Technology have given our age more of its unique characteristic and coloring than they have any other age. They have done so by altering nearly all the basic components which make up the life of modern man, and altering them in important ways" (Walker, 1968, p. 9).

The pace of technological change is accelerating. The typical time between a technical discovery and recognition of its commercial usefulness and application has decreased from 30 years at the beginning of the century to less than 10 years. Scientific and technological changes are more rapidly diffused through the economy, as exemplified by the development and utilization of new generations of computers. Transistor radios and pocket calculators were developed, produced, and distributed worldwide over a short time period. The quartz crystal watch has revolutionized a traditional industry.

Certainly the changes brought about by science and technology are not limited to the United States and other industrialized countries. Many of the developing and semi-industrialized countries of the world are gearing their national policies toward increasing industrialization and technical development. One of the manifestations of this is a convergence of sociocultural systems. For example, there is an emphasis on education. A basic requirement of modern technology is a high level of literacy and specialized training. The effective utilization of technology requires the development of complex organizations that are quite similar, in spite of different cultures, economic systems, and political ideologies.

But Don't Forget the Past

We should not overemphasize the accelerating technology of the present and forget the tremendous heritage of knowledge from the past. The invention and development of language, the domestication of animals, agriculture, irrigation systems, and processes for preservation of foods are products of past technological development (Darlington, 1969). The invention of writing by someone or some group "some 5,000 years ago set mankind on the road we are still traveling today" (Leikind, 1971, p. 9). Lewis Mumford suggests that the technological development of the mechanical clock during the thirteenth century had a more profound effect on society than any other development (Mumford, 1934, pp. 12–18). The clock regimented human activities, disassociating them from natural biological and sociological processes. The clock determines when we eat, sleep, go to classes, and work. It provides the basic means for the integration of human activities and is a measuring device for them: output per work hour (productivity); the four-minute mile; the minutes we have available for our computer program; and the 55 mph we drive on freeways.

We have come to underestimate these vital technological developments from the past because they are so commonplace. But they have had a profound effect on the ways in which our societies and cultures have developed.

Conflicting Attitudes Toward Technology

For much of our history, we have had positive attitudes toward technology. It was the primary means by which we could minimize human toil, increase productivity, and have a better quality of life. More recently, we have begun to question this assumption and have stressed the negative side of technological "improvements." Many suggest that technology has become an end in itself, and, unabated, it will ultimately drive out humanistic and social considerations. It will dominate and control humankind and reduce us to victims of the machine.

Some people have advocated a return to a less sophisticated technological society. However, this could have many adverse consequences. In our view, a dismantling of technology and a return to the past is neither likely, feasible, nor desirable. Science and technology will continue to be primary forces for change. Technology can be controlled, but not without some fundamental changes in values and goals. We agree with Mesthene (1970, p. 34), who suggests that advancing technology should not be viewed as an "unalloyed blessing for man and society" or an "unmitigated curse."

Technology is created by people and it can be controlled by them. In the past, Americans have emphasized the economic advantages of technology. In the future, we will develop a greater understanding of the environmental, sociologi-

cal, and psychological consequences of technological changes. We agree with Bell (1973, pp. 165–265) who suggests that the post-industrial society will increasingly be based on the utilization of knowledge. This knowledge will be used not only to create new technology but also to utilize and control it for greater social benefit.

ORGANIZATIONS AS CREATORS AND APPLIERS OF TECHNOLOGY

A phenomenon of modern industrial society is the development of large-scale, complex organizations for the accomplishment of specific purposes. This development is closely related to technological change. "Technical progress and organizational development are aspects of one and the same trend in human affairs" (Burns & Stalker, 1961, pp. 19–20).

It is difficult to determine which comes first—the social structure or the technology. Some would argue that developments in social structure are a necessary prerequisite to advancing science and technology. Others suggest that developments in technology create the necessity for new social organizations. Most likely, they are codeterminant forces. It is obvious that individuals and informal groups alone cannot accomplish certain results. "Large-scale organizations have evolved to achieve goals which are beyond the capacities of the individual or the small group. They make possible the application of many and diverse skills and resources to complex systems of producing goods and services. Large-scale organizations, therefore, are particularly adapted to complicated *technologies,* that is to those sets of man-machine activities which together produce a desired good or service" (Thompson & Bates, 1957, p. 325). Organizations have become the primary creators and users of technology. They are, in effect, the social mechanism for the utilization of knowledge.

In the economic sector, corporations are the means for the creation and utilization of industrial technology. They are the vehicle for combining large amounts of capital, extensive mechanization, and comprehensive planning that advanced technology requires. By adapting to and utilizing new technology, the corporation has developed means for growth and diversification, and expanded its role in society. This movement toward technological virtuosity has been implemented by the increasing number of scientists, professionals, and technical personnel who are aggressively seeking outlets for their creativity.

Other types of organizations are also involved in this process. Large hospitals, with treatment, research, and training functions, are engaged in utilization and creation of advanced technologies. Universities are geared to the two major functions of transmission of knowledge (teaching) and the creation of knowledge (research). The National Aeronautics and Space Administration has engaged in many advanced programs that have severely taxed our technical skills.

Organizations as an Example of Social Technology

In a broad sense, the development of large-scale organization represents an advancement in social technology. The ability to bring together the material, human, and information resources necessary to accomplish complex tasks is a major achievement. The development of appropriate structures and information systems, integrated planning and control processes, and programs for more effective selection, training, development, and motivation of human participants is part of this social technology.

Organizations of the type that we have today were not possible at the beginning of the twentieth century. The social structure would not have been able to support our modern institutions (Stinchcombe, 1965). This is readily apparent today. It is impossible to transplant the physical manifestations of technology (plant and equipment) to a developing country without first developing the requisite social technologies of organization and management. And in many cases the social structure of these developing countries is not capable of providing them. They, too, have to be imported (in the form of managers, specialists, information, etc.). Frequently, these advanced organizational forms conflict with many of the cultural values and social structures of the developing country.

It is obvious that knowledge about how to organize and manage complex systems is as much a social technology as engineering and design of plant and equipment are a physical technology. Both are manifestations of technology—the rational utilization of knowledge to accomplish human purposes.

A VARIETY OF TECHNOLOGIES

The broad definition of organizational technology as the knowledge, equipment, skills, and techniques used in transforming inputs into outputs implies that many technologies can be utilized by organizations. It would be desirable to have some classification scheme or typology that would array this wide variety of technologies into broad categories. We could then test the central hypothesis set forth by Thompson (1967, p. 1): "Those organizations with similar technological and environmental problems should exhibit similar behavior; patterns should appear." Unfortunately, a classification scheme appropriate for all types of organizational technologies has not been developed.

Joan Woodward (1965) developed a classification scheme based on chronological development of industrial technology and increased complexity. Basically, this is a three-fold classification: (1) unit and small-batch production such as custom furniture and special purpose equipment; (2) large-batch and mass production such as a large commercial bakery and automobile assembly line; and (3) continuous-process industries such as manufacturing of chemicals and oil refining.

This classification scheme is appropriate for looking at manufacturing processes and has been used by a number of researchers. This scheme tends to emphasize the observable machine and layout production technology and does not give sufficient recognition to knowledge technology. While the Woodward model is an appropriate classification in some circumstances, it does not appear to be sufficiently broad to cover all types of technologies such as those used in hospitals, universities, and service industries.

Classification Based on Complexities and Dynamics

In considering organizational technologies there appear to be two major issues: (1) the degree of complexity of the technology; and (2) whether the technology is stable or dynamic. We have used these two dimensions to suggest a continuum ranging from a stable and relatively simple technology, such as basic person-tool, to a dynamic and complex technology (see Figure 9.2). Others have utilized similar classifications (Perrow, 1967; Lynch, 1974; and Withey, Daft, & Cooper, 1983).

There are a number of possible combinations along this continuum. At the lower left is the organization that uses simple and uniform person-tool technology. At the other extreme is the organization that has a dynamic and complex knowledge-based technology, such as an aerospace company, a graduate program in a university, or a research and development laboratory. Obviously, within any complex organization, there may be different departments that are at various positions along this continuum. In a hospital, for example, many custodial functions are based on uniform procedures and stable technology. However, at the other end of the spectrum, the hospital research activities and the diagnosis and treatment of many patients involve dynamic and nonuniform technologies.

Although the illustration in Figure 9.2 suggests industrial examples, this view of a technological continuum can be used for describing all types of organizations. Perrow, for example, has used a similar model to investigate the impact of technical systems in general hospitals, mental institutions, correctional institutions and large corporations (Perrow, 1970). We will use this model to consider the impact of these various types of technologies upon organizations and their members.

TECHNOLOGY AND ORGANIZATIONAL STRUCTURE

Technology has received increasing attention in the study of organizations. In general, technology was neglected by traditional management theorists and early human relationists alike. But it is increasingly recognized that the nature of the

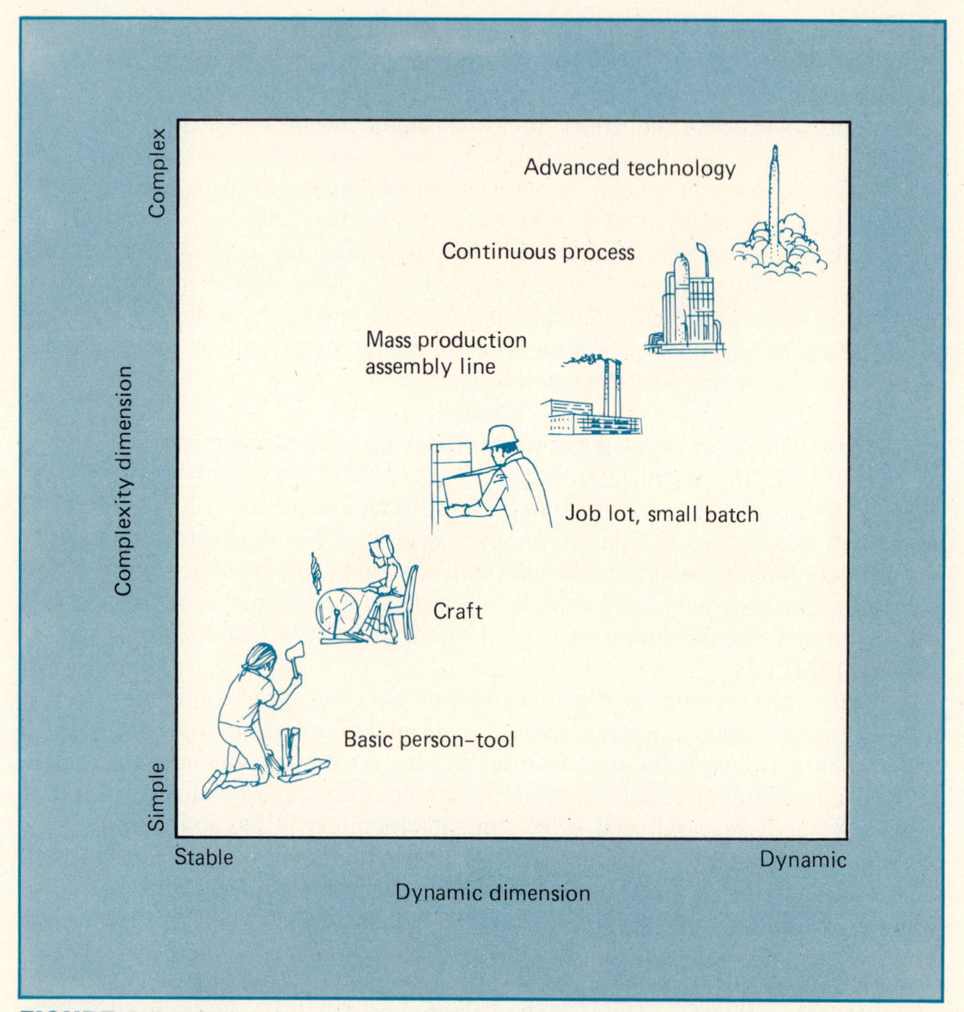

FIGURE 9.2 Different Types of Technology. **Source:** Fremont E. Kast and James E. Rosenzweig, *Organization and Management: A Systems and Contingency Approach,* 3d ed. (New York: McGraw-Hill, 1979), p. 184. © 1979. Reproduced with permission.

technology can have a major effect upon the goals and values, structural characteristics, managerial processes, and human relationships in the organization. In this section, we will consider its impact on goals, structure, processes, and management. In the following two sections we will look in more detail at its effect upon people.

The technical system is directly related to the environmental suprasystem. As a subsystem of the society in which it exists, the organization utilizes the available technical knowledge in its transformational processes. However, new technology is also created by organizations and is made available as an output to society.

The nature of the technical system also has an important relationship to the goals and values of the organization. The value of striving for *technical rationality* is apparent in most organizations. The very goals that the organization attempts to accomplish are frequently determined by the available technology. We could not adopt a goal of transformation from hydroelectric and fossil fuel generation of electrical energy to nuclear power generation without having the available technology. At the operating level in the organization, technology is one of the prime forces in determining specific goals and the means for their accomplishment.

There have been many studies of the relationships between technology and organizational structure (Fry, 1982). One of the most important was Joan Woodward's extensive research in 100 industrial firms in Great Britain. She classified these firms along the continuum discussed previously, unit or small-batch, large-batch and mass production, and continuous processes. She found a direct relationship between technology and structure. The study also found a close relationship between successful performance and the organizational structure of companies within each industry. This finding is of key importance; there tended to be an appropriate structure for each type of technology. "The fact that organizational characteristics, technology, and success were linked together in this way suggested that not only was the system of production an important variable in the determination of organizational structure, but also that one particular form of organization was most appropriate to each system of production" (Woodward, 1965, pp. 69–70). A replication of the Woodward study by Zwerman (1970) in the United States using 56 firms in the Minneapolis area generally corroborated her findings.

A later series of studies carried out by the Industrial Administration Research Unit of the University of Aston in England provided additional information concerning the impact of the technical system. They classified technology into three components: *operations technology* includes the techniques used in the work flow activities; *materials technology* refers to the nature of the materials used in the transformation process; *knowledge technology* refers to the characteristics of the knowledge used in the organization.

The Aston group found that the effect of operations technology upon structural variables was most apparent on the production line, but it did not have significant impact upon higher levels in the organization (Hickson, Pugh, & Pheysey, 1969). In their view, the size of the organization had more of an effect upon the overall structure than did the technology. However, this study considered only operations technology and did not include materials and knowledge technology. It is likely that these two components of technology would have an effect on structure at all levels.

Other research studies have attempted to understand the differences in concepts and findings between the Woodward studies and those at Aston (Aldrich, 1972; Child & Mansfield, 1972). It is apparent that at least a good part of the disagreement stems from problems associated with the definition and measurement of all the technological and structural variables.

Technology and the Managerial System

In many ways, the impact of technology on the managerial system of planning, coordinating, and controlling has been even more dramatic than on the other organizational subsystems. We marvel at the obvious technological advancement required to develop a manned space station. However, the managerial skills required to plan for and integrate all the diverse activities for successful mission accomplishment are equally important.

One of the major consequences of changing technology has been the increasing specialization of knowledge. The managerial system in most organizations includes many participants with specialized skills and training: operations researchers, personnel specialists, research and development engineers, communications experts, planning experts, environmental specialists, and many others. The modern managerial system is composed of a complex team of trained specialists who are contributing their technical knowledge.

Many research studies have considered the effects of changing technology on managerial systems. One of the more comprehensive was conducted by Burns and Stalker (1961) in their investigation of English and Scottish firms. They examined a number of firms with a stable technology and environment that were attempting to move into the electronics field with a rapidly changing technology. "We hoped to be able to observe how management systems changed in accordance with changes in the technical and commercial tasks of the firm, especially the substantial changes in the rate of technical advance which new interests in electronic development and application would mean" (p. 4). It was their hypothesis, substantiated by the research findings, that a different managerial system was appropriate for concerns involved in a stable technology and environment as compared with those adapting to rapidly changing technology.

Managerial systems adapted to a stable technology were termed *mechanistic*. Such a system was characterized as having a rigidly prescribed structure. By contrast, *organic* managerial systems are best adapted to conditions of rapidly changing technology and environment. It has a more flexible structure and dynamic managerial process.

Burns and Stalker also emphasized the difficulties involved in making the transition from the mechanistic to the organic system by firms that were trying to move into the electronics industry. The unstructured and highly dynamic nature of the organic system often created anxiety and insecurity on the part of the managers who had been used to working in the structured, mechanistic system.

The Fit Between Technology and Organization

We have briefly reviewed a few of the many research studies concerning the relationship between the technical system and the goals and values, structure, and managerial processes in organizations. Because of the newness of this line of research and the problems of clear definition of the technological and other variables, the exact nature of these interrelationships is still not known. However, based on the existing knowledge in this field we will venture the following generalizations:

The *bureaucratic-mechanistic* organization form is more appropriate where:

1. The environment is relatively stable and certain.
2. The goals are well defined and stable.
3. There are routine activities where productivity is the major objective.
4. The technology is relatively uniform, stable, and routine.
5. Decision making is relatively certain and routine.
6. Coordination and control processes tend to make a tightly structured, hierarchical system possible.

The *adaptive-organic* organizational form is more appropriate where:

1. The environment is relatively uncertain and turbulent.
2. The goals are diverse and changing.
3. The technology is complex and dynamic.
4. There are many nonroutine activities where creativity and innovation are important.
5. Judgmental decision-making processes are utilized.
6. Coordination and control occurs through reciprocal adjustments. The system is less hierarchical and more flexible.

IMPACT OF TECHNOLOGY ON PEOPLE IN ORGANIZATIONS

The effect of technology on the human participants in organizations has been implied in the previous discussion. Technology has both direct and indirect effects on people via its influence on goals and values, structure, and managerial processes. For example, the introduction of new, mechanized equipment into a factory, or of a computerized information processing system into the office, will generally require major changes in the structuring of activities, planning and control processes, and coordination of tasks. These, in turn, influence employees.

Traditional management theory gave little consideration to the ways in which technology affected people. The technical system was considered given and invariable, and the assumption was made that the people would adapt. Fortunately, human beings are adaptable and have responded to rapidly changing technologies. Technological progress in organizations over the past century has required major adjustments on the part of social systems. The techniques of bureaucracy, scientific management, and mass production required fundamental changes. The newer innovations of automation and computerized information systems are currently having significant effects; yet little consideration has been given to the relationship between these technologies and the people in the organization.

> Our industrial production layouts are built to utilize the production technique, the machine's characteristics, and the material's qualities to the utmost. The operator is considered the dependent variable. He is expected to (and fortunately does) bend and adjust. It is interesting to spec-

> ulate on what might happen if we were to build a production line designed to maximize the human resources and motivations of the operators, and then consider the machines as dependent variables which must be built to conform to the requirements of a system designed to maximize the human's potentialities (Haire, 1964, pp. 6–7).

This was written a number of years ago. Later, we will discuss several examples of where Haire's speculation has come true; where technologies are being modified to fit humans. But, these instances remain the rare exception.

Technology affects people in organizations in many ways. It is influential in setting the specific design of each employee's task: from the variety of activities performed and the modes of interaction with others to the amount of discretion and autonomy allowed. It is a key determinant of the general climate of the workplace. A trip through a lumber mill, tire factory, clothing factory, or computer service center readily suggests how the technology has influenced all aspects of the work situation.

Technology affects the network of social relationship among workers. It often determines the size and composition of the immediate work group and the frequency and range of contacts with fellow workers and supervisors. Employees working for eight hours each day on an isolated machine have very different social interactions from the repair team that moves throughout the plant. Technology frequently proscribes the extent of physical mobility. It affects the various roles and status positions of people in organizations: generally the possession of higher technical skills meaning more status, pay, and other rewards. The engineer and systems analyst are paid more and have higher-level positions than machine operators and workers on the assembly line.

Technology, particularly in assembly-line operations imposes a time dimension on workers. It requires punctuality in being there to start the process and requires a steady work pace. Technology can have a major effect on almost every dimension of the workers' activities. However, it doesn't stop there, but carries over to off-the-job life. The technology of the automobile plant (*Assembly Line* vignette) affects Eric Sorenson's life in many ways.

The importance of technology is frequently highlighted during periods of change. Technology changes may create job insecurities and anxieties. Skills developed over a long period may become outmoded, vitally affecting the self-image and motivation of the worker. The skilled linotype operator in the printing plant may face major changes with the introduction of computerized equipment. The secretary with the standard electric typewriter will have to learn many new skills to operate new word-processing equipment. The high degree of specialization required in many mass-production operations may reduce the worker's task to one of great simplicity. Increased specialization of production leads to a greater need for predictability of work behavior, and therefore to increased discipline in the work place.

We frequently underestimate or fail to perceive the effect of the technical system on people. With stable operations, the interaction often goes unnoticed.

BOX 9.1
TECHNOLOGY AND WORK SYSTEMS

The industrial era began with the catalytic discovery that machines are more than ancillary devices; they could be combined with particularly conceived tasks for people to create a powerful new social means for overcoming the historical specter of scarcity. . . . The history of jobs and their design evolved from this social technology set in the positivistic, optimistic ethos of technological determinism. The material consequences in overcoming scarcity were enormous. The social consequences, however, were work performed under social compulsion and regimentation, and work so organized that people became interchangeable spare parts.

A central question of the now-waning industrial era remains unanswered: How do we design or redesign organizations and work systems that can satisfy the needs of society, its organizations, and their members *without* dehumanizing work?

Source: From *Design of Jobs,* edited by Louis E. Davis and James C. Taylor. © 1979 Scott, Foresman and Company. Reprinted by permission.

However, a major change in the technology component will often highlight this interdependence. Many of the most important studies showing the relationship between the technical system and people have been conducted during periods of change, when these relationships become more dramatic and observable.

Members of the Tavistock Institute in England have engaged in a number of important research studies showing the relationship between technical and human systems (Trist, 1981). Of key importance in these studies was the finding that change in a work organization determined only by engineering considerations can disrupt the social system to the extent that the new technology will not work effectively. These studies emphasized another important factor. A given technical system does not automatically lead to one and only one social system. There may be alternatives in designing the total sociotechnical system that lead both to increased productivity and to more personal satisfaction.

These studies are just a few of many that have investigated the impact of changing technology on people. Increasing evidence suggests that technological change should no longer be considered purely from the mechanistic-engineering viewpoint. Although the requirements of technology may set broad constraints, there are alternate ways of adapting so that human satisfaction can be maintained, or even enhanced. We will consider some of these alternatives later, but for now it is important to recognize that improved productivity through technological progress, and greater participant satisfaction, are not necessarily contradictory goals. Considering both factors as dynamic variables can lead to a better accommodation of people and technology.

WORK AND SATISFACTION IN DIFFERING TECHNOLOGIES

The classification of different technologies as shown in Figure 9.2 represents an approximation of chronological developments. Prior to the industrial revolution, person-tool and craft technologies were of primary importance. In this stage of development, tools and simple machines were used as adjuncts and supplements to the skill of the craftsperson. It was primarily the workers' abilities, and not the equipment, that determined the output. The mass-production technologies of the late nineteenth and early twentieth centuries fundamentally changed this relationship. The tools and equipment became the primary factors of production, and the workers' tasks were highly specialized. The worker fed the machine or performed specialized functions on the assembly line, but the pace of work and the quality and quantity of the output were determined largely by the machine and the assembly line. The assembly line was the most important industrial technology during the early part of the twentieth century.

Advances in technology led to continuous-process operation and automation. This again changed the nature of workers' tasks. Rather than machine tenders and specialists on the assembly line, they became monitors of a number of special-purpose machines and integrated-production systems. Rather than being highly specialized, their tasks became more generalized. Machine monitoring and maintenance became the primary function. Workers had to have a broader range of skills and were involved in a number of different activities. Continuous-process and automated production became the most important industrial technologies after World War II.

Advanced technologies utilizing a high level of employee skill and knowledge have been a more recent phenomenon. These are the technologies utilized in sophisticated medical research, aerospace industries, the computer field, electronics, and in most research and development laboratories. Skilled technicians require a high level of professional training and expertise. The biostatistician, the space engineer, the environmental scientist, and the computer programmer are examples.

Obviously all of these technologies are currently present in various industries. However, there has been a general evolutionary trend toward continuous processes, automation, and the advanced technologies. Let us look at the issue of worker satisfaction in these various technologies in more detail.

Craft Technology

Craft technology generally requires a high level of worker skills. Carpenters, machinists, tool and die makers, and other craft workers have long-term apprenticeship training and there is usually some means for certification of the individual's competency. Workers generally have substantial autonomy and are responsible for the final product. To a large extent they control the way the tasks are performed and the pace of the work. They usually have substantial amounts of mobility on the job—not tied to the machine—and have much social interaction with other workers. The craftsperson usually has a strong sense of identity with the work. Fellow workers and the community recognize their skills.

Although we may think of craft technology in terms of blue-collar workers and the trades, there are many examples among white collar office and service workers. The skilled laboratory technician, legal secretary, real estate broker, and interior designer are examples. They also have significant job autonomy, a sense of accomplishment, and responsibility for the total job.

Mass Production—Assembly Line Operations

In many industries mass production and assembly-line operations were substitutions for existing craft technologies. The custom shoemaker or tailor were replaced by the shoe or clothing factory. The individual shopkeeper was replaced by the supermarket, which has many characteristics of an assembly line. Fast-food services, such as McDonald's and Kentucky Fried Chicken, utilize assembly line techniques.

Mass-production assembly lines are characterized by a high level of mechanization. Special-purpose tools and equipment perform sophisticated operations on standardized products. Workers are no longer autonomous, nor do they perform all the work on the product. In most cases, their tasks are highly specialized and the work pace is controlled by the machine or the assembly line. Tasks tend to be highly repetitious and never-ending. Generally an elaborate system of coordination and control is developed to ensure that the tasks fit together and the assembly line is balanced. The individual worker has nothing to do with these planning and integrating processes. The activities are performed by industrial engineers, time-and-motion experts, and other specialists. Once established, the machine and the assembly line become the central control mechanism. Even the supervisors have little to say; it is their job to keep the line moving. These machine-tending and assembly-line jobs provide little opportunity for initiative, autonomy, and job interest. It is difficult for the employee to have a sense of accomplishment or achievement. "What did you do at work today?" "I spent eight hours soldering three red, white, and blue wires on the thingumajig." Or, "I spent ten hours today putting peaches in the peeling-and-pitting machine."

One of the advantages of mass-production and assembly-line operations is the utilization of relatively low-skilled labor. But, there are obviously many problems. "Management pays a price for the work simplification, routinization, and ease of supervision inherent in mass-production work. The cost is largely in terms of apathy and boredom as positive satisfactions are engineered out of jobs" (Sayles & Strauss, 1966, p. 47). We would add that the workers pay an even higher price in terms of their own sense of achievement and satisfaction.

Again, there are many similarities between blue-collar machine-tending and assembly-line jobs and white-collar office or service activities. The secretaries in the central typing pool, the bookkeeper performing a highly specialized and standardized task in the paperwork system, the worker in a Wendy's Hamburger stand, and the key punch operator are examples.

Continuous Process and Automated Technologies

Continuous-process and automated technologies are exemplified by chemical plants, oil refineries, automated transistor factories, and nuclear electrical plants. These processes involve a higher level of mechanization than do mass-production and assembly-line operations. Generally, in these technologies the workers do not actually work on the product directly. Rather they maintain and monitor the equipment and keep records of operations. This is a basic change in the man-machine relationship. One of the effects is to reverse the long-term trend toward task specialization. Employees have a wider variety of activities and need a higher level of overall skills. They must do more than perform the physical operations and thus need mental and psychological involvement. "The dominant job requirement is no longer manual skill but responsibility. In the place of the *able workman,* required when the worker's role in the productive process is to provide skills, a *reliable employee,* capable of accepting a considerable load of responsibility, is needed in the automated industries" (Blauner, 1964, p. 167).

Workers in process industries are likely to have a good deal of free time when the process is running smoothly and there are opportunities for social interaction. An emergency or breakdown in the process will involve intense activity and excitement. Recent accounts of emergency problems in nuclear generating plants are good, if upsetting, examples of a change of pace that relieves boredom and maintains interest.

Because of the high degree of skill and commitment involved in many of these tasks, the training and investment in human-resource development is frequently high.

Advanced-Knowledge-Based Technologies

In the technological continuum shown in Figure 9.2, advanced-knowledge-based technologies represent the more recent development. These are popularly referred to as the high-tech industries. Large research-oriented hospitals; the aerospace, computer, electronics, robotics, and biotechnology industries; industrial research and development laboratories; the National Aeronautics and Space Administration; large research-oriented universities: all are examples of organizations utilizing these technologies. Although these organizations do have sophisticated equipment and facilities, their key characteristic is that they are knowledge intensive and utilize a high proportion of skilled technical, scientific, and professional employees.

One of the main characteristics of modern industrial societies is their greater reliance on scientific, technical, and professional workers. There has been a significant increase in professional and technical workers from under 7.5 million, or 11.4 percent of the total labor force, in 1960 to over 17 million, or 17 percent of the labor force in the 1980s. This has been the fastest-growing occupational group over the past 25 years.

The employment of technical, scientific, and professional personnel in organizations has created numerous problems of conflict and accommodation. They have certain characteristics, values, and needs that may conflict with the prescribed status and role systems or behavior norms of the organization. They are frequently the source of innovation and creativity. They place high value on intellectual pursuits and autonomy in the work environment. They are frequently much influenced by their professional reference groups, which provide status and prestige. They generally have a high need for achievement and accomplishment in their work environment.

These values and characteristics may create problems within the organization. There is often conflict between administrative authority, based upon hierarchical position, and authority based upon the expertise of the individual. Workers of the latter type frequently demand sufficient autonomy to fulfill their role, yet their activities must be integrated with others and contribute to achieving the overall goals of the organization. In many organizations with a large number of these knowledge-oriented employees, new forms of teamwork have developed. These forms emphasize a collegial relationship that depends on the mutual contribution of the members.

These employees tend to be mobile and not as closely tied to the organization as other workers. Frequently their loyalty is to their profession rather than to the organization. They seek employment opportunities which will increase their knowledge, broaden their skills, and provide a sense of accomplishment. Above all, one of the major sources of job satisfaction is a sense of doing work which is important and recognized both by the organization and by professional colleagues.

Comparative Analysis of Satisfaction in Different Technologies

The above discussion suggests that there might be important differences in worker satisfaction under different technologies. Many research studies tend to support this view. Generally satisfaction tends to be highest in craft and process industries and lowest in mass-production, machine-tending, and assembly-line operations.

Robert Blauner (1964) conducted an extensive study of worker alienation and dissatisfaction in the printing (craft), textile and automobile (mass production), and chemical (process) industries. He investigated four types of alienation: *powerlessness; meaninglessness; social isolation;* and *self-estrangement*. His findings support the view that alienation and dissatisfaction were highest in mass-production and assembly-line operations.

> In the early period, dominated by craft industry, alienation is at its lowest level and the worker's freedom at a maximum. Freedom declines and the curve of alienation (particularly in its powerlessness dimension) raises sharply in the period of machine industry. The alienation curve continues upward to its highest point in the assembly-line industries of the twentieth century. . . . But with automated industry there is a counter trend, one that we can fortunately expect to become even more important in the future. The case of the continuous-process industries, particularly the chemical industry, shows that automation increases the worker's control over his work process and checks the further division of labor and the

> growth of large factories. The result is meaningful work in a more cohesive, integrated industrial climate. The alienation curves begin to decline from its previous height as employees in automated industries gain a new dignity from responsibility and a sense of individual function—thus the inverted *U* (p. 182).

Michael Fullan (1970) reported similar findings for workers in the printing, automobile, and oil industries. He used integration as the dependent variable in his study as defined by: (1) relationship with other workers; (2) relationship with first line supervisors; (3) labor-management relations; (4) the status structure; and (5) evaluation of the company. He found that oil workers had the highest level of integration, automobile workers the lowest, and that printers fell in between.

These findings of different degrees of worker satisfaction in differing technologies have generally been supported by other research results in the United States and other countries. The nature of the technology is obviously a key factor in determining worker satisfaction, motivation, and a sense of self-worth.

There have not been comprehensive studies comparing employee satisfaction in advanced-knowledge-based technologies with those in other types of technologies. However, there are a number of survey findings that suggest some differences. Generally, technical, scientific, and professional personnel do indicate a relatively high degree of job satisfaction. But they also have significant criticisms of their organizational environments. How do we explain this apparent contradiction? Most of these employees express a high level of satisfaction with their career choices; they would enter the same field again if they had it to do over, and they feel positively about their profession. However, there appear to be many conflicts between their professional orientation and the requirements of the organizational role. We might hypothesize that these employees have higher expectations of the organization than workers in less sophisticated technologies. They want a significant degree of autonomy, discretion over their task assignments, professional recognition, and a high sense of personal worth from their work. In a sense they display characteristics of craft workers, but to a stronger degree. Organizations often have difficulty in providing a climate that meets all of these needs—hence the conflict. These issues of providing sufficient motivation and satisfaction for employees utilizing advanced technologies will become even more important in the future.

Major Job Dimensions Affecting Satisfaction

Although there appear to be important differences in worker motivation and satisfaction under differing technologies, it has not been easy to determine the contributing factors. Hackman and Oldham (1976) have developed a job characteristics model, which helps clarify this relationship. They suggest the five major job dimensions shown in Figure 9.3.

This listing of major job dimensions helps us to put the issue of worker satisfaction in different technologies into a historical perspective. In the tradi-

Skill Variety. The degree to which a job requires a variety of different activities in carrying out the work, which involve the use of a number of different skills and talents of the person.

Task Identity. The degree to which the job requires completion of a "whole" and identifiable piece of work—that is, doing a job from beginning to end with a visible outcome.

Task Significance. The degree to which the job has a substantial impact on the lives or work of other people, whether in the immediate organization or in the external environment.

Autonomy. The degree to which the job provides substantial freedom, independence, and discretion to the individual in scheduling the work and in determining the procedures to be used in carrying it out.

Feedback. The degree to which carrying out the work activities required by the job results in the individual obtaining direct and clear information about the effectiveness of his or her performance.

FIGURE 9.3 Major Job Dimensions. **Source:** J. Richard Hackman and Greg R. Oldham, "Motivation through the Design of Work: Test of a Theory," *Organizational Behavior and Human Performance* 16/2 (August 1976): 250–79. Reprinted with permission.

tional craft technologies, jobs ranked high on these five dimensions. However, craft technologies could not meet the increasing demands for products and services in a rapidly growing society. The rise of mass-production technologies at the turn of the century emphasized greatly increased productivity of standardized products. They provided employment opportunities for many foreign immigrants and rural migrants who were moving to industrial centers. These people were basically unskilled and untrained in craft technologies and it was necessary to design jobs in machine-tending and assembly-line work that utilized the available skills. Specialization, routinization, and tight controls were the answers. However, these jobs ranked low on the dimensions set forth in Figure 9.3 and tended to decrease motivation and satisfaction.

Changing educational levels and increasing aspirations for greater work satisfaction made this approach both less necessary and less acceptable. The new technologies—continuous process, automation, and advance-knowledge-based—require more skill and provide a work climate that is more satisfying. Work in these technologies typically ranks high among the five job dimensions.

As our labor force has become better educated and trained, the United States no longer needs to rely on technologies geared to unskilled workers. Rather, the level of skills available should affect the selection of the appropriate technologies. We would carry this one step further and suggest that the issue of human satisfaction may also be an increasing determinant of the type of technology employed. Our society may be entering an age in which people no longer are forced to adjust to technology; rather technology will be adapted to people. This may be the most important characteristic of future industrial revolutions. Improved productivity through technological progress and greater participant satisfaction are not necessarily contradictory goals. Considering both factors as dynamic variables will lead to increased organizational effectiveness, efficiency, and participant satisfaction.

A Period of Transition

The decade of the 1980s will see important shifts in America's industrial structure and in the nature of jobs and work to be performed. There will be further declines in the number of jobs in mass-production industries, such as the automobile, and growing employment opportunities in the high-tech and service industries. The technology of robotics will expand rapidly and robots will take over many functions previously performed by humans. Millions of routine manufacturing jobs will disappear from the scene. Newer employment opportunities will be found in a wide variety of fields such as microelectronics, computers, business and financial services, communications, and biotechnology. This very significant restructuring of work will result in the devaluation of the current work skills for millions of workers. It will also create new and more sophisticated skill requirements for the emerging industries. In order to make this transition successful, renewed emphasis will have to be placed on education and training to provide these job skills. It will also involve large-scale retraining to help people make the transition.

This transition of industries and jobs will also have a major impact on the location of facilities. The quality of life is the most important factor in attracting a skilled work force for a high-tech plant. The proximity of superior educational facilities, including top universities, is a key location determinant. These factors were very important in the earlier location of high-tech industries along Boston's Route 128 and in the Silicon Valley in California.

These dramatic shifts in industrial America will bring many dislocations for organizations and individuals. However, they provide the major hope for revitalizing the nation's industrial complex. Fortunately, these new technologies and industries provide jobs with a high level of personal satisfaction. This transition offers the opportunity to create a new, more effective integration between work and human satisfaction.

Current reality, however, somewhat tempers the enthusiasm of our long-range predictions. Different societies are at different stages of their social and technological evolutions. In other countries, the primary emphasis may be on technological improvements with little consideration of the issue of human satisfaction. The United States must compete in the international marketplace with these other countries. We must continue to emphasize the use of technology to improve productivity *and also* to conserve energy and material resources *and at the same time* to direct it toward the end of human betterment. These combined demands upon technology are a very tall order.

SOCIAL AND BEHAVIORAL TECHNOLOGIES IN ORGANIZATIONS

Much of the previous discussion has been concerned with the technology utilized directly in production processes. In addition, organizations utilize a wide variety of social and behavioral technologies in the design of the structure, in planning and controlling operations, in selection, training, and motivating employees, and in decision-making processes. Many of these techniques are incorporated into our existing knowledge about how to organize and manage large, complex socio-technical systems. Bell (1973) calls this knowledge, the "new intellectual technology." He says:

> The major intellectual and sociological problems of the post-industrial society are those of 'organized complexity'—the management of large-scale systems, with a large number of interacting variables, which have to be coordinated to achieve specific goals (p. 29).

The organization of a large corporation, professional association, hospital, or accounting firm represents a *social* technology just as an assembly-line or computer-controlled tool is a *machine* technology.

In management, new social technologies are introduced through research, serendipity, and practice. Budgetary controls, personnel selection, training and development programs, organization charts and position descriptions, and long-range planning have been with us for some time. But there is an emergence of other technologies, such as quality circles, human-factors engineering, management-by-objectives programs, human asset accounting, management assessment centers, planning-programming-budgeting systems, job design/enrichment techniques, and a variety of organization change strategies. The management science have also contributed many new technologies, such as systems analysis, operations research, and computerized systems.

Organizations are utilizing new behavioral technologies to influence directly individuals and groups: sensitivity training, transactional analysis, and behavior modification, for example.

It is impossible to cover all of the newer social technologies in this unit. However, we can illustrate their importance by briefly considering two applications; job design/enrichment and behavior modification. Many other social technologies are covered in other units of this book.

Job Design/Enrichment

Substantial research, experimentation, and actual application of behavioral science concepts have focused on job design and the relationship between technology, task, productivity, and worker satisfaction. It is based on certain value premises:

> Many managers and behavioral scientists have come to recognize that the missing element of motivation to work may lie in the character of the work itself. For the mature individual, work may be a means of personal growth; it may satisfy his need for achievement, creativity and self-fulfillment. Work, then, becomes more than a means for economic survival, and it is apparent that in this age of affluence with its more sophisticated population, people won't work long or well at a job that offers no challenge or meaning (Rush, 1971, p. ii).

We use the term *job design* to include a broad spectrum of approaches, including job enlargement, job enrichment, job restructuring, work reform, autonomous work groups, and sociotechnical systems analysis. Generally speaking, these approaches also include an increased element of worker participation in the job design processes.

More specifically, "job design means specification of the contents, methods, and relationships of jobs in order to satisfy technological and organizational requirements as well as the social and personal requirements of the jobholder" (Davis, 1966, p. 21). Under this concept, the goal of job design is to enhance productivity/performance *and* to improve the quality of an employee's working life and job satisfaction.

It focuses directly on the actual work that people perform in organizations and assumes that many of the problems of unsatisfactory relationships between people and their jobs can be remedied by restructuring the jobs and the way work is accomplished (Hackman & Oldham, 1980, p. x).

Modern job-design concepts consider all aspects of jobs as variables. More specifically, the production technologies and the structural relationships may be modified and redesigned to fit the *needs of the workers.* Rather than increased specialization of tasks, job redesign may advocate job enlargement by increasing the scope of the task, or job enrichment by giving the employee greater discretion for planning and control functions. Rather than the worker performing highly specialized work in an assembly-line process, job redesign may call for the creation of autonomous work units that are responsible for a complete assembly operation and have substantial leeway in assigning and scheduling tasks among group members. In effect, job design approaches attempt to improve all those job characteristics listed in Figure 9.3.

There have been many different approaches to job design, and this social technology is being used throughout the world. There seem to be various approaches used, based on differing sociocultural factors. What works in one country may not be appropriate in another setting (Foy & Gadon, 1976). Nevertheless, there is a common theme: "How do we design jobs and reform work to increase productivity *and* satisfaction?" This is a common problem for all industrialized countries.

Some of the more comprehensive projects have been undertaken in Sweden and other Scandinavian countries. The development of the new Volvo automobile assembly line at Kalmar, based on autonomous work groups, has received the most publicity. However, there have been more than 500 other experimental work-reform projects carried out by several hundred Swedish companies over the past several years.

Job design and all of its complementary approaches represent a relatively new social technology, and it is apparent that there are many problems. Although there have been many reported successes on experimental projects in job design, these approaches are slow to spread, even within the same organization (Walton, 1975).

It is obvious that this is a social technology with much broader ramifications

BOX 9.2
MANAGING TECHNOLOGICAL CHANGE

In the 1980s technological changes will undoubtedly affect working environments massively, powerfully, often unpredictably, often perniciously. In these ways, technology will run according to form. Nevertheless, some new forces may begin to alter the consistent historical pattern, a pattern in which technology has been an irresistible prime mover that inevitably defines working tasks and working environments.

Many companies have recently begun to try to manage this process instead of simply letting it happen. As they do, and as the purposes for which technology is developed expand, these companies are likely to have an increasing variety of technologies from which to choose. For example, the need for technologies that save materials and energy is rising relative to the traditional labor-saving motive. At the same time, management assumptions, values, and techniques may be shifting in the direction of no longer taking for granted that the quality of working life (QWL) must be subordinated to the choice of equipment and process.

Source: Wickham Skinner, "The Impact of Changing Technology on the Working Environment," in Clark Kerr and Jerome M. Rosow (Eds.) *Work in America: The Decade Ahead.* New York: Van Nostrand Reinhold Co., 1978, p. 204.

than just the individual's job productivity and satisfaction. Comprehensive programs may not only require modifications in technologies, structure, and superior-subordinate relationships but in all other aspects of the organizational climate as well. Several such programs have had difficulties because of the failure to recognize and deal with these broader consequences.

Job design is still a developing technology and we do not understand all of the complex interrelationships. It is a soft social technology that is strongly influenced by values and attitudes. The goal of job and work redesign—to increase both organizational performance and employee satisfaction—is well worth striving for and will become an increasingly important consideration for the future. Some of the more specific approaches to job design will be discussed in Chapter 13.

Behavior Modification

Another behavioral technology which may have important implications for organizations and their participants is behavior modification. Obviously, managers have always attempted to influence the behavior of their subordinates so that they would work toward organizational objectives. So what's new about behavioral modification? It is an attempt to apply techniques more scientifically to modify human behavior in an organizational situation—techniques based on underlying theories of learning, operant conditioning, and behaviorism. These theoretical concepts have been developed over many years of experimentation with animal and human subjects. It would be impossible to discuss all aspects of behavioral modification theories. We can present only the most fundamental ideas and then illustrate some of their actual applications in organizations.

What causes people to behave as they do? Traditional motivation theories explained human behavior in terms of internal states; people behave in certain ways because they are attempting to satisfy certain needs. These cognitive explanations were discussed in Chapter 4 and emphasized that humans have needs, desires, and expectations that affect their behavior. People are continually engaged in feeling, thinking, and deciding in the attempt to satisfy their needs. These cognitive explanations suggest that human beings are highly aware and self-directing and make many choices among alternatives. These cognitive explanations provide a foundation for understanding and predicting motivation and behavior.

Another view, based on learning theory, considers overt, *observable* behavior as the most fundamental aspect for consideration. Rather than being overly concerned about "inner" drives that cannot be observed or measured, the *behaviorists* have concentrated on the study of actual observable behavior. They have focused their attention on how to modify more scientifically and effectively the environment of the organism (animal or human) in order to affect behavior. The behavioral psychology of B. F. Skinner and his followers suggests that these behavior-modification approaches provide the primary basis for the development of a more effective technology for changing behavior (Skinner, 1971). Walter Nord and others suggest that Skinner's behavioral psychology has been neglected in management and organizational literature (Nord, 1969). Writers in the field have tended to emphasize the work of other behavioral scientists, such as Maslow, McGregor, and Herzberg without recognizing the potential contributions of Skinner and the behavioral psychologists.

Just what are the basic concepts of behavior modification? In very simple terms, it suggests that behavior is dependent on the external conditions in which the behavior takes place. It stresses the importance of the administration of rewards and punishments imposed by the environment to elicit desired behavior. Behavior is a function of its consequences. The primary means is through conditioning, wherein desired behavior is reinforced and undesired behavior is ignored. In concept, if an individual behaves in a certain way and that behavior is immediately rewarded or reinforced, there is an increased probability that the individual will behave in the desired way in the future. A simple example will help illustrate this approach. At Valleyfair, a family entertainment center near Minneapolis, management wanted to ensure that all of the employees treated customers and guests in a friendly and helpful manner. They set about to develop a workplace culture dedicated to good human relations between guests and employees. They wanted to provide positive reinforcement for employees to behave in the desired ways. Customers entering the park are given cards saying

"Nice Going Award" and are asked to give them to Valleyfair employees who help make their day more pleasant. Supervisors carry and award "Fuzzy Tickets" which are given to employees for good performance. These tickets are then redeemable by the employees for various prizes. Management reports that this system, together with several other programs, has led to high ratings for friendliness, helpfulness, and service by guests.

Note that this program utilizes many of the basic aspects of behavior modification. It provides positive rewards for desired behavior. It emphasizes positive reinforcement rather than negative punishments. It provides immediate performance feedback to the employees.

Behavior modification programs tend to emphasize the use of positive reinforcers rather than negative punishment as a means of improving performance. In the past, many managers have tended to utilize punishments or withdrawal of rewards. Punishment is appropriate under certain circumstances, but it has often been overused. Quite frequently, punishment doesn't have a predictable effect on behavior. And the natural tendency is for punishment to increase because (1) the negative consequences of punishment are hidden; (2) the punisher is reinforced by directly observing the results of the action (the child cries when hit); and (3) the individual punished learns to retaliate and the punishment gets tougher. Thus, generally it has been found that positive reinforcement and performance feedback have longer-run, more predictable, and favorable results in improving performance than does punishment.

There has been a growing interest in using behavior-modification techniques to improve organization performance. Luthans and Kreitner (1975) use the term *organizational behavior modification* to suggest the integration of operant learning theory and the principles of behavior modification with the management field of organizational behavior. They define organizational behavior modification (O.B. Mod.) as follows:

> Broadly based on behavioral or operant learning theory and more precisely based on the body of theoretical and practical knowledge known as behavior modification, O.B. Mod. attempts to systematically relate the impact that the environment has on organizational behavior. The overriding assumption is that organizational behavior depends on its consequence (pp. 12–13).

Various terms are used to describe such programs: performance management; positive reinforcement management; behavioral engineering; operant conditioning; behavior modification; and contingency management.

In the past, behavior modification programs have been used by many different types of organizations to improve individual performance. For example, reward systems using tokens as direct reinforcements have been used in schools and correctional agencies. There is an increasing trend toward the use of such programs in business and other work organizations. Ford, United Airlines, IBM, ITT, Procter & Gamble, Questor, 3M, and Emery Air Freight are a few of the large corporations that have developed programs based on behavior-modification concepts (Hamner & Hamner, 1976). Although there are many variations among these programs, the common emphasis is on direct performance feedback to employees and the use of positive reinforcements to improve performance.

These programs, like most other applications of behavioral science technologies in organizations, are not simply and easily applied. Rather, successful applications require intensive retraining of management and supervisory personnel in the utilization of behavior-modification techniques. Frequently, behavior modification is part of a broader program for developing and improving the organization. Although the number of organizations using formal programs applying behavioral technologies is still relatively small, we anticipate that they will be utilized more extensively in the future as the approaches and techniques are refined.

We have briefly discussed two of the social technologies utilized by organizations. Our primary purpose was to suggest the importance of these in organizational endeavors so as not to overemphasize machine technology. In our view, these various social technologies will become increasingly important in the future. And, just as we will have new inventions of machinery and processes, we will also develop new social inventions—social and behavioral technologies—to deal with our organizational problems and opportunities.

SO WHAT? IMPLICATIONS FOR YOU

As a Member of an Organization

Generalizations	Implications
1. Technology is the application of knowledge for the achievement of practical purposes. It includes physical manifestations such as tools and machines but also the mental processes used in solving problems.	1. Recognize the broad concept of technology. Think about the technology in the organization where you have worked or where you will have your career.
2. Organizations, themselves the result of social technology, are creators and appliers of technology.	2. Observe this phenomenon in your daily contacts with organizations.
3. Organizations use a wide variety of technologies and require many different technical skills.	3. Be aware of the technical knowledge and skills that you bring into the organization. Assess how your skills match the organization's requirements.

Generalization	Implications
4. The nature of the technology has a major effect on the goals and values, structure, managerial process, and human relationships within the organization.	4. Recognize that as an employee you will be interfacing with various technical systems. Be aware of how they affect your performance and satisfaction.
5. In order to perform effectively there needs to be an appropriate fit between the technology and the organization. Some organizations are highly bureaucratic/mechanistic and others are more adaptive/organic.	5. Assess yourself and your interests. Which type will provide the best fit between you and the organization? Don't apply for *any* job but try to understand the technical constraints of various positions and seek the best accommodation.
6. The organizational climate and satisfaction with work is often dependent on the nature of the technical system.	6. In your career planning you should look beyond your first job and try to determine what influences the various technologies have on possible future positions.

As a Current or Future Manager

Generalizations	Implications
1. There should be congruence among the technology, structure, managerial practices, and social systems. An appropriate fit leads to better performance as well as participant satisfaction.	1. Develop a conceptual model of these relationships. For example, does the nature of the technology indicate a bureaucratic/mechanistic form or an adaptive/organic form? Try to develop the appropriate fit.
2. The organization is a sociotechnical system. It makes use of various technologies, but humans are the vital ingredient in making the technologies work.	2. Recognize the importance of this interface. Always consider the interrelationships between the technical and social systems.
3. New technologies may require changes in structure, processes, social relationships, and other characteristics of the organization.	3. Recognize the impact of changing technologies on other factors. Do not assume that new technologies can be introduced without ramifications.

Generalization	Implications
4. Employees frequently appear to resist technological change. They have many uncertainties about how the change will affect their roles, status, and social relationships.	4. Be prepared for resistance and work to minimize the adverse social consequences of the change. Anticipating and planning ahead can make the change process more successful. Explain the reasons for the changes and the potential consequences.
5. The way in which jobs are designed in relationship to the available technologies has an important effect on both performance and satisfaction.	5. Be aware that within your area of responsibility as a manager you can design jobs to increase performance and satisfaction. Don't take the traditional way of doing things as given. There may be opportunities for experimentation and improvement.
6. Frequently the technology is not given or fixed. There is flexibility to adapt the technology to meet other requirements.	6. Do not take a purely engineering view of technology. It may be desirable to modify the technology to meet other goals. Think about tradeoffs. Will you be willing to redesign jobs when the primary outcome is greater employee satisfaction?
7. Organizations utilize a wide variety of social and behavioral technologies in the design of the structure, in planning and controlling operations, in selecting, training, and motivating employees, and in decision-making processes.	7. Recognize that these technologies are all part of the art of management. Be continually aware of their potential usefulness and their effect on other aspects of your organization.

LEARNING APPLICATION ACTIVITIES

1. Write a vignette, similar to those at the beginning of the chapter, that illustrates your experience with the technical system in an organization. Specifically, describe how this technical system affected your behavior.

2. *Step 1:* Scan your local newspaper or current periodicals to find examples of the impact of technology on people in work organizations (similar to the *Assembly Line* or the *Operating Room* vignettes).

Step 2: Share your findings in groups of four to six. Do these incidents illustrate machine technology or the broader concept of technology as the application of knowledge?

3. *Step 1:* In groups of three or four visit a local fast-food outlet, such as McDonald's, Wendy's, or Kentucky Fried Chicken, and observe how the technology affects the operations and particularly the behavior of the employees. Note how technology affects almost every task and action from the preparation of the food to the ringing up of the sale.

Step 2: Briefly outline your observations and be prepared to share your observations with the entire class.

4. Pick a particular technological advancement, such as the development of television, nuclear power, or home computers, and list the positive and negative effects of the technology on (a) individuals and (b) organizations.

5. Think back to your own work experiences and consider how the technology affected the network of social relationships.

a. Make a list of ways technology affected the people individually.
b. Make a list of ways technology affected intragroup and intergroup relationships.

6. *Step 1:* Meet in groups of four to six and consider the issue of job satisfaction in organizations (or subparts of organizations) with different technologies. Based on the individual experiences within the group, were certain types of technologies related to (a) more or (b) less job satisfaction?

Step 2: Share your observations with the entire class. Is there general agreement as to types of technology that are related to higher/lower levels of satisfaction?

7. *Step 1:* Think of a number of social technologies that are used in organizations. The examples listed in the chapter can help get you started.

Step 2: Select one of these social technologies and describe in detail its impact on the organization and its people.

8. Investigate the impact of technological change on an organization (similar to *The New Executive VP: D. Computer* vignette). For example, what happened when the organization introduced a new computer or a strategic planning system? Talk with several managers and trace through the effects of the changing technology.

REFERENCES

Aldrich, Howard E. "Technology and Organizational Structure: A Reexamination of the Findings of the Aston Group." *Administrative Science Quarterly* 17/1 (March 1972): 26–43.

Bell, Daniel. *The Coming of Post-Industrial Society*. New York: Basic Books, 1973.

Blauner, Robert. *Alienation and Freedom*. Chicago: University of Chicago Press, 1964.

Burns, Tom, and G. M. Stalker. *The Management of Innovation*. London: Tavistock, 1961.

Child, John, and Roger Mansfield. "Technology, Size and Organization Structure." *Sociology* 6 (September 1972): 369–393.

Darlington, C. D. *The Evolution of Man and Society*. New York: Simon & Schuster, 1969.

Davis, Louis E. "The Design of Jobs." *Industrial Relations* 6/1 (October 1966): 21–45.

Davis, Louis E., and James C. Taylor, 2d ed. *Design of Jobs*. Santa Monica, Calif: Goodyear, 1979.

Ellul, Jacques. *The Technological Society*. Transcribed by John Wilkinson. New York: Knopf, 1964.

Foy, Nancy, and Herman Gadon. "Worker Participation: Contrasts in Three Counties." *Harvard Busines Review* 54/3 (May-June): 71–83.

Fry, Louis W. "Technology-Structure Research: Three Critical Issues." *Academy of Management Journal* 25 (September 1982): 532–552.

Fullan, Michael. "Industrial Technology and Worker Integration in the Organization." *American Sociological Review* 35/6 (December 1970): 1028–1039.

Hackman, J. Richard, and Greg R. Oldham. "Motivation through the Design of Work: Test of a Theory." *Organizational Behavior and Human Performance* 16/2 (August 1976): 250–279.

———. *Work Redesign*. Reading, Mass.: Addison-Wesley, 1980.

Haire, Mason. *Psychology in Management,* 2d ed. New York: McGraw-Hill, 1964.

Hamner, W. Clay, and Ellen Hamner, "Behavior Modification on the Bottom Line." *Organizational Dynamics* 4/4 (Spring 1976): 2–49.

Hickson, David J., D. S. Pugh, and Diana C. Pheysey. "Operations Technology and Organization Structure: An Empirical Reappraisal. "*Administrative Science Quarterly* 14/3 (September 1969): 378–397.

Kast, Fremont E., and James E. Rosenzweig. *Organization and Management: A Systems and Contingency Approach,* 3d ed. New York: McGraw-Hill, 1979.

Leikind, Morris C. "The History of Technology: Man's Search for Labor Saving Devices." In Donald P. Lauda and Robert D. Ryan (Eds.), *Advancing Technology: Its Impact on Society*. Dubuque, Iowa: Brown, 1971, pp. 8–16.

Luthans, Fred, and Robert Kreitner. *Organizational Behavior Modification*. Glenview, Ill.: Scott, Foresman, 1975.

Lynch, Beverly P. "An Empirical Assessment of Perrow's Technology Construct." *Administrative Science Quarterly* 19/3 (September 1974): 338–356.

Mesthene, Emmanuel G. *Technological Change*. New York: New American Library (Mentor Books), 1970.

Mumford, Lewis. *Technics and Civilization*. New York: Harcourt Brace Jovanovich, 1934.

Nord, Walter R. "Beyond the Teaching Machine: The Neglected Area of Operant Conditioning in the Theory and Practice of Management." *Organizational Behavior and Human Performance* 4 (November 1969): 375–401.

Perrow, Charles. "A Framework for the Comparative Analysis of Organizations." *American Sociological Review* 32/2 (April 1967): 194–208.

———. *Organizational Analysis: A Sociological View*. Belmont, Calif.: Wadsworth, 1970.

Rush, Harold M. F. *Job Design for Motivation*. New York: Conference Board, 1971.

Sayles, Leonard, and George Strauss. *Human Relations in Organizations*. Englewood Cliffs, N.J.: Prentice-Hall, 1966.

Skinner, B. F. *Beyond Freedom and Dignity*. New York: Knopf, 1971.

Skinner, Wickham. "The Impact of Changing Technology on the Working Environment." In Clark Kerr and Jerome M. Rosow (Eds.), *Work in America: The Decade Ahead*. New York: Van Nostrand Reinhold, 1979, pp. 204–230.

Stinchcombe, Arthur L. "Social Structure and Organizations." In James G. March (Ed.), *Handbook of Organizations*. Chicago: Rand McNally, 1965, pp. 142–193.

Thompson, James D. *Organizations in Action*. New York: McGraw-Hill, 1967.

Thompson, James D., and Frederick L. Bates. "Technology, Organization, and Administration." *Administrative Science Quarterly* 2/3 (December 1957): 325–343.
Trist, Eric L. "The Sociotechnical Perspective." In Andrew H. Van de Ven and William F. Joyce (Eds.), *Perspectives on Organizational Design and Behavior.* New York: Wiley, 1981, pp. 19–75.
Walker, Charles R., ed. *Technology, Industry and Man*. New York: McGraw-Hill, 1968.
Walton, Richard E. "The Diffusion of New Work Structures: Explaining Why Success Didn't Take." *Organizational Dynamics,* 3/3 (Winter 1975): 3–22.
Withey, Michael, Richard L. Daft, and William H. Cooper. "Measures of Perrow's Work Unit Technology: An Empirical Assessment and A New Scale." *Academy of Management Journal* 26/1 (March 1983): 45–63.
Woodward, Joan. *Industrial Organization: Theory and Practice*. London: Oxford University Press, 1965.
Zwerman, William L. *New Perspectives on Organization Theory.* Westport, Conn.: Greenwood, 1970.

10
Structure

LEARNING OBJECTIVES

After reading this chapter you should be able to:

1. Define organization structure and describe its key characteristics.
2. Recognize the interrelationship between structure and the environment and other subsystems.
3. Identify the key issues and considerations in designing an organization's structure.
4. Understand traditional concepts about structure and the emergence of new organizational forms.
5. Outline the ways that structural characteristics affect the attitudes and behavior of people in organizations.
6. Recognize the need for congruence among various factors, such as environment, technology, structure, and behavior.

AN ENCOUNTER WITH BUREAUCRACY

George Kozlov had a problem. He had preregistered for 15 hours, but, when his registration sheet came back his Sociology 101 class was scheduled for M-W from 10:00-12:00 A.M. instead of T-Th 10:00-12:00. And that was the time he was taking a class in his major, Accounting 463. Didn't sound too complicated. He could return to the registrar's office and get it corrected. But the registration clerk told him that the T-Th, 10:00-12:00 Sociology 101 class was already filled and he couldn't get it changed without approval of the department. "Why don't you talk with the sociology department. They have jurisdiction; I can't make the change without their approval." George protested, "The computer made the error, why can't we just readjust it according to my original schedule?" But to no avail. The secretary in the sociology department informed him that the class was already filled and that no exceptions could be made except for sociology majors. Again, George protested, "I really don't want to take the damned course, but it is the only way I can satisfy my distribution requirements for the social sciences." This didn't impress the secretary, who suggested that inasmuch as he really wasn't majoring in sociology, he should take his problem back to the School of Business because he was under their jurisdiction. On to the advisor in the School of Business, where he was informed that Accounting 463 was only being taught during that hour and would not be scheduled again for the rest of the year. George responded, "What am I to do? Go another complete year to get that class? I should graduate this quarter. Can't you help me out to get into the right Sociology 101 class?" The advisor responded that this matter was completely under the control of the sociology department. He did suggest that George talk with the instructor teaching the Sociology 101 class to see if she would make an exception and take him as an overload.

George went back to the registrar's office and got a class change card. He hoped that the sociology instructor would sign it as an overload and let him in. To make certain, he decided to attend the class and then get the instructor's signature. Unfortunately, there were 10 other people trying to get in as overloads and the instructor only took the first five. George was number six. He asked the instructor, "What do I do now?" The instructor was sympathetic, but still wouldn't let him in. She did suggest, however, that the evening class in Sociology 101 was not overloaded and that George might attend that. George didn't particularly like the idea, but it was the only alternative. So, back to the sociology department for their approval. The secretary agreed that this was a good idea, but informed him that they didn't have any jurisdiction over the registration of evening class students. He would have to go to the evening division office to make the change. George finally got his Sociology 101 class on M-W from 7:30-9:30 P.M. He had spent two days making the change, had talked with five different departments or agents of the university and had missed out on the first two days of his other classes. "What a helluva organization!"

HOW MUCH DECENTRALIZATION?

Elizabeth Fotheringill, manager of the Westgate branch, tore open the confidential memorandum from William Cook, president of Central Savings and Loan Association. The memo explained that the failure to keep expenses in line with declining revenues had caused the association to record a loss in the first six months of the year. It would be necessary to impose stringent controls on expenditures, especially on personnel, during the second half. Department heads in headquarters and the branch managers were to reduce staff by 10 percent from the current level. A list of those to be laid off must be on the president's desk by next Friday. A total ban was imposed on new or temporary hiring and salary increases.

Before she had completed reading the memo, Elizabeth was on her way to see William Cook. "Surely, this doesn't apply to my branch," she said. "I'm afraid it does," Cook replied. "If I exempt you from these economy measures, then everyone will want a special case. That was the problem two months ago when we told everyone to bring spending into line with revenues. It simply didn't work. That is why I decided on prescribing action that is certain to reduce our expenditures."

Elizabeth didn't buy these arguments. "You have continually told us that we are a decentralized organization and that each branch has responsibility to maintain profits. I have built the Westgate branch to the largest and most efficient unit in the association. In my mind we are really carrying some of the less efficient branches."

William Cook thought for a moment and then responded. "Yes, Elizabeth, you have done a great job with the Westgate branch. But, we all have to face this difficulty together and do our share. It's up to you which 10 percent of your force to cut. You can cut secretaries, tellers, or supervisors, but you must comply with the directive."

Elizabeth persisted, "But as long as we meet and exceed our savings and loan goals and keep within our expense ratios, which I assure you we can do, we should be exempt from cutbacks. Ever since I have been a branch manager, I have met or exceeded my targets. My branch is the biggest profit contributor to the association. Some of the other branches have been losing money for two or three years now. I can see the logic of making them adhere to these cutbacks. But surely it's madness to penalize a prosperous branch to subsidize money-losing ones. Your cutbacks would wreck the morale and efficiency of my branch. I have worked hard to make it profitable. My people have a real commitment to the association and I have an obligation to them. So don't expect a list from me on your desk. I don't intend to fire anyone. If there are any layoffs in my branch you will have to start with me," Elizabeth said and strode out.

"That is exactly what I will do," Cook thought. But as he began to consider how he would explain to the board his reasons for firing the manager of the association's most profitable branch he had second thoughts. Perhaps he should simply look the other way if Elizabeth did not comply.

THE PROGRAM MANAGER

James Casey was the manager for Project Pluto, a major component of an advanced space system under contract with the U.S. government. At the start of the project two years earlier, there were many conflicts and uncertainties. There had been a major issue over how to organize Project Pluto and where it would fit into the existing organizational structure. Richard Donaldson, vice president and head of engineering, had wanted the project assigned directly to his department. However, Project Pluto required integrating the activities of a number of different departments, and the president of the company had decided that it would be more appropriate to establish a separate project management office, which would have the responsibility for the overall planning, control, and coordination of the project. The actual work would be performed by the existing departments.

James Casey was selected as the project manager. His staff was composed of a small group of engineers, planners, and coordinators who were assigned to his office from the various departments. They would be members of his team until completion of the project.

Casey had many problems in making this approach work. He had the responsibility for seeing that Project Pluto met the time schedules and kept within the cost constraints. But he didn't have the authority to get the work done. He seemed continually to be negotiating and pressuring the various department heads to give his project higher priority. They seemed to give his project less emphasis than the work assigned directly to their departments.

Members of his project staff worked reasonably well together. It had been difficult to assign specific authority to each of the members of his staff because of the dynamic nature of the project. Rather than having strict and clearly defined authority and roles, Casey had tried to develop a team spirit to encourage his staff to work together. In order to coordinate their activities they had frequent meetings to iron out difficulties. But Casey recognized that some of them had conflicts trying to satisfy the needs of the Project Pluto and still remain in the good graces of their permanent bosses, the department heads. After all, when the project was over they would have to go back to work in their previous departments.

After two years, the project was moving along fairly well. Because they were dealing with advancing the state of the art, they had to make frequent design changes and the customer was continually modifying the specifications. They had kept costs under reasonable control. But now he was having another battle—with Richard Donaldson, head of the engineering department. Donaldson was arguing about meeting the specifications and wanted an extension of time and a larger budget to work out some design bugs. This would get the project behind schedule and lead to cost overruns. Casey didn't know how to deal with the impasse. Perhaps he should take the problem to the president for resolution, but he hated to go over Donaldson's head. He needed his continuing cooperation and didn't want to alienate him completely.

Casey sat in his office thinking about the project. He would be glad when it was over. Sure, it had been a very exciting assignment. But the conflicts and problems of coordinating all the activities and meeting the needs of the customer had been a real strain. He had put in 10 to 12 hours a day, six days a week for over two years, and even his wife and kids were grumbling. Nor was his future all that certain. He knew that if the project was successfully completed, it would be a big feather in his cap, but if things went wrong he would get the blame. His career with the company was on the line.

THE EMERGENCY ROOM

Dr. Nancy Reynolds had been an emergency room doctor at City Hospital for five years and was regarded by the staff as very competent: able to make quick, accurate diagnoses and to keep the emergency room running smoothly. Unlike the doctors with private practices who used the facilities of the hospital, emergency room doctors were hired under contract directly by the hospital and were full-time employees.

Doctors with private practices were on the medical staff but were not under contract as employees of the hospital. However, they were required to adhere to specific medical staff by-laws that governed the nature and quality of patient care. One of these doctors is assigned by the board of directors of the hospital as chief of staff, whose duties, as stated in the by-laws include "responsibility for the enforcement and implementation of medical staff by-laws and rules and regulations and for the supervision of all medical staff activities of the hospital." Dr. Richard Blackstone, a surgeon, was appointed as the chief of staff and served as the intermediary between the hospital administration and the medical staff. Dr. Blackstone was very busy with his successful private practice and left most routine administrative matters to the hospital administrator, Henry Thorson. Henry was also appointed by the board of directors. He was not a doctor, but had a master's degree in hospital administration. He relied on Dr. Blackstone to see that medical practices and ethics were maintained in the best interests of patients and the hospital.

During her fourth year at City Hospital, Dr. Nancy Reynolds encountered many problems in her personal life. She went through a lengthy divorce process and lost large sums of money on investments. It was rumored that she had become quite intoxicated at the Christmas party and on other social occasions. The hospital administrator, Henry Thorson, was concerned over her behavior and suggested that Dr. Blackstone have a conference with her. Blackstone replied, "I try not to get involved in the personal lives of our staff. Dr. Reynolds' work here at the hospital emergency room is just fine and I see no reason to interfere."

During the next month, Dr. Reynolds called in sick two or three times a week, creating problems in obtaining substitute doctors. The head nurse of the emergency room complained that Dr. Reynolds was behind in her paperwork and was creating many other "difficulties." One Friday afternoon, the head nurse called Mr. Thorson to inform him that Dr. Reynolds had shown up for work intoxicated. The nurse had tried to contact Dr. Blackstone, but he could not be reached. "That's the straw that broke the camel's back," said Thorson as he slammed down the telephone. He immediately went to the emergency room and, finding Dr. Reynolds obviously drunk, fired her on the spot. He told her to get her things and never return to the hospital.

The following morning the board of directors received a letter of resignation from Dr. Blackstone which stated, "I have learned of the action Thorson took regarding Dr. Reynolds. I am infuriated that such action was taken without my prior consent or knowledge. If this is the way City Hospital is going to deal with problems, I resign as chief of staff and will take all my own patients to Memorial Hospital."

INTRODUCTION

Structure is often considered to be one of the most theoretical aspects of organizations, perhaps because some of its aspects are abstract and not directly observable. Leadership styles and group dynamics, for example, can be observed directly, and we can experience their effects. Even technology is apparent. But, organization structure? It is related to organization charts and operations manuals, position descriptions, procedures, rules, regulations, departmentalization of activities, and issues of authority and responsibility. No one has seen an "organization structure." It has to be inferred from the processes and activities of the organization.

But, consider. Even the smallest unit of organization, the family, has a structure. To be sure, it is an informal structure and it is doubtful that your family has charts and manuals to guide its activities. Yet, typically, families do have a hierarchical structure: parents having greater power, authority, and influence than children. Families do have specialization of activities as well as rules and regulations (typically unwritten) to guide behavior of members.

Organizational structures are social inventions. They are created by people as the means for integrating, coordinating, and controlling cooperative activities. Obviously, there is little that is absolute or predetermined about structures. They are created by, and can be changed by, people. Organizational structures have a decided affect on our lives. The four incidents opening the chapter illustrate some of these influences. George Kozlov was dealing with the effect of structural relationships in trying to get his course schedule corrected. His university was departmentalized into academic areas that had jurisdiction over certain courses. He had to find the right *authority* to make the course change. He dealt with five different units within the university's structure.

Elizabeth Fotheringill was also dealing with a structure problem. How much autonomy should she have to operate her branch? The issue of centralization of authority versus decentralization is important in most organizations. President Cook was faced with the questions of how much autonomy he should allow and what type of control he should maintain over the different operations. Should he use the authority of his position to enforce compliance with his directive? What are the limits to his authority? This issue was on the line when Elizabeth threatened to quit.

James Casey, as the Pluto Project manager, faced an even more complex set of structural issues. How should he organize his team to accomplish the project's objectives? How much real power did he have and how could he resolve conflicts when he didn't have positional authority over everyone working on his project? The effectiveness of the structure could contribute to the project's success (or failure) and affect his career.

The emergency room incident represents a classic issue in organization structure. There was confusion and differences in perception as to who had authority and responsibility to handle a problem situation. The hospital administrator felt he had to take strong action to protect the integrity of the hospital, but Dr. Blackstone thought he was meddling in medical staff affairs.

These people were all involved in problems related to structure. Structure has a significant effect on the behavior of people in organizations. It determines their tasks and roles, their relationships with other people, groups, and departments, and is a primary determinant of authority and influence. In this chapter we will discuss structure under the following topics:

The Concept of Organizational Structure
Structure: The Connection Between Environment and Other Subsystems
Key Considerations in Structure
The Dynamics of Structure
Emerging Organizational Forms
Effect of Structure on People
Congruence Between Structure and Behavior
So What? Implications for You

THE CONCEPT OF ORGANIZATIONAL STRUCTURE

Structure affects everyone in the organization. When you walk into an unfamiliar store, the person at the information desk helps you find shoes or furniture, depending on your needs. From the customers' viewpoint the entire organization is structured around various departments. This structure is convenient for customers because we have come to associate products and services with given departments. (On the other hand, when some product or service doesn't fit into a department, confusion results. Try finding the men's restroom in Gum's Department Store in Moscow, U.S.S.R.!)

The new employee in his first assignment is told, "You will work under Mary Smith in internal auditing." He may be shown an organization chart and the policies and procedures manual. One of the more difficult things for the new employee to learn is the name and function of the various departments, the superior-subordinate relationships, and "who does what."

Definitions of Structure

Very simply, *structure is the established pattern of relationships among the parts of the organization*. It reflects the way in which the tasks of the organization are divided (differentiated) and the activities coordinated (integration). In a formal sense, structure can be set forth by organization charts, job descriptions, policies, procedures, and rules. It is concerned with patterns of authority, communication, and work flow. The structure of a social system is not visible in the same way as a biological or mechanical system. It cannot be seen but is inferred from the actual operations and behavior of the organization.

In the complex organization, structure is set forth initially by the design of the major components or subsystems, and then by the establishment of patterns of relationship among these subsystems. It is this internal differentiation and

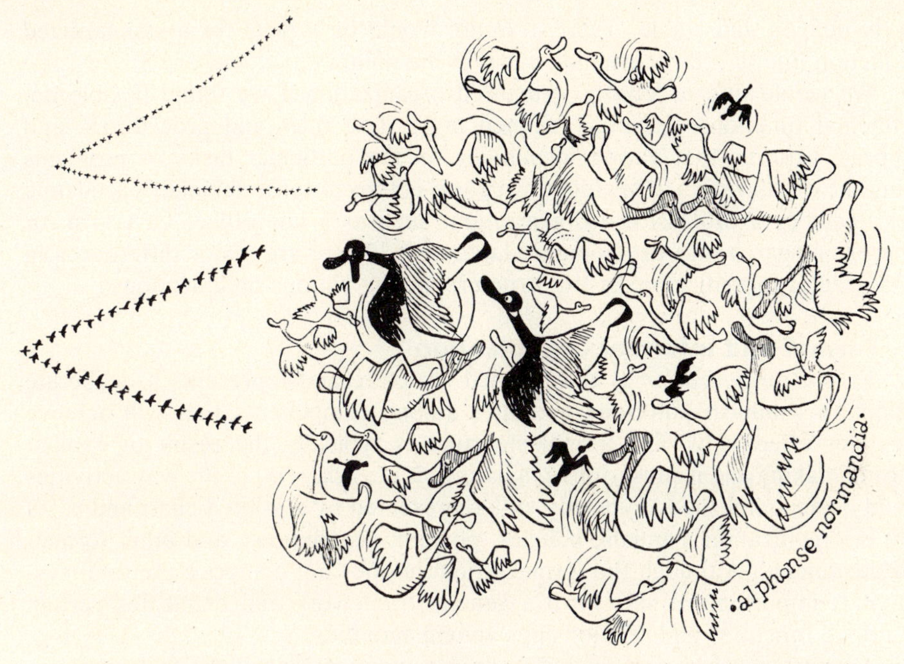

"There are times when I wish we had a somewhat stronger organization."

patterning of relationships with some degree of permanency that is referred to as structure. The formal structure is frequently defined in terms of the following:

1. The pattern of formal relationships and duties—the organization chart plus job descriptions or position guides.
2. The way in which the various activities or tasks are assigned to different departments and people in the organization (differentiation).
3. The way in which these separate activities or tasks are coordinated (integration).
4. The power, status, and hierarchical relationships within the organization (authority system).
5. The planned and formalized policies, procedures, and controls that guide the activities and relationships of people in the organization (administrative system).

Obviously, we cannot find any one measure of the *degree* of structure in an organization. We do know that there are important differences among organizations; some are tightly structured, while others are loosely structured. For example, we would infer a tightly structured organization if it had well-defined departments or work units, if the tasks were specialized and prescribed in detail, if there were well-established policies and procedures for how people and functions were to be interrelated, and if the authority and status relationships were clearly defined and stable. Tight structure would be typical for a standardized production line or a basic-training camp in the military.

We would infer a loosely structured organization if we found flexible departmental functions, generally defined tasks, few rules and procedures, and authority patterns that varied, depending on the particular tasks or problems facing the organization. This loose structure is typical for a university academic department or a professional organization, such as a law office, CPA firm, or nonprofit research and development laboratory. There are major differences in the degree of formalization of the structure among various organizations.

Formal and Informal Organization

Formal organization is the planned structure and represents a deliberate attempt to establish patterned activities among components that will achieve objectives effectively. The formal structure is typically the result of explicit decision making and is prescriptive in nature. It is a *blueprint* of the way activities should be accomplished. Typically, it is represented by a printed chart and is set forth in organization manuals, policies, position descriptions, and other formalized documents. Although the formal structure does not comprise the total system, it is important. It sets forth a general framework and delineates certain prescribed functions and relationships among activities.

Anyone who has participated in an organization recognizes that many interactions occur that are not prescribed by the formal structure. In your university, there is much informal communication concerning classes, instructors, and procedures that are not part of the formal system. You learn informal procedures, such as "Don't be late for registration or you get stuck with 7:30 P.M. classes." You can probably think of many ways that students use to beat the formal system. The *informal organization* refers to those patterns of relationships that are not planned explicitly but arise spontaneously out of the activities and interactions of the participants.

Informal relationships are vital for the effective functioning of the organization. Frequently, groups develop new means for dealing with important activities. When the formal organization is slow in responding to external and internal forces, informal relationships develop to deal with problems. Thus, the organization may be adaptive and serve to perform innovative activities that are adequately being met by the formal structure. On the other hand, there are occasions when the informal organization may operate to the detriment of goals: when work groups slow down or sabotage production, for example.

Traditional management theorists concentrated on the formal organizational structure. The human relationists, in contrast, were concerned primarily with informal relationships. This diversity of interest led to the view that there is an actual separation between the formal and the informal structures. In actuality, they are intermeshed. "It is impossible to understand the nature of a formal organization without investigating the networks of informal relations and the unofficial norms as well as the formal hierarchy of authority and the official body of rules, since the formally instituted and the informally emerging patterns are inextricably intertwined'' (Blau & Scott, 1962, p. 6). In this chapter we will be emphasizing the formal organizational structure and its effect on participants.

STRUCTURE: THE CONNECTION BETWEEN ENVIRONMENT AND OTHER SUBSYSTEMS

It is useful to think of structure as the connection or linkage between the organization's environment and the internal subsystems. This would include the technology utilized in the transformation processes, the relationships among people performing various tasks, and the managerial system of planning and control. Each of these systems is an important determinant of various structural characteristics belonging to the organization. In turn, the structure is a binding element for the integration of these systems.

The fact that an organization is an open system and must receive support from its environment has an important effect on its internal structure. Organizations establish departments to deal with inputs from, and outputs to, specific sectors of its environment. In business enterprises, many departments interact directly with specific sectors of the environment. Purchasing is concerned with material inputs; personnel departments recruit and select employees; market research obtains information from the outside. On the output side, sales departments maintain relationships with distributors, advertising departments attempt to influence customers, and public relations departments disseminate information that will enhance the reputation and image of the corporation. A university's structure is similarly affected by environmental relationships. Separate units may be established to attract and select students, negotiate with the legislature, interact with alumni and donors of resources, attract research funds from the government, place graduates, and engage in many other activities relating to specific environmental forces.

We can generalize by suggesting that the more heterogeneous, dynamic, and uncertain the environment, the more complex and differentiated the internal structuring of the organization. We see many examples of this. With increased pressure from governmental agencies, many organizations respond by establishing lobbying units. Pressure from environmentalists and consumers has resulted in new internal departments. Increasing emphasis on equal employment opportunities for minorities and women has led to new departments to deal with these issues. Obviously, movement into new environments through product diversification or geographic dispersion (e.g., multinational organizations) results in restructuring.

Technology affects most directly those structural characteristics closely related to the transformation process. For example, the technical system is the prime determinant of the structure of the production line, the machine shop, the operating room in the hospital, and the food-processing plant. At these operating levels, the technology is a major determinant of the specialization and differentiation of activities, the means of integration, the authority relationships, the procedures and rules, and the degree of formalization.

The psychosocial system both affects, and is strongly influenced by, the structure. For example, people with different educational and work experiences will often respond differently to various structural arrangements. The professional or technical specialist may seek autonomy and freedom from tight structure. This is true, for example, of doctors in hospitals, professors, design engineers, and many other professionals. Factory employees may be conditioned to accept a high degree of control over their activities. However, this situation may be changing. The desire for more meaningful work and greater participation has led to job redesign, autonomous work groups, and other approaches that affect structure.

Taken together, environmental influences, technological requirements, and psychosocial factors are key determinants of structure. But the cause-effect relationships are not easily determined, nor is there substantial agreement about which of these forces is the most important. They are all interactive and interdependent.

Management's Role in Organization Design

One key managerial function is to design the organization in response to various contextual and internal forces. Managers make strategic choices that are fundamental in the determination of organizational design. "Strategic choice extends to the context within which the organization is operating, to the standards of performance against which the pressure of economic constraints has to be evaluated, and to the design of the organization's structure itself" (Child, 1972, p. 1).

It is not the objective environment to which managerial decision makers respond, but the environment as *they perceive it*. Furthermore, managers often have an important say as to which environment will be relevant; they select an organizational domain. For example, the corporation decides which markets it will enter on the basis of products, or geographical areas, or both. Managers also make strategic choices concerning the goals of the organization, the nature of the technology, and the internal climate. Although the environment and internal subsystems may place constraints on how managers design the structure of organizations, the importance of managerial decision making should not be underestimated. "Depending on perceptions of both environmental and internal properties, managers have considerable leeway in making strategic choices to meet various contingencies" (Anderson & Paine, 1975, p. 811). Figure 10.1 illustrates these determinants and the design process.

Environmental Influences on Structure

One of the most comprehensive studies of the relationship between environment and structure was conducted by Burns and Stalker (1961) in their investigation of English and Scottish firms. They examined a number of firms with a stable environment that were attempting to move into the electronics field—a dynamic environment. They found that different organizational structures and managerial systems were appropriate in different environments.

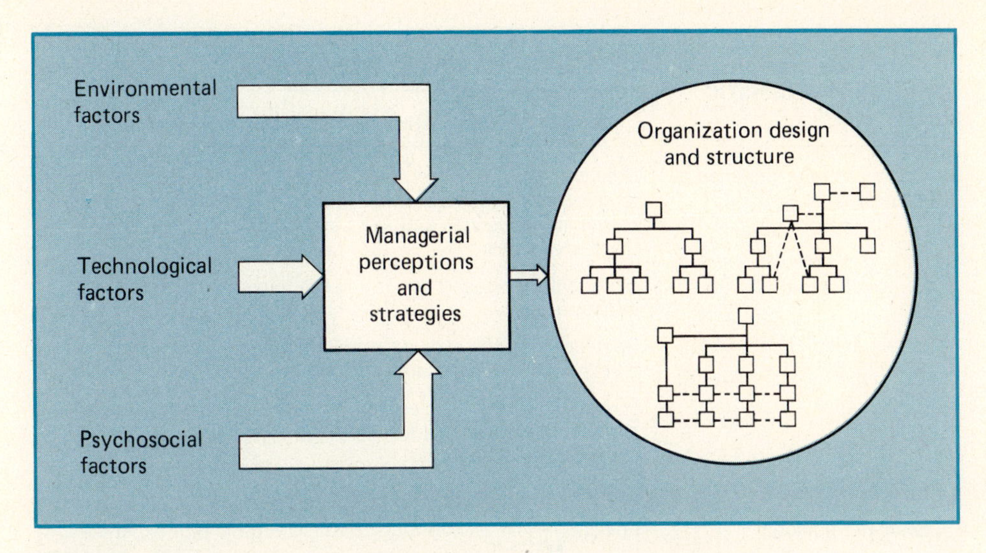

FIGURE 10.1 Managerial Strategies and Organizational Design

Lawrence and Lorsch (1967) studied the relationship between environmental forces and the internal structural characteristics of ten organizations in three distinct industrial environments: plastics, packaged food, and standardized containers. They were seeking to answer the fundamental question: "What kind of organization does it take to deal with various economic and market conditions?" The found that effective firms operating in a dynamic and complex environment (the plastics industry) tended to have a more complex internal structure. In contrast, firms in a stable environment (the container industry) tended to have a less complex structure. Firms that did not develop the appropriate structures to match their environments were less effective in achieving organizational goals. Organizations designed to match environmental characteristics performed more effectively. Furthermore, these studies and a number of others support the view that complex, dynamic environments require more highly differentiated and complex structures (Duncan, 1972; Khandwalla, 1973; Baldridge and Burnham, 1975).

Figure 10.2 suggests two distinct types of organizational structures, the *stable/mechanistic* and the *adaptive/organic*. There appears to be a movement toward dynamic, flexible structures, and away from rigid mechanistic forms. Instead of providing for permanent, structured positions, as characteristic of the stable/mechanistic system, the adaptive/organic system has less structuring, more frequent changes of positions and roles, and more dynamic interplay among the various functions. The adaptive-organic system requires more time and effort toward integration of diverse activities. These two structural forms are appropriate under different environmental circumstances. Let's take an example from government.

The postal system operates in a relatively stable and simple environment. It is most appropriately organized along *stable/mechanistic* lines with a high

ORGANIZATIONAL CHARACTERISTIC	TYPES OF STRUCTURE	
	Stable-Mechanistic	**Adaptive-Organic**
Openness to environmental influences	Relatively closed. Attempts to select and minimize environmental influences and reduce uncertainty	Relatively open. Designed to adapt to environmental influences and cope with uncertainty
Formalization of activities	More formality based on structure	Less formality based on structure
Differentiation and specialization of activities	Specific, mutually exclusive functions and departments	General, sometimes overlapping activities
Coordination	Primarily through the hierarchy and well-defined administrative procedures	Multiple means and interpersonal interaction
Authority structure	Concentrated, hierarchic	Dispersed, multiple
Source of authority	Position	Knowledge and/or expertise
Responsibility	Attached to specific positions and/or roles	Shared by many participants
Tasks, roles, and functions	Clearly defined and specified in organization charts, position descriptions, and so on	Loosely defined and determined by circumstances, mutual expectations, and so on
Interaction-influence patterns	Superior → subordinate, hierarchical	Superior ⇌ subordinate, horizontal and diagonal
Procedures and rules	Many and specific, usually written and formal	Few and general, often unwritten and informal
Stratification (in terms of power, status, compensation, and so on)	More difference between levels	Less difference between levels
Decision making	Centralized, concentrated toward the top	Decentralized, shared throughout the organization
Permanency of structural form	Tends to be relatively fixed	Continually adapting to new situations

FIGURE 10.2 Organizational Characteristics of Stable-Mechanistic and Adaptive-Organic Structures. **Source:** Fremont E. Kast and James Rosenzweig, *Organization and Management: A Systems and Contingency Approach,* 3d ed. (New York: McGraw-Hill, 1979), p. 230. © 1979. Reproduced with permission.

degree of formalization, well-defined rules and procedures, a hierarchical chain of command, and centralization of authority. There is limited differentiation of functional activities; integration and coordination is relatively simple. In contrast, the National Aeronautics and Space Administration operates in a very complex and dynamic environment. It has a much more complex and differentiated structure than the post office. It is effectively organized as an *adaptive/organic* system.

It has a high degree of differentiation and specialization of activities and critical problems of integration. There is substantial decentralization of authority, emphasis upon horizontal integration of activities, and less formal rules and procedures. Flexibility and adaptability are emphasized. For example, in its space shuttle program, NASA had to develop a flexible structure to deal with a wide variety of environmental contingencies.

We should not overemphasize the view of organizations as passively accommodating to their environments. Many organizations are proactive rather than reactive. Managers influence their environments (Weick, 1979, pp. 149–169; Aldrich, 1979, pp. 144–149; Pfeffer & Salancik, 1978, pp. 71–88). Most organizations endeavor to reduce the uncertainties and adverse effects of their environments. For example, business organizations will spend vast sums of money to advertise their products and to create a stable demand. They establish long-range contracts with suppliers of materials and fabricated parts in order to reduce uncertainties. They actively seek to influence governmental agencies to provide a favorable business climate. Universities seek to influence their legislators, alumni, and potential donors to provide resources. The military does not just accept the appropriations that Congress provides; it actively tries to influence legislation.

Organizations frequently determine the environments within which they operate. "Organizations' environments are largely invented by organizations themselves. Organizations select their environments from ranges of alternatives, then they subjectively perceive the environments they inhabit" (Starbuck, 1976, p. 1069). This is most obvious for business firms when they make decisions on product lines, pricing, and distribution channels. Managers make strategic choices that help determine the environment in which the organization operates. These strategic choices about the environment set the framework for the design of the appropriate organizational structure.

Chandler found that as firms developed new strategies in response to the changing social and economic environment, basic changes in structure were required. In an intensive study of four large corporations—E.I. du Pont de Nemours & Company, General Motors Corporation, Standard Oil of New Jersey, and Sears, Roebuck & Company—which was supported by a survey of seventy other large industrial firms, he found certain evolutionary patterns of structure. Changing population, income, technology and other forces in the environment led to the expansion of these firms into new fields. This strategy of diversification and expansion required major modifications in structure. "A new strategy required a new or at least refashioned structure if the enlarged enterprise was to operate efficiently" (Chandler, 1962, p. 15).

We can summarize our discussion by suggesting that organizations do have some control over their environments and do make strategic choices. However, once these choices are made, the environmental characteristics seem to influence structure. Increased turbulence, uncertainty, and complexity in the environment results in more complex organizational structures. In turn, this complexity creates difficult problems for planning, decision making, and integration of activities.

Influences of Technology on Structure

The impact of technology on structure was first discussed in Chapter 9. Simple and stable technology leads to a high degree of formalization with task specialization, rigid procedures and rules, centralization of authority, and emphasis on vertical hierarchy as a means of integration. In contrast, when the technology is dynamic and complex there tends to be a more general task orientation, fewer procedures and rules, and more adaptive responses to problems. Authority and influence are less related to position and more to knowledge and emphasis is on lateral rather than vertical relationships.

The evidence from various research studies suggests that technology has the greatest influence on structural relationships at the operating levels in organizations. It has less of an impact on structure at higher levels, where environmental influences are likely to be more important determinants of the structural characteristics.

Characteristics of the Psychosocial System

The nature of the psychosocial system can affect structure. One of the key issues concerns size—the number of people in the organization. Stated simply, Are there major differences in the ways in which small and large organizations are structured? Some researchers have found that size is one of the key factors determining organizational structure (Pugh et al., 1969; Blau & Schoenherr, 1971). Large organizations tend to be more formal. The evidence for this view is substantial. However, it is not clear that size alone is the key factor; rather, complexity of operations may be a more important determinant of structure. These two variables often go together. Large organizations tend to have more complexity and diversity of operations than do small organizations. For example, large multidivisional corporations tend to operate in diverse and heterogeneous environments and to utilize a wider variety of technologies than do one-industry firms. Large universities are more complex than small colleges. Our reference to the structural differences between the post office and NASA illustrates this idea. They are both very large organizations but they differ significantly in their degree of complexity and have different structures. Here are some tentative generalizations concerning the effect of size and complexity on structure.

1. With increased size, organizations tend to differentiate their activities in order to gain the advantages of specialization. They establish functionalized departments to deal with specific environmental and internal problems.
2. Policies and procedures tend to become more formalized in order to guide the activities of participants.
3. Increased specialization creates problems of integration and an administrative structure is established to meet the problems of coordination.
4. It is difficult for top management to exercise personal leadership and control; thus a more clearly defined role and authority system is developed.

5. It is impossible to control all of the operations from the top; thus there is a movement toward decentralization of authority.

There is another commonly held view that as organizations increase in size, the number of administrative personnel increases more than proportionately. Large organizations become top-heavy with managers, staff personnel, and white-collar workers, showing proportionately fewer direct workers. However, research findings suggest that the ratio of administrative personnel to operative personnel decreases or is curvilinear with increasing size (Hall, 1972, pp. 124–128). Again, the issue of complexity enters in. More complex operations result in a greater proportion of administrative and staff personnel. As the managerial problems of planning and coordination increase, the organization requires more specialized knowledge from staff and technical groups. The post office has a relatively high proportion of operative personnel as compared with NASA, which has many more people engaged in administrative and specialized staff functions. In standardized automobile production, there is a low ratio of administrative to operative personnel. In the aerospace industries the ratio is much higher. (That may partially explain why one large commercial jet airplane costs as much as 3000 Chevrolets.) The space system or modern jetliner represents a tremendous investment in specialized technical and administrative skills.

KEY CONSIDERATIONS IN STRUCTURE

The key considerations of organization structure are (1) differentiation, (2) integration, (3) authority and responsibility relationships, and (4) the development of an administrative system. An organization, by definition, involves two or more people working toward a common goal. This requirement implies a division of labor, and a means of integrating activities and results into a composite whole. It also suggests that the authority of the people involved should be delineated, responsibilities assigned, and some administrative system of policies, procedures, regulations, and rules developed. In the small organization, these aspects are frequently informal; in the larger organization, they tend to be more formalized.

Differentiation

All organizations are characterized by some degree of task specialization. In the small organization, this may be rather general and informal. In larger organizations, this differentiation is carried much further. For example, a large university can afford more specialization in course offerings and faculty personnel than a small liberal-arts college that concentrates on more general, less specialized subject matter. The total task of the organization is differentiated so that particular departments and units are responsible for the performance of specialized activities. "*Differentiation* is defined as the state of segmentation of the organization system into subsystems, each of which tends to develop particular attributes in relation to the requirements posed by its relevant external environment" (Lawrence & Lorsch, 1967, pp. 3–4).

In organizations, this differentiation occurs in two directions: the vertical specialization of activities, represented by the hierarchy; and the horizontal differentiation of activities, called departmentalization.

The vertical division of labor establishes the hierarchy and the number of levels in the organization. This hierarchy sets the basic communication and authority structure—the chain of command. Vertical positions in a business organization typically range from hourly employees to first-line supervisors, middle managers, and top executives. These levels are fairly well defined, with major differences in functions and status for the various positions.

Substantial rewards accrue for moving up the hierarchy. Position determines the authority and influence, privilege, status, and remunerations enjoyed by the incumbent. Theoretically, the further up the vertical hierarchy, the broader the perspective and the more strategic the decisions one makes.

Organizations also typically have some basis for horizontal differentiation of activities. Even in a small retail store, one partner often performs certain functions, such as purchasing and inventory control, with the other in charge of advertising and sales promotion. In larger organizations, this differentiation is usually associated with the creation of departments, branches, or divisions to perform certain specialized functions.

The three primary bases of departmentalization are (1) function, (2) product, and (3) location. Departmentalization by function is one of the more commonly used approaches; for example, dividing activities into manufacturing, marketing, engineering, personnel relations, and finance. This arrangement has the advantage of specialization and concentration of similar activities within a departmental unit. Product departmentalization has become increasingly important, especially for large organizations. For example, companies such as General Electric, General Motors, and DuPont have major product divisions (appliances, turbines, aircraft engines), each having substantial autonomy. The third primary basis of departmentalization is location. All the organizational activities performed in a particular geographic area are brought together and integrated into a single unit. This has been the pattern adopted by chain stores in establishing regional offices. It has also been used by many multinational corporations, such as IBM, Nestle, and Unilever.

Frequently, organizations also differentiate activities that require specialized knowledge and expertise. *Staff* units are established to perform these specialized functions. We see many examples such as corporate planning, market research, environmental and consumer affairs, legal counsel, and public relations. The staff expert, because of technical competence in a particular area of specialization, is frequently viewed as a source of knowledge and influence.

Integration

The second overall consideration in the design of organization structures is that of coordination of activities. "*Integration* is defined as the process of achieving unity of effort among the various subsystems in the accomplishment of organization's task'' (Lawrence & Lorsch, 1967, p. 4). It is important to recognize the interaction between the need to specialize activities and the requirements for intergration. The more differentiation of activities and specialization of tasks, the more difficult the problems of coordination.

> Both horizontal and vertical differentiation present organizations with control, communication, and coordination problems. Subunits along either axis are nuclei that are differentiated from adjacent units and the total organization according to horizontal or vertical factors. The greater the differentiation, the greater the potential for difficulties in control, coordination, and communications (Hall, 1972, p. 146).

Organizations typically establish several different mechanisms for achieving integration. One means of integration is through the formal hierarchy. The president integrates the producing and selling functions. The vice president of marketing integrates the advertising and selling functions. The advertising director integrates the direct mail, newspaper, magazine, radio, and television advertising.

Formal policies, procedures, and rules are also means of integrating activities: making behavior reasonably consistent throughout the organization. Long-range, comprehensive plans provide a means for integrating activities over time and among subunits in the organization. Strategic plans are translated into medium-range tactics and short-range operational steps. The technology—from automation to detailed procedures and specifications—often provides the means of integrating the many steps in a manufacturing process. General rules, such as a nine-to-six workday, are also a means of integration.

With the development of more complex activities and structures, many new devices to achieve integration have developed. Standing committees, ad hoc committees, task forces, project teams, and staff meetings are examples.

Formal approaches cannot provide all of the integration for complex organizational activities. As suggested earlier, informal voluntary coordination often takes place. When the situation is dynamic and changing it is often necessary to make immediate decisions that affect several individuals or departments. Coordination is often achieved via an informal discussion over coffee or lunch. Achieving voluntary coordination is one of the most important, yet difficult, problems for the manager. Voluntary coordination requires that the individuals have sufficient knowledge of organizational goals, adequate information concerning the specific problem of coordination, and the motivation to do something on their own.

Different organizations require different means of integration. The problems of integration for the organization with a stable environment, a constant technology, and routine activities are substantially different from those for the organization facing rapidly changing environmental and technological forces. The stable organization can rely on the hierarchical structure and established policies and procedures to ensure coordination. The organization in a changing context must develop other, more complex mechanisms for integration.

Authority and Responsibility

There is a direct interrelationship between organizational structure and patterns of authority. Authority refers to the influence that various positions have in the organization and is not an attribute of one individual. Authority is institutionalized power: the legal right to influence behavior. The authority structure provides the basis for assigning tasks to the various elements in the organization, and for developing a control mechanism to ensure that these tasks are performed according to plan. It provides for the establishment of formalized influence transactions among the members of the organization.

The concept of authority is closely related to the idea of *legitimate exercise of power* of a position and depends on the willingness of subordinates to comply with certain directives of superiors. Obviously, the structure and the positioning of participants in a hierarchical arrangement facilitate the exercise of authority.

Authority relates to differentiation and is most commonly associated with vertical levels: as in the president having positional authority over the vice presidents. It is also related to *departmentalization:* the granting of authority to perform certain functional activities. A vice president of marketing operates on this kind of delegated authority. But authority is equally a means of achieving integration. A boss may have to settle a dispute between two subordinates (when all else fails) by *ordering* them to cooperate.

Authority relationships differ greatly in organizations. In relatively simple, stable, and standardized operations, it tends to be concentrated at the top. The top executives have the training, knowledge, and means to exercise authority. However, in more dynamic and complex organizations, authority is often decentralized to positions within the organization where participants have specialized knowledge and expertise.

Structure is directly related to the assignment of responsibility and accountability to various organizational units. Control systems are based on the delegation of responsibility. Most organizations develop some means to determine the effectiveness and efficiency of the performance of these assigned functions and create control processes to ensure that these responsibilities are carried out. In simple structures, authority and responsibility can clearly be defined and assigned to specific departments that can then be held exclusively accountable for results. In more complex organizations, where substantial integration and coordination are required between departments, both authority and responsibility may be shared by several units.

Administrative System

Most organizations develop some system for the coordination of repetitive, routine activities. "A great deal of coordinative effort in the organization is concerned with a horizontal flow of work of a routine nature. *Administrative systems* are formal procedures designed to carry out much of this routine coordinative work automatically" (Litterer, 1973, p. 466). Organizations develop purchasing procedures, procedures for handling customers' orders, and production, scheduling and control systems. Universities develop procedures for registration: typically better, we hope, than those facing George Kozlov *(An Encounter with Bureaucracy)*. These policies, procedures, and regulations are all part of the planned structure.

Frequently, administrative procedures extend beyond the boundaries of the organization, and are tied in with other people or organizations in the environment. Imagine for a moment that you are ordering an around-the-world ticket from your travel agent. Think of the administrative system—the people, the computers, and other resources—that help to create that twenty-page ticket. With scheduling involving ten to twenty countries and a number of different airlines, each with their own fluid pricing index, assuring accuracy of destination, price, and time is no simple affair. But this marvel (when it works) of fixed planning may not meet your need. Say you really like Hong Kong and decide to stay over for a few extra days. You will want to ask the airline representative to reschedule the flight, perhaps even change the itinerary for the remainder of your trip. Without an integrated and smoothly running administrative system, such transactions would be impossible.

There are differences in administrative systems among organizations. It is much easier to establish an effective administrative system when the organization is dealing with relatively routine activities (your world trip was a routine activity for the travel agent and airlines). It is much more difficult to develop administrative systems to deal with changing circumstances. In fact, that is one of the major problems with administrative systems—they tend to become relatively inflexible (remember George Kozlov's problems). A dilemma for organizations is how to design administrative systems that handle repetitive, routine activities efficiently but still maintain the flexibility to deal with more unusual circumstances.

THE DYNAMICS OF STRUCTURE

The primary issues concerning structure have changed significantly during this century. With the growth of large-scale organizations during the latter part of the nineteenth century and early part of the twentieth, the basic trend was the movement from highly personalized systems based on the dynamic leadership and personal influence of the owner-manager to a formalized, rational, and impersonal structure. The early concepts of structure were geared to making all activities rational, predictable, clearly defined, and efficient. This model worked well for the organizations at that time and was the primary basis of organizing mass-production industries, stable government operations, and the military.

However, this same structural model did not work as effectively for many organizations emerging during the second half of the twentieth century. These organizations were more complex, had a diversity of operations, were faced with turbulent environments, and utilized dynamic and complex technologies. For example, Bell Laboratories, the research and development arm of American Telephone & Telegraph Company, has been on the forefront in basic scientific research and has achieved major technological breakthroughs in transistors, semiconductor chips, lasers, and microelectronics. It has 10,000 patents in effect and has several hundred licensing agreements with U.S. and international companies. Bell Laboratories is organized around individual laboratory operations in 21 locations with nearly 25,000 employees. Its structure is very different from traditional organizations. Companies such as Xerox, Hewlett Packard, Atari, Burroughs, Texas Instruments, Apple Computer, Inc., Honeywell, and the Tandy Corporation in the personal computer, video game, and information-processing industries are also facing a turbulent environment with complex and changing technologies. The organizational forms advocated for the more stable organizations are not appropriate. As suggested in Box 10.1, these new organizations emphasize innovation, change, and adaptability rather than routinization and standardization. In order to understand how these different orientations have affected structural relationships, we will briefly review some of the design prescriptions for more traditional organizations and then discuss newer organizational forms.

The Bureaucratic Model

One of the major pillars in the development of classical concepts of organization was provided by Max Weber's bureaucratic model. The term *bureaucracy* as developed by Weber and his followers is not used in the popular, emotionally charged sense of red tape and inefficiency. The bureaucratic model

BOX 10.1
DESIGNING THE INNOVATING ORGANIZATION

Innovation requires an organization specifically designed for that purpose—that is, such an organization's structure, processes, rewards, and people must be combined in a special way to create an innovating organization, one that is designed to do something for the first time. The point to be emphasized here is that the innovating organization's components are completely different from and often contrary to those of existing organizations, which are generally operating organizations. The latter are designed to efficiently process the millionth loan, produce the millionth automobile or serve the millionth client. An organization that is designed to do something well for the millionth time is not good at doing something for the first time. Therefore, organizations that want to innovate or revitalize themselves need two organizations, an operating organization and an innovating organization. In addition, if the ideas produced by the innovating organization are to be implemented by the operating organization, they need a transition process to transfer ideas from the innovating organization to the operating organization.

Source: Adapted by permission from "Designing the Innovating Organization," by Jay R. Galbraith, pp. 5–6, *Organizational Dynamics,* Winter 1982 © 1982 by Jay R. Galbraith.

possesses certain structural characteristics that are found in every complex organization. The concept of bureaucracy used herein is neither good nor bad but, rather, refers to certain characteristics of organizational design. Weber viewed bureaucracy as the most efficient form that could be used for complex organizations—business, government, military, for example—arising out of the needs of modern society.

The view of rational/legal authority was basic to Weber's concept of bureaucracy. It is the right to exercise authority based on position. "In the case of legal authority, obedience is owed to the legally established impersonal order. It extends to the persons exercising the authority of office under it only by virture of the formal legality of their commands and only within the scope of the authority of the office" (Weber, 1964, p. 328). Rational/legal authority is based on position within the organization, and when it evolves into an organized administrative staff, it assumes the form of a bureaucratic structure. Within this structure, each member of the administrative staff occupies a position with a specific delineation of power: positions are organized into a hierarchy of authority; compensation is in the form of a fixed salary; fitness for office determined by technical competence; and the entire organization governed by rules and regulations. Essentially, the bureaucratic form attempts to restrain human variables and personal idiosyncrasies and to develop a rational, structured, mechanistic structure. The characteristics shown for the stable/mechanistic structure in Figure 10.2 are typical of the bureaucratic form.

Traditional Applications

This view of structure was reinforced by many traditional management theorists who were primarily concerned with the design of efficient organizations. They also emphasized such concepts as objectivity and impersonality. The organizational structure was designed for the most efficient allocation and coordination of activities. The positions in the structure, not the people, had the authority and responsibility for getting tasks accomplished. The structure was emphasized as the most important and enduring characteristic of the organization. Many of the traditional concepts were based on experiences with stable organizations, such as the military, church, and established public bureaucracies. The traditional theorists developed principles of organization: (1) a high degree of task specialization and division of labor; (2) a well-defined scalar hierarchy with authority and responsibility flowing in a direct line from the highest level of the organization to the lowest level; (3) emphasis on authority as the legitimate right of command, with subordinates having the duty to obey; (4) a narrow span of control or supervision to ensure that the superior would coordinate activities of subordinates; and (5) the line and staff concept, with the line managers having the authority and the staff providing advice and support.

These principles were appropriate for organizations with stable environments, technology, and operations, and they are still appropriate for many organizations today. However, they *are not* general principles that are appropriate for *all* organizations.

EMERGING ORGANIZATIONAL FORMS

We have seen the emergence of many new organizational forms to deal with problems of increased size and complexity, environmental uncertainties, new technologies, and geographic dispersion of activities. These new, more dynamic forms have departed significantly from the bureaucratic model and the principles of the traditionalist.

Multidivisional, Conglomerate, and Multinational Organizations

One of the most important developments has been the growth of large multidivisional organizations. The Chandler study referred to earlier traced this development for many U.S. corporations. This pattern of development led to the adoption of a multidivisional structure, where the central corporate office plans and coordinates the activities of a number of operating divisions and makes allocations of personnel, facilities, funds, and other resources. The actual operations of the organization are decentralized to the operating divisions, which have substantial autonomy.

A further extension is the development of what Peter Drucker (1974) calls federal decentralization. "In 'federal decentralization' a company is organized in a number of autonomous businesses. Each unit has responsibility for its own performance, its own results, and its own contribution to the total company. Each unit has its own management which, in effect, runs its own 'autonomous business' " (p. 572). The major advantages of federal decentralization is that it allows each of the separate divisions to develop structures that are appropriate to its own environment, technologies, and internal characteristics. It also provides for a clear delineation of the goals of each division and gives managers the authority and responsibility for achieving them.

General Electric provides an excellent example of a large multidivisional company. In 1977, this company used its strategic planning system to identify the strongest growth opportunities and then developed an organizational structure that would be appropriate for the 1980s. The company established a new sector organizational structure that allowed the company to operate effectively in different markets and environments. Currently, General Electric has seven major sectors: Technical Systems, Services and Materials, Power Systems, Industrial Products, Consumer Products, Natural Resources, and the Aircraft Engines Group. Several of these sectors represent the basic core activities of GE, whereas others are geared to new, fast-growth businesses. These core businesses serve as the solid, income-producing foundations that provide the resources for developing strong positions in the more vital sectors of the world economy, such as engineered materials, information services, financial services, construction services, medical systems, and natural resources. General Electric has continually restructured its organization to meet changing environmental and technological circumstances.

The development of large-scale conglomerates in recent years has resulted in further structural modifications. Organizations such as International Telephone and Telegraph (ITT), Gulf and Western Industries, Litton Industries, and Textron have grown by encompassing within their structures a number of previously unrelated businesses in different industries. They have accumulated vast financial resources and have spread their risks through expansion into many diverse fields. The structural forms of these conglomerates are usually different from the older diversified organizations, such as General Motors and General Electric. Typically, they have a much smaller corporate headquarters staff and do not attempt to control tightly the operating units or to coordinate activities among them. Allen (1970) suggests the following characteristics for conglomerates:

> Conglomerates have several organizational characteristics which make them a unique corporate form: diversity, comparatively simple integrative devices, pooled interdependence, major subunits which are both self-contained and autonomous to a considerble degree, and interunit coordinative requirements that center mainly around corporate-divisional relationships (p. 22).

The conglomerates have carried differentiation of activities to an extreme. They have generally adopted a loose structure that does not require substantial coordination between the different operating units. The basic strategy is to achieve integration over broad financial policies at the strategic level, with limited attempts to achieve division-to-division integration.

Large corporations are operating increasingly in many countries. Corporations that have their home in one country, but which operate and live under the laws and customs of other countries as well, have been termed *multinational corporations*. These multinational corporations have increased greatly in number and size over the past several decades, and this trend will continue. Many U.S. firms are becoming more dependent on international markets. In 1981, General Motors had international sales of $20.7 billion, nearly 30 percent of its total sales. General Electric reported that in 1981 international operations contributed 40 percent of corporate earnings.

There are many problems associated with developing appropriate structures for these multinational organizations. "The multinational corporation raises diversity and complexity to new levels and makes new and unprecedented demands on top management with respect to business strategy as well as structure and behavior" (Drucker, 1974, p. 728). The multinational corporation has significantly changed the boundaries of its activities and the diversity of its environment. It must operate in new sociocultural settings and must maintain dynamic flexibility. This geographic dispersion leads to greater differentiation of organizational activities and creates many new problems of integration. The multinationals cannot simply transfer the home-office organizational structure and design to foreign environments and expect them to work. Rather, it is necessary to adapt the structure to fit different sociocultural environments.

Project Management and the Matrix Structural Form

Another major modification from traditional bureaucratic structures has been the development of project management and matrix structural forms. These approaches have been used where dynamic environmental and technological forces make traditional functional departmentation inappropriate. The major emphasis of these forms is to provide more effective integration of all the activities necessary to complete a specific project. The project manager acts as the focal point and center of the information network for all of the activities related to the project. A project team, under the project manager, is usually composed of individuals from diverse functional specialities that contribute to the project. The project organization is temporary in nature and is usually superimposed on the permanent organization.

Project managers are responsible for organizing and controlling all activities involved in achieving the ultimate objective: development of a new space craft; construction of a dam; development of a new automobile design; or introduction of a new product line. Projects are usually superimposed on the functional organization, creating new and complex relationships. This structural approach requires organizational modifications and substantial changes in the attitudes and behaviors of the people in the organization. Instead of an organization operating under the traditional view, with well defined hierarchical structure, a unity of command, and clear-cut relationships of authority and responsibility, the system is much more dynamic and much less structured.

The project manager cannot operate effectively by relying solely on the formal authority of position. Success is more likely to depend on the ability to influence other organizational members. Because the project manager is a focal point in the operation, he or she does have informational inputs that provide a strong basis of influence.

From this brief description, it is easy to see why Project Pluto's James Casey (*the Project Manager*) was having difficulties. With such problems, you might wonder, why adopt this structural form at all. First, you should recognize that the approach is not the culprit. Rather, the dynamic environment, the technologies, and the internal complexities create the problems. The project form is one approach that attempts to deal with these issues. It may not be the perfect answer, but it is the best available to meet certain conditions. From our observations, people have to learn to work within this type of system; and they do. The first major project is often a traumatic learning experience for the entire organization, but the next one is easier. People do adapt successfully to a variety of structural approaches.

The *matrix organization form* has evolved from project management (Kolodny, 1979). The matrix design is a permanent structural form that integrates the functional and project/product needs of the organization as shown in Figure 10.3. Essentially, the matrix form is a structural design geared to two primary organizational needs: (1) the need to specialize activities into functional departments that develop technical expertise and provide a permanent home base for employees; and (2) the need to have units that integrate the activities of these specialized departments on a program, project, product, or system basis. This form is a compromise between the traditional functional organization and the autonomous project organization. There are permanently established functional departments that maintain a stable base for specialized activities. Integrative units that have

BOX 10.2

WHAT IS A MATRIX?

The identifying feature of a matrix organization is that some managers report to two bosses rather than to the traditional single chain of command.

Companies tend to turn to matrix forms:

1. when it is absolutely essential that they be highly responsive to two sectors simultaneously, such as markets and technology;
2. when they face uncertainties that generate very high information processing requirements; and
3. when they must deal with strong constraints on financial and/or human resources.

Matrix structures can help provide both flexibility and balanced decision making, but at the price of complexity.

Matrix organization is more than a matrix structure. It must be reinforced by matrix systems such as dual control and evaluation systems, by leaders who operate comfortably with lateral decison making, and by a culture that can negotiate open conflict and balance of power.

In most matrix organizations there are dual command responsibilities assigned to functional departments (marketing, production, engineering, and so forth) and to product or market departments. The former are oriented to specialized in-house resources while the latter focus on outputs. Other matrices are split between area-based departments and either products or functions.

Every matrix contains three unique and critical roles; the top manager who heads up and balances the dual chains of command, the matrix bosses (functional, product, or area) who share subordinates, and the managers who report to two different matrix bosses. Each of these roles has its special requirements.

Aerospace companies were the first to adopt the matrix form, but now companies in many industries (chemical, banking, insurance, packaged goods, electronics, computer, and so forth) and in different fields (hospitals, government agencies, and professional organizations) are adapting different forms of the matrix.

Source: Reprinted by permission of the Harvard Business Review. Excerpt from "Problems of Matrix Organizations," by Stanley M. Davis and Paul R. Lawrence [May-June 1978].

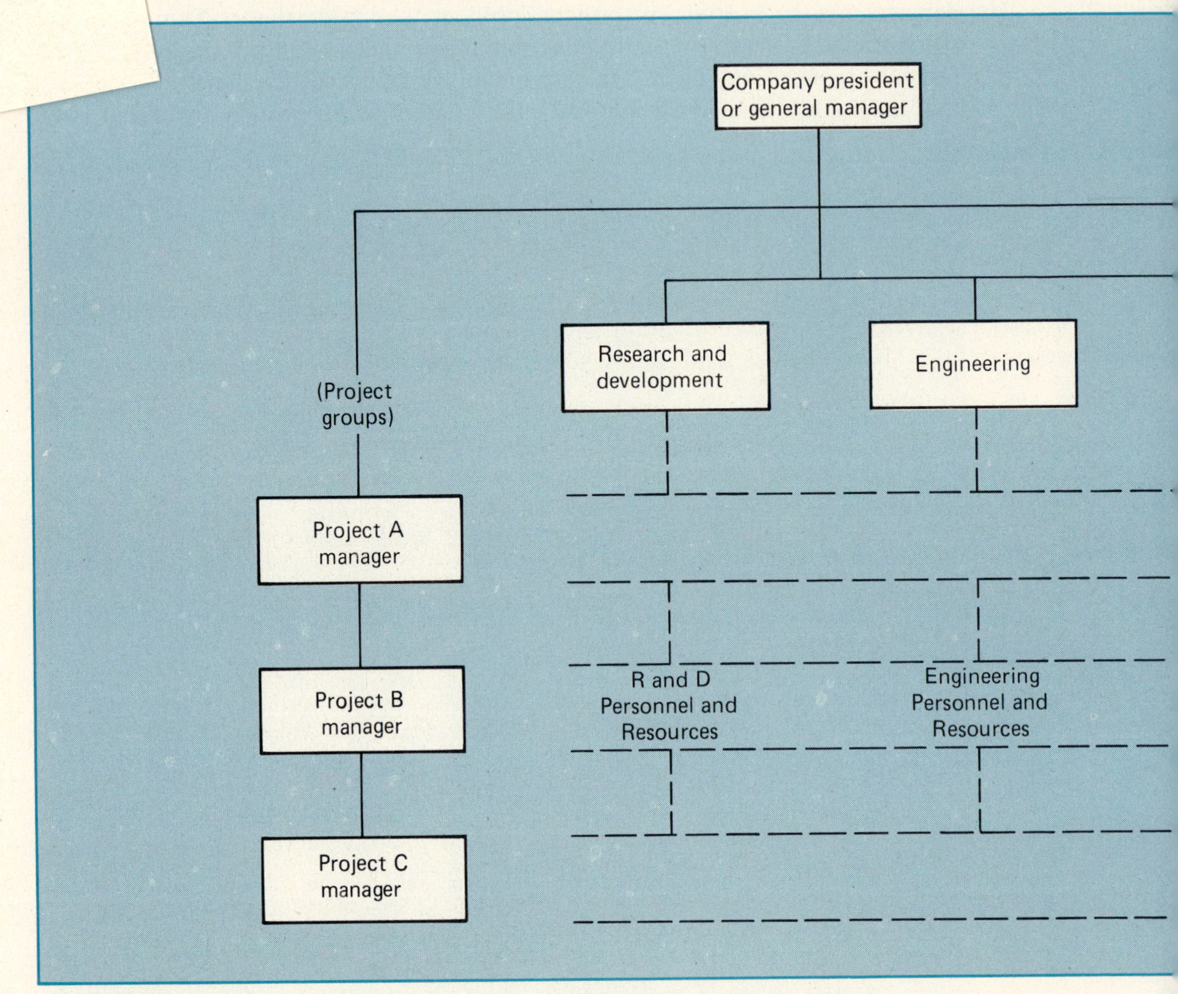

FIGURE 10.3 Illustrative Matrix Organization Structure

the prime role for coordination of activities are superimposed over this functional structure. The matrix form results in dual authority and responsibility.

The matrix form has been used in a variety of companies. In a major reorganization, Dow Corning Company changed from a conventional divisionalized organization to a matrix form. The matrix structure was separated into cost centers, which were the functional activities (marketing, manufacturing, technical service and development, research, and supportive activities) and into profit centers, which were the product lines (rubber, resins and chemicals, consumer, medical, and semiconductors). Under this arrangement, a business board was established for each of the company's ten businesses. The managers of the businesses have the direct responsibility for profits, but they rely on the resources allocated from the functional managers. The majority of the company's profes-

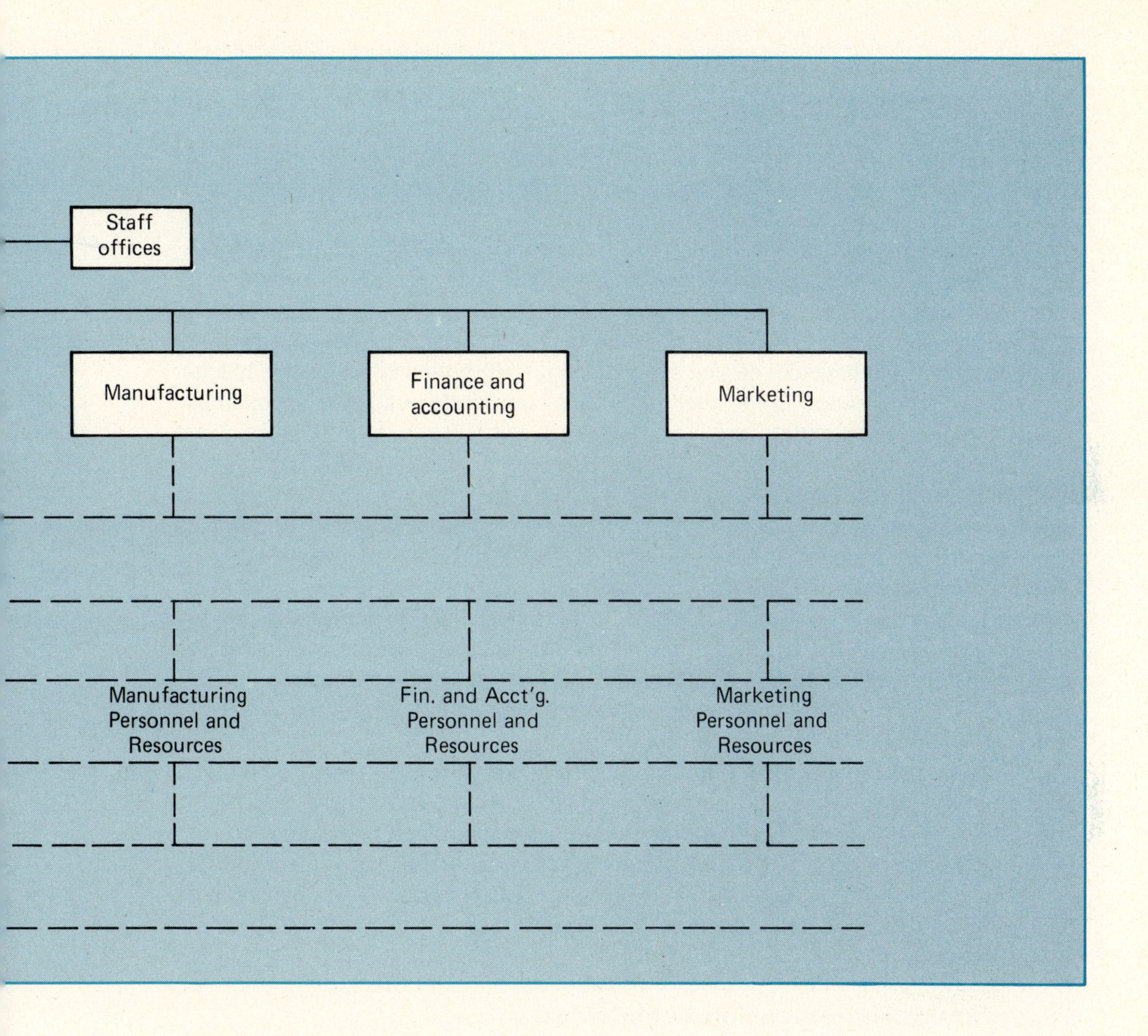

sional and managerial personnel work in a dual authority relationship. They report to the business manager and to their functional manager. Dow Corning has extended this matrix to reflect the different geographic regions in which the company operates. In reporting on the success of this multidimensional form, William Goggin (1974), board chairman and chief executive officer suggests that this structural form is not appropriate for all organizations but fits those that meet all or most of the following conditions (p.64):

Developing, manufacturing, and marketing many diverse but interrelated technological products and materials.
Having market interests that span virtually every major industry.
Becoming multinational with a rapidly expanding global business.

Working in a business environment of rapid and drastic change, together with strong competition.

A company operating with a limited product line, mainly in the United States, serving a single industry, and having a relatively stable environment and technology would not find this form appropriate.

Hospitals have developed matrix type structures. Departments (nursing, social work, dietary, physical therapy, and medical staff specialists) provide for functional specialization; laterally organized units, such as patient care teams, integrate these activities. Universities have functionally organized academic departments, but also have developed specialized interdisciplinary institutes, teaching and research centers, and other units that coordinate academic specialities around programmatic endeavors.

There are many variations of the matrix form in industry and government, but a key common characteristic is that each matrix involves a set of systems managers sharing or contending for resources controlled by a set of functional managers. This approach differs significantly from traditional concepts and requires new attitudes and behavior. "The matrix is a far cry from the organizations most managers have read about and idealized. Clean lines of authority; unambiguous resource allocation to each problem or goal; clear boundaries separating jobs, divisions, organizations, and loyalties are all part of that simpler life that we need to forsake in a dynamic world of overlapping and contradictory interests and goals" (Sayles, 1976, p. 17).

The matrix organization requires managers at all levels—top, functional, and integrative—and their subordinates to develop new approaches, leadership styles, and ways of operating. It is a more complex and difficult form and requires human flexibility in order to provide organizational adaptability. This form should not be used indiscriminately, but only in situations where environmental and technological dynamics make it more appropriate than more traditional organizational structures.

Information-Processing Technologies

One of the key issues in the appropriate design of organizational structures is the obtaining and processing of information for effective decision making. In the open-systems view, information is continually flowing between the organization and its environment and an effective structure must be designed to transmit this information. As organizations have become more complex, they must also be designed to handle internal exchanges of information. Many structural relationships are associated with the communication and processing of information.

Galbraith (1973) suggests that the key issue in designing organizational structures is related to the processing of information. If all tasks are well understood prior to their performance, it is possible to preplan activities effectively. The bureaucratic structure is appropriate under these circumstances. However, organizations operating in a dynamic environment with complex and changing technologies must have information to make continuous adaptations in activities.

"The greater the task uncertainty" writes Galbraith, "the greater the amount of information that must be processed among decision makers during task execution in order to achieve a given level of performance" (p. 4).

In the mass production of standardized products there is a high degree of certainty concerning the tasks to be performed. In contrast, when the National Aeronautics and Space Administration is developing a new space shuttle, the tasks are highly uncertain and a great deal of information will have to be developed and exchanged during the execution of the project. The organization coping with uncertainty must be more adaptive and flexible in order to be effective.

Computers and other technological advancements in information gathering and processing have contributed greatly to organizations' capacity for information processing. However, these information technologies cannot replace the role of the communications network created through the organizational structure. A great deal of important information is obtained, shared, processed, and acted on by the key people working together to coordinate their activities—this is the essence of structure.

The information-processing view emphasizes the importance of knowledge in organizations. With more complex and dynamic environments, organizations need to become more effective learning/adapting systems. Just as it is important to understand how individuals learn and adapt to their circumstances, it is important to understand how organizations use knowledge and learn (Duncan & Weiss, 1979). Our current knowledge concerning information processing and organizational learning suggests that structural characteristics are vital in these processes.

EFFECT OF STRUCTURE ON PEOPLE

There is a commonly held view that people cannot find satisfaction in the formal, highly structured organization. Some people apparently long for a return to nature and more informal work and social relationships. Students frequently say they would prefer careers as entrepreneurs or in smaller organizations, but reality dictates that most will work in large, complex, and formally structured organizations. This view implies a basic conflict between individual needs and satisfactions and large, formal organizations. If this conflict actually exists, our society has a basic dilemma. Environmental, technological and other forces require the creation and utilization of larger, more complex, and formalized organizations with higher degrees of differentiation, integration, formalized authority relationships, and a highly elaborate administrative system of policies and procedures. We are faced with the dilemma of conflict between individual satisfactions and organizational performance.

Let's not be quick to accept this conflict between people and structure absolutely. We see evidence of dedication and apparent satisfaction by members of athletic teams in relatively structured situations. In team sports, there is an interdependence among the members and a reliance on structured relationships. The star quarterback would not be very successful without an effective offensive line and good receivers. The entire offensive unit might be highly effective if it scores 40 points per game, but the *team* is not successful if the defensive unit allows the competitor to score 56 points. The entire team is successful only when members effectively perform roles that are coordinated. This requires structure. The rules of the game, the playbook, the differentiation into offensive and defensive units, the game plan, and the authority/influence system of coaches and scouts are all part of this structure.

Even more dramatic are examples of men's and women's intercollegiate crews. To be successful, this sport requires a high degree of coordination of effort on the part of all eight members and the coxwain. It may entail tremendous amounts of personal effort; rowing between 5:30 and 7:30 A.M. for six months and rigid diets to maintain weight. And the payoff in terms of recognition may be relatively small compared to other sporting events. Yet, many crew members do find a significant amount of personal satisfaction in this relatively structured situation.

Sometimes we fail to recognize how dependent we are on the structuring of situations in our daily lives. Hampton, Summer, and Webber (1982) provide an interesting example to illustrate how we may be less resentful of authority and control by administrative processes than power exercised by a person.

> We resent a traffic light much less than we would resent hundreds of cars with no rules of the road, or a policeman who had no rules to go by other than what he sees and decides himself. This is another way of saying that structural systems in one sense actually permit more delegation, and they do not require so much of one person meddling into another's work affairs (p. 506).

One has only to have driven in those foreign countries where there are few stoplights and where people pay little attention to the rules of the road, to appreciate the value of *some* structure. So perhaps it isn't so much that people resent structured situations as that they resent inappropriate or excessive structuring of their behavior. Until a few years ago, there was one traffic light in the small community of North Bend, Washington. It was reputed to be the only traffic light for the entire distance of I-90, which crosses the country. During summer weekends when many Seattleites went to the Cascades and Eastern Washington, the line of cars, campers, and trucks was five to six miles, with waits of several hours to get through the stoplight. There was little happiness and satisfaction among the travelers. The situation brought out the worst human behavior. The people felt that this structuring of behavior was totally inappropriate.

Sometimes we attribute problems and our dissatisfaction to too much structure when in actuality there really may not be enough. The vignette of George Kozlov attempting to change his registration is an example. Rather than being too tightly structured, perhaps the university did not have an administrative system that was efficient (structured) enough to handle his situation. If similar problems are faced by a number of students, the best answer may be to develop a more comprehensive system of integration between various departments in the university. More, rather than less, structure may be the better answer.

Take another example, the routine physical examination. Would you prefer to make all of your own arrangements for visits to the cardiologist, internist, laboratory, and X-ray technicians—an unstructured situation—or would you prefer to turn yourself in for a day to a clinic where the entire physical examination was arranged, necessary specialists were available for consultation, X-ray and laboratory facilities were scheduled, and the entire endeavor was well planned, structured, and integrated? We prefer the latter approach. It saves a great deal of time and we think it is more efficient. Others may prefer a less structured approach with more options and self-control.

This brings up the point of individual differences in responses. People are different in the degree to which they tolerate structure. Even more complicated, the same person may have different attitudes concerning the structuring of various work and life activities. For example, we may tolerate and even welcome the structure imposed on us by the clinic for physical examinations. As professors we may appreciate a well-structured registration system that assigns students to classes efficiently, and an effective bookstore that ensures that textbooks are available. At the same time, we may resent the imposition of external authority and controls over our classroom teaching and research activities.

We suggest that people both welcome and resent structure. They do have an implicit recognition that any organized system requires some structuring of their behavior. But, generally they would prefer that the system structure the behavior of other participants rather than their own.

Effect of Structure on Attitudes and Behavior

Substantial research has been focused on the relationship between structural characteristics and attitudes (such as job satisfaction and need fulfillment) and behavior (such as performance, absenteeism, and turnover). (For a review of this research see Berger & Cummings, 1979 and Dalton et al., 1980.) Unfortunately, many research results are contradictory or specifically related to individual organizations and are not generalizable to other situations and organizations. However, there is agreement that structural characteristics do have significant impact upon both attitudes and behavior. Some of the structural characteristics that seem to influence people the most are shown in Figure 10.4.

When these structural characteristics are appropriate, and fit the environmental, technological, and internal requirements, they have a positive impact upon individual satisfaction and performance. However, major deficiencies in structure can lead to many major organizational problems. Some of the consequences of structural deficiencies are suggested in Box 10.3. It is evident that "bad" structural relationships can create many organizational and individual problems. It should not be inferred that either a low or high degree of structure is bad or good per se. Actually there are often adverse individual or organizational consequences of either too much or too little structure. For example, people perform poorly and are dissatisfied when tasks and roles are poorly defined, or

BOX 10.3
CONSEQUENCES OF STRUCTURAL DEFICIENCIES

Among the features which so often mark the struggling organization are low motivation and morale, late and inappropriate decisions, conflict and lack of co-ordination, rising costs and a generally poor response to new opportunities and external change. Structural deficiencies can play a part in exacerbating all these problems.

1. Motivation and morale may be depressed because:
   a. Decisions appear to be inconsistent and arbitrary in the absence of standardized rules.
   b. People perceive that they have little responsibility, opportunity for achievement and recognition of their worth because there is insufficient delegation of decision-making. This may be connected with narrow spans of control.
   c. There is a lack of clarity as to what is expected of people and how their performance is assessed. This is due to inadequate job definition.
   d. People are subject to competing pressures from different parts of the organization due to the absence of clearly defined priorities, decision rules or work programmes.
   e. People are overloaded because their support systems are not adequate.
2. Decision-making may be delayed and lacking in quality because:
   a. Necessary information is not transmitted on time to the appropriate people. This may be due to an over-extended hierarchy.
   b. Decision-makers are too segmented into separate units and there is inadequate provision to co-ordinate them.
   c. Decision-makers are overloaded due to insufficient delegation on their part.
   d. There are no adequate procedures for evaluating the results of similar decisions made in the past.
3. There may be conflict and a lack of co-ordination because:
   a. There are conflicting goals which have not been structured into a single set of objectives and priorities. People are acting at cross purposes.
   b. People are working out of step with each other because they are not brought together into teams or because mechanisms for liaison have not been laid down.
   c. The people who are actually carrying out operational work and who are in touch with changing contingencies are not permitted to participate in the planning of the work. There is therefore a breakdown between planning and operations.

4. An organization may not respond innovatively to changing circumstances because:
   a. It has not established specialized jobs concerned with forecasting and scanning the environment.
   b. There is a failure to ensure that innovation and planning of change are mainstream activities backed up by top management through appropriate procedures.
   c. There is inadequate co-ordination between the part of an organization identifying changing market needs and the research area working on possible technological solutions.
5. Costs may be rising rapidly, particularly in the administrative area because:
   a. The organization has a long hierarchy with a high ratio of 'chiefs' to 'indians.'
   b. There is an excess of procedure and paperwork distracting people's attention away from productive work and requiring additional staff personnel to administer.

Source: John Child, *Organisation: A Guide to Problems and Practices*. London: Harper & Row, 1977, pp. 10–12.

when there is a total lack of policy guidelines, or when nobody understands who is supposed to do what. On the other hand, where tasks and roles are overly specialized, where rules cover every activity, and where the hierarchy and authority patterns are extremely rigid, there is decidedly too much structure: which also tends to create dissatisfaction and lack of motivation. Obviously, the key issue of organization design is to find the most appropriate structure *to fit the situation*.

Effect of Specific Structural Characteristics

So far we have discussed rather general relationships between structure and human attitudes and behavior. We might look at more specific structural characteristics and their impact. For example, do people perform better and are they more satisfied in small or large organizations, in tall or flat structures, in line or staff positions, at different levels in the hierarchy, and under centralization or decentralization? These are good questions, but unfortunately there do not appear to be any clearcut answers from the research findings. In fact there has not been an abundance of research on these relationships as compared to other issues of human behavior in organizations, such as motivation and leadership (Porter & Lawler, 1965; Berger & Cummings, 1979).

One study relating employee behavior and satisfaction to organizational shape and size was conducted by James Worthy (1950) in his investigation of nearly 100,000 employees of Sears Roebuck over a 12-year period. He concluded that larger organizations with complex and tall structures (many levels) had lower

Structural Characteristics	Explanation
Design of Tasks	How different tasks are designed and assigned to individuals and units within the organization.
Definition of Roles	Specification of role requirements and demands of the position.
Composition of Work Units and Departments	How tasks, functions, and positions are grouped together to form the hierarchical structure.
Authority and Responsibility Relationships	Who has the authority and responsibility for performance and who reports to whom.
Communications Patterns	The information flow between individuals, work units, and departments in the organization.
Formalization of Activities	The degree to which various tasks, activities, and processes are formalized through policies, rules, and procedures.
Centralization/Decentralization	Who makes the decisions and at what level in the hierarchy. The degree of autonomy and discretion at various levels.
Planning and Control Systems	The systems of decision making and control processes to ensure and measure organizational performance.
Compensation Systems	Designing compensation systems to fit tasks, positions, and responsibilities and to reward effective performance.
Recruitment, Selection, Training and Career Development	Developing a system to ensure that people are available and capable of filling positional requirements.

FIGURE 10.4 Structural Characteristics That Influence Human Behavior

employee productivity and satisfaction than smaller ones with flatter structures. "Flatter, less complex structures, with a maximum of administrative decentralization, tend to create a potential for improved attitudes, more effective supervision, and greater individual responsibility and initiative among employees" (p. 179). Other researchers have reached similar conclusions in different organization settings (Ivancevich and Donnelly, 1975). In contrast, some have found the reverse to be true, or that no relationship between structural shape and employee satisfaction and performance could be found (Carzo and Yanouzas, 1969). Porter and Lawler (1964) found the relationship between organizational structure and satisfaction to be even more complex. They concluded that there was "no overall superiority of flat over tall organizations in producing greater need satisfaction for managers" (p. 146). However, they did find that in companies with fewer than 5000 employees, managerial satisfaction was greater in flat rather than tall organizations. But, for companies with more than 5000 employees the relationship was reverse. Furthermore, they concluded that the effects of organizational structure on satisfaction appeared to vary with the type of psychological need being considered. A tall structure seems to satisfy the security and social needs better, whereas a flat structure is superior in influencing self-actualizational satisfactions. These conclusions are interesting because they reflect one of the most apparent relationships between structure and human satisfaction: that different structures create climates in which different psychological needs can be satisfied. We should be cautious about absolute statements on the relationship between structural characteristics and participant satisfactions. There are, however, some tentative generalizations, based on the best available evidence, that we can put forward.

Generally, there is evidence that employee satisfaction is slightly higher in small and medium-sized organizations than in larger organizations. However, there does not appear to be any clear relationship between organization size and performance. There is stronger evidence suggesting that employees have high satisfaction and performance when working in smaller departments or subunits (Dalton et al., 1980). For example, employees in large stenographic pools, draftsmen working with 100 others in the same room, and clerical workers in large units in insurance companies seem to have lower satisfaction (and likely lower performance) than employees in smaller, more personal units. Large task units seem to make it more difficult for employees to develop social interactions, an overall perspective of the work, and a sense of contribution and achievement. We also sense this in the university setting. Many share a distaste for sitting in large lecture classes with 500 to 700 other students and with little opportunity for interpersonal contact.

There is greater job satisfaction as people move up the hierarchy. Superiors are more satisfied than subordinates at all levels. In opinion surveys of approximately 175,000 employees in 159 companies taken since 1950, there has been a consistent pattern of more positive attitudes and job satisfaction on the part of managers, as compared with clerical and hourly employees. "There is a consistent difference of opinion expressed by employees at many levels in organizations. We call this consistent difference, in which managers are usually more satisfied than clerical and hourly employees, the 'hierarchy gap.' This gap is usually greatest between managers and hourly employees" (Cooper et al., 1979, p. 117).

These differentials in satisfaction by levels seem natural. Totally alienated people are likely to leave the organization and those that move up the hierarchy receive greater status and rewards, reinforcing their behavior and satisfactions. However, there is also evidence of different types of satisfactions at different levels. At lower levels, satisfaction of physiological, security, and social needs seem most important, whereas, as one moves up the hierarchy, status and self-actualization become more important.

Managers in line positions in organizations appear to have higher satisfaction than employees in staff positions. Theoretically, line functions are basic and the manager has authority, whereas staffs are supportive and provide advice. The distinction between line and staff is no longer clearcut in many organizations. Yet the image of staff as secondary in importance and subservient to the line still hangs on (Browne and Golembiewski, 1974). Participants see staff units as having less status, power and influence, and effects on organizational activities. Staff units tend to have a higher level of frustration and uncertainty about their operations. Frequently, staff members are not as well rewarded in terms of status and remunerations. The climate is less supportive of staffs, and their satisfaction and sense of achievement is less. To a large extent, the distinction between line and staff and the low recognition of the importance of staff activities is a holdover from traditional organizational structures. In many dynamic and complex organizations, staff units have a vital function. They are frequently the major source of innovation and adaptation for the organization, creating, and pressing for the utilization of new knowledge. Their importance will be recognized more in the future than it has been in the past, but the structural relationships, climate, and perceived importance of various organizational activities can, of course, be slow to change.

It does appear that the popular notion of low satisfaction and performance in large, formally structured organizations is not necessarily true. Nor is it true that everyone finds satisfaction in the less formal, decentralized, and dynamic organization. For example, there is evidence of many human problems in project and matrix organizational forms (Sayles, 1976; Lawrence, Kolodny, & Davis, 1977). Project managers and their staffs seem to be in stressful positions and have a high level of anxiety and uncertainty as compared with functional managers. Engineers and scientists working for NASA or an aerospace firm on an exciting new program may find work interesting and have the opportunity for real involvement. But, what happens when the project is terminated and, after 20 years with the company, they wait every Friday in anticipation of a layoff notice? Many wish they had started their careers in more stable industries. Work life may be somewhat boring in the mechanistic/stable organizations, but it can be uncertain and stressful in the dynamic, change-oriented organization. There is evidence to suggest that people with different attitudes, personality traits, and needs find satisfaction and motivation to perform well in different types of organizations.

Organizational Boundary Roles

Environmental forces have a direct effect on the way the organization structures its activities. When the environment is dynamic and heterogeneous it is usually necessary to establish functional departments within the organization to deal with a specific set of environmental inputs or outputs (Aldrich & Herker, 1977). Many staff departments have been established as boundary-spanning components. These positions are often stressful and the incumbents have significant role conflict. For example, the sales department may have continual conflicts in responding to the needs of customers, while recognizing the requirement for production efficiency. The press secretary may have problems in playing a supportive role for the president of the United States, and still retaining credibility and effective relationships with the news media. The general manager of a multinational division may have difficulty in both responding to the expectations from corporate headquarters and adapting to the local environment. The university football coach may have difficulty in attending to the internal-system requirements of players, other students, and faculty as well as to those of the alumni, press, and general public.

> Boundary positions have a number of unique properties deriving from their structural relationship to other roles and from the fact that the occupants of these positions must effect transactions with external agents. First, the occupant of such a position—named here the boundary role person or BRP—is more distant, psychologically, organizationally, and often physically, from other members of his organization than they are from each other, and he is closer to the external environment and to the agents of outside organizations; second, he represents his organization to the external environment; and, third, he is his organization's agent of influence over the external environment (Adams, 1976, p. 1176).

The boundary role person may find her own organization suspicious of her activities. She may have to arbitrate conflicts between the environmental forces and her organization. She is subject to substantial role conflicts. "In effect, the BRP is both the influencer and the recipient of influence from insiders and outsiders. This basic characteristic leads potentially to higher levels of role conflict and tension for the BRP than for other organization members" (Adams, 1976, p. 1178). This may affect her own level of satisfaction significantly.

CONGRUENCE BETWEEN STRUCTURE AND BEHAVIOR

The research findings suggests the need for congruence among various factors, if an organization is to perform effectively. We have discussed the need for congruence between environment, technology, and structure earlier in this chapter and now need to integrate another vital factor—human behavior. Figure 10.5 suggests this interrelationship.

Different structures create different organizational internal climates, which, in turn, require different attitudes and behavior. Effective organizations have a high level of congruence among these factors (Lorsch & Morse, 1974). People do adapt to different organization structures and can perform effectively with high levels of satisfaction in different types. This is particularly true when they recognize that a particular structure is appropriate for meeting the organization's goals. However, there are individual differences; people vary in terms of the types of organizational structures and climates in which they are effective. This suggests the need for some matching between personality and organizational types. Figure 10.6 depicts how the dominant behaviors of people would differ in the two major forms.

Organizations need to have a clear assessment of how the structure affects attitudes and behavior of people. This assessment is vital in determining the types of individuals who are selected and trained, the nature of the compensation and

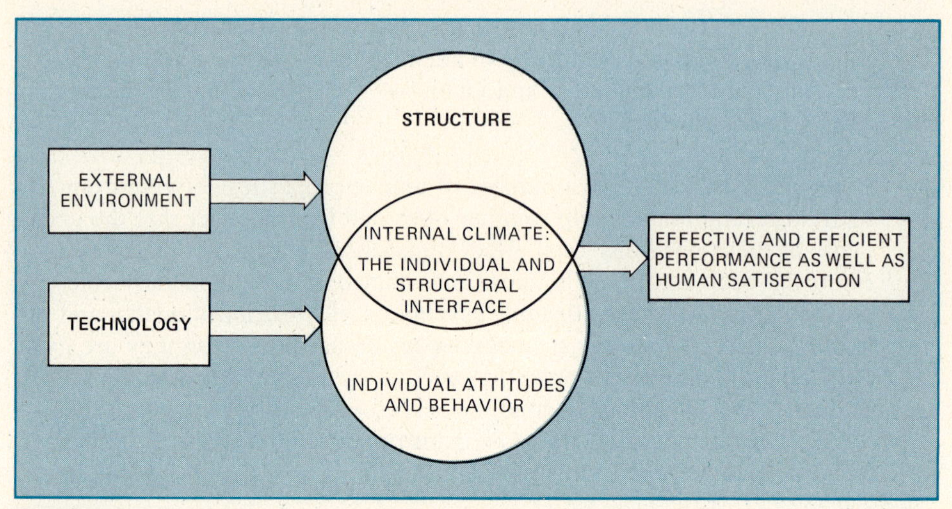

FIGURE 10.5 Congruence Among Environment, Technology, Structure, and Individual Attitudes and Behavior.

reward system, and many other personnel policies and procedures. It is unrealistic, however, to conceive of the matching of structure and human behavior as a one-way process: as if the manager should design the structure first and then find the appropriate people whose attitudes and behavior match that structure. It is both necessary and proper to look at the other direction: which starts with human attitudes and behavior and then moves toward designing a structure that will maximize both performance and human satisfaction. This view is prominent in many of the experiments on work redesign. The middle-ground approach holds that both structural characteristics and human attitudes and behavior are *variables* that are adaptable within limits. The manager can make adaptations in structure to fit human factors and people can adapt to different structural characteristics. The managerial task is to develop congruence between structure and attitudes and behavior.

This leads us back to our original premise. There is little evidence to suggest that *all* people respond the same way to any particular type of organizational structure. There are differences in personality characteristics. Some people prefer a tightly structured, more formal situation, while others are more effective in informal relationships. Environment and technology are obvious determinants of structure and cannot be ignored in organizational design. Evidently, people have a sense of competence and satisfaction when the internal structure is appropriately designed to fit the situation. Working in an effective organization may in itself provide a source of motivation and satisfaction for participants.

One last idea relates to organizational change and improvement. If there is an inappropriate fit between environment, structure, and the predisposition of

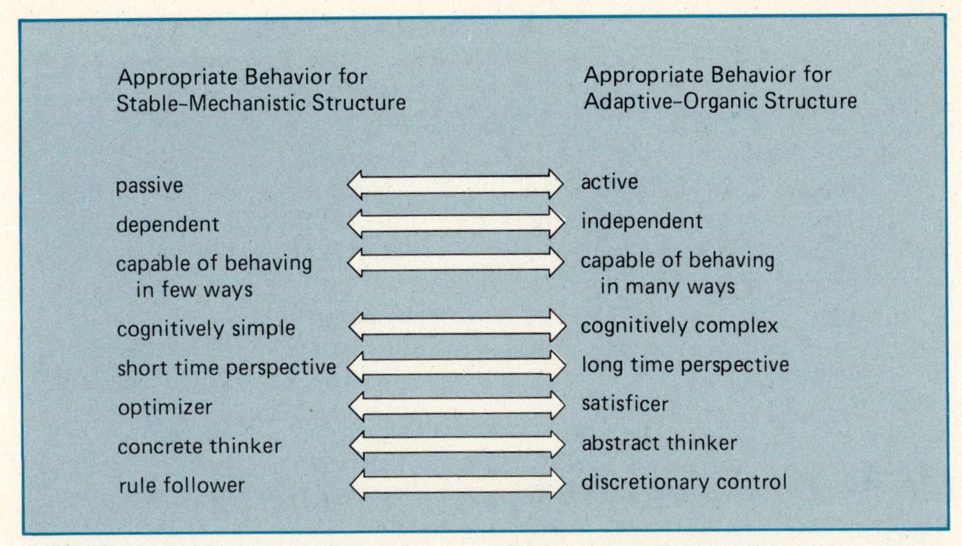

FIGURE 10.6 Behavior Appropriate in Different Organization Structures. **Source:** Adapted from Laird W. Mealiea and Dennis Lee, "An Alternative to Macro-Micro Contingency Theories: An Integrative Model," *Academy of Management Review,* July 1979, p. 338.

members, how do managers go about making changes and improvements? One way might be to attempt to modify the environment and the technology. As we have suggested, this may be possible, but only to a limited extent since managers usually do not have much control over these forces. Another way might be to attempt to change the attitudes and behavior of the people—shape the people to fit the situation. Again, this can be done within limits. However, it is not easy for the manager to make significant changes in the personality characteristics and behavior of people. They can be modified, certainly, but in many cases only within a narrow range.

In actual practice, it may be easier and more efficient for the manager to make changes in organizational structure and climate than in the other two variables. In Chapter 9, we discussed one such structural modification—job redesign. There are many others. For example, managers can look more closely at the issue of centralization or decentralization of authority. They can make adjustments in administrative procedures and control processes. They can determine the degree of differentiation, both vertically and horizontally. They can develop alternative means for achieving integration. In effect, working on structural issues may be one of the most effective means for improving organizational performance *and* for increasing the satisfaction of individual members. Chapter 16 will discuss some of organizational improvement strategies that use structural approaches.

SO WHAT? IMPLICATIONS FOR YOU

As a Member in an Organization

Generalization	Implications
1. Structure affects the behavior of people in organizations. It determines their tasks and roles, their relationship with other people, groups, and departments, and authority and influence systems.	1. When joining an organization, make an effort to learn about the basic structural relationships. Find out (1) how the work is divided, (2) who has authority for what, and (3) who is responsible for what. Understand how your assigned position and functions fit into the structure.
2. Formal organization is the planned structure and represents the deliberate attempt to establish the pattern of relationships.	2. Recognize that the formal structure affects you. It typically provides the framework for the hierarchy, the compensation system, and various career paths.
3. Typically, formal organization is represented by an organization chart and described in policy statements, position descriptions, and procedures manuals.	3. Obtain an organization chart and other written representation of your organization. Study these structural relationships.
4. Many interactions occur which are not prescribed by the formal structure. The *informal* structure plays a vital part in the functioning of most organizations. The informal structure refers to those aspects of the system that are not planned explicitly but arise spontaneously out of the activities and interactions of the participants.	4. Be aware of and use the informal structure. Try to determine the informal communications networks and group dynamics that seem to facilitate the accomplishment of the organization's goals.
5. Environmental influences, technological requirements and psychosocial factors help determine structure.	5. Be aware of the interactions and interrelationships between these various components in the organizational system.
6. Many newer organization forms, such as project and matrix structures, are dynamic and	6. Recognize that these new forms must deal with conflict and that this is normal. You will need to

Generalization

flexible. They can also lead to conflicts and may be stressful to participants.

Implications

be adaptable to meet the requirements of these forms.

Generalization

7. Conflict (or compatibility) between individual need satisfaction and organizational structure is not inherent.

Implications

7. Recognize that you really welcome a certain degree of structure in your life and that there is no inherent conflict between this inclination and the achievement of personal satisfaction. The issue is one of having the appropriate structure to fit the situation.

Generalization

8. Different structures create internal climates that require different attitudes and behavior. The stable/mechanistic and the adaptive/organic forms, for example, require quite different behaviors.

Implications

8. Assess your own attitudes and behavior. In what kind of organization will you operate best? Recognize that no structure is perfect. Each will have advantages and disadvantages for the participants.

As a Current or Future Manager

Generalization

1. Environmental, technological, and psychosocial factors help determine structure. One of management's key functions is to design the organization in response to various contextual and internal forces.

Implications

1. Recognize the importance of managerial choice in designing structure. Be aware of the interrelationships among the various factors that influence structure.

Generalization

2. Organizations designed to match environmental characteristics and technological requirements perform more effectively.

Implications

2. Structure should be designed to link the environment and internal subsystems.

Generalization

3. Increased turbulence, uncertainty, and complexity in the environment results in the need for more complex and differentiated organization structures. In turn, this complexity creates

Implications

3. Recognize that the environment may require a more complex structure, and this may bring additional managerial problems. Pay particular attention to the need for designing, planning,

Generalization	Implications
problems for planning, decision making, and the integration of activities.	and implementing structural changes.
4. Differentiation and integration are two of the most important aspects in designing organization structure.	4. Recognize that the move toward greater differentiation, either vertically or horizontally, generally leads to the need for more effective integration. Do not create separate units, departments, or groups without giving due consideration to the need for integration.
5. Many newer organizational forms, such as multidivisional, multinational, project, and matrix structures, are significant departures from traditional stable/mechanistic structures.	5. Recognize that structure has to be adapted to meet specific situations. Be prepared to review your structure and make necessary changes.
6. Managers probably have more control over structural relationships than they have over other variables (such as the environment, technology, or human attitudes and behavior).	6. Use this control judiciously to design your organization. However, recognize that control over structure is never absolute and must be used with an awareness of the effect on other subsystems.
7. Structural characteristics affect the attitudes and behavior of people in your organization.	7. Continually review the effect of structural characteristics on the people in your organization. Be aware that any structural change is likely to affect their attitudes and behavior.
8. Because structural characteristics are semipermanent, they may become inappropriate for current circumstances. It is easy to develop rigid, inflexible structures that were effective for "yesterday's organization."	8. Continually review to ensure that structural characteristics are functional and meet the needs of the contemporary organization.
9. Many of today's decisions (such as selection and training of per-	9. Develop long-range concepts and plans concerning how your

Generalization	Implications
sonnel) can affect future organization design and structure.	organization will be structured five to ten years in the future. Your current decisions should build toward this desired future.

LEARNING APPLICATION ACTIVITIES

1. Write a short vignette based on your own experience that illustrates the effects of structure on people in an organization.

2. a. Review the vignette *How Much Decentralization?* What do you think William Cook should do?
b. Share your recommended actions in groups of four to six.
c. As an alternative select one person to play the role of William Cook and another to play the role of Elizabeth Fotheringill. The rest of the group should act as observers.

3. *Step 1.* Prepare a list of factors that contribute to the problems in the vignette *The Emergency Room*. How might these problems have been avoided?
Step 2. Meet in groups of four to six and share your lists of factors and suggested solutions. Acting as the board of trustees of City Hospital, what changes in organization structure would you implement?

4. *Step 1.* Scan you local newspaper, the *Wall Street Journal*, or other periodicals to find an incident illustrating issues in organizational structure.
Step 2. Share your incidents in groups of four to six.

5. a. Pick any organization that you're familiar with and describe the formal structure. Draw its organization chart.
b. For the same organization, describe the informal structure. In what ways are the formal and informal structure compatible? In what ways are they in conflict?

6. Choose an organization that you are familiar with and briefly describe (a) the way in which activities are differentiated, (b) the means of integration, (c) the authority and responsibility relationships, and (d) the nature of the administrative system.

7. *Step 1.* In groups of three to four visit a convenient organization, such as an automobile dealership, bank, or department store. Interview the owner/manager (or other key employees) with the objective of finding out about how the business is organized and managed.
a. Develop an organization chart that indicates the formal di-

vision of work, both horizontally (e.g., departments) and vertically (superior-subordinate relationships).

b. Write a brief job description of each of the key roles in the organization. The description should include the following: (1) functions and responsibilities (work activities) and (2) authority relationships (reports to. . . supervises. . . interacts with. . .).

c. Determine in your interview what are the major problems associated with the organization structure (e.g., too much concentration of authority or lack of understanding of roles and responsibilities).

Step 2. Be prepared to put your organization chart on the blackboard and share your observations with the entire class.

8. Based on your experience in an organization (using Figure 10.4 as a frame of reference) describe the structural characteristics that seem to have a significant effect on the attitudes and behavior of the people.

9. *Step 1.* Assess your own attitudes and preferred ways of behaving. Do you think you will be more satisfied and productive in a stable/mechanistic or an adaptive/organic structure?

Step 2. Share your observations in groups of four to six. Does your self-assessment match others in your group?

REFERENCES

Adams, J. Stacy. "The Structure and Dynamics of Behavior in Organizational Boundary Roles." In Marvin D. Dunnette (Ed.), *Handbook of Industrial and Organizational Psychology*. Chicago, Ill.: Rand McNally, 1976, pp. 1175–1199.

Aldrich, Howard. *Organizations and Environments*. Englewood Cliffs, N.J.: Prentice-Hall, 1979.

Aldrich, Howard, and Diane Herker. "Boundary Spanning Roles and Organization Structure." *Academy of Management Review* 2 (April 1977): 217–230.

Allen, Stephen A. III. "Corporate-Divisional Relationships in Highly Diversified Firms." In Jay W. Lorsch and Paul R. Lawrence (Eds.), *Studies in Organization Design*. Homewood Ill.: Dorsey Press/Irwin, 1970, pp. 16–35.

Anderson, Carl R., and Frank T. Paine, "Managerial Perceptions and Strategic Behavior." *Academy of Management Journal* 18 (December 1975): 811–823.

Baldridge, J. Victor, and Robert A. Burnham. "Organizational Innovation: Individual, Organizational, and Environmental Inputs." *Administrative Science Quarterly* 20 (June 1975): 165–176.

Berger, Chris J., and L. L. Cummings. "Organizational Structure, Attitudes, and Behaviors." In Barry M. Staw (Ed.), *Research in Organization Behavior*. Vol. 1. Greenwich, Conn.: 1979, pp. 169–208.

Blau, Peter M., and Richard A. Schoenherr. *The Structure of Organizations*. New York: Basic Books, 1971.

Blau, Peter M., and W. Richard Scott. *Formal Organizations: A Comparative Approach*. San Francisco, Calif.: Chandler, 1962.

Browne, Philip J., and Robert T. Golembiewski. "The Line-Staff Concept Revisited: An Empirical Study of Organizational Images." *Academy of Management Journal* 17 (September 1974): 406–417.

Burns, Tom, and G. M. Stalker. *The Management of Innovation*. London: Tavistock, 1961.

Carzo, Rocco, Jr., and John N. Yanouzas. "Effects of Flat and Tall Organization Structure." *Administrative Science Quarterly* 14 (June 1969): 178–191.

Chandler, Alfred D., Jr. *Strategy and Structure*. Cambridge, Mass.: M.I.T. Press, 1962.

Child, John. *Organization: A Guide to Problems and Practice*. London: Harper & Row, 1977.

———. "Organizational Structure, Environment and Performance: The Role of Strategic Choice." *Sociology* 6/1 (January 1972): 1–22.

Cooper, Michael R., Brian S. Morgan, Patricia Mortenson Foley, and Leon B. Kaplan. "Changing Employee Values: Deepening Discontent?" *Harvard Business Review,* 57/1 (January-February 1979): 117–125.

Dalton, Dan R., William D. Todor, Michael J. Spendolini, Gordon J. Fielding, and Lyman W. Porter. "Organization Structure and Performance: A Critical Review." *Academy of Management Review* 5 (January 1980): 49–64.

Davis, Stanley M., and Paul R. Lawrence. "Problems of Matrix Organizations." *Harvard Business Review* 56/3 (May-June 1978): 131–142.

Drucker, Peter F. *Management: Task, Responsibilities, Practices*. New York: Harper & Row, 1974.

Duncan, Robert. "Characteristics of Organizational Environments and Perceived Environmental Uncertainty." *Administrative Science Quarterly* 17 (September 1972): 313–327.

Duncan, Robert, and Andrew Weiss. "Organizational Learning: Implications for Organizational Design." In Barry M. Staw (Ed.), *Research in Organizational Behavior*. Vol. 1. Greenwich, Conn.: JAI Press, 1979, pp. 75–123.

Galbraith, Jay. *Designing Complex Organizations*. Reading, Mass.: Addison-Wesley, 1973.

———. "Designing the Innovating Organization." *Organizational Dynamics,* Winter 1982, pp. 5–25.

Goggin, William C. "How the Multidimensional Structure Works at Dow Corning." *Harvard Business Review* 52/1 (January-February 1974): 54–65.

Hall, Richard H. *Organizations: Structure and Process*. Englewood Cliffs, N.J.: Prentice-Hall, 1972.

Hampton, David R., Charles E. Summer, and Ross A. Webber. *Organizational Behavior and the Practice of Management*. 4th ed. Glenview, Ill.: Scott, Foresman, 1982.

Ivancevich, John M., and James H. Donnelly, Jr., "Relation of Organizational Structure to Job Satisfaction, Anxiety-Stress, and Performance." *Administrative Science Quarterly* 20 (June 1975): 272–280.

Kast, Fremont E., and James E. Rosenzweig. *Organization and Management*. 3d ed. New York: McGraw-Hill, 1979.

Khandwalla, Pradip N. "Viable and Effective Organizational Design of Firms." *Academy of Management Journal* 16 (September 1973): 481–495.

Kolodny, Harvey F. "Evolution to a Matrix Organization." *Academy of Management Review* 4 (October 1979): 543–553.

Lawrence, Paul R., Harvey F. Kolodny, and Stanley M. Davis. "The Human Side of the Matrix." *Organizational Dynamics* 6/1 (Summer 1977): 43–61.

Lawrence, Paul R., and Jay W. Lorsch. "Differentiation and Integration in Complex Organizations." *Administrative Science Quarterly* 12 (June 1967): 1–47.

———. *Organization and Environment*. Boston, Mass.: Division of Research, Graduate School of Business Administration, Harvard University, 1967.

Litterer, Joseph A. *The Analysis of Organizations*. 2d ed., New York: Wiley, 1973.

Lorsch, Jay W., and John J. Morse. *Organizations and their Members: A Contingency Approach*. New York: Harper & Row, 1974.

Mealiea, Laird W., and Dennis Lee. ''An Alternative to Macro-Micro Contingency Theories: An Integrative Model.'' *Academy of Management Review* 4/3 (July 1979): 33–46.

Pfeffer, Jeffrey, and Gerald R. Salancik, *The External Control of Organizations*. New York: Harper & Row, 1978.

Porter, Lyman W., and Edward E. Lawler III. ''The Effect of 'Tall' Versus 'Flat' Organization Structures on Managerial Job Satisfaction.'' *Personnel Psychology* 17 (Summer 1964): 135–148.

———. ''Properties of Organization Structure in Relation to Job Attitudes and Job Behavior.'' *Psychological Bulletin* 64 (July 1965): 23–51.

Pugh, D. S., D. J. Hickson, C. R. Hinings, and C. Turner. ''The Context of Organization Structure.'' *Administrative Science Quarterly* 14 (March 1969): 91–114.

Sayles, Leonard R. ''Matrix Management: The Structure with a Future.'' *Organizational Dynamics* 5/2 (Autumn 1976): 2–17.

Starbuck, William H. ''Organizations and Their Environments.'' In Marvin D. Dunnette (Ed.) *Handbook of Industrial and Organizational Psychology*. Chicago: Rand McNally, 1976, pp. 1069–1123.

Weber, Max. *The Theory of Social and Economic Organization*. Translated by A. M. Henderson and Talcott Parsons. N.Y.: Free Press, 1964.

Weick, Karl E. *The Social Psychology of Organizing*. 2d ed. Reading, Mass.: Addison-Wesley, 1979.

Worthy, James C. ''Organizational Structure and Employee Morale.'' *American Sociological Review* 15 (April 1950): 169–179.

11
Decision-Making Processes

LEARNING OBJECTIVES

After reading this chapter you should be able to:

1. Explain why decision making is a good focus of attention for understanding human behavior in organizations.
2. Illustrate the decision-making process (from problem sensing through following up) by referring to a real decision you have made.
3. Describe the role of information (and information processing) in the decision-making process.
4. Compare and contrast beliefs and values; illustrate their effect on decision making with a personal example.
5. Discuss the advantages and disadvantages of group decision making (vis à vis individuals) and the role of leadership in making the process effective, efficient, and satisfying for participants.
6. Outline a managerial approach for facilitating improved decision-making processes in organizations, with reference to both the rationality and creativity of decisions.

SEMICONSCIOUS

The alarm sounded at 6:00 A.M. and Alex reached over, turned it off, and promptly went back to sleep. He stirred again at 7:00 A.M.; remembered he had an exam in his 7:30 class; forced himself to get out of the sack; and groped unsteadily toward the bathroom. He dressed quickly, skipping breakfast, and headed out the door for class.

Fortunately, traffic was light at this time of the day and he was able to cover the distance from his apartment to school in near record time. His mind was on the exam as he exceeded the speed limit a little and unknowingly slipped by two amber lights. Alex reached the classroom at 7:31, only to find the room deserted. Panic! Then he remembered; the exam was scheduled for the auditorium at the other end of the building.

After the exam Alex climbed into his 280Z and drove out of the parking lot. When he drove into his stall in the parking garage of his apartment, he remembered that he had agreed to meet with Debbie and Chuck this morning, at Debbie's place, to study for tomorrow's accounting final.

AL'S DILEMMA

Al had a real dilemma. He worked part-time in the produce department of a large supermarket with two full-time employees and several other part-time employees. Charlie, one of his part-time co-workers, was not doing his share of the work. He tended to take extra time on coffee breaks and he spent a lot of time talking with other employees or customers. Al hadn't been too upset until he realized that he was doing a considerable amount of Charlie's work.

Al needed the job and hoped to keep it two more years until he finished college. He assumed that Charlie would be there another year or so—until he completed his degree in psychology. Charlie was a likeable sort of guy who seemed to "organize" the after-work recreation, and he always included Al.

The situation was complex and Al had mixed emotions about what to do. He wondered whether he should say something to the department manager, talk to Charlie directly, or do nothing at all.

WIN OR TIE?

Pete was the quarterback at State University. During the final minute of last week's football game, State scored a touchdown to come within one point of their opponents, 20 to 19. Pete's problem was whether or not to go for one point and a tie or two points and a win. The probability of kicking an extra point was about 80 percent, based on past experience. The probability of scoring two points with a run or pass was about 50 percent. Pete had made up his mind to try for two, when the coach sent in the place kicker. The kick was blocked. Since the game, everyone has been offering Pete free advice on what he should have done.

TO DANTE'S OR NOT?

Gary, Dennis, and Sam were discussing the relative merits of studying for tomorrow's final exam or cutting out for Dante's for several hours of rest and relaxation. Gary, who usually had little trouble taking tests, was a strong advocate of the tavern alternative. Sam, who knew he wasn't as well prepared as he might be, was trying to convince the other two that more review time was crucial. Dennis was literally in the middle: he felt reasonably well prepared; knew some more group study would be helpful; but usually tended to follow Gary's lead.

In these situations, the three of them tended to act as a group; they rarely set off on their own. Somehow they would have to decide.

A MERGER OR ACQUISITION

Tony Romano, an outside member of the board of directors of Fidelity Bank, was reflecting on a recent meeting in which the board became virtually deadlocked on the issue of whether or not to recommend, to Fidelity's shareholders, a merger with Westcorp. The financial services holding company had made an offer for all of the stock of Fidelity Bank and it seemed quite reasonable. Several board members made strong arguments for the increased strength and viability of the combined organizations—not to mention the increased marketability and potential growth in value of Westcorp's stock. Others reported mixed reactions from current shareholders; some eager to sell and some firmly against the change. The officer-directors of Fidelity Bank were concerned about their managerial futures if the merger were to take place. It was difficult for them to say so in the board meeting (such concerns seemed too personal, maybe even unbusinesslike) so, instead, they talked about preserving the high quality of service to clients that resulted from a small, well-run organization. Tony was unsure how he would vote at next week's meeting.

Norman Calderwood, president and chief executive officer of Fidelity, was also unsure how he would vote. He had been hired from the outside by the chairman and founder just five years ago. He owned only 100 shares of Fidelity's stock, but he had options on 5,000 shares at $20 (Westcorp's offer was for $30). Whether he would have a future in the merged system was problematical. Westcorp officials indicated that Fidelity executives would continue to fill key roles. However, Calderwood was well aware that the top management of many acquired companies seemed to fade away after several years. The offer from the National Bank of Anchorage, to become president and CEO (including a 20-percent increase over his current salary) was still in his desk drawer—unanswered.

INTRODUCTION

These individual, group, and organizational incidents are all examples of decision-making activity. They involve choosing a particular point of view or course of action from among two or more alternatives at a point in time. They vary in complexity: some are fairly routine and well-structured; others are non-routine and ill-structured. In this unit we will focus on decision making as a means of understanding human behavior in organizations. Although our approach to individual decision making could encompass relatively unconscious (highly programmed) behavior such as breathing, walking, and reflex actions of various kinds, we will concentrate on relatively more conscious activity. This includes habits for individuals and standard operating procedures for organizations.

Several dimensions are important in studying decision making in organizations. A major distinction is that between *descriptions of* behavior and *prescriptions for* behavior. We will be concerned with both aspects: first, with describing decision-making behavior (including consideration of the numerous factors or forces influencing decision makers and decision processes) and second, with increased understanding of what does happen, we can begin to consider prescriptions for how decision makers can improve the processes used and choices made.

A key dimension is the decision maker. We will begin by focusing on individuals, then broaden our coverage to consider groups as decision makers, and finally look at organizational systems for making decisions. As indicated in the vignettes, we will illustrate the discussion with examples of specific types of decisions in a variety of settings. The following topics will be covered:

Levels and Pervasiveness
The Decision-Making Process
Knowledge, Uncertainty, and Information
Decision Making and Behavior
Characteristics of Decision Makers
Group Decision Making
Organizational Decision-Making Systems
Techniques for Improving Decision Making
So What? Implications for You

LEVELS AND PERVASIVENESS

To *decide* means to make up one's mind. It implies the consideration of two or more alternatives leading up to an individual's making a choice. Choosing may have the implication of overt action, such as taking a new job, buying a new typewriter, or publishing a new administrative procedure. Or, it may involve only the intent to behave in a certain way at some future time. For example, a person may decide to be a Democrat or decide that the Ajax Company is a poor credit risk. These latter decisions give birth to a propensity in individuals and organizations to decide a certain way if a particular issue should arise in the future.

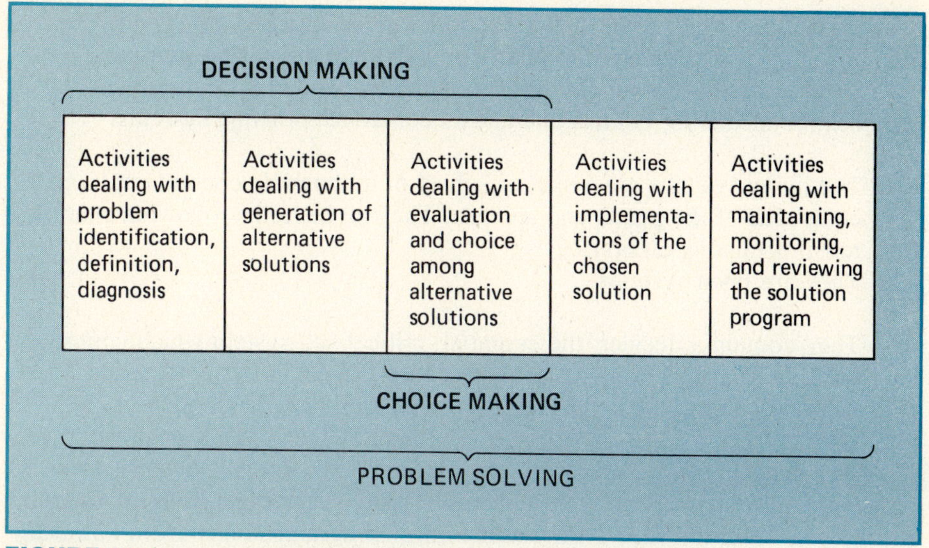

FIGURE 11.1 Decision Making Related to Choice Making and Problem Solving. **Source:** From *Managerial Decision Making,* George P. Huber. © 1980 by Scott, Foresman and Company. Reprinted by permission.

Words such as *determine, settle, conclude,* and *resolve* are often used as synonyms for "decide."

Several elements are involved in all decisions: a decision maker, the need for a decision, and a context or situation. Deciding is one phase of an overall process that includes (1) recognition of the need for a decision, (2) analysis of the situation, (3) choice of a particular alternative, (4) implementation of appropriate steps, and (5) follow-up or review. As shown in Figure 11.1, where parts of the process are highlighted for attention, problem solving is typically considered to be broader than decision making. We will tend to use the two terms interchangeably, however, particularly when referring to the process as a whole. If the need for a distinction arises, problem solving will be considered the more global process, with decisions (choices) present throughout.

Thinking involves using the mind to reflect, draw inferences, arrive at conclusions, make decisions, and form opinions, beliefs, and expectations. Thus, thinking is closely related to decision making. It is a mental process, particularly when we emphasize conscious, deliberative decisions rather than unconscious, reflexive behavior.

Perception is basic to understanding behavior because it is the means by which stimuli affect individuals; that is, they indicate the need for a decision to be made. Stimuli that are not perceived by people have no effect on their behavior. Individuals have *cognitive* systems that represent what they know about themselves and the world about them. These systems are developed through cognitive processes that include perceiving, imagining, thinking, reasoning, and decision making. The urge to take action can be touched off by an external stimulus or can be generated internally in individual thought processes.

Decision making is fundamental to individual and organization behavior. It provides the means for control and allows coherence in living systems.

> The living systems are a special subset of all possible concrete systems, composed of the plants and animals. They all have the following characteristics (among others):
> They are open systems. . . .
>
> They contain a decider, the essential, critical sub-system which controls the entire system, causing its subsystems and components to co-act, without which there is no system (Miller, 1965, pp. 203–204).

This concept of a *decider* for every living system suggests the pervasiveness of decision-making processes for individuals, groups, and organizations. Decision making and behavior vary on a continuum of programmability from automatic physiological process, reflex actions, and habits, to conscious, deliberate choices in complex situations.

Think about your own behavior and the number of decisions made during any one day. When to get up, what pair of shoes to wear, what to eat for breakfast, what route to take to school or work, how to perform a particular task, how hard to work, where to go for lunch, whether to go to the bank on the way home or cash a check at the supermarket after dinner, what television program to watch, and when to go to bed. Everything we do is the result of a decision: some unconscious, some semiconscious (like Alex's in the vignette), and some conscious.

The job of managing can be viewed as decision making. It includes a variety of kinds of decisions made at various levels in organizations (bottom, middle, and top), in various functions (production, engineering, marketing, industrial relations, etc.), and in various processes (goal setting, planning, implementing, and controlling). The pervasiveness of decision making at every level of organizational activity suggests that the phenomenon deserves further study as we progress in our understanding of human behavior in organizations.

THE DECISION-MAKING PROCESS

The basic problem-solving process is simply this: What is the problem? What are the alternatives? Which alternative is best? (Dewey, 1910). This same basic three-part model can be used in describing the decision-making process (Simon, 1960, p. 2).

> The first phase of the decision-making process—searching the environment for conditions calling for a decision—I shall call *intelligence* activity (borrowing from the military meaning of intelligence).

HAGAR

> The second phase—inventing, developing, and analyzing possible courses of action—I shall call *design* activity.
>
> The third phase—selecting a particular course of action from those available—I shall call *choice* activity.

In our discussion, we will elaborate on this basic process and include eight phases: sensing, defining, generating alternatives, evaluating alternatives, choosing a solution, planning action steps, implementing, and following up (see Figure 11.2). Much of the research, writing, and teaching concerning decision making has focused primarily on evaluating alternatives and choosing. The problems are given and little attention is paid to implementing solutions that result from the diagnostic phase. The bulk of the effort has been normative, prescribing what decision makers ought to do in certain situations. Our discussion will be primarily descriptive, but with a plea for balanced consideration of the eight phases in order to improve decision making by individuals, groups, and organizations. In a later section, we will turn to a more explicit consideration of decision aids: techniques designed to improve decision-making processes.

Sensing

Most of us use the word *problem* to indicate "something wrong": a connotation focusing on past behavior that has fallen short of some standard or expectation and must thus be remedied. This is not inappropriate but should be broadened to mean "opportunity" as well. The generalized approach is to view a problem/opportunity as the difference between expected and actual results or current and desired conditions; that is, as gaps that initiate decision-making processes. Perception plays an important part in sensing, as Figure 11.3 illustrates. With this in mind, our definition can be sharpened. A problem/opportunity is *the difference between the perceived present situation and the perceived desired situation*. It can be major or minor, depending on the degree of this difference. Part of the sensing process is to ascertain the actual present situation. If there is a mismatch between the real and the perceived, we may very well be addressing ourselves to the wrong problem. Or, we may be attending to, and trying to alter, symptoms rather than causes. For example, if we perceive that

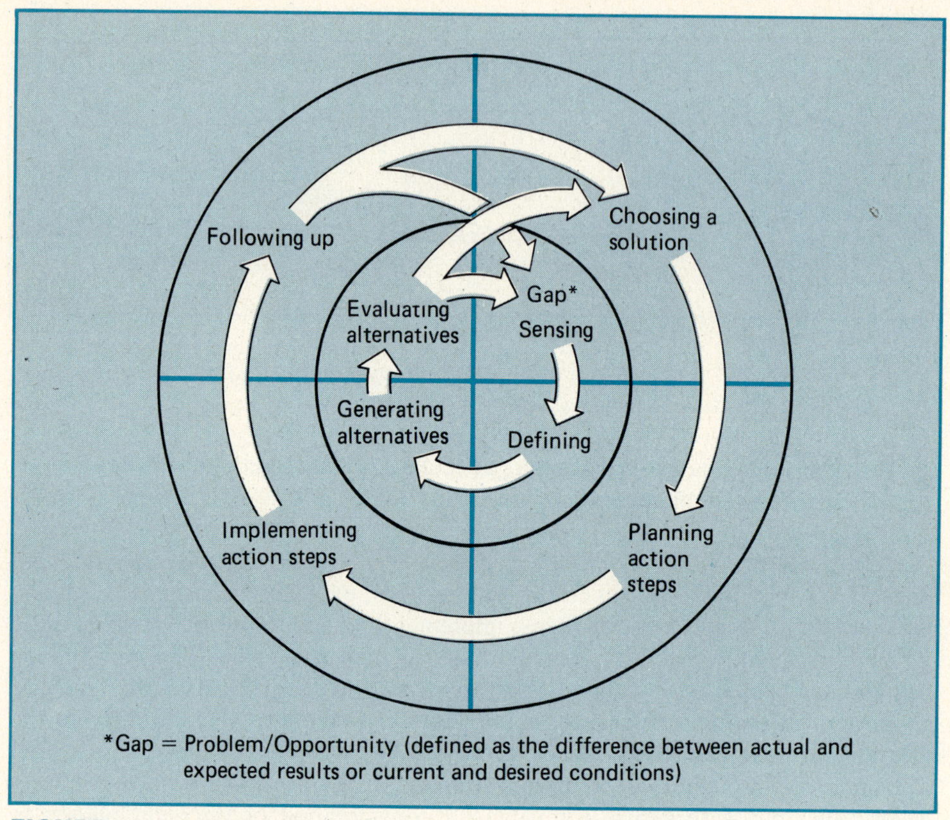

FIGURE 11.2 The Decision-Making Process—Diagnosis and Action

employees are not putting in a day's work, we might install time clocks and assume that people punching in at eight and out at five means they will have worked eight hours. In fact, they may only be in attendance for eight hours. Ensuring productive effort while on the job is a basic problem; ensuring attendance for eight hours a day is more superficial in its implications. The situation requires more penetrating diagnosis and a more focused plan of action.

As a prelude to decision making in an organizational context, sensing a problem/opportunity can occur in a variety of ways: contrasting operating results with plans; soliciting feedback from customers or employees; or receiving input from the boss. For example, your boss might call you to report that he had received 73 letters last week from owners of the new, improved Wizard Widget II—all complaining that it fizzled the first time they used it. It is now your problem and you must decide what to do about it. Many problems come up routinely; others are crises, such as the death of a chief executive, a startling innovation by a competitor, or the failure of a critical element in the production process. Problems, as we have defined the term, occur when new or unfamiliar opportunities present themselves. In all of these cases, a decision-making process is initiated.

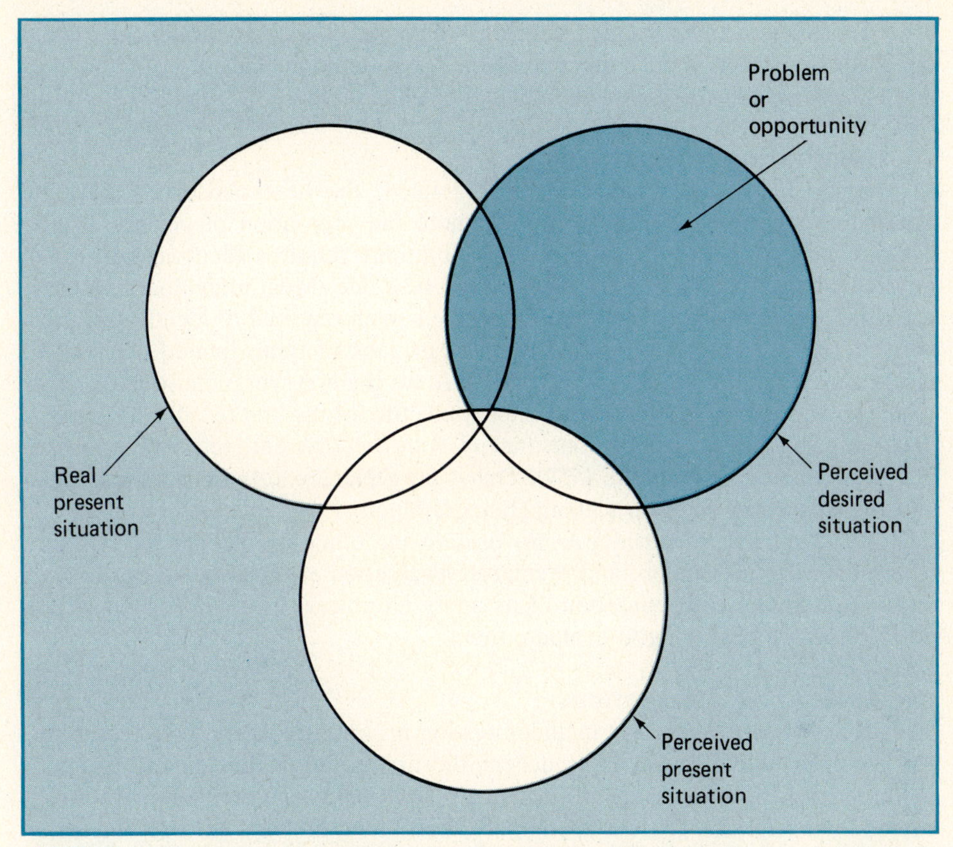

FIGURE 11.3 Problem/Opportunity Sensing. **Source:** Edwin M. Bartee, "A Holistic View of Problem Solving," *Management Science,* December 1973, Part I, p. 440.

Defining

Have you ever been involved in what was slated to be a decision-making meeting and were forced to conclude after several hours that the lack of progress was due to the fact that the participants were each trying to solve different problems? Such an impasse exemplifies the need to describe the problem/opportunity thoroughly enough to ensure that organization members agree on the definition. Defining involves explicit attention to several dimensions:

1. Who is involved—an individual, a group or groups, the total organization?
2. Who is causing it—a few people, a specific department or function, top management?
3. What kind of problem is it—a lack of skills, unclear goals, intergroup conflict?
4. What is the goal for improvement?
5. How can we evaluate results?

The answers to questions 1–3 help develop an accurate picture of the current condition; questions 4 and 5 relate to the desired condition. This process identifies and makes explicit the gap to be reduced or eliminated.

Generating Alternatives

Once the problem has been well defined, the next phase is generating alternative solutions. It is important to note the separation of generation and evaluation. In theory, reaching optimal solutions requires identification of all possible alternatives and then selecting the best one. Most individual and organizational situations preclude the exhaustive search required to identify all alternatives. We are bound by limited knowledge, lack of time, limited capacity to process information, and a tendency to settle for the first workable solution. This "satisficing" approach is typical; we tend to settle for the first feasible alternative that we can identify, usually one that is *good enough* and relatively close to previous behavior (Lindblom, 1959). This is the typical pattern for both individual and organizational decision making (Janis & Mann, 1977). In order to offset this tendency, we need to consider *brainstorming* and other approaches to creativity where habit, tunnel vision, and premature evaluation are forestalled or offset in order to facilitate the generation of as many alternatives (however unusual) as possible before beginning to evaluate them.

Evaluating Alternatives

The evaluation process includes testing proposed solutions for feasibility. As indicated above, we tend to accept the first solution that meets minimum requirements. This is particularly true for relatively routine problems. We rarely extend the evaluation process to compare alternatives in detail unless it is a major problem with potentially crucial consequences. Hiring a new filing clerk usually involves less extensive search and evaluation than selecting a new vice president. On the other hand, research has shown that even for major decisions, organizations often do not pursue the evaluation process beyond minimal feasibility before making choices (Cyert & March, 1963; Huber, 1980). Although optimality is a utopian goal, because of limited knowledge and existing uncertainty we usually do a reasonably good job of checking the feasibility of one or two alternatives in terms of costs (time, effort, resources) and benefits. Evaluation also involves anticipating the impact of potential solutions on the people in the system.

Choosing a Solution

The choice of a solution is the culmination of the diagnostic phase of the decision-making process. It may or may not have immediately practical implications (in terms of specific action to be taken). At least in the short run, the problem may be purely a mental one, such as your attitude toward capital punishment, abortion, euthanasia, affirmative action, or communism. Your private solution in such deliberations results in an attitude that may merely condition your thinking and behavior in the future. This special case aside, however, the decision-making process leads to the taking of certain actions, publicly verifiable steps, by those who have been involved in the deliberations and for others inside or outside the organization. Thus, it is important to develop plans for implementing solutions.

Planning Action Steps

A plan is a predetermined course of action. It involves identifying the human and material resources necessary to accomplish an objective: moving from current condition, as perceived, to a desired future condition. It also requires proper sequencing in instances where initiating some steps depends on prior completion of other steps. For example, if you have chosen to become a certified public accountant, there is a preferred sequence of actions leading toward your goal. You must be accepted as a major, take the designated courses in the required sequence, pass a series of examinations, and acquire a certain amount of relevant experience.

Suppose your problem is one of being overworked and you decide to hire an administrative assistant to ease your burden. You need to attract applicants, evaluate them, and select someone for the job. Then, you need to train the new person to absorb a significant amount of your workload. A well-developed plan for implementing the solution you have reached will facilitate accomplishing that goal. Without it, your workload may actually increase.

Implementing and Following Up

These phases involve carrying out the decided-upon plan of action and checking periodically to see if you are on target (controlling). If so, you proceed accordingly; if not, you have in effect, sensed a problem and the decision-making process begins anew. When realization of the plan requires only action on the part of you and your fellow decision makers, the implementation phase is relatively easy to manage—unless significant behavioral change is called for. Implementing a decision to stop smoking because of suspicious dark spots on your chest X-ray is theoretically quite within your control; however, it is difficult to accomplish. A resolution to prioritize your workload and concentrate only on the most important tasks may, granting that it is even under your control and not the function of others' decisions, still be stymied by long-standing habits that cause you to involve yourself with inconsequential, minor tasks and avoid the sticky, major issues.

Implementing a solution that requires the approval or involvement of people other than the decision makers themselves presents a situation much more complex. A good deal of work has been done toward improving the quality of decision making by means of quantitative techniques that help decision makers evaluate alternatives more thoroughly and make better choices. Relatively less has been done on the issue of acceptance and implementation. Being involved in (or at least aware of) the deliberations in a decision-making process that will ultimately affect you will usually increase the chances that you can understand and carry out the steps required. Most of us like to feel we have some influence in the organizational context, and if we perceive our influence to be effective we are more willing to help implement the resulting plan. The degree of willingness usually varies with the degree of perceived influence (White, Dittrich, & Lang, 1980).

KNOWLEDGE, UNCERTAINTY, AND INFORMATION

Knowledge and information are the raw materials for the decision-making process. At each stage of the process we seek more or less information, depending on our knowledge of the situation. The more routine the problem, or the more experience we have had in similar situations, the more we rely on existing knowledge. In new or complex situations, we tend to seek more information in order to understand the problem and deal with it effectively. Information usually increases our knowledge and may lead to changes in beliefs, values, and attitudes.

Pete, the quarterback in the vignette *Win or Tie?,* knew the probabilities of success for the alternatives of going for one or two points after his team had scored a touchdown. His attitude (an aversion to a tie) was reflected in his decision to go for two. He didn't seek additional opinions (more information) from his teammates or the coach. Based on a longer-range perspective, and perhaps with more at stake, the coach reasoned that a tie would be satisfactory. He may have solicited ideas from his assistant coaches, but the primary difference in this case was not knowledge or information—it was the value attached to potential outcomes. The perspectives of player and coach were different enough to lead to different conclusions. In another situation, Gary, Dennis, and Sam (*To Dante's or Not?*) had all the information they needed to decide whether to study or go to the tavern. The key element in resolving this dilemma would be their collective value judgment about which course of action was best.

If we are uncertain, we want more information in order to clarify the situation and make the correct choice more apparent. In the vignette *Al's Dilemma,* Al may wait awhile to see if Charlie continues to slack off, thus confirming his diagnosis. Or, he might try a hypothetical question on the department manager in order to check her expectations for part-time employees. Both actions would yield more information and change the picture for Al. He might become more certain or less certain about what to do after obtaining more information.

Many using quantitative techniques to aid in decision making have sought to make the process more rational: emphasizing logic more than intuition, reason more than emotion, certain knowledge more than a venturing into uncertainty. However, we find that *confounding*, as well as *confirming,* is helpful to decision makers. Certitude (subjective certainty) may lead to a course of action that is dead wrong. Information that makes a situation less certain may lead to a delay, but it may thereby forestall an inopportune action. The vignette *A Merger or Acquisition* illustrates this point. By asking shareholders for their opinion, the board sought information that would confirm a tentative decision to merge. Mixed reactions made the tentative decision less of an obvious good; the situation had become more uncertain. Thus, *information* is best thought of as anything (facts, opinions, etc.) that *changes the degree of uncertainty* in decision-making situa-

tions. This is an important concept because human beings tend to seek certainty and to avoid ambiguity, thus leading to behavior that limits and distorts information processing.

Limiting and Distorting

The more open-minded one is regarding a given situation, the greater the amount of information that is likely to be admitted into the decision-making process. The closed-minded tend to shut out information, simplifying in a reductionistic way their picture of a situation in order to contrive straightforward solutions. "Don't confuse me with facts; my mind is made up." Most people seek relative certainty even when the facts do not warrant it. Given our definition of information as anything that changes the degree of uncertainty in a situation, it is easy to see why closed-mindedness is such a pervasive phenomenon.

Individuals vary in terms of cognitive complexity. Some can cope with conflicting information and sort it out in complex situations. Others need to keep their world in a neater package. Once they have developed a model of a particular situation or formed an opinion about a particular issue, they are prone to ignore information that would cause them to adjust their thinking or action. Some people are simply better at the physical and mental processes of assimilating and using information. This ability is a sign of maturity as well as a measure of intelligence.

The cost of an information search (in time and money) should be compared to the potential benefits to be derived. If the potential difference in outcome from action *A* versus action *B* is minimal, it probably does not pay to spend much time and effort in seeking information that will corroborate or adjust our first approximation. However, if significantly different outcomes are possible, it is worth the investment to continue the search for relevant information in order to achieve the best possible solution.

People perceive and interpret stimuli in different ways, based on past experience, beliefs, values, and attitudes. The same process can be used to describe the way information is distorted by decision makers. In large measure, this is an unconscious process entailing no deliberate intent to distort. However, we tend to notice (even embellish) favorable information that fits our model of the situation, reinforces beliefs, values, or attitudes, or, in general, makes us more comfortable or confident. Likewise, we tend to fill in gaps in order to complete the picture and decrease ambiguity. On the contrary, we tend to miss signals and discount information that does not fit our model of the situation, that might cause adjustments in beliefs, attitudes, or values, or that would, in general, make us uncomfortable or less confident.

Conscious filtering may occur when we have a stake in the outcome of the decision process. In his letter of resignation to the president, the staff member of a large utility stated, "I have been amazed time and again at how casually your staff can bend figures to create the fact or twist arguments to fit the preconception. Having held positions at two other levels of government, I cannot say this is unique, but I have never been witness to such callous disregard, even contempt, of professional integrity."

The filtering process goes on in all directions in organizations. The role of administrative assistant is a virtual embodiment of this process. Often, the role description (probably informal) calls for a screening of information before it reaches the boss. The screenings have the effect of determining what information is called to the boss's attention, or who gets to see the boss. On a more formal level, it may involve the drafting of summaries of more detailed studies. Because of time pressure, many executives require that reports, position papers, and other similar sources of information be summarized on one page, if they are to get any attention at all. This may solve the time problem, but it may very well destroy a message's flavor or essence, which could be crucial for making a decision.

In sending messages down through the organization, top managers have a tendency to be concise, even terse. Again, this may be because of time pressure, but it often leads to lack of understanding, misinterpretation, and foot dragging. For example, the implementation of a plan or new process may be forestalled because of a lack of relevant information necessary for understanding the what, why, and how of action steps.

Information is distorted on the way up in organizations for a variety of reasons. Often subordinates provide only the information they think the boss wants to hear. "No use getting the boss upset. Maybe the situation will be better the next time he asks for a report." This tendency is affected by the boss's reaction to bad news. That is, if the messenger (not necessarily the cause of the problem) is punished, the probability increases that potentially upsetting news will be stifled. Also, information is distorted according to how it makes subordinates look in the eyes of the boss. The embellishing and discounting process is at work here. All of the good points will be noted and forwarded while some of the negative aspects may get lost in the shuffle. This tendency typically varies with the seriousness of the problem and perhaps with the degree of upward aspiration. Middle managers who have high aspiration levels are likely to filter information in ways that will enhance their upward mobility.

Disconfirming Information

Information can have a direct impact on beliefs by uncovering new facts that make prior convictions questionable. Assume you are the chief of the State Patrol. Several times in the past the Teamsters have attempted to organize your people but have not succeeded. A third attempt is now under way and you believe it will also fail. Then the leader of your southeast unit calls to say he took an informal poll and seven out of ten of the people indicated they would join the union. Such information should alter your expectations with regard to success or failure of an attempt to unionize the employees.

Your attitude toward the union has tended to be negative and you have tried to build a professional image for the State Patrol. You don't condone strikes as appropriate for emergency services, even if collective bargaining were to be approved. However, the fact that the legislature has turned a deaf ear to your pleas for increased wages, better working conditions, and equipment improvement is causing you to adjust your attitude somewhat. Maybe a collective approach would be better and maybe a strike would get their attention.

You are faced with a dilemma concerning goals for your organization and appropriate means for attaining them. The information you are receiving (some requested and some unrequested) is causing some changes in your beliefs and attitudes. This is a never-ending process for you as chief of the State Patrol. And it is a never-ending process for all of us in organizational contexts as we move sequentially from one decision to the next. Now that we have looked at the general role of knowledge and information in the decision-making process, we can consider some specific factors that affect decision making and behavior in organizations.

DECISION MAKING AND BEHAVIOR

All behavior is goal oriented. Think about this statement in terms of your own behavior. Can you think of anything you do that does not have some purpose? Breathing, eating, studying (or not studying), walking, obtaining a job, filing correspondence, loading box cars, reviewing loan applications, asking for a raise, taking a vacation, changing jobs, retiring: all are purposeful behaviors. Granted, some seem more purposeful than others—typing versus daydreaming, for example—but the notion of behavior as goal-oriented is a necessary axiom, without which we would be faced with explaining completely random activity. While we may have difficulty understanding the purpose underlying the behavior at times, it is safe to say that from the point of view of the individual, as a person and as an organism, any behavior is purposeful.

Motivation to exert effort toward a goal occurs when there is disequilibrium: a gap between a current condition and a desired condition (see Chapter 4). Recognition of a gap is the stimulus that initiates the decision-making process and choice of what action to take. The gap concept expands on the stimulus-response approach to understanding behavior by allowing an intervening decision process between stimulus and response. In contradistinction, the strict *behaviorists* contend that the physiological pattern of the *reflex arc* explains the stimulus-response relationship. This school of thought explains behavior in terms of learning new conditioned responses through experience. While it may explain the relatively unconscious or highly programmed decision processes of reflex actions and habitual behavior, it does not provide a good explanation of more complex decision making and behavior.

A Mental Process

As indicated in Figure 11.4, the view of the *cognitive theorist* includes an intervening mental process between stimulus and response. The gap concept is basic to this approach. Individuals are always testing mentally their current situation for congruity and incongruity. If congruity exists—that is, if the situation is consonant with some plan or expectation—no further action is called for. If there is incongruity, some active, sequenced operation (action steps) will be invoked. For example, let's say you plan to watch a football game on television. You proceed step by step to turn on the set and check to see if the game is on Channel 4. If so, that operation is completed and you proceed to another phase

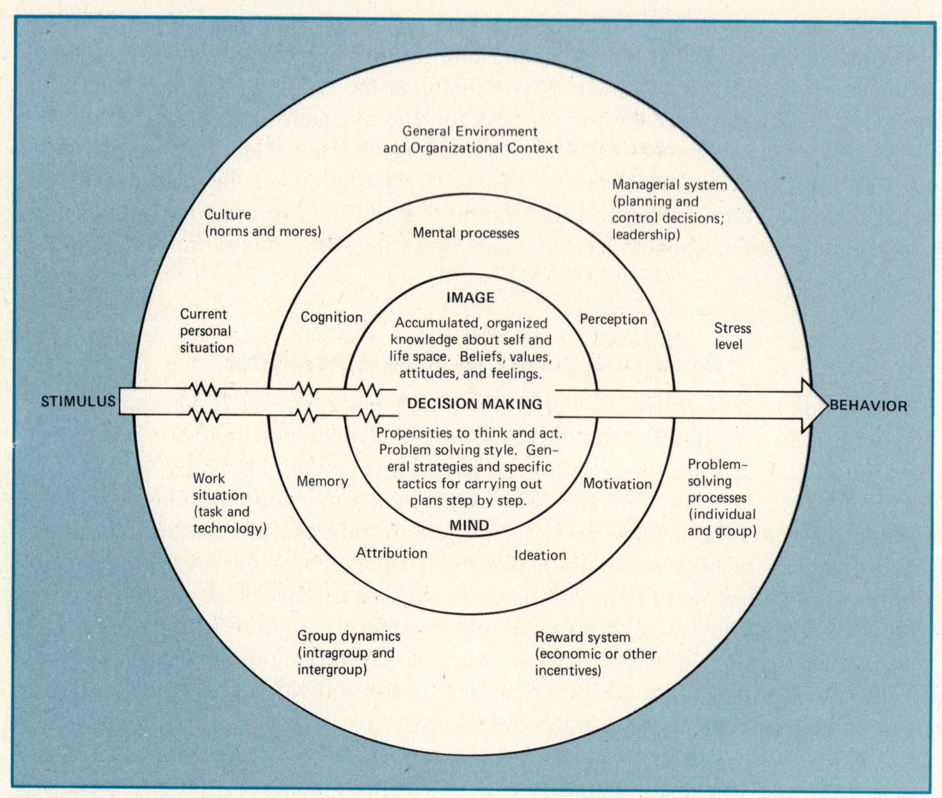

FIGURE 11.4 Potential Factors Affecting Decision Making and Behavior

of your overall plan. If not, you switch to Channel 8 to repeat the test. Once the current situation coincides with the desired situation, you are ready to move on to another test. Perhaps you feel a need for something to eat or drink (another type of gap). If the decision is yes, the question of what to eat or drink comes into play. Perhaps the alternatives are beer and pretzels or milk and cookies. Once this decision is made and executed another test might be made for congruity-incongruity. If an incongruity persists, you decide to have another beer and more pretzels.

Writing a term paper can be analyzed by means of the same model of decision making and subsequent behavior. You might test the appropriateness of the topic against a list provided by the instructor. You might test the research phase in terms of your own feeling of having enough information. You may make a rough test during the writing process to see if you have at least 2,500 words, the minimum for the particular assignment. (There should of course be tests of quality as well as quantity!) If, after several revisions, it meets your own standards, plus those externally imposed, you will close out the process by turning in the paper.

In deciding whether or not to approve a loan application, a bank officer will make similar tests against preestablished criteria. Ordinarily, a fairly routine procedure is followed in order to ensure as much consistency in loan decisions as possible. The same approach is followed when making personnel hiring decisions and checking candidate qualifications against requirements for various jobs.

The basic process of recognizing the need for a decision (a gap or incongruity; problem or opportunity), diagnosing the situation, choosing a course of action, and implementing it is relatively simple and straightforward. Much of our behavior is highly programmed and the testing and decision making occurs automatically. For most conscious decisions, the process is much more complex; we operate in an uncertain environment, with many factors and forces affecting the basic process.

The Context of Decision Making

Suppose your boss has just said, "We've got to get this done today." This is a *stimulus;* that is, a gap is opened between a current condition and a desired condition. How do you respond? The answer to this depends on a number of factors, some of which are illustrated in Figure 11.4. As an individual, and as a member of a group and an organization, you are part of an overall culture that includes norms for behavior. Your behavior in this specific instance is affected by a general attitude toward achieving goals. In some cultures achievement is highly valued; in others, "Do your best" is good enough. The work situation, the specific task and its technology, also affect the response to this stimulus. If you are a writer for a monthly news magazine with critical deadlines that have always been met, the odds are that you will respond accordingly. A sense of urgency that is internalized (e.g., defense production during wartime or month-end statements in the accounting department) affects an individual's decision to behave in a certain way. On the other hand, if you are a member of a work group that has traditionally resisted efforts to improve productivity and has not responded to managerial pressure, you are not likely to do so now.

Group relationships may play an important role in your decision to respond. As indicated above, there may be pressure to ignore the request and maintain the pace that has been traditional for the group. However, there may be a general consensus and commitment to perform well and this force will have an effect on you as an individual. The boss may present the request in the context of competition with another organization or another subgroup within your own organization, and the competitive aspect may affect your behavior.

The overall managerial system in the organization is part of the environment, or setting, for this particular situation. How are activities planned and controlled? Who makes the decisions? How much influence do you have in this process? How are leadership functions carried out? The answer to these questions can serve as background for understanding and predicting behavior in a specific situation. If you have a lack of confidence in the overall planning process or if your boss seems to manage by crisis when you are convinced that none really exists, your response to this request is likely to be relatively negative. On the other hand, if you are convinced that management in general is pretty good and that the boss doesn't call for extra effort unless it's really needed, your response is likely to be relatively favorable.

The reward system in your organization is also likely to affect your behavior. What happens if you do turn out six tractors by the end of the day, or get all of the freight unloaded before dark, or produce a grabber television commercial that the client is ecstatic about? Or, on the contrary what happens if you produce only five tractors, don't finish unloading the freight, or don't create an acceptable version of the commercial? Does your behavior make any difference? Are there economic or other incentives for good performance? Are there sanctions for poor performance? If various degrees of performance are not distinguished and rewarded accordingly, there is no reason to expect that your or anyone else's behavior will change in any appreciable way. The punishment/reward system will have considerable effect on your decision-making process and subsequent behavior.

An institutional punishment/reward system is not exhaustive in its coverage, however. Your current personal situation will also affect your response to the boss's call for action. For example, suppose you are a waiter or waitress at a restaurant where the manager says, "Today we've got to have harmony between the cooks and the servers." You think this is a fine objective in general but today you have a terrible hangover and last night you had to return four meals to the kitchen because the customers said they were unfit for human consumption. Moreover, you received a speeding ticket on the way to work, thus being later than you would have been otherwise, and the boss said, "This is the last time I'm going to warn you about being late." Immediate personal concerns will undoubtedly affect your response in this particular situation.

The forces operating on you in the environment do obviously affect one's behavior. These forces will differ in their degree of susceptibility to control. For instance a cultural norm is less amenable to change than the net effect of one's immediate personal concerns. A host of environmental forces and personal factors help shape the premises and constraints operating in the individual's decision-making process. Sometimes they are involved explicitly, as the givens of a particular situation; often they might be said to exist solely in the mind of the individual decision maker.

CHARACTERISTICS OF DECISION MAKERS

As indicated in Figure 11.4, mental processes mediate between stimuli and their effect on a decision maker. The most global factor *in* the decision maker is the *image,* the accumulated, organized knowledge about self and life space (Boulding, 1956). This includes beliefs, values, attitudes, and feelings that contribute to the propensity to think or act in a certain way. Problem-solving style—the way people acquire and use information in making decisions—is another relevant characteristic that helps us understand human behavior.

Beliefs

Beliefs are an important aspect of the image and are particularly relevant to decision making. *Beliefs* are convictions that certain things are true or real.

They include opinions, expectations, or judgments and usually have some (often assumed) factual basis but not absolute certainty. Beliefs reflect an individual's view of the interrelationship of events—either past, present, or future (Ebert & Mitchell, 1975, p. 51). Related terms are faith, trust, confidence, and credence. Beliefs are obviously important in decision making, but it is difficult to identify them explicitly. We often have to reason backward from behavior in order to ascertain what are our underlying beliefs. If a manager expresses a belief that most workers are responsible and yet behaves in an overly controlling manner, it suggests that her statement does not represent basic, gut-level beliefs. Once acquired, beliefs are persistent, often standing in the face of conflicting evidence.

> Another barrier to educational attempts is that people's beliefs change slowly and are extraordinarily resistant to new information. Research in social psychology has often demonstrated that once formed, people's initial impressions tend to structure the way they interpret subsequent information. They give full weight to evidence that is consistent with their initial beliefs while dismissing contrary evidence as unreliable, erroneous, or unrepresentative (Slovic, Fischoff, & Lichtenstein, 1980, p. 48).

Most fire engines are still red in spite of evidence that lemon green is the most visible color. If a decision to have red fire trucks is based on a value judgment that fire trucks should be red (maybe even because they've always been red), it may be justifiable. However, if it is a belief that red fire trucks are the most functional in terms of preventing accidents, we have a different kind of problem: one in which more attention to facts might lead to adjusted beliefs and a decision to change.

Expectations are beliefs about future conditions. Such beliefs can be viewed in terms of probabilities. Much of our decision making is based on what we believe about the future and what will be the outcome for various courses of action. If the future is certain, we can make relatively straightforward determinations pertaining to the effect of various alternatives. But ultimate outcomes are by no means certain, because we are not sure that an alternative that is selected will be carried out precisely. This is illustrated in the *Win or Tie?* vignette.

The other end of the spectrum is a theoretical condition that is called complete uncertainty. With absolutely no information or knowledge, there can be no belief on which to base a choice of action. While a number of theorists have toyed with a variety of ways of dealing with complete uncertainty, it is not a very realistic notion. We would rather consider a continuum from relative uncertainty to relative certainty and integrate the concept of beliefs with probability and risk. When there is considerable past experience that is believed to reflect the future, we enjoy relative certainty in assigning levels of risk based on objective probabilities. Without much past experience—that is, for new, nonroutine decision situations—we still develop beliefs about risk based on subjective probabilities. We make *guestimates*. Human beings are intuitive statisticians basing their estimates on beliefs about the interrelationships of past, present, and future events (Beach & Peterson, 1967). We tend to overestimate the probability of good outcomes. We tend to discount very high and very low probabilities even though objective evidence warrants their consideration. We eliminate complexity and ambiguity in our assumptions because they are uncomfortable. In so doing, the sense we have of a situation prior to decision making becomes more tolerable but less realistic.

Values and Attitudes

The importance of values and attitudes for understanding decision making and behavior is central, but the concept is difficult to define in unambiguous terms. Total past experience provides a framework—one might also say a propensity—by which an individual appraises or evaluates the relative merit, usefulness, or importance of things, ideas, and alternative courses of action.

> A value is a conception, explicit or implicit, distinctive of an individual or characteristic of a group, of the desirable which influences the selection of available modes, means, and ends of action. . . . Value may be defined as that aspect of motivation which is referable to standards, personal and cultural, that do not arise solely out of immediate tensions or immediate situations (Kluckhohn et al., 1951, pp. 395, 425).

Values are reflected in statements of what is preferable, best, or good, as well as what should or ought to be. Many values that we as decision makers hold are implicit to us. We rarely, if ever, become consciously introspective enough to identify our own value system and its impact on our decision-making processes. In some cases, where decisions are particularly important and visible, we may consciously consider the values we hold to be important. Value systems develop bit by bit over one's life and are intricately interwoven with instinctual and habitual behavior as well as with more cogitative decision-making activity.

There are at least two ways of categorizing values—by their nature and their generality (England, Olsen, & Agarwal, 1971). We can have specific personal preferences (needs and desires), specific prescriptions for behavior (shoulds and oughts), general preferences (likes and interests), or general philosophies (morals and ethics). Ethics might be considered relatively specific normative values if they represent a system or code of behavior for a particular person, religion, group, or profession. They spell out principles, standards, or habits with respect to right or wrong in conduct. For example, ethical lawyers traditionally do not advertise. Recently, this particular issue has been challenged from the standpoint of free speech and free competition. Those wanting to abrogate the code point to the benefit for the consumer in terms of more complete information being available prior to selection of a firm and of lower prices resulting from competitive advertising. These, they say, net overall benefit for the public good.

Attitudes reflect our disposition, opinion, or mental set. They result in a propensity to respond in a favorable or unfavorable way to objects, persons, or ideas. Value systems include sets of attitudes and perhaps feelings, those relatively vague indications of like and dislike.

Values (pertaining to what is good) and beliefs (pertaining to what is true) are related concepts, but there is an important difference. Because they have some factual basis (often assumed rather than proved), beliefs can be confirmed or disconfirmed. An ad campaign or TV show based on past success patterns may fizzle and lead to some rethinking about cause-effect relationships. In addition to beliefs and values, most decision-related situations involve some factual aspects—those that can be verified by testing. Thus we have a range of elements in most decisions: (1) facts that can be established beyond the shadow of a doubt; (2) beliefs that might be adjusted based on evidence that is not necessarily proof; and (3) values that reflect what is good or desirable and remain personal judgments that cannot be changed easily, if at all.

Problem-Solving Styles

Another important characteristic for helping us understand human behavior in organizations is the general approach individuals take in solving problems and making decisions. It is a deep-seated aspect of the mind shown as the core in Figure 11.4. As you think about the problem-solving behavior of people you know, it is likely that a variety of labels come to mind: logical-nonlogical, objective-subjective, toughminded-softheaded, analytic-synthetic, scientific-artistic, and reasoning-intuiting. Obviously, people have these characteristics in varying degrees and combinations. However, it is likely that we label them based on their most typical behavior.

In recent years the focus has intensified, going beyond differences between individuals to include differences within the mind of one individual. The contrasting terms set forth above are used most often to describe differences among people, but recent neurophysiological research points to the existence of such differences within the mind of each person. "The two hemispheres of the brain process information in different ways. For most people verbal and analytical thought processes are located in the left hemisphere, and the right hemisphere is responsible for spatial and intuitive thinking" (Taggart & Robey, 1981, p. 187). Three aspects of this general approach are important for understanding human behavior: (1) showing differences among people; (2) showing different orientations within individuals that may vary according to the situation or over time; and (3) showing how individuals acquire and use information to solve problems and make decisions. This last aspect may be most helpful for us to consider.

In our previous discussion of perception, we described how some people are closed-minded and narrow in their perspective, tending to limit both the amount of information they acquire and the breadth of their interest. Those free of these limitations will, of habit, seek multiple sources and conduct an exhaustive search in order to have as much relevant information as possible. McKenny and Keen (1974) elaborated on this propensity to gather and evaluate information by noting that gathering could be categorized as relatively receptive versus relatively preceptive and that evaluating could be categorized as relatively intuitive versus relatively systematic. Receptive people suspend judgment and avoid preconceptions, while trying to get as much detailed information as possible. Preceptive thinkers tend to be more selective, look for cues, and fit information into preconceived frameworks. Their description of the evaluation process is as follows (p. 83):

> *Systematic thinkers tend to:*
> look for a method and make a plan for solving a problem,
> be very conscious of their approach,
> defend the quality of a solution largely in terms of the method,
> define the specific constraints of the problem early in the process,
> discard alternatives quickly,
> move through a process of increasing refinement of analysis,
> conduct an ordered search for additional information, and
> complete any discrete step in analysis that they begin.
>
> *Intuitive thinkers tend to:*
> keep the overall problem continuously in mind,
> redefine the problem frequently as they proceed,
> rely on verbalized cues, even hunches,
> defend a solution in terms of fit,
> consider a number of alternatives and options simultaneously,
> jump from one step in analysis or search to another and back again, and
> explore and abandon alternatives very quickly.

Much of the focus of our attention in education and training—public schools, universities, and professional programs—has been focused on preceptive information gathering and systematic evaluation facilitated by analytical techniques. We have emphasized the development of left-brain thinking and perhaps become unbalanced in terms of attitudes and skills. We are taught to be decisive; this tends to mean to define the problem quickly, apply operational decision rules, quantify the process whenever possible, and find *the* answer. Although it is difficult to argue against being systematic and analytical, it is important to recognize that there are some costs involved. Right-brain attributes could be helpful in facilitating a more meaningful problem-solving process: from finding the right problems to the solution phase and its culmination in enthusiastic implementation of decisions. Two serious concerns have been voiced (Leavitt, 1975 [part I]):

> In industry much of the new criticism of the analysts centers on their insensitivity to shades of gray, on what they have missed. . . .
>
> Inside an organization, the analysts have been accused of setting up their own versions of problems and solving those, rather than the problems that were really there.

Mintzberg (1976) takes the split-brain and beyond-the-analytical-manager ideas a little further by suggesting that the left side should control planning while the right side should control managing, particularly at the policy-making level. Specifically (p. 53):

> I propose that there may be a fundamental difference between formal planning and informal managing, a difference akin to that between the two hemispheres of the human brain. The techniques of planning and management science are sequential and systematic; above all, articulated. Planners and management scientists are expected to proceed in their work through a series of logical, ordered steps, each one involving explicit analysis. . . .
>
> But I believe there is more than that to the effective managing of an organization. I hypothesize, therefore, that the important policy processes of managing an organization rely to a considerable extent on the faculties identified with the brain's right hemisphere. Effective managers seem to revel in ambiguity; in complex, mysterious systems with relatively little order.

This suggests the need for receptive information gathering and more intuitive evaluation in managerial decision-making processes.

Taggart and Robey (1981) build on the various dimensions discussed above—human information processing, left- and right-brain activity, and managerial skills—to develop the composite model of decision styles shown in Figure 11.5. Gathering information (perception) and using it (judgment) are the two

	LEFT HEMISPHERE ← DECISION STYLE → RIGHT HEMISPHERE			
	ST Sensation/Thinking	NT Intuition/Thinking	SF Sensation/Feeling	NF Intuition/Feeling
Focus of Attention	Facts	Possibilities	Facts	Possibilities
Method of Handling Things	Impersonal analysis	Impersonal analysis	Personal warmth	Personal warmth
Tendency to Become	Practical and matter of fact	Logical and ingenious	Sympathetic and friendly	Enthusiastic and insightful
Expression of Abilities	Technical skills with facts and objects	Theoretical and technical developments	Practical help and services for people	Understanding and communicating with people
Representative Occupation	Technician	Planner	Teacher	Artist
	← Manager →			

FIGURE 11.5 The Range of Styles in Human Information Processing. **Source:** William Taggert and Daniel Robey, "Minds and Managers: On the Dual Nature of Human Information Processing and Management," *Academy of Management Review,* April 1981, p. 190.

BOX 11.1
AN ILLUSTRATION OF MANAGERIAL MINDS IN ACTION

How the Types Shown in Figure 11.5 Might Behave in a Typical Organizational Situation

Consider a manager who has rated a subordinate's performance as marginal. How the manager might handle the situation illustrates the range of styles. An ST manager responds with "Improve your performance or you're fired!" (factual, impersonal, practical). The NT manager's attitude moderates a bit with "If your performance does not improve, you will be transferred to another position" (possibilities, impersonal, ingenious). The SF manager approaches the problem with "You need to change, what can we do to help you?" (factual, personal, sympathetic). And the NF manager suggests "You can improve your performance, let me suggest an approach" (possibilities, personal, insightful). Any one of the responses may be best, depending on situational factors, such as who the subordinate is, the pressure of time, and group norms. The flexible manager recognizes the contingencies and chooses the most appropriate style.

Source: William Taggart and Daniel Robey, "Minds and Managers: On the Dual Nature of Human Information Processing and Management," *Academy of Management Review,* April 1981, p. 191.)

primary dimensions. Assessment instruments can provide feedback for individuals with regard to their strengths; that is, how they tend to approach problem solving and decision making. Our experience indicates that, as you might expect, the results vary widely.

It is important to note that there are no right or wrong results. It depends on who you are and how you behave compared to what you would like to be and do. A contingency view has considerable merit in this regard. The more flexible managers can be in adapting the style to the situation, the more appropriate their behavior is likely to be. This holds true equally for technician and planner as for teacher and artist. It introduces a concept that will be important later in this chapter, when we discuss techniques that can improve the processes used and the quality of the decisions made in organizational problem solving.

GROUP DECISION MAKING

In organizational contexts, groups play a pervasive role in problem solving and decision making. This is true in spite of all the bad publicity, such as "Too many cooks spoil the broth," or "A camel is a horse put together by a committee," or "The best way to forestall action is to appoint a study group or fact-finding commission." For, at the same time, common wisdom has it that "two heads are better than one." We have institutionalized this last view in the jury system, which communally renders judgment on matters involving complex legal questions, and in the board of directors, which is the first legal requisite for a corporation. Our view is that group approaches to problem solving and decision making are here to stay. Groups are not bad per se. The kernel of the issue is that *bad* groups are bad. We need to understand why, and we need to design processes that will accentuate the positive aspects and eliminate, or decrease the effect of negative aspects.

Whether to use a group in organizational decision making depends on the particular situation, the participants, and the leadership. Box 11.2 sets forth a procedure and some considerations for determining when a group approach would be appropriate. (Note how it is similar to the diagnostic approach for determining the appropriate degree of subordinate participation in decision making—Chapter 6, page 211.) The answers to the diagnostic questions can help a manager decide if a group is called for and, if so, whether it should serve in a decision-making capacity or as a decision-aiding (advisory) body.

Our primary concern is with groups in the role of decision maker. We want to describe the characteristics of groups and identify the factors that influence their behavior. We are also concerned with developing prescriptions for how groups ought to behave to improve as decision makers. Our focus is on group decision processes: both what actually happens and what ought to happen to improve performance.

The basic concepts that we considered with regard to individual decision making and behavior (Figure 11.4) can be applied to groups as well. The same external and internal factors or forces are at work. Gaps and incongruities, strategic and tactical plans, beliefs, values and attitudes, and a composite image are useful constructs for understanding group behavior. However, because of the sometimes unstable mixture that results when a number of personal propensities to think and act along certain lines meet head on, the situation is much more problematical for a group than for an individual.

In considering the dimensions of group decision making, we need to keep in mind three basic concerns of organizational well being: (1) effectiveness; (2) efficiency; and (3) participant satisfaction. We will compare individual and group approaches and consider the impact of a number of factors on group decision making in terms of these three fundamental issues.

Quality and Effectiveness

The primary reason for using groups to solve problems and make decisions is to get better solutions or decisions. This is the effectiveness issue: the goal being the best possible solution to the given problem; the presumption being that a group approach will produce the best results. Best in this sense is related to the achievement of overall group or organizational goals. This view of quality is related to the concept of rationality: making choices that, from the decision maker's point of view, move the system toward desired conditions (goals). Of

BOX 11.2

A PROCEDURE AND CONSIDERATIONS FOR DETERMINING WHEN AND HOW TO USE GROUPS IN DECISION MAKING

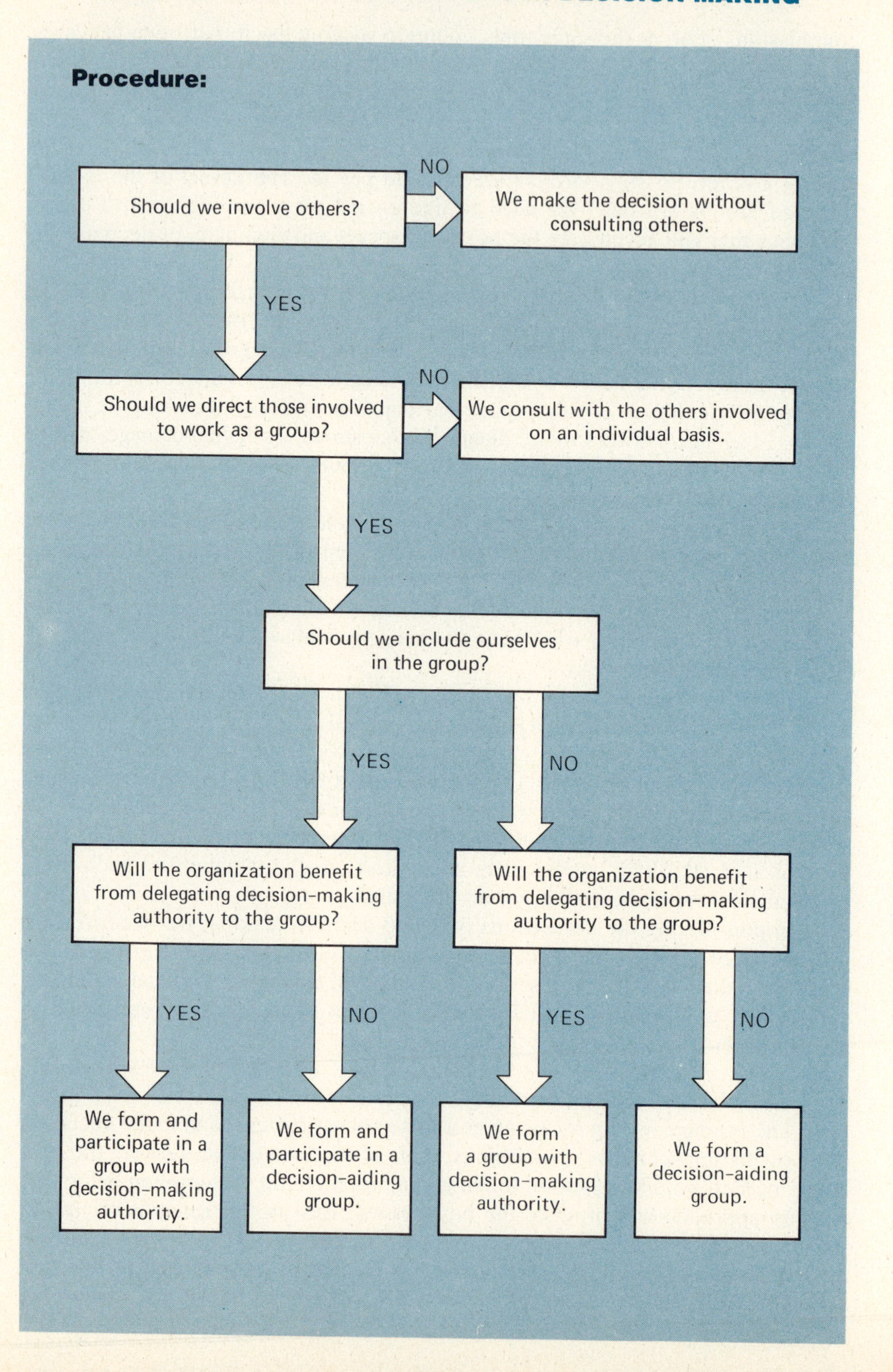

Considerations:

A. *Considerations in Deciding Whether to Involve Others*
1. Would involvement increase quality?
2. Would involvement increase acceptance or understanding?
3. Would involvement develop personnel?
4. Would involvement waste time?
5. Would involvement damage subordinates' relationships?

B. *Considerations in Deciding Whether a Group Should Be Formed*
1. Would interaction help quality?
2. Would interaction increase motivation?
3. Would disagreement be useful or damaging?
4. Would interaction conserve or waste time?

C. *Considerations in Deciding Whether to Include Ourselves*
1. Can anyone else provide sufficiently strong leadership?
2. Can anyone else answer unanticipated questions?
3. Would our participation inhibit the surfacing of sensitive (but important) information?

D. *Considerations in Deciding Whether to Delegate Final Decision-Making Authority*
1. Would delegation save time?
2. Would delegation increase motivation?
3. Could the goals or abilities of the group members lead to a choice of less than adequate quality?

Source: George P. Huber, *Managerial Decision Making*. © 1980 Scott, Foresman and Company. Reprinted by permission.

course, in most organizational contexts there are multiple goals and, therefore, it is difficult to take action that is consistently positive for all of them. In some situations it is difficult to ascertain, even after the fact, the quality of a particular decision.

For example, assume you are trying to determine the quality of a specific personnel selection decision. You pick Sam Jones and he turns out to be an excellent department manager. However, you are never quite sure that Bill Robbins, who came in second in the selection process, would not have done even better. On this particular issue there is some evidence based on longitudinal research, with control groups, that group approaches in assessment centers lead to better decisions concerning long-run managerial potential (Howard, 1974). Decisions about promotability are made by a group of assessors based on a wide variety of information generated by candidates in exercises designed to predict managerial potential. The result of the group approach to decision making has been measured against more traditional approaches—past records and the subjective evaluation of superiors.

A number of methods are used by groups to make decisions: (1) *lack of response,* to a proposed solution by one or a few members; (2) *authority rule,* the leader announcing the decision; (3) *minority rule,* a few people with assumed expertise or dominating presence; (4) *majority rule,* "let's take a vote"; (5) *consensus,* the most acceptable (not necessarily optimal) solution for all members; and (6) *unanimity,* a possible, but not probable, condition in complex situations. Research has shown that on complex, problem-solving tasks where there is a single, correct answer (based on objective facts or expert judgment), groups using a consensus mode have been more effective than those using averaging techniques, voting, and, except in rare cases, the authority of a single individual (Hall, 1971). Solution quality increases with the degree of interaction. The strength of the consensus approach is that differences of opinion are used creatively; they are assumed to be natural and are expected. Different points of view are sought out, heard, and encouraged. Disagreement is considered functional because it brings a variety of expertise and information to bear on the problem. A consensus mode facilitates the identification and utilization of resources available in the group.

Cost and Efficiency

With regard to efficiency, it seems obvious that more total hours are spent in group decision making than in sessions where an individual tackles the problem alone. Yet, an individual could spend more time in analyzing a problem because of the need for gathering diverse information. From this point of view, concentrated group attention to the problem may be more efficient. The efficiency of specialization can also be brought to bear in a group approach. A face-to-face confrontation is usually the most expeditious way to resolve intragroup conflict.

The probability that an adequate decision be reached increases with the amount of interaction in group processes. Minority rule shows minimal interaction and tends to be more rapid than majority rule (voting) or consensus. For complex issues, achieving consensus can be an extremely time-consuming process. The authors have had instances of groups not being able to reach a decision during the allotted time in classroom exercises. You have probably been involved in meetings that have ended in a stalemate from which no action resulted. Thus, there are significant trade-offs in terms of quality and the amount of time and energy devoted to the problem. In an organizational context, time translates into money; therefore, we need to be aware of the costs involved in achieving better solutions. It seems apparent that a contingency view is called for, wherein we at least attempt to ascertain the payoff from improved quality and measure it against the resources that will be consumed. A variety of individual and group approaches to problem solving may be most appropriate depending on the specific situation.

Concern for efficiency has typically focused on the solution phase, with little attention to the problem-sensing or implementation phases. If a group approach helps us in sensing and defining the *right* problems, it improves overall organizational effectiveness and efficiency. There is nothing as wasteful as time-consuming processes that result in sophisticated solutions to the wrong problems. Moreover, quality solutions that are not implemented represent wasted time and effort. If a group approach enhances the probability of acceptance and implementation of solutions, then it improves the efficiency of the overall decision-making process and, ultimately, of organizational endeavor.

Participant Satisfaction

By and large, we are all interested in having some influence in planning our own destiny. In an organizational context we can do this by participating in the problem-solving processes that lead to decisions that affect us. Research and experience seem to indicate rather clearly that participation in the process increases the probability that solutions will be accepted and implemented. This does not necessarily mean direct involvement in the face-to-face deliberations of a committee or task force. Influence can be exerted in a number of ways, such as identifying important problems, being asked to react to tentative solutions, or other means of secondary involvement.

Figure 11.6 shows several kinds of group problem-solving behavior that, in varying degrees, reflect the concern for decision adequacy and the commitment of participants. Eye-to-eye decision making reflects emphasis on both these aspects. The most influence is wielded in the consensus mode of group problem solving wherein members feel satisfied that their points of view have been heard and that the ultimate solution is acceptable (if not optimal) from their point of view. The greater the opportunity to influence the process, the higher the degree of confidence in the decisions made. Those involved *own* the solution and readily implement it. However, it is possible that realistic appraisal of our own lack of expertise in a given situation could lead us to seek less involvement in order to ensure decision quality based on the expertise of others. This mature an approach is not prevalent in most organizations. Participation is often inversely proportional to expertise.

Other factors can help us understand behavior in decision-making groups. Several were covered in Chapter 7, "Group Dynamics": size of group, physical arrangements, and groupthink (the phenomenon whereby too much cohesiveness becomes dysfunctional). A particularly important aspect of groupthink is the propensity for groups to take undue risks, those that individuals probably would not take.

Risk Propensity

It appears that groups often take more risks than individuals in similar situations. In part, this can be explained by the concept of spreading the risk. If one individual is solely responsible for a risky venture, she may balk. If a group is involved in making the decision, the responsibility is effectively diffused and no one individual feels under the gun. Therefore groups may, in fact, engage in more risky decision-making behavior than individuals. Of course, in all these instances we are considering averages or tendencies. Some individuals will act

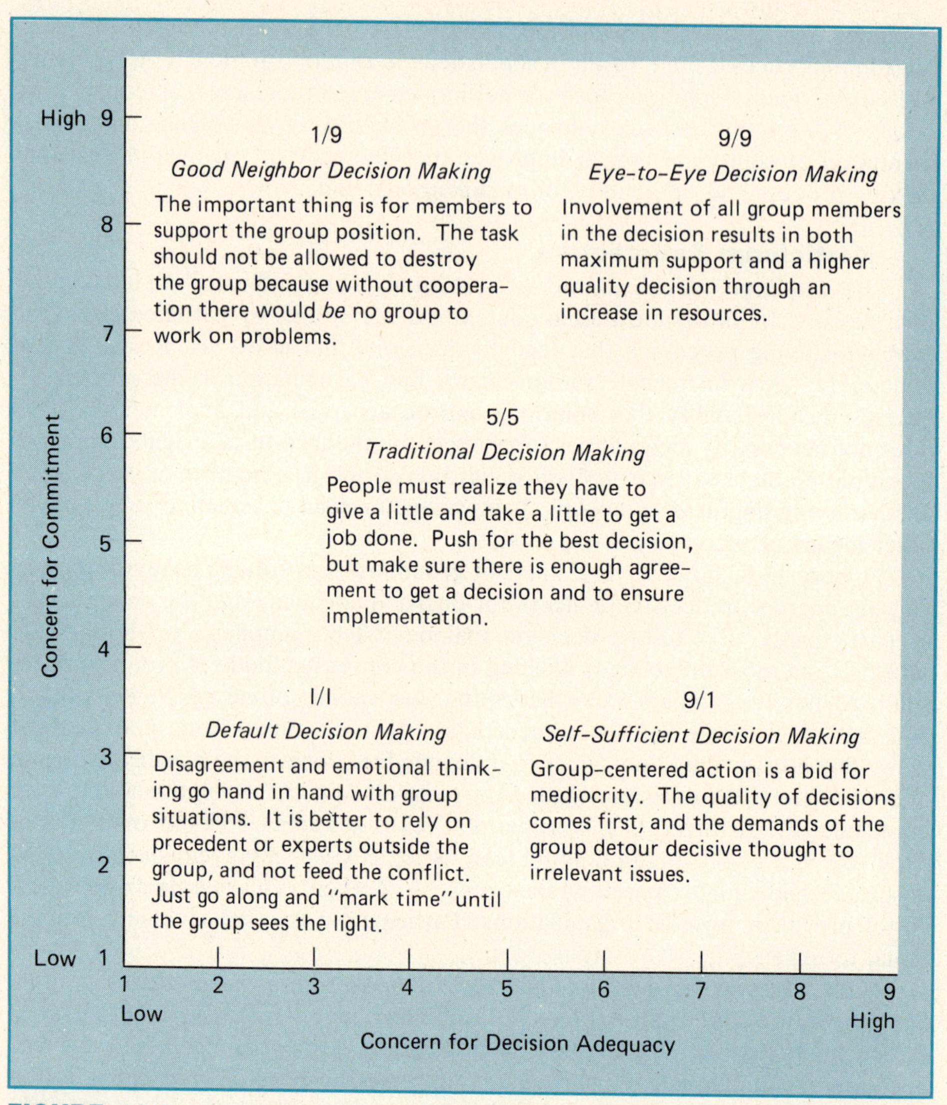

FIGURE 11.6 The Decision-Making Grid. **Source:** Jay Hall, Vincent O'Leary, and Martha Williams, "The Decision-Making Grid: A Model of Decision-Making Styles," © 1964 by the Regents of the University of California. Reprinted from *California Management Review* 7/2 (Winter 1964): 46, by permission of the Regents.

in much more risky a manner than almost any group; some groups, because of the composite of individual value systems, may be much more conservative than most individuals.

Some research indicates that group processes can result in both more risky *and* more cautious behavior, depending on the perceived societal values in a particular problem situation (Stoner, 1968). That is, if there is a societal consensus tending toward risk, individuals will move in that direction after discussing the problem, and the group's decision will be riskier than the average of individual decisions prior to that discussion. An example might be the difficult choice between retaining a secure position in an established company and accepting a new opportunity in an entrepreneurial venture. There tends to be a shift toward the risky new job after a group discussion.

Similarly, where the prevailing societal value is weighted toward caution, group discussion leads to more cautious choices. An example of this phenomenon is a person of moderate means considering whether or not to borrow money to invest in a stock that may grow substantially in value. Here the shift is toward not borrowing money.

Accounting for risky or cautious shifts in group decision making by reference to the prevailing social value is intuitively appealing. However, there are many situations where prevailing social values are not evident. In any case we need to be aware of a number of countervailing forces affecting group decision processes.

Facilitative Leadership

Our discussion has indicated a number of assets and liabilities apparent with group approaches to decision making (see Box 11.3). With groups, more knowledge and information can be brought to bear and more creative ideas can be generated. There is likely to be more comprehension and acceptance of solutions, thus increasing the likelihood of implementation. On the other hand, social pressure may inhibit some individuals. A few people, because of status and power differentials, may dominate group processes, perhaps offsetting quality with *weight*. Some people may be caught up in winning the argument rather than solving the problem. Other factors come into play that are neither clearly assets or liabilities. Disagreement can be functional or dysfunctional depending on how it is managed. Conflicting interests bring out different points of view but may forestall meaningful resolution. On the other hand, interests may be too mutual; that is, where there is an assumption of unanimity and hence no attempt to consider alternative courses of action. Finally, the amount of time and effort involved may be an asset or a liability depending on how wisely it is invested.

In order both to bring out the positive aspects and deemphasize the negative, group decision making needs to be facilitated. This may be provided by a formal leader, or it can be the responsibility of all group members from time to time. Some examples of effective and ineffective behavior in groups were covered in Chapter 7 (see Figure 7.5). We need to recognize the importance of task functions, process issues, and personal relations: all of which are essential for long-run effectiveness, efficiency, and participant satisfaction. Explicit attention to process issues will help the group improve. Overemphasis on the task (solving the specific problem at hand) without regard for maintaining and improving the group's ability to solve problems is rather shortsighted. Some explicit attention should be paid to how the group works by encouraging helpful behavior and discouraging be-

BOX 11.3
ASSETS AND LIABILITIES IN GROUP PROBLEM SOLVING: THE NEED FOR AN INTEGRATIVE FUNCTION

Assets

There is more knowledge and information in a group than in any of its members.

A greater number of ideas and approaches to a problem emerge.

Participation in the problem-solving process increases acceptance.

Direct involvement facilitates better comprehension of the decision.

Liabilities

Social pressure reduces disagreement and leads to conformity.

Solutions that pass a threshold of acceptance tend to be adopted regardless of their quality, thus shutting out other alternatives.

Dominant individuals have more than their share of influence.

Winning the argument may become more important than finding a high-quality solution.

Uncertain: Value Depending on Leadership

Disagreement can lead to stalemate and hard feelings or it can lead to conflict resolution and innovative solutions.

Conflicting interests regarding goals, obstacles, and solutions can be overwhelming unless mutual interests are identified.

Groups may be more willing to take risks than individuals faced with the same problem, but not always.

Groups may take more time to reach a decision than individuals faced with the same problem, but not always. Does more time pay off in terms of decision quality?

Who changes in order to reach consensus, or at least agreement? Those with the most constructive views? Or, those with the least constructive views?

Source: Norman R. F. Maier, "Assets and Liabilities in Group Problem Solving: The Need for an Integrative Function," *Psychological Review* 74 (1967):230–249.

havior that is dysfunctional. This approach is easier to propose than to carry out. We find that groups seldom address the issue of their own inner workings. They are almost completely task-oriented, except perhaps when the members disperse into pockets of dissatisfaction, lamenting how bad the meeting was. If some time could be spent trying to understand why it was bad, and in making improvements, such an investment would likely pay off in the future.

ORGANIZATIONAL DECISION-MAKING SYSTEMS

So far we have looked at individuals and groups as decision makers. Now we turn our attention to the macro-level aspects of problem solving and decision making in organizations.

The decisions underlying the actions of the total organization are made by key people such as chairpersons, presidents, and directors, or high-level groups such as boards, commissions, and executive committees. Examples of such decisions might be a general price increase, a new product or service, a revised retirement system, a formalized affirmative action program, or a merger with another organization such as described in the vignette *A Merger or Acquisition*.

The model we have used to describe individual and group decision-making processes can be used for organizations as well. The concepts are not as clear because of the complexity of environmental and internal forces, plus inconsistent behavior on the part of individual participants and subgroups, but they do provide a useful means of understanding organizational behavior. Organizations have a total past experience, or image, that is recognized and often promoted to employees, stockholders, suppliers, and customers. Statements of mission or purpose, objectives, and policies provide an indication of a generalized system of beliefs, values, and attitudes. These formal statements, viewed along with actual past behavior, provide an indication of generally shared propensities in an organization to think and act in certain ways.

From the outsider's point of view, organizations each have a certain image and may even fall into a stereotype. For example, one department store may have an image of high prices/quality, soft sell, and a liberal return policy. Another department store, located across the street, may have an image of medium prices/quality, hard sell, and a sticky return policy. An aerospace company may have an image of engineering excellence, innovation, and cost overruns. For many years railroads had an image of status-quo complacency, featherbedding, and inefficiency. Images are also attached to large sectors of society, such as business organizations, governmental agencies, political parties, educational institutions, unions, and consumer groups. Often the image held by outsiders does not coincide with that held by insiders.

An organization's total past experience, culture, and propensity to behave in certain ways provides the background for plans and their execution. Strategic and tactical plans guide organizational behavior. The decision-making process is initiated by identifying problems or opportunities: gaps between current conditions and expected or desired conditions.

Managerial System

Managers plan and control organizational activities toward objective accomplishment by making decisions. A number of factors affect managerial decision-making processes. The external environment includes a general societal milieu plus the specific forces related to the basic task (see Figures 1.2 and 1.3). Internal subsystems include goals and values, structure, technology, and psychological aspects. These contextual variables in the organizational setting affect managerial decisions and actions. Decisions are made with regard to goals, structure, technology, and a number of psychosocial issues, such as reward systems, leadership styles, and training.

Managerial decision making varies considerably in a number of key dimensions: formal-informal, routine-nonroutine, programmable-nonprogrammable, and computational-judgmental. For routine problems, decisional processes can often be programmed and carried out computationally. For example, processes related to production are often monitored and adjusted automatically by comparing actual conditions with specifications for weight, size, or color. Humans may be involved in the process of interpreting results and making adjustments. Even so, the procedures used can be structured so that minimal judgment is involved (Bylinsky, 1983).

For nonroutine problems, the decisional process is less likely to be programmable and considerably more personal judgment is involved. Selecting a new branch manager, an advertising campaign, or an external consultant are examples of such problems. Obviously, organizational problems and the appropriate processes for solving them vary considerably between these polar examples. A measure of the effectiveness of the managerial system is the degree to which decision-making processes are designed to match the problems they are applied to.

A good deal of managerial decision making occurs informally on a day-to-day basis. In many organizations, particularly small or medium-sized ones, the process tends to be almost entirely informal. In other cases, particularly for a large, complex organization, the process is formalized for nonprogrammable as well as programmable decisions. Explicit processes are often designed for complex issues such as goal setting and long-range planning (LRP). Many organizations have highly formalized processes for managing by objectives and results (MBO/R). For project organizations the critical path method (CPM) or performance evaluation review technique (PERT) are used to guide planning and control decisions. Within the context of overall planning and control processes, management information systems (MIS) are designed to provide raw material for decision making.

Information-Decision Systems

Information-decision systems are part of all managerial systems. They vary considerably in terms of design and degree of formality. Informal, ad hoc, intuitive, seat-of-the-pants approaches to decisions making make heavy use of existing beliefs or expectations, values and attitudes, and knowledge. More formalized processes of decision making require considerable attention to the design of systems of information flow that facilitate a more thorough, systematic process for the organization. This does not necessarily mean a computerized system; rather, it means determining the kinds of decisions made, identifying the decision makers (individuals or groups), and finding out what information would be relevant and useful in the decision-making process. Sources of information may be internal or external, oral or written, past history or predictions of the future. Detailed data may be most useful in some cases, while the opinions of key participants may be most useful in others. The primary concern is to design a system that facilitates a careful, exhaustive search to provide as much relevant information as possible, keeping in mind the relationship between its value and its cost.

TECHNIQUES FOR IMPROVING DECISION MAKING

Focal points for improving decision making in organizations are the quality, acceptance, and implementation of decisions. Interest in improving is not automatic because the approaches we use seem to work. We survive. "Decision making is a process in which everyone has already acquired a good deal of experience. . . . Much of that experience has been reasonably successful. . . . However, past experience in decision making is no guarantee that our experiences have taught us the best possible methods. . . . It is only training in systematic method which enables us to correctly analyze situations so that we can truly learn from experience in those situations" (Elbing, 1970, pp. 13–14). The common tendency is to underestimate the potential for improvement in the way we do things—making decisions, for example. Assuming we could do better, as individuals and organizations, how can we go about it?

The methods for improving decision making relate to the following questions:

1. What is an optimal decision?
2. How should a rational decision maker behave?
3. How should decisions be made in an organization?

Many quantitative techniques are available for calculating optimal choices when the alternatives are known and all of the relevant information is available and quantifiable. Most problems are not so clear cut; therefore, the methods used must be less precise, more realistic, and adapted to the situation.

Another approach to improvement focuses on questions two and three above: on human limitations that affect our ability to make good decisions that will be implemented enthusiastically. This involves decision aides that make organizational processes (1) as objectively *rational as possible,* by overcoming cognitive limitations of individuals and (2) as *creative as possible,* by overcoming the counterproductive behaviors that are part of group dynamics (Huber, 1980, p. 214). When we don't recognize these inherent limitations we handicap ourselves in the long run by oversimplifying situations unduly, by ignoring readily available and relevant information, and by accepting the status quo or embracing only incremental changes.

Rationality

In reviewing all of the potential factors affecting individual decision making and behavior (Figure 11.4), it is easy to see why there is so much concern about rational decision making. Rationality in this sense is concerned with the choice of a decision maker who has clear-cut alternatives. A consensual yardstick is assumed: "What would a prudent person do in this particular situation?" By noting the complexity illustrated in Figure 11.4 it seems obvious that we rarely have clear-cut conditions: (1) complete knowledge of the environment; (2) every alternative delineated for analysis; (3) a straightforward means of determining preferences (i.e., some clear way to measure utility, usually money); and (4) the ability to choose the alternative that maximizes the decision maker's utility. If such situations are rare, what do we have in organizations? We have *bounded rationality,* wherein we recognize that cognitive limits (acquiring and remembering information isn't easy) of human beings, coupled with the vast amount of potentially useful data that is theoretically available, means that we must settle for something less than perfection.

Simon (1965) outlines a number of ways to view rationality:

> A decision may be called "objectively" rational if *in fact* it is the correct behavior for maximizing given values in a given situation. It is "subjectively" rational if it maximizes attainment relative to the actual knowledge of the subject. It is "consciously" rational to the degree that the adjustment of means to ends is a conscious process. It is "deliberately" rational to the degree that the adjustment of means to ends has been deliberately brought about (by the individual or by the organization). A decision is "organizationally" rational if it is oriented to the organization's goals; it is "personally" rational if it is oriented to the individual's goals (pp. 76–77).

Objective rationality is a rather utopian goal, but it is worth striving for: the aim of decision aides, such as utility tables, payoff matrices, and decision trees. Although we may never achieve perfection, these techniques enhance and extend human capabilities by facilitating the acquisition, storing, and manipulation of as much relevant information as possible.

Ensuring that *personally rational* decisions (made in an organizational context) are also *organizationally rational* is a managerial challenge. Values and beliefs are highly personal. Consideration of what is "good" might differ significantly from person to person. This suggests that what is rational for Smith might not be rational for Jones. Philosophers have been concerned about the problem for centuries and there has been little progress. "Goodness remained a philosophical, theological, and personal matter. Individual truth came to be viewed as the property of cerebral-sensory systems; universal truth was approachable but openly unknowable. And so an operational philosophy of decisions developed, wherein the goodness of a decision would be measured by the extent to which its results satisfied the decision maker's objectives" (Miller & Starr, 1967, p. 23).

Thus the question of rationality should be approached with certain preliminary ground rules. If we speak of a choice from the point of view of the decision maker, it must always be *intendedly rational*. A decision to jump from the Golden Gate Bridge is perfectly rational if it achieves the objective of suicide. From an outsider's point of view—or the consensus of society—the rationality of such a choice is questionable. In this example there may be a question of irrationality (insanity) in a medical or legal sense. In work organizations, we assume that decision makers are all within what we fuzzily refer to as the normal range on the sanity continuum. This presumes an acceptable degree of rationality from a medical-legal point of view. Within this normal range, however, we sometimes make decisions that are questioned by peers, superiors, and subordinates. They might even describe our choice as "crazy."

It seems that disagreements over the rationality of choices is almost inevitable, given the differences in experience, values, and points of view that individuals bring to organizational contexts. More progress is likely to be made if the focus of attention is on making the decision-making process as objectively rational as possible. While some people will always question the ultimate choice, they may accept it on the basis that it was arrived at via a systematic, thorough, analytical method of diagnosis and action planning.

Explicit, formal techniques, such as linear programming or networking, facilitate rational processes and choices as long as the assumptions made in order to apply them are realistic. The development of models to aid in decision making forces explicit identification of important variables and their relationships. Moreover, the disciplines of model building can be beneficial even though a computational approach to solving the problem is not feasible. Quantification and mathematical techniques have been most useful for computational problem solving where few variables have to be considered and issues of value are relatively unimportant. As managers face decisions that encompass more territory, involve numerous variables, and include nonquantifiable aspects, such methods lose their usefulness and judgment plays a more important role. Wise decisions makers recognize those circumstances where different approaches will be appropriate. A problem may be made up of numerous subproblems, all of which can be solved with computational techniques. However, implementation may require integrating the fragmentary and partial solutions from subproblems into a total system. Often, a larger system will be relatively open and complex because it includes more environmental inputs and relies on the judgments of decision makers. When groups are involved in decision making, the process is even more complex.

Creativity

Is creativity an inherent capability? Do a few of us have it and most of us not have it? Unfortunately, this latter notion is a widespread assumption that has a detrimental effect on both individuals and organizations. If we assume that we can't improve, we don't try, and uncreative behavior becomes a self-fulfilling prophecy. Fortunately, some people start with the more positive assumption and have been able to demonstrate that all of us have creative abilities that can be improved with practice (Prince, 1972; Adams, 1974). The key seems to be to enhance our capabilities to offset or forestall counterproductive thinking and behavior. Routine, habitual thinking may be appropriate in many cases, but we need to get beyond safe (correctness, certainty, accuracy, for example) approaches to more risky behavior (wrongness, uncertainty, approximateness, for example) in other cases. We must be willing to tolerate confusion and ambiguity, at least in the initial stages of problem-solving processes.

> Few people like problems. Hence the natural tendency in problem solving is to pick the first solution that comes to mind and run with it. The disadvantage of this approach is that one may run either off a cliff or into a worse problem than one started with. A better strategy . . . is to select the most attractive path from many ideas (Adams, 1974, p. xi).

In the material that follows we will be focusing on methods of making groups more creative. However, the same principles apply to individuals. The goal is to first generate lots of ideas, thus increasing the probability of having a really good (innovative) idea that can be refined and implemented. Personal inhibitions (against looking foolish, troublesome, or extreme) have to be broken down in either individual or group problem-solving endeavors.

Organizational socialization (Chapter 2), cultural or societal norms, and group pressure on individual decision makers to conform might lead us to conclude that problem-solving groups are not particularly creative. The mechanism in group processes offers the opportunity to generate many ideas, but it is not automatic. Creative individuals may be stifled in a group context. Unless explicitly encouraged to do otherwise, groups, similar to individual decision makers, tend to accept the first satisfactory solution rather than engage in an exhaustive search for new and better ways. Changes to close the gap between perceived current conditions and desired future conditions are typically incremental in nature, not dramatically different from tried and true behavior patterns.

Think of your own experience in meetings. What are some typical responses to a new idea?

> What a crazy notion!
> That'll never work.
> We tried that in 1979.
> They tried it at Ajax and it didn't work.
> People won't accept it.
> The boss won't buy it.
> We've never done it that way.
> It'll cost too much.
> etc.

Several responses of this sort to your ideas will decrease the probability that you offer any in the future. If such an atmosphere is traditional it makes the probability of creative problem solving by a standing committee or staff group extremely low. On the other hand, if evaluation is delayed and suggestions encouraged with positive reactions, we tend to become more venturesome. In a group setting new ideas trigger other new ideas; there is a process of building on the contributions of others.

If we recognize the potential pitfalls in group processes, we can encourage creativity via relatively simple and practical techniques. For example, the rules for *brainstorming* usually involve something like:

Say what you're thinking
Be as nonevaluative as possible (don't laugh, criticize, or groan)
Try to get as many ideas as possible
Build on the ideas of others
Try to be enthusiastic
Try to be innovative and creative
Encourage far out ideas
Evaluate quality after idea generation is exhausted

If everyone in the group is encouraged to make suggestions, regardless of how bizarre they may appear on the surface, the number of ideas can increase dramatically. Forestalling evaluation until the generation of ideas is exhausted increases the probability of creative solutions.

Encouraging brainstorming in face-to-face groups can be effective. However, there are still a number of counterproductive behaviors that need attention: dominant members, ultraquiet members, and conservative members. Some of these forces can be offset by using the *nominal group technique* (NGT) described in Box 11.4. The problem is introduced in a group setting; discussion is encouraged to get agreement on the definition and to explore the various aspects of the problem. The next phase involves individual effort to generate as many ideas as possible. Then all of the individual contributions are made public in the group setting where they can be augmented and embellished. Suggestions are made in round-robin fashion, one idea per person until the list is completed. This approach typically generates more ideas than a face-to-face discussion with no groundrules (Van de Ven, 1974).

Structured decision-making processes such as NGT and brainstorming outperform ordinary face-to-face group meetings in terms of number and quality of ideas and hence increase the probability of creative solutions (Murnighan, 1981). Structured processes do not necessarily require more time or money; they may even be more efficient than typical meetings by focusing time and attention on relevant issues. Other important factors are commitment to the solution, feelings of accomplishment, and group cohesiveness. Managers should take all of these criteria into account when designing groups and structuring their decision processes. People grow and develop by being involved; they tend to feel rewarded and satisfied when they are part of processes that result in high-quality decisions that are implemented successfully.

BOX 11.4
FACILITATIVE ASPECTS OF THE NOMINAL GROUP TECHNIQUE

During the first stage of the nominal process (silent generation of ideas in writing), members have time for uninterrupted thought. By allowing members to think and to record their ideas first, without interacting with others, the inhibitory factors of conformity pressures, polarization on a few ideas, status incongruities, and premature closure are immediately avoided. The nominal process also allows for the positive effects of "social facilitation" which may occur when one is working in the presence of others.

During the next stage of the nominal process (round-robin listing of ideas on newsprint), an opportunity is provided for all members to influence the group's decision. Because all ideas are revealed in writing, minority opinions and ideas are represented and conflicting ideas are tolerated. Again, the problems of individual domination and social conformity—which can hinder interacting group functioning—are alleviated. This listing of items also provides visual and aural concentration on ideas. Since many interacting groups deluge members with more ideas than they can handle or remember, this second stage of the nominal process is very useful.

The third stage (discussion of ideas) and the last stage (ranking) of the process provide clarification of items and give each idea a hearing.

By encouraging an attitude of "problem mindedness" in group members as opposed to "solution mindedness" (the latter being characteristic of conventional interacting groups), the nominal process improves group decision making and problem solving. Further, the round-robin process facilitates self-disclosure of ideas—even by reticent members. In the conventional interacting group, in which a critical group atmosphere may exist, such members may hesitate to raise their ideas.

It should be noted, however, that a critical atmosphere can be both functional and dysfunctional, depending on the context of the situation. In the process of finalizing and evaluating the group's solution, a critical atmosphere can prompt members to reject inferior ideas and synthesize more useful ones, thus upgrading the final product of the decision-making procedure. On the other hand, in such an atmosphere, a good idea may be rejected before it is fully explained or understood.

Source: David L. Ford, Jr. and Paul Nemiroff, "Applied Group Problem Solving: The Nominal Group Technique." In J. William Pfeiffer and John E. Jones (eds.), *The 1975 Handbook for Group Facilitators* (San Diego, Calif.: University Associates Publishers, Inc. 1975), p. 181.

SO WHAT? IMPLICATIONS FOR YOU

Increased knowledge of what does happen (description) and what ought to happen (prescription) helps us understand human behavior in organizations. Perfection in problem solving and decision making is unlikely because of incomplete information, cognitive limitations, multiple points of view, counterproductive behavior, and changing conditions over time. However, better use of existing knowledge can lead to increased skill and ultimate improvement in the quality of organizational decisions and the likelihood of their acceptance and implementation. The following generalizations and their implications for individual behavior and organization design illustrate the process of applying what we know and believe.

As a Member in an Organization

Generalizations	Implications
1. Individuals have an image of their total life space. This includes beliefs and expectations, as well as values, attitudes, and feelings. Our respective images give each of us a propensity to think and act in certain ways, a problem-solving style.	1. Know yourself. Use available factual data to ascertain the realism of beliefs and expectations. Make a conscious effort to understand how your values, attitudes, and feelings affect your decisions. Know others. Empathizing with other points of view (reflecting different images) can improve your understanding of human behavior in organizations.
2. Perception is critical; we decide and behave on the basis of perceived stimuli. Our images tend to distort reality by adding or subtracting meaning in order to fill in gaps or make new information fit beliefs.	2. Strive for fidelity in perception. Perfection is impossible, but recognizing potential pitfalls and using available information accurately can close the gap between initial perceptions and actual conditions.
3. Individuals tend subjectively to increase the probability of good outcomes in evaluating alternative choices.	3. Guard against wishful thinking in anticipating future conditions, including the actions of others. Check first impressions for realism.
4. All behavior is intendedly rational from the point of view of the decision maker at a particular point in time. Rationality is bounded by existing knowledge	4. Go easy on second guessing after the fact. "If I knew then what I know now" is an oft-heard lament. Such feelings are inevitable, but don't be too

Generalizations	Implications
and readily available information.	harsh on yourself because you didn't "know" then. Similarly, be aware of the propensity to judge other decision makers as irrational when their knowledge, information, and perception of the situation may just be quite different than yours.
5. Individuals tend to develop habits, accept satisfactory solutions, and make slight incremental changes in problematic situations. In short, creative solutions are not the most likely to occur.	5. Make a conscious effort to push beyond immediately "obvious" solutions. Generate as many ideas as possible in order to increase the probability that some really good, creative ideas will occur.
6. Numerous factors, forces, and pressures are part of the general environment and organizational context for individual decision making. They vary in their degree of controllability. For example, culture is probably less controllable from the individual's point of view than intragroup relationships.	6. Be aware of the complexity in decision situations. Don't ignore factors for the sake of simplifying the situation. On the other hand, concentrate on relevant concerns only; don't make the problem unnecessarily complex.
7. Problems vary from well structured to ill structured, from programmable to nonprogrammable, and from routine to nonroutine.	7. Adjust your approach to decision making accordingly to the situation. Straightforward, computational techniques can be applied to relatively routine, programmable decisions. More elaborate, judgmental approaches are more appropriate for novel, ill-structured problems. Strike an appropriate balance between the importance of the decision and the time, effort, and money invested in making it.
8. Most people desire influence through participation in organizational decision-making pro-	8. As a follower, try to match your natural desire to be influential with appropriate opportunities.

Generalizations

cesses. Participation is particularly useful in sensing and defining the right problems and in facilitating the implementation of solutions.

Implications

Concentrate on high-priority issues; don't waste time on less important problems. As a leader, recognize the desire of others to be influential and design processes to accommodate them. Be flexible and adjust the degree of participation according to the needs of the situation, keeping in mind effectiveness, efficiency, and participant satisfaction.

As a Current or Future Manager

Generalizations

1. Managing organizational activity is accomplished by means of decisions in goal setting, planning, and controlling. Problem-solving and decision-making processes are the means of coordinating organizational behavior across departments and functions, as well as over time.

Implications

1. Given the importance of decision making in management, attention should be devoted to designing systems that recognize key decision points and provide relevant, timely information. Programmatic efforts, such as management by objectives and results (MBO/R), can be developed accordingly. Explicit attention should be given to issues such as centralization versus decentralization of decision making and the degree of participation at various levels and for different issues.

Generalizations

2. Organizations tend to emphasize analysis of readily evident problems and workable solutions. Less emphasis seems to be spent on finding and defining the right problems and in ensuring the implementation of high quality solutions.

Implications

2. Considerable attention should be devoted to designing overall problem-solving processes with balanced attention to sensing, defining, generating alternatives, evaluating alternatives, choosing a solution, planning steps to be taken, implementing, and following up. If such an approach is designed into the man-

Generalizations	Implications
	agerial system and the organization focuses on high priority issues, the probability of continuing success will increase.
3. Information flow is vital for decision making. Organizations tend to rely heavily on past experience and do not seek new information.	3. Concerted efforts should be made to increase the breadth and depth of the search for information relevant to problem situations. However, the cost of such information should be recognized and a balance maintained with potential benefit from more adequate decisions.
4. Information tends to be filtered in organizations through both conscious and unconscious behavior. Organizations, as groups of individuals, tend to see and hear what they want to see and hear, and there is a tendency for messages to be distorted via embellishment or omission. In some cases, information is adjusted in terms of what the recipient supposedly wants or in terms of what will make the sender look good.	4. Organizations need to be aware of the propensity for information to be filtered. This in itself is a step in the right direction. Multiple channels of information flow with feedback loops for checking can also be effective in offsetting the potentially harmful aspects of filtering. Some filtering is probably necessary in terms of coping with information overload. The goal, obviously, is to provide appropriate amounts of relevant information on a timely basis and with as much fidelity as possible.
5. Groups are involved in much organizational problem solving and decision making. Effectiveness, efficiency, and participant satisfaction vary widely.	5. Given the pervasiveness of group decision making, it is important to devote considerable attention to improving group processes. One approach to facilitating group effectiveness is to train appointed leaders to use processes that lead to improved effectiveness, efficiency, and participant satisfaction. Another approach is to encourage all group members to be aware

Generalizations	Implications
	of the need for facilitating group progress and to fill the role from time to time.
6. Numerous techniques have been developed to aid in organizational decision making. Modeling can be used to aid in analysis and synthesis in a variety of situations. Quantification and computational methods can often be beneficial.	6. In designing organizational decision-making processes it is important to recognize when various techniques are most appropriate. This calls for a thorough understanding of problem situations as well as a thorough understanding of relevant techniques. The key issue is matching problems and techniques in order to maximize the contributions of both the human decision maker and available technology. Even if techniques are not used in a computational mode, the modeling process can be beneficial in helping decision makers understand the situation better because of the need to be explicit about the variables involved and their interrelationships.

LEARNING APPLICATION ACTIVITIES

1. Write a vignette based on your own experience that illustrates effective or ineffective (or both) decision making by either an individual or a group.

2. List examples of problems or situations where routine thinking is appropriate and where creative thinking is appropriate. How do they differ?

3. Describe a situation from your own experience where you may have (unconsciously?) overestimated the probability of a good outcome and underestimated the probability of a bad outcome where making an important decision. Share your examples with two or three colleagues. List some suggestions for making subjective probability estimates more realistic.

4. Write out, in detail, all the factors you would consider in deciding to make a career move to another city. What kind of information would you need for each factor? Where would you get the necessary information?

5. Imagine that you have to cut three people from your staff of 30. What steps would you take in preparing for that decision? What factors would you consider?

6. *Step 1:* With two or three colleagues, talk to a manager about what decisions he or she makes during a typical day. Find out what kind of information is sought/used for making various decisions. What are the sources of information and how is it obtained?

   Step 2: Report your findings to the class.

7. Assume you are Al (vignette *Al's Dilemma*).
   a. Describe the problem as you see it.
   b. List at least three alternative courses of action for you.
   c. What are the pros and cons of each alternative?
   d. Which alternative would you choose?
   e. What do you think will happen when you take the action you have chosen?

8. *Step 1:* Describe a personal or organizational problem/opportunity that you would like to work on. Use the steps set forth in Figure 11.2 to diagnose the situation, choose a tentative solution, and plan some action steps.

   Step 2: Share your analysis with two or three colleagues and invite their reactions in order to get different perspectives and refine your thinking.

9. Describe several situations where your self-censorship has inhibited creative thinking.

10. *Step 1.* List your favorite idea-killer phrases.

    Step 2. Share your list with four or five colleagues and develop a master list.

    Step 3. Identify a problem/opportunity that is shared by the group members (perhaps some issue of concern in the course).

    Step 4. Use the nominal group technique and brainstorming to generate as many solutions as possible.
    a. Jot down ideas individually.
    b. Share ideas in round-robin fashion (one idea per person per round).
    c. *Do not use* any of the idea-killer phrases from the master list developed in Step 2 (or groan or laugh)
    d. Say something positive about each idea presented—no matter how far out it seems.

    Step 5. Compare the process used in Step 4 with other problem-solving meetings you've engaged in.

REFERENCES

Adams, James L. *Conceptual Block Busting*. San Francisco: Freeman, 1974.

Bartee, Edwin M. "A Holistic View of Problem Solving." *Management Science* 20/4 (December 1973, Part I): 439–448.

Beach, Lee Roy, and Cameron R. Peterson. "Man as an Intuitive Statistician." *Psychological Bulletin* 68 (July 1967): 29–46.

Boulding, Kenneth E. *The Image*. Ann Arbor: University of Michigan Press, 1956.

Bylinsky, Gene. "The Race to the Automatic Factory." *Fortune,* 21 February 1983, pp. 52–64.

Cyert, Richard M., and James G. March. *A Behavioral Theory of the Firm.* Englewood Cliffs, N.J.: Prentice-Hall, 1963.

Dewey, John. *How We Think.* Boston: Heath, 1910.

Ebert, Ronald J., and Terence R. Mitchell. *Organizational Decision Processes.* New York: Crane, Russak, 1975.

Elbing, Alvar O. *Behavioral Decisions in Organizations.* Glenview, Ill.: Scott, Foresman, 1970.

England, G. W., K. Olsen, and N. Agarwal. "A Manual of Development and Research for the Personal Values Questionnaire." Duplicated. Minneapolis: University of Minnesota, October 1971.

Ford, David L., Jr., and Paul Nemiroff. "Applied Group Problem Solving: The Nominal Group Technique." In J. William Pfeiffer and John E. Jones (Eds.), *The 1975 Handbook for Group Facilitators.* LaJolla, Calif.: University Associates Publishers, 1975, pp 179–182.

Hall, Jay. "Decisions, Decisions, Decisions." *Psychology Today,* November 1971, pp. 51–54.

Hall, Jay, Vincent O'Leary, and Martha Williams. "The Decision-Making Grid: A Model of Decision-Making Styles." *California Management Review,* 7/2 (Winter 1964): 43–54.

Howard, Ann. "An Assessment of Assessment Centers." *Academy of Management Journal* 17/1 (March 1974): 115–134.

Huber, George P. *Managerial Decision Making.* Glenview, Ill.: Scott, Foresman, 1980.

Janis, Irving L., and Leon Mann. *Decision Making.* New York: Free Press, 1977.

Kluckhohn, Clyde, et al. "Values and Value-Orientations in the Theory of Action." In Talcott Parsons and Edward A. Shils (Eds.), *Toward a General Theory of Action.* Cambridge, Mass.: Harvard University Press, 1951.

Leavitt, Harold J. "Beyond the Analytic Manager." *California Management Review* 17/3 (Spring 1975, Part I): 5–12 and 17/4 (Summer 1975, Part II): 11–21.

Lindblom, Charles E. "The Science of 'Muddling' Through." *Public Administration Review* 19/2 (Spring 1959): 78–88.

Maier, Norman R. F. "Assets and Liabilities in Group Problem Solving: The Need for an Integrative Function." *Psychological Review* 74 (July 1967): 239–249.

McKenny, James L., and Peter G. W. Keen. "How Managers' Minds Work." *Harvard Business Review* 52/3 (May-June 1974): 79–90.

Miller, David W., and Martin K. Starr. *The Structure of Human Decisions.* Englewood Cliffs, N.J.: Prentice-Hall, 1967.

Miller, George A., Eugene Galanter, and Karl H. Pribram. *Plans and the Structure of Behavior.* New York: Holt, Rinehart & Winston, 1960.

Miller, James G. "Living Systems: Basic Concepts." *Behavioral Science,* July 1965, pp. 193–237.

Mintzberg, Henry "Planning on the Left Side and Managing on the Right." *Harvard Business Review* 54/4 (July-August 1976): 49–58.

Murnighan, J. Keith "Group Decision Making: What Strategies Should You Use." *Management Review,* February 1981, pp. 55–62.

Prince, George M. *The Practice of Creativity.* New York: Collier, 1972.

Simon, Herbert A. *Administrative Behavior,* 2d ed. New York: Free Press, 1965.

———. *The New Science of Management Decision.* New York: Harper & Row, 1960.

Slovic, Paul, Baruch Fischoff, and Sarah Lichtenstein. "Risky Assumptions." *Psychology Today,* June 1980, pp. 44–48.

Stoner, James A. F. "Risky and Cautious Shifts in Group Decisions: The Influence of Widely Held Values." *Journal of Experimental Social Psychology* 4 (October 1968): 442–459.

Taggart, William, and Daniel Robey. "Minds and Managers: On the Dual Nature of Human Information Processing and Management." *Academy of Management Review* 6/2 (April 1981): 187–195.

Van de Ven, Andrew H. *Group Decision Making and Effectiveness*. Kent, Ohio: Kent State University Press, 1974.

White, Sam E., John E. Dittrich, and James R. Lang. "The Effects of Group Decision-Making Process and Problem-Situation Complexity on Implementation Attempts." *Administrative Science Quarterly* 25 (September 1980): 428–440.

12
Planning and Control

LEARNING OBJECTIVES

After reading this chapter you should be able to:

1. Show how organization assessment and goal setting are related to planning.
2. Compare and contrast strategic and operational planning as components of an overall planning process.
3. Explain the role of premises in the planning process and give an example of how a prediction of future conditions has affected your plans.
4. Illustrate the basic elements of control and the control cycle with examples of direct and indirect control from your own experience.
5. Describe how planning and control processes facilitate the integration of organizational activities across levels and functions.
6. Outline the MBO/R process and explain the purposes that an organization aims for as part of an ideal system.

A PRIZE-WINNING STRATEGY

Dale Patterson adjusted his sunglasses and settled into the deck chair for another nap in the sun. It was March and he wondered how deep the snow was in Minneapolis where he was branch manager for Aladin Systems, manufacturers of small-scale computers and related office equipment. A two-week Caribbean cruise seemed like an impossible dream, but he had won the trip for two as a prize for the best performance of any Aladin branch during 1982. What was even more surprising was that Dale's branch had improved their sales and profit over 1981, in spite of a deepening recession that affected every segment of their market. He recalled their strategy formulation sessions during mid-1981.

The two-day session started with several key branch people making suggestions about how to justify a sales and profit decrease for the coming year. Although there was some support for this tactic, the majority—including Dale—favored moderate increases in the forecast as a means of stimulating creative planning. Once the group accepted this premise, they turned enthusiastically to the task of developing a strategy that would allow them to achieve their goals. Three major elements emerged: (1) focus maximum attention on banks as the primary source of new business; (2) place considerable emphasis on government agencies and educational institutions as customers; (3) maintain reasonable contact with all other segments of the economy. The general plan was to concentrate about 80 percent of the branch's time and resources on the three highest potential markets.

Dale knew that it was important to maintain relationships with all current and potential customers so that the long-run future of the branch would not be jeopardized. However, he did recognize the need for significant changes in order to cope with the recession that was leading to financial problems and bankruptcy for many customers. The strategy paid off. The branch was number one in improvement for 1982 over 1981 in both sales and profits. Most of the account representatives had earned substantial bonuses; all employees had participated in Aladin's profit-sharing program; and Dale's compensation had increased significantly. Moreover, he was cruising around the Caribbean for two weeks trying to keep his mind off the changes that would be needed to make 1983 a better year than 1982.

TO OUR SHAREHOLDERS AND EMPLOYEES

"We are pleased to report that fiscal 1981 was another record year for Standun Inc. Sales and net operating income were the highest in the company's history, reflecting a five-year pattern of operating improvement. Furthermore, Standun's potential for future growth was enhanced by the continued expansion of our products, markets and technology and the strengthening of the Company's financial position. . . .

"In this volatile economy, the improved operating results demonstrate the effectiveness of Standun's long-term strategy. Our principal objective continues to be the development of profitable growth opportunities within specialized manufacturing markets—through development of new products, creation of new applications for existing products, and specialized acquisitions.

"As evidenced by the Company's recent performance, this focus has resulted in greater stability through diversification while providing new opportunity for the future. . . . These operations, in keeping with Standun's planned diversification strategy, more than offset the cyclical downturn experienced by the Machine Technology Division. . . .

"Another advancement of Standun's technology was marked by an agreement in July 1981 for the purchase by a major steel producer from Standun of a new generation, two-piece food can manufacturing system. The seamless food can system, employing the 'draw/redraw' process, is capable of manufacturing a wide range of food can sizes. It is designed to meet anticipated changes by the industry in replacing the present soldered three-piece food cans. Standun's previous food can system has been limited to production of shallow can sizes. The new system, scheduled for general market introduction in late 1982, is expected to expand the market for Standun's technology and equipment beyond its historic concentration in the beverage industry.

"Increased research and development activities continue to focus on other potential applications for our technology in such diverse fields as energy, military and automotive markets. . . .

"Standun entered into an exciting new market with the acquisition of CLS Industries Inc. in January 1982. Based in Los Angeles, CLS manufacturers lasers and related instruments used as alignment devices in the construction and agriculture industries. Sales of CLS are expected to be in excess of $6 million in 1982.

"The acquisition of CLS adds an important dimension to Standun and is consistent with our objective of achieving significant positions in selected markets. CLS is a leader in its specialized technology, having developed the world's first electronically self-leveling rotating lasers. . . .

"Although operating results for the first six months of fiscal 1982 will be adversely impacted due to softness in certain markets and recessionary purposes, we remain optimisitc about Standun's ability to resume its growth rate over the long term. This confidence is based on the company's established reputation in its specialized technologies, the diverse opportunities afforded by new markets and products, a strong financial position and experienced management.

"These resources provide a substantial base for Standun's continued progress as we look to the future."

(signed) Harold I. Rice
President and Chief Executive Officer
February 19, 1982
Annual Report for Fiscal 1981

THE SUM IS LESS THAN THE TOTAL

For several years, Infomatics Ltd. had enjoyed 17- to 19-percent annual increases in sales. For the next year, John Barrington, managing director, wanted to make it an even 20%. But he faced a delicate situation. In the past, the sales forecast and the planning premises for the company as a whole were built up from branch and regional estimates. He was aware that clear, difficult goals were helpful in motivating employees. They had to be challenging but reasonable and accepted. If they were imposed and unrealistic, efforts might decrease and grumbling might increase.

Charles Wilkins, Western Region manager, got the message that a 20% increase was expected for next year. He interpreted it as a quota rather than a wish. When he added up the forecasts from his 11 branches, the increases averaged a little less than 16%. This reflected the branch managers' consensus that the recent high levels of growth could not be sustained indefinitely. It was important to have a considerable degree of agreement on the forecast, at all levels in the organization, because it provided the foundation for strategic and operational planning.

Charles wondered what to do next. Should he talk to Barrington about how 20 percent might be unrealistic? Or, should he talk to his 11 branch managers and encourage (order?) them to increase their estimates?

FORM OR SUBSTANCE?

During the 17 years Dave Larsen had been director of central services, the unit had been marked by an unusually high degree of effectiveness and efficiency. The employees liked working in central services and their clients throughout the organization seemed to think they were doing a good job. The response to requests was prompt and the work was of high quality. The people in the office always seemed to be congenial. To an outsider, however, the office might have seemed a little chaotic. People came to work at various times but someone always opened the office on time. Employees drank coffee or Coke at their desks and seemed to celebrate a birthday or an anniversary or something almost every week. Dave tolerated the apparent mess because he knew that when work needed to be done it got done.

Then Larsen retired. The new director, Dick Oldham, and the office manager, Mary Combs, agreed that the organization needed to "shape up." Mary began recording the times when people arrived at work and began reminding people that the workday was eight to five. After Sarah spilled coffee on some outgoing correspondence that had to be redone, Dick wrote a memo that said, in part, "Beverages will not be permitted in the work area. Please confine coffee and Coke consumption to the back room during break periods." Indeed, the organization appeared tidier and more businesslike during the next several weeks.

Then a strange thing happened. People began leaving promptly at five o'clock whether the day's work was done or not. Customers complained about both the quality and timeliness of the service. Mary and Dick were quite disturbed and wondered what they should do next in order to control the behavior of their employees.

BUY NOW: PAY LATER

Stan Barnett, president of the Metropolitan Athletic Club, was reading a letter signed by 66 dissident members. The letter questioned the need for expanding and remodeling the bar and the cardroom. The letter suggested that other projects be given higher priority; specifically, it called attention to the need for at least two more racquetball courts. In addition, the letter suggested allowing all members to participate in identifying and prioritizing projects requiring capital expenditures. Finally, the members who signed the letter were concerned about the $400 assessment. They suggested, instead, that the cost of such improvement projects be capitalized and amortized over a long period so that future members could help pay for major improvements.

Stan thought, "This will kick off a lively discussion at the next board meeting on Wednesday." The vote had been 6 to 3 to proceed with the assessment and remodeling. But the three who voted no had argued long and hard against the motion. Cal had been against any changes that caused a dues increase or an assessment. "It is important to keep the club within the means of young professional people." Gordie made several impassioned pleas for two new racquetball courts in the space designated for expanding the bar/cardroom. Jim pushed for more involvement of all 422 members in major decisions such as the one under consideration. However, the majority of the board kept harping on the idea that nine people were elected by their peers to make such decisions. Stan anticipated that the 66 petitioners would be dismissed as chronic malcontents who were not representative of the membership as a whole.

INTRODUCTION

The above examples of individual, group, and organizational activities reflect planning, implementing, and controlling behavior in a variety of settings. A number of common elements are evident. The foundation for planning includes premises about what is feasible (forecasting) and what is desirable (goal setting). Harold Rice's message to stockholders includes estimates of future conditions, references to primary objectives, and some strategic decisions concerning acquisitions. John Barrington (Infomatics Ltd.) may have allowed his desires to distort objectivity in his forecast of next year's sales. Dale Patterson's approach was to concentrate the branch's resources on a few markets in order to overcome adverse conditions and still achieve success.

Premises lead to plans that provide a framework for controlling individual and organizational activities. In the case of central services the performance and well-being of the unit began to deteriorate as control measures were made more explicit, focusing on irrelevant factors. Stan Barnett's dilemma, as president of the Metropolitan Athletic Club, derives from the issue of who should be involved in planning and controlling organizational endeavors.

In Chapter 3, "Individual and Organizational Goals," and Chapter 11, "Decision-Making Processes," we have provided the foundation and background for our discussion of planning and controlling—especially their effect on human behavior in organizations. In Chapter 3, we stated that goals set the framework for the planning and control system. In Chapter 11, we discuss how gaps or incongruities induce decisions for closing those gaps or moving toward congruity. Planning is the activity or function that is focused on closing gaps, moving individuals and organizations from current conditions toward desirable conditions, or from actual toward expected results. The planning process involves developing general guidelines and a series of specific actions that will result in a particular set of future conditions.

The managerial task, among other things, includes setting goals, planning a means of achieving them, implementing the decided-upon steps, and controlling organizational endeavor to maintain current conditions within desirable limits, as set forth in goals and plans. These activities are an inherent part of all organization behavior. In this chapter we will discuss these concepts in more detail under the following topics:

Role of Planning and Control
The Planning Process
Implementing Strategies and Plans
Controlling Organizational Endeavor
Management by Objectives and Results
So What? Implications for You

ROLE OF PLANNING AND CONTROL

A *plan* is any detailed method, formulated beforehand, for doing or making something. *Planning* is the process of deciding in advance what is to be done and how. It involves determining overall missions, identifying areas in which key results will take place, and setting specific objectives. It also involves developing policies, programs, and procedures for achieving these objectives. Planning provides a framework for integrating decision making throughout the organization and over time. At the *strategic level,* long-range, comprehensive plans are developed to achieve overall missions. Short-range, tactical plans are used at the *operating level* and their implementation is more detail oriented. In between, at the *coordinative level,* management is involved in translating strategy into tactics, developing policies and procedures, and coordinating the planning activity. Planning provides the means by which individuals and organizations cope with a complex, dynamic external environment and an ever-changing internal context.

Control is the phase of the managerial process concerned with maintaining organizational activity within allowable limits, as measured from expectations. It is intertwined with, and dependent on, planning. Plans provide the framework against which the control process works. At the same time, feedback from the control phase often identifies the need for new plans or at least adjustments to existing ones. Organizations are controlling when they evaluate overall performance against a five-year strategic plan or specific performance against a production quota of 25 units per hour. Control is a relevant concern for both ends (outputs/results) and means (inputs/transformation processes/procedures).

Explicit attention to planning and control encourages individuals and organizations to focus on relevant results rather than endless activities. Managers sometimes are lulled into a sense of satisfaction because they are busy; their day is filled with routine, programmed activity that may or may not be essential for success (Odiorne, 1974; Morrisey, 1976). A planning process that permeates the entire organization can provide guidelines for more appropriate behavior at all levels. At the top, a cabinet, board of directors, general staff, or executive committee sets goals and develops an overall strategy to accomplish them. Defining a mission or purpose is a starting point for strategy formulation; long-range, comprehensive plans subsume more specific objectives, programs, and tactics. And all anticipatory planning decisions provide a framework for follow-up and control decisions.

Planning provides a means for individuals and organizations to cope with changes in their environment. The accelerating pace of change in political, technological, economic, and other factors highlights the needs for continuing attention to strategy reformulation.

> An organization is both an articulated purpose and an established mechanism for achieving it. Most organizations engage in an ongoing process of evaluating their purposes—questioning, verifying, and redefining the manner in which they interact with their environments. . . . Organizations must also constantly modify and refine the mechanism by which they achieve their purpose—rearranging their structure of roles and relationships and their decision making and control processes (Miles & Snow, 1978, p. 3).

The coping process is reflected in Box 12.1 and others placed throughout this chapter that describe management's attempts to redefine missions, find new market niches, and adjust operating tactics. The strategy that is developed affects the organization's structure and processes. For example, a strategy of diversification probably leads to decentralization of decision making and functional departments (manufacturing, marketing, personnel, etc.) within product organizations or product groups. In turn, the structure and processes that exist in an organization constrain strategic options. Competence and resources must be considered in testing the feasibility of strategic alternatives. For example, a history of minimal delegation could lead to a condition where there are few trained, experienced managers. Such a condition would make it difficult to im-

BOX 12.1

MATSUSHITA: SEEKING INDUSTRIAL MARKETS WHILE STAYING STRONG IN HOME PRODUCTS

Traditionally, Matsushita Electric Industrial Co. has been known as the world's largest maker of home electric appliances. Consumers almost everywhere know its National, Panasonic, Technics, and Quasar brand products, which range from vacuum cleaners to videotapes. Its 26,500 retail shops saturate the Japanese consumer market, selling well over one-third of Japan's irons and clothes dryers, for example, as part of the company's consolidated $13.4 billion sales last year.

But for all its dominance in its consumer markets, Matsushita also acquired the reputation of being a conservative, noninnovative plodder. To be sure, its technical prowess and marketing skills were given very high marks, but at the same time it was rarely known as a trailblazer. Even so, the company's sales increased 18% as its profits jumped 26%, to $709 million, during the 1981 recession.

Broader production base. Recently, however, in an unusual reversal of its stodgy style, management started to alter the company's image. A "long-term vision" completed last year at the behest of President Toshihiko Yamashita projects that by 1990 fully half of the conglomerate's sales will come from nonconsumer goods. By then the company wants to be a powerhouse in factory and office automation, data communications, and several other fields of industrial electronics. At the same time, with almost half of its products already sold overseas; . . . , Matsushita plans to expand its foreign production base.

In an almost textbook explication of planning at Matsushita, the chief executive says: "Technological change is getting severe, and vast new fields are opening up. It's impossible for Matsushita to enter all of them, and it would be inefficient just to move instinctively. We examined our strengths to help determine which directions to move in."

But not just casebook theory is involved. Matsushita has reorganized its research staff, established its financial base, and is already building on manufacturing efficiencies gained as the major consumer electronics maker. Within a short period the company has made some striking inroads into industrial fields thought to be the province of the first competitors in these businesses.

A bellwether. Matsushita is not the only consumer electronics company eying an industrial electronics strategy, but its plan so far is the most concrete, ambitious, and extensive. "Matsushita is actually moving," says Yoshio Suzuki, deputy general manager of the industrial research department at Industrial Bank of Japan Ltd. Matsushita will probably emerge as a bellwether of the consumer electronics industry's fortunes.

The reasons for the strategic change are clear: Alone among such mainstay markets as television, stereo, and home appliances, only videotape recorders (VTRs) are a bright spot. U.S. stereo sales are actually declining, and industry sources say only two Japanese producers are making money in color TV, so severe is price-slashing. Suzuki expects growth of consumer electronics to remain at the 5%-to-6% annual level of the past five years. In contrast, anticipated annual growth in commercial electronics will be 21% and in robots it will be 25%, through 1985. Since "Matsushita is especially reliant on consumer electronics, it is nearing a crisis point," Suzuki says.

That prediction may be rather melodramatic, but with fully 70% of sales coming from consumer products, Yamashita agrees that "there is a limit to consumer electronics, so we have to shift accordingly." Knowing where and how to shift for growth is the trick, of course. Until recently, Matsushita was ill-prepared to find out.

Rejuvenation. Not until 1979, for example, did the company, founded in 1918, start making even three-year plans. The credit for expanding beyond mere one-year plans goes to Yamashita, who became president in 1977. He is the first non-family member to run the company, which was headed until 1973 by founder and current executive adviser Konosuke Matsushita, 87.

Intending to "rejuvenate" the stodgy behemoth, Yamashita almost immediately ordered a three-year plan and established a new five-man section in the corporate planning office to devise a long-range strategy. After four years of toil, they presented Yamashita with a 10-year projection last year.

The overall plan for reducing Matsushita's reliance on consumer electronics entails expanding the company's product mix and geographic scope. By 1990, Yamashita predicts sales will balloon to $39 billion, assuming average annual growth of 13%, with half of those revenues generated from nonconsumer sales.

Source: Reprinted from the September 27, 1982 issue of *Business Week* by special permission,

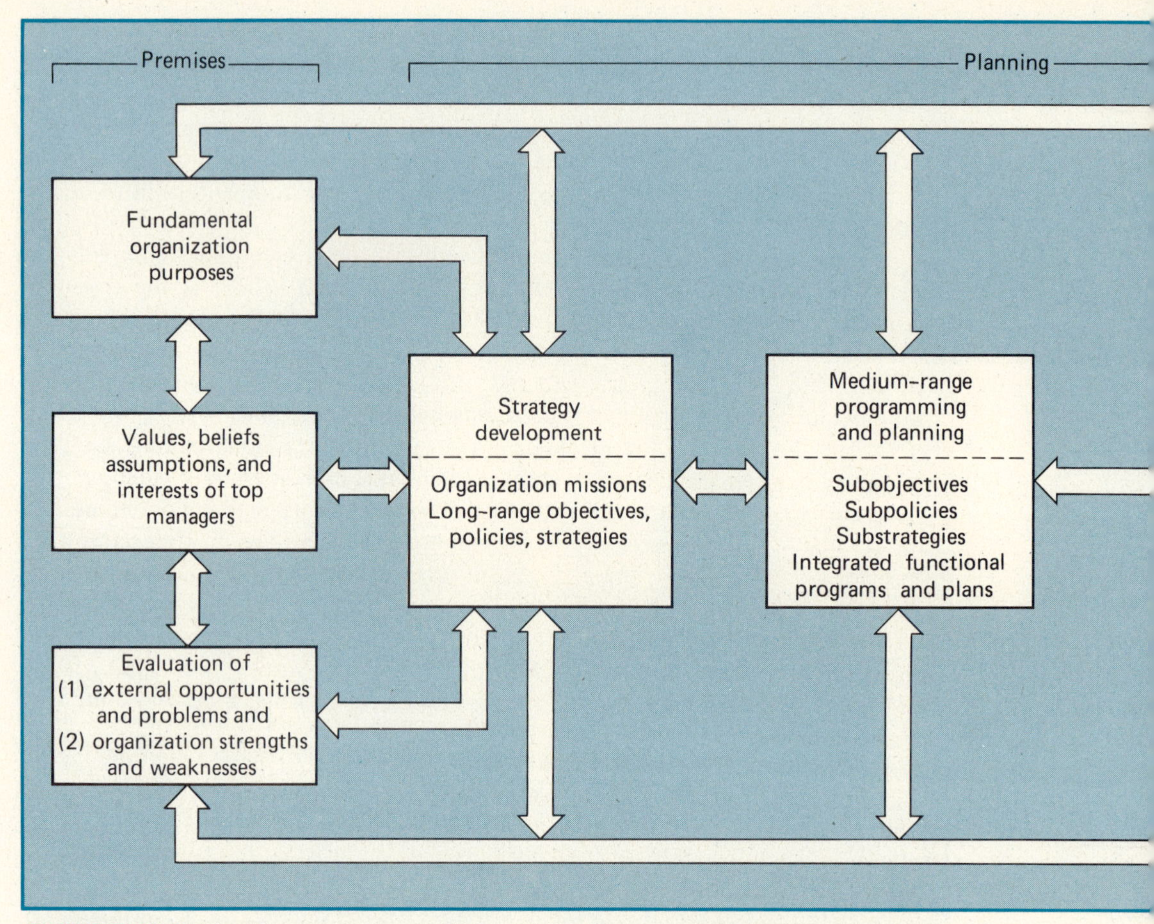

FIGURE 12.1 The Planning Process. **Source:** Adapted and Reprinted with Permission of Macmillan Publishing Company from George A. Steiner, *Top Management Planning,* p. 33. © 1969 by The Trustees of Columbia University in the City of New York.

plement a strategy of rapid expansion from within. If growth were a paramount goal, then acquisition would probably become part of the strategy.

Behavior in organizations is affected by several kinds of strategies (Mintzberg & Waters, 1982). The intended, explicit, announced strategy sets a tone, focuses attention, and encourages action. The Standun Inc. annual report provides some examples (vignette entitled *To Our Stockholders and Employees*). In many cases, part of the intended strategy is unrealized; unintended elements emerge; and the realized strategy is comprised of deliberate and emergent elements. This is similar to formal and informal structure and processes. They both affect behavior: sometimes the informal more so than the formal. Thus, to understand the behavior of individuals and organizations it is important to go beyond intent and to infer strategy from practice. The behavior of people will be guided

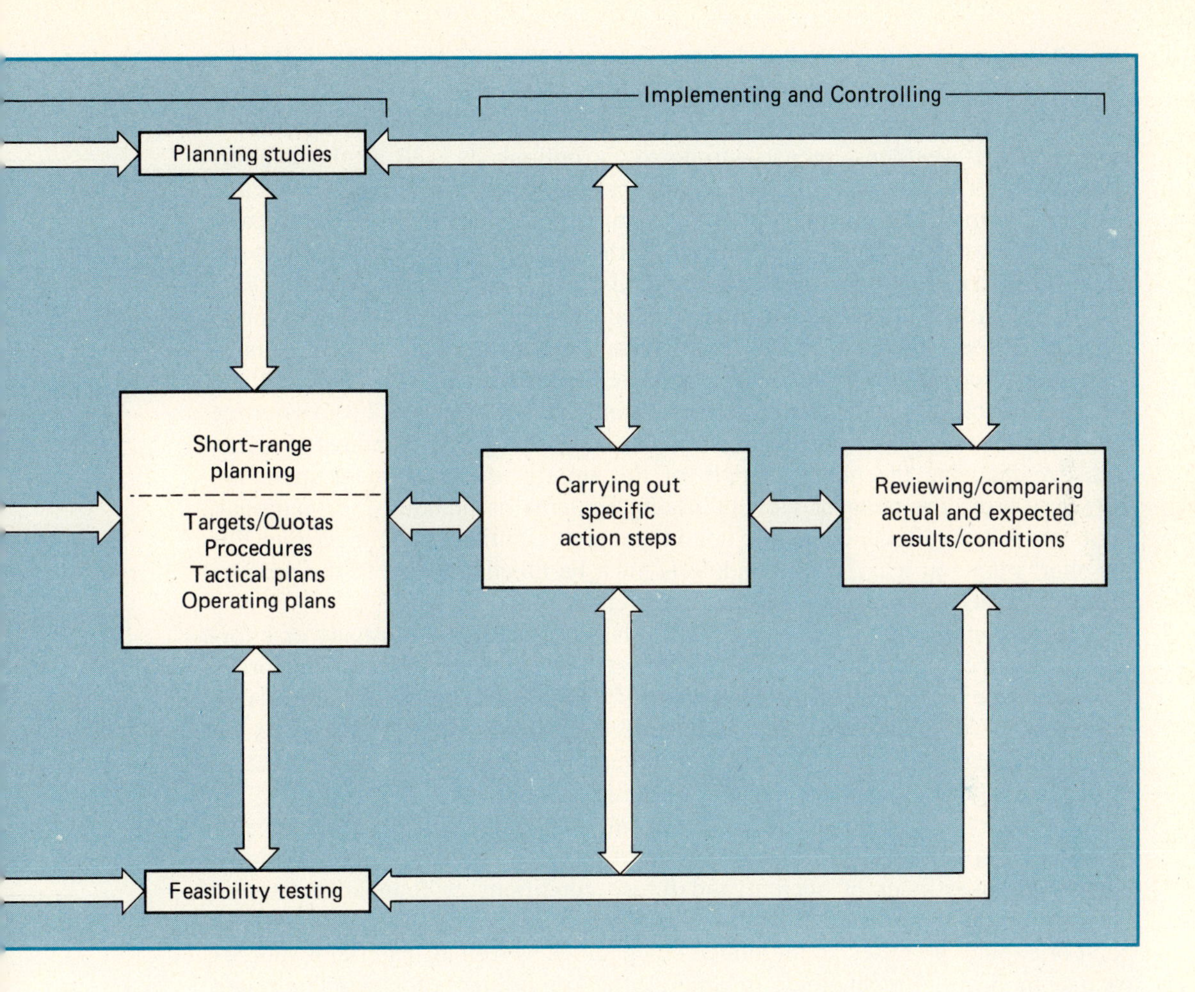

by their perceptions of approved goals, plans, and tactics. Even when they are stated explicitly, differences in interpretation, degree of commitment, and restraining forces mediate between intention and behavior.

THE PLANNING PROCESS

Figure 12.1 shows the planning process used by individuals and organizations. Premises about the future underlie the planning process that starts with strategy development, including mission statements and long-range objectives. Next comes medium-range programming, which integrates functional plans and translates strategy into tactical plans. Operating plans are implemented via specific action steps. Control is maintained by reviewing actual conditions, comparing them with expected results, and initiating corrective action if need be. Let's look at each of these phases in more detail.

Premises

Human beings spend considerable time and effort *forecasting the future.* The front page of most daily newspapers, as well as television and radio broadcasts, include weather forecasts—tomorrow's outlook as well as the five-day guesstimate. The *Farmer's Almanac* contains a long-range forecast, enunciated in general terms. Many business periodicals make continual reference to forecasts of general economic conditions as well as the outlook for specific subsectors, such as construction, consumer durable goods, or aerospace industries.

Expectations about the future are based on past trends and current conditions. *Beliefs* are mixed with *desires* to form the background for setting goals. Some future conditions, like the weather, are essentially uncontrollable. Others are controllable to a degree and thus warrant explicit attention in goal-setting and planning processes. For example, economic activity can be adjusted somewhat by changing the money supply or the amount of government spending. However, from the point of view of Aladin Systems or Standun Inc., national, regional, and even local economic conditions are essentially uncontrollable. For the short range, at least, such conditions must be taken as given in the process of setting goals and planning organizational endeavor.

Assumptions and *assertions* are also planning premises. Formally or informally, we develop notions about the future, at least about those factors or forces that seem relevant to organizational activity. *Values* and *attitudes* are important premises as well. Our view of what is good and desirable affects the goals we set and the means we use to try to achieve them. (See Box 12.2 for an illustration of how management's values can affect strategic planning.)

Premises about the external environment are coupled with premises regarding internal conditions, particularly strengths and weaknesses. This provides a composite assessment of current and future conditions, a foundation for the planning process. For individual and organizational planning, we also have implicit or explicit premises about human competence as well as material resources such as money and technology. In general, the key premises for planning relate to identification of legitimate, wholesome opportunities plus determination of existing or potential capacity (individual or organizational) to exploit them. Although it is unlikely, managerial interests and desires may be strong enough to compensate for lack of competence and opportunity. Fortunes have been made by entrepreneurs who didn't understand that there was no opportunity or that they weren't qualified according to some traditional criteria.

Strategy Development

The strategy development process can be described in terms of four major components: (1) environmental opportunity—what the organization *might do;* (2) competence and resources—what the organization realistically *can do;* (3) managerial interests and desires—what the organization *wants to do;* and (4) responsibility to society—what the organization *should do* (Andrews, 1971, pp. 37–38). Consideration of each and all of the components should lead to a viable strategic plan: one that has a reasonable probability of success. This approach reflects a contingency view because it recognizes the interrelationships among the various

BOX 12.2
IT WAS FIDELITY RIGHT TO THE END

Philip Kuharski has a desk, a telephone and secretary to find a new job to replace the one that he was ordered by the Federal Deposit Insurance Corp. to give up.

In the meantime, Kuharski can reflect on the reasons why Fidelity Mutual Savings Bank became only the second thrift institution in the nation to merge with a commercial bank.

"We were so damned fair," says Kuharski, who until recently was Fidelity's executive vice president and chief economist.

"Our position was to pay the highest rate possible to savers and charge the lowest on loans," Kuharski said. "Because of it, we tended to have a lower earnings ratio than other institutions. We were the top mortgage lender in Spokane 80 percent of the time.

It's the Law

"It is sort of a case of the good guys finishing last," he said.

Both Kuharski and Fidelity President E. J. McWilliams were required by law to quit when Fidelity merged March 15 with First Interstate Bank of Washington.

For McWilliams, it was particularly disappointing because it was his grandfather who founded Fidelity in 1907.

Kuharski said the McWilliams family had always viewed the role of Fidelity as a sort of "corner store" for mortgage financing and servicing.

"Management had strong feelings about staying very loyal to our own market," said Kuharski in explaining the bank's reluctance to sell new loans at a profit to outside investors in the secondary market.

"By the time management changed its mind, there weren't that many loans being made and there wasn't that much of a market to sell to," Kuharski said.

Low-Yield Loans

Because it suffered losses of more than $15 million during the past two years, Fidelity was forced to merge with First Interstate in a deal that cost the FDIC an estimated $47 million.

Fidelity, like other thrift institutions, had too much of its money locked up in long-term, fixed-rate, low-yield loans at a time when the cost of money was increasing sharply.

Fidelity had 22 offices statewide, with deposits of $542 million and assets of $700 million. First Interstate is a subsidiary of First Interstate Bancorp., the holding company for 21 affiliated banks in 11 western states.

First Interstate Bancorp. came into the merger with assets of more than $73 billion.

Source: United Press International. Printed in *Seattle Post-Intelligencer,* 29 March, 1982.

components. An organization may not be able to capitalize on an environmental opportunity (e.g., market demand) if in fact it does not have the competence or resources to do so. Similarly, an organization is unlikely to succeed if its strategic plan is based on managerial interests, without reference to competence, opportunity, or societal responsibilities. Integrating these four components of strategy development is a delicate and complex task. Being aware of them is an important first step; reconciling their implications and combining them into a viable strategy is considerably more difficult.

Obviously, some managers and some organizations are successful without explicit, time-consuming attention to strategic planning. Their intuitive feelings about what to do and when to do it may fit the situation. They may be lucky. On the other hand, it is more likely that they have gone through some unconscious strategy-formulation process that leads to an appropriate response, even though they cannot articulate their rationale. While such success stories are not uncommon, it is our view that the *long-run probability of success* is enhanced with a more careful, explicit approach to thinking through the various factors involved.

Explicit strategy development has a proactive flavor that suggests innovation rather than merely reaction and adaptation. It provides the means for an organization to influence its environment and carve out a niche that is suited to its particular strengths and interests. Some managers shy away from explicit strategy development because they are apprehensive about the rigidity that may be implied. However, *long range* and *comprehensive* are not synonymous with *singleness of purpose* or *rigidity*. Organization strategy can be both firm and resilient. Strategic planning is a continuous process of refinement based on past trends, current conditions, and estimates of the future. A visible strategy serves to focus organizational effort, to facilitate commitment on the part of the participants (and perhaps motivate them), and to increase the probability of self-control in subunits and individuals.

Directional Planning

In most discussions of planning, there is an emphasis on the need for clear, specific goals as the first step in the planning process. We should note, however, that there is some virtue in vagueness, particularly in situations in which either the complexity or a long-run time perspective causes considerable uncertainty from the point of view of the decision maker. McCaskey (1974) takes this notion a step further by describing two types of planning, each of which can be appropriate in particular situations. The situations' characteristics are summarized in Figure 12.2. Planning with goals is appropriate in many situations described in the left-hand column. However, the right-hand column describes a significant number of situations that should also be considered. Directional planning, or *planning from thrust* does not mean planning without goals. The goals are merely less clear or more vague than is typical in stable/mechanistic organizations. In adaptive organic situations it may be enough to have a sense of the domain of relevant activities and an intuitive feeling for appropriate direction. One goal in such an approach is to be ready to take advantage of opportunities that may present themselves at any point in time. Short-range plans can then be contingent

PLANNING WITH GOALS	DIRECTIONAL PLANNING
Characteristics	
Teleological, directed toward external goals	Directional, moving from internal preferences
Goals are specific and measurable	Domain is sometimes hard to define
Rational, analytic	Intuitive, use unquantifiable elements
Focused, narrowed perception of task	Broad perception of task
Lower requirements to process novel information	Greater need to process novel information
More efficient use of energy	Possible redundancy, false leads
Separate planning and acting phases	Planning and acting not separate phases
Contingent Upon	
People who prefer well-defined tasks	People who prefer variety, change, and complexity
Tasks and industries that are quantifiable and relatively stable	Tasks and industries not amenable to quantification and which are rapidly changing
Mechanistic organization forms, "closed" systems	Organic organization forms, "open" systems
"Tightening up the ship" phase of a project	"Unfreezing" phase of a project

FIGURE 12.2 Contrast between Planning with Goals and Directional Planning. **Source:** Michael B. McCaskey, "A Contingency Approach to Planning with Goals and Planning without Goals," *Academy of Management Journal,* June 1974, p. 290.

on current conditions in a particular situation. A contingency view is important in order that the planning process be appropriately matched with the situation. To impose a process that calls for specific measurable goals on a situation that is dynamic and uncertain may lead to oversimplification, a false sense of security, undue rigidity, inability to adapt to internal and external changes, and frustration. On the other hand, failure to develop, when it is possible, a conscious strategy with specific and measurable goals is also inappropriate. Just rolling along with the tide is not good management.

Organizations can compromise on the rigidity-versus-flexibility issue by developing relatively fixed, short-range plans under the general umbrella of more flexible, long-range plans. The result is a comprehensive plan that covers the foreseeable future—whatever length of time is affected by current decisions.

Operating Plans

In day-to-day operations, planning and plans take on quite a different character. This is the part of the organization that produces the goods or services for which it was designed and developed. The planning process is more routine and programmable because some of the turbulence and uncertainty of the environment has been screened out by top management or taken into account in the guidelines set forth in long-range strategy and mid-range programs. In effect, top management serves as a buffer. The time perspective is typically short run, and there is at least a possibility that plans can be developed for optimizing performance with regard to objectives (quotas, deadlines, etc.) that have been established. Operating plans tend to be repetitive and inflexible over the short run. Change comes only when it is obvious that plans and specific steps are not working. Identification of such a problem is part of the more comprehensive strategic planning and medium-range programming processes or an outcome of controlling activity. Standard operating procedures, rules, and regulations are part of organizational life in the day-to-day operations. These phenomena have a direct effect on human behavior and attitudes, including morale.

Planning and plans in the middle levels of organizations are more difficult to conceptualize than in either strategic or operating functions. However, part of the managerial task is to translate top management's strategy into programs and tactics and see that they are realized in day-to-day operations. Thus, planning and plans must be coordinated across *levels* in organizations. In addition to this, they must be coordinated across *functions:* engineering and production, advertising and sales, or nursing and medical staff. Sometimes coordination is achieved through the planning process itself, if it is integrated by one individual or perhaps a team approach.

An important part of planning is scheduling the sequence of activities or tasks that must be completed for a particular project; for example, constructing a building, introducing a new product, or designing a management information system. Making the plan visible by means of a bar chart or network diagram (Figure 12.3) helps to coordinate the efforts of many people. Explicit identification of important milestones on a chart or diagram can induce the effort required to achieve the goal or goals. Note that in the bar chart subtasks A–2 and C–1 are behind schedule and will require extra effort in order to catch up. A network diagram provides more information than a bar chart because it shows more interrelationships, particularly the precedence of different tasks. It is also possible to identify the critical path: the sequence of activities (double line) and events with the longest completion time (times are shown on each activity arrow). It represents the shortest possible time to complete the project; any delay on the critical path causes a delay in the project as a whole. Slack time on other paths in our scheme is identified by dotted lines. A dashed line is used for dummy activities (0 time) in order to connect an appropriate sequence of tasks. The techniques can be very elaborate and sophisticated, with, for instance, probability estimates and computer programs for adjusting schedules and for keeping a complete picture of planned and actual progress. However, the primary benefit can be obtained with simple charts and diagrams that help coordinate activities and encourage effort.

Example of Planning

In order to illustrate the nature of plans and the planning process, let us look at a specific example where prescribed goals are achieved by design. The

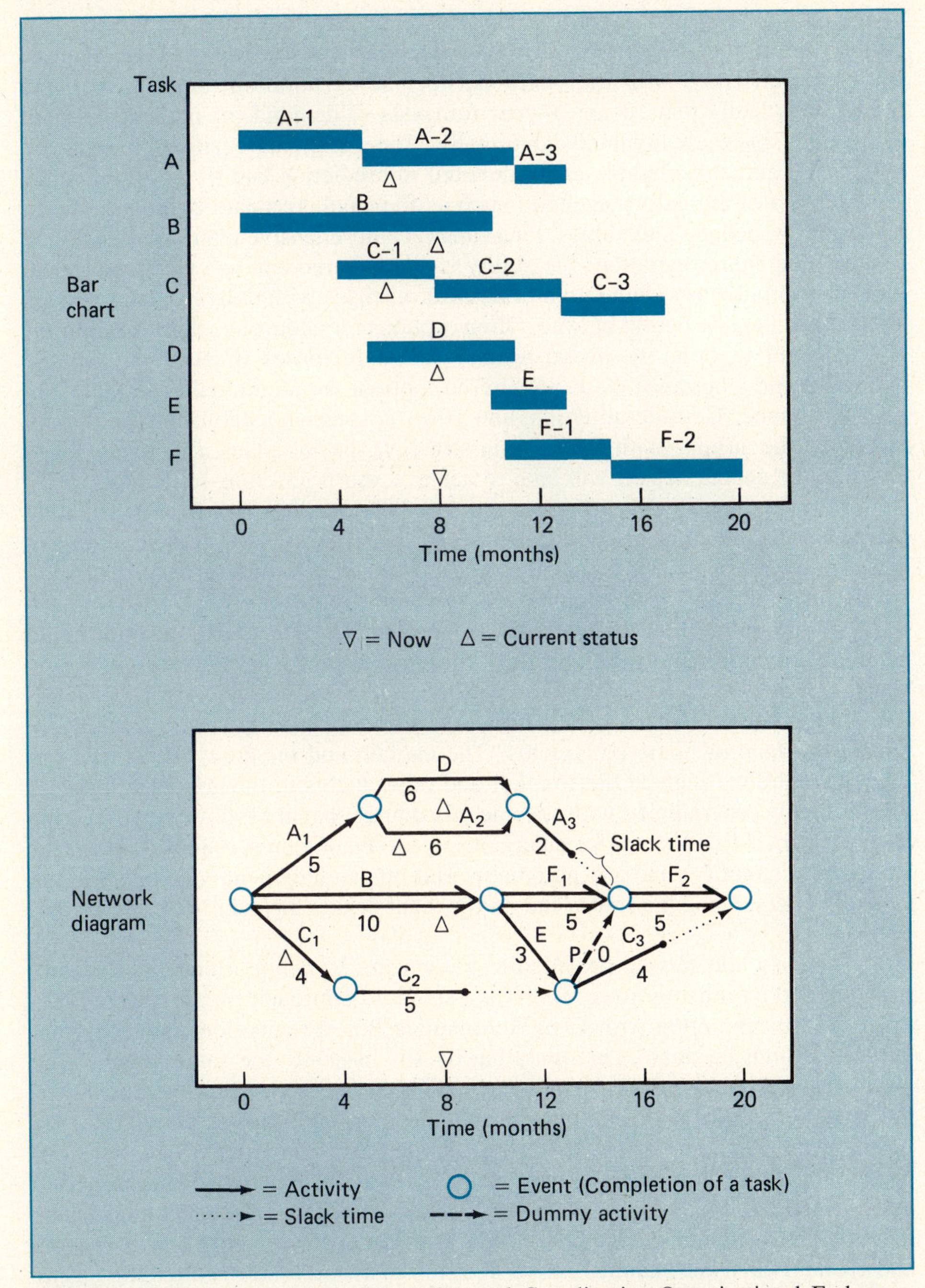

FIGURE 12.3 Techniques for Scheduling and Coordinating Organizational Endeavor. **Source:** Adapted from *Successful Project Management,* by Milton D. Rosenau, Jr. © 1981 by Lifetime Learning Publications, Belmont, California 94002, a division of Wadsworth, Inc. Reprinted and adapted by permission of the publisher.

board of directors and executive committee of an airline are responsible for strategy development. The president and vice presidents, along with the planning staff, are concerned with the world outside the corporation, both current and future. It is likely that 10- or 20-year forecasts of demand for passenger travel and cargo space are updated continually. The competitive situation must be anticipated and considerable effort devoted to predicting and trying to influence the behavior of regulatory agencies such as the Civil Aeronautics Board. Based on forecasts, beliefs, and values, long-range, comprehensive plans are developed to cover the entire operation. Flexibility is a key ingredient, as evidenced by the tendency to purchase a minimum of aircraft outright, with delivery dates spaced over a considerable period of time. Often, options for acquiring additional aircraft are arranged in order to hedge against future increases in need. If demand decreases and long-range plans are altered, options for additional equipment can be relinquished. Considerable time and effort is spent in establishing an overall image for the airline. Within this basic strategy, specific plans are developed to program the actual steps it will take to achieve short- and long-term goals.

Planning also involves the development of specific plans for coordinating the people and equipment necessary to provide the service as designed. Appropriate numbers of people must be hired and trained. A variety of aircraft may have to be purchased and maintained over time. Routes are developed and the level of service between points must be determined. A network diagram could be useful in coordinating all the tasks that are involved in inaugurating a new route.

In the operation of a specific flight, the planning process covers a relatively short time span of hours or minutes. The captain and his crew check environmental conditions such as the weather and other flights in the area. The process used is highly programmed with specific procedures that are followed by referring to a basic checklist. Except for emergencies, the flight plan is followed on a step-by-step basis that is relatively automatic. But human judgment is involved in the control towers, along the route, and on the flight deck, particularly during takeoff and landing.

Similarly, the service provided to passengers by cabin attendants is highly programmed on most airlines. There is a standard approach for serving refreshments and meals, often with Civil Aeronautics Board regulations defining what can and cannot be done. The operating plan is basically the same whether the aircraft is 25 percent full or carrying a capacity load. At another level, however, the data concerning load factors is used to determine current conditions and future trends. The results are fed into planning processes that include decisions concerning the number of flights per week to be scheduled between San Francisco and Chicago. A regulation limiting the sale of alcohol to passengers could have a direct effect on human behavior in the operational setting—both for passengers and crew. A Civil Aeronautics Board decision to award a new route to an airline would obviously affect overall strategy but would not affect the operation of a flight from Boston to Miami.

In this example we can see the role of managers in planning general strategy

and specific tactics. Long-range, comprehensive planning is carried out by top management. The planning process progresses through the organization to result in specific plans that can be carried out step by step. As the process works its way down through the organization, it becomes more detailed, often spelling out operating procedures as well as rules and regulations that obviously affect human behavior.

Effect of Planning on Behavior

Our discussion of planning was not meant to be exhaustive, nor to provide specific guidelines on what is a good planning process or what is a good plan. Our purpose is to reflect on the effect of planning and plans on human behavior in organizations. For example, how do goals, strategies, tactics, and procedures affect your behavior? Your long-range goal might be a successful career as a stockbroker. A first step is to be hired by Smith-Barney or Kidder, Peabody & Company, or E.F. Hutton, or some similar firm. Your strategy development process involves assessing your opportunities as realistically as possible. Will your competence (knowledge, skill, aptitude, attitude, etc.) fit the requirements of the firms you are interested in? Your overall strategy may include elements of education (a degree in finance with emphasis on investments and a minor in marketing), experience (a summer doing miscellaneous jobs at a local brokerage), and contacts (checking with Uncle Henry, a broker for 25 years, to see if he has any suggestions or leads).

Your medium-range program is focused primarily on a degree in business administration with a major in finance. This approach will allow you some flexibility to pursue other careers if the stockbroker goal is unobtainable. Given the demand for operations analysts and computer specialists, your quantitative skills may allow you to take advantage of opportunities in those areas. Your degree program affects your behavior by requiring certain courses, recommending others, and leaving some credits to your complete discretion (except you've heard via the grapevine that successful applicants in the recent past have had good communication skills, implying that courses in speaking and writing may be good insurance).

Your short-range objective is to finish the quarter with 15 more credits and a G.P.A. of 3.5 or better. Your behavior is governed by the requirements of each class, some of which are explicit in terms of exams to take and papers to write. Other "requirements" are implicit. For example, is it important to attend regularly? Is it important to participate by asking good questions? Is it better to be seen and not heard? Will it help or hinder (in terms of a final grade) if you visit the professor during office hours? These elements of a short-range plan affect specific behavior every day. Your behavior is guided by general intentions and specific action steps that may be written down on your daily reminder list.

Goals, strategies, and plans also serve as guidelines for organizational behavior. Long-range, comprehensive strategy has little effect on day-to-day activities of participants in the operating subsystem. Plans to double sales over a five-year period may not affect existing operations at all if the primary tactic is acquisition of three new companies. However, if the plan includes significant changes for existing products and facilities, there will be a direct effect on existing personnel. (See Box 12.3.)

The degree of involvement in the planning process usually has a substantial effect on subsequent behavior in carrying out the plans that are developed. If there is a wide zone of acceptance, plans made at the top and handed down may be accepted and implemented wholeheartedly. On the other hand, the results of such a process may create resentment and half-hearted efforts in the implementation phase. In many organizations participants are taking more interest in both what goals are established and what means are designed to accomplish them (Main, 1983). Being involved in and influencing the planning process seems to increase the probability that plans will be implemented (Pasmore & Friedlander, 1982).

Most of us would like to increase the proportion of *planning to doing* in our work situation. That is, to have little or no influence over how our work is to be done is not very palatable. Of course, the planning phase cannot be increased to the point where there is no time left for doing the job. However, in most cases this is not a significant problem. Typically there is room to expand the amount of influence, if not time, in the planning process without usurping an inordinate amount of time required for implementing the resultant plans and procedures. As indicated above, involvement enhances the probability of implementation in a way that is functional for the organization. This also increases the likelihood that participants exercise self-control, which makes managing less onerous and can eventually lead to more effectiveness, efficiency, and participant satisfaction.

IMPLEMENTING STRATEGIES AND PLANS

Many of the topics covered in other parts in this book relate to implementing activity. Some topics such as socialization, culture-climate, and contingency views provide background information or *flavor*. Other topics are more directly related to the process of implementing plans or carrying out organizational tasks. Of particular concern are technology, structure, communication, conflict resolution, group dynamics, and organizational improvement. Because so much attention is devoted to various aspects of implementing in other chapters, we will cover the subject only briefly here.

In general, more attention has been devoted to planning than implementing. The former is an intellectual or thinking activity; the latter is more action oriented.

> Planning is one of the two major functions of management and is associated with the "deciding" aspects of the manager's job. The other function—execution—involves implementing decisions. Thus, "deciding" and "doing" are inseparable parts of the manager's job; indeed, developing and operating a comprehensive planning system involves these two parts; deciding what to do—and then doing it. It is much easier to design a planning system than it is to implement it (Cleland, 1974).

Implementation involves mobilizing resources, structuring their relationships, integrating diverse activities, and controlling activities in light of policies, plans, and procedures. Accomplishing goals in human systems requires effective personal leadership. Strategies may be successful because of drive, verve, and brilliant leadership that elicits commitment and effort. (See Chapter 6, "Influence and Leadership," particularly Box 6.3.) It is also possible that a sound strategy can be subverted because leadership is lacking and organizational participants merely go through the motions. The obvious goal is to couple sound strategy and skillful implementation via effective leadership.

Implementation is the doing phase of organizational activity. To be sure, goal setting, planning, and controlling require human behavior. In a sense, however, they are facilitative rather than basic. They provide focus, guidance, and feedback concerning the basic task of any organization.

Implementing accounts for a large share of total organizational activity. Goals, plans, and controls are often set for relatively long periods of time. Repetitive plans that cover routine production processes (newspapers, milk, or cigarettes) are implemented without much variation from day to day. Of course, this description varies across organizations and would not be true for dynamic situations where single-use plans (advertising, space shuttle, or football) are the rule rather than the exception. In such cases strategic planning represents a somewhat larger share of total human behavior and organizational activity.

Two major considerations in implementing plans are (1) technology and (2) human effort. This assumes that key resources such as time and money are available.

Technology

As indicated in Chapter 9, technology refers to the *knowledge* about performing tasks or activities. It is far more than just hardware; it refers to standardized means for attaining objectives or results. Technology helps convert spontaneous, unreflective, and uncoordinated behavior into deliberate and rationalized action through the instrumentality of plans. By organizational technology we mean the techniques used in the transformation of input into output.

BOX 12.3
CLARK EQUIPMENT: A SURVIVAL EFFORT THAT DEPENDS ON STREAMLINING

Four years ago, Clark Equipment Co. was chasing a booming market for its two primary product lines: lift trucks and heavy construction equipment. Clark, headquartered on the outskirts of rural Buchanan, Mich., had been missing out on sales because management's attention had been diverted. In the 1960s it went on a buying spree designed to insulate it from the cyclicality of the heavy machinery business. Reversing that strategy in the late 1970s, Bert E. Phillips, chief executive officer, orchestrated a $300 million divest-and-invest program that doubled the number of Clark's heavy machinery factories in the U.S., boosted worldwide capacity by 35%, and increased its work force by 3,600 (BW—Sept. 4, 1978). "To those who have doubts about the company's future," said Phillips, "I just say, 'Wait and find out.' "

Those who waited saw a sad situation. Instead of enjoying heady growth, Clark is now battling what it admits is the "grave possibility" of collapse. The company is midway through a 15-month "survival" strategy directed by new Chairman and CEO James R. Rinehart. The strategy—designed to avert a severe cash shortage, cut worldwide capacity by 25%, slash plants' breakeven points, and pare salaried employees by a third—has a simple goal: to enable Clark to hang on until another long-range plan can be found.

Early in 1981, former Chairman Phillips, 63, belatedly realized that his plan, directed exclusively toward growth, left his company ill-prepared to cope with a recession. He persuaded Rinehart, 52, to leave the presidency of General Motors of Canada Ltd. and take over as Clark's president and CEO last November. Rinehart's strong suits were his solid operations background and his flair for long-range strategic planning. His challenge was clear: Clark's 21% drop in sales from 1979 to 1981 and a 1981 earnings decline of 42.3% offered him a chance to strut his stuff. "It is very helpful to have a crisis," he deadpans. "It opens management's mind to change."

Change is exactly what Rinehart, who was named chairman in May, is starting to make. Seeing no growth ahead for Clark's traditional industrial products, he has based his short-term strategy on cutting the manufacturing breakeven point from a sales level of $1.4 billion to $925 million. At its current sales level of $1 billion, Clark can operate at only 35% of its worldwide capacity. And it expects to report an aftertax loss of $147 million for 1982. If Rinehart had not reduced the company's inventories 35% this year, Clark would have lost even more. Next year he will phase out three of his company's 11 North American plants, eliminating 1,700 hourly jobs, while shifting some of the capacity to newer facilities. Some 1,600 salaried employees have already been cut this year under a zero-based staffing process that requires justification of every position at Clark.

Two-in-one jobs. To slim down what he acknowledges is an "overstaffed and overlayered" company, Rinehart has combined staff and operating functions. Now Clark's various divisions report to one of four group vice-presidents, each of whom also has staff duties. Thus the company's top financial officer heads Clark Equipment Credit Corp.—one of the few bright spots on the company's balance sheet these days. But he also oversees Clark's handling systems and loader-manufacturing divisions as well as the treasurer's office.

Rinehart believes the fundamental problem at Clark in the past decade was poor planning. Until now, he notes, divisions worked out five-year plans with almost no regard for what other parts of the company were proposing. "It was divisional and additive," he says. "And nobody except the chief executive knew how it all added up." Now Rinehart is rushing to implement a two- to five-year "viability" plan and a five- to 10-year "growth" plan, predicated on the short-term survival strategy, for each division and for the company as a whole. He argues that Clark—just like any other well-managed company—needs a two-year survival plan ready at all times so it can respond positively to disaster rather than react to it willy-nilly. But to prosper, he says, it needs all three plans.

Clark officials concede that more red ink may flow in 1983, in part because the company is still a year away from introducing a new, lower-priced lift truck that will use automotive rather than costlier, industrial-grade components. Seen as the first step in Rinehart's viability strategy, it will compete directly with Japanese imports, which have captured 30% of the U.S. market.

An emotional lesson? Meanwhile, to survive, Clark has cut prices on its premium models as much as 30%. While the long-term strategy has not been set, the purchase in September of White Motor Credit Corp. is a signal that acquisitions could again be part of Clark's future. So sure is Rinehart that his simpler organization and better planning will solve Clark's shortcomings that he has resisted bringing in his own team, betting his changes will maximize the "human effectiveness" of existing management. "Doing that," he declares, "is what it's all about."

Analysts give Rinehart good marks for his efforts so far, but they worry that Clark's dilatory tactics have permanently shrunk its market share. One says: "They should have realized years ago they were in a no-growth industry with lots of foreign competition." Adds a Michigan banker: "Clark's problems go beyond the business cycle. A lot of the companies they serve will never be the same size again, and neither will Clark."

Even Rinehart concedes that the real test of his handiwork at Clark will not come until the next business upturn. "Have we learned anything philosophically, emotionally, and intellectually?" he asks. "That will be the key."

Source: Reprinted from the December 6, 1982 issue of *Business Week* by special permission,

Industrial firms, for example, utilize both machine and knowledge-based techniques to accomplish this task. The computer is part of technology, as are the programs written by humans to be used in the processing of data. Selling activities are typically facilitated by equipment such as automobiles and telephones, but they are also carried out via certain techniques (such as prospecting, interacting with potential customers, and closing) adapted from the behavioral sciences. Thus it is easy to see that the implementation of plans in an organizational context is dependent on technology to varying degrees. It may involve automated equipment with minimal involvement of human actors. On the other hand, the plan may be designed to provide social services in a crisis clinic where implementation depends almost entirely on human effort.

Human Effort

As indicated above, performance in a work setting is dependent on technology. However, when equipment and knowledge are reasonably equal in two departments, there still may be a large difference in their performance. This is particularly true if human behavior is involved to a considerable extent. The degree to which plans are implemented by people depends on two basic variables: capacity and inclination. Capacity can be further subdivided into physical, mental, and emotional components. Intelligence, knowledge, strength, and agility can be measured with relative ease. Certain ranges of performance can be identified, beyond which it is unlikely that people can go, regardless of their intentions. They may be extremely interested in running a mile in less than four minutes and yet their physiological capacity is such that six minutes is a much more realistic goal.

Within work organizations, consideration of what people are inclined to accomplish, by and beyond themselves, is typically much more relevant. Capacity is similar over a reasonable range for individuals at a given level or in a particular function. Consequently, differences in performance are, in large part, a measure of the degree to which people are inclined (motivated) to implement plans. A number of factors and forces are at work in organizational settings. Two fundamental issues are motivation and leadership, each of which were covered in detail (Chapters 4 and 6). It is sufficient at this point to call attention to the importance of understanding motivation and effective leadership and analyzing the degree to which established plans are implemented. Problems in implementation may occur in a variety of ways, deriving from faulty premises, inappropriate plans, or poor execution. The problem may be the result of improper technology, or a mismatch of human-technical factors. And, in the latter case, it may be a question of inadequate resources, bad organizational design, or ineffective leadership.

Effect on Behavior: Examples

In the airline example covered previously, we described how planning is supposed to happen and how plans are supposed to be carried out. Routine implementation for a flight can be interrupted by irregular influences, such as bad weather, equipment malfunction, or hijackers. When such things occur it is necessary to use alternative procedures and common sense. For top management, major problems (world-wide recession, high interest rates, or high fuel costs) and opportunities (deregulation of routes and service levels by the Civil Aeronautics Board) cause significant adjustments in implementation that in turn lead to strategy reformulation, refined plans, and new action steps.

Implementing plans to achieve goals is the most pervasive activity in organizations. Similarly, individuals implement action steps based on implicit or explicit goals and plans. For example, you carry out specific action steps (see Figure 12.1) to meet course requirements in Finance 301; to fulfill degree requirements—MBA with a major in finance; and to satisfy any other requirements for getting a job with a brokerage firm. Because the degree to which plans are implemented is often a function of involvement in planning as well as doing, influence over decisions, and commitment to courses of action, you may find that some action steps come easier than others. Required courses, particularly those outside your major area, can be a source of irritation. An elective, on the other hand, is often more interesting and even fun. Similarly, writing reports on required subjects is often more tedious than when you are able to pick a topic closer to your interests.

The degree to which plans are implemented is also a function of the zone of acceptance for operating personnel. Footdragging or outright refusal to implement plans can occur when people either (1) do not agree with goals and the means to achieve them or (2) do not understand what is to be done and how to do it. If people think that stated goals are inappropriate or that the methods are unsound, they lose confidence and decrease commitment. Charismatic leadership may provide the needed impetus in the short run. However, over the long run it would be wise to note problems in implementation, to analyze causes and effects, and to overcome them in future planning processes.

CONTROLLING ORGANIZATIONAL ENDEAVOR

Monitoring the degree to which plans are implemented and goals are achieved is the role of *control* in organizations. It is essential for both organizational and individual well-being.

> Characterizing an organization in terms of its patterns of control is to describe an essential and universal aspect of organization which every member must face and to which he must adjust. Organization implies control. A social organization has an ordered arrangement of individual human interactions. Control processes help circumscribe idiosyncratic behaviors and keep them conformant with the rational plan of the organization. Organizations require a certain amount of conformity as well as the integration of diverse activities. It is the function of control to bring about conformance to organizational requirements and achievement of the ultimate purposes of the organization. The coordination and order created out of the diverse interests and potentially diffuse behaviors of

> members is largely a function of control. It is at this point that many of the problems of organizational functioning and of individual adjustment arise (Tannenbaum, 1968, p. 3).

The curbing or restraining side of control is often saddled with bad associations. On reflection, we see that, besides being a normal and pervasive activity, it is essential to keeping individual and organizational activity on target—directed toward established goals. Driving an automobile requires control behavior in order to stay on the highway. A map provides information to develop a plan (route) for getting from point A to point B. Comparing house numbers with the address listed tells us whether or not we have reached our destination. We verify the balance in the checking account before writing a sizable check. And we watch the progress of steaks cooking on the charcoal broiler to ensure that they come out medium rare.

Thus, control has a very basic and positive function in all behavior—individual and organizational. It is the means of regulating activity by verifying or checking actual conditions with desired conditions. Goals (ends) and plans (means) serve as standards in the control phase of behavior (see Figure 12.1). If actual results are different from expected results, some adjustment is made to close the gap. This might be more intense activity (working harder or differently) or it might call for a change in goals.

The Control Process

A general model of the control process is shown in Figure 12.4. Goals and strategies are determined, programs planned, resources allocated, and work performed. The ability to control any endeavor depends on four elements: (1) a controllable characteristic for which standards are known; (2) a means of measuring the characteristic; (3) a means of comparing actual results to standards and evaluating differences; and (4) a means of effecting changes in the system in order to adjust the pertinent characteristics. If the elements are present, the cycle can be completed and related to higher- and lower-level control processes. If any element is missing, the process may be meaningless. For example, goals of a department being unclear, achievement will be difficult to evaluate. If a manager lacks the authority to make adjustments in work plans or resource allocations, feedback on performance won't be very useful.

The process shown in Figure 12.4 applies to any control system regardless of the degree of sophistication in the various steps outlined. The *means* used to measure, compare, and adjust the process may be highly programmed, mechanistic, and computerized, or subjective human beings may be involved in each step. The inclusion of human decision makers in the process tends to make the control system more flexible and capable of using a variety of information in the feedback loop. In many production processes, measuring and comparing can be relatively objective and use means such as counting or weighing. Food processing is an example of this approach. The control phase can be relatively subjective, however, with results depending on the perceptions of human beings. Controlling

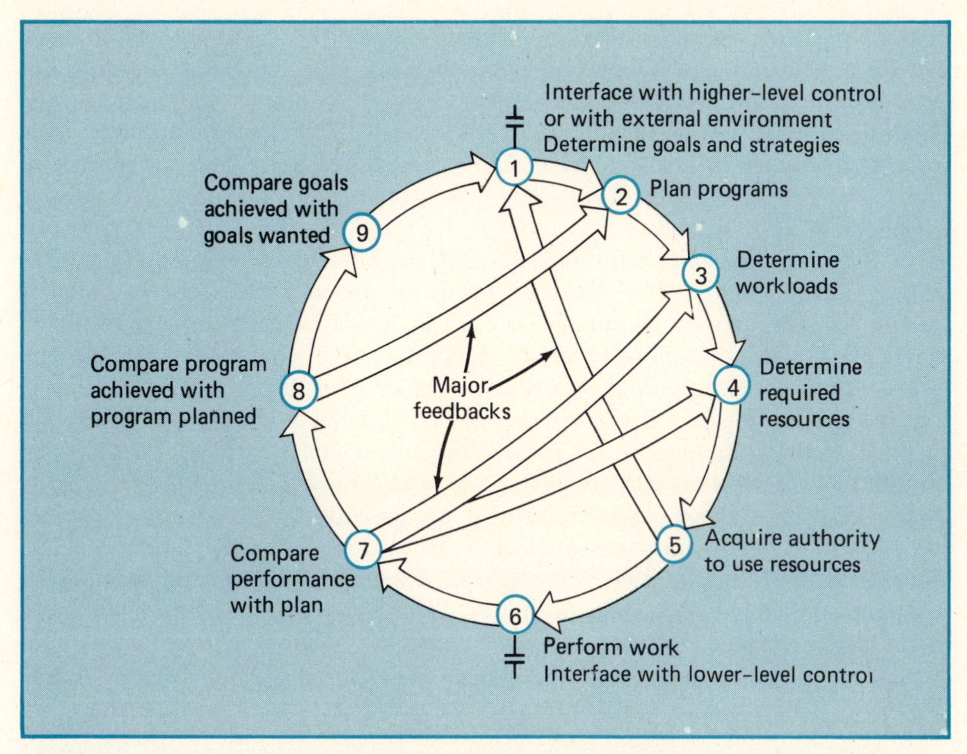

FIGURE 12.4 The Cycle of Control. **Source:** Adapted from Marvin E. Mundel, *A Conceptual Framework for the Management Sciences* (New York: McGraw-Hill, 1967), p. 162. Reproduced with permission.

the quality of service in a bank or restaurant is an example; subjective perception plays a major role in checking current conditions against expectations.

An important phase in the control process is the selecting of characteristics to be monitored and regulated. These characteristics should be within the orbit of key goals and the plans of action developed for them. The control function requires valid and reliable information, the obtaining of which, in turn, requires vast amounts of time and energy. One aim of this selection phase is to see that costly attention is not wasted on meaningless characteristics, behaviors, or outcomes. (We will address this issue more fully in discussing management by objectives and results in a following section.)

Another issue is the relative emphasis to be placed on ends versus means. Are we truly satisfied with results only, or are we concerned with checking to verify that appropriate means are being used? In dealing with organizational control, both output control and behavior control are legitimate concerns (Ouchi & McGuire, 1975). It is important to match the degree of emphasis on either aspect with the particular situation. If output measures are relatively simple and straightforward, they can be used to good advantage. In large, complex organizations they are probably the only realistic means of comparing performance across similar units. Behavior control is much less transferable across divisions based on function, because of the subjective nature of standards that reflect the values and beliefs of particular managers (Ouchi, 1978). However, where goals or output standards are somewhat fuzzy, it may be appropriate to put more emphasis on behavior control. Examples are research and development or service functions of various kinds.

Behavior control usually implies emphasis on subjective perceptions, thus raising several issues. Who decides what is appropriate behavior? Some of us have clear ideas of what is right and hence can determine gaps between expected and actual behavior relatively easily. In other cases, fuzzy output goals and unclear behavior expectations lead to an extremely complex situation for carrying out the control phase of individual or organizational activity. However, whether implicit or explicit, the control phase does occur and provides at least some indication of whether or not activity is within allowable limits.

The effects of control exercised by key individuals can persist even after they have left the organization. William S. Paley, founder and chairman of CBS, Inc., officially retired in 1982. For several years before that he had been relinquishing some day-to-day responsibilities. But his departure was probably more form than substance. He was no longer a member of management, but he continued as a director and was on the scene. In fact, Paley retained his office in the New York headquarters. One report describes the situation as follows:

> Certainly, Paley's influence was pervasive. "Every decision at CBS was affected by 'the Paley Factor'," recalls one company executive. Such dominance can hamper management development. At RCA Corp., General David Sarnoff controlled the company so totally that when he finally left, there were no upper- or middle-management executives with an unobstructed view of RCA.
>
> Paley may be trying to avoid just that by giving Wyman [Thomas H. Wyman, the new CEO] more of a chance to make his own mark and to establish a management team. Yet by keeping some power, Paley has made it clear that he has not made his final bow (Paley, 1982, p. 42).

The examples in Figure 12.5 illustrate the control process for individuals, informal groups, and the organization as a whole. In each case there is a relevant characteristic and means of measuring performance, comparing the actual versus the expected, and adjusting both goals and actions. For example, an airline might take advantage of deregulation of routes to develop a strategy of selective coverage of a larger area. Sales targets would be established for an appropriate period of time and results would be monitored. If the anticipated sales do not materialize, the variance will have to be explained by the sales manager and adjustments made in the goal or the plan or both. Performance may be so bad that the sales manager and others are fired. On the other hand, performance may be so good that the key people are commended, given bonuses, and tagged as promotable (see the vignette *A Prize-Winning Strategy*).

Controls Administered by:	Direction for Controls Deriving From:	Behavioral and Performance Measures:	Signal for Corrective Action	Reinforcements or Rewards for Compliance:	Sanctions or Punishments for Noncompliance
Organization	Organizational plans, strategies, responses to competitive demands	Budgets, standard costs, sales targets	Variance	Management commendation ↓ Monetary incentives, promotions	Request for explanation ↓ Dismissal
Informal group	Mutual commitments, group ideals	Group norms	Deviance	Peer-approval, membership, leadership	Kidding, ↓ Ostracism, hostility
Individual	Individual goals, aspirations	Self-expectations, intermediate targets	Perceived impending failure, missed targets	Satisfaction of "being in control" ↓ Elation	Sense of disappointment ↓ Feeling of failure

FIGURE 12.5 Types of Control in Organizations. **Source:** Gene W. Dalton, "Motivation and Control in Organizations," in Gene W. Dalton and Paul Lawrence (Eds.), *Motivation and Control in Organizations* (Homewood, Ill.: Irwin, 1971). © 1971. Reprinted by permission.

For an individual example, we can refer to our previous case of a person with career aspirations to be a stockbroker. If you achieve your goal of 15 credits this quarter with an average G.P.A. of 3.57, you will be elated and feel that your degree program and career plan is in control. However, if you flunk a core investments course, you will undoubtedly be disappointed. Moreover, missing such a significant target will probably cause you to reassess your overall strategy—unless you feel you can get back on track by working harder and smarter.

Indirect Control

Societal values, norms, mores, and laws all serve as background for control processes in organizations. They affect individual propensities to behave in certain ways and underlie the general dilemma of individualism versus collaboration in group and organizational endeavors. Note the references to informal group norms and peer approval in Figure 12.5. In general, society seeks to develop mature individuals who progress from dependence to independence, from self-centeredness to cooperation, from subjective thinking to objective thinking, and from control by others to self-control. Obviously, these are countervailing tendencies that are present in all situations. Homogeneous value systems, internalization of group norms, and knowledge and acceptance of laws should lead to self-control and behavior that is within appropriate limits for a given situation.

All of these forces are designed to develop precontrol and provide built-in means for adjusting behavior according to current conditions. Checking after the fact—exercising postcontrol—often involves others and is beneficial if future behavior is more in line the next time a similar situation arises.

Direct Control

Organizational socialization can be an explicit process of selecting, training, developing, and promoting individuals who seem to internalize the goals and plans that prevail. This condition suggests that implementation will be relatively straightforward and that control, particularly after the fact, will be relatively easy. Because we tend to hire and promote people in our own image there is a tendency to make the organizational setting as comfortable as possible and thereby facilitate the managerial processes of goal setting, planning, implementing, and controlling.

Regardless of this human tendency toward comfort, the size and complexity of many organizations make the establishment of desired conditions on all levels unlikely. Even when this is not the case, the socialization process, which is never complete, and individuals changing over time would still complicate the picture. Moreover, work organizations represent only one portion of our activities; outside factors introduce an element of unpredictability that can alter the course of an operation. Therefore it is necessary to establish explicit processes that allow for and facilitate control in organizations. As indicated above, goals and plans represent characteristics that can be checked to ensure that results and activities come close enough to expectations.

In many organizations the *budget* becomes the primary tool for controlling organizational activities. For business enterprises, objectives are typically expressed in terms of dollar sales. Sales forecasts are developed in the light of both external and internal information, with the results providing a foundation for all organizational activity. An advertising budget is drawn up to fit the sales forecast. The wage and salary budget is designed in view of the number of people required to accomplish the objectives as established. Throughout the organization, future activity is spelled out in dollar terms.

The budgeting process forces management to consider future plans explicitly and attach dollar values to them. By asking organization members at all levels to develop subparts of the budget, a sense of participation and organizational involvement is often achieved. Self-generated plans for budgets often are easier to control than those imposed by others.

Once the various parts of the budget are integrated into a comprehensive financial plan, it becomes a standard against which performance can be measured during the ensuing period. In most cases budgets are flexible enough that adjustments can be made, if need be, according to the way circumstances develop. It is not necessarily a rigid constraining device.

Budgetary control in many organizations involves dollar allocations whereby a total amount of money is divided and earmarked for certain functions over a period of time. In this sense, the budget is a constraining device because activities dependent on available funds must be curtailed if the funds run out. Therefore, the control process is typically one of ascertaining expenditures over time as measured against some planned rate.

A typical problem in organizations of this type is that of running out of funds before the budget period expires. Either funds must be transferred from other endeavors, or activity in this phase of the organization must be curtailed. A less typical, but evident, problem is that of coming to the end of a budgetary period with excess funds on hand. At this point there is often a mad scramble to expend the funds in order that the budget officer or appropriating agency (legislative body) will not interpret efficient performance as a lack of need and hence cut off the supply of funds in the future. In large, complex organizations, the allocation process is difficult. Matching needs with resources is an important function, and the process should be flexible enough to adjust according to changes in the environment. In most cases, however, changes are rather slow in coming, thus resulting in a continuation of expenditures in relatively obsolete activities and undersupporting new and growing areas of need.

Whether done formally or informally, *performance appraisal* is a phenomenon inherent in organizations. Superiors, subordinates, and peers all form perceptions of each other. Because of its relationship to the reward system, performance appraisal by superiors of subordinates is of primary concern and often formalized, at least in decisions such as hiring, firing, promoting, and reviewing merit for pay increases. Responsibility for performance appraisal gives superiors considerable potential power to control the behavior of subordinates unless there are overriding considerations based on union contracts, automatic step increases, or other built-in means of fairly automatic rewards.

Of crucial importance in formal performance appraisal systems is identification of appropriate criteria. For example, performance on the job should carry more weight than appearance or personality attributes. When results can be measured relatively objectively, appraisal and control are straightforward. When subjective judgments are necessary, the process is facilitated by high levels of trust between superiors and subordinates. Performance appraisal can be functional for the individual and the organization if performance criteria are established jointly, appropriate on-the-job behavior is mutually understood, and the review is a continual process focused on growth and development. It can be highly motivating if it taps inherent needs, builds on expectations of appropriate effort leading to desired performance, and includes positive reinforcement via both intrinsic and extrinsic rewards that are equitable in the eyes of all parties concerned.

It is easy to understand, however, how performance appraisal has become dysfunctional in many organizations. Low levels of trust, application of inappropriate criteria, mutual recriminations long after the fact, and emphasis on shortcomings rather than on accomplishments all work together to create a poor atmosphere, employee dissatisfaction, and decreased organizational efficiency and effectiveness.

Feedback and Timing

As shown in Figure 12.4, feedback is an essential ingredient in any control process. In relatively closed systems, feedback leads to automatic adjustments in the system. In relatively open systems, information is received by human beings who process it and decide on appropriate action. Many kinds of feedback systems can be designed to facilitate control. Managers may desire a continual flow of information to monitor the system. Or, they may assume that no news is good news and hence require information in only exceptional situations.

The time dimension is important to the control function in several ways. Organizations develop precontrol by means of policies, procedures, and rules or regulations. The development of relatively uniform value systems among organizational members provides valuable precontrol. Emphasis is focused on preventing the system from deviating too far from preconceived norms. Considerable organizational effort goes into maintaining the system within designated limits—preventing undesirable occurrences. Education of the citizenry with regard to traffic laws and the consequences of breaking them is an attempt at precontrol of driving behavior. However, it is apparent that precontrol is often not sufficient to maintain systems within desirable limits (Hassett, 1981). Therefore, considerable effort must also be devoted to postcontrol: ascertaining the results of behavior, evaluating it, and taking action that is designed to correct or adjust behavior in future situations. For example, a flashing red light, a siren, and a $50 fine are elements of a postcontrol process designed to persuade a person to drive within the posted speed limit. In such a case, the precontrol effort of education outlining a set of rules did not prove effective. Therefore postcontrol in the form of punitive action is invoked. Suspending someone without pay or withholding a merit increase are typical organizational responses for doing something wrong or not doing enough right.

There is considerable disagreement concerning the relative weight that should be placed on pre- and postcontrol. The most extreme position suggests that if enough effort is given to precontrol, there will be no need for postcontrol. That is, if group value systems were internalized completely, all individual and organizational actions would fall within desirable limits and the system would be self-regulating. So far, however, this concept appears to be utopian, and considerable attention continues to be devoted to postcontrol. Many examples of postcontrol in organizations could be cited: reviewing profit performance as related to established goals; checking the reject or scrap rate at the end of the week; or checking a sales agent's expense account at the end of the month. In each case the difference between actual and expected would be ascertained, and a decision would be made concerning appropriate corrective action which, if successful, would lead toward improved performance in the future.

Effect of Control on Behavior

Figure 12.6 indicates two alternative views of control—traditional and behavioral. A widespread belief among managers is that the amount of control is fixed. This leads to the assumption that if subordinates have more control over

Classical Assumptions (traditional base)	**Contemporary Assumptions** (behavioral base)
Control is:	Control is:
1. a fixed amount	1. a variable amount
2. a *f* (structure and authority)	2. a *f* (interpersonal influence)
3. unilateral	3. performed via mutual understanding
4. vertical	4. horizontal, vertical, and diagonal

FIGURE 12.6 Two Views of Control. **Source:** Adapted from J. Timothy McMahon and John Ivancevich, "A Study of Control in a Manufacturing Organization: Managers and Nonmanagers," *Administrative Science Quarterly,* March 1976, p. 67.

their actions, the boss necessarily has less control as a manager. However, the proper emphasis is on maintaining performance within desired limits, and in this sense the amount of control is variable and increases directly with the amount of concern collectively shown by participants for achieving organizational objectives. Thus, delegation, involvement, motivation, and loyalty may contribute to an increased total amount of control.

A prevalent traditional view is that control is a function of the formal structure and authority (right to command) relationship. An alternative view is that control is a function of interpersonal influence. This suggests that real control takes place via an interaction influence system that flows in all directions and depends on mutual understanding and acceptance of desired outcomes.

Substantial research evidence suggests that the amount of control and performance are related. Overcontrol can lead to feelings of helplessness, dissatisfaction, and a decrease in productivity (see *Form or Substance* vignette). On the other hand, absence of control can lead to anarchy and an individual sense of uncertainty, anxiety, and frustration (Lawler, 1976, p. 1265). People do respond positively to clearly defined objectives *and* to feedback concerning their performance. Furthermore, when there is concordance among organizational members regarding the nature of controls and influence processes, performance is enhanced (McMahon & Ivancevich, 1976).

Even though the control system may be reasonably well designed, controls over behavior may be resented, and resistance should be anticipated. Lawler (1976, p. 1274) lists the occasions when resistance to control systems is more likely:

1. The control system measures performance in a new area.
2. The control system replaces a system that people have a high investment in maintaining.
3. The standards are set without participation.
4. The results from the control system are not fed back to the people whose performance is measured.

5. The results from the control system are fed to higher levels in the organization and are used by the reward system.
6. The people who are affected by the system are relatively satisfied with things as they are and they see themselves as committed to the organization.
7. The people who are affected by the system are low in self-esteem and authoritarianism.

The controlling function typically has a direct effect on behavior because it leads toward reinforcing existing behavior patterns or adjusting them if there is a gap between expected and actual. Determining the characteristics to be checked is a crucial aspect of controlling behavior. In organizations we tend to get from subordinates what we measure and reward accordingly. Therefore, it is important that we measure and reward the right things. What is it that will lead to success? What aspects are substantive for organizational performance? What aspects are superficial? Obviously, managers with different values will disagree on these questions. Some will stress results only, or at least primarily, without worrrying too much about the means used. Others are concerned to see that satisfactory results are obtained by appropriate means. The actions of managers should be legal and ethical. Physical or human resources should not be squandered to achieve short-run objectives. But the concern about *how* can be overdone. For example, is it appropriate for a manager to state that he is interested "only in results," and then question a subordinate about the amount of time spent on the job or about when the normal amount of working time is put in during the week? Or, should the expense account be a focus of attention if the bottom-line profits for the unit are exemplary?

These issues are crucial and it is important for managers to think through what sort of behavior they want that is in line with overall goals and plans. Substantive aspects should be emphasized, regardless of measurement difficulties. Superficial indicators should not be used just because they are more accessible. To do so causes behavior to gravitate in those directions and hinder the pursuit of substantive goals.

Another major issue is the degree of self-control that is encouraged in organizations. Emphasis on external control in terms of procedures and rules may foster a self-fulfilling prophecy to the effect that people lose the ability to control themselves. If they don't have the opportunity to practice self-control, the ability will probably wither and die. However, if people are given ample opportunity for this, and get progressively better at it, the result could be significant savings of time and effort on the part of managers in the system.

MANAGEMENT BY OBJECTIVES AND RESULTS

A formal system of MBO/R, as shown in Figure 12.7 provides a framework for the essential managerial functions discussed in this chapter: goal setting, planning, implementing, and controlling. The rationale for this comprehensive, integrated

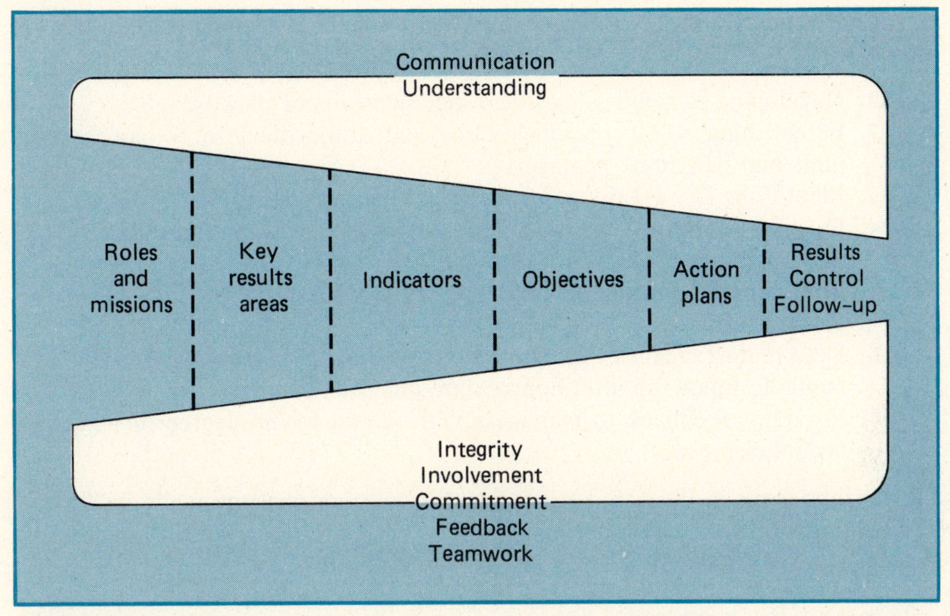

FIGURE 12.7 MBO/R Approach to Planning and Controlling Organizational Endeavor. **Source:** Adapted from George L. Morrisey, *Management by Objectives and Results in the Public Sector.* (Reading, MA: Addison-Wesley, 1976), p. 23.

managerial system is based on a number of findings from the behavioral sciences that are focused on improving individual and organizational performance (Carroll & Tosi, 1973; Odiorne, 1978; McConkie, 1979; Locke & Latham, 1979). Unfortunately, there are many examples of unsuccessful MBO/R programs. Failure typically stems from unbalanced emphasis on the various purposes or elements involved or lack of skill (particularly autocratic behavior) in carrying out the essential steps in the process (Levinson, 1970; Kondrasuk, 1981).

Many organizations use some form of MBO/R adapted to their specific circumstances. Because all behavior is goal-oriented or purposeful, focusing on objectives and comparing actual results with expected results is common and expected. It happens informally for each of us in our personal and organizational lives. MBO/R as a managerial system is designed to (1) make the process that is shown in Figure 12.7 more explicit; (2) emphasize results rather than activities; and (3) encourage attention to high-priority objectives and plans of action.

MBO/R Process

MBO/R is a programmatic means of carrying out the managerial functions of goal setting, planning, implementing and controlling. It provides a framework for managing at any level in an organization. It is a specific program that fits the general planning process set forth in Figure 12.1. If it is organization-wide, MBO/R provides a framework for consistent, coordinated behavior on the part of participants. The number of steps and their specific procedures will vary by organization, but they include essentially the following:

1. Developing or reaffirming long-range missions or purposes.
2. Establishing roles (responsibilities and authorities) for organizational units and individual managers.
3. Identifying key results areas and performance indicators.
4. Specifying short-range objectives within key results areas (prioritized and related to resource utilization).
5. Programming overall plans and specific steps required to achieve the desired results.
6. Determining means of measuring and evaluating performance in order to facilitate follow-up after appropriate intervals of time.
7. Providing feedback to managers with regard to the degree of objective accomplishment.

The various steps in the MBO/R process typically go on continually in day-to-day organizational endeavors. However, it is easier to illustrate the process by looking at a specific example with a time frame of one year.

Example of MBO/R

Let's look at the branch office of a nationwide firm of certified public accountants. We can assume that the firm as a whole has developed or reaffirmed its basic mission and established roles for subparts of the organization such as auditing or consulting services. The top management of the regional office typically would meet to discuss overall company goals and translate them into meaningful terms for local operations.

Within these general guidelines individual managers of subunits in the regional office would develop objectives to be accomplished in the next year. For example, in the consulting services area, objectives might include a specific number of new accounts, a target for dollars billed, and a projected net profit figure for the unit. In addition, there might be an objective of providing an entirely new and different type of consulting service. These objectives would be reviewed between the managing partner and each department head, leading to refinements and ultimate agreement on mutual expectations. At this stage, it may also be appropriate for a meeting of all managers on the same level to check for overlaps, gaps, and interdependent activities required to achieve desired results (French & Hollmann, 1975).

The next step in the process is the development of strategic plans and tactical action steps for achieving the objectives. Here again it may be appropriate to discuss such planning both vertically and horizontally (units, teams, or task forces) in order to coordinate activity and resource utilization.

Measures of performance would be agreed on between superiors and subordinates in order to facilitate follow-up, evaluation, and feedback. A key element in this phase is self-evaluation by each manager before discussing the results with his or her superior. This approach facilitates the development of internalized self-control and allows the superior to react to the subordinate's perception rather than being forced to play the heavy in the evaluation process. In some cases it may be useful for a work team to evaluate the results of group efforts.

A Multipurpose System

Ideal MBO/R programs are designed to provide a means for the following activities:

Goal setting. Identifying and prioritizing missions, key results areas, and objectives
Program planning. Designing means for implementing action
Participation. Involving organization members on a one-to-one (superior-subordinate) and work team basis in the planning process
Development. Improving managerial skill in decision making, planning, and controlling
Motivation. Tapping latent capability through involvement in setting challenging, realistic objectives
Control. Measuring and evaluating results
Performance appraisal. Providing feedback to individuals and work teams concerning actual versus expected results
Compensation. Designing reward systems that recognize results *and* the behavior deemed appropriate for specific roles

These elements comprise a total system requiring balanced attention if potential benefits are to be realized. However, the use of a framework such as MBO/R does not ensure success. There is no guarantee that the right objectives will be identified or that appropriate plans of action will be developed. However, a systematic MBO/R process at least ensures that important issues are considered and discussed. It provides a means for shifting the emphasis from activities toward results and for coordinating objectives and action plans among various individuals and subunits.

As shown in Figure 12.7, communication and understanding are important factors in the overall process. As the various elements are made explicit between superiors and subordinates and among team members, communication and understanding are enhanced. Mutual expectations become apparent and coordination of organizational endeavor is facilitated.

Effect of MBO/R on Behavior

Depending on how MBO/R is introduced and implemented, it can lead to improvement in a number of key dimensions that underlie improved and sustained performance. Participation of each manager (indeed each employee) in the process of both setting objectives and designing action steps is important for several reasons. Involvement leads to commitment, both publicly and privately. Clear, challenging goals that are accepted by individuals lead to improved performance. Explicit performance objectives make it easier to identify good performance and hence reward it appropriately. Such positive reinforcement increases satisfaction and the probability that desired behavior will be repeated in the future. Explicit objectives also provide an opportunity for specific feedback concerning results. Feedback, responsibility, and meaningful work are central ingredients in enriched jobs. Focusing on key results increases task identity and enhances task significance, two aspects of meaningful work. A properly implemented MBO/R program can enrich jobs while simultaneously emphasizing relevant, challenging, and realistic goals (accepted by participants) that lead to improved performance (Umstot, 1977).

The MBO/R process also allows emphasis on the dimensions of effective leader behavior discussed in Chapter 6: support, interaction facilitation, goal emphasis, and work facilitation. Development of subordinates is a key area for managers in terms of results, but the degree of attainment may be difficult to measure. In such cases, evaluation, feedback, and coaching should focus on behavior that has been determined appropriate for achieving objectives; that is, guidelines for *how* results are to be achieved (Beer & Ruh, 1976; Levinson, 1976). There is a fine line between giving people an opportunity to do it themselves and providing appropriate guidance. In any case, expectations should be explicit; people should know whether they are to be concerned with results only or appropriate behavior or both.

Teamwork can be improved through the process of sharing objectives and action plans among team members, particularly when interdependent activities are involved. The public commitment in a group setting also increases the probability of improved performance. Integrity is a key element in the success or failure of management by objectives and results programs. The process should be approached with genuine respect for the ability of participants to set challenging, realistic objectives that are organizationally relevant. Similarly, each participant must approach the process as a meaningful way to carry out the managerial task. If it is a hollow exercise, it will not be very effective. Developing the proper overall organizational climate and individual attitudes takes adequate preparation and patience.

The potential benefits can be negated in a variety of ways. Half-hearted support (lip service) by top management can cause managers at lower levels to view the program as another passing fad rather than as something basic to the managerial process. Autocratic, top-down objective setting may result in active or passive resistance. Overemphasis on quantification for ease of measurement can lead to concentration on results that are not particularly meaningful for organizational success. Lack of follow-up, appraisal, and feedback leaves managers wondering if results make any difference. Lack of recognition and undifferentiated rewards for improvement suggest that the primary purpose is increasing productivity over the short run or that MBO/R is just additional paperwork with little relation to actual operations.

Implementing a meaningful MBO/R program requires skill and understanding; it is not a panacea. Everyone involved should understand the basic philosophy, process, advantages, and potential pitfalls. Adequate preparation and training in skills such as developing meaningful objectives and conducting functional appraisal feedback sessions should be part of any program. The success of MBO/R programs is not due to the technique itself. Rather, it is dependent on enlightened, skillful managers using a framework to enhance the probability that a basic, natural process will lead to improved performance and increased satisfaction for everyone involved.

SO WHAT? IMPLICATIONS FOR YOU

Planning and controlling are pervasive personal and organizational activities. They are primary managerial functions. Knowledge about planning and controlling should help you understand more about human behavior in work organizations—your own and others.

As a Member in an Organization

Generalizations	Implications
1. Goals and plans—whether explicit or implicit—structure behavior. Individual and organizational behavior is not random; it is directed toward some purpose or desired end.	1. Be cognizant of your goals (desired future conditions) and how they affect your plans and your behavior. Be as explicit as possible, but remember they should be guidelines, not a strait jacket.
2. Explicit attention to planning and control encourages individuals to focus on relevant results rather than endless activities.	2. Beware of the activity trap—just keeping yourself busy with routine matters. Focus on key results so that your time and energy are devoted to major issues and not taken up by low-priority "squeaky wheels."
3. Premises underlie individual planning processes. Forecasts, predictions, assumptions, and assertions about environmental conditions, organizational strengths and weaknesses, and personal interests and inclinations are somehow fused into premises about what is feasible and desirable.	3. Strive for realism in your premises. Don't let your desires affect your predictions and assumptions unduly. Assess the external and internal environments thoroughly, using multiple sources of information and the opinions of knowledgeable others.
4. The planning process is the same at all levels in organizations, but the resulting strategies, coordinative programs,	4. Know the planning process and plans that directly affect you and your work. Be aware of your organization's overall

Generalizations	Implications
and operating plans are different in terms of comprehensiveness, time span, and flexibility. To be really effective the various plans must be part of an integrated system.	planning process so that you can relate effectively with others whose tasks are interdependent with yours.
5. Good planning and plans are only half of the battle. Implementation of action steps is crucial to success. This requires adequate financial, technical, and human resources. Knowledge and skill are important, but inclination to exert the necessary effort may be most important. Good effort can overcome bad plans; poor effort can negate good plans.	5. Do a reality check on your own plans to be sure that the necessary resources are available before making commitments that can't be met. Recognize the role your effort plays in carrying out the organization's plans of action. Give it your best shot or air misgivings openly. Don't surreptitiously drag your feet and then say, "I knew it would never work."
6. Unobtrusive control in organizations comes indirectly, through selection, orientation, and training processes. From the organization's point of view, if the "right" people have the proper experiences, they will behave in such a way that operations and activities will be satisfactorily under control.	6. Recognize how indirect controls work through your beliefs, values, and attitudes. Check periodically to see if you are comfortable with the goals, plans, and tactics that are proposed, particularly those that directly affect your behavior.
7. Precontrol and in-process feedback tend to be more effective and efficient in the long run than postcontrol for keeping individual and organizational behavior within tolerable limits.	7. Emphasize precontrol and in-process feedback as much as possible in order to avoid the hassles and costs of postcontrol. Build in unobtrusive processes that allow monitoring without the ill feeling that checking up sometimes generates. Of course, one way to get attention is to make a really big mistake.
8. Organizational control can focus on output or behavior or both. Output measures are usu-	8. Know whether good results are sufficient for you to be considered in control, or if you are ex-

Generalizations	Implications
ally more objective and can be used throughout large, complex organizations. Behavior control is more subjective and related to the values of particular managers in specific situations.	pected to behave in certain ways as well. Determine a set of control criteria that is comfortable for you and, if you have the opportunity, communicate your ideas to your boss.
9. Management by objectives and results (MBO/R) can be a useful way to approach the managerial task. It is a basic process of goal setting, planning, implementing, and controlling organizational endeavor that can serve many purposes if done right.	9. Know the philosophy, purpose, and process of MBO/R. Concentrate your attention on the basics, even though your organization may deviate from good practice as you understand it. Develop your skill by using the basic ideas and techniques and then learning from your mistakes.

As a Current or Future Manager

Generalizations	Implications
1. Organizational behavior is goal-oriented. General strategies direct behavior toward desired future states; specific plans direct behavior toward particular objectives.	1. Be explicit about organizational planning processes and plans. Provide guidelines for people to follow, but keep enough flexibility in plans to allow adaptation to changing circumstances.
2. Planning and control systems help organizations focus on high priority issues and results rather than routine activities. Managerial inattention allows programmed activity to fill available time.	2. Establish a means of monitoring the system so that people become aware of high priority issues that need attention. Focus on areas where key results are expected so that organizational time, energy, and resources can be devoted to important concerns and not taken up putting out fires in chronic but unimportant problem areas.
3. Premises underlie organizational planning processes. Forecasts, predictions, assumptions, and assertions about environmental conditions, organizational strengths and weak-	3. Develop planning processes that lead to realistic premises. Caution people not to let hopes affect their predictions and assumptions unduly, but recognize that overly optimistic

Generalizations	Implications
nesses, and human interests and inclinations are somehow fused into premises about what is feasible and desirable for the organization or a subunit.	premises may be natural. Design a system for assessing the external and internal environments thoroughly, using multiple sources of information—including knowledgeable people from inside and outside the organization.
4. The same basic planning process is appropriate at all levels in organizatins, but the resulting strategies, coordinative programs, and operating plans are different in terms of comprehensiveness, time span, and flexibility. Effective planning results in plans that are part of a system that is integrated vertically and horizontally.	4. Use a planning process that integrates plans across levels (top, middle, and operating) as well as across functions and departments. Tie interdependent tasks together with tactical plans (action steps) that require joint effort to develop. Fit short-range subunit plans into the long-range, comprehensive plan for the organization as a whole.
5. Organizations that have good planning and plans increase their probability of success. However, implementation of action steps is necessary to achieve objectives. This requires adequate financial, technical, and human resources. Knowledge and skill are important, but inclination to exert the necessary effort may be the most important.	5. Include a reality check as a routine part of the planning process in order to ensure that objectives and action steps are challenging, but realistic and acceptable to those who must implement them. Don't overcommit; repeated failure leads to disillusioned participants. Recognize how important inspiration and effort are in the implementation of action steps. As a leader, you may be able to overcome bad planning—on the part of others—by means of super effort on the part of your group.
6. Managers tend to hire and promote people who are most like themselves. And some control in organizations comes indirectly through selection, orien-	6. Recognize how indirect controls work through the beliefs, values, and attitudes of organization members. Try to get people to think alike enough so that de-

Generalizations	Implications
tation, and training processes. From the organization's point of view, if the right people have the proper experiences they will behave in such a way that activities will be satisfactorily under control.	cisions can be made and actions taken. But don't stifle creativity or dissent by overusing indirect controls. Check periodically to see if expressed organizational values and actual behavior are in sync. Work toward keeping them aligned.
7. Precontrol and in-process feedback tend to be more effective and efficient in the long run than postcontrol for keeping individual and organizational behavior within tolerable limits. Control processes that are designed to monitor subsystems as well as total system performance provide the means to correct small problems before they become major disasters.	7. Encourage timely feedback throughout the system as a means of keeping on top of situations. Build in unobtrusive processes that allow monitoring without the ill will that checking up sometimes generates. Emphasize pre-control and in-process feedback as much as possible in order to avoid the problems and costs of postcontrol.
8. Control systems can be designed to monitor output or behavior or both. Appropriate emphasis depends on the relative importance of ends (outputs or results) and means (methods or behavior) in determining success. Valid and reliable information is necessary for the criteria that are selected.	8. Design control systems to focus on relevant criteria for which valid and reliable information is available. Emphasize results if methods or behavior are of little or no concern. However, if *how* things are done is important to you, be explicit about your expectations. Let people know how you will monitor and evaluate their behavior.
9. Management by objectives and results (MBO/R) can be a useful framework for organizations to use in programming the managerial task. As a basic process of goal setting, planning, implementing, and controlling organizational endeavor it serves many purposes if designed and implemented ideally.	9. Know the philosophy, purpose and process of MBO/R. Use it as an explicit means of carrying out the managerial task that builds on natural tendencies. Be patient in implementing a system like MBO/R; caution people to have realistic expectations and to be patient. It may take several years for it to become a way of managerial life.

LEARNING APPLICATION ACTIVITIES

1. Write a vignette based on your experience that illustrates the effect of managerial planning or control on human behavior in a work organization.

2. Review the vignette *The Sum Is Less than the Total*. If you were Charles Wilkins, what would you do? What are some potential consequences of your decision? What action steps would you plan in order to increase the probability of a good outcome?

3. Using a (a) might do, (b) can do, (c) want to do, and (d) should do framework for strategy development, develop a personal five-year strategy. As part of your overall strategy, identify two or three objectives for the next six months along with tactics (plans of action) for achieving them.

4. Develop a network diagram for writing a term paper. Specify the starting and finishing dates and then list all of the activities or tasks that must be completed. Estimate the time needed for each activity and arrange them in a logical pattern of concurrent and sequential tasks. Identify the critical path—the minimum time to complete your project.

5. Think of your class as a learning organization. What are the (a) direct and (b) indirect controls on your behavior?

6. *Step 1:* Write out a policy and regulations regarding employee appearance (i.e., clothes and hair style) for an organization of your choice.

Step 2: Share your policy statement with three or four colleagues who have chosen different kinds of organizations. Note similarities and differences.

Step 3: As a group, develop guidelines or key criteria to consider in establishing appearance standards for organizations.

Step 4: Report your results to the class and discuss. Also report how easy or difficult it was for your group to reach consensus.

7. *Step 1:* Review the vignette *Form or Substance*. Assume you are Mary or Dick, and think about what you would do next.

Step 2: With three or four colleagues playing the roles of your subordinates (plus one or more observers), have a meeting (15-20 minutes) to solve the problem.

Step 3: Have the observers report their conclusions concerning the group's progress during the meeting. Have the participants report their feelings and thoughts about their experience during the meeting. Have a general discussion of the control issues implied in the vignette.

8. Browse through current newspapers or magazines for examples that illustrate the effects of (a) lack of control or (b) too much control on human behavior in organizations. Share your examples with two or three colleagues.

9. With a colleague, interview a manager in a work organization. Ask about control issues: Is control a problem? Why or why not? Where is the emphasis, output or behavior?

REFERENCES

Andrews, Kenneth R. *The Concept of Corporate Strategy.* Homewood, Ill.: Dow Jones Irwin, 1971.

Beer, Michael, and Robert A. Ruh. "Employee Growth Through Performance Management." *Harvard Business Review* 54/4 (July-August 1970): 59–66.

Business Week. 27 December 1982.

———. 6 December 1982.

Carroll, Stephen J., and Henry L. Tosi. *Management by Objectives: Applications and Research.* New York: Macmillan, 1973.

"Clark Equipment: A Survival Effort that Depends on Streamlining." *Business Week,* 6 December 1982, p. 93.

Dalton, Gene W., and Paul R. Lawrence (Eds). *Motivation and Control in Organizations.* Homewood, Ill.: Irwin, 1971.

French, Wendell L., and Robert W. Hollmann. "Management by Objectives: The Team Approach." *California Management Review* 17/3 (Spring 1975): 13–22.

Hassett, James. "But That Would Be Wrong." *Psychology Today,* November 1981, pp. 34–50.

"It Was Fidelity Right to the End." *Seattle Post-Intelligencer,* 29 March 1982.

Kondrasuk, Jack N. "Studies in MBO Effectiveness." *Academy of Management Review* 6/3 (July 1981): 419–430.

Lawler, Edward E. "Control Systems in Organizations." In Marvin D. Dunnette (Ed.), *Handbook of Industrial and Organizational Psychology.* Chicago: Rand-McNally, 1976.

Levinson, Harry. "Management by Whose Objectives?" *Harvard Business Review* 48/4 (July-August 1970): 1125–1134.

———. "Appraisal of *What* Performance?" *Harvard Business Review* 54/4 (July-August 1976): 30–48.

Locke, Edwin A., and Gary P. Latham. "Goal Setting—A Motivation Technique that Works." *Organizational Dynamics* 7/2 (Autumn 1979): 68–80.

Main, Jeremy. "Ford's Drive for Quality." *Fortune,* 18 April 1983, pp. 62–70.

"Matsushita: Seeking Industrial Markets While Staying Strong in Home Products." *Business Week,* 27 September 1982, p. 72.

McCaskey, Michael B. "A Contingency Approach to Planning: Planning with Goals and Planning Without Goals." *Academy of Management Journal* 17/2 (June 1974): 281–291.

McConkie, Mark L. "A Clarification of the Goal Setting and Appraisal Processes in MBO." *Academy of Management Review* 4/1 (January 1979): 129–140.

McMahon, J. Timothy, and John M. Ivancevich. "A Study of Control in a Manufacturing Organization: Managers and Nonmanagers." *Administrative Science Quarterly* 21/1 (March 1976): 166–183.

Miles, Raymond E., and Charles C. Snow. *Organizational Strategy, Structure, and Process.* New York: McGraw-Hill, 1978.

Mintzberg, Henry, and James A. Waters. "Tracking Strategy in an Entrepreneurial Firm." *Academy of Management Journal* 25/3 (September 1982): 465–499.

Morrisey, George L. *Management by Objectives and Results in the Public Sector.* Reading, Mass.: Addison-Wesley, 1976.

Mundel, Marvin E. *A Conceptual Framework for the Management Sciences.* New York: McGraw-Hill, 1967.

Odiorne, George S. *Management and the Activity Trap.* New York: Harper & Row, 1974.

———. "MBO: A Backward Glance." *Business Horizons* 21/5 (October 1978): 14–24.

Ouchi, William G. "The Transmission of Control Through Organizational Hierarchy." *Academy of Management Journal* 21/2 (June 1978): 173–192.

Ouchi, William G., and Mary Ann Maguire. "Organizational Control: Two Functions." *Administrative Science Quarterly* 20/4 (December 1975): 559–569.

"Paley Decides To Move Aside—at Least Partway." *Business Week,* 20 September, 1982, p. 42.

Pasmore, William, and Frank Friedlander. "An Action-Research Program for Increasing Employee Involvement in Problem Solving." *Administrative Science Quarterly* 27 (September 1982): 343–362.

Rosenau, Milton D., Jr. *Successful Project Management.* Belmont, Calif.: Lifetime Learning, 1981.

Seattle Post-Intelligencer, 29 March 1982.

Steiner, George A. "Comprehensive Managerial Planning." In Joseph W. McGuire (Ed.), *Contemporary Management,* Englewood Cliffs, N.J.: Prentice-Hall, 1974.

Tannenbaum, Arnold S. *Control in Organizations.* New York: McGraw-Hill, 1968.

Umstot, Denis. "MBO + Job Enrichment: How to Have Your Cake and Eat It Too." *Management Review* 66/2 (February 1977): 21–26.

13
Personnel Policies and Practices

LEARNING OBJECTIVES

After reading this chapter you should be able to:

1. Illustrate how personnel policies and practices can affect relationships between people and can affect individual and group performance.
2. Give examples of how management's assumptions about human resources get acted out in (a) staffing, (b) training and development, and (c) collective bargaining.
3. Explain the assumptions underlying job enrichment, and discuss some of the consequences of a job enrichment program.
4. Discuss some reasons why performance appraisal is usually very troublesome and possible strategies for minimizing some of the problems associated with it.
5. Explain what is meant by "fair treatment."
6. Discuss some of the consequences that come from lack of organizational due process.

MERIT OR COST OF LIVING?

Ruth was the president of a small manufacturing firm. Her company had been in business for four years and had weathered two years of losses but was now beginning to show a reasonable profit. Ruth was worried about inflation and what she could do, and not do, relative to pay increases for her employees.

She sat in her office, thinking: "I have only 8 percent to add to salaries, inflation is eroding my employees' purchasing power at 12 percent per year, but I don't see any way I can make up this difference."

She thought about various individuals and how they had been performing. "While they vary in terms of performance from satisfactory to outstanding," she mused to herself, "I want to keep them all. They make a strong team and I want to keep them all motivated. How in the world do I allocate money? If I help everybody keep up with inflation to some extent, I won't have enough money for differentials, but if I allocate a lot of merit money to the best performers, everybody else will fall even further behind. They are also going to feel very unappreciated."

THE NOTICE ON THE DOOR

This morning, George Atwood, president of a small electronics firm, had seen several office employees drinking coffee at their desks and chatting. Furthermore, somebody had spilled coffee in one of the aisles and had not cleaned it up. A large backlog of orders was waiting for processing, and George was boiling mad.

He went back to his office and wrote the following memo, which he had his secretary type and post on the inside of the front door.

> Effective immediately, there will be no coffee drinking and socializing in the office. Coffee drinking and socializing are to occur only during the 15-minute morning and afternoon breaks.
>
> (Signed) George Atwood

Within a few minutes after the notice had been posted, most of the employees in the office had expressed their irritation and anger to one another. Some were whispering about the need for a union. One person went out and got a cup of tea and brought it back; another person brought in a can of Pepsi. A number of people made telephone calls to friends or spouses that started with the theme, "Guess what George did this time. . . ."

THE ENGINE THAT COULDN'T

Art Jones was an abrasive, technically effective employee who tended to taunt his supervisors. He was a mechanic in a small company that sold and repaired marine engines for both fishing vessels and pleasure craft. He had been with the firm for more than twenty years. The shop supervisor, Dan Gulbrandson, did not like him, but his fellow workers were generally tolerant and took some pleasure in Art's baiting the supervisory staff.

One day, Dan received a call from the general manager saying there had been a complaint that a part had been installed incorrectly in the engine of a large sailboat: the engine was cutting out and the owner was furious. Art Jones was the mechanic who had been assigned to repair the engine.

Dan summoned Art to his office, and used some strong language in accusing Art of installing the part upsidedown. Art vehemently denied that he had installed the part incorrectly and used some strong language of his own. He went on to indicate that the management staff was too busy drinking coffee and talking about their social lives to know what was going on. Dan ended the interview by saying, "Get the hell out of here. We'll see. . . ." Art went back to his work station. Dan went down to the general manager's office.

The next day, Art was handed a discharge slip by his foreman, who said, "I'm sorry about this, but that's the way it's got to be." Art locked up his tools, went home, telephoned the representative of the international union, and filed a grievance.

Over the next few days a good deal of time was spent by the mechanics in the shop discussing Art's discharge and commiserating with each other about a wide range of things they didn't like about their working conditions. By the end of a week, Art's grievance had become a cause célèbre.

As the grievance went through several steps, the company insisted that Jones had been properly discharged for unsatisfactory work and a bad attitude, and furthermore, that he probably should have been discharged long before. The union was equally insistent that the discharge was improper. The case went to arbitration.

The arbitrator held that there had been no progressive discipline, such as warnings in the file, that Art was not aware that the meeting in Dan's office could lead to discharge, and that discharge was too severe a penalty under the circumstances. The arbitrator ordered Art reinstated, but without back pay and with an implied admonition to him to shape up.

THE APPRAISAL INTERVIEW

Sharon Goldberg was nervously waiting to talk with her boss, Louise Todd. It was one of their regular biweekly meetings, but this time she was sure that her performance would be reviewed and Louise would discuss her salary for the coming year.

Sharon believed that she had been working hard and generally doing a good job. She liked her job and found it challenging as well as satisfying in many ways. Recently, however, it seemed to her that Louise had been somewhat distant and occasionally abrupt. "I wonder what I'll do if she gives me a below-average pay increase," thought Sharon. "I know I'm going to be awfully upset."

Sharon knew a little about the ground rules for compensation. She knew that the maximum pay raises were going to be about 8 percent, that there was going to be no across-the-board increase even though inflation had been about 10 percent during the past year, and that the company's profits had been down somewhat. Sharon also knew that she had spent a lot of time helping her co-workers, and wondered if that had been noticed. "They had better take that into account, or I'll stop helping new people," she thought.

Within a few moments, the secretary ushered Sharon into Louise's office where she was cordially asked to be seated. After chatting with her briefly about the weather and their golf scores, Louise said, "Sharon, it seems to me that generally you have been doing quite a good job and I think we have a pretty good pay increase for you. Your salary is going up from $1,800 a month to $1,926, effective the first of the month. Keep up the good work.'' Louise paused for a moment and then changed the subject to a problem the department was having with purchasing.

Sharon didn't know whether to be pleased or not. She had quickly figured in her head that this meant a $126 per month pay increase, but she hadn't calculated it in percentages. Further, she wondered whether this was one of the higher pay increases in the unit, or just average, or below average. She felt confused and anxious. When Louise started talking about the purchasing department problem, Sharon nodded a few times and made one or two brief comments.

After the short meeting, Louise thought, ''I wonder what was bothering Sharon; she didn't seem very pleased with the pay increase, even though only one other person got more than she did. Well, at least I got a chance to help her shape up her relationship with purchasing, which is about the only area where she needs improvement.''

WHY IS HE PAID MORE THAN I AM?

Ilse had been employed in a responsible middle-management job for several years. She had just come from a meeting involving several other managers, including Keith. As Ilse walked back to her office from the meeting, she passed Keith's office, and pondered something that had been irritating her for some time. It wasn't just that Keith's office was larger and better furnished than hers, it was that she was convinced that her own job was more complex and required more judgment than Keith's job, and that she was being paid less than he. Although individual salaries were not published, salary ranges were available, and Ruth's job was slotted into a lower pay bracket than Keith's. There was some overlap between the ranges, however.

''I think it's time I did something about this,'' she thought. ''But what?''

INTRODUCTION

These vignettes suggest that the policies and practices of personnel management have a powerful influence on the behavior, attitudes, and satisfactions of organizational participants. This holds true for the president and vice presidents on the top floor of the main office building as well as the workers on the assembly line in the factory.

In these vignettes, Ruth was worried about how to allocate pay for merit increases when inflation was running higher than the amount she could add to the payroll; she knew her decisions would affect morale and motivation. George tried to establish a rule about no coffee drinking or socializing in the office and had the beginnings of a rebellion on his hands. Dan fired Art, perhaps for good reason, but the procedures that were followed were not proper, and an arbitrator ultimately reinstated Art. Sharon, who had been doing good work, had a performance interview with her boss; but she was confused and anxious at the outcome. Ilse was convinced that she was underpaid, relative to Keith, and was trying to figure out what to do about it.

As suggested by the vignettes, management's attitudes and assumptions about dealing with people are acted out through the medium of formalized personnel policies and practices as well as through day-to-day leadership style. For example, George's behavior suggested that he assumes the way to be an effective leader is to issue edicts. Some personnel policies and practices are influenced by external forces, such as federal and state laws and court decisions pertaining to discrimination. Ordinarily, however, a great deal of discretion can be exercised by management across a wide range of personnel matters.

This chapter will deal with the consequences of selected personnel practices on organizational behavior. To some extent, we will also comment on consequences that stem from different leadership styles and from assumptions that managers make about human behavior. It is not our intent to cover personnel and labor relations in a comprehensive way, but to focus on topics that are of current interest or that represent some particularly troublesome areas:

Definitions
Human Resources Planning
Staffing
Job and Working-Conditions Design
Performance Appraisal
Training and Development
Organization Development
Compensation and Rewards
Labor Relations
Justice Determination
So What? Implications for You

DEFINITIONS

Personnel management refers to the design and administration of personnel systems. *Personnel systems* are particular linkages of policies, procedures, and techniques either consciously or inadvertently designed to facilitate processes pertaining to human resources that are inherent in most organizations. *Processes* are flows of events moving toward some identifiable end or consequence. For example, staffing is a broad, continuous process in organizations through which people are brought into the organization, transferred, promoted, and ultimately separated (French, 1982).

The *personnel department,* which typically emerges when organizations reach a certain level of complexity, say from 150 to 200 employees, has the task of being concerned about the design and administration of personnel systems. However, many of the decisions and the carrying out of policy will be shared with a number of managers across the organization. All supervisors and managers are heavily involved in personnel management. In a sense, every manager is a personnel manager. Thus, a particular personnel system is typically managed by many more people than just those in the personnel department. The latter have a key role, however, in the coordination of personnel policies and practices and in the quality of personnel management across the organization.

The major personnel processes are included in Figure 13.1 and are shown as overlapping and interdependent because each interacts with the others. However, we need to discuss them separately in order to focus our attention and increase our understanding.

HUMAN RESOURCES PLANNING

Human resources planning is shown as a central component of personnel management in Figure 13.1, because all personnel processes, to be effective, need to be planned. This planning typically includes an analysis of expected curtailment or growth in various units of the organization; an analysis of current and needed skill levels in the various units (called a ''skills inventory''); and an analysis of present and anticipated vacancies due to retirements, transfers, promotions, leaves of absence, and other reasons. Human resources planning must also be responsive to both voluntary and legal requirements with respect to the employment of minorities, women, the handicapped, people between the ages of 40 and 70, and veterans. Plans are then made for appropriate action, such as recruitment, transfer, promotion, or training.

Broadly conceived, human resources planning goes far beyond needs forecasting and includes program planning in all aspects of personnel management. Ideally, it is future oriented and proactive, rather than reactive.

STAFFING

One major personnel process is *staffing,* a flow of events that results in the movement of people into and out of the various jobs through an organization.

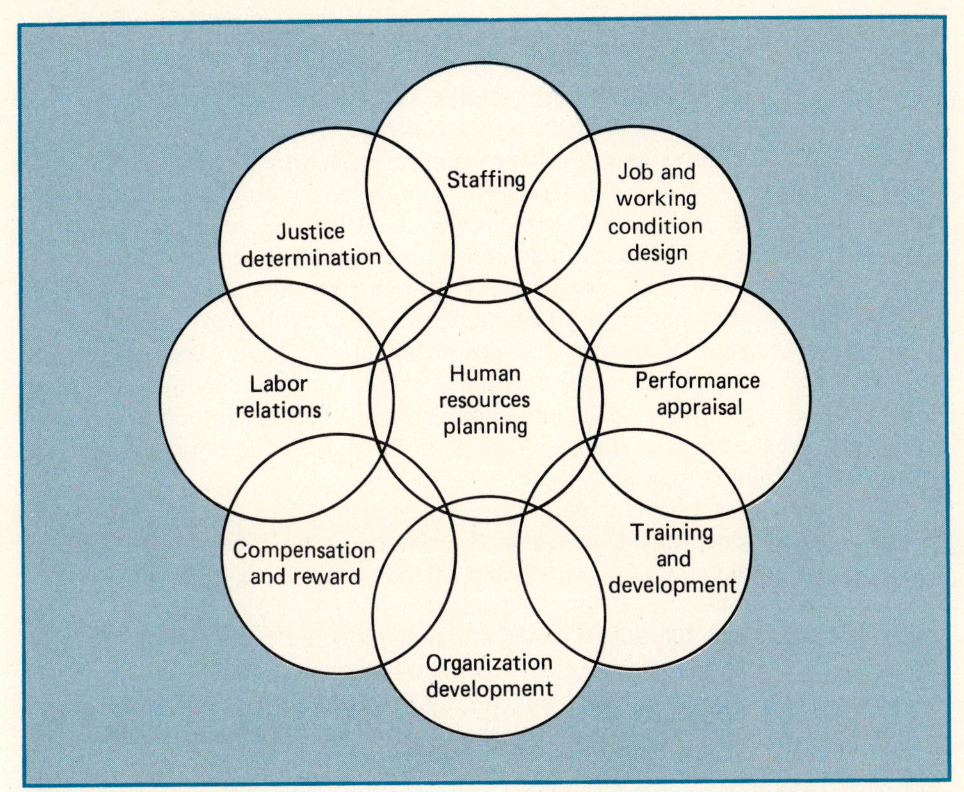

FIGURE 13.1 Major Personnel Processes. **Source:** Adapted from Wendell L. French, *The Personnel Management Process,* 5th ed. (Boston, Mass.: Houghton Mifflin, 1982), p. 51.

This process typically includes recruitment and selection, induction and orientation, transfers, promotion, demotions, and various kinds of separations, such as layoffs, discharges, retirements, or deaths. People are brought into organizations, people leave them, and there is usually considerable mobility upward, laterally, and sometimes downward. Each of these areas of activity tends to be systematized to some extent in some organizations.

The quality of the staffing procedures and decisions is important to the success of an organization. This holds true across a wide array of activities, including bringing people into the organizations, arranging how they are to be utilized, and determining under what circumstances they leave. Let's look at some of these matters in more detail.

Employment

The recruitment and selection of new organization members must be carefully planned and systematically implemented. The skills, talents, and potential of the people recruited by an organization have wide-ranging and long-term effects on the resulting behaviors of people in the organization. To state the case in extremes, well-trained, skilled people will create fewer technical problems in an organization than untrained, unskilled people. People oriented toward cooperation with others will precipitate fewer interpersonal and intergroup problems than people predisposed to resist direction from others. In general, a mismatch of qualifications can create unnecessary problems in groups and organizations. Some of the consequences can be lower morale, unnecessary conflict, lower performance, and higher turnover. For example, the employment of an autocratic supervisor can create havoc in a machinists' unit that has had a tradition of, and successful experience with, participative approaches. Similarly, there can be dysfunctional consequences to assigning a supervisor with a participative style to a group consisting of people who are unskilled and have expectations of a great deal of direction. The employment of a professional with high-quality group dynamics and participation skills into a unit supervised by an autocratic manager can lead to frustration and disillusionment on the part of the person employed, and probably conflict as well.

The hiring of women and minorities, as part of an affirmative action program or as a voluntary departure from earlier discriminatory practices, can change the dynamics of interpersonal and intergroup relationships. Long-standing attitudes are likely to emerge, and, if not confronted and worked through, can lead to outright conflict or to subtle acts aimed at humiliation and exclusion. As a result, people can still feel cut off from their work groups, even if employed. There can also be resentment surrounding policies and practices that are perceived as reverse discrimination. Obviously, these attitudes and feelings can affect communication and cooperation within the organization.

There should be careful analysis of task requirements (job analysis), careful development of the qualifications necessary to perform the various jobs (job specifications), and careful attention to the psychosocial aspects of the setting before people are recruited. But employment should not be viewed as an isolated event; preparation of the group for a new member and follow-up to see how the parties adjust to each other are also important.

Induction and Orientation

When people are employed, there is an induction and orientation procedure of some sort: sometimes of high quality and sometimes not. There are usually people to meet, forms to fill out, instructions to receive, and a work station to experience (to say nothing of learning the location of the restrooms, the cafeteria, and the first-aid station). How this is handled, and by whom, can affect subsequent relationships and reflect assumptions about what newcomers want and need during the first hours and days on the job.

In traditional induction and orientation practice, information is dispensed either in one-way communications to individuals or, in large companies, to groups of new employees, sometimes in a lecture hall or the company cafeteria. These practices are undoubtedly helpful, but probably do little to reduce the anxieties of the new people and may not result in as much useful learning as other approaches.

Some experimentation with group discussion methods has resulted in a substantial lowering of anxiety and higher retention of introductory information on the job in contrast to more traditional modes. One such experiment in a large electronics manufacturing company found the following about new employees:

> The first few days on the job were anxious, disturbing ones to new employees.
> Initiation practices instigated by peers increased anxiety.
> The anxiety experienced by new employees greatly interfered with training.
> Substantial turnover of newly hired employees was caused primarily by anxiety.
> New employees were reluctant to discuss problems with their supervisors.

Interviews with supervisors and middle managers produced the following information about supervisors:

> The supervisors were experiencing about as much anxiety as the new employees.
> Supervisors felt inadequate when new employees were seasoned, experienced people.
> Supervisors curtailed their downward communications to the new people to conceal their own ignorance.
> Supervisors tended to be defensive, which discouraged upward communication.

In possession of these findings, the company devised an experiment in which a group of new employees attended the usual two-hour orientation seminar but was then sent to a special *anxiety-reduction seminar* for the rest of the day. This seminar focused on information about the job, the job environment, and the supervisors, and permitted extensive opportunity for questions, answers, and discussion. The inductees were given statistics indicating the high probability of their success and were told what to expect in the way of rumors, hazing, and initiation practices on the part of the present employees. They were also urged to take the initiative in asking questions of supervisors and they were given information about the management styles and personalities of the supervisors. The result? At the end of four weeks, the experimental group was performing significantly better than a control group that had undergone the more traditional induction and orientation (Gomersall & Myers, 1966, pp. 62–72).

Transfer and Promotion

The transfer and promotion of employees is another aspect of personnel management where leadership style and assumptions about people are acted out. In many organizations, opportunities for transfer or promotion are kept secret, thus giving managers maximum control over these activities and reducing the number of applicants with whom to deal. However, organizational members may think the organization has few opportunities for advancement and may see transfer and promotion practices as fraught with favoritism. Present employees may resent new people who are hired under semisecret circumstances, simply because they have not been informed that outsiders were under consideration or because they were not involved in the screening process. They may also view hiring from the outside as unfair on the assumption that the contributions and qualifications of present employees should have been given open consideration. (More about perceptions of equity and inequity later.) Conversely, opening up opportunities for present employees to apply for transfer or promotion leads to higher mobility and morale and enhanced employee development.

Layoffs

Management policy and practice with respect to budgetary crises can have a powerful influence on the attitudes and behavior of employees at all levels. Suppose, for example, that it is necessary to reduce expenditures by ten percent. One strategy might simply be to terminate enough low seniority people so that the desired savings result. Although employees might be accustomed to such practices, one can assume that a wide range of dysfunctional attitudes and behaviors will result. By contrast, if the stated policy and well-known practice of the organization is to shrink the work force gradually and only through the normal attrition that occurs through resignations and retirements, one can assume that fewer dysfunctional attitudes and behaviors will result.

Let's take a look at a few of the consequences of fear and anxiety about losing one's job. Some may be positive, but most are negative.

One of the positive consequences, if layoff is determined partly on the basis of performance, might be that people work harder. (However, for people already under considerable stress, working harder may be precisely what they do *not* need for maintaining health and long-run effective performance.) Another consequence might be more and better work, individually or in cooperation with others, in order to help the organization survive and thus protect one's job. Still another positive consequence might be more appreciation of one's employment opportunity.

There are likely to be many more negative consequences than positive, at least in the aggregate, across the work force. Among the dysfunctional consequences can be intrapersonal, interpersonal, group, and intergroup reactions and behavior that can severely restrict performance.

One of the intrapersonal consequences can be preoccupation with fears of losing one's job and thus lack of concentration and attention to one's work and to others, or reduced flexibility and creativity. There can be difficulties in sleeping, nightmares, or physical ailments. Another of the consequences can be suspicion and mistrust of what other people are saying and planning relative to one's job situation. Are they planning to lay me off? Is that meeting going on in the supervisor's office about me? Bill and Joan quit talking when I approached them in the cafeteria; do they know something I don't know?

This suspicion and mistrust, then carries over into interpersonal and group behaviors. People can become more guarded, more careful, less friendly, and less cooperative. Rumors abound. Some people begin to lie low: avoid being

HAGAR

conspicuous, and avoid making mistakes that can be used as reasons or excuses for termination (Shepard & Davis, 1972, p. 70). These behaviors detract from group effectiveness.

Probably the most destructive attitudes and behaviors can occur in intergroup behavior. If programs or units are to be affected differentially, then the classic we-they syndrome can emerge, including trying to undermine the "enemy." If that other unit gets cut, then maybe my unit and I will survive. All of the other intergroup conflict phenomena, such as distortion in perceptions and reduction in communications with the other group or groups can emerge.

What can be done to avoid the dysfunctional consequences of potential layoffs? One way to proceed, would be to present the problem to employees and seek opinions and suggestions about possible solutions. Management is not immune to being inflexible and unimaginative in a budgetary crisis, and extensive employee input is likely to surface a much wider range of realistic options than would otherwise emerge.

We have already alluded to shrinking the work force on the basis of normal attrition as a desirable option to consider. Another option might be temporary wage or salary reductions for everyone. This is by no means a perfect solution; implications relative to retirement pay of those nearing retirement would need to be considered, and people with high job security or who see themselves as highly mobile might object strenuously. On the other hand, such persons might appreciate the maintenance of the present group and intergroup fabric of the organization. Another option might be to shorten the work week or the work month temporarily, or to lay off large groups of employees for several days adjacent to one or more holidays. Other options might include a reexamination of plans for capital expenditures. An organization might decide, for example, to postpone the construction of a new office building for a year or two in order to protect what is seen as a more valuable asset—the human resources of the organization. On the other hand, it might be that the purchase of new equipment would be essential to the survival of the organization, in which case opportunities might be provided for part-time work as an alternative to layoff, and incentives offered for early retirement. Obviously, there are tradeoffs.

One general practice that can assist in minimizing the dysfunctional human consequences of budgetary cutbacks is the more frequent and accurate dispensing of information about the organization's or the unit's condition, backed up with an open invitation to ask questions and raise issues. Other practices that can assist are the development and dissemination of thoughtful criteria for making layoff decisions. Going a step further, organizations can do much to minimize the impact of layoffs on individuals by providing severance payments, giving laid-off employees priority in being rehired when conditions improve, and offering *outplacement services*. The latter refers to using internal or external counselors to help the person work through the shock of the layoff, to make plans for finding new employment, and to assist in arranging for interviews with other organizations.

Retirement

Preretirement and retirement policies and practices can strongly influence the attitude and performance of employees, particularly on those who have just a few years of employment left. People who are approaching retirement typically have many concerns and anxieties: about finances, health, future activities, the loss of influence, the changing relationship with spouses, the giving up of certain goals, or the leaving behind of tasks and circles of friends that have provided a sense of identity and competence. If these concerns and anxieties are not dealt with, there is bound to be a negative result relative to attitudes and performance. On the other hand, if an organization develops opportunities for people to plan their retirement strategies, to share their concerns, and to develop support groups, there can be a salutary effect on performance as well as mental health.

Management can also do much to set norms pertaining to older employees. If management and peers assume that the older employee has less to offer and is over the hill, conditions are likely to be created that will validate these assumptions. On the other hand, if the older employees are valued for their knowledge and wisdom, and given opportunities to continue to develop, performance levels and job satisfaction among the senior people are likely to be enhanced.

JOB AND WORKING-CONDITIONS DESIGN

Job and working-conditions design is another broad process inherent in organizations. We will define it here as a complex flow of events that subdivides the total work to be done into separate jobs and creates working conditions for individuals and groups. While the nature of the tasks to be performed will influence the motivation and satisfaction of organization members, the rules and conditions surrounding that job will also have a major effect, and can be considered a part of the broad process.

As discussed in Chapters 4 and 9, there has been considerable theorizing and research in recent years about the consequences of job structure on people. The central argument is that while people have become better educated and expectations for job satisfaction have increased, pressures for technological efficiency have also intensified with the result that jobs are insufficiently challenging

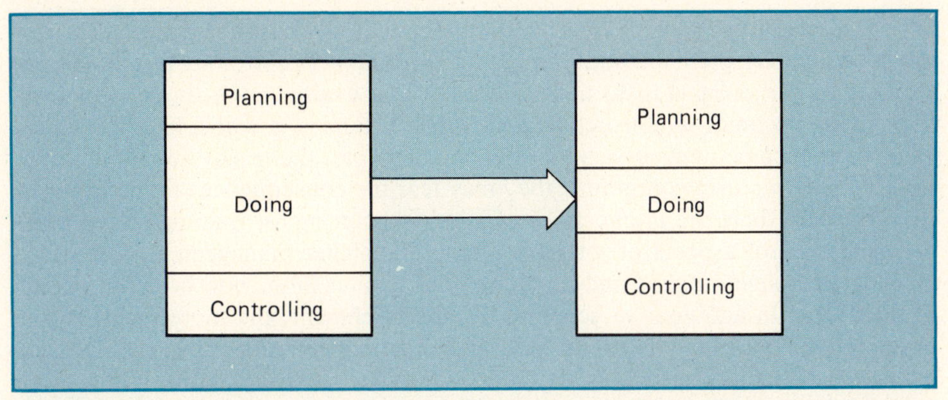

FIGURE 13.2 Job Enrichment. **Source:** M. Scott Myers, ''Every Employee a Manager,'' © 1968 by the Regents of the University of California. Adapted from *California Management Review* 10/3 (Spring 1968): 9–20, by permission of the Regents.

and meaningful. The result, it is argued, is low motivation and low productivity. While there is widespread agreement that there are job-design problems in our contemporary organizations, there is substantial disagreement about the extent of the problem. Some see worker alienation in the United States as a massive crisis, while others see the need for careful diagnosis of morale and productivity on a case by case basis (Hackman & Oldhan, 1980, pp. 3–21). Whether there is a crisis or not, it is clear that millions of jobs could probably be restructured to provide for greater challenge and responsibility.

Job Structure

One approach to job design views jobs as consisting of planning, doing, and controlling aspects. The goal, in this view, is to design jobs with a higher proportion of planning and controlling aspects than is typically the case (Myers, 1968). (See Figure 13.2.) In so doing, the job characteristics that lead to increased job satisfaction—skill variety, task identity, task significance, and autonomy—are enhanced. (See Figure 5, Chapter 4, and Figure 1, Chapter 16.)

The assumption underlying such job design is that working on challenging tasks, being permitted more self-direction, and assuming more responsibility are inherently motivating for people, thus leading to better job performance and more job satisfaction. This assumption finds support in Herzberg's motivation-hygiene theory, in Masow's need-hierarchy theory, and in McGregor's Theory Y.

Whether this underlying assumption is universally applicable has been questioned on the grounds that not everyone wants a significant amount of challenge and self-direction in her or his job, and that some jobs are already too complex and stressful. Furthermore, there may have to be tradeoffs between efficiency and satisfaction; it may be that a certain amount of boring work is the price that must be paid in order to maximize the usefulness of machines and methods of material and information flow.

It is also important to realize that individual jobs are not designed in isolation. Whenever the planning, doing, and controlling proportions of one job are adjusted, other jobs and tasks need alteration. For example, the supervisor's role in planning becomes diminished and, in some instances, a whole layer of supervision can become unnecessary. It is understandable, then, why some managers resist job restructuring programs; they may fear the consequences to themselves.

Further, there are implications of job restructuring for training. If the planning and control aspects of jobs are increased, higher management now has a much larger role in training and coaching subordinates in the new broader aspects of their jobs. In addition, to accomplish job enrichment, the more menial tasks or operations must be put into the jobs of less skilled employees or accomplished by machines. There also may be implications for compensation. While more complex jobs may be intrinsically more motivating and satisfying, equity theory (to be discussed later in the chapter), suggests that people may expect more compensation along with their increased responsibilities, at least if the job responsibilities go significantly beyond just removing the boredom factor.

In recent years there have been numerous experiments in job design and redesign that have focused on groups or teams. Generally, the approach has been to assign some large task to a team, such as assembling an entire engine, and give the team members broad responsibilities for planning the work, for work assignments, and for inventory and quality control. Usually, team members are paid according to how many of the different tasks of the total effort they can perform.

Given the above, then, there are at least three basic questions to be considered in job design:

1. How can jobs be designed to optimize motivation and satisfaction of organization members and at the same time overall effectiveness and efficiency of the organization? There are many compromises and trade-offs to be considered.
2. What are the implications of job design for different hierarchical levels in terms of what happens to supervisory and other jobs, what happens to structure of the organization and what effects are there on the staffing, compensation, training, and other personnel systems? Job restructuring at one level will affect people at other levels and will affect various personnel systems.
3. Should job design focus on individual jobs or on jobs for people in groups? Which approach is used will depend on a number of assumptions including assumptions about the utility of teams as motivating, energizing devices and about what leadership style fits the particular technology and circumstances.

Work Rules

The working rules and conditions that are created, largely by management, are also part of the broad process of job and working-conditions design. It is obvious to experienced employees and managers that some rules are necessary in order for there to be coordinated effort toward common purposes. For example, there needs to be predictability as to when employees start and stop work, how absences are to be regulated, and who can authorize expenditures from the organization's treasury. Most organizations have rules prohibiting fighting, intoxication, and gross insubordination; such rules usually include penalties for infractions.

It is also obvious that a long list of do's and don'ts that are perceived as unnecessary can be oppressive and will be resented. There can be widespread circumvention of such rules by employees, including groups conspiring to do so. The vignette *The Notice on the Door* is an example.

Many people, when forced to comply with rules that they consider demeaning or stifling, tend to be resentful toward both management and themselves. Under these circumstances, people will deprecate themselves for being ineffective in taking on their oppressors—either the offending supervisor or management in general. This condition is particularly prevalent when supervisors or managers punish people for dissent—for being openly critical in a meeting, to take an example. Punishment might take the form of some immediate sarcasm in front of one's peers, or a session of behind-the-scenes complaining that what's-his-name is a real troublemaker and therefore not to be trusted or much communicated with, or the withholding of rewards. This is not to say that these punishments are always unwarranted; sometimes dissent goes beyond the bounds of being constructive. However, rather than punishing the employee, a better approach, as a first step, might be for the supervisor to confront the extreme behavior in private discussions with the subordinate.

Excessive or unreasonable work rules are probably becoming less prevalent, due to the influence of labor unions in contract negotiations and through the use of grievance procedures in both union and nonunion situations, and perhaps because of a general shift toward more participatory leadership styles. But we have had enough exposure to organizations to suspect that there are thousands upon thousands of instances of demeaning rules, procedures, and controls across the spectrum of contemporary organizations.

Work Rule Innovations

A significant number of organizations have experimented—successfully, in many cases—with approaches to work rules that depart from the traditional, fixed, eight-hour shift occurring five days per week. Among these innovations are the compressed workweek, flextime, permanent part-time work, and job sharing. All can contribute to employee satisfactions and productivity if they meet both employee and organization needs and if managed properly.

The *compressed workweek* usually takes the form of a four-day, forty-hour workweek for all employees or for certain units in the organization. Some of the desirable consequences have been increased morale, reduced absenteeism, improvements in traffic flow, increased productivity, and enhanced recruiting. However, under some circumstances the compressed workweek has created problems for working parents who do not want to be away from their children for ten hours plus commuting time. There have also been instances of less effective service being given to customers and reports of more worker fatigue (Wheeler, Gurman, & Tarnowieski, 1972, pp. 13–15). An experiment with the compressed workweek at a Chrysler plant one summer was abandoned when employees found that three-day trips with children were no longer possible when school started in the fall (Bornstein, 1974).

Flextime is another fairly recent innovation. Flextime essentially permits employees to manage their own starting and ending times each day within broad guidelines. For example, employees might be permitted to arrive any time between six and nine a.m., take a lunch period any time between ten and two, and leave any time between three and six p.m., providing a full eight hours is worked. This results in some core periods when everyone is present. Time is monitored by everyone clocking in and out or filling out daily time cards. This includes executives. Flextime has been adopted by such organizations as Hewlett-Packard, Digital Equipment, and Corning Glass.

Some of the reported advantages have been employees and work teams enjoying more autonomy over their own schedules and accommodating more to their own life styles, less stress stemming from tardiness due to traffic problems or other factors beyond one's control, and ability to manage personal matters such as doctor or dentist appointments. Disciplinary problems associated with tardiness almost disappear.

One disadvantage of flextime appears to be the lack of availability of employees during the flexible work periods. This can be frustrating to other employees in the organization and to customers or suppliers. Other disadvantages include problems in compliance with wage and hour laws, the need to make sure that vital communications jobs such as switchboard operator are continuously staffed, and the need for units to keep each other informed of unit availability (Fleuter, 1975, pp. 77–84; and Golembiewski, Hilles, and Kagno, 1974).

Other innovations that are appearing with more frequency are *permanent part-time work* and *job sharing*. In both types of arrangements, the job incumbents tend to be people who wish to pursue other interests or who have responsibilities that preclude a full work week. The essential difference is that in job sharing the incumbents split a job into two four-hour segments or divide up the work week in some way but hold down one full-time job between them. Organizations frequently find that these part-time employees are more productive than their fraction of a job would have suggested (Clutterbuck, 1979).

Working Conditions

Working conditions, such as high noise levels, toxicity, or extreme temperatures, can have an impact on attitudes, morale, and health. The wearing of ear-protection devices by airline ground crew members shows a recognition of this fact.

The physical layout of plants and offices does much either to inhibit or to facilitate communications. Many organizations have moved toward more open

arrangements in offices in recent years in order to make communications easier. The ability to socialize with other employees—schmoozing—clearly contributes to morale if it is not indulged in to such an extreme as to result in reduced performance. Each situation is probably unique in terms of balancing ease of communication and coordination against the need for quiet and privacy.

PERFORMANCE APPRAISAL

Another broad process that is found in all organizations is *performance appraisal,* the evaluation of the contribution of individuals (and sometimes groups) to the objectives of the enterprise. Such evaluations are typically made for a wide variety of purposes, including job assignments, compensation, coaching, training and development, promotion, discipline, and separation. While this process is universal, effective management of this process is by no means universal. Most managers have trouble with it, particularly in talking about appraisals with subordinates.

Problems with Appraisal

One of the greatest areas of anxiety and tension and potential conflict in organizations is the matter of evaluation of performance and the communication of that evaluation. An exception may be when an evaluation is all, or nearly all, positive. But even when performance is clearly above the norm, the job incumbent may project worries and anxieties carried over from other situations into the appraisal situation, or incomplete communications from superiors can create anxiety. *The Appraisal Interview* vignette is an example of the latter.

Communications following evaluation can occur in various forms, typically through an interview but sometimes only through the rewards and punishments dispensed. Research on appraisal interviews has shown that supervisors are often so anxious about these interviews that there are cases when, after an appraisal interview had presumably occurred, the employee was not aware that his or her performance had been reviewed.

Why is there so much anxiety about this process? Perhaps, people do not, in general, like to play God and, in particular, do not like to communicate negative judgments.

> Managers experience their appraisal of others as a hostile, aggressive act that unconsciously is felt to be hurting or destroying the other person. The appraisal situation, therefore, gives rise to powerful, paralyzing feelings of guilt (Levinson, 1970, p. 127).

This judgmental aspect is particularly evident in appraisal forms that emphasize traits or subjective factors. Box 13.1 contains a sarcastic response to some of the items that appeared on an appraisal form used by Chief of Staff Hamilton Jordan during Jimmy Carter's administration. That appraisal form had items on it like self-confidence, maturity, flexibility, stability, and intelligence (*Time,* 1979).

BOX 13.1

YET ANOTHER PERFORMANCE APPRAISAL FORM

TO: Those in Power and/or Who Need to Evaluate Others
FROM: Staff Chief Jerdin
SUBJECT: Staff Shape-Up or Shake-Up

Please answer the following questions about each of your staffs:

1. On the average, does this person . . .
   arrive at work: early ______ late ______ seldom ______
   leave work: early ______ soon after arrival ______
   can't notice the difference ______

2. Pace of work: 1 - 2 - 3 - 4 - 5 - 6
   slow (1) · slower (3–4) · immobile (6)

3. What is he/she best at? (rank 1 to 5)
   ______Passing the buck
   ______Raising extraneous questions
   ______Writing memos
   ______Shelling peanuts
   ______Planning for others

4. Does this person have the skills to do the job he/she was hired to do?:
   Yes ______ No ______
   No observable evidence on which to draw a conclusion ______

5. Would the slot be better filled by someone else?
   Yes, even *I* could do it better ______
   No, he/she is the best slot-filler on the staff ______

6. How confident is this person? 1 - 2 - 3 - 4 - 5 - 6
   Self-Doubting (1) · Confident (3) · Doubts Everyone Else (6)

7. How flexible is this person: 1 - 2 - 3 - 4 - 5 - 6
   Can Bend Around in a Circle (1) · Firm as the Stock Market (3) · Stiff as a Tenure Ad Hoc Committee (6)

8. How would you characterize this person's impact on other people?
   ______ Devastating
   ______ Like an impacted tooth
   ______ Sweeping
   ______ Yuk

9. Give a balanced picture of this person's strengths and weaknesses:

Strengths:	*Weaknesses:*		
1.	1.	4.	7.
	2.	5.	8.
	3.	6.	9.

FEEDBACK REPORT:

I have shown the above evaluation to the person being rated whose response was:

1. He/she took me out to dinner _____
2. He/she burst into tears _____
3. He/she broke my arm so I can't sign below _____

Signature: __________________________

Source: *The Industrial-Organizational Psychologist* 17/2 [February 1980]:35.

A second reason for anxiety about performance reviews, in addition to the judgmental aspects, may be that both parties are aware that there is little reciprocity in the process, and this gives rise to all sorts of contradictory feelings. The manager is judging the subordinate's performance, but prevailing norms and practices do not usually permit the subordinate to judge the manager's performance, at least in an overt sense. Thus, typical appraisal procedures may either foster a high degree of dependency, or leave the subordinate inwardly angry at the lack of reciprocity, or both. Furthermore, appraising the subordinate may leave the superior feeling guilty about the lack of reciprocity, and paradoxically, fearful that reciprocity could emerge with some unknown consequences. The supervisor may well wonder, "What if the subordinate appraises me?" and, "What if the appraisal goes to my boss?" The supervisor and perhaps the subordinate may have deep reservations about giving the subordinate the power that comes from legitimizing upward judgments, which would be contrary to traditional notions about how work organizations should be run. Is not a subordinate evaluating superiors inconsistent with property and ownership rights, and inconsistent with superiors being held accountable for performance of their units? This ambivalence about wanting reciprocity versus fearing it is a troublesome matter.

The third reason why there may be high anxiety about appraisals is that supervisors and managers probably intuitively know that all or most of their subordinates are important to the ongoing stability and success of their particular unit. To communicate, or imply, through conversation or rewards, that any sizable proportion of the work group's performance is less than acceptable—or even below average, whatever that may mean—threatens to undermine the very foundations of the unit. Such signals create a kind of zero-sum climate that is frequently destructive to morale.

Finally, many managers and subordinates may intuitively realize that the subordinate's performance is a function of a complex constellation of variables, and that deficient performance frequently cannot be attributed solely to deficiencies in the subordinate. Those outside variables may include the manager's own performance, the behavior of peers, and other factors in the organization over which the subordinate has little control. (See the discussion on attribution theory, Chapter 6.)

In short, both parties may feel that the process is inherently unfair, in spite of the fact that formalized appraisal and review procedures are typically required, and in spite of the fact that there is no escaping the evaluative process entirely if there are to be differentials in rewards and in assignments. But both the superior and the subordinate try to submerge a whole range of ambivalent and troublesome feelings about such evaluations. No wonder there is so much uneasiness about the whole process!

The dynamics described above may not come into play, or will at least be minimized, if the supervisor and subordinate have an extended history of mutually supportive signals and if evaluations have been consistently positive and enthusiastic. But we hypothesize that some of the above dynamics underlie most appraiser-appraisee relationships, even though outwardly the procedure may appear as routine.

Zero-Sum Climates

We commented earlier on zero-sum climates in organizations. Many rating techniques, such as forced distribution, rank order, or peer-comparison methods, help create such a climate. Under such systems, everyone feels trapped in an environment in which half of the employees in a unit must be considered below average, and half above average. If someone's performance improves relative to others and that person moves out of the below-average category, it means that someone else must be relegated to that lower condition. Such zero-sum situations frequently lead to "wide-spread discouragement, cynicism, and alienation" (Thompson & Dalton, 1970, pp. 149–157).

While there does not seem to be any easy way out of this dilemma, a deemphasis on ranking or comparison techniques plus emphasis on other approaches can be helpful. There may be no escaping the ranking of people—for example, in making promotion decisions and in allocating differential rewards—but there may be some practices that will temper the adverse effects of ranking and direct comparisons and reduce the anxiety surrounding appraisals. A focus on goals and results, joint problem solving, the use of many kinds of feedback, and participative and supportive leadership styles may be partial ways out of the above dilemmas. Let's take a look at some of these approaches.

Some Partial Solutions

The more the manager and his or her subordinates can create an open, problem-solving approach to the achievement of goals, including personal goals, the more that the mutual interdependency that is inherent in the situation can openly be talked about and acknowledged. If they can both talk openly about how they may each contribute to the achievement of common goals, with either one or both of them showing a willingness to modify behavior or tactics, much of the ambivalence about performance review can be reduced.

While management by objectives programs can help avoid some of the problems we have discussed, different versions of MBO programs can have highly divergent results. One version, for example, can be highly autocratic and reinforce a one-on-one kind of leadership style. Another version might be highly participative and reinforce a team leadership style (French & Hollman, 1975). As an example of an autocratic approach, the manager might unilaterally develop next year's objectives for a subordinate. This does happen in some organizations. Or, as an example of a participative approach, a manager might request the subordinate to develop next year's objectives, the manager may make some notes as to what she or he would like to see the subordinate accomplish over the next year, and the two might sit down to an open exploration about what the goals should be and how they might be achieved. This discussion could include how the manager could contribute to meeting the subordinate's objectives. In still another version, there might be an additional dimension of sharing of individual goals and getting reactions and discussion from peers in a team situation. There has been some experimentation with this approach, including discussions about how the whole team can contribute to the achievement of each member's goals, and subsequent group review of the extent to which goals were met (Likert, 1979, pp. 22–24).

Support is also important; for example, the supervisor might be very supportive or just the opposite. A study at General Electric found that the more critical the supervisor was in the interview, the less likely it was that the person would develop plans to improve and the less frequent the cases of actual improvement (Meyer, Kay, & French, 1965, pp. 123–129). Another study found that goals set in a participative way, in contrast to assigning them, led to better performance. Further, it was found that supportive behavior resulted in higher goals being set (Latham and Saari, 1979, pp. 151–156). Research results about the consequences of participation in goal setting are not conclusive, but the evidence tends to point to the superiority of participative approaches under certain conditions.

Terminology is also important. Labels can be insidious. For example, instead of using the category of *average* in a three-point scale of exceptional, average, and below standard, a rating scale might substitute the terms *effective* or *meets expectations*. These terms may be closer to what is intended, and are probably seen as more supportive than the term *average*.

In summary, while there is no escaping comparisons if differential rewards and assignments are to be made, the more that appraisal practices acknowledge interdependency and mutuality, the less ambivalence and resistance to performance appraisal there is likely to be. The more there is a supportive, coaching, development, and problem-solving approach in contrast to an emphasis on ranking people, the higher the levels of motivation and cooperation in the organization are likely to be. Some of the anxiety and destructive consequences surrounding performance appraisal may be reduced with such approaches.

TRAINING AND DEVELOPMENT

Another broad process that one can infer in organizations is *training and development*. This is a complex mixture of many things aimed at increasing the ability of individuals and groups to contribute to the achievement of organizational goals. Included in this process might be formal training programs, coaching, appraisal interviews (these processes overlap), and job reassignments. Self-initiated activities, such as voluntary enrollment in university technical or management seminars, would be a part of this process.

Training and development is a pervasive process, even though it may be unplanned and the quality low. Most organizations are conscious of the need to do some training, but how much they do will be a function of available resources, the type of industry, and assumptions about people acted upon.

Organizational workers can be viewed as passive, interchangeable components to be hired, transferred, promoted, or separated depending on their particular skills and the particular needs of the organization. Or, they can be viewed as in process: as changing; as amenable to skill development and personal growth; as capable of contributing to the effective design of jobs and of the organization.

Adherence to the first view would probably take an organization in the direction of minimal expenditures of time and money on training and development. Those expenditures that would be made would probably occur in the area of operator and technician training to ensure that specific tasks were carried out satisfactorily and that equipment was utilized properly. Managers, supervisors, and professionals in the organization would probably be subject to a sink-or-swim policy. An attitude of "we hired you because we thought you would perform well" might be considered sufficient. Inadequate performance would probably be dealt with in a directive, telling manner.

Adherence to the second point of view would probably lead an organization in the direction of skill training *plus* more attention to the long-range development needs of the individual and the organization. We would expect to see training and development activities above and beyond immediate job requirements on the assumption that jobs will change, that incumbents have a role in improving jobs so that more productivity and job satisfaction can result, and that many people will want to transfer or be promoted to jobs requiring additional skills and knowledge. Underlying supervisory and management courses would be an implicit, if not explicit, question: How can the participant use the knowledge of this particular seminar or course to become more effective in this organization in the future? Deficiencies in performance would be confronted, but in the context of ongoing coaching, which would be of a supportive and give-and-take nature. Individual employees' long-range careers would be of concern to top management, and managers would encourage open discussion of career and development aspirations and opportunities.

ORGANIZATION DEVELOPMENT

Organization development is another broad personnel process, but will be discussed in some detail in Chapter 16 on "Improvement Strategies." In general, it has to do with how the people in an organization can learn to work collaboratively to continually renew the organization's vitality and purposes.

COMPENSATION AND REWARDS

Still another broad personnel process is *compensation and reward*. This is the complex flow of events that determines the type and level of wages, supplemental benefits, and nonfinancial rewards received by organizational members. Typically in this broad process we see procedures for assessing wage levels in the labor market (wage surveys), for determining relative worth of jobs (job evaluation), for establishing wage rates or salary ranges, and for allocating rewards based on criteria such as differential performance (merit) or length of service (seniority). Other criteria might include direct measures of productivity, sales, or cost savings. Procedures of this sort might include individual or group piece-rate plans, commissions, or some kind of a plantwide productivity or profit bonus plan. Praise, recognition, and signs of status are some of the nonfinancial rewards conferred upon organization members.

Intuitively, we all know that people need to receive some minimal level of reward if membership in organizations is to be sustained. However, we may not be aware of the complexities in designing and managing a compensation and reward system that is at once motivating and satisfying as well as within the means of the organization. The more one digs into this topic, the more complex it becomes, but there are some theoretical notions and research results that help us understand why people react as they do to certain compensation and reward practices. First let us look at equity theory, which was introduced briefly in Chapter 4 on ''Motivation and Performance.''

Equity Theory

Underlying the management of compensation and rewards in organizations are assumptions and perceptions about fairness and equity. A great deal of human attention and energy goes into determining what is fair, in dealing with different perceptions of fairness, and in correcting mistakes in the allocation of rewards and punishments.

People tend to react intuitively to many things that happen to them as being fair or unfair, just or unjust, equitable or inequitable. According to the theory of distributive justice, one's perceptions of being treated fairly depends on whether one's *investments,* such as effort or seniority or experience, are in line with the *profits* in the situation. Profits consist of rewards minus costs. Rewards are such things as wages, status, and intrinsic interest in the job; costs are aspects such as responsibility, discomfort, and danger. For people to feel fairly treated, according to the theory, they need to feel that there is a proper alignment of investments, rewards, and costs, but always in relationship to other people. Those with whom we compare ourselves—*comparison others*—may be either individuals or groups. According to the theory, if a person does not feel fairly treated relative to comparison others, the minimum result is anger, with the person probably taking some action beyond that (Homans, 1961, pp. 232–264). We don't know what Ilse is going to do beyond being irritated in the *Why Is He Paid More Than I Am?* vignette, but we do know that she perceives her investments and job costs relative to her rewards to be out of line with Keith's.

A modification of this theory translates the terminology of investments and profits into inputs and outcomes. Basically, the central hypothesis of the theory, sometimes called equity theory, states, "Inequity exists for Person whenever his perceived job inputs and/or outcomes stands psychologically in an obverse relation to what he perceives are the inputs and/or outcomes of Other" (Adams, 1963, p. 424). As with the theory of distributive justice, equity theory suggests that if people feel unfairly treated, they tend to do something to bring matters into balance again. In addition to the immediate reaction of anger, there are likely to be other consequences, including lowered performance, absenteeism, or quitting.

There have been a number of studies that tend to confirm these theories. For example, a study in an oil refinery investigated the relationship between absenteeism (attendance was considered an input) and employees' feelings about how fairly they had been treated in terms of promotion and pay (outcomes). The study found that workers who felt they had been unfairly treated with respect to either promotion or pay increases had a significantly higher rate of absenteeism than those who felt fairly treated (Patchen, 1960, pp. 349–360).

In another study, two groups of students were hired to conduct interviews at a fixed rate of $3.50 per hour. The experiment was conducted so that one group was induced to feel fairly paid and the other group to feel overpaid. The consequence was that the group that felt overpaid conducted more interviews in the allotted time. Apparently they worked harder to set right the overpayment (Adams, 1963, pp. 422–424).

In another study where the subjects were paid on a piece-work basis, subjects who were induced to believe that they were overpaid tended to restrict their production and thus their pay, apparently in order to minimize the inequity. The researchers further hypothesized that the overpaid subjects were probably improving the quality of their work in order to create more equity, and this turned out to be true. It appeared that the subjects could not reduce feelings of inequity by increasing production so they improved the quality of their work (Adams, 1963, pp. 434–435).

Research and experience suggest that a wide range of variables are likely to be included in the notions people have about whether they are being treated fairly. Figure 13.3 lists a number of potential inputs and outcomes that are likely to affect feelings of equity or inequity. You could undoubtedly add more, and some of these variables could be broken down into more specifics. For example, a wide range of dimensions probably enters into people's notions about level of responsibility: from the number of people supervised to the size of the budget administered to the value of the equipment the person is responsible for.

Three dimensions now deemed illegal for use in such matters as hiring and reward allocations—sex, race and national origin—enter into perceptions of equity and inequity when managers have biases in these areas. It appears, for example, that in many organizations being a female has been considered a lesser input or investment than being male when decisions about salary scales and promotions have been made. The same has held true for older age and handi-

Input Variables

(Investments and Costs One is Likely to Consider)

Age	Total time spent on each assignment, shift, day, etc.
Sex	Comfort/discomfort in working conditions
Experience	Travel to work (ease/difficulty)
Education	Monotony
Reputation	Attendance record and predictability
Contacts of worth to organization	Honesty, reliability
Seniority in organization or unit	One's intentions (good vs. evil)
Accumulated investments and costs over time	Level of responsibility
Skill/quality of work	Number and qualifications of subordinates
Effort	Budget responsibilities
Cooperation, wilingness	Equipment responsibilities
Loyalty	Impact of decisions
Hours of work	

Outcome Variables

(Rewards and Punishments One Is Likely to Consider)

Dollar amount of wage and salary	Transfer to a particular job
Size of pay increase	Job security
Frequency of pay increase	Punishments; extent and type for a particular offense
Size and type of fringe benefits	Recognition
Salary vs. wage status	Inclusion/exclusion By work groups By peers in general By management By admired others
Opportunity for advancement	Type and size of furniture or equipment
Promotion/demotion to a particular job	Privileges
Parking location and space	
Time off	

FIGURE 13.3 What People Consider in Fair Treatment: Inputs and Outcomes Likely to Affect Feelings of Equity/Inequity. **Source:** Adapted from Wendell L. French, *The Personnel Management Process,* 5th Edition, Houghton Mifflin, Boston, Massachusetts 1982, p. 135.

Peers in work group
People in comparable jobs in other groups within the organization
People in comparable jobs in other organizations
One's boss
One's subordinates
One's spouse

FIGURE 13.4 Potential Comparison Others

capped status; laws are attempting to remove or reduce the weight of these variables in decision making on personnel matters. Equal Employment Opportunity Commission hearings and lawsuits centering on the use of these variables in personnel decisions have led to numerous out-of-court settlements or court awards in recent years.

We want to stress that perceptions or feelings of equity or inequity also relate to how one sees others treated. Some potential comparison others are shown in Figure 13.4. There are undoubtedly wide variations in who are the comparison others for different people, but one can be fairly sure that most people compare their job inputs and job outcomes to some of the people on the list. Comparisons between spouses are becoming more common as more and more women enter the work force.

Wage and Salary Administration

It is clear that managers must pay attention to matters such as compensation levels, the determination of relative worth of the jobs in the organization, differentials between hierarchical levels, and rules about frequency of pay increases and criteria for wage and salary advancement. Systematic attention to these matters is imperative if motivation is to be sustained and counterproductive levels of dissatisfaction avoided. Such devices as wage and salary surveys (to determine current wage levels in a particular industry or geographical area), job evaluation (to determine relative job worth), and merit rating (one purpose of which is to assist in determining differential rewards) are widely used.

Wage and salary administration is particularly troublesome in periods of rapid inflation. When the rate of inflation exceeds the rate at which an organization can raise compensation, management is faced with deciding which employees will have their purchasing ability reduced the least and which ones the most, if there are to be pay differentials. Issues such as how much to allocate across the board versus how much to allocate on the basis of merit become more sensitive than usual and considerable conflict can emerge around such problems. In the *Merit or Cost of Living?* vignette, Ruth, the president of the company, was faced with some troublesome dilemmas in this regard. Similar dilemmas arise when an organization is faced with severe budget cuts and decisions must be made about how the few dollars available will be allocated. Perceived inequities in the allocation of a 2-percent fund can create as much anger and dissension as perceived inequities involving amounts of five or ten times as much.

Conflict is also likely to emerge when pay or other reward differentials between levels or groups within an organization get too far out of line. For example, if subordinates begin to make about as much money or more money than the supervisor, the supervisor becomes resentful. In another example, extremely high pay for the top executive group with a tremendous gap between that group and the next level of management can result in great resentment and high turnover at those levels. Or, plant workers who see office workers enjoying many more privileges tend to complain and sometimes bargain collectively about their perceived inequities.

The issue of relative job worth underlies some of the problems in pay differentials we have mentioned. This issue has been surfacing with considerable intensity in recent years as a sex discrimination issue under the label of *comparable worth*. Job evaluation practices, in particular, are the focal points in this controversy.

There are several methods of job evaluation, but they all basically produce a ranking of jobs in terms of worth based on selected criteria. Dollar amounts can then be attached to these relative rankings. The point method is by far the most widely used method. In this approach, points are allocated for several selected factors that are considered to be of worth to the organization, such as technical skills required, responsibility, human-relations skill required, and the like. All jobs within the purview of the particular job evaluation plan are measured with the same yardsticks, and the different points resulting are used as a basis for assigning different dollar amounts.

Critics say that many organizations traditionally apply job evaluation separately to several different job clusters, such as plant workers, office workers, supervisory employees, and professional employees. Pay plans are then developed separately for these groupings, and if one or more of these groups is predominantly comprised of women, salary scales tend to be depressed. *All* jobs within the organization should be compared with each other, so the argument goes.

But even when the same job evaluation plan is used for all jobs, the critics argue that the members on the job-evaluation committee can be biased, subjectively assigning lower points to tasks traditionally performed by women. Or, the job-evaluation scheme itself may be biased, with terminology and dimensions skewing the results in the direction of fewer points for job elements predominantly done by women.

Those on the other side of the argument say that there are labor market, collective bargaining, and other conditions that give rise to differences between major categories of employees, and that job evaluation techniques are only one means of determining relative pay within an organization. Further, they would argue that, while there may be some areas of bias in job-evaluation schemes, that terminology can be corrected and that these schemes are really aimed at minimizing bias.

Such controversy stems from differing perceptions of relative investments, costs, and rewards. Again referring to the vignette *Why Is He Paid More Than I?,* Ilse is questioning decisions that have been made about the relative worth of her job versus other middle management jobs.

Incentive Pay Plans

Most plans which provide incentives to individuals are one of two types. One type, the piece-rate plan, provides for payments based on the quantity of units produced. Sales-commission plans that provide payments based on some percentage of gross sales are comparable. The other prevalent type, the production-bonus plan, basically provides payments based on the extent of production beyond the number of units considered standard for a given period of time. Sometimes such plans are established for teams of employees where cooperation is particularly important or where individual contribution is hard to measure.

Plantwide incentive plans are frequently called productivity plans, and feature considerable worker participation. Employees participate on committees that study problems and suggestions and make recommendations about such matters as materials, methods, scrap reduction, plant layout, and machinery. One of the most famous to result is the Scanlon Plan, which features employees sharing in cost savings.

There is considerable evidence that individual, group and plantwide incentive payment systems can result in higher productivity and higher wages than in the case of employees working for straight hourly wage payments. However, there can be many problems associated with incentive systems. In addition to the problems of establishing and changing standards and reaching agreement with union representatives, there are deeper and more pervasive problems that frequently occur in the social system of the organizations when incentive systems are introduced. One problem is an almost universal fear on the part of employees that the higher one's productivity rises under the incentive system, the more likely that standards will be raised, and the more that one's real reward for increasing productivity is ultimately going to be either harder work or conditions where fewer employees will be needed, or both. There are many documented cases of individuals restricting their productivity and of group pressures exerted to keep people in line for such reasons (see Chapter 7). Further, there are many documented cases of employees hiding work in order to be able to demonstrate acceptable production on days when they are unable to keep pace or on days when they wish to coast. Even 30-foot propeller shafts have been buried in order to be dug up when advantageous to employees! (See Box 7.5.)

Plantwide productivity-incentive systems seem to have an advantage over individual group incentive systems by allowing and encouraging employee participation and cooperation in solving production problems that are broader in scope than the individual worker's particular task. When this participation is coupled with extensive participation in the design of the incentive plan itself, such approaches seem to reduce fears of exploitation and to tap into the widely held expertise in the work force. In general, it would seem that trust—between a group of employees and the supervisor, between employees and management, between the union and management—is a major ingredient in successful incentive systems. It appears that incentive systems are more likely to be successful and to have fewer dysfunctional consequences when the following conditions are present: (1) there is participation in the design of the system and in the administration of the system; (2) employees and supervisors understand and agree with the measurements and standards that are used; (3) management is careful to ensure that employees share substantially in the gains that occur; and (4) the incentive system is linked to broader, participative problem solving in the organization.

LABOR RELATIONS

Another broad process in many organizations is *labor relations*. It involves management-employee negotiations over wages, hours, and working conditions, the grievance-arbitration process, and the day-to-day administration of the labor contract. This process is in existence whenever there is a labor union representing some segment of the employees in an organization. We can also infer some such process where there is any kind of collective influence being exercised by organizational members. For example, an engineer's association might be attempting to influence top management about working conditions, or a faculty council in a university or a public school system might be attempting to influence top management or a governing board about compensation policies.

Unions and employee organizations, such as professional associations and councils, serve other purposes in addition to collective bargaining. For example, the union provides a means of socialization and influence for organization members. The labor contract also typically provides a formal mechanism for organizational due process.

Recent years have seen a wide expansion of the kinds of occupations influenced by collective bargaining as well as an increased militancy among some occupational groups. There have been more and more collective bargaining agreements involving bank employees, teachers, nurses, and government employees. Professional groups, such as nurses' associations, have in some instances become instruments for collective bargaining and for taking strike action. The number of teacher strikes has increased greatly, and there have been strikes of physicians employed in public hospitals. In 1981 there was a general strike of professional baseball players that interrupted the regular season for an extended period. In general, however, strike action has not increased in recent years (*Monthly Labor Review,* 1982).

This increasing militancy and use of strikes by some organized groups has its influence on individual attitudes and on interpersonal relationships. The more that union-management relationships are of an adversary nature—in contrast to what has been called integrative bargaining (Walton & McKersie, 1965, pp. 4–6)—the more subordinates and superiors will display the behavior and attitudes toward each other that were described in the chapter on conflict. The behavior includes the we-they syndrome, the withholding of information, distortion in perceptions and judgments, and the use of information to erode the position of the other party. While peer group solidarity and some aspects of cooperation and morale might increase, there is always the possibility that solidarity and cooperation may be aimed at subverting organizational effectiveness and efficiency.

Contract negotiations and informal interactions on the job are only part of the scene in which union-management relationships are acted out. The grievance-arbitration process also becomes the focal point for either reinforcing an adversary stance or reinforcing a problem-solving approach. Management or the union may hang tough in terms of their position on a grievance, thus sending the problem on to arbitration, even though they know they are in the wrong. In extreme situations, grievances are filed simply to harass supervisors or top management.

Whatever collective-bargaining climate is prevalent—whether adversary or problem solving—will be transmitted down from the top union official to shop stewards and to the employees in the plants and offices. Similarly, managers and supervisors will transmit their attitudes to subordinates. If the climate is essentially adversary and of a win-lose nature, management will be much more cautious in what information it dispenses, will tend to see grievances and complaints as harassment, and will tend to see ulterior motives in suggestions for change. If the climate emphasizes problem solving and cooperation, grievances and suggestions for change will be seen as opportunities for working through issues at all levels.

JUSTICE DETERMINATION

Finally, there is a broad process that we might call *justice determination*. This is a complex flow of events that allocates rewards and penalties to members of the organization in some relationship to the worth of their contribution, and provides means for the correction of mistakes in the allocation of rewards and penalties. This process extensively overlaps labor relations in unionized settings where grievance-arbitration procedures are usually in place to assist in remedying mistakes in the treatment of employees. Determining where justice lies in a particular situation is a task that overlaps a good deal with matters of compensation and reward that we have already discussed under the topic of equity theory. The aspect of correcting mistakes in rewards and penalties we have only mentioned, however, and we will briefly deal with that topic here. We will also extend our discussion of the allocation of rewards and penalties by focusing on disciplinary actions.

Organizational Due Process

Leadership styles that permit and encourage organizational members to express current concerns and frustrations can be a safety valve whereby problems are aired before their consequences become dysfunctional. In addition, procedures that permit grievances to be aired and worked through, and that protect the person bringing the grievance forward, are also mechanisms for constructive conflict resolution. The use of such procedures has been called organizational due process, defined as follows:

> Organizational due process consists of established procedures for handling complaints and grievances, protection against punitive action for using such established procedures, and careful, systematic, and thorough review of the substance of the complaints and grievances by unbiased or neutral parties (French, 1982, p. 145).

Sometimes management establishes and supports such means for nonsupervisory workers but acts as though supervisors, middle managers, or higher echelon executives are immune from feelings of unfair or inequitable treatment, which, of course, they are not. Formal grievance procedures for middle and higher managers, in particular, are rarely found.

Progressive Discipline

Reprimands, disciplinary layoffs or discharges that are imposed without preliminaries are widely reacted to as being arbitrary and capricious. In the vignette *The Engine That Couldn't,* Art was not performing well, but the actions of his supervisor, Dan, were nonetheless too impulsive and too unexpected. Such actions lead to anger, various forms of fighting back, and can create considerable insecurity and resentment among employees.

Many contemporary organizations have adopted a philosophy of progressive discipline that is not so precipitant and allows for remedial action. Under such a philosophy, ineffective performance or offenses against rules result in a sequence such as follows: *first,* an oral warning; *second,* if performance does not improve adequately, a written warning stating the consequences of future offenses or below-standard performance; *third,* if performance is not corrected, disciplinary layoff or demotion; and *fourth,* discharge. If the deficiencies are severe enough, discharge might occur at the third step. Such an approach signals to employees and supervisors that the organization adheres to a developmental and remedial approach to performance, and serves to curb precipitant punishment by supervisors. Some offenses are so disruptive, of course, that immediate suspension followed by review of the circumstances and then discharge is warranted. These offenses are usually stated in writing in organizational work rules.

All of these processes described above are largely inherent to organizations, are interrelated, and are vital to organizational success. The quality of the systems designed to facilitate these processes will have consequences on the motivation and satisfaction and development of organizational members, as well as consequences in the relationships between people. In many ways, the nature of the personnel policies and practices in an organization contributes extensively to what we have discussed previously as *organizational climate*—the overall tone of the organization.

SO WHAT? IMPLICATIONS FOR YOU

We believe that understanding how personnel practices affect human behavior can lead to more effective personnel policies and procedures. In many ways, personnel practices help weave the fabric of human relationships in organizations, and the result can be either a harmonious whole or a jumble of incongruous scenes. The following are some generalizations that we believe are warranted, and some possible implications for you as an organizational member or manager.

As a Member in an Organization

Generalizations	Implications
1. Personnel policies and practices affect behavior, performance, and satisfaction.	1. You should find out as much as you can about the personnel policies and practices of any organization to which you are applying for employment. These policies and practices can greatly affect your work life.
2. Jobs have different mixes of planning, doing, and controlling components; these mixes affect motivation and satisfaction.	2. Search out jobs that have the mix of components that will lead to your objectives, such as job interest, satisfaction, and development.
3. Rules are necessary, but people tend to circumvent and resent rules that seem unnecessary or oppressive; group collusion often occurs.	3. Discuss with your supervisor problems you have with rules that are getting in the way of effective work.
4. Supervisors and subordinates alike tend to be anxious about performance appraisal.	4. Seek feedback about your performance; do not wait until pay adjustment time comes around. Recognize that this may be an uncomfortable process for your supervisor.
5. You and your peers will probably assess almost anything that happens as fair or unfair relative to each other and to other groups.	5. You will need to decide how far to depart from group norms in terms of working toward securing higher rewards for yourself. If group rewards are not already there, you may want to press for changes in practices to provide group rewards for cooperative effort.

Generalizations	Implications
6. Organizations differ in the training and development opportunities available.	6. Utilize training opportunities for both personal and organizational improvement.
7. If there is an adversary labor-management relationship where you work, there are likely to be widespread symptoms of the kind associated with groups in conflict.	7. Be aware of the conflict dynamics. Sort out inaccurate perceptions, fantasies, and scapegoating behavior on either management's or labor's part, so that you can be more in control of the flow of events.
8. Organizations vary in terms of the openness of channels for presenting suggestions and complaints.	8. Press for fair treatment, but use approved procedures and attempt to create a problem-solving climate rather than an adversarial one.

As a Current or Future Manager

Generalizations	Implications
1. Personnel policies and practices affect the motivation of employees and relationships between people.	1. Develop personnel policies and practices that create the kind of organizational culture you want.
2. Skills and interaction style of people newly hired, transferred, or promoted into a unit will affect interrelationships and probably morale and performance.	2. Staffing decisions need to be based on a diagnosis of unit characteristics, strengths, and weaknesses, and on applicant qualifications.
3. Newly hired people are anxious and their supervisors may be anxious.	3. Consider using participative approaches to bringing people aboard; this can help reduce anxieties and result in more rapid assimilation.
4. Layoffs tend to have many dysfunctional personal, interpersonal, group and organizational consequences.	4. Provide as much information and support as possible in a budgetary cutback situation; press for looking at a wide range of options that include ways to minimize the human consequences of layoffs.

Generalizations	Implications
5. People approaching retirement have many concerns and anxieties.	5. Be sensitive to the various needs of people approaching retirement, including their needs to feel included and competent; help foster constructive group norms about older employees. Provide opportunities for preretirees to plan their retirement strategies and to develop support groups.
6. The opportunity for mobility within the organization enhances overall morale.	6. Press for promotion-from-within practices that are in balance with the need to bring in outside people. Encourage subordinates who are ready for more responsible positions to apply for such openings.
7. The mix of planning, doing, and controlling aspects in a job can affect motivation, effort, and job satisfaction.	7. Work with subordinates in developing jobs more tailored to their qualifications, but keep in mind that such changes may require the wage and salary structure to be changed and may require changes in your role.
8. Excessive or unreasonable rules create resentment and covert behavior on the part of subordinates to circumvent them.	8. Do not try to solve all problems with more rules; look and listen for unnecessary constraints on people and work to remove these constraints.
9. Supervisors, almost universally, are anxious about performance appraisal.	9. Acknowledge your anxiety to yourself (and perhaps to your subordinates). The clearer you are as to your purposes in reviewing performance, the more objective job performance data you have and the more skilled you are at giving constructive feedback, probably the easier the process will be.

Generalizations	Implications
10. Performance appraisal can have different purposes and these purposes should govern practices that are used.	10. Think through what kind of a climate you want to create in your unit and what the purposes are of the appraisal. If an important aspect is development, try to get as much involvement of subordinates as possible and try to create a give-and-take climate.
11. Appraisal should be frequent and continuous.	11. Don't wait until pay adjustment time comes around; discuss positive and problem performance as it occurs. Try to include discussion of your role in the person's performance.
12. The training and development of employees has long-range implications for the success of an organization.	12. Develop a training and development strategy for your unit. This requires planning and discussions with subordinates and liaison with the training and personnel department.
13. A wide range of items affects employees' perceptions about whether they are being treated fairly.	13. Assess the probable input/output variables that may be perceived as relevant to equity or inequity in any treatment of people, such as changes in duties, compensation, or working conditions.
14. Attempts to increase employee output are frequently met with widespread distrust of management's motives and cynicism about the consequences.	14. Work with other managers and employees to develop reward systems in which there is an increased reward to individuals and groups when they contribute to higher quality and productivity.
15. Union-management collective-bargaining stances—whether adversary or problem-solving—will be acted out within and between groups: subordinates vis à vis supervisors, in	15. Try to help shift the collective-bargaining stance toward joint problem solving. In an adversary situation, you will need to be even more alert in managing frequent and effective com-

Generalizations	Implications
particular. In an adversary climate one can expect distortions of perceptions, we-they attitudes, unreasonable grievances, and scapegoating within a losing group.	munications that will minimize distortions in perceptions.
16. Precipitant discipline produces anger and fear and frequently some form of individual or group retaliation.	16. Develop progressive discipline procedures aimed at correcting behavior. This will tend to minimize the dysfunctional consequences of precipitant discipline, and will help develop people.
17. Established procedures for handling complaints and grievances have been found helpful in many organizations. The approachability of supervisors is a major factor in remedying mistakes in treatment.	17. Permit people to come to you with complaints. Be aware of formal channels for processing problems beyond your level; be oriented toward due process in matters of discipline.

LEARNING APPLICATION ACTIVITIES

1. Write a vignette based on your experience that illustrates how some personnel practice affected the behavior of employees in an organization.

2. Analyze the vignette *The Notice on the Door.* How might George Atwood have handled the matter more effectively? Share your ideas in a group of four to six colleagues. Report group conclusions to the total class.

3. Review the vignette *The Appraisal Interview.* In what way was the interview deficient from the point of view of Sharon Goldberg? From the point of view of Louise Todd? If you were Sharon, how would you want to be treated? If you were Louise? Compare your likes and dislikes with four to six class members; note similarities and differences.

4. With one or two colleagues, interview a personnel director and ask that person (among other questions) what personnel problems are currently particularly troublesome. Share the results with your class and see what common themes emerge, if any. (An alternative may be to invite, via your instructor, a personnel director to visit class to be a resource person.)

5. *Step 1:* Think about the adjustment problems, if any, that someone you know has had when he or she has been fired or laid off.

Step 2: On a voluntary basis, discuss aspects of your reflections to your class.

Step 3: As a class, discuss any common themes.

6. Think about a job you have held that you particularly liked; note those job attributes that made the job particularly desirable. Share your notes with four or five colleagues and make a common list. Repeat for a job you particularly disliked. Report to the total class and discuss commonalities.

7. *Step 1:* Describe in writing a work incident in which you felt unfairly treated.

Step 2: Share the incident with four or five colleagues and have them assist you in analyzing (a) those with whom you were adversely comparing yourself and (b) how the incident affected your behavior. Listen to and analyze the incidents of your colleagues.

Step 3: Record and report to the total class the different kinds of comparison groups or persons that people mention and the various kinds of consequent behaviors that people described in your group discussion.

8. With one or two colleagues, interview a labor union official about the biggest challenges currently facing his or her union. Share with your class, and discuss how contemporary union objectives would probably influence human behavior within organizations.

9. List some examples of the policies and procedures that would be in effect if an organization were adhering to the notion of organizational due process.

10. Describe progressive discipline. In a group with four or five colleagues, develop a consensus description and illustrate with good examples. Share experiences that group members have had when the concept was not followed, noting the consequences.

REFERENCES

Adams, J. Stacy. "Towards an Understanding of Inequity." *Journal of Abnormal and Social Psychology* 67/5 (November 1963): 422–424.

Bornstein, Leon. "Developments in Industrial Relations." *Monthly Labor Review* 97/12 (December 1974): 72–73.

Clutterbuck, David. "Why a Job Shared is Not a Job Halved." *International Management* 34/10 (October 1979): 45–47.

Fleuter, Douglas L. *The Workweek Revolution: A Guide to the Changing Workweek.* Reading, Mass.: Addison-Wesley, 1975.

French, Wendell L. *The Personnel Management Process: Human Resources Administration and Development,* 5th ed. Boston: Houghton Mifflin, 1982.

French, Wendell L., and Robert W. Hollman. "Management by Objectives: The Team Approach." *California Management Review* 17(3) (Spring 1975): 18–19.

Golembiewski, Robert T., Rick Hilles, and Munro S. Kagno. "A Longitudinal Study of Flex-time Effects." *Journal of Applied Behavioral Science* 10/40 (October 1974): 503–532.

Gomersall, Earl R., and M. Scott Myers. "Breakthrough in On-the-Job Training." *Harvard Business Review* 44/4 (July-August): 62–72.

Hackman, J. Richard, and Greg R. Oldham. *Work Redesign.* Reading, Mass.: Addison-Wesley, 1980.

Homans, George C. *Social Behavior: Its Elementary Forms.* New York: Harcourt Brace Jovanovich, 1961.

Industrial-Organizational Psychologist 17 (February 1980): 35.

Latham, Gary P., and Lise M. Saari. "Importance of Supportive Relationships in Goal Setting." *Journal of Applied Psychology* 64/2 (April 1979): 151–156.

Levinson, Harry. "Management by Whose Objectives." *Harvard Business Review* 48/4 (July-August 1970): 125–134.

Likert, Rensis. "No Manager is an Island." *International Management* 34/1 (January 1979): 22–24.

Meyer, Herbert H., Emanuel Kay, and John R. P. French Jr. "Split Roles in Performance Appraisal." *Harvard Business Review* 43/1 (January-February 1965): 123–129.

Monthly Labor Review 105/6 (June 1982): 111.

Myers, M. Scott. "Every Employee a Manager." *California Management Review* 10/3 (Spring 1968): 9–29.

Patchen, Martin. "Absence and Employee Feelings About Fair Treatment." *Personnel Psychology* 13/3 (Autumn 1960): 349–360.

Shepard, Herbert A., and Sheldon Davis. "Organization Development in Good Times and Bad." *Journal of Contemporary Business* 1/3 (Summer 1972): 65–73.

Thompson, Paul H., and Gene W. Dalton. "Performance Appraisal: Managers Beware." *Harvard Business Review* 48/1 (January-February 1970): 149–157.

"If Jimmy Took Ham's Test." *Time,* 30 July 1979, p. 19.

Walton, Richard E., and Robert B. McKersie. *A Behavioral Theory of Labor Negotiations*. New York: McGraw-Hill, 1965.

Wheeler, Kenneth E., Richard Gurman, and Dale Tarnowieski. *The Four-Day Week*. New York: American Management Association, 1972 (pamphlet).

14
Organizational Culture and Climate

LEARNING OBJECTIVES

After reading this chapter you should be able to:

1. Define the concept of organizational culture.
2. Give some illustrations of aspects of organizational culture.
3. Define the concept of organizational climate.
4. Describe the variables that are typically measured in organizational climate studies.
5. Identify potential consequences of different climates.
6. State several practical uses of organizational climate surveys.

EXECUTIVE SUITE

To Irv Green, assistant to the vice-president for finance, assignment to an office on the top floor of corporate headquarters was an exciting development. His boss's office was there, as were the offices of the president, the board chairman, and a few other vice presidents and their assistants and immediate staffs.

It didn't take Irv long to be aware of some of the things he could and could not do. For example, it seemed to be all right to read the Wall Street Journal at his desk early in the morning, but not after any of the officers of the company came in. It was not all right to read any other journals on the job; the first time he tried that he was advised by a more experienced co-worker that the officers expected anyone who was serious about their career to do their "nonbusiness" reading at home. Coats and ties were clearly the rule except in the hottest summer months, although there was nothing written down or said about it.

Irv would have thought that research and manufacturing would be equally important to the company, but over a period of weeks on the top floor it became evident to him that research was the most highly valued. The director of research and the research scientists seemed to get pretty much what they asked for, but the manufacturing vice president and plant managers were put off more frequently or had their requests questioned in much more detail. Handbooks and brochures clearly showed that the company took great pride in the succession of high-quality products that had been developed in the laboratories. Scientists and engineers were supported in attending seminars and conferences; it was rare for a manufacturing supervisor or general foreman to attend a seminar on management or on manufacturing equipment.

Written reports seemed to be important: probably stemming, it was said, from the chairman's frequent assertion in earlier years that "any suggestion worth making is worth documenting." In short, very little discussion of ideas occurred between Irv's level and the level above until a great deal of information had been gathered and the case made in a formal, written proposal. And then, frequently, the proposal was side-tracked or completely scuttled by a vice president's comment, such as "that idea was tried out here a long time ago, and it didn't work" or "*X* department would never go for it." Project progress reports had to be in writing and submitted quarterly, which seemed to Irv to be very time consuming. Irv did a lot of his report writing on Saturday morning when the telephones were quieter. The chairman frequently came in on Saturday mornings, and it was assumed among the top executives that getting ahead in the company meant coming in also. The only thing that made Saturday mornings tolerable to Irv was that the dress was informal and he could come in wearing a sport shirt, slacks, and jogging shoes—that, and the fact that he was mostly left alone to work.

POWER POLITICS

To Don, assistant plant engineer, the Morrison Company was a lot different from Carston Products Ltd. People seemed much less friendly at Morrison; there was more gossip and backbiting, and there appeared to be many more edicts issuing from headquarters. Some of these struck Don as petty; for example, no one in the plant could use a telephone to call home (although the office employees and the engineers could). And, other than plant workers, men were expected to wear ties, even in summer. It was generally understood that top management had little faith in group meetings and the word committee was almost taboo. It also appeared that top management gave out little information about company plans. It seemed, too, that there was insufficient delegation; at least Don's boss complained about it a lot. These matters weren't all that important to Don, but they were irritating, and he heard a lot of complaining about them and about other practices.

But what was really getting to Don was the behind-the-scenes maneuvering. Power politics were rampant. The previous vice president-controller had been forced out by the vice president of finance, and there seemed to be hard feelings in the accounting department because of it. Now there was a rumor that the director of research and the personnel director were feuding, with each one trying to rally support. The trouble was that subordinates got caught up in the politics, and Don really resented it.

On the other hand, Morrison's products were as well received by consumers as Carston's. New products were emerging from the laboratories at reasonable intervals, although Don suspected that costs were much higher at Morrison. In any event, Don didn't feel as happy about working at the Morrison Company as he had at Carston. "This is a real 'dog-eat-dog' place," he thought, "This move was a big promotion and more money for me, but maybe it was a mistake."

THE JIC FILE

Tom was still angry when he came back to his office. His boss, Joan, had just remarked in a meeting with six other people that one of Tom's assistants "had goofed again" in sending out a report with errors in it. Joan's tone had been accusatory and sarcastic, and Tom had begun a slow burn, although he had tried to hide it. Incidents like this had happened several times before, and usually in the presence of others. Further, this kind of behavior wasn't restricted to Joan. Tom had heard that the division manager was prone to grill department heads unmercifully in front of their peers and staff people in their monthly meetings, particularly if he sensed any indecisiveness on anyone's part. Some department heads found the process challenging; others found it demeaning or embarrassing.

Tom had heard of JIC (just-in-case) files and had scoffed at the idea of making a record of things that occurred in order to defend himself or his unit in case of some future flap. To Tom, a JIC file was symptomatic of either a gross distrust or blatant opportunism. He had decided that he would prefer forcing issues into the open rather than resorting to a JIC file. But in a meeting with a crowded agenda, there seemed to be no way to respond to the kind of remark Joan had made.

Tom pulled a new file holder out of his desk drawer, marked it JIC, and made the following entries:

Month of June—Joan's assistant wrote a notation on my request for travel funds, which I accidentally saw, implying that the trip was not strictly business.

Week of July 10—Joan, or Joan's secretary, twice failed to notify me of meeting changes. When I showed up, her secretary's response was, "Oh, didn't you know the meeting had been postponed?"

Week of July 17—Joan held up a report so long that there was no way I could correct it properly in time for publication. Later she complained about how the report was written.

Month of July—In my last two meetings with Joan, her own crises completely preempted the agenda, and we never got around to my items. On at least two occasions, I've had to move ahead without advice from Joan, and subsequently, she indirectly complained about the action I took.

Tom put the sheet with these entries into the file, placed it in his desk drawer, slammed the drawer shut, and locked it. "This place is a damned jungle," he thought to himself. "I'm going to keep a record of things that happen, and if Joan pushes me too far, I'll give her some of her own medicine."

THE FACTORY

The first thing Jocelyn sensed when she applied for a job at Valley Electronics was that the place was cheerful. The receptionist was cheerful and made her feel at home. The interviewer was enthusiastic about the company and seemed to be enthusiastic about his job. The department head who was to interview her was just winding up a meeting with a group of people, and they all seemed to be friendly and in good spirits. The telephone rang twice in succession as the interview was starting, whereupon the department head asked her secretary to take calls and suggested the interview continue in the adjacent conference room.

Later, on a plant tour with the department head, Jocelyn was struck with the friendly interaction between the production employees and the department head. It was clear that people were very busy, yet there was an easy informality about the place. It was clean and well painted, too. Jocelyn had never seen large, potted plants in a factory before, yet there they were. It dawned on her later that the dress was very casual, and that she would not have been able to distinguish managers, engineers, machine operators, and office employees by what they wore. Her overall reaction was that she liked the atmosphere of Valley Electronics in contrast to other places where she had interviewed.

THE TEAM

Margaret had never worked so hard in her life, but she was feeling good. She had just come out of a meeting with her boss, Stan, and the other managers who reported to him. They had spent all day refining group objectives for the year, and there was strong consensus about the final document. In a similar session the previous week, each manager had reviewed his or her unit achievements and problems of the past year, and there had been substantial give and take of a problem-solving nature.

It seemed to Margaret that there was a great deal of support and help offered among the managers, in contrast to the company where she had previously worked. There, people had tended to be protective of their own domains and frequently blamed others for problems that had occurred. Here it was different. "By a quantum jump," thought Margaret. "People express concerns, but there is a minimum of blaming. What I particularly like here is the way people build on others' ideas instead of putting them down. We work the problems through."

INTRODUCTION

Organizations differ in their customs and traditions, in what is valued, in the way they feel to us, and in the way they operate. We might find it hard to describe the various differences between Company *A* and Company *B*, but we *know* they are different. Some of these differences we evaluate as favorable or unfavorable; some we may simply be descriptive about. For example, friendliness is usually evaluated as favorable; observing that an aircraft assembly plant is huge may simply be a description without evaluation.

In the above vignettes, there appear to be patterns of organizational characteristics that we might refer to as part of organizational culture or as organizational climate. Culture is a broader concept than climate, as we will see. But both have to do with patterns.

One can also think in terms of divisional, or departmental, or group cultures and climates. While there tend to be broad consistencies throughout a given organization, there can be major differences between units within organizations.

Organizational or unit cultures in the above vignettes were having strong influence on organizational members; if one assumes that the feelings and perceptions of these people about these cultures were irrelevant to their performances, the incidents might be considered trivial. Our view, however, is that these anecdotes are anything but trivial. Perceptions and feelings and behavioral responses to organizational culture are powerful forces influencing organizational end results. Incidents such as we have described are frequently indications of functional and dysfunctional currents that run deep in organizations. We would want to be much more thorough in our analysis, of course, before reaching conclusions and making recommendations for change. For example, we might want to find out how other organization members perceived the organization as well as looking at a broader range of phenomena.

In this chapter we will consider these general issues via the following topics:

Organizational Culture: The Concept
Some Examples of Different Organizational Cultures
Organizational Climate: The Concept
How Organizational Climate is Measured
Some Key Questions About Organizational Climate
Organizational Climate Studies
Organizational Climate in Subunits
So What? Implications for You

ORGANIZATIONAL CULTURE: THE CONCEPT

Based largely on definitions from anthropology, we define organizational culture as *the prevailing pattern of values, myths, beliefs, assumptions, and norms; and their embodiment in language, symbols, and artifacts, including technology, in management goals and practices, and in participant sentiments, attitudes, activities, and interactions* (Kroeber & Kluckhohn, 1952, p. 357; Baker, 1980, p. 8).

"Who sets the tone here?"

Although some of the terms in our definition overlap, we include them because they tend to provide some additional, subtle meanings. A *myth,* for example, is "a traditional or legendary story . . . any invented story, idea, or concept . . . an unproved collective belief that is accepted uncritically" (Stein, 1967, p. 946). A *norm* is an idea shared in a group about what group members should do under certain circumstances (see Chapter 7 on "Group Dynamics"), and can include the notion of standards. An assumption is something taken for granted, or an hypothesis or conjecture, while a belief is much stronger than that, and has the connotation of certainty and conviction.

In a sense, the concept of culture overlaps or includes all of the organizational variables we have described in earlier chapters, including the concept of the formal and the informal system. It is different, however, in that the concept calls attention, in particular, to the prevailing pattern of values, beliefs, and assumptions about how things should be done. This helps focus our attention on such matters as management philosophy, assumptions that managers make about what motivates people and on patterns of norms that influence behavior.

By including such dimensions as language and technology in the definition, the concept of organizational culture reminds us that what may be familiar and understandable to members of one organizational culture or subculture may be strange and puzzling to members of another. For example, the language and technology of a high-technology electronics firm initially might have some puzzling aspects to a person who had worked for several years in the restaurant industry, or who had just graduated from a liberal arts program. The language of the hospital controller's office might initially be very puzzling to nursing supervisors who are being asked to negotiate and manage their departmental budgets. The terminology valued by the controller, and the underlying assumptions and values of that terminology, might seem alien to the culture of the nursing staff. Allocating time to direct or indirect costs, or to categories like general patient care, physician assistance, record keeping, staff meetings, and training might be both puzzling to and resisted by people preoccupied with saving lives and helping people get well.

There are at least four major questions to which the concept of organizational culture leads us. *One question:* What is the pattern that characterizes Organization A (or unit A) as similar to, or different from, Organization B (or unit B)? In the *Power Politics* vignette, Don found the culture of the Morrison Company to be quite different from Carston Products. He found the Morrison Company valuing high control and devaluing committees and extensive delegation. He also saw a pattern of less friendliness, more internal competition, more politics, and more conflict than at Carston Products. But there was also higher pay. These weren't isolated matters; to Don, the same set of characteristics seemed to appear in a variety of ways. While these may have been only surface manifestations of deeply held assumptions and beliefs about managing people and organizations, they nevertheless formed a discernible pattern. When Don thought about the situation further, he may have surmised that it was a relatively high pay structure—and maybe fear of losing that pay—that was the glue that held the Morrison Company together.

In *The Factory* vignette, Jocelyn sensed a pattern of behaviors and customs at Valley Electronics that made the place seem cheerful and to her liking. While she had not had the opportunity or the time to analyze the organization in any depth, she had begun to notice such dimensions as norms about dress and communications, leadership style, interviewing practices, the use of groups, cleanliness and maintenance, and decor. This pattern was inconsistent with her values and beliefs.

The *second question* that the concept of organizational culture leads us to is this: What is functional and what is dysfunctional in the culture of Organization *A* (or Organization *B*) in terms of such outcomes as effectiveness, efficiency, and participant satisfaction, both short and long range? In the *Executive Suite* vignette, the value placed on written reports had gone so far as to close off preliminary discussion of ideas and was undoubtedly highly dysfunctional in terms of innovation and morale. It may have been functional in saving some top executive time, but that is debatable.

In a sense, much of this book has been addressing the question of functionality and dysfunctionality of aspects of organizational culture, at least in terms of one or a few variables at a time. In Chapters 6 and 7, for example, we indicated that a norm that says a leader should be responsible for all of the effective leadership behaviors of a group is often dysfunctional. In several chapters we have emphasized the importance of active listening and checking on meaning if people are to be optimally effective in diagnosing and solving problems. In this chapter we will look at a wider pattern of variables and patterns.

A *third question:* What are the origins of these functional and dysfunctional aspects of organizational culture? Some of the factors that can influence a specific culture might be the philosophy and behavior of the present (or past) CEO, the organization's history of successes and failures (Schwartz & Davis, 1981, p. 35), the values held by employees (new employees may differ in their's), and personnel policies and practices pertaining to such matters as recruitment and selection, training, appraisal, and reward. In the *Executive Suite* vignette, the overemphasis on written reports apparently stemmed from the chairman's emphasis, some years past, on documentation. Some sense of the origin of various aspects of organizational culture can be useful in planning how to change those that are dysfunctional and keeping those that are functional.

The *fourth question* is as follows: How can we change organizational culture, assuming we want to do so? This we will address in Chapter 15, "Organizational Change Processes," and Chapter 16, "Organizational Improvement Strategies." To give a preliminary response to the question, however, and to be only partly facetious, we will suggest two answers: *Carefully,* and *slowly.* Organizational culture—in particular, basic assumptions held by organizational members—helps "to avoid or reduce anxiety by reducing uncertainty and cognitive overload" (Schein, 1981, p. 22). The organization itself is seen by some psychoanalytic theorists, as a defense mechanism against anxieties (Faucheux, Amado, & Laurent, 1982, p. 372). If these statements are true, trying to make changes in organizations is likely to raise anxieties and create resistance. We will say more about this in subsequent chapters.

SOME EXAMPLES OF DIFFERENT ORGANIZATIONAL CULTURES

Pascale and Athos (1981) provide us with some interesting examples of organizational culture in their book, *The Art of Japanese Management,* which is really about both American and Japanese firms. They pay particular attention to Matsushita Electric Company, whose products appear under such brand names as Panasonic and Quasar, to International Telephone and Telegraph (ITT), and to United Airlines. We will not attempt to summarize all of the rich detail they provide, which includes such important aspects as product and marketing strategy, but will focus primarily on philosophy and practices pertaining to human resources.

As is often the case, the values, beliefs, assumptions, and norms in these companies must be inferred to a certain extent. In some instances, however, the governing values and beliefs are stated overtly. This is the case with Matsushita.

Under the guidance of founder Konosuke Matsushita, Matsushita Electric considers people to be the most critical resource. This attitude is reflected in certain practices: the headquarters staff maintaining active interest in, and involvement with, recruitment, hiring, and promotions; a heavy emphasis put on both job-skills training and training in Matsushita values. Harmony, cooperation, fairness, and "struggle for betterment" are values openly expounded and practiced.

While there are strong financial and planning controls, divisional managers have wide latitude to be entrepreneurs. Financial controllers in each of the divisions report jointly to the division manager and to corporate headquarters and are evaluated on how well the division does. Division managers meet on a quarterly basis and share their operating results with each other and top management. Although performance ranking is evident in the order in which presentations are made (the outstanding ones go first), no one is otherwise deliberately singled out or embarrassed. Troubleshooting sessions with subordinates involve much probing and the asking of difficult questions, but these interventions are seen as, and intended to be, training-and-development experiences for subordinates. *Acceptance time* is built into discussions so that conflict between points of view can be worked through.

The firm essentially adheres to a concept of lifetime employment. People who are not performing well are likely to be asked to analyze where else they might better contribute to the organization, if on-the-job corrections and coaching do not suffice. Thus, planned transfer is used instead of discharge. Praise and positive reinforcements such as recognition are used extensively. Employee recommendations are viewed as vital for making product and shop-floor improvements. The firm has been very successful, and is seen by Pascale and Athos as having high resiliency and ability to replicate itself in the growth of new divisions.

ITT, in the era when Harold Geneen was CEO, is described as having a very different culture. We will focus only on some of the more salient differences that contrasted ITT with Matsushita. At ITT, there was much stronger emphasis on systematic employee evaluation and the bonus system for the top 500 managers and staff members, and less emphasis on training and management development. Controllers reported directly to corporate headquarters to assist Geneen in a multiple-source information-reporting system. Conflicting information and points of view flowed to the top to be reconciled by Geneen.

Great value was placed on producing *unshakeable facts*. The top 50 managers from all over the world were regularly assembled by Geneen for reporting purposes. These meetings were essentially interrogations by Geneen and his headquarters staff. An important dynamic in these meetings seems to have been fear of being humiliated or punished. Inadequate performance throughout the managerial ranks was typically handled by discharge. ITT, as described by Pascale and Athos, was highly successful in an economic sense during Geneen's tenure, but it's fortunes declined significantly after his retirement. Geneen was not seen as successful in building a corporation that could persist at a high level of performance. Further, the authors see a great deal of wasteful conflict between line and staff people during those years, wasted time at meetings when Geneen was not there to run them, and lack of development of senior executives who could take over the corporation. Turnover was very high in the executive ranks.

During the period when Ed Carlson was president of United Airlines, strong emphasis was placed on financial results and the development of people, but also on employee satisfaction. Carlson spent a great deal of time traveling, meeting with, and listening to people from all ranks and specialties in the organization. Meetings with groups of top managers were frequently used to generate ideas and to develop a consensus approach to strategy. *Base touching*—checking out an idea with a lot of people—became standard practice. (See vignette NETMA, Chapter 5.)

Task forces, comprised of people representing different departments, were used to make major studies and make recommendations for change; for example, in the accounting system. Retention of executives was valued, but rotation of executives was used to develop generalists whose perspective extended beyond one specialty. A team approach, consensus decision making, and sensitivity to people were valued. Disagreement was encouraged, but in a way that people would, according to Carlson's rule, "disagree without being disagreeable." Carlson and United Airlines were seen as highly successful during Carlson's tenure by Pascale and Athos, but less than fully successful in establishing the conditions that would perpetuate the culture. Carlson's successor behaved differently, and some of the patterns, such as listening and accessibility, began to break down.

While the above descriptions are not complete, they do permit us to begin making inferences about the differing values, beliefs, assumptions, and norms in these different organizations. For example, strong values pertaining to the development of people were evident at Matsushita and United Airlines; high value was placed on unshakeable facts at ITT. Some values were overtly stated and taught; for example, the values of harmony and cooperation at Matsushita. In each case, these differing features of organizational culture contributed to a unique fabric of management practices and participant sentiments, attitudes, activities, and interactions.

Frequently, organizational culture can only be inferred, because basic values, beliefs, assumptions, and norms have not been articulated. One study found less than one-third of nearly 80 companies studied to have beliefs that were clearly articulated (Deal & Kennedy, 1982, p. 7). However, a sizable number of organizations do have well-developed statements of management philosophy, or mission statements, or statements in manuals about "how we work" that include clear value statements. For example, Hewlett-Packard's statement of corporate objectives includes these statements pertaining to "Our People": "The company has been built around the individual, the personal dignity of each, and the recognition of personal achievements . . . the opportunity to share in the success of the company is evidenced by our above-average wage and salary level, our profit-sharing and stock purchase plans . . . The objective of job security is

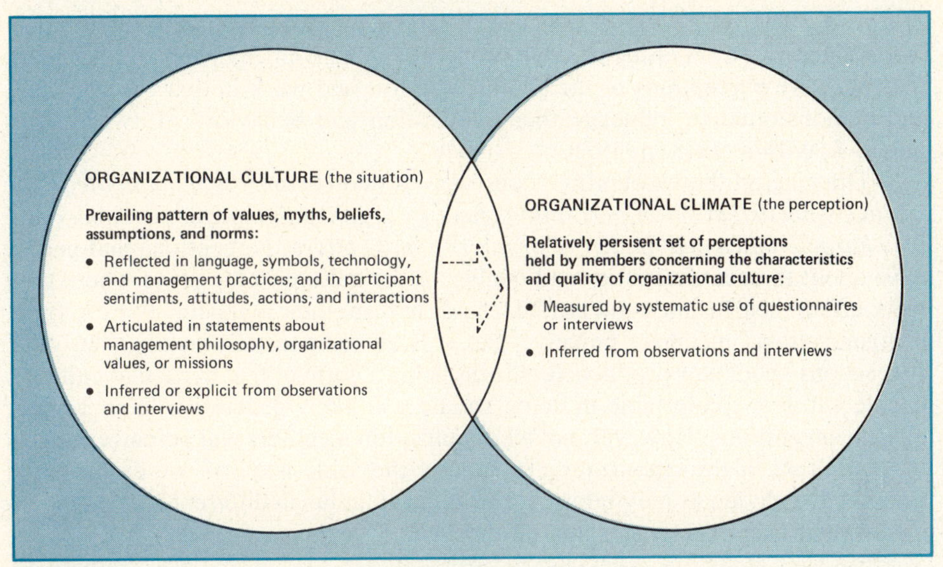

FIGURE 14.1 The Relationship of Organizational Culture and Climate

illustrated by our policy of avoiding large ups and downs in our production schedules'' (Ouchi, 1981, p. 230).

ORGANIZATIONAL CLIMATE: THE CONCEPT

Organizational climate is less encompassing than the concept of organizational culture and is more readily measured. Organizational climate is how organization members perceive (see and feel about) the culture that has been created and perpetuated in their unit or organization. (See Figure 14.1 for a diagram showing the relationship of the two concepts.)

Conceptualization and research about the concept of organizational climate has been sufficient for it to have considerable utility in understanding human behavior in organizations. Further ''research has demonstrated that climate dramatically affects not only the people but also the performance and growth of the organization'' (Litwin, Humphrey & Wilson 1978, p. 87). We will focus on the conceptualizations provided by Renato Taguiri, George Litwin and colleagues (1965), and Rensis Likert and his colleagues (1961, 1967, 1976). A number of other authors and researchers have conceptualizations that are comparable (Payne & Pugh, 1976, pp. 1125–1173; Campbell, Dunnette, Lawler, & Weick, 1970, p. 393; Schneider, 1975; and DeCotiis & Koys, 1980).

Organizational climate has been defined as ''a relatively enduring quality of the internal environment of an organization that (a) is experienced by its members, (b) influences their behavior, and (c) can be described in terms of the values of a particular set of characteristics (or attributes) of the organization'' (Taguiri

& Litwin, 1965, p. 27). In a similar, but later definition, organizational climate was defined as "a set of measurable properties of a given environment, based on the collective perceptions of the people who live and work in that environment, and demonstrated to influence their motivation and behavior" (Litwin, Humphrey, & Wilson, 1978, p. 187).

Drawing on these definitions, our view is that *organizational climate is the relatively persistent set of perceptions held by organization members concerning the characteristics and quality of organizational culture.* Perceptions that people have about the characteristics and quality of the culture in the place where they work affect their feelings and attitudes and, in turn, their behavior. For example, if organizational members perceive that it is all right to risk making "far out" suggestions about new products (boldness being a norm of that particular culture), people will feel comfortable in doing so and will likely generate a large number of such suggestions. However, not all organization members will perceive aspects of the culture of the organization in exactly the same way. As we discussed in Chapter 5, individuals may interpret the same stimulus in different ways depending on their past experiences and on their value systems.

HOW ORGANIZATIONAL CLIMATE IS MEASURED

In their early research, Litwin and Stringer (1968) measured climate by asking organization members to respond to questionnaire items pertaining to nine categories. Although they refer to these categories as assessing "feelings," in reality they seem to be perceptions that are likely to have feeling or attitudinal overtones (pp. 81–82). Perceptions and feelings are obviously interrelated; perceptions give rise to feelings, and feelings affect perceptions. The categories are:

1. *Structure*—the feeling that employees have about the constraints in the group—how many rules, regulations, procedures there are; is there an emphasis on red tape and going through channels, or is there a loose and informal atmosphere?
2. *Responsibility*—the feeling of being your own boss; not having to double check all your decisions; when you have a job to do, knowing that it is *your job*.
3. *Reward*—the feeling of being rewarded for a job done; emphasizing positive rewards rather than punishments; the perceived fairness of the pay and promotion policies.
4. *Risk*—the sense of riskiness and challenge in the job and in the organization; is there an emphasis on taking calculated risks, or is playing it safe the best way to operate.
5. *Warmth*—the feeling of general good fellowship that prevails in the work group atmosphere; the emphasis on being well liked; the prevalence of friendly and informal social groups.
6. *Support*—the perceived helpfulness of the managers and other employees in the group, emphasis on mutual support from above and below.

7. *Standards*—the perceived importance of implicit and explicit goals and performance standards; the emphasis on doing a good job; the challenge represented in personal and group goals.
8. *Conflict*—the feeling that managers and other workers *want* to hear different opinions; the emphasis placed on getting problems out in the open, rather than smoothing them over or ignoring them.
9. *Identity*—the feeling that you belong to a company and you are a valuable member of a working team; the importance placed on this kind of spirit.

These categories are then used to develop some 50 specific items for a questionnaire. For each item, a four-point scale of *definitely agree, inclined to agree, inclined to disagree,* and *definitely disagree* is used (Muchinsky, 1976, p. 373). When administered to the members of an organization, or to those in some major unit of an organization, the tabulated results are then considered to be a measure of the perceived climate of that organization or unit at that point in time.

Climate questionnaires administered in the organizations featured in the vignettes at the beginning of the chapter would provide more extensive data than the situation as seen through the eyes of one person. In the *JIC File* vignette, for example, it appears that we might find a widespread pattern of emphasizing punishment, lack of risk taking, lack of warmth and support, and a great deal of submerged conflict. If there is such a pattern, the division is probably paying a big price for it in terms of motivation and morale. If we are to trust Margaret's perceptions in *The Team* vignette, we could expect that a climate survey would show a pattern of extensive support and warmth, a healthy sense of identity, a working-through approach to conflict, and, quite likely, a sharing of high standards. Such information could be important to the department head and department members, giving them an understanding of some of the basic strengths of the system.

The Survey of Organizations and Systems 1–4

The dimensions included by Rensis Likert and others to measure the human/social characteristics of organizations include, in large part, the dimensions assessed by the Litwin and Stringer categories. The long form of the Likert questionnaire has 105 items and is called the *Survey of Organizations*. The survey includes categories pertaining to leadership, organizational climate, and satisfaction, as shown in Figure 14.2. Items relating to the first two categories can be considered largely under the category of organizational climate, because they relate to perceptions of organizational phenomena. The items included in the satisfaction category, however, are not climate categories, strictly speaking, because they focus more on the feeling or attitude results of climate.

A short questionnaire based on the survey is shown in Figure 14.3. It is largely an organizational climate questionnaire. The profiles shown are the aggregate perceptions of the top 52 managers of a plant, at two different times, of the climate created by a plant manager (Likert & Likert, 1976, p. 75).

The *Survey of Organizations,* as well as the shorter forms, are used to

Leadership

1. Managerial support
2. Managerial goal emphasis
3. Managerial work facilitation
4. Managerial interaction facilitation
5. Peer support
6. Peer goal-emphasis
7. Peer work facilitation
8. Peer interaction facilitation

Organizational Climate

9. Communication with company
10. Motivation
11. Decision-making
12. Control within company
13. Coordination between departments
14. General management

Satisfaction

15. Satisfaction with company
16. Satisfaction with supervisor
17. Satisfaction with job
18. Satisfaction with pay
19. Satisfaction with work group

FIGURE 14.2 Dimensions of the Survey of Organizations Questionnaire. **Source:** James C. Taylor and David G. Bowers, *Survey of Organizations: A Machine-Scored Standardized Questionnaire Instrument,* Institute for Social Research (Ann Arbor, Mich.: University of Michigan, 1972), pp. 3-4. © 1972. Reprinted by permission.

assess the degree to which organizations are perceived as System 1 as opposed to System 2, System 3, or System 4, all of which are classification types of organizations that can be applied by the people employed in them. (See the labels at the top of the four columns in Figure 14.3.) In his earlier writings, Likert called these types *Exploitive Authoritative, Benevolent Authoritative, Consultative,* and *Participative Group*. In later works, only the Systems 1–4 terms were used, probably because of the heavily evaluative connotations of the other terms.

Some would argue that the terminology of some of the scales is also too value laden. This argument suggests that the wording of the scales might be inducing respondents, if asked, to indicate that they would prefer the climate to shift toward the right hand side of the scale. This is one of the reasons why some organization improvement approaches feature thorough group discussions, unit by unit, with all of those who participated in the survey centered on what the patterns of responses mean and what the implications might be. (See the "Survey Feedback" section in Chapter 16.)

In the Likert model, each type of organization (Systems 1–4) is seen as having internally consistent characteristics of which organizational climate is a major part. A description of each type of system follows. (This discussion is

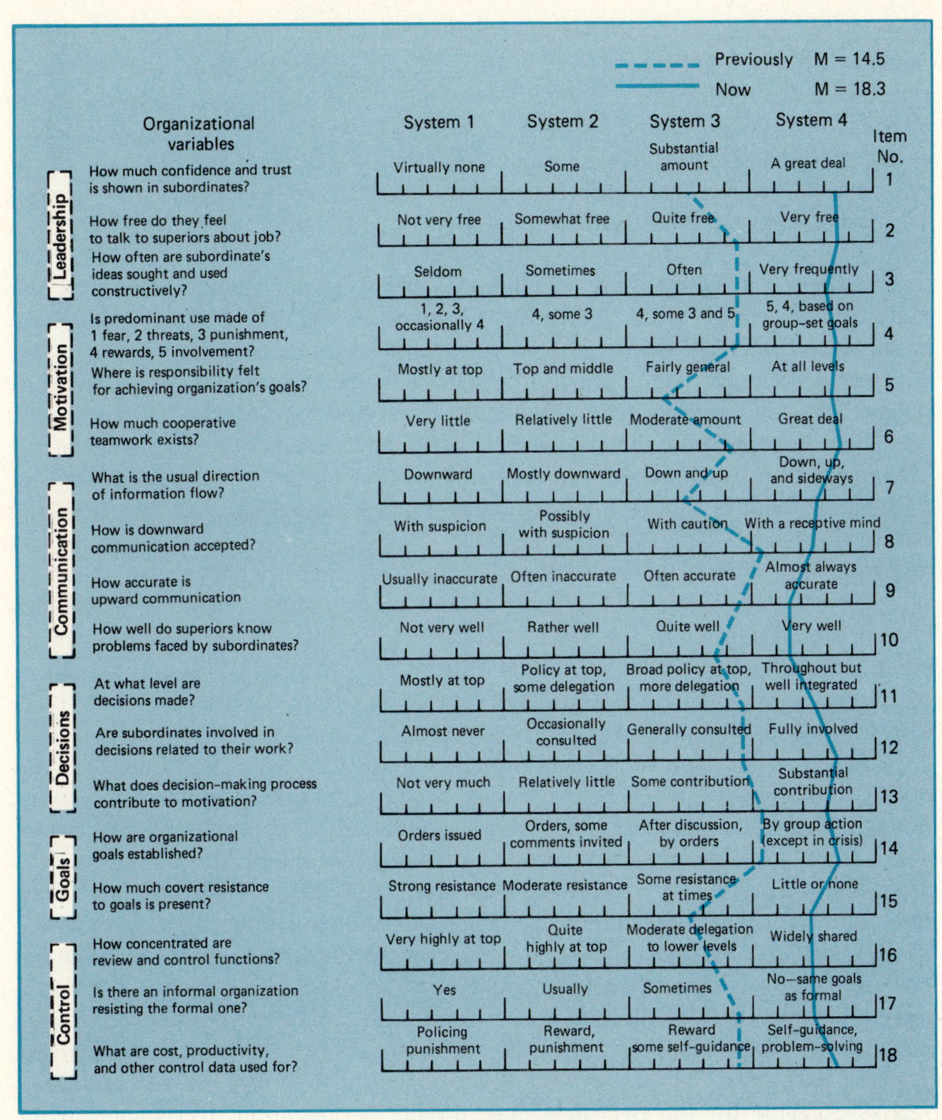

FIGURE 14.3 Profile of Organizational Climate at Different Time Periods. **Source:** Rensis Likert and Jane Gibson Likert, *New Ways of Managing Conflict.* (New York: McGraw-Hill, 1976), p. 75. © Reprinted with permission.

based on the questionnaires in Likert & Likert, 1976, pp. 21–32; Likert, 1967, pp. 3–10; Likert, 1961, pp. 223–233; and Bowers, 1976, pp. 101–107.)

In the System 1 type of organization, control, goal setting, and decision making are concentrated at the top. There is practically no seeking of subordinates' ideas, and subordinates are not involved in decisions related to their work.

In general, little or no confidence is shown in subordinates. Extensive use is made of threats, punishment, and fear. Cost and productivity data are used for policing and punishment. Communication is largely downward. There is little lateral communication and upward communication is minimal and frequently distorted. Mistrust, hostility, and dissatisfaction are extensive, and there is considerable resistance in the informal system to the directives of the formal organization. Teamwork is essentially nonexistent. Motivation, except at the top, is low.

System 2 is slightly more participative. In this system, control and direction and decision making are perceived as largely concentrated at the top but there is some delegating of decision making relative to implementing policies; some comment is invited about organizational goals. Subordinates' ideas are sometimes sought and subordinates are occasionally consulted before decisions are made about their work. Communication is mostly downward, there is some lateral communication; and upward communication is frequently filtered for superiors. Some confidence is shown in subordinates, but it tends to be of a condescending nature. Extensive use is made of monetary awards; some use is made of threats and punishment, but there is generally less fear than in System 1. Cost and productivity data are used for rewards and punishments. There is sometimes considerable hostility in the organization, but at times favorable attitudes do exist. Generally, there is substantial dissatisfaction, with and considerable covert resistance to, the formal system. Little teamwork exists. Motivation is relatively low, but higher than in System 1.

System 3 is significantly more participative than Systems 1 and 2. Broad policy is decided at the top, but there is substantial delegation of decision making down through the organization. Goals are formulated at the top after consultation. There is moderate delegation of review and control activities. Subordinates' ideas are usually sought, and subordinates are generally consulted about decisions related to their work. Substantial confidence is shown in subordinates. Communication tends to be both downward and upward without much distortion; lateral communication is common and encouraged. Extensive use is made of involvement and rewards as motivating forces, and little use is made of fear. Cost and productivity data and other controls are used for rewards and some self-guidance. There is little hostility, and attitudes are generally favorable; most individuals feel responsible for the overall welfare of the organization. Resistance in the informal system is generally low. Teamwork exists in moderate amounts.

System 4 is the most participative and is highly group-process oriented. As viewed by organization members, goals are established through participation and many decisions are made by consensus. Group interaction is facilitated by superiors who are the linking pins between work groups and by task force members from various relevant units. Subordinates' ideas are sought as a matter of course and they are fully involved in decisions related to their work. A high level of confidence is shown in subordinates. Communication flow is downward, upward, and lateral, and there is little distortion. No use is made of coercion or fear, and high motivation is based on extensive involvement, group goals, and compensation systems developed through participation. Cost, productivity, and other control data are used for self-guidance and problem solving. Attitudes are generally quite favorable. People at all levels feel responsible for achieving the organization's goals and there is little or no covert resistance to unit goals and policies. Teamwork is evident throughout the organization.

Each of these systems works, although there is considerable evidence to show that System 1 organizations usually pay a heavy price in terms of resistance of all kinds and low morale and commitment. In general, there is more and more expectation among managers and employees alike that organizations should shift toward Systems 3 or 4 modes in contrast to System 1.

SOME KEY QUESTIONS ABOUT ORGANIZATIONAL CLIMATE

Research suggests that there are some important contingencies, such as technology and mission, to be considered relative to organizational climate. For example, research in less effective and more effective manufacturing plants (two of each) and in less effective and more effective research laboratories (three of each) found that the more effective in each category of organization shared certain patterns of characteristics. The more effective manufacturing plants had a relatively high degree of structure, a directive supervisory style, and influence mostly concentrated at the top, in contrast to the less effective plants. The more effective research laboratories, in contrast to the less effective, showed a relatively low degree of structure, a participative style of supervision, and a broad distribution of influence (Lorsch & Morse, 1974, pp. 80–83, 105–107). In all of the effective organizations, in contrast to the less effective, organizational members displayed considerable skill in working through conflict (French & Bell, 1984, p. 263). Thus, it may be that there is an optimal pattern of the exercise of authority and influence and of decision making for organizations depending upon the business they are in and what technology is being used.

Therefore, the key question for managers may not be: Do we have a System 1 or a System 4? The key question may be: Does the culture we have and its reflection in climate measures contribute appropriately to the outcomes we want? Some of the important subquestions for a particular organization, then, are: What kind of a climate do we have?; What are the consequences for us?; What kind of a culture—values, beliefs, assumptions, and norms—do we have that contributes to the climate we have?; What do we want to change? Organizational climate surveys, followed by extensive dialogue about the results, can make a major contribution to the answering of these questions. As Litwin and colleagues say, such a process "does not purport to tell managers how to manage":

> It does not say that they should be . . . "System 4," "participative," "authentic," or whatever. The manager determines the kind of climate required for high performance, receives specific data on where his or her unit stands in relation to the required climate, and chooses from a variety

> of actions those necessary to achieve this requirement (Litwin, Humphrey, & Wilson, 1978, p. 205).

We will describe this process further in Chapter 16 under the topic of "Survey Feedback."

ORGANIZATIONAL CLIMATE STUDIES

The concept of organizational climate is sufficiently practical for many organizations to use climate surveys. There is a growing trend for organizations to use climate surveys at regular intervals to identify problem areas, to assess trends, and to measure progress in improving climate. Some of the latter kinds of studies have been published, and we will report briefly on two. One study is a report on a quality of work life (QWL) project at a General Motors' plant. The other is an earlier study of a comprehensive organization improvement effort at the Weldon Company.

GM's Lakewood Plant

In 1969, in collaboration with the Institute for Social Research at the University of Michigan, General Motors surveyed organizational climate and performance indicators of two plants, Doraville and Lakewood (Dowling, 1975, pp. 23–38; Likert & Likert, 1976, pp. 71–86). As was suspected, the measures confirmed that Doraville was a "sweetheart" operation, while Lakewood was a "disaster" in terms of productivity, quality, costs, and labor relations. Organizational climate measures indicated that Doraville was essentially a System 4 operation, while Lakewood was a System 2 organization. The manager at Doraville, who had been successful in helping improve the plant's performance, was transferred to Lakewood to try to repeat the success. A number of changes were initiated under the new plant manager.

First, training sessions were held for managers and supervisors in such areas as team building (see Chapter 16), goal setting, and communications. Teamwork, mutual understanding, and trust were stressed. Training for all employees was made available and encouraged.

Second, hourly employees were regularly provided information on plant operations and problems, including data on labor costs, quality and efficiency, plans for future products or changes in facilities, and data comparing costs at Lakewood with other plants.

Third, the foreman's job was redefined to put more emphasis on direct contact with subordinates. Each foreman was provided with a *utility trainer* to assist with such matters as picking up supplies and tools from storerooms, trouble shooting, training new employees, and controlling salvage.

Fourth, about one year before a new model of automobile was to go into production, employees were provided with detailed information about both the new model and the facilities changes that would be required. Employees were then encouraged to participate in planning changes in work flow, physical arrangements, and job design.

As typically found in such projects (Bowers, 1976, pp. 95–100), productivity and costs deteriorated during the first few months as the human organization was improving.

> The reason seems to be a combination of factors: First, improvements in the human organization required initially heavy dollar outlays in increased manpower and training and facility changes. Second, and more important, it simply takes time for improvement management practices to be reflected in improved employee attitudes, and still more time for these improved attitudes to be reflected in improved performance (Dowling, 1975, p. 29).
>
> Over a three-year period, however, substantial improvements in productivity, costs, profits, and organizational climate occurred at the Lakewood plant. Improvements in labor efficiency alone resulted in a $5-million . . . savings (Likert & Likert, 1976, p. 74).

The Weldon Company Research

Other interesting longitudinal research has been done using the Systems 1–4 conceptualization and its organizational climate aspects. One detailed and careful study compared two manufacturing companies and spanned a number of years. (This discussion is based on Marrow, Bowers & Seashore, 1967; Seashore & Bowers, 1970, pp. 227–233; and Likert & Likert, 1976, p. 86).

The Harwood Manufacturing Company purchased its major competitor, the Weldon Company. The companies had striking similarities; they both manufactured pajamas, employed about 1,000 people, had similar volumes, were single-plant operations about thirty years old, had similar growth histories, had good reputations in the industry, and were family owned and managed. But the similarities ended there. At the time of purchase, Harwood was aspiring to be a System 4 organization—participative, open, and team-oriented—and, in the eyes of employees, had largely attained this objective. The Weldon Company, on the other hand, had not formulated a desired organizational system, but was de facto a System 1 or 2 organization with a management style and organizational processes perceived to be autocratic, secretive, and obedience oriented (see Figure 14.4).

The Harwood Company was in sound shape generally—a relatively high return on investment, low absenteeism and turnover, and high productivity. Weldon was in deep trouble—the company was losing money, absenteeism and turnover were high, and productivity was low. The new owners determined to correct the problems at Weldon partly by gradually shifting the organization from System 1 toward System 4. Leadership style and the resulting organizational climate were to be major aspects of the shift. The change program had three main phases although there was considerable overlap.

The *first phase* of the change effort was called protecting the human investment and commenced with assurances to affected employees that operations would continue and that there were no immediate plans to terminate any em-

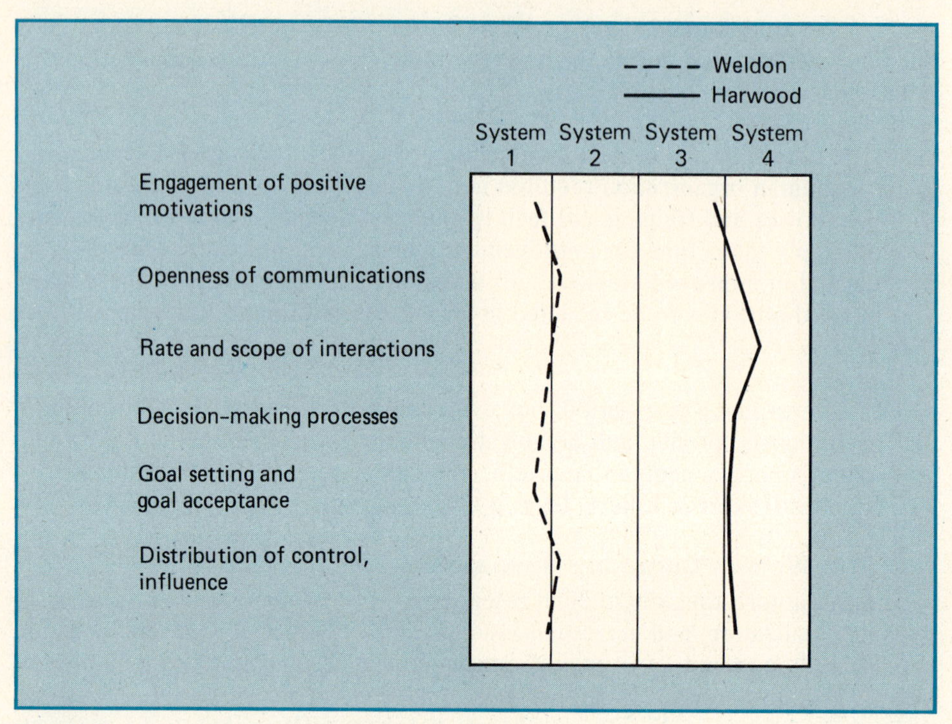

FIGURE 14.4 Operating Characteristics: Harwood and Weldon, 1962. **Source:** Alfred J. Marrow, David G. Bowers, and Stanley E. Seashore, *Management by Participation.* (New York: Harper & Row, 1967), p. 56. Reprinted with permission.

ployees. A personnel department was formed and an experienced personnel manager was hired. All Weldon supervisors and managers were interviewed about matters such as morale and interpersonal relations; and a climate survey was conducted among nonsupervisory employees.

In the *second phase,* the plant was converted to a *unit system of production* from a plantwide mixed-batch system. Other changes included revision of record systems and a restructuring of the shipping department and the cutting room. Work standards and incentive pay were introduced in the latter two departments, with some eventual termination of employees who were chronically substandard performers and who were excessively absent.

The *third phase* was aimed directly at shifting toward a more *participative mode* and attempting to create a System 4 organizational climate. This was accomplished through the help of consultant-facilitators, by top managers and consultants using participative approaches, by providing training programs for supervisors and managers in participative approaches, and by emphasizing group problem solving at all levels. There was a conscious effort to distribute influence and responsibility downward throughout the organization.

After two years, a number of significant improvements had been made. A sharp rise in profits at Weldon had occurred, production efficiency was up significantly; and both operator turnover and absenteeism had declined substantially. Employees had a more positive view of the company and were more satisfied with their pay in spite of feeling that they were working harder. Paradoxically, there was a decrease in satisfaction with their immediate supervisors in terms of goal emphasis and work facilitation, but questionnaires indicated that, overall, operators were experiencing more support, more goal emphasis (things done by supervisors to stimulate enthusiasm for the tasks to be done), and more work facilitation (things to help the employee get the job done) from the supervisory/engineering/managerial/consulting staff in general. The organization had shifted significantly from a System 1 organization to a System 3 organization.

After another five years, a follow-up study found these changes to have been sustained or enhanced, including improvements in profits and productivity. Further, satisfaction with immediate superiors was substantially higher in terms of both goal emphasis and work facilitation (Seashore & Bowers, 1970).

We interpret these two research studies to mean, in part, that a participative, supportive, yet challenging leadership style, when coupled with certain other conditions, can produce improvements in both organizational climate and productivity in manufacturing plants. The style needs to be pervasive and sustained, and reinforced by such support as appropriate engineering help, and by training in both technical skills and group process matters. The improved organizational climate appears to be linked to improvements in organizational outcomes, including effectiveness, efficiency, participant satisfaction, and individual and group development.

ORGANIZATIONAL CLIMATE IN SUBUNITS

While organizational climate is usually considered in the context of the total organization, it can also be helpful to think of it in terms of various subunits of the organization (Johnston, 1970, pp. 95–103). Each supervisor or manager is likely to have some control over the rules and procedures within the unit, the extent to which he or she delegates, the recognition given people, the warmth and support extended to people, and the expected levels of performance.

Thus, there can be subclimates in the organization, and each individual manager can have a strategy for moving toward a particular climate. We need to recognize, however, that managerial practices at the top are particularly powerful in establishing organizational climate, and that it is very difficult for an individual supervisor to depart very far from the culture created at the top. This is borne out by research results indicating that, while there can be differences between units, there is typically a great deal of consistency as to climate within the total organization (Drexler, 1977; Jones & James, 1979).

Further, the concept of climate can be extended to perceptions by such important groups as customers and suppliers. For example, customers in a department store will be more likely to come back if treated with warmth and support. Bank customers who perceive a positive service climate are less likely to take their accounts to another bank (Schneider, 1980, p. 63). Organizational climate, then, has implications beyond the boundaries of a particular unit or organization.

PRACTICAL APPLICATIONS OF THE CONCEPTS

It appears that the culture of an organization and perceptions of people in organizations as to that culture are associated with important consequences. Although there is some overlap in the concepts, organizational culture—that is, the prevailing pattern of values, myths, beliefs, assumptions, and norms—leads to or contributes to a pattern of perceptions that can be called organizational climate. Perceptions about such aspects as the degree of participation, the degree of support on the part of supervisors, the friendliness of people, standards, and the way conflict is handled in the organization, are all a reflection of organizational culture and seem to be associated with human satisfactions. When coupled with skill training and appropriate technical and managerial support, positive assessments of these climate conditions by employees appear to be associated with relatively high productivity and quality.

It also appears that some climate characteristics tend to cluster together. Organizational climate dimensions such as perceived confidence shown in subordinates, the way control data are used, and the accuracy of upward communication tend to be mutually reinforcing. Managers need to tackle many dimensions simultaneously, although gradually, if they wish to make significant changes.

The concept of organizational culture directs our attention to that pattern of fundamental values, myths, beliefs, assumptions, and norms that exist in an organization. Organizational culture has powerful consequences in terms of influence on individual and group behavior and on organizational performance. A wise top management group will periodically examine the culture of its organization to assess its functionality and dysfunctionality in terms of present and future challenges and opportunities.

We think that there is enough evidence to support the usefulness of the organizational climate concept to suggest that managers would do well to take periodic climate readings. We want to add a major proviso, however: Managers must also be prepared to work skillfully with subordinates in making improvements suggested by such readings. Asking people to give their perceptions of how things are going in the organization and then not using this information is to raise expectations and then create resentment and cynicism.

SO WHAT? IMPLICATIONS FOR YOU

Here are some implications in more detail:

As a Member of the Organization

Generalizations	Implications
1. Organizational culture is the basic pattern of values, myths, beliefs, assumptions, and norms that is fundamental to the behavior of people in the organization.	1. You are not likely to make major changes in organization culture single-handedly; the fabric probably has enough functionality to it so that changes will be strongly resisted.

Generalizations	Implications
2. Organizational culture and climate factors can affect your job performance and satisfaction.	2. When applying for a job, try to tune into the prevailing culture and climate and assess what its effect on you is likely to be.
3. Organizational climate is largely created and sustained by management practices.	3. If you see climate aspects in your organization that are dysfunctional, consider discussing them with your superior.
4. Nonmanagers also have influence on climate.	4. Your behavior toward other employees—for example, the friendliness and support shown to co-workers and superiors—will influence climate and, thus, organizational results.

As a Current or Future Manager

Generalizations	Implications
1. Consciously or unconsciously, organizational culture is created by organizational members, with the values, philosophy, beliefs, assumptions, and norms of top management playing a dominant role.	1. Organizational culture can be changed. A fundamental place to start is (a) through a description of that culture and an analysis of its functional and dysfunctional aspects; (b) through an exploration of what culture you wish to help create and sustain.
2. Management practices largely create the quality of the climate that exists in organizations.	2. Do not treat organizational climate as a given. Think about the climate you want to create and sustain in your unit. Develop a strategy for saying and doing things that are consistent with creating that climate.
3. Organizational climate can be measured. Periodic surveys can help measure trends and serve as a basis for diagnosing problems and for dialogue.	3. Consider measuring climate periodically; but be prepared to take action or resentment will result. You may be able to have considerable influence on top management in encouraging them to take a periodic reading on the climate in the organization and to make plans to help

Generalizations	Implications
	shift the climate in desired directions. At the least, you may be able to obtain their support for you to survey climate in your unit.
4. The different types of organizations—for example, Systems 1 through 4—tend to have internally consistent characteristics that reinforce each other.	4. To shift from System 2 to System 4 requires simultaneous attention to a wide range of organizational variables, including leadership style, training in participative skills, and changes in reward and control systems.
5. Typically, there are some differences in organizational climates between subunits of organizations.	5. You will have some influence, perhaps considerable, over the climate in your unit, but there are likely to be some limits on your ability to make changes, largely because of the climate created by the top managers of the organization.
6. The higher you go in the organization, the more influence you will have on organizational culture and climate.	6. The higher you go, the more important it is that you periodically review your fundamental values, beliefs, and assumptions about managing people and assess the consequences in terms of the climate that is being created.

LEARNING APPLICATION ACTIVITIES

1. Write a vignette based on your experience that describes some aspects of the culture of an organization. In particular, focus on values, beliefs, norms. Speculate on the source (driving forces) of the prevailing norms. List ways that cultural aspects (values, beliefs, norms) were (a) functional or (b) dysfunctional for the organization.

2. Write a vignette based on your experience that describes the organizational climate of an organization. Be prepared to comment, in class discussion of the vignette, in what ways the climate of the organization seemed to affect the behavior of organizational members.

3. Review the *Executive Suite* vignette.

a. What aspects of the culture of this particular organization were probably functional and what aspects dysfunctional for the corporation?

b. What aspects were probably functional and what aspects were dysfunctional for Irv Green's career?

c. Compare and contrast your answers to (a) and (b).

4. Review the *Power Politics* vignette and, using Litwin and Stringer's categories, analyze the organizational climate of the Morrison Company.

5. *Step 1:* Use Likert's descriptions of System 1 through 4 to analyze Matsushita, United Airlines, and ITT as described in the chapter.

Step 2: Share your analysis in a group with four or five colleagues and focus on similarities and differences between companies.

Step 3: Report the highlights of your group discussion to the class.

6. List the purposes for which the organizational climate questionnaires appear to have been used at (a) the Lakewood Plant of General Motors and (b) the Weldon Company. Compare the lists; discuss any differences.

REFERENCES

Baker, Edwin L. "Managing Organizational Culture." *Management Review* 69/7 (July 1980): 8–13.

Bowers, David G. *Systems of Organization*. Ann Arbor, Mich.: University of Michigan Press, 1976.

Campbell, John P., Marvin D. Dunnette, Edward E. Lawler III, and Karl E. Weick, Jr. *Managerial Behavior, Performance, and Effectiveness*. New York: McGraw-Hill, 1970.

Deal, Terrence E., and Allan A. Kennedy. *Corporate Cultures: The Rites and Rituals of Corporate Life*. Reading, Mass.: Addison-Wesley, 1982.

Dowling, William F. "At General Motors: System 4 Builds Performance and Profits." *Organizational Dynamics* 4 (Winter, 1975): 23–38.

Drexler, John A., Jr. "Organizational Climate: Its Homogeneity Within Organizations." *Journal of Applied Psychology* 62 (February 1977): 38–42.

DeCotiis, Thomas A., and Daniel J. Koys. "The Identification and Measurement of the Dimensions of Organizational Climate." *Proceedings, Academy of Management,* 1980, pp. 171–175.

Faucheux, Claude, Gilles Amado, and Andre Laurent. "Organizational Development and Change." In Mark R. Rosenzweig and Lyman W. Porter (Eds.), *Annual Review of Psychology* 33 (1982): 343–370.

French, Wendell L., and Cecil H. Bell, Jr. *Organization Development: Behavioral Science Interventions for Organization Improvement,* 3d ed. Englewood Cliffs, N.J. Prentice-Hall, 1984.

Johnston, H. Russel. "A New Conceptualization of Source of Organizational Climate." *Administrative Science Quarterly* 21 (March 1970): 95–103.

Jones, Allan P., and Lawrence R. James, "Psychological Climate," *Organizational Behavior and Human Performance,* 23 (April 1979): 201–250.

Kroeber, A. L., and Clyde Kluckhohn. *Culture: A Critical Review of Concepts and Definitions*. New York: Random House, 1952.

Likert, Rensis. *New Patterns of Management*. New York: McGraw-Hill, 1961.

______. *The Human Organization: Its Management and Value*. New York: McGraw-Hill, 1967.

Likert, Rensis, and Jane Gibson Likert. *New Ways of Managing Conflict*. New York: McGraw-Hill, 1976.

Litwin, George H., John W. Humphrey, and Thomas B. Wilson. "Organizational Climate: A Proven Tool for Improving Performance. In W. Warner Burke (Ed.), *The Cutting*

Edge: Current Theory and Practice in Organization Development. La Jolla, Calif.: University Associates, 1978, pp. 187–205.

Litwin, George H., and Robert A. Stringer, Jr. *Motivation and Organizational Climate*. Boston, Mass.: Graduate School of Business Administration, Harvard University, 1968.

Lorsch, Jay W., and John J. Morse. *Organizations and Their Members: A Contingency Approach*. New York: Harper & Row, 1974.

Marrow, Alfred J., David G. Bowers, and Stanley E. Seashore. *Management by Participation: Creating a Climate for Personal and Organizational Development*. New York: Harper & Row, 1967.

Muchinsky, Paul M. "An Assessment of the Litwin and Stringer Organizational Climate Questionnaire." *Personnel Psychology* 29/3 (Autumn 1976): 371–392.

Ouchi, William G. *Theory Z: How American Business Can Meet the Japanese Challenge*. Reading, Mass.: Addison-Wesley, 1981.

Pascale, Richard T., and Anthony G. Athos. *The Art of Japanese Management: Applications for American Executives*. New York: Warner Books, 1981.

Payne, Roy, and Derek S. Pugh. "Organizational Structure and Climate." In Marvin D. Dunnette, (Ed.). *Handbook of Industrial and Organizational Psychology*, pp. 1125–1173. Chicago: Rand McNally, 1976.

Schein, Edgar. "On Organizational Culture." Working Paper, Sloan School of Management, MIT, June 1981, Duplicated.

Schneider, Benjamin. "Organizational Climates: An Essay." *Personnel Psychology* 28 (Winter 1975): 447–479.

———. "The Source Organization: Climate is Crucial." *Organizational Dynamics* 9 (Autumn 1980): 52–65.

Schwartz, Howard, and Stanley M. Davis. "Matching Corporate Culture and Business Strategy." *Organizational Dynamics* 10 (Summer 1981): 30–48.

Seashore, Stanley E., and David G. Bowers. "Durability of Organizational Change." *American Psychologist* 25 (March 1970): 227–233.

Stein, Jess, ed. *The Random House Dictionary of The English Language*. New York: Random House, 1967.

Taguiri, Renato, and G. J. Litwin, eds. *Organizational Climate: Explorations of a Concept*. Boston, Mass.: Graduate School of Business Administration, Harvard University, 1968.

Taylor, James C., and David G. Bowers. *Survey of Organizations: A Machine-Scored Standardized Questionnaire Instrument*. Ann Arbor, Mich.: Institute for Social Research, University of Michigan, 1972.

PART FIVE

INDIVIDUAL, GROUP, AND ORGANIZATIONAL CHANGE

Part Five is concerned with the practical application of concepts developed throughout the book to individual and organizational improvement. Individual behavior, interpersonal, intragroup, and intergroup relationships, and organizational factors all contribute to results, outputs, and performance. But we are not concerned with short-term output only. We are also interested in *development* processes; that is, the building of a better system, wherein individuals, groups, and the total organization can achieve their potential and continue to improve performance over the long run. In this part we will look specifically at individual, group, and organizational change strategies and processes.

Chapter 15 discusses change processes. Individuals and organizations must adapt to and plan for rapid and dramatic changes resulting from environmental and internal forces. Planned change is a deliberate effort to modify the organizational system to respond to these forces. It is important to consider each of the key organizational subsystems in any process of planned change and to be aware that there are intended and unintended consequences of the endeavor to change. The chapter suggests ways to develop more effective processes by which change can occur.

Chapter 16 considers various individual, group, and organizational improvement strategies. It starts by looking at strategies for improving individual performance, such as job enrichment and positive reinforcement, and then moves to more comprehensive, organization-wide strategies, such as quality-of-work-life programs (QWL) and organization development (OD). These various improvement strategies are aimed at improving the results of individual and organizational activities in terms of effectiveness, efficiency, and participant satisfaction.

Chapter 17 focuses on career development with the perspective that there is a continual matching process between individuals and organizations. Career planning requires substantial self-assessment, as well as analysis of challenges and opportunities. People want different things from their careers and there are various career paths that can lead to a successful and satisfying work life. The chapter considers many of the career problems faced by people and discusses individual and organizational strategies for career development.

Chapter 18 looks at managerial philosophy and style and explains how they affect managerial behavior in organizations. In this capstone chapter we are concerned with how managerial actions affect the behavior of others. A primary goal of the chapter is to get you, the reader, to consider issues of philosophy and style explicitly enough so that you can begin to develop guidelines for your own managerial behavior. We express our opinions on a variety of key concerns, emphasize a contingency view of management, and stress the importance of flexibility and adaptability in achieving both productivity and quality of work life.

15
Organizational Change Processes

LEARNING OBJECTIVES

After reading this chapter, you should be able to:

1. List and describe five major categories of variables (subsystems) that are potential targets of change in an organization's change effort.
2. Define the concepts of *causal, emergent,* and *end-result* phenomena, including their interaction, and identify several variables that logically can be included in each of the three categories.
3. Contrast and use the concepts of *functional* and *dysfunctional* in the context of organizational effectiveness.
4. Describe the diagnostic and action-planning technique of force/field analysis and its underlying assumptions.
5. Define Lewin's concepts of *unfreezing, moving,* and *freezing,* relative to improving organizational performance.
6. Outline the important steps in a planned change effort.
7. List and elaborate upon several critical dimensions to consider in a planned change effort.

ENOUGH IS ENOUGH

Andy Erickson, vice president of personnel in a chemical manufacturing company, sat with his feet on his desk in the mostly darkened building. It was past time to go home, and he was tired. "I wonder what's going to happen next?" he mused.

On Monday, the vice president for purchasing had unexpectedly announced his decision to retire for health reasons. People in the purchasing department were understandably upset and the air was thick with rumors that it might be absorbed by the manufacturing department.

On Wednesday, the National Labor Relations Board had served notice on the company that approximately one-third of the technicians in the laboratories had signed authorization cards for a union-representation election. The same day, the most successful salesman in the company, a man in his middle twenties who had been salesperson of the year for three years in a row, had given one month's notice to go into business for himself. The marketing VP had been thinking of promoting him to district sales manager, but had neglected to share his intentions with the young man.

On Thursday, the company president had announced a 30-percent cut in the hourly and salaried work force at the Riverbend Plant because of declining orders. Andy had suggested a different procedure involving furloughs of one week per month for most of the affected employees, but he had been overruled.

Now, practically the whole work force was upset, community leaders were protesting, and the union was threatening to go to court. Andy had spent the entire day today trying to keep things from getting worse. "I wish things would stand still for awhile," he thought.

THE WORD PROCESSOR

Trudy Zalenovich was anxious and annoyed. The "wonderful" new word processor that her boss had so benevolently bestowed on her was not easy to operate. Furthermore, the printer seemed to have a mind of its own and she was convinced that she could do a better job with her old, faithful Underwood typewriter.

There was something else that she didn't dare mention to her boss. As she confessed to a friend at lunch, she was terribly worried that once she learned how to operate the new equipment she wouldn't have enough to do and would be forced to fill in the time with filing, which she detested. Worse still, her boss might be tempted to combine two jobs and eliminate hers.

A SLOW START

On February 1, the president of Amalgamated Manufacturing Company issued the following memorandum:

To All Management Personnel:

As we all know, a focus on objectives makes smart business sense. We need to be more systematic about defining our objectives and carrying them out. Therefore, effective immediately, Amalgamated Manufacturing will begin to implement a Management by Objectives program. Charles Nelson, Vice President of Personnel and Industrial Relations, will coordinate the effort. Our target is to have written statements of objectives completed for every managerial person down through the foremen level by August 15. I know you will all give Charles Nelson your complete cooperation.

(Signed)
Alan Winthrop
President

When Charles Nelson saw the memo, which he had helped write, he was pleased, but a bit apprehensive. A few of the senior top executives had talked about MBO on and off for some time, and the president had finally concluded that such a program really was necessary. The others had concurred, although James Kelly, vice president for research, had said right along that he didn't think MBO would work in a research organization. It was Jim Kelly's attitude, in particular, that made Charles Nelson apprehensive.

By November 1, only a few managers in manufacturing had made efforts at writing statements of objectives, and not much had happened elsewhere. To Charles, there seemed to be a lot of excuse making and foot dragging, as well as some grumbling about all of the paper work. Charles had had some success in getting his own subordinates to write their objectives, but it was taking much more time than he had expected. Jim Kelly reported that, while he wanted to cooperate, his department heads were very much opposed to the whole idea.

"YOU'RE FIRED"

It was common knowledge among the employees of Bobbitt Electronics Ltd. that morale had been very low in the accounting department for the past few months. The controller, John Dalton, was prone to occasional outbursts of temper and to making scathing comments to supervisors or employees in front of their peers or subordinates. His critical and caustic remarks also carried over into private meetings, where he would often castigate someone who was absent. At the same time, he was prone to lavish praise on some employees and to make pay increase decisions consistent with both his praise and his criticisms.

Productivity in the accounting department was substantially below what the president, Mike Greene, had been expecting, and on two occasions he had expressed his concern to Dalton. John's responses tended to focus on technical problems with a new computer system and on the ineptness of some of the old-time supervisors.

One Friday afternoon, as he was getting ready to leave for the day, the assistant controller, Fred Gibson, saw John Dalton summoned to the president's office and observed what seemed to be a heated discussion. About ten minutes later, John emerged, slammed the door behind him, went into his own office, and departed shortly thereafter, without any comment to the few people still around. Dalton was obviously upset.

Mike beckoned Fred into his office, told him that he had just asked for John's resignation, and offered Fred the job of acting controller, effective immediately. Within two weeks, productivity in the accounting department had risen sharply. Fred was pleased with his new responsibilities and hoped he would be appointed controller. He wondered, though, if Dalton's firing hadn't been too precipitant and whether the president and the company had made sufficient effort to help Dalton improve his performance. He was also worried about Dalton, who was reputedly having difficulties relocating and was beginning to drink heavily.

THE DISAPPEARING BACKLOG

A series of budget cuts had resulted in staff reductions in the central stores operation of Enormous State University. The number of order pickers had been reduced from seven to six through attrition. During high-demand periods some of the office staff helped out in the warehouse temporarily.

George Connor was the senior member of the crew, with 17 years of service. When it appeared that he would be off for an extended period on sick leave with a nagging back problem, the boss, Wilma Bowers, asked for a volunteer from the office staff to fill in full time. The backlog of unfilled orders had increased to five days and she had been getting complaints from users. Linda Murray quickly volunteered. She was bored with office work and welcomed the change of pace and the opportunity to move around and get some physical exercise.

Late the first day, Wilma stopped by to ask how things were going. She noticed that Linda tallied (made a check mark on her calendar) each order filled. Wilma asked, "Why are you keeping track like that? It's not required." "I know," Linda answered, "but I'd like to know how many orders I fill each day." Maybe this could be useful information, thought Wilma, but she also wondered what the other pickers would think. "That's a good idea," she said, "why don't you let me know how you do each day." "O.K.," Linda replied.

The next day, Walt Peters asked Linda what she was doing with the check marks. After she explained, he growled, "Did the boss tell you to do it?" "No, it was my own idea," Linda answered. Over the next several days Linda noticed that all of the order pickers were keeping track of the number of orders filled and reporting the results to Wilma each day. She wasn't sure (none of the results were posted), but she had a hunch that the number of orders filled per person had gone up significantly. Wilma liked what was happening and complimented everyone for their good work.

By the middle of the second week Wilma was truly amazed. The backlog had disappeared. Orders were being filled on the day received, or at least by the very next day. Complaints had also decreased significantly.

PRESIDENT JANE

Jane Ilgen, fairly new in the presidency of a small, high-quality dinnerware manufacturing company, was both pleased and worried. She was pleased because demand by prestige department stores for the company's products was growing rapidly, the company had recently moved into a larger facility, and start-up problems were being solved. She also felt confident that most of the employees liked her and respected her ability. But she was worried about research and development. Changes were needed, but what changes?

No new product had emerged from the company for several months, in spite of the fact that the company employed a designer on a retainer fee. Department-store buyers and her own sales people were pressing for new items for the product line. Foreign competition was increasing, and there was always the possibility that some manufacturer would copy one or more of the company's products.

One new product that had looked promising had failed because of inadequate early development and testing. Because of structural and glazing problems, it simply could not be manufactured with a low-enough reject rate. This had been disillusioning for both Jane and some of her key employees; the latter now seemed more motivated to try to improve existing pieces than to develop new ones. But the lack of new products was affecting the morale of the total group.

Steve, who wore two hats as production manager and glazing supervisor, was also new to his positions. He was preoccupied with ironing out problems in the production process, some of which stemmed from the move to a new facility. Furthermore, problems in the forming division were causing extra work for the glazing-division employees, who were beginning to resent the work being pushed off on them. Some employees in the glazing division had ideas about new products, but the extra work load was precluding much effort toward any new-product development. Besides, Steve believed that more attention should be given to production-process development than had occurred heretofore.

As a kind of fringe benefit, the president and board had approved the idea of a small studio where employees could work on their own art or craft projects after regular working hours. The studio had been furnished with a kiln and other equipment, and could be reached in about a five-minute drive by car. New-product development was not a requirement for use of the studio, but there was a hope that some new products might emerge. So far, this had not happened. There was no policy to pay royalties on any new products that might be developed by employees, although the subject had surfaced several times. At the new manufacturing facility, no space had been set aside strictly for design work, and no centralized technical library had emerged.

Most of the employees were young and relatively inexperienced, but they were highly motivated to make quality products and to make the company go. Many had been employed as a result of referrals by friends working in the company and felt deficient in technical skills. A few were taking night courses in local trade schools. Two were leaving soon, one because of family ties in another region, and another because of a desire to gain other kinds of experiences. One imminent departure was particularly worrisome to Jane, who wondered if the person's understudy had really learned all of the techniques and nuances of the craft. Little had been written down, and there hadn't been good communications between the understudy and the employee who was leaving. It seemed to Jane that things were constantly changing, that she had no control over many of the changes, but that she and her employees were going to have to do some things differently.

INTRODUCTION

Change, or attempted change, is a common theme in all of the above vignettes. Much of it was unplanned and unanticipated, like the resignation of the salesperson of the year in the chemical company and the improved productivity in the central stores department of the university. Some changes, like the development of a new product by the dinnerware company, were planned but had not come to fruition. Some changes, like the retirement of the vice president of purchasing, were inevitable, but this one occurred a few years earlier than expected. One change, the firing of John Dalton, was brought about because of *changes that did not occur* in Dalton's performance. In the *Slow Start* vignette, the president's memo that called for a change (the MBO effort) created more resistance than real change. Most, if not all, of the changes set off secondary, unanticipated consequences that needed attention. Many of the changes got one or more people upset. Some changes, like the cutback at Riverbend Plant, drastically affected the lives of many people.

Some of the managers—Andy Erickson, the vice president in a chemical company, and Jane Ilgen, the president of the small dinnerware manufacturing company—were trying to manage many changes simultaneously. Andy, along with the president and other executives of the firm, needed to solve both a problem of succession and a morale problem in the purchasing department. Further, they needed to replace a key salesman and perhaps modify company strategy with respect to retaining the most promising people, to respond to a change in company relationships with technicians, and to respond to serious employee morale and community- and labor-relations problems stemming from a plant layoff. Jane, also, was coping with many interrelated dilemmas; the way she responded to one would affect the way she could respond to another. If, for example, the organization allocated more time and money to new product development, fewer resources could be applied to solving problems in production.

The question in situations like these is not whether there will be change: all life is change; all organizational life is change; all management can be considered the management of change. The question is: How do we cope with change? Can it be managed? Can change be managed in careful, thoughtful, planned ways so that organizational performance improves and human needs and aspirations are fulfilled? Or will there be missed opportunities—as well as unnecessary stress, pain, effort, and other dysfunctional consequences—that lead to less than optimal individual, group, or organizational success?

The 1980s have seen rapid and drastic changes in the external environment that have required people in organizations to adapt and to plan counterchanges in order to compete and to survive. For example, rapid rises in oil prices and highly successful Japanese design and manufacturing approaches forced American automobile companies to change the design of their products and their methods of manufacture in order to compete domestically and internationally. High interest rates, combined with an economic recession and high fuel costs, contributed to the bankruptcy of Braniff Airlines and the demise or merger of other airlines. Budget cutbacks in federal and state governments resulted in major reorganizations and layoffs. Economic conditions forced public schools, colleges, and universities to eliminate some programs (and jobs) and restructure others. And all of these changes affected people: their feelings; their families; their careers; their opportunities.

This chapter is about what dimensions to look for in understanding and planning change, including responses to unanticipated changes in the external environment. What are the key variables to be alert to? What is cause and what is effect? How can we conceptualize change processes? What are the steps in effective planned change? We will cover the following topics:

The Concept of Planned Change
Key Subsystems to Consider in Change Efforts
Emergent Psychosocial Dimensions
Functional and Dysfunctional Phenomena
Change Dynamics
Steps in Planned Change
Critical Dimensions of Planned Change
So What? Implications for You

THE CONCEPT OF PLANNED CHANGE

Planned change is any premeditated, deliberate attempt to alter the status quo. Another definition, as related to organizations, is provided by Zaltman and Duncan (1977, p. 10): "Planned change . . . is a deliberate effort with a stated goal on the part of a change agent to create a modification in the structure and process of a social system such that it requires members of that system to relearn how they perform their roles."

The broader goals underlying planned-change efforts might include such hoped-for outcomes as improved product quality, increased productivity, the development of new products or services, reduced costs, increased job satisfaction, or just plain surviving. The change agent—the person who is the prime mover in bringing about change or acts as a catalyst in the change process—could be a manager, a group of managers, one or more subordinates acting in cooperation with others or with higher management, someone acting in the role of a consultant who is a member of the organization or who has been brought in from the outside, a board of directors, or a labor union. How the change agent goes about trying to make changes is an extremely important matter. For example, the different approaches to change illustrated in the previous chapter produced different results. Ed Carlson's listening and consensus approach at United Airlines resulted in high morale and high commitment to the changes that were being made. The group discussion approach and "acceptance time" at Mastsushita Electric contributed to proposed changes being well understood and planned, conflict being worked through at all levels, and high commitment to changes.

The interrogation tactics of Harold Geneen at ITT, while perhaps producing "unshakeable facts," produced fear and alienation. Similarly, how two subordinates plan a proposal and how they approach their supervisor will partially determine their success as agents of change. How a consultant goes about collecting information will partially determine how acceptable his or her recommendations will be. Whether a board of directors views its role as reacting to proposals from the CEO, or as assuming responsibility for leadership in articulating the organization's mission and its management philosophy, will be important in determining how much influence that board will have.

KEY SUBSYSTEMS TO CONSIDER IN CHANGE EFFORTS

In Chapter 1 we described organizations as goal-oriented systems interacting with their environments and consisting of five major subsystems: a goals and values subsystem, a technical subsystem, a structural subsystem, a psychosocial subsystem, and a managerial subsystem. Each of these major subsystems, in turn, can be thought of as consisting of a number of key variables or dimensions that might be a target in some planned change effort (see Figure 1.2).

The Goals and Values Subsystem

The hierarchy of goals ranges from broad statements of missions or purposes down to more specific operational objectives (Chapter 3). These goals tend to be connected within the organization in the sense that the goals at one level determine the goals (subgoals) of the units below, and so on. The goals (assigned goals, at least) of individuals are presumed to be a subaspect of the goals of their units. This cascading of goals from overall mission statements to unit goals to individual goals can be viewed as the goal subsystem. Assuming that goals affect behavior—and this is a reasonable assumption—changes in goals at higher levels, will in particular have a cascading effect on the expected behaviors of people down through the organization. Underlying the mission and the goals of the organization are the basic values held by the members of the organization—and the top management group, in particular. Further, these basic values and the assumptions that are made by key persons about managing people will have a profound effect on all of the subsystems.

The Slow Start vignette describes an attempt to modify the goal subsystem of an organization by trying to make it more systematic, having managers write down explicit goals and stand prepared to review both the goals and progress toward them with their superiors. The resistance to this effort was a symptom of the complex interplay between the goal system and other subsystems, such as the psychosocial subsystem. Writing down goals and reviewing them with one's superior requires a variety of adjustments; one's goal statements must be coordinated with those of others and activities guided more surely by goals long operative but only now made explicit.

The recent experience of several of the large oil companies in redefining themselves as being in the energy business is an example of how changes in goals affect how organizations are structured and what people do. All of a sudden, there may be a new coal-mining division or a synthetic fuels research laboratory. Company geologists may be expected to have a perspective encompassing more than potential sources of oil; scientists may find themselves transferred or studying different problems.

The Technical Subsystem

The technical subsystem, as described in Chapters 1 and 9, consists of people using knowledge, techniques, equipment, and facilities. An example of a change in the technical system in a chemical company would be the discovery and use of a new formula leading to the manufacture of a new product. Another example would be revision in the sequence in which chemicals are added to a mixing tank. Any such changes require changes in human behavior. Some changes in the technical subsystem, such as the rearrangement of manufacturing facilities, offices, storage rooms, shower and restrooms, and the like, would probably require changes in individual behavior. These changes would also produce changes in the customary interactions with others. Thus, changes in the technical system usually, if not always, have an impact on the psychosocial subsystem.

The vignette in Chapter 6, *Computer Task Force,* was an example of planning for organizational change involving the introduction of new equipment, in this case a computer. The change was successful, largely because Ann had both technical expertise and an awareness of the needs of various managers. Quality circles, to be discussed in the next chapter are planned-change efforts focusing extensively on the technical system, but they also represent changes in other subsystems, as we will see. Box 15.1 is a statement about the extent to which robots, as well as computers, will affect people's jobs in the future.

The Structural Subsystem

The structural subsystem consists of dimensions such as the many tasks that need to be done in the organization, the grouping of tasks and people into units, departments, and divisions, and the flow of work among units. Authority relationships are also aspects of the structural subsystem; that is, who reports to whom, who can reward and punish whom, work rules, and rewards or punishments that channel behavior. The design of the communications and information flow and the number of reporting levels are also parts of the structural subsystem. Changes in these dimensions tend to have far-reaching effects on the psychosocial subsystem.

The vignette in Chapter 10, *The Program Manager,* is an example of a change in the structural subsystem to a program or matrix-type organization that sets off many changes in relationships and created numerous intergroup and motivational problems. Job enrichment and sociotechnical systems, to be discussed in the next chapter, are planned efforts at change focusing largely on the structural subsystem but having many ramifications in other subsystems. Management by objectives (MBO) programs, also to be discussed in the next chapter, are efforts directed at changing the goal subsystem, but can also be viewed as

BOX 15.1
WORK WON'T BE THE SAME AGAIN

The U.S. is well launched on the voyage from the industrial age into the information age. What happens in the next decade or two will perhaps change the way Americans work as much as the industrial revolution did in the last century. The application of computer technology to office and factory "will affect almost every job and almost every aspect of work," says James O'Toole, a professor at the University of Southern California's graduate school of business and a student of the future of work.

Such a revolution would be hard to deal with under normal circumstances, but these enormous changes in the work force are coming on top of an already high level of unemployment. Even after the recovery takes hold, millions of manufacturing jobs—many of them in the auto, steel, and rubber industries—will vanish because of foreign competition and automation.

Millions of new jobs will be created, mostly in information systems, but they'll be so different that today's laid-off workers will be hard pressed to fill them. The net outcome will be more jobs, probably better jobs at better pay; but getting there is going to be painful for many Americans.

U.S. businesses have, of course, been working with computers and robots for years. Banks have long had automated check processing, for instance, and many plants use computer-controlled robot welders. But these are stand-alone systems that have taken over single functions, and their impact has been "very modest" in the view of Professor Wickham Skinner of the Harvard Business School. Now companies are moving to integrated office and factory systems with hierarchies of computers and robots. The number of robots will grow from a few thousand today to an estimated 100,000 by 1990, and the number of electronic work stations from four million to 25 million to 30 million. As a result, says Skinner, "in a five- to 15-year period profound and dramatic changes will occur in factories and many service operations."

Source: Jeremy Main, "Work Won't Be The Same Again," *Fortune*, 28 June 1982, pp. 58-59.

modifying the structural and psychosocial subsystems. Box 15.2, "Canaries at Texas Instruments," suggests how changes in structure can affect the feelings of people, their relationships, and their careers. The "canary theory" of motivation is seen as motivation through anxiety.

The Psychosocial Subsystem

The psychosocial subsystem consists of the individuals in the organization, their technical skills and abilities, and their particular leadership and followership skills. In addition, this subsystem includes boss-subordinate, intragroup, and intergroup interactions and the norms governing these interactions. It also includes the feelings, perceptions, goals and motivations of individuals. Furthermore, the psychosocial subsystem includes the phenomenon we discussed in the previous chapter, organizational climate.

The vignette in Chapter 13 in which the president of a company tried to stop coffee drinking and conversation in the office (*The Notice on the Door*) offered an example of an unsuccessful attempt by a manager to control norms and interactions by an edict. At least two of the vignettes in this chapter—*The Word Processor* and *The Slow Start*—are examples of efforts toward change that ran into difficulty in the psychosocial subsystem. Organization development (OD) and team building, discussed in the next chapter, are essentially planned change efforts that focus initially on the psychosocial subsystem—on perceptions, feelings, and norms, in particular. The Quality of Work Life (QWL) program at General Motors, aspects of which were described in Chapter 14 and will be described more fully in Chapter 16, is an example of a change-directed effort that has emphasized changes in the psychosocial subsystem but has included changes in the other subsystems as well.

The Managerial Subsystem

Finally, the managerial subsystem consists of planning, coordinating, and controlling the overall organization and its activities. In addition, managerial philosophy and leadership style can be considered part of this subsystem because of the pervasive impact they have on the organization. Again, this subsystem is interdependent with the others.

The vignette in Chapter 10, *How Much Decentralization?,* is an example of top management's attempts to make improvements through changing the managerial subsystem's control mechanisms. The vignette in the current chapter, *You're Fired,* is partly an example of the president trying to change the leadership style in a unit by removing the top person and replacing him with a subordinate. In Chapter 14, "Organizational Culture and Climate," we saw how Ed Carlson of United Airlines changed the planning, control, and leadership processes of the company through the use of task forces, consensus decision making, and his own extensive travel during which he engaged in extensive listening and dialogue.

Organizational Change and the Subsystems

Any one of the subsystems described above might be the central target in a planned-change effort, or the source of unplanned change in other subsystems. Seldom does a change-directed effort affect only the subsystem or subsystems to which it is directed. For example, top management might change the psychosocial subsystem by hiring new people with new skills, but this would probably have the further result of effecting changes in the technical and structural subsystems because of new techniques or tasks created by the new people. Or, if top management alters the structural subsystem by eliminating a layer of supervision, the pattern of relationships in the psychosocial system is bound to be altered. All of a sudden, some people will be reporting to new supervisors and new work groups will be formed. Furthermore, unless well planned and implemented, such a change could create unwanted changes in the psychosocial subsystem, such as the emergence of informal coalitions that resist the changes or the channeling off of employee time and energy into dealings with anxiety.

In planning changes it is important not only to analyze what subsystem requires changing, but to be aware of the secondary changes that will occur in other aspects of organizational life. Further, we need to have an understanding of how the various subsystems and their parts interact. For example, some aspects of the psychosocial system tend to be heavily influenced by changes in the structural, technical, and managerial subsystems, but are not so readily changed themselves. To illustrate more specifically, low morale or excessive conflict cannot be eliminated by mandate or by statements that everything is all right. Organizational climate is largely a result of many managerial practices, and major shifts tend to require presistent, long-term attention to a wide variety of matters.

EMERGENT PSYCHOSOCIAL DIMENSIONS

As suggested above, some organizational dimensions are more subject to direct managerial control and change than others. We now want to emphasize this and to separate a number of the variables shown in Figure 1.2 into the causal, emergent, and outcome phenomena as shown in Figure 15.1.

Causal variables are variables over which the management of an organization has substantial (not total) control. (In particular, the term "causal" needs qualifying because of the process of *reciprocal determinism* (Craighead, Kazdin, & Mahoney, 1976, p. 175). *Emergent* variables are aspects of the organization over which management has much less direct control and which tend to emerge out of the causal dimensions. These emergent phenomena tend to reinforce, modify, or block the causal variables that management sets in motion, and have powerful influences on overall organizational performance. The latter, overall organizational performance, we are calling *outcomes*. Subcategories of outcomes are effectiveness, efficiency, participant satisfaction, and individual, group, and organization improvement. (In a similar way, Likert has written about causal, intervening, and end-result variables. Likert & Likert, 1976, pp. 46–48, 74.)

Three Emergent Categories

The emergent phenomena have been separated out into three categories: individual, group, and organizational phenomena. The *emergent individual phenomena* are individual feelings, perceptions, attitudes, performance goals, motivation, effort, job performance, and actions beyond job requirements. An example of the latter would be reading a novel while on extended breaks in the company washroom (not likely to contribute much to organizational effectiveness). Another example, from *The Disappearing Backlog* vignette, was Linda's voluntarily establishing a procedure for keeping track of productivity (which did contribute to organizational effectiveness). This emergent individual behavior

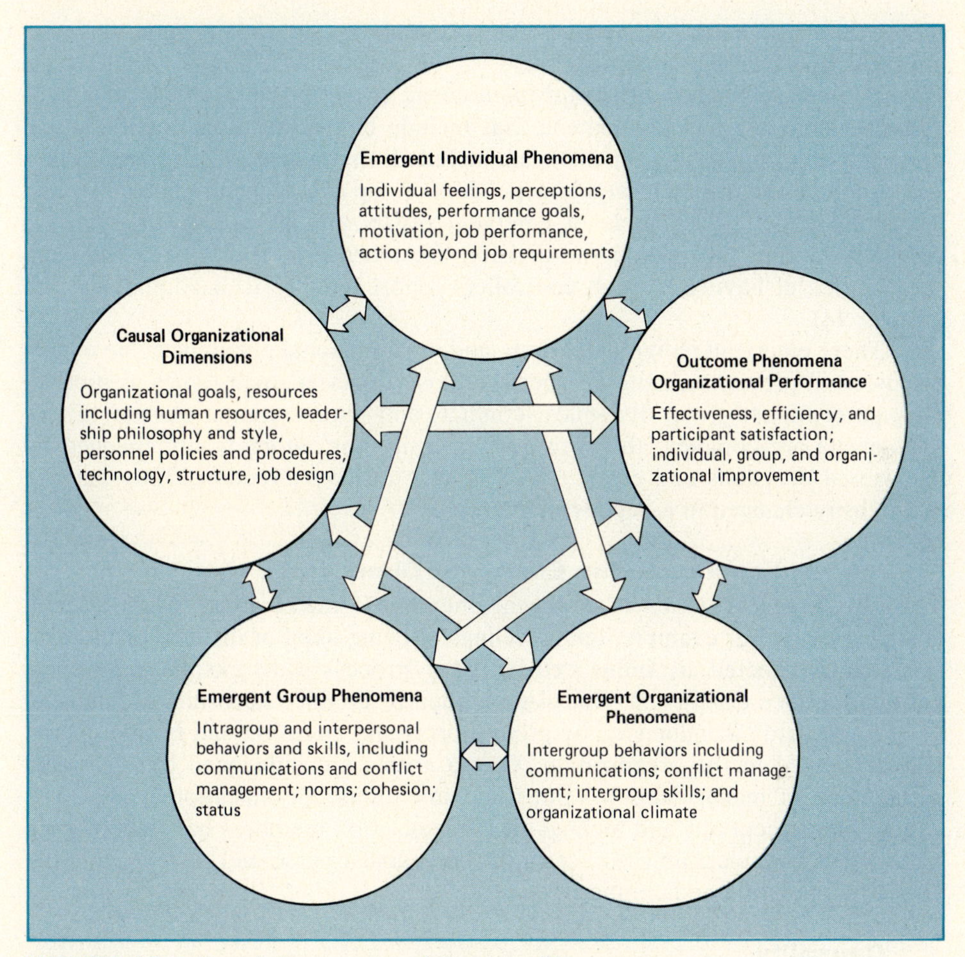

FIGURE 15.1 Causal, Emergent, and Outcome Phenomena

partly stemmed from Wilma's leadership style (a causal variable), which was to encourage and support Linda in Linda's innovative approach to her job.

The *emergent group phenomena* are intragroup and interpersonal behaviors and phenomena, including communications, conflict, norms, cohesion, and status. Group and intergroup skills are also included, because whether they are developed is largely a result of managerial philosophy and style. Recall the vignette in Chapter 13 in which the president of a small electronics firm posted a notice saying "effective immediately, there will be no coffee drinking and socializing in the office"? His leadership behavior immediately produced some emergent individual and group behavior he had not bargained for, including one person bringing in a Pepsi and another a cup of tea, a general buzz of whispering about a union, and phone calls to people outside about "What George did this time.'' George intended to improve office productivity, but the emergent feelings, attitudes, and interactions lowered it.

The *emergent organizational phenomena* are intergroup and transorganizational behaviors and phenomena that include communications, conflict, and organizational climate. Again, skills are included—in this case intergroup skills—because their emergence is largely dependent on top management philosophy and leadership style. An example of emergent organizational phenomena was the conflict between staff people and division line managers at ITT stemming from the practice of having division controllers report directly to headquarters (see Chapter 14).

These emergent individual, group, and organizational phenomena have been discussed in previous chapters, when we have discussed such topics as motivation, perceptions, group dynamics, conflict, and organizational climate. These phenomena are complex; they are neither easily nor automatically changed by managerial decisions and edicts, at least in a positive direction. They may be more easily changed in a negative direction.

Interaction among the Emergent Dimensions

The three categories of emergent phenomena interact with each other in complex ways. For example, one's feelings of being liked or disliked or of being accepted or rejected are influenced by group process skills exercised by one's work group (see Chapter 7). One's motivation to produce according to management's standards is influenced by group norms and cohesion and by the overall climate sensed in the organization. Group norms are influenced by individual perceptions of management's values and intentions. Organizational climate is largely the perceptions and feelings that organization members have about such dimensions as leadership style, organizational goals, personnel policies, and degree of cooperation and conflict.

Causality

Note that, in Figure 15.1, there are arrows pointing in both directions between all five categories. While the direction of causality is generally in the direction of the causal to the emergent phenomena, and subsequently to the outcome phenomena, all five categories influence each other. For example, group effectiveness can influence leadership style (the lower the group's capabilities in participation, the more the leader is likely to be autocratic). Similarly, the success of the organization is likely to influence factors in organizational climate such as feelings of identity with the organization (people like to be on a winning team and in a successful organization). And, of course, overall organizational performance will influence top management goal setting and planning.

A Note about Outcome Phenomena

We include participant satisfaction and individual, group, and organization improvement under the category of outcome phenomena, although these dimensions overlap with the various emergent phenomena. Participant satisfaction, as reflected in organizational climate, can be considered an emergent variable; it is also frequently a desired end result along with effectiveness and efficiency. Similarly, enhanced individual, group, and intergroup skills are emergent variables, but they may also be desired outcomes in their own right. In short, the board of directors and top management of an organization may value the development of human capabilities as one of several outcomes they are seeking.

FUNCTIONAL AND DYSFUNCTIONAL PHENOMENA

We have alluded to ineffective behaviors and to unfortunate or unintended outcomes. A useful way of thinking is to look at the degree to which a given phenomenon (e.g., events or conditions such as a particular leadership behavior, a particular personnel policy, a particular employee skill, or a particular group norm) is functional or dysfunctional vis à vis the attainment of some particular unit or organizational goal (Seiler, 1967). For example, a *flextime* policy under which employees may use considerable discretion in arriving at work and leaving may be highly *functional* for employee morale. A group norm of always deferring to the opinions of the formal leader may be highly *dysfunctional* for effective decision making. Sometimes a given phenomenon can be functional for one outcome and dysfunctional for another. Referring to flextime again, flexible working hours may be functional for morale and for reducing traffic congestion, but may be dysfunctional in terms of employees' being available for telephone calls from customers and for meetings.

The vignette *President Jane* provides some illustrations of functional and dysfunctional phenomena. For example, the retainer fee for the designer may have been dysfunctional in contrast to some compensation scheme based on performance. The failure of the new product was dysfunctional to morale. Work being pushed off from the glazing division was dysfunctional to performance and morale in the forming division. The studio concept was functional for morale, but an unanticipated consequence was that it intensified the dilemma as to whether employees should be rewarded for new product development. This ambivalence was probably dysfunctional in terms of innovation and moving ahead on product development. The successful move to the new facility was functional for morale and for long-term productivity. The overall motivation of employees and their loyalty to the company was functional for both productivity and employee satisfaction. Lack of written procedures may have been functional for the skilled workers when there was continuity in the workplace, but dysfunctional when turnover occurred.

Thus, a particular causal or emergent phenomenon can be analyzed in terms of its functionality or dysfunctionality, but always in terms of some particular goal. Further, consequences can sometimes be unintended, and it is important to analyze probable effects of a course of action. A given action can have a ripple effect in an organization. This way of thinking about situations—in terms of functional and dysfunctional consequences and in terms of intended and unintended consequences—can be useful in analyzing human problems in organiza-

Early Warning Analysis

This system is designed to help decision makers become aware of and make plans for coping with the potential problems resulting from their decisions (or a decision they are considering).

The first step is to brainstorm a list of *potential problems* that may (will) result from the decision. Who will not support it? What will they do about it? What are all of the negative consequences; e.g., monetary, morale, credibility, etc.? The more specifically each of these can be stated the better. In fact, *no general statements* should be accepted; they should be broken apart into *very specific increments*.

When the most significant potential problems have been identified, the next step is to estimate the likelihood of each one happening. Is it sure to happen? Then give it a 100% probability. Is it quite unlikely? Then give it 5%. And so on until all potential problems are assigned probabilities.

Next, estimate the *impact* (on the individual, group, or organization) if the worst happened, i.e., the *force* of the problem if it should come about. This can be done on a scale of 1 to 100, and every item should be rated. Multiply the probability times the degree of impact in order to determine the degree of risk.

Discussion should then be focused on ways to prevent (forestall) the occurrence of the problems with the highest impact, and to devise (design) (invent) ways (actions) that could be taken should they occur. What could we do? How could we survive? What steps could we take?

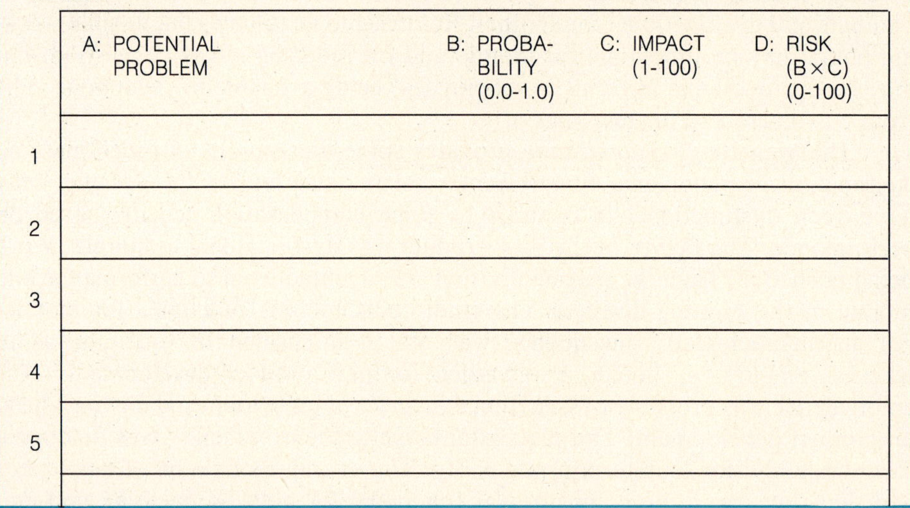

	A: POTENTIAL PROBLEM	B: PROBA-BILITY (0.0-1.0)	C: IMPACT (1-100)	D: RISK (B × C) (0-100)
1				
2				
3				
4				
5				

FIGURE 15.2 Early Warning Analysis

tions and in choosing the most appropriate courses of action. (See Figure 15.2 for a procedure to anticipate dysfunctional outcomes.)

CHANGE DYNAMICS

In addition to deciding what organizational outcomes we wish to improve in any change-directed effort, and what subsystem we plan to change—goals, technical, structural, psychosocial, managerial—to reach those objectives, it is important to have some general notions about why change does or does not occur in the desired directions. The emergent variables will either reinforce, modify, or block changes set in motion by management. We will now look at some concepts developed by Kurt Lewin about the dynamics of change. These concepts have had wide acceptance and are relevant in understanding processes of change in organizations.

Force-Field Analysis

Lewin viewed any present situation—the status quo—as being maintained in a field of forces, or in what he called a condition of "quasi-stationary equilibrium" (Lewin, 1951, p. 172). To Lewin there were two types of forces—driving forces and restraining forces. A driving force is one which helps move events in a given direction; a restraining force is experienced in terms of physical or social obstacles to the events' moving in that particular direction (p. 259). From these ideas grew the diagnostic technique called force-field analysis, which has been refined and utilized widely in recent years. The technique has four basic assumptions:

1. Most conditions, such as turnover in a factory or a given kind of behavior on the part of an employee, are held in a state of quasiequilibrium in a field of forces. That is, most conditions tend to stay much as they are and are a result of multiple forces operating simultaneously. The notions of equilibrium and multiple causation are important concepts to keep in mind.
2. It is useful to conceptualize any present condition as held in equilibrium between two sets of forces: (a) forces driving toward a desired change and (b) forces restraining movement toward the desired change. Driving and restraining forces can also be thought of as positive or negative relative to a particular goal, or one could use the terms functional or dysfunctional relative to a desired outcome. (See Figure 15.3 for a fictional example of the forces operating on a student who wishes to improve her grade-point average.)
3. It is useful to identify the forces operating in a given situation before making action plans.
4. Although action planning will often involve modifying both driving and restraining forces, it is frequently preferable (at least initially) to reduce the restraining forces rather than to add to the driving forces. (For example, parental lectures about poor grades may precipitate additional restraining or resisting forces.)

Remember that President Jane (in the vignette of that same name) was faced with a large number of problems all occurring simultaneously. Figure 15.4 shows the forces affecting the research-and-development effort in that company. Although names have been disguised, this is an actual analysis recorded on flipchart paper and conducted in a workshop setting with all of the management people and key employees of the company present. The problem these people were wrestling with was how to enhance the research-and-development effort, and

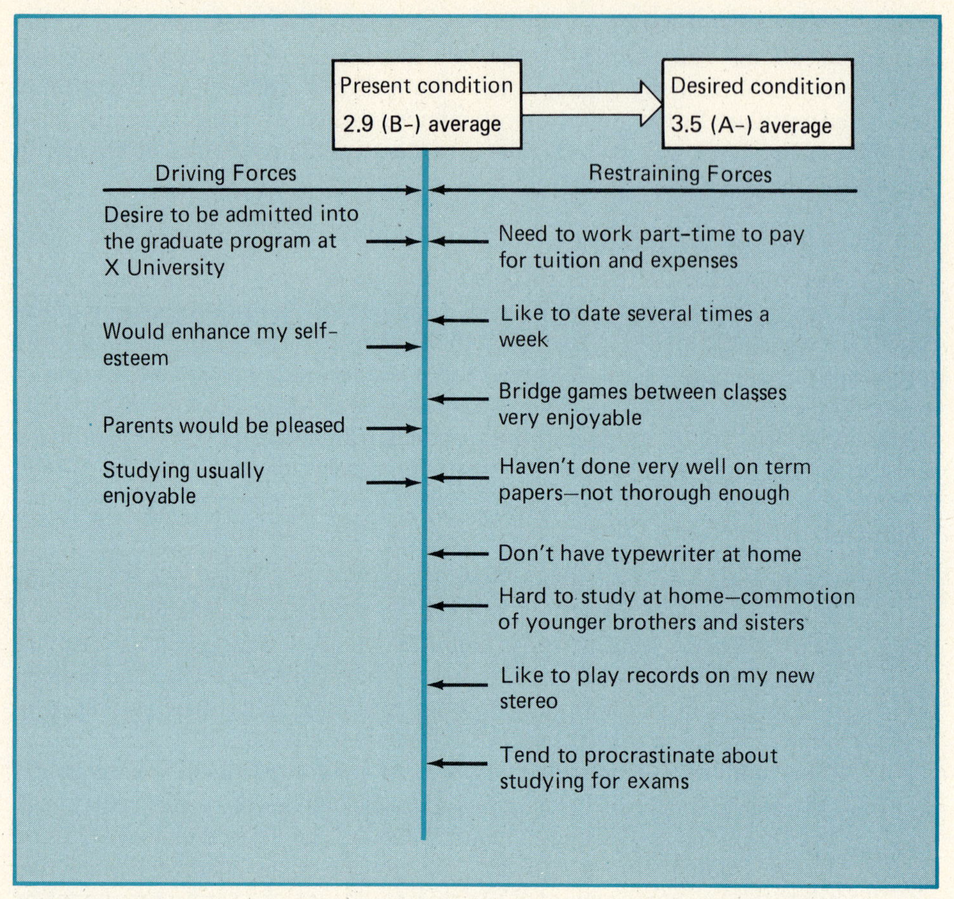

FIGURE 15.3 Why Is My G.P.A. Lower Than Desired? A Force Field Analysis

how to do it in a way that would involve most of the employees and generally enhance the quality of work life in the organization.

After the forces that people perceived to be operating were listed, the group then proceeded to identify forces over which they had control or significant forces that seemed to be particularly susceptible to modification. They then made action plans for beginning to modify a few of the forces (the latter items were marked with an asterisk). In subsequent weeks, task forces met many times to facilitate progress in several areas. The total group met in a follow-up session three months after the first workshop to check progress and to develop additional action plans. The important thing is that they analyzed the forces that were helping and restraining the research-and-development effort. They then made plans of action to modify the restraining forces and reinforce some of the driving forces and began to carry out these plans.

Note that many of the variables shown in Figures 1.2 and 15.1 appeared on the flipchart. For example, quality of present products (end-result phenomenon),

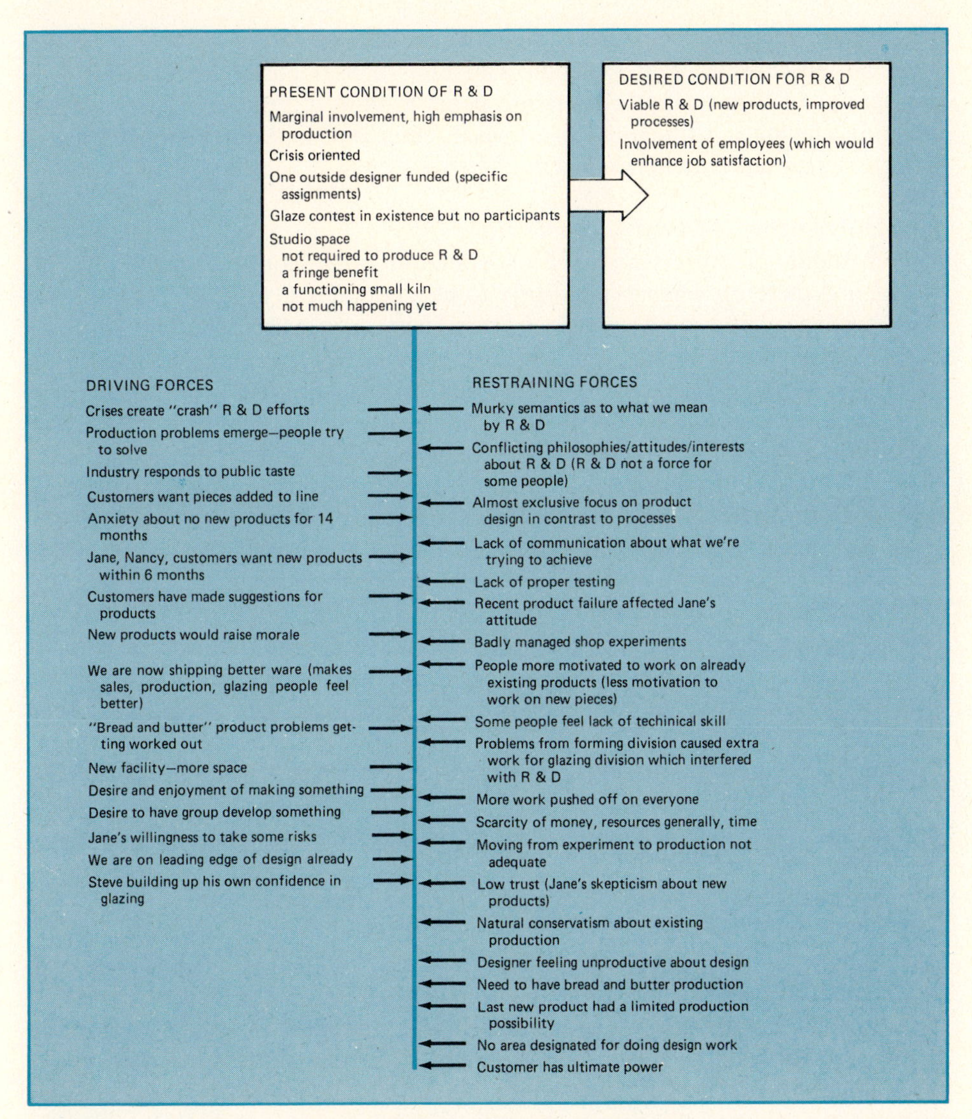

FIGURE 15.4 Why Is Our R & D Unsatisfactory and What Can We Do about It? Use of Force Field Analysis in a High-Quality Dinnerware Company

the new factory (technological/causal), self confidence (attitudinal/emergent), murky semantics (communication/causal and emergent), lack of skill (human resources/causal), problems in one division causing more work for another (intergroup/emergent), and scarcity of money (resources/causal) were all cited as active forces in the present circumstance. The group clearly saw these forces as critical to their future success or failure and set out to reduce the restraining (negative) forces. To have focused on only one force or variable would probably have been futile.

Notice also that the cause-and-effect sequence is not simple. For example, what can be considered an outcome variable, such as customer and employee perceptions of high-quality dinnerware being produced, was having a favorable effect on employee attitudes. Thus, causal, emergent, and outcome phenomena are interacting and interdependent.

Unfreezing, Moving, Freezing

In addition to observing that most conditions are a consequence of multiple forces, and therefore change was likely to be a complex matter, Lewin observed that improved performance required three steps: unfreezing, moving, and then freezing again on a new level. Further, improved performance could occur through a "shot in the arm," but that performance frequently returned to its previous level unless the new field of forces was made relatively stable and secure (Lewin, 1951, 228–229). An example with which we are all familiar is the New Year's resolution to eat fewer calories or to exercise regularly. The resolution may result in changed behavior for a short time, but unless we do several things like enlisting the support of the people around us, measuring our progress, and changing the way we reward ourselves, we are likely to lapse back into our old ways. Thus, it is important to manage effectively the entire process of change. This includes making changes involving several (sometimes many) variables simultaneously and managing the new equilibrium that occurs.

It is generally recognized that, for improvement to occur, there needs to be a perception by someone, or some group, that things are not going as well as they might and that some change must occur (unfreezing). Further, it is generally recognized that, after changes have been implemented (moving), considerable reinforcement of the changes needs to occur as well as attention to spinoffs of the change process (freezing).

We can refer to some of our vignettes to provide illustrations of these concepts. In the *Slow Start* vignette, the vice president for research, James Kelly, really didn't see the need for a change, and little unfreezing occurred, at least with respect to his departments. In the *You're Fired* episode, we can assume that the controller's leadership style had never been directly confronted as an issue by his superior: and that, with the exception of an indirect approach on the part of his superior who had expressed concerns about productivity on two occasions, no substantial disconfirming (unfreezing) incident had occurred. In the illustration of the key employees of the dinnerware company using force-field analysis in a group setting, we can assume that the joint identification of driving and restraining forces was an unfreezing process, and that the plans of action resulting took the group well into the moving phase.

STEPS IN PLANNED CHANGE

Given the above notions about what variables are to be addressed, the multiplicity of variables that are usually involved in a change effort, and some notions about unfreezing, moving, and freezing, we might now look at some specific compo-

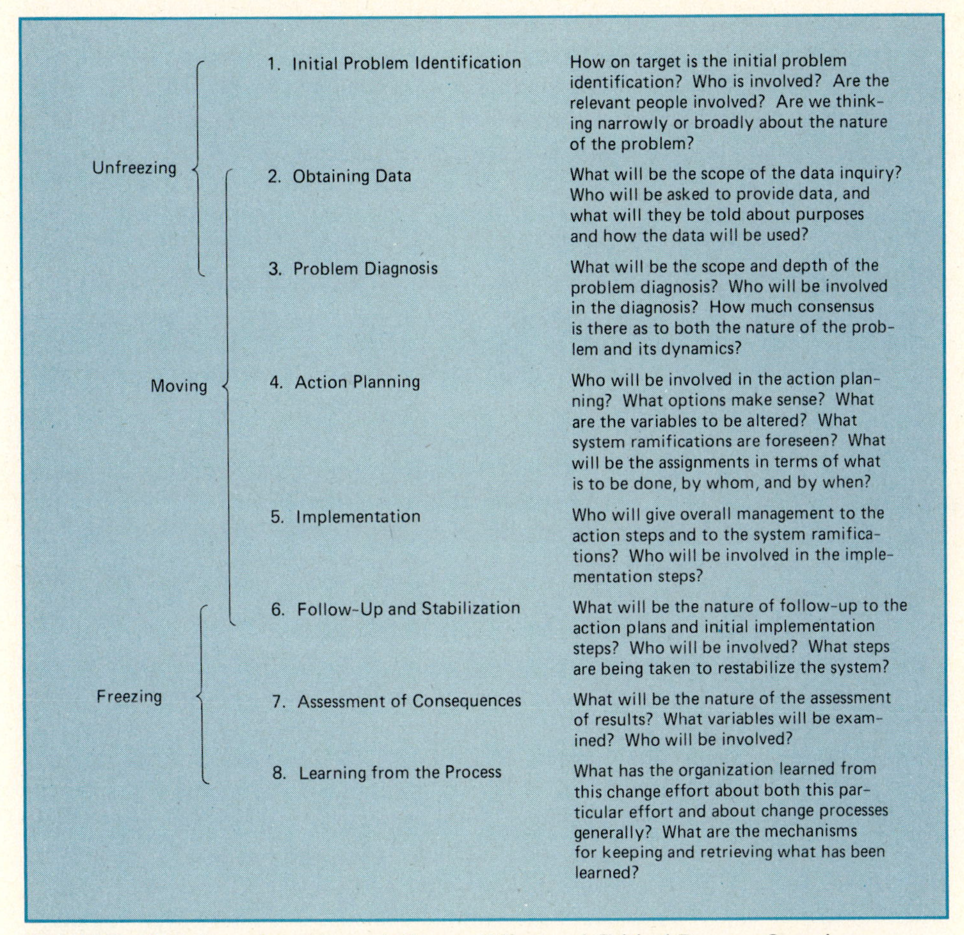

FIGURE 15.5 Steps in a Planned-Change Effort and Critical Process Questions

nents or steps of a planned-change effort. The steps are important in themselves, but there are some critical *process* questions that need to be asked about each. By process we mean how one goes about accomplishing the change, who is involved, and the quality of the interactions that occur. In other words, what are the means by which the change occurs?

Figure 15.5 lists eight steps in a planned-change effort, and some of the critical process questions pertaining to each step. Most problem solving and attempts to improve things tend to approximate this sequence, at least steps one through five. The quality of what occurs in each step can vary tremendously, however, and in some situations one or more steps may be left out entirely—frequently with unfortunate results. (The steps listed here follow the general pattern of the decision-making process described in Chapter 11.)

In *step one,* by *problem* we mean "the discrepancy between what is expected or desired and the present situation." The delineation of the problem can be on target or off target, of course, depending on such matters as the frame of reference of the viewer or the amount of quality of information available. Who is involved can also be important. Obviously, the quality of problem identification can be enhanced by having the relevant people participate. As to frame of reference, it can be useful to assess whether one is thinking narrowly or broadly about the problem. That is, is the problem initially identified really one aspect of a much larger problem? What are the implications of solving the narrow one?

We may be engaged in *single-loop learning:* corrective action that does no more than keep a system operating. In identifying a problem, however, we may better be served engaging in *double-loop learning,* a process requiring us to address broader questions, such as those pertaining to the basic purposes or assumptions of the broader system in which the immediate problem is immersed (Argyris, 1977, pp. 115–125). For example, we might identify a problem having to do with test validation in an employee selection system, but maybe we need to be looking at the broader selection system and asking questions about the fundamental objectives of that system and how those objectives fit into a total program of the management of human resources.

In *step two*—obtaining data—the question arises: Once a problem has been reasonably well defined, how broad or how narrow will the solicitation of data be? Obviously, we can collect far more data than is practical under the circumstances. But data can also be collected too narrowly. If Charles Nelson, in the *Slow Start* vignette, had involved all of the top managers, and perhaps some subordinate managers as well, in collecting data about the need for some target-setting system, the subsequent problem diagnosis and action planning might have been much different. It can be inferred that obtaining data, problem diagnosis, and action planning were not adequate in this case.

Another important question relative to the obtaining of data is this: What will people be told about purposes of the data and how it will be used? Many efforts at improvement have floundered on the mistrust caused by previous data-collecting episodes in which people were either deceived, or never told about the results, or which came to nothing. Obviously, trust is an important dimension in change efforts.

Step three, problem diagnosis, is closely related to the data-gathering phase. Problem diagnosis involves an examination of the forces giving rise to the present situation and the obstacles to improvement, as well as of factors that support a move in the desired direction. This step is frequently executed in too superficial a manner with respect to the human dimensions of problems. For example, new techniques or technologies—a computer system is a prime example—are too frequently added without adequate examination of the implications for the training and job reassignment of the people involved. Who it is that is involved in the diagnosis can affect both the depth of understanding of the problem and the acceptance of the nature of the problem. People are more inclined to *own* a problem if they have been involved in its diagnosis, as well as in the information-gathering phase preceeding diagnosis. If there is consensus among key people as to the dynamics of the problem, it is likely to be on the way to a solution.

Action planning, *step four*, is broader than decision making alone. It requires looking at various options and their consequences, deciding what will be done, who will do it, and by when. And action planning frequently involves planning various stages of implementation.

Implementation, *step five*, requires attention to managing the action steps and any ramifications for the system as a whole. Many of these may have been planned for, but some will be unanticipated.

Follow-up and stabilization, *step six*, is really a part of implementation, but is so important that we consider it separately. A great deal of research and experience suggests that follow-up during any improvement program is necessary to avoid allowing the organization to return to its previous equilibrium. Usually, changes must be reinforced in many ways. In short, we can't set a program of change into motion and then ignore it. Efforts at improvement, to be successful, invariably require careful shepherding as the process unfolds.

The phases of planned-change effort will not be complete without *step seven*—the assessment of consequences. Here, data need to be gathered to determine whether the intended consequences are actually occurring and to determine the extent to which dysfunctional side effects are likely to occur across a range of variables. For example, a program of job enrichment may reduce the need for supervision. This, in turn, has consequences for organizational structure, for morale, and for staffing. A related broad question is: What has the effort done to attitudes and perceptions of those affected by the change? What has the effort done to relationships between people?

And finally, we have the issues arising in *step eight*. What has the organization learned from the change effort? What have we learned about the particular program or techniques that were attempted? What modifications would improve such programs or techniques? What are the implications of all we have discovered about attitudes and morale and relationships? What have we learned about change-directed processes in general? What are the organizational mechanisms for keeping and retrieving what has been learned? Does, for example, the organization's statement of philosophy about managing people and its training programs reflect what has been learned? These kinds of questions are extremely important if an organization is not to repeat the same mistakes every time a new improvement effort is attempted. Thus, the concept of organizational learning is important (Hedberg, 1981).

CRITICAL DIMENSIONS OF PLANNED CHANGE

Several dimensions shown in Figure 15.6 are important in understanding human behavior as it relates to organizational improvement efforts. The advantages and disadvantages of change-directed efforts with different mixes of characteristics are also shown. One dimension is whether the improvement effort is largely unilateral or autocratic versus being participative. A second is whether the agent of change, the person acting as a catalyst in the current effort to alter the status quo, is acting in the role of an expert or in the role of a facilitator. A third

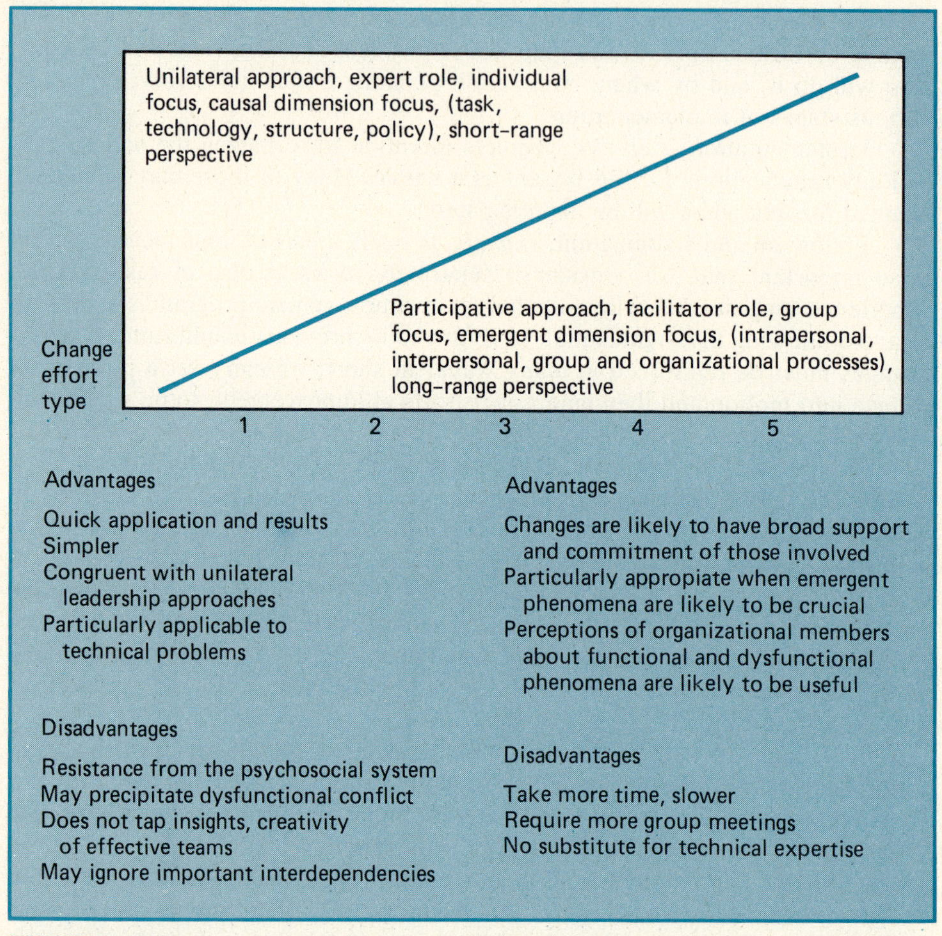

FIGURE 15.6 Some Critical Dimensions of Planned Change: Advantages and Disadvantages of Polar Types

dimension is whether the focus is on intact teams of the boss and subordinates together, on task forces with members drawn from different units, or on individuals. A fourth dimension is whether the focus is largely on causal variables, or whether a deeper level of organizational culture is brought into focus: with emergent (irreducible to cause and effect) phenomena, such as norms, informal interactions, perceptions, attitudes, and feelings, entering into the picture. A fifth dimension relates to the time frame of the improvement effort. Some organizational improvement strategies assume rapid implementation; others assume several months or years for effective implementation. And finally, some improvement strategies have an educational focus in contrast to more direct attempts to change the way the organization works.

Different change-directed efforts show different mixtures of these characteristics, although they tend to cluster together, as implied in Figure 15.6. Efforts falling under the Type-1 classification tend to feature a unilateral approach, an expert mode of consultation, a one-on-one (individual) approach. They tend to also focus on causal dimensions and to have a short-range time perspective. Type-5 efforts tend to be participative: featuring the use of the facilitator role, a team approach, a focus on emergent dimensions, and occupation with a time perspective that is fairly long. (We will discuss this clustering further in Chapter 16.)

Unilateral versus Participative Approaches

Change-directed efforts can be attempted unilaterally or can be participative. Unilateral changes usually involve the exercise of power, while participative approaches feature shared power and influence. There are many degrees of participation, of course. As discussed in Chapters 6 and 11, a manager's behavior can vary all the way from making a decision and announcing it to permitting subordinates to function within broad limits defined by the superior (Tannenbaum & Schmidt, 1973). Still another highly participative mode would be the superior working with subordinates as a group to reach a team consensus on some matter.

To illustrate further, a manager, with or without consultant help, might unilaterally plan and announce a restructuring of her organization as an attempt at organizational improvement (see Box 15.2). Or she might engage others in an extensive dialogue about the merits of reorganization to solve certain problems and be open to suggestions about how to proceed. Or, in an even more participative mode, the manager, together with immediate subordinates (and with input from lower echelons), might push toward a genuine consensus about reorganization—a decision that all would *buy into* and help implement. Advantages of a unilateral approach include speed of application and results—people with power can initiate some program more or less immediately and with quick results. Disadvantages include the possibility of resistance from people and groups, the possibility of conflict, and the likelihood that the change effort does not capitalize on the insights, creativity, and synergy that can emerge from effective teams.

Not all change efforts of a unilateral kind are top-down. A wildcat strike of machinists in a foundry occurring because of poor working conditions could be considered an upward-directed, unilateral attempt at change. A rebellious clique of subordinates going over the head of a manager and seeking his ouster would be another illustration of an upward-directed unilateral attempt at change. While we will not discuss these in detail, such efforts frequently precipitate an acrimonious power struggle, which is probably why Lippitt gives the advice stated in Box 15.3 on "Advice to Insurgents."

Expert versus Facilitator Approaches

Probably all organizations use some kind of consultants as agents of change to help improve things from time to time, whether or not they are recognized as such. Informal consulting help from within the organization is nearly universal. Most managers act as consultants to other managers, subordinates and superiors

BOX 15.2
THE "CANARY THEORY" OF MOTIVATION

Trying to forge ahead too quickly, TI was swamped by what Bucy called a bow wave of demand for money and people to support new products. Corporate resources were stretched so thin that most programs were delayed. The company, Bucy announced, had lost its ability to focus "on the right products, for the right growth markets, at the right time."

To regain those skills, TI is reorganizing from top to bottom, seeking to give its managers enough resources to get their jobs done. In March the company shook up the semiconductor group, reassigning over a dozen vice presidents and operating managers. A new executive for marketing, technology development, and strategy took over in May, as did a chief financial officer and managers for semiconductors and consumer products. More turmoil is in store: a Texas Instruments spokesman says that Bucy and Mark Shepherd, 59, chairman and chief executive, see no end to the restructuring.

Keep the canaries flying

Industry analysts and company veterans doubt that regrouping alone will solve TI's problems. TI habitually reorganizes when business turns bad; it has shifted executives at least once a year since 1979 in its hard-pressed computer memory operations. Some former TIers, as they call themselves, ascribe such shifts to a "canary theory" of motivation through anxiety: when you've got ten tons of canaries—or executives—in a five-ton truck, you beat on the roof now and then to make sure at least half of them are up and flying.

Source: Bro Uttal, "Texas Instruments Regroups," *Fortune,* 9 August 1982, p. 40.

frequently act as consultants to each other, and units frequently draw on the expertise of specialists from other units within the same organization. Many organizations supplement this informal consultation by formalizing internal-consultant roles and utilizing outside consultants.

Consultation help—whether informal or formal, from outside the organization or from within—can vary dramatically in terms of consultant behavior. Although there can be mixtures of behavior types, we want to focus on two contrasting approaches: the expert approach and the facilitator approach.

The behavior of the consultant who plays the expert role has frequently been likened to a doctor treating a patient. The patient presents some symptoms, the doctor makes a diagnosis and prescribes some treatment. In the organizational context, the expert listens to the set of problems being presented, makes a

BOX 15.3
ADVICE TO INSURGENTS

I would propose changing the insurgents' guideline . . . "Never fight a battle if there is a chance of losing it," to "Never fight a battle if there is a chance of initiating collaborative problem-solving."

Source: Ronald Lippitt, in preface to Herman Resnick and Reno J. Patti (Eds.), *Change From Within* (Philadelphia: Temple University Press, 1980), p. xii.

diagnosis, and prescribes some solutions. Examples would be a consultant studying a chemical manufacturing problem and recommending new equipment, or a consultant studying organizational problems and recommending a more decentralized structure or the creation or elimination of a department. The expert role usually involves studying the situation and writing a report that includes recommendations. The expert mode of consultation is particularly appropriate when the problem is essentially technological or when time constraints are severe.

By contrast, the consultant who plays the facilitator role tends to avoid making many substantive recommendations, but works with the manager in such a way that organization members can do a more effective job of diagnosing and solving their own problems. For example, the facilitator might recommend a two-day conference attended by representatives of all of the departments who are to be involved in the building of a new plant, with the purposes of clarifying the overall task and respective roles. Or, the facilitator might be asked to sit in on department head meetings and to comment on how the group appears to be working together. The facilitator role is particularly appropriate when emergent phenomena are likely to be crucial in the success of the change.

The facilitator tends to focus on the processes used by the organization, while the expert focuses on making substantive recommendations. These two roles are not perfectly distinct; nevertheless, consultants using these modalities tend in large part to behave differently. (We will describe the facilitator role in more detail in Chapter 16.)

Individual versus Team Approaches

Some change strategies deliberately focus on what we call intact work teams; that is, the boss and subordinates as an interdependent group. Some group approaches use task forces with membership drawn from several units. Other strategies deal with either individuals or individual jobs; examples would be skill-advancement and training programs and some forms of job enrichment. Such individual approaches may pay little, if any, attention to team dynamics. Individual approaches may be less time consuming and not require others to be present. On the other hand, they may ignore important interdependencies.

Focus on Causal versus Emergent Variables

Some change strategies focus largely on causal dimensions of organizations (see Figure 15.2) such as buildings, plant layout, equipment, order of rank and responsibility, control processes, and hiring and reward practices. Other strategies focus on the more subtle, emergent aspects of organizational culture, such as interpersonal and group processes, intergroup relationships, and climate. Further, some strategies start with the emergent dimensions of perceptions and feelings as a way of beginning to diagnose the total system. There may not be any inherent advantage of one focus over another; the problem that needs to be solved is what is important. However, a case can frequently be made for the wisdom of capitalizing on the perceptions of organizational members in making a diagnosis of what causal aspects are functional or dysfunctional. However, participative group approaches are no substitute for technical expertise. What is frequently needed is technical *and* social-system skill.

Short-range versus Long-range Time Perspective

Organizational change efforts vary a great deal in terms of the time perspective held by those proposing or implementing the particular program. For example, Frederick Taylor and his clients, in the early days of the scientific-management movement, assumed that there could be some almost immediate, major improvements in productivity if tasks, equipment, employee training, and compensation practices were redesigned. These assumptions proved largely true and continue to hold true (Locke, 1982). Wofac Company and other consulting firms in recent times have claimed largely the same thing and appear to be able to offset their fees with immediate savings (see Box 15.4, Main, 1981, p. 56). In

BOX 15.4
ONE METHOD OF COST CUTTING

In their first step forward, Hootnick and Calhoun called in Wofac Co., a New Jersey consulting firm that specializes in a system for improving productivity marked under the name VeFac. The process is a variation of the old time-and-motion studies devised at the turn of the century by Frederick W. Taylor. A Wofac consultant studies a unit like the supply department for several weeks, determines how long each job should take and how often it is performed, and then estimates how many workers the unit needs—usually fewer than it has.

Wofac attacked several areas of Intel, mainly inventory and supply functions, and quickly produced results. David J. Hamilton, one of Nevin's deputies, says that Wofac had already saved Intel its $240,000 fee by the time the fee was paid. Following the Wofac plan, the company made fixes that eliminated 122 jobs and now save $1.9 million a year.

But VeFac is a canned, standard system that has its limits. Supervisors were sometimes infuriated by it. One complained: "That [Wofac] guy comes in here and takes notes for a couple of days and he comes back a week later and says, 'You need five less people.' What the hell does he know?"

Source: Jeremy Main, "How to Battle Your Own Bureaucracy," *Fortune*, 29 June, 1981, p. 56.

contrast, many facilitators and managers involved in such contemporary efforts as quality-of-work-life or organization-development programs (to be discussed in the next chapter) have a time frame of several years in mind, relative to major, sustained improvements. This is particularly true with respect to such matters as teamwork effectiveness or the management of major structural change where a minimum of dysfunctional consequences in terms of employee morale and development is permissible.

SO WHAT? IMPLICATIONS FOR YOU

Because all management can be considered the management of change, it is important to understand change processes. This includes what to look for in terms of what is being changed, what the instruments or techniques of the change process might be, and what the effect might be on individuals, groups, and the total organization. Thus, we can act more intelligently and wisely as organization members or managers in responding to change and in initiating and managing change. Some of the specific implications of the material in this chapter are treated on the next few pages.

As a Member in an Organization

Generalizations	Implications
1. The environment external to organizations is always changing; organizations change; relationships change.	1. Anticipate change. View changes as opportunities rather than problems. Learn about the dynamics of change to be able to anticipate intended and unintended effects.
2. Organizational improvement may occur through changes in one or more of the following subsystems: goals and values, technical, structural, psychosocial, or managerial.	2. Don't be preoccupied with one or more favorite variables like communication, motivation, or decision making. They can blind you to the wide range of possibilities for constructive change.
3. Most changes in the goal, technical, structural, and managerial subsystems are likely to have repercussions in psychosocial subsystems—particularly in the areas of feelings, perceptions, motivations, and interactions.	3. Be aware of the multiple consequences that are usually produced by almost any change.
4. Individual phenomena, such as feelings, perceptions, performance goals, and motivation tend to be influenced by the causal phenomena that management sets in motion. Your feelings, perceptions, and attitudes have an effect on your performance and subsequently on the performance of the organization.	4. An issue for you is the extent to which it would be functional to share your perceptions and feelings about your job and your working environment with your work group or superior. This will depend partly on the norms of the group. It is important to sort out the feelings and attitudes you *bring* to the organization from those feelings and attitudes caused by what is going on in the organization. The former are probably more appropriately explored outside the organization with friends, counselors, and the like.
5. Group phenomena have a powerful effect on organizational outcomes, and are major factors	5. Issues for you are whether the norms of your group are functional for you and for the orga-

Generalizations	Implications
in change and resistance to change.	nization, and how much initiative to take in demonstrating effective interpersonal and group skills and in surfacing any dysfunctional norms.

As a Current or Future Manager

Generalizations	Implications
1. It is frequently difficult to solve major problems because most situations are held in equilibrium between forces resisting change and forces driving toward change.	1. Sense, define, and diagnose the forces operating in your situation.
2. The forces operating in most situations are multiple.	2. Be aware of the wide range of variables in the various subsystems that may be operating in a given situation. Keep in mind the notion of multiple causation.
3. Change tends to occur more readily by removing restraining forces than by adding to the driving forces.	3. Avoid adding to the driving forces; for example, by coercive means. This would usually create more restraining forces.
4. Many individual and group phenomena are largely "unplanned" in the sense that, as a manager, you have no direct control over them.	4. A major part of your task is to create an environment in which functional individual and group behaviors can emerge and constructive change can occur.
5. Intergroup behaviors and organizational climate are largely emergent phenomena that are set in motion by such dimensions as leadership style and philosophy and personnel policies and procedures.	5. An issue for you is the extent to which your leadership behaviors are congruent with the desired overall leadership style in the organization and are congruent with effective intergroup behavior.
6. As a leader of a group, you can do much to help create changes in the direction of constructive relationships with other leaders and groups.	6. While your behavior undoubtedly will be influenced by your superiors, you may have significant latitude in helping create constructive relationships.

Generalizations	**Implications**
7. Some changes can be functional for some organizational outcomes but dysfunctional for other end results.	7. Anticipate as many consequences of proposed changes as possible, and make decisions accordingly.
8. To be effective, planned change requires attention to initial problem identification, data gathering, problem diagnosis, action planning, implementation, follow-up and stabilization, assessment of consequences, and learning from the process.	8. The omission of one or more of these steps may result in no change or in negative change.
9. Planned-change efforts vary a great deal along such dimensions as whether the consultant role used is the expert or facilitator mode, whether the change effort is unilateral or participative, or whether there is a focus on individuals versus teams, causal or emergent variables, short-range or long-range time perspective.	9. Be alert to these dimensions and consider them in planning the processes.

LEARNING APPLICATION ACTIVITIES

1. Write a vignette based on your experience that describes some major change that was attempted in an organization. Include a description of how the change effort affected different people.

2. List several conditions or circumstances under which it is easy for you to change your behavior, and list several conditions or circumstances under which you tend to resist changing your behavior. Share with a subgroup of the class, and then ask a member of your group to report out common themes to the total class.

3. Study *The Word Processor* vignette and analyze why Trudy was anxious and annoyed. List several actions that might have been taken so that she would have been better prepared for the change. Share with subgroup and/or total class and discuss.

4. Analyze the vignette *The Disappearing Backlog* using the concepts listed in Figure 15.2, "Causal, Emergent, and Outcome Phenomena," to explain why the positive changes occurred.

5. Analyze the *President Jane* vignette and identify the causal, emergent, and outcome phenomena that were functional and those that were dysfunctional in terms of achieving Jane's goals for the organization.

6. In subgroups, discuss the external changes that have occurred in your lifetime—technological, political, and economic—that have affected the organization(s) where you have been employed. Share with the total class.

7. Analyze the vignette *A Slow Start* using Figure 15.5, "Steps in a Planned Change Effort." To what extent were the various critical process questions followed? What might have been done differently in order for the change effort to succeed? Where would you place this MBO effort on the continuum shown in Figure 15.6?

8. In subgroups, discuss any contact you have had with consultants. Describe the approach they used and discuss the extent to which they worked in a facilitator mode vs. the expert mode. Share the descriptions of the different consulting modes with the total class.

REFERENCES

Argyris, Chris. "Double Loop Learning in Organizations." *Harvard Business Review* 55/5 (September-October 1977): 115–125.

Craighead, E., A. E. Kazdin, and M. J. Mahoney. *Behavior Modification*. Boston, Mass.: Houghton Mifflin, 1976.

Hedberg, Bo. "How Organizations Learn and Unlearn." In Paul C. Nystrom and William H. Starbuck (Eds.); *Handbook of Organizational Design,* vol. 1. New York: Oxford University Press, 1981.

Lewin, Kurt. *Field Theory in Social Science*. New York: Harper & Row, 1951.

Likert, Rensis, and Jane Gibson Likert. *New Ways of Managing Conflict*. New York: McGraw-Hill, 1976.

Locke, Edwin A. "The Ideas of Frederick W. Taylor: An Evaluation." *Academy of Management Review* 7/1 (January 1982): 14–24.

Main, Jeremy. "How to Battle Your Own Bureaucracy." *Fortune* 103/13 (29 June, 1981): 54–58.

Resnick, Herman, and Reno J. Patti, eds. *Change from Within*. Philadelphia: Temple University Press, 1980.

Seiler, John A. *Systems Analysis in Organizational Behavior.* Homewood, Ill.: Irwin, 1967.

Tannenbaum, Robert, and Warren H. Schmidt. "How to Choose a Leadership Pattern." *Harvard Business Review* 36/2 (March-April 1958): 96.

Uttal, Bro. "Texas Instruments Regroups." *Fortune,* 9 August 1982, p. 40.

Zaltman, Gerald, and Robert Duncan. *Strategies for Planned Change*. New York: Wiley, 1977.

16 Organization-Improvement Strategies

LEARNING OBJECTIVES

After reading this chapter you should be able to:

1. Describe seven of the organization improvement strategies discussed in this chapter.
2. Compare and contrast these seven improvement strategies in terms of the critical dimensions of planned change discussed in Chapter 15; that is, unilateral versus participative, expert versus facilitator, individual versus team, causal versus emergent, or short-range versus long-range approaches.
3. Illustrate how the various improvement strategies relate to organizational subsystems. Give examples, from your own experience, if possible.
4. Identify the key ingredients in quality-of-work-life programs (QWL) and organization-development (OD) efforts.
5. Show how the strategies for interpersonal- and intergroup-conflict management draw on what is known about groups and individuals in conflict (Chapter 8).
6. Demonstrate how improvement strategies are reflective of particular leadership styles.

SEVEN DIVISIONS!

Weldon McNaughton, marketing manager, Agricultural Chemicals Division, located at corporate headquarters in New York City, was shocked and anxious. A memo addressed to all management personnel from the president of the company had just arrived. The memo started out as follows:

> The Board of Directors has just approved a reorganization of the company. The management believes a new structure will be advantageous to all of us. This reorganization plan, based on a lengthy study by Smith & Cooper, has been under review and modification in my office for several months, and we now believe it to be timely to move ahead.
>
> Effective July 1 the Company will be organized into seven regional divisions: Southeast, Northeast, Midwest, Southwest, Pacific West, Gulf, and Northwest. Each will be a cost center under an Executive Vice President for Operations who reports to the president's office. Headquarters for each region will be in the following cities, listed by respective regions: Miami, Boston, Chicago, Phoenix, Los Angeles, New Orleans, and Seattle.
>
> While this reorganization will involve a number of relocations, transfers, and/or reassignments, we hope there will be a minimum of disruption in the careers of most of our employees. As quickly as details are worked out division by division, you will be kept informed. Your immediate superior will be meeting with you within the next few days to provide you with some information about how the changes will effect you and your unit.

The memo was disturbing to Weldon in at least two respects. In the first place, it was not at all clear whether or not the company was going to retain overall corporate marketing on a major product basis or whether marketing would be grouped together on a regional basis. Secondly, since most of the company's agricultural chemical business was in the Midwest, in the southern Gulf States, and in California, it appeared to Weldon that a specialist like himself could wind up in any one of three cities, Chicago, Los Angeles, or New Orleans. Or, he might be kept on at headquarters. "As a southern boy, New Orleans would be O.K., but I'm not keen on going to Chicago or L.A.," he thought. "Furthermore, if this means a demotion, I may quit. This going from five product divisions to seven geographical divisions may be a crazy idea, with a bunch of capable people getting hurt in the process. I guess I'll call up Charlie in finance and see if we can get together for lunch—maybe he knows what is going to happen."

TASK REALIGNMENT

Jobs had become so specialized in the order department that Nancy Dittrich, manager, discussed with her staff the possibility of reorganizing some of the activities associated with them. The general notion was to give each employee more of a total "package" of tasks involving seeing matters through several steps—including the planning and final checking phases—rather than having some people doing the planning and others the checking. Most of the department members seemed to agree with the idea. The question of salary realignment came up indirectly, but was not pushed as an issue by anyone.

After extensive analysis of the various jobs and a series of group discussions about each one, with Nancy as moderator, agreement was reached about how the majority of them were to be restructured. Morale improved markedly, and it seemed to Nancy that productivity had gone up. She wondered if there were going to be requests for reevaluating these jobs into higher pay grades on the grounds that they were more complex, but by the end of the first six months no such requests had been made.

THE T-GROUP

Barbara was shocked at the consequences of what she had done. She had just criticized Don, one of eleven other T-group members, as follows:

"That's the way all of you rigid engineers think. You've got to reduce everything to some kind of mathematical formula. You'd think the universities could do a better job of turning out engineers who weren't just slide-rule jocks."

Don had flushed, started to respond, then stopped. Another group member had intervened, with considerable irritation, "Barbara, I get very angry with you when you pin labels on someone like that. You've done it to me and I don't like it."

Barbara had been visibly taken aback. After some give and take for a few minutes, the trainer had said, "Barbara, I'd like for you to describe your feelings right now, and then try to recall the feelings you were experiencing just before your comment to Don about slide rules and rigid engineers." As Barbara talked about her feelings, she began to realize that she had been feeling dominated by Don, resented the domination, and had wanted to punish him in some way.

As the T-group progressed, Barbara became more open in dealing with her feelings. In one or two instances when she started giving someone an unflattering label, she corrected herself, and explored her feelings about the other person's behavior or statement.

A CHANGE OF COMMAND

Captain Blumenthal had made a major effort to improve both the extent and the quality of participation at the large naval facility. He believed that the old dictatorial styles were out of fashion and did not tap the potential of the people in the organization. Personally, he preferred to use a participative approach, and his style was gradually emulated by several of the key department heads.

To further this approach, Captain Blumenthal, with the general concurrence of his key subordinate officers and civilian department heads, had employed two outside professionals with strong backgrounds in organization-development consulting and in group dynamics. These people were used to facilitate problem-solving workshops and as instructors in the management-development programs. They were later joined by a naval officer who had had extensive training in organization-development consulting.

At the end of a two-year tour of duty, Captain Blumenthal was promoted and transferred to Washington D.C. He was replaced by an officer with a more traditional approach to authority and directing people. The outside consultants were no longer used, and their Navy colleague requested a transfer. Problem-solving workshops were abandoned, relationships became more formal and somewhat strained, and department heads became a little less open in their dealings with each other. As one subordinate officer commented in private, "People are beginning to play competitive games with the budget again. And they'll say one thing in a meeting, and something else behind your back."

A DATA-GATHERING, FEEDBACK PROCESS

Consultant Ed Morris had been involved in a series of lunches with the division manager, Kay Sorensen, and then two meetings with Kay and her subordinate managers together. At the end of this last meeting, Kay, Ed, and the group agreed to a three-day workshop away from the office. During the preliminary discussions, the managers had talked about the need for improvements in communications, priority setting, and cooperation between departments. Ed had also discussed with the group the process he would use if the improvement effort materialized.

Two of the managers, Harold and Gwen, had started out with suspicions of Kay's motives, thinking that there was some hidden reason why Kay was bringing in the consultant. But after one of the preliminary discussions, Harold said: "Kay seems to really want to create better teamwork and to let people be more frank and open. I think I can trust Ed—he seems to be saying he wants to consult with the total team and not be a lackey for the boss." Gwen replied, "I agree, but a lot depends on how Kay behaves in the workshop. If she springs some grand scheme on us about how things ought to be, people will start dragging their feet right away, including me."

A few days before the workshop, Ed interviewed all the members of the management team, including Kay. He opened the interview by saying that the information from the interviews would be kept anonymous, but that he would report on any themes that emerged, and that those themes would be used to develop the agenda for the workshop. He then went on to say, "I'd like you to answer two broad questions while I take notes: (1) What things are going well within this top management team?; (2) What things are getting in the way of getting the job done the way you think it should be done? In other words, what are the strengths and what are the problems?"

THE ACTING MEDICAL DIRECTOR

Robert MacMaster, M.D., was acting medical director of Central States Group Health Cooperative, one of the largest health maintenance organizations in the country. He agreed to be acting director for a year while the executive council searched for a permanent medical director. The council was comprised of three members who were automatically included because of their roles as medical directors of the three geographic regions served by the cooperative. One other representative was elected from each of the regions. These six, plus the medical director, comprised the seven-person council.

It was a fairly complex arrangement because the medical director reported to the executive council, three of whose members were his subordinates in the day-to-day operation of the organization. That is, the three regional medical directors reported to the medical director on a day-to-day basis.

Performance evaluation was a primary concern in this complex arrangement. Evaluation of professional competence had long been a thorn in the side of Central States as well as other medical organizations. This reluctance to evaluate carried over into the managerial roles that needed to be carried out. Thus, the whole concept of performance planning and evaluation had to be approached rather carefully.

Accordingly, Dr. MacMaster took advantage of a one-day workshop at the university on the subject of motivation and performance. He liked a number of the ideas set forth by Professor Tom Owens, and sought him out after the workshop in order to see if he would be willing to discuss Central States' specific problem. Tom was intrigued by the issues involved and agreed to a series of meetings: (1) with Bob and his administrative assistant, Joe Burghoff; (2) with the executive council to explain some of the ideas involved in performance planning and evaluation; and (3) a half-day workshop session to actually demonstrate what might be done. Much of what was covered was new ground for most of the people involved.

Professor Owens suggested focusing on roles rather than persons as a first step in the process. As a start, the group spent several hours working on the role of a member of the executive council. They tried to determine what an effective council member would do; that is, how would he or she behave if performing successfully. This served as a warm-up for doing the same thing with the role of the medical director. The expectations were summarized and prioritized in order to identify the key dimensions that seemed important for success or failure as a medical director in the eyes of the executive council. In the process of discussing these expectations, the council in effect evaluated the performance of the acting medical director without the process becoming overly personal.

A by-product of this process was a set of criteria that the council could use in evaluating candidates for the permanent position of medical director. The council members seemed quite relieved that they had established a meaningful process and had developed some relevant criteria by which to judge candidates and to make a decision.

INTRODUCTION

This chapter is chiefly about *nontechnical interventions* into the various subsystems in order to bring about organizational improvement. To intervene means to impose or interject some programmatic activities into the ongoing processes of an organization in a deliberate attempt to improve organizational outcomes (French & Bell, 1984, p. 77). By *non-technical* we mean interventions that focus more on the psychosocial, structural, managerial, and goal subsystems than on the technical subsystem. However, at least one intervention we will describe, the use of quality-control circles, can be a direct intervention into the technical subsystem as well as other subsystems.

In this chapter we will discuss the nature of specific improvement programs, noting what variables are changed and what some of the human reactions and dilemmas are that can arise. We will also draw on our discussion of what critical dimensions to look for in a planned-change effort (Chapter 15) and will consider some of the probable consequences of alternative ways of going about organizational-improvement efforts. The following topics will be covered:

Different Improvement Strategies
Individual-Performance Improvement Strategies
Group-Performance Improvement Strategies
Intergroup-Performance Improvement Strategies
Comprehensive Organization-Improvement Strategies
Emphases in Different Improvement Strategies
So What? Implications for You

DIFFERENT IMPROVEMENT STRATEGIES

The vignettes in this chapter and *The Slow Start* vignette (about MBO/R) in Chapter 15 are examples of managerial strategies aimed at improving organizations. Some were successful, others not. By improving, we mean better organizational outcomes in areas such as effectiveness, efficiency, and participant satisfaction. Some focus largely on causal dimensions; others focus, at least at the beginning, on emergent dimensions. There are, of course, many improvement strategies other than what we will cover in this one chapter. A research-and-development (R&D) effort in an organization is, in a broad sense, an organization-improvement strategy. As another example, top management might try to improve the effectiveness of an organization through careful and elaborate recruiting practices. Or, top management and a board of directors might try to improve organizational performance by the installation of a key-executive-bonus and stock-option plan. And, obviously, a number of strategies might be attempted concurrently.

Improvement efforts also vary in terms of what organizational subsystems are being altered. Sometimes several are changed; sometimes all are changed to some extent. In the vignettes *Seven Regional Divisions!* and *Task Realignment,* attempts were being made to improve the organization by altering the *structural* subsystem—the overall structure of the company in one instance and, in the other, the structure of individual jobs within a department. In the *Change of Command* vignette, there had been an attempt to improve the organization by changes in the managerial subsystem: more specifically, in the prevailing leadership style. But patterns of behavior began to revert to the old ways when the innovative commanding officer was transferred. In the *Data-Gathering, Feedback Process* vignette, a process was being started to improve the organization by focusing on the perceptions of key managers as to problems and opportunities.

In the *Acting Medical Director* vignette, an attempt was being made to improve organizational functioning by drawing on the perceptions of the executive council relative to their expectations of the medical director role. This was an intervention in both the psychosocial and the structural subsystem. The focus was initially on the psychosocial system in the sense that perceptions were

BOX 16.1
AVOID EITHER-OR CONCEPTIONS OF WORK ORGANIZATIONS

An example of this faulty thinking relates to the sources and types of controls: "Traditional systems rely on hierarchical controls. The innovative system is the opposite; therefore, it must rely on individual or team self-management." Another example of this thinking is: "If we need to rely on self-discipline and peer group pressure to minimize counterproductive behavior, then there is no place for management-administered discipline."

Indeed, as managers in these work systems have sooner or later discovered, a selective emphasis and sensible mixture of management techniques are called for. A number of organizations have had to go through a period of permissiveness before management discovered the need to set and enforce certain boundaries on the behavior of members of the company.

Managers make a related mistake when they assume that an organization at start-up can be at an idealized, advanced state of development. Some plans for new plant organization neglect the important distinction between conceiving of the steady state design and designing the initial organization. These plans start up with workers and supervisors having roles and responsibilities that reflect the planners' idealized view of the mature organization. Workers lack the technical and human skills as well as the problem-solving capacities to perform effectively. Supervisors cannot merely "facilitate"—they must provide directive supervision.

Source: Reprinted by permission of the *Harvard Business Review*. Excerpt from "Work Innovations in the United States," by Richard E. Walton [July-August 1979]

brought to the surface and shared and that the issues were to be worked on in a group setting. However, we can assume that other subsystems would also be addressed since the way priorities and goals were being set seemed to be a problem. In *The Word Processor* vignette of Chapter 15, an attempt was being made to improve organizational performance through technology, at least in one unit. In the *Slow Start* vignette, an attempt was made to improve the organization by focusing on the goal and managerial subsystems by introducing an MBO/R program that laid heavy emphasis on goal setting and control.

Some of the vignettes in this and the preceding chapter involve managers bringing in consultants from outside or from elsewhere in the organization. A majority of the change-directed efforts did not involve consultants. In the instances when they were used, the mode of consulting varied a great deal. In the *Seven Divisions!* vignette, for example, a consulting firm recommended changes in structure; in the *Data Gathering, Feedback Process* vignette, a consultant was used to gather anonymous data and facilitate a process of feedback, diagnosing problems, and making action plans.

All did not go smoothly in all of these efforts. For example, in the *Slow Start* vignette, there was a great deal of resistance. In the *Change of Command* vignette, turnover at the top level negated most of the changes that had occurred during the previous two years. In the *Word Processor* vignette, anxiety, uncertainty, and annoyance were probably reducing the productivity of an employee. In *Seven Divisions!* we may suspect that there was a great deal of anxiety and misdirected effort after the president's memo appeared, at least until people found out how they would be affected by the reorganization.

Organization-improvement efforts can also be classified, roughly, by the complexity of the social system being changed. The focus might be on individuals as entities, on two-person relationships (such as between boss and subordinate), on work-groups (including the supervisor), on intergroup relationships, or on the total organization. The effort might be even more broadly focused—on the organization-environment relationship. Or, it might be on several of these systems' levels simultaneously.

INDIVIDUAL PERFORMANCE IMPROVEMENT STRATEGIES

Many contemporary improvement strategies focus on the performance or the tasks of individuals. The individual, or the individual's job, is the target of change. However, most such strategies require changes in the behavior or roles of other persons if the strategy is to be successful, as we shall see.

It should be noted that most training programs in organizations, and the encouragement of employees to take courses offered by schools and universities and other institutions, are organizational-improvement strategies aimed at the individual. The assumption is usually made that the individual can make a more valuable contribution to the organization as a result of the training. Again, this assumption may be only partially valid, in that the attitudes or awareness of others may need to change if the training is to be utilized effectively. Four individual performance improvement strategies, in particular, have received considerable publicity in recent years. They are job enrichment, positive reinforcement, management by objectives, and the T-group.

Job Enrichment

Job enrichment, discussed briefly in Chapter 9, is one form of job design. Job enrichment involves redesigning jobs to provide a more meaningful package for each employee. The *Task Realignment* vignette is an example of such an approach. Rather than simply adding additional tasks to a job to provide more variety (called job enlargement), a conscious effort is made to include more planning and controlling activities, thus providing more autonomy and challenge for the person. An attempt is made to automate repetitive aspects of the job or to push them to lower job classifications (Myers, 1970, pp. 55–95; Ford, 1973, pp. 96–106).

Hackman and Oldham (1980, pp. 71–90) have a different conceptualization of job components than that above, and see the core job characteristics as skill variety, task identity, task significance, autonomy, and feedback. These core job characteristics are seen as important to certain "critical psychological states." As shown in Figure 16.1, the first three job characteristics—skill variety, task identity, and task significance—are important for experiencing the meaningfulness of the work. Autonomy is important for a sense of responsibility for job outcomes and feedback from the job is necessary for a person to know the results of his or her work efforts. These critical psychological states, in turn, are seen as leading to high motivation, satisfaction, and work performance.

Of considerable consequence is whether or not such job enrichment is unilateral or participative. Experts disagree on which approach is best. Herzberg and colleagues, for example, seem to suggest that the incumbent is not in the best position to see how to enrich a job (Paul, Robertson, & Herzberg, 1969, p. 75). Myers, on the other hand, clearly favors a team, participative approach, this reflecting his stint at Texas Instruments. In Myers' approach, a team of workers under an elected team captain is presented with a manufacturing challenge in terms of costs, delivery time, and other dimensions and allowed to plan and control the work and work flow in any way that makes sense (Myers, 1970, pp. 55–95).

Participation can also be analyzed in terms of the points at which participation occurs. In the Herzberg approach, there may be no participation in the diagnosis of the problem, in the adoption of the job-enrichment plan, nor in any of the subsequent steps (see Figure 15.5). Or, there may be participation in any one or more of those steps. In the Myers approach, there may or may not be participation in adopting the broad program, but there is considerable employee participation in problem diagnosis and action planning. In the *Task Realignment* vignette, Nancy involved her subordinates throughout the process.

In the more unilateral approaches to job enrichment, consultants tend to be of the expert variety. In the participative approaches, consultants tend to be facilitators who involve supervisors in examining the utility of the approach and

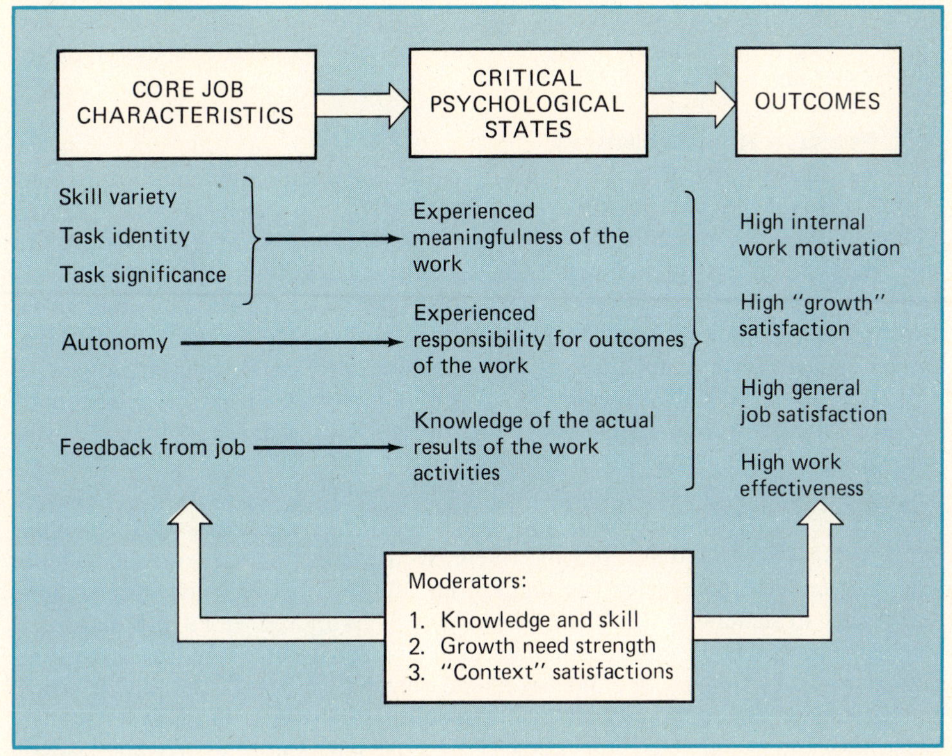

FIGURE 16.1 Job Characteristics Model. **Source:** J. Richard Hackman and Greg R. Oldham, *Work Redesign* (Reading, MA: Addison-Wesley, 1980), p. 90. Reprinted with permission.

who provide help to supervisors and employees in running problem-solving meetings. The time frame for implementing unilateral versions of job enrichment appears to be fairly short, while the more participative approaches require more time for training—for group and leadership skills to be developed.

Job-enrichment efforts frequently have by-products beyond the immediate people and jobs involved. An entire layer of supervision is sometimes eliminated. At a minimum, the role of the immediate supervisor changes as a result of some supervisory responsibilities being pulled down into the jobs below. The resulting role might involve further training of subordinates and seeing to it that the flow of materials and information is expedited.

Clearly, there will be resistance to such programs on the part of supervisors if their job security, status, and feelings are not taken into account. Immediate issues that arise are whether or not supervisors have any job protection, whether the changes will be gradual, whether any reductions in staff will be accomplished through normal attrition, and how much training supervisors and employees are to receive in order to prepare themselves for new responsibilities. Further, experience suggests that there are additional ramifications for the system that need to be managed, including the way jobs are clustered together and the layout of offices and plants (Ford, 1973).

Positive Reinforcement

As discussed in Chapter 9, positive reinforcement programs, sometimes called *behavior-modification* programs, have become more conspicuous in recent years, but do not appear to be widespread. The approach is to emphasize praise and the avoidance of punishment. The steps in starting and maintaining such a program include (a) describing the behavior expected on the job and conducting a performance audit: (b) establishing specific performance goals for each employee (a participative approach is recommended); (c) permitting employees to keep records of their own work; and (d) providing praise for positive aspects of performance and withholding praise when work is substandard (Hamner & Hamner, 1976, pp. 8–9).

There may be participation in setting goals, but little participation elsewhere in the process. Consultant help appears to be of the expert variety. The time frame is fairly short in that rapid improvements are expected. Several subsystems are changed simultaneously. The managerial subsystem is changed in that there is a change in leadership style. The goal subsystem is altered with a high emphasis on goal setting. The psychosocial subsystem changes in the sense that the norms change toward praise being emphasized and punishment being discredited. While the aspect of monetary rewards (the structural subsystem) is played down in these programs, compensation tends to become an issue after a while. When company profitability increases, employees begin to question whether or not they are getting a fair return for their improved performance.

Management by Objectives and Results

MBO/R programs can be considered strategies for improving individual performance, and for that reason we include a discussion here in addition to the brief discussion in Chapter 12. If conceptualized more broadly, however, MBO/R programs can be considered goal-setting and control systems that link all managers, and conceivably all employees, in an integrated, interactive process of mutual influence about unit and organizational objectives.

MBO/R programs feature (a) periodic agreements between a superior and a subordinate as to the subordinate's objectives for a stated period of time; (b) an interim review of progress; and then (c) review at the end of the period of time as to the degree of success in meeting the objectives. An attempt is usually made to state objectives in measurable terms; for example, "Will obtain 20 new customers for product line X by 30 December," or "Will complete building modifications on Plant B within budgeted amounts on or before 1 July, complying with all building codes and environmental standards." Not all objectives can be stated in quantitative terms; it is important to include all relevant objectives, even if they are written in qualitative terms. For example: "Will improve my staff meetings, as perceived by those attending."

MBO/R programs are interventions in both the goal and managerial subsystems. They vary widely in terms of the degree of real participation between subordinate and superior in the setting of objectives; some applications clearly have been highly autocratic. Such approaches have a high-control aspect; on the other hand, participative approaches can provide the opportunity for much more supportive, helpful interaction between subordinate and superior.

The consultant role in MBO/R programs varies, depending on the extent to which consultants conceive of themselves as group facilitators versus traditional experts: the latter's function being to insist on a standardized procedure. Usually the consulting mode traffics in a mixture of *advisory* (to managers about procedures) and *workshop* (affording practice in writing objectives) information and guidance.

While it is hard to quarrel with the desirability of a focus on objectives, many problems have been found to occur in the implementation of MBO/R programs. These problems include a neglect of the spontaneous or creative aspects of the job that have not been reduced to formal goal statements, a feeling on the part of the subordinate of being overcontrolled, or a lack of emphasis on the interdependency and teamwork aspects of jobs (Levinson, 1970, pp. 128–129).

These problems, coupled with difficulties inherent to the work of clarifying objectives, writing them in measurable terms, and getting agreement, usually mean that a great deal of time and effort needs to be spent on the MBO/R program. Many managers have found to their chagrin that a successful implementation of an MBO/R effort has taken three or four years instead of a few months as was originally hoped. The *Slow Start* vignette in the previous chapter reflects some of the problems that can be encountered.

MBO/R programs vary in the extent to which there is a focus on one-to-one relationships versus team approach. Theory and experience suggest that a team approach to MBO/R might have many advantages (French & Hollman, 1975; Likert & Fisher, 1977). However, it is clear that such an approach would require the development of some desirable level of skill in group dynamics and would require a commitment to teamwork as well as to a participative approach.

T-Groups

The T (training)-group is one form of laboratory training. Laboratory training refers to an educational experience in which the participant draws practical and theoretical knowledge from the dynamics of the seminar of the workshop itself. The learning mode is first and foremost *experiential;* that is, one learns by experiencing an event or process and only then analyzing it and conceptualizing about it. Forms of laboratory training have been widely used in the U.S. and abroad since the mid-1940s, but use of the T-group appears to have decreased somewhat in recent years. Instrumented labs make extensive use of participant involvement in group or organizational exercises, followed by the use of scored questionnaires or scales pertaining to personal, interpersonal, or group behavior.

Typically, the T-group involves approximately 12 participants plus a trainer and features examination of the emergent phenomena in the group. Objectives include learning more about group dynamics, becoming more aware of one's own feelings and impact on others, and increased competence in interpersonal and group relationships. Sessions are usually unstructured, in the sense that there is no formal agenda. However, under the guidance of the trainer, the focus tends to be on dealing with feelings, achieving clarity in communications between members of the group, sharing perceptions about the evolving group dynamics, and learning from the experience. Emphasis is on learning from the here-and-now dynamics of the interaction rather than dealing with past or outside events of a personal nature. The *T-group* vignette is an example of the kind of learning that can occur in a T-group.

Attendance by an individual in a T-group experience is not an organizational-improvement strategy per se, but may be used as an educational supplement to a broader improvement strategy. In the early days of T-groups, a number of organizations and trainers experimented with intact work teams (superior and subordinates together) participating in a T-group (called *family* T-groups), but this practice has declined. The emphasis now is more on the involvement of work groups in team building sessions that have more of a task orientation. Individuals attend *stranger* labs; that is, with people from other organizations.

One of the difficulties with T-groups is the problem of transferring what is learned back to the job setting. It often happens that people go back to their jobs only to find the culture of the work group or organization is not supportive or clearer, more direct communications, of dealing with group process and maintenance issues, and of dealing with feelings. As a result, what has been learned begins to fade, or the emotional investment in the experience gives way to cynicism. Thus, it is important that managers consider the kind of an organizational culture they want. If they want to build a culture more congruent with T-group insights, several key people should attend laboratory-training sessions in order to gain understanding and increased support for a new approach.

GROUP PERFORMANCE IMPROVEMENT STRATEGIES

A number of interventions in current use focus directly on work groups. We believe that the remainder of the 1980s and the 1990s will see an intensified interest in organization-improvement strategies that have a strong team emphasis.

While some of the individual interventions described above have group versions—for example, the group problem-solving approach to job enrichment and team forms of MBO/R—some improvement efforts have been developed that relate specifically to groups. These interventions assume that there is a great deal of latent problem-solving capability and motivation that can be unlocked through the development and support of effective work teams. Of particular importance are sociotechnical systems, quality circles, and variants of team building, including a top-management problem-solving conference called the *confrontation meeting*. In addition to describing these, we will also briefly discuss a technique called *sensing*.

Sociotechnical Systems

The creation and use of semiautonomous work groups largely grew out of experiments conducted by the Tavistock Institute in England and subsequently by universities such as U.C.L.A. in the United States. The approach developed by Tavistock, under the general title sociotechnical systems, is an organization-improvement strategy in which there is an attempt to create a better fit between organizational structure, the task to be done, the technology used, and the social/psychological needs of employees.

An experiment in the U.S. stemming from Tavistock approaches may be illustrative. This organization improvement effort was conducted at the Rushton coal mine in Pennsylvania with the initial cooperation of both management and the union, and had the following features (Mills, 1970):

1. The employment of consultants who served as experts in the sense of recommending a particular approach and as facilitators in the sense of helping guide the improvement effort, in giving assistance to various committees, managers, and union officials, and in training production crews in problem solving.
2. The appointment of a steering committee composed of local union officials and managers who met once a week for several months to diagnose problems in overall performance of the mine and to make recommendations.
3. Ratification of the overall improvement plan by union members.
4. The creation of an experimental section in the mine, composed of a crew of nine volunteers from each of three shifts.
5. Retaining specialization of tasks, but training all crew members in all jobs of the section.
6. Providing top pay for all of the crew members, since they would eventually all learn all of the jobs including the higher-paid specialties.
7. Turning over direct supervision of production and the handling of grievances to each crew, with the foreman now responsible for training, safety, and planning.
8. Discussions as to how any gains would be shared by the workers.

The essential change was the creation of a team of workers who now managed their equipment and tasks in an interdependent, cooperative way and who diagnosed and solved problems as a group. In addition, the role of the foreman was changed to more of a planning and expediting role instead of direct supervision.

At the end of one year, productivity and safety data indicated the experiment in one section to be generally successful. Partly because of lack of adequate information to, and involvement of, employees in the rest of the mine, and attempts by the management to extend the concept unilaterally to a newly created unit, union members voted down a proposal to extend the experiment to the entire mine. However, in a few months, because of employee and supervisor interest, the concept was extended to other parts of the mine, but not to all sections. A few years later, the program was essentially stalled because of lack of consensus within management and within the union as to its benefits (Goodman, 1979).

Although the Rushton experiment stalled, there have been enough successes with the sociotechnical approach—for example, at the Topeka General Foods plant (Walton, 1977) and Donnelly Mirrors (Iman, 1975)—for the issue is no longer to be whether the approach will work. The issues now are how to sustain the successes and how to provide further challenges and developmental opportunities for individuals and groups once the program matures. The next steps appear to be helping work teams gradually become responsible for managing more of the business aspects of their units: monitoring and controlling costs; managing maintenance and quality assurance; and machine replacement (Miles & Rosenberg, 1982, p. 38).

The ingredients that appear to be associated with successful sociotechnical approaches include (Miles & Rosenberg, 1982, pp. 29–30):

1. A philosophy that states the desirability of optimizing outcomes for both the organization and the employees.
2. Relatively autonomous teams at the operating level, "responsible for significant processes or products."
3. Within-team job assignments that are challenging.
4. Facilitative leadership—a role that is gradually assumed by the team itself.
5. Careful hiring and extensive training at induction.
6. Pay and promotion practices that reward learning additional skills of relevance to the unit and plant.
7. Participative decision making and a relatively egalitarian culture.
8. Physical facilities and norms that enhance communications within and across units.
9. Profit-sharing or bonus plans that are plantwide.

These ingredients are comparable to those to be described later in this chapter under the category of quality-of-work-life (QWL) programs.

Quality Circles

The quality circle (or quality-control circle, see Box 16.2) is similar to the form of job enrichment described above in which a work group is extensively involved in problem diagnosis and problem solving. The essential difference in the quality circle is that there is a strong emphasis on improving and maintaining product or service quality. The statistical aspects of quality control were introduced to Japanese firms by Edward Deming and other Americans in the 1950s and 1960s with the Japanese introducing the techniques into group settings. The approach spread rapidly in Japan and then spread to American firms in the late 1970s and early 1980s. The Lockheed Missile and Space Company was the first American company to study and implement the approach on an extensive scale (Cole, 1979).

BOX 16.2
LOCKHEED SHIPBUILDING AND CONSTRUCTION COMPANY QUALITY CIRCLES

"A small group of employees, meeting regularly, to manage their work"

Employee participation in decision making, problem solving, and other creative tasks is a prerequisite to a healthy business enterprise. The knowledge represented by employee education and experience is vast and largely untapped. The objective of quality circles is to create the proper medium and process to utilize this knowledge.

Our single statement to quality circles is to find ways of improving our daily operations to reduce costs and improve our competitive position.

We view quality circles as an inherent component of the management structure. For this reason, supervisors actively participate in and frequently lead quality circles. Quality circles are the mechanism by which the concepts of participative management are activated at the level of individual workers. Quality circles work with the existing management structure. Circles make and enact decisions appropriate to the level of management present in the circle, keeping higher-level management informed. Decisions requiring higher-level approval are referred to that level with recommendations and reasons for the recommendation. Such recommendations are accepted or rejected. However, if rejected, higher level management must justify the rejection to the circle.

Source: Used with permission of the Lockheed Shipbuilding and Construction Company.

In one version, quality circles are composed of seven to ten employees from a unit who volunteer to meet regularly to diagnose product quality and other problems and to make recommendations about solving those problems. Recommendations are usually forwarded to a coordinating or steering committee. Meetings, which are typically held once a week on company time, are usually chaired by the supervisor, although circles are sometimes chaired by an employee elected from the group or on a rotating basis. Facilitators are sometimes invited to sit in on the meetings to assist groups with procedures and group processes.

In another version, such as at the Lockheed Shipbuilding and Construction Company, quality circles may have as many as four hierarchical levels represented at a meeting. In these instances, participants are volunteers from subunits of a larger unit, and the meetings are chaired by the top manager of that unit. Circle activities are reported through the regular management-reporting structure, with higher management, including the shipyard president, simultaneously receiving minutes of the quality-circle meetings (Hayes & Swanson, 1982).

Before the formation of the quality circle groups, volunteer supervisors are trained by facilitators and quality control experts in such areas as leading participative discussions, in group-dynamics and communications skills, and in quality-control concepts and statistical tools. The facilitators are frequently internal consultants or training people who have organization development skills (see the following sections on team building and OD). Once trained, the supervisors, with the help of facilitators, train those subordinates who volunteer to participate. The facilitators also assist the groups in linking to other groups dealing with overlapping problems and in linking to the overall steering committee. The quality circle groups are encouraged to utilize experts from anywhere within the organization in solving problems, and are sometimes authorized by management to make changes without higher approval whenever feasible. Some member of top management usually meets with each group at least once a year (Zippo, 1980; Cole, 1979; Yager, 1979).

Thus, the introduction of quality circles into an organization is an intervention in several subsystems simultaneously. There is a change in the structural subsystem, in the sense that the jobs of the volunteer participants are changed to include working with the quality circle group. There is a further change in the structural subsystem when several hierarchical levels are represented at problem-solving meetings. There is a change in the managerial subsystem in that there is more emphasis on a participative leadership style. The technical subsystem is changed through the sharing of production and quality-control techniques. The goal subsystem is affected through group development of specific quality-control objectives. Finally, the psychosocial subsystem is changed by managers tuning into the perceptions of employees and by increased linkage between groups.

The adoption of the quality circle concept appears to be a long-range strategy because of the time required to train employees in quality-control and group-dynamics techniques, and the time required to accomplish a real shift in leadership style. Time is also required for the concept to spread and for people to gain confidence in its utility.

Team Building

The central activity in many organization development (OD) efforts is frequently called *team building*. Team building, in essence, involves the members of a formal work team, including the supervisor, collaboratively examining the functional and dysfunctional aspects of their work-group culture as well as addressing the issues and challenges that have not been adequately addressed to date, and making plans to correct deficiencies and achieve their objectives. Team building is applicable to task forces and committees as well as to the more traditional work group.

The term team building probably emerged because of the origin of the process in so-called family laboratories that focused on interpersonal and group relationships. The label probably remains because of the heightened sense of teamness and teamwork that usually emerges through collaborative problem-solving experiences.

The vignette at the beginning of the chapter, *A Data-Gathering, Feedback Process,* describes some of the typical preliminary activities in the team-building process. Based on interviews with each member of the group, the facilitator extracts the themes that emerge—both the strengths that people see and the areas where problems are perceived—and feeds this data back to the group during a workshop. Groups are typically asked to prioritize the themes in terms of which areas are the most important to be worked on, and the facilitator works with the group to help them diagnose the problems, evaluate alternative solutions, and make actions plans. The problems that are worked on may have to do with interpersonal relationships, role expectations, goals, leadership style, norms, external forces that are influencing group effectiveness—any causal or emergent phenomena that are dysfunctional.

The general approach is also applicable to assisting task forces or special-project groups in getting off to a rapid start and in their ongoing effectiveness as teams. Task forces and project teams frequently have unique problems in terms of members representing a sort of *constituency* in a home department, and need to work through issues pertaining to loyalty, leadership, and goals. Task forces or project groups may also have problems of motivation if rewards are perceived as coming through one's regular job and superior, not through performance in the task force or project group. Team building is also applicable to newly formed groups assigned to start up a new plant or other facility or to design or build a prototype product. Aerospace executives in one firm told us that the use of team building had saved the corporation many weeks of start-up time on new projects and thus millions of dollars. Team building can also be applicable in situations like the *Seven Divisions!* vignette when new teams result from reorganizing the work force.

The dimension of trust is particularly important in successful team building. The facilitator must be seen as being potentially helpful and concerned about the interests and feelings of all members of the group, the superior must be trusted enough so that people have some belief the intervention will be useful, and group members must trust each other enough so that people can begin to become more open about what they see as functional and dysfunctional. The process succeeds as trust is gradually earned and increases. This requires skill and integrity on the part of the facilitator, sufficient commitment on the part of group members to work through differences and make the process work, and the periodic reinforcement that successful endeavor brings as the process unfolds.

For major shifts in team culture and major improvements in group performance to occur, a long-range view is necessary. However, most team building tends to result in a number of short-term, immediate benefits, such as a better understanding on the part of participants of how others perceive strengths and problem areas, the discovery of solutions to some of the easier problems, and increased morale.

Team building is a direct intervention in the psychosocial subsystem because it initially focuses on the perceptions and feelings that people have about what is going on in their group and the broader organization. Further, team building focuses on both causal and emergent variables. For example, in a team-building session, group members might discuss problems in interpersonal communications and group norms along with concerns about equipment or how tasks have been assigned.

Role-Analysis Technique

When unclear expectations is a high priority issue, the *role-analysis technique* can be used effectively in the context of team building (French & Bell, 1984, pp. 146–148; Dayal & Thomas, 1968). The procedure assumes that there is a need for clarifying or renegotiating the activities carried out by one or more members of the team. Ideally, it is a voluntary process, with job incumbents volunteering their jobs to be the focal point for discussion. With a job incumbent listening—the district sales manager, let us say—group members answer this question: "If the sales manager were operating in an optimally effective way, what would he or she be doing?" All responses are listed on newsprint (flipchart paper), including disagreements between members of the group. After an appropriate period, twenty minutes or so, the job incumbent is then asked to respond. This is followed by group discussion and interchange between the incumbent and other members of the group, including the boss. The superior's role is often discussed using this technique (see Box 16.3).

What typically emerges through this discussion is a modified and agreed-upon set of expectations about the carrying out of the particular role: both (a) *what* should be done and (b) *how* it should be done. Obviously, the technique should not be used as a mechanism for venting hostility on a group member. It requires commitment to a process of sharing expectations, listening effectively, and working through conflicting ideas.

The Confrontation Meeting

Beckhard (1967) describes a one-day intervention involving most or all of the managerial group in a small or medium-sized organization. This approach, which involves a facilitator who coordinates the process, Beckhard calls a *confrontation meeting*. The confrontation meeting is more complex than team building in that several levels of management and several groups are present. Beckhard sees the intervention as appropriate when the following pertains (p. 150):

> There is a need for the total management group to examine its own workings.
> Very limited time is available for the activity.
> Top management wishes to improve the conditions quickly.
> There is enough cohesion in the top teams to ensure follow-up.
> There is real commitment to resolving the issues on the part of top management.
> The organization is experiencing, or has recently experienced, some major change.

BOX 16.3
ROLE ANALYSIS TECHNIQUE

"If the ____________ were operating in an optimally effective way, what would
Focal Role
he or she be doing?"

Procedure

1. Select a volunteer who wishes his/her role (Focal Role) to be analyzed and/or clarified. (Ideally, several persons, in an interdependent group wish to take turns being in the Focal Role.)
2. While the Focal Role person listens, the group members respond to the above question with their expectations and understandings of the Focal Role. (The Focal Role person may only ask questions for clarification, not discuss the points raised.)
3. Have one of the group members list the expectations on a sheet of newsprint.
4. Conclude the role analysis in about 15 to 20 minutes, at which time the Focal Role person responds to the list with his/her own expectations and reactions (e.g., agreement, disagreement, needs further study, needs negotiation).

The steps in the intervention are as follows (pp. 154–155):

Step 1—*Climate Setting* (45 minutes to one hour). The top manager communicates his or her goals and hopes for the meeting, including open and free discussion, and assures the group that there will be no punitive consequences of open confrontation of issues. The consultant or the top manager might then talk about such matters as communications problems in organizations, concepts of shared responsibility, and the opportunity for influencing the organization.

Step 2—*Information Collecting* (one hour). Heterogeneous subgroups of seven or eight people each are formed. No boss-subordinate pairs are permitted in these groups, and each group includes someone from each of the functional areas represented, such as accounting, manufacturing, personnel, marketing, and the like. If a top management group has been meeting regularly, it meets as a separate subgroup.

The subgroups are asked to select a recorder and a reporter and report back their deliberations on an assignment something like the following:

"Think of yourself as an individual with needs and goals. Also think as a person concerned about the total organization. What are the obstacles, demotivators, poor procedures or policies, unclear goals, or poor attitudes that exist today? What different conditions, if any, would make the organization more effective and make life in the organization better?'' (Beckhard, 1967, p. 154).

Step 3—*Information Sharing* (one hour). Reporters present their subgroups' deliberations, which are displayed on newsprint posted around the room. The consultant makes suggestions for categorizing the data into a few categories, such as communication difficulties, problems with top management, or problems in the mechanical department.

Step 4—*Priority Setting and Group Action Planning* (one hour and 15 minutes). After a break (lunch, or overnight if the meeting started in the evening), during which the data on the newsprint has been typed and duplicated, the total group is reassembled. The consultant and the group now put category numbers by each item.

People are now assigned to meet with their regular work units—manufacturing people, marketing people, and so on. Requests are made of each unit:

(a) Discuss the issues and problems affecting its area, decide on priorities and fairly immediate actions to which the group is prepared to commit itself.

(b) Identify the problems or issues to which the top management group should give high priority.

(c) Plan how to communicate the results of the confrontation meeting with their subordinates.

Step 5—*Organization Action Planning* (one to two hours). The total group is next reassembled and each unit reports on the results of its discussions, including the list of items for top management to consider as high priority. The top manager reacts to the priority lists and makes commitments by assigning task forces, and timetables for specific progress. Each unit shares how it plans to communicate the results of the meeting to subordinates. The top manager makes some closing remarks, and this concludes the session except for the top management group.

Step 6—*Immediate Follow-Up by Top Team* (one to three hours). The top management group reconvenes immediately to plan the first follow-up action steps, which are to be reported back to the total group within the next few days.

Step 7—*Progress Review* (two hours). The total management group and the consultant reassemble four to six weeks later to review progress to date.

The confrontation meeting is simultaneously an intervention in the psychosocial subsystem, the structural subsystem, and the managerial subsystem. It is an intervention in the psychosocial subsystem because it focuses directly on the perceptions and feelings of managers. It is an intervention in the structural subsystem because it alters the traditional chain-of-command information flow by asking people across unit lines and from several hierarchical levels to collaborate in diagnosing problems and in making recommendations for action steps.

It is an intervention in the managerial subsystem because it alters traditional planning procedures and may alter leadership style toward a more participative mode.

Sensing

Sensing is aimed at giving a top manager a better understanding of the perceptions and feelings of employees with whom he or she has limited contact. Although the groups that are involved are not intact work groups, the individuals involved may have some interdependency and certainly will have common areas of interest.

Fordyce and Weil (1971) describe the process by giving the example of a general manager of an organization with 200 employees who wants to find out what aspects about the business are of most concern to employees so that he can talk to them more effectively when he presents his annual report in a large general session. The personnel manager is asked to schedule four meetings, each with a group of 12 employees, and each meeting to be two hours in length. One group is selected from nonsupervisory technical, office, and plant employees. Another is selected from among professional employees and staff specialists. A third group is made up of supervisors. The fourth group is selected from a diagonal slice of employees at all levels across different departments. Superiors of those to be contacted are informed first so that they will understand and support the purpose of the meetings.

Immediately prior to the general manager's meeting with these employees, the personnel manager meets with each group and helps them prepare for the process by involving them in a discussion of some of the kinds of things they want to say when the general manager appears. During the meeting, the general manager mostly listens, but occasionally asks questions to make sure he understands what is being said. He also expresses his own thoughts and intentions regarding some of the matters raised.

As Fordyce and Weil indicate, the process will work only if there is considerable trust in the organization. Obviously, the manager needs to be skilled in listening and relating effectively to people at different levels. Some of the limitations of the approach include the possibility of employees hiding or disguising their real concerns. Other limitations include the possible perception by supervisors that they are being by-passed, or the danger of the manager making commitments to employees before problems have been diagnosed thoroughly and optional solutions considered.

Sensing is an intervention in the psychosocial subsystem, and is aimed directly at the perceptions of people about what is going on in the organization. Although group methods are used, in a way it is an individual intervention because a cross-section of employees is usually interviewed in contrast to a higher manager meeting with intact work teams. It is a short-range, participative intervention, but the approach can be congruent with a longer-range shift toward, or maintenance of, a participative mode of managing.

INTERGROUP PERFORMANCE IMPROVEMENT STRATEGIES

The intergroup and interpersonal interventions we will describe have their theoretical base in intergroup conflict research and insights from nondirective counseling described in Chapter 7. The three interventions to be discussed—*third-party peacemaking, intergroup team building,* and *the organization mirror*—have some common elements; namely, careful structuring by the facilitator, sharing of perceptions between the parties, active listening, exploration of the implications, and action planning. These techniques are applicable when there is serious conflict disrupting effective working relationships, but they are also applicable when there are only minor problems and the managers and groups involved wish to analyze present strengths and potential problems in their interactions. They require a desire on the part of both groups or parties to improve the relationship and the availability of a trusted facilitator (third party). Ideally, the parties have had some training in group progress skills and in giving feedback in a constructive manner. In addition, it can be helpful if two groups wanting to improve their interactions have had some experience with their own team buildings.

BOX 16.4
ON CONFLICT MANAGEMENT

The distinction between substantive and emotional issues is important because the substantive conflict requires bargaining and problem solving between the principals and mediative interventions by the third party, whereas emotional conflict requires a restructuring of a person's perceptions and the working through of feelings between the principals, as well as conciliative interventions by the third party. The former processes are basically cognitive, the latter processes more affective.

Source: Richard E. Walton, *Interpersonal Peacemaking: Confrontations and Third Party Consultation* [Reading, Mass.: Addison-Wesley 1969], p. 75.

Third-Party Peacemaking

When two people are in conflict and wish to improve the relationship, a procedure frequently used by facilitators is third-party peacemaking (Fordyce & Weil, 1971). For example, such a procedure would be applicable where there is conflict between the director of purchasing and the quality-control manager. The procedure is as follows:

Step 1—The facilitator requests each person to make three lists. The first list is positive feedback about ways in which the two have interacted. The second list includes those things not liked about the interaction. The third list is a prediction of what the other person has on his or her lists.

Step 2—Each person presents the three lists. The facilitator encourages active listening and discourages any arguing or debate. The emphasis is on understanding the other party's perceptions of what is going on. (Understanding is not the same as agreement, as discussed in Chapter 5.)

Step 3—Each person is encouraged to offer any information that might clarify matters. Again, general discussion is discouraged.

Step 4—The facilitator encourages the two parties to negotiate changes they want and decide how to bring those about. The facilitator records agreements and lists any unresolved issues, encouraging the two people to decide how and when to deal with the unresolved matters.

A facilitator needs three attributes if the above kind of intervention is to be successful. One is high professional expertise. A second is a low degree of power over the fate of the principals. Having any power over one or both of the parties reduces the chance that they will take risks and increases the likelihood that one or both will attempt to behave in ways that will elicit the facilitator's approval. A third attribute is high control over the physical setting and the process. This is necessary to create conditions to deescalate the conflict, one of which is to minimize any power differentials between the parties (Walton, 1969, pp. 131–142).

Conflicts are sometimes worked out in the context of a team-building workshop, particularly if several people need to improve their working relationships. In addition to the role-analysis technique, various exercises have been devised to help members of a group clarify their expectations of each other and negotiate new ways of working together (see Box 16.5). Such techniques can also be used in third-party peacemaking when only two people and the third party are present.

Intergroup Team Building

Widely used procedures for intergroup conflict management and improving teamwork between units are similar to the third-party peacemaking techniques described above. The first two steps are essentially the same, with the exception that in intergroup team building two separate groups generate the three lists which are recorded on newsprint and reported out in a joint session. Again, as in third-party peacemaking, the facilitator establishes ground rules prohibiting arguing and debate but encouraging explanation and understanding. The next

BOX 16.5

NEGOTIATION FORM

From ____

To ____

1. It would help me to be more effective if you were to do the following things *more* or *better*:

2. It would help me to be more effective if you were to do the following things *less,* or were to *stop* doing them:

3. Please *continue* doing the following things that have helped my effectiveness:

steps are as follows (Blake, Shepard, & Mouton, 1964; Beckhard, 1969, pp. 33–35; Fordyce & Weil, 1971, pp. 124–130; and French & Bell, 1984, pp. 156–159):

Step 3—The groups again meet separately, this time to reflect on what they have heard and on its implications. Frequently, it is found that differences are not as large as imagined and that some disagreements and frictions have been based on spurious perceptions and poor communications. Each group develops a list of priority issues that still need to be resolved.

Step 4—The two groups meet again and share their new lists. After clarifying and comparing the lists, they are then asked to make one list that combines the issues and problems to be resolved. With the facilitator's help, the total group decides on priorities and specific actions to continue the problem-solving process and makes assignments as to who will do what and by when.

Step 5—A follow-up session is scheduled in which the two groups or their leaders meet to review progress and to make further plans if necessary. Continued follow-up is necessary to maintain momentum.

Intergroup team building and third-party peacemaking are interventions in the psychosocial subsystem. As dysfunctional emergent phenomena shift toward the functional end of the spectrum—for example, misperceptions shifting to more accurate perceptions—individuals and groups can make a corresponding shift in their dealings with other organizational problems and challenges, expanding the range of competence and increasing the degree of effectiveness in these areas.

The Organization Mirror

The organization mirror is a name for a session similar to that of intergroup team building, except in this instance the effort focuses on one unit obtaining feedback from a number of other units in order to improve relationships. An example might be the staff of a purchasing department desiring to improve services to other departments within the organization. It can be used between a company and, say, key suppliers or customers, but it is important that all parties be sympathetic to and understand the process, or there could be considerable resistance and thus minimal or even negative results. Further, all parties involved need to have at least some reasonable level of skill in constructive feedback so that the session can be helpful.

In one version of the organization mirror (Fordyce & Weil, 1971, pp. 101–105), the host group invites two representatives from each of the other key units to a one-day meeting for the purpose of improving services. Prior to the meeting, the facilitator interviews each person singly or in groups to obtain data about problems and to prepare people for the meeting.

At the outset of the meeting, the facilitator reports on the interview data. The outsiders are then requested to pull their chairs into a circle to discuss the data (this is called a *fishbowl*) while the host group members listen and take notes. The host-group members then assemble in the fishbowl mode to discuss the data and review what the guests have said. All participants are then convened in a general session to summarize what has happened thus far.

After lunch, subgroups are formed, each including both host-group members and outsiders. These groups are given the task of identifying the five most important changes that would be needed to improve the effectiveness of the host organization. The subgroups report back to the total group, which synthesizes the lists. Subgroups are then assigned to meet for two hours on specific problem areas and to make plans for changes. These action plans are then reported to the total group and assignments made.

The organization mirror is at once an intervention in the psychosocial system and in the structural subsystem. There is a focus on perceptions and intergroup behavior, but there is also a temporary altering of the traditional authority hierarchy and channels of information flow. Instead of problems between groups going to a higher level, problems are shared directly between the groups involved. At another level of analysis, the organization mirror is an intervention into emergent organizational phenomena in that it deals with many unplanned and unanticipated conditions that have developed.

COMPREHENSIVE ORGANIZATION-IMPROVEMENT STRATEGIES

A number of contemporary organization-improvement strategies are more comprehensive in scope than the individual, interpersonal, group, and intergroup interventions discussed so far. Some of these strategies include the techniques we have discussed, but the ones to which we will now turn our attention are usually much broader in scope. More subsystems are involved; more organizational dimensions are modified. The strategies we will examine are quality-of-work-life (QWL) programs, survey feedback, *Grid* organization development, and comprehensive organization development (OD) efforts.

Quality of Work Life

The label *quality of work life* (QWL) has been adopted for a wide variety of organization-improvement efforts and it is therefore difficult to discuss QWL projects in general. Some have emphasized job enrichment, some have utilized team building, some have a sociotechnical thrust, and some have included quality circles. Most have included several such features.

What would high-quality work life be like? Walton (1975) provides eight categories that he says "provide a framework for analysis of the salient features that together make up the quality of working life." If an organization used a questionnaire to measure employees' perceptions of these categories, it could be considered an organizational-climate survey (see Chapter 14). Walton's categories are as follows (pp. 93–97):

1. Safe and healthy conditions of work (reasonable hours and working conditions that minimize injury and health risks)
2. Adequate and fair compensation (what is adequate is a subjective, relative matter; fairness can be measured somewhat more objectively by job evaluation and wage surveys; one could argue that fairness requires that higher profits resulting from changes in work rules be shared with employees)
3. Opportunity to use and develop one's human capacities (access to information, autonomy, opportunity for enriched jobs)
4. Opportunity for security and continued growth (job and income security, individual development, advancement opportunities)
5. Social integration in the work organization (the experience of supportive groups and sense of community, interpersonal openness, opportunity for mobility, freedom from prejudice)
6. Constitutionalism (rights of due process, free speech, equity and privacy)
7. Appropriate balance between work and other life spheres such as family life (the individual's responsibilities versus the organization's responsibilities in this matter is a complex, debatable issue)

8. Socially relevant work (the social contribution of the work and the work organization)

An examination of the QWL-labeled projects at some General Motors plants suggests a general strategy to meet some of the above criteria. Some of these projects have included the following features (Fuller, 1980; Bluestone, 1980):

Union agreement with the process and participation in the process
Voluntary employee participation
Assurance of job security (no loss of jobs because of the program)
Employee and supervisory training in team problem solving
Use of quality-control circles where teams of employees meet to discuss quality and other problems in the plant's performance and in the work environment
Encouragement of skill development and job rotation within work teams
Availability of skill training for employees
Work-team involvement in team-member and team-leader selection, in forecasting and work planning
Regular plant and team meetings to discuss quality, safety, and customer orders
Responsiveness to employee concerns

Although specifics vary from one QWL project to another in American business and industry, several factors tend to be common to these projects. Union involvement is one. A focus on work teams is another. One might also expect to see these elements contributing: problem-solving sessions by work teams in which the work team tackles many aspects of work life, including safety, product quality, and productivity; increased autonomy in planning work; the availability of training; increased responsiveness on the part of supervisors.

Facilitators from within the organization, or consultants employed from outside, are frequently used in these programs, particularly in the initial stages. Their responsibilities are likely to include training supervisors and employees in participative methods, sitting in on meetings when invited to act as consultants on group decision making, and advising on the overall process.

QWL projects that are comprehensive as those at General Motors involve a simultaneous intervention in most or all of the major organizational subsystems. For example, the managerial subsystem is altered because of a change in leadership style and a shift toward participative planning, coordinating, and controlling. The goal subsystem is altered because procedures for establishing quality and productivity goals shift toward more frequent team participation in goal setting. The technical subsystem is altered because of the introduction of new knowledge about such matters as quality control and boardroom skills. The structural subsystem is altered because the information flow changes and because personnel policies are changed (prevention of job loss because of the program, for instance). The psychosocial subsystem is altered through an emphasis on team problem solving, changes in interaction patterns, and work-team selection of new members and leaders.

Both causal and emergent phenomena are directly addressed in QWL projects. Along with changes in the causal dimensions of the organization—leadership style, personnel policies, technology—planned change occurs in emergent variables such as group skills and intergroup behavior.

Survey Feedback

In *survey feedback,* data is collected from employees in all units of an organization and the results are fed back into what Mann has called an "interlocking chain of conferences" (Mann, 1961, p. 609). Facilitators, who have assisted in the data-collection process, then assist work groups, including the supervisor, in guiding them through a process of diagnosing problems and making action plans. The unit manager is the linking pin to the unit in which he or she is a subordinate, thus enabling the organization to solve those problems that involve more than one group either laterally or vertically in the organization.

Questionnaires used in survey-feedback approaches frequently include categories of items pertaining to job satisfaction, organizational climate, and leadership; they may also include items pertaining to such matters as employee benefits or working conditions (see Chapter 14). Tailoring the questionnaire to a particular organization provides management and employees with the opportunity to assess perceptions of a specific practice or a condition of particular interest. For example, management may wish to assess employee reaction to a new flexible-hours work schedule.

Once a problem has been identified through the questionnaire, it then becomes the task of the various groups to explore the meaning of the data and to provide enough information for meaningful problem solving to occur. The design of the questionnaire and the questionnaire results are only the preliminary phases of group-problem diagnosis and eventual action planning.

Grid OD

Grid OD is a six-phase organization-development program lasting from three to five years and was developed by Robert Blake and Jane Mouton (Blake & Mouton, 1975; 1969). It includes a focus on work teams, coordination by internal consultants (who are organization members and who have been trained by external consultants), intergroup problem solving, and, eventually, the creation of an "ideal strategic corporate model." The word "organizational" can be substituted for "corporate" because the process is applicable to government and service organizations as well as business and industrial firms. The phases are as follows.

Pre-Phase—*Grid Seminar.* Prior to Phase 1, key managers are selected to be instructors and attend the one-week *Grid Seminar.* At this laboratory training experience, the managers study management concepts and assess their own leadership styles using the *Managerial Grid* questionnaire.

Developed by Blake and Mouton, it is an instrument designed to assess managerial behavior along two dimensions, *concern for people,* and *concern for production.* These dimensions are not conceptualized as polar opposites but as dimensions that can occur in different degrees along a scale from 1 to 9 and in different combinations. The ideal managerial behavior is seen as a strong combination of concern for both people and production (9,9). Other aspects of pre-Phase 1 include an instructors' seminar where potential instructors learn how to conduct a Phase-1 program and the seminars for other phases.

Phase 1—*The Managerial Grid.* All managers in the organization attend a grid seminar conducted by one of the organization's instructors. In this seminar each manager assesses his or her leadership style, works on problem-solving and communications skills, and practices 9,9 behaviors.

Phase 2—*Teamwork Development.* This phase is conducted with actual work teams that include the manager. Work-team culture is jointly diagnosed, issues are worked through, and feedback is shared between members as to their team behavior.

Phase 3—*Intergroup Development.* In this phase, teams that are particularly interdependent and have issues to work on relative to the way they are working or not working together join together in a workshop. Dynamics of intergroup competition and conflict are explored, and each group analyzes and shares what an ideal relationship with the other group would be like. Action plans are then made to move in the direction of the ideal state.

Phase 4—*Developing the Ideal Strategic Corporate Model.* In this phase, the top management team engages in corporate strategic planning through a process of jointly designing a model of what the organization would be like if it were truly excellent. Ideas of this top group are tested in conjunction with other organizational members, and the top group draws on the resources of any organization member or group when relevant to do so.

Phase 5—*Implementing the Ideal Strategic Model.* In this phase, the model is implemented through planning teams whose task it is to make plans for bringing practices within their respective divisions, product lines, and functional areas in line with the ideal strategic model. Action steps are then undertaken after the planning is complete.

Phase 6—*Systematic Critique.* In this phase, the results of Phase 5 and the other phases are measured and critiqued. New problems and challenges are identified, and new action plans are made. Ideally, the process would now have been built into the culture of the organization, and the collaborative, team, problem-solving, 9,9 approach will continue.

Organization Development

A number of the interventions discussed thus far are frequently only partial aspects of more comprehensive organization-development (OD) efforts, while some we have described are comprehensive in their own right. Grid OD, for example, can be considered a comprehensive effort if all of the phases are utilized. Similarly, survey feedback, if it results in extensive group and intergroup work with the data, can be considered a comprehensive OD effort.

Team building, while central to systematic and comprehensive OD, needs to be accompanied by other interventions, including intergroup team building, if the organizational-improvement effort is to be considered comprehensive OD. Some interventions, like the role-analysis technique, third-party peacemaking, the organization mirror, and the confrontation meeting are usually only components of a broader, longer-range process.

A significant number of organizations, both in the U.S. and abroad, have been involved in comprehensive organization development efforts in recent years. Government organizations, such as the U.S. Army and the U.S. Bureau of Reclamation, have utilized the process along with a number of public schools, hospitals, churches, and business and industrial organizations both small and large. Among some of the large firms have been Digital Equipment, Esso, and TRW Systems Group. Terminology varies, for example, the broad process we will describe is called organizational effectiveness (OE) in the U.S. Army. Evaluation studies of OD programs have generally showed positive results (French, Bell, & Zawacki, 1983, pp. 519–522), although the research is not as extensive as we would like to see.

Definition of OD. Organization development can be defined as "a long-range effort to improve an organization's problem-solving and renewal processes, particularly through a more effective and collaborative management of organization culture—with special emphasis on the culture of formal work teams" (French & Bell, 1984, p. 17). This definition includes some of the features of OD.

Characteristics of OD. A broad organization-development process includes the following features. Some of the features are implicit in the definition of OD given under the topic of team building (French & Bell, 1984, pp. 17–22):

A focus on face-to-face work groups. This would include intact work teams—subordinates and supervisor together—as well as any use of task forces, committees, and project teams;
A focus on intergroup effectiveness;
A focus on diagnosing the functional and dysfunctional aspects of group, intergroup, and organizational culture, and on participative problem solving;
The use of a participant action research model (to be discussed further below);
The use of facilitators;
Viewing the process in long-range terms;
Managing the systems ramifications of the process.

Action Research. The participant-action research model underlies the process that was being used in the *A Data-Gathering, Feedback Process* vignette and underlies most OD interventions. Its steps are essentially as follows: (1) a preliminary, joint diagnosis of problems between key people in a unit or between organization and the facilitator; (2) data gathering from the client group (this could be in the form of interviews or questionnaires; (3) data feedback to the client group by the facilitator; (4) problem exploration and diagnosis by the client group with the facilitator's help; (5) action planning by the client group; (6) action by the client group; and (7) follow-up. The action-research process is cyclical and can be repeated at appropriate intervals (French & Bell, 1984, p. 21).

Participant-action research is similar to the steps in a planned-change effort shown in the previous chapter (Figure 15.5). The essential difference is that the questions of who will be involved is essentially answered by the use of interdependent work groups. It is also consistent with Lewin's three-phase model in that the participative data gathering and problem diagnosis typically assists in the *unfreezing* process; the action planning and action are the *moving* aspects; and the action and follow-up phases serve to *refreeze* the organization at a new level of stability and equilibrium.

OD Facilitators. The facilitator, in OD efforts, is there in large part to help those in the client system learn new modes of diagnosis, problem solving, and group interaction. Because of the facilitator's professional qualifications and personal investment in serving the group, and also because the facilitator is from *outside* the particular system, he or she can help surface dysfunctional phenomena that otherwise would remain frozen in the particular group or organizational culture. The facilitator need only be from outside the particular unit being served, however, not the entire organization; a specialist from some other unit in the organization, such as an OD unit, the human resources department, or a line manager specially trained in the facilitator role might serve as well as an outside consultant. Although we see the facilitated training groups as a means for organization members to help themselves more effectively, we also see a role for the facilitator as a resource to be drawn on periodically: to facilitate repeat team-building sessions (perhaps once a year or so) and to help manage the broader OD effort as it unfolds.

Time Perspective. Although short-range gains can be realized from OD interventions, major, sustained gains usually require long-range attention. As discussed in the previous chapter, problems or conditions tend to be held in equilibrium between many forces. Further, changes in one subsystem can set off changes in other subsystems, as we have seen. This leads us to a final point about the nature of comprehensive OD efforts.

System Ramifications. A long-range OD effort is likely to be an intervention into all organizational subsystems. While the initial intervention is in the psychosocial subsystem and focuses extensively on emergent phenomena, very quickly the effort carries over into addressing problems in any of the other subsystems. A successful, comprehensive OD effort, then, requires management of the effort's many ramifications for the system. Not only must the multiple changes that began to emerge in the various subsystems be managed, but many practices need to change to support the emerging process. For example, to be congruent and supportive of the OD effort, the training-and-development activities need to include training in communications and leadership skills, group dynamics, and problem solving. Recruitment and orientation activities require information for prospective and new employees about the type of organizational culture that exists and that is emerging.

There is a potential for new participative modes to precipitate suggestions for change that could affect the job security of employees and supervisors. Thus, personnel policies may need to be changed in the direction of more job protection if people are going to feel free to make suggestions pertaining to their own and others' jobs. Work rules may need changing from restrictive, punitive rules to much more open, flexible rules. For example, at the Lockheed Shipbuilding and Construction Company, many of the old rules, as well as the signs admonishing employees to abide by them, were removed when management shifted to a more participative problem-solving approach.

EMPHASES IN DIFFERENT IMPROVEMENT STRATEGIES

Figure 16.2 summarizes how the various intervention strategies we have discussed tend to be arrayed in terms of the degree to which they (1) are unilaterally determined by management in contrast to being participative, (2) use the expert mode of consultation in contrast to the facilitator mode, (3) focus on individuals in contrast to groups, (4) focus on causal variables in contrast to emergent variables, and (5) have a short-range orientation in contrast to a long-range perspective. These dimensions were discussed in Chapter 15.

Some intervention strategies, such as the time-and-motion study, which is usually aimed at making the execution of individual tasks more efficient, tend to have the features clustered toward the left-hand side of the diagram. Typical use of attitude surveys and MBO/R and unilateral forms of job enrichment tend to have features clustered toward the left-hand side also. (However, we should note that unilateral job enrichment and one-on-one MBO programs may take extended periods to implement.) Others, such as comprehensive OD, Grid OD, and quality-of-work-life programs tend to have the features clustered toward the right-hand side of the figure. Others have different mixtures of features and we have arrayed them along a scale to suggest approximately where they might fall in terms of being more like one or the other end of the continuum.

Note that the diagonal line does not go all the way to the top right-hand corner of the diagram. The line is drawn this way to suggest that the highly participative organizational-improvement strategies typically address causal variables such as technology, task, structure, and policy as the process unfolds. Further, such strategies do not ignore the individual. Mechanisms like quality circles and team building, for example, frequently provide avenues for the expression of individuality that have not been present before. We believe these to be important dimensions in considering and analyzing improvement strategies. Although there are circumstances, such as an unanticipated financial emergency, when the characteristics to the left of the scale may be the ones to choose, we believe that, in general, improvement strategies that have mixtures of the char-

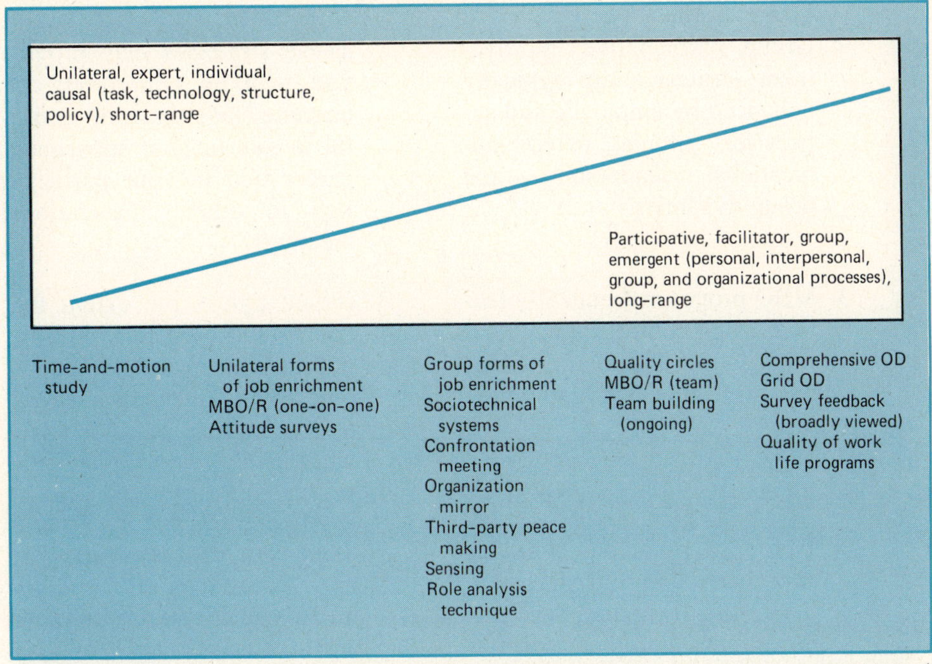

FIGURE 16.2 Emphases in Various Improvement Strategies. **Source:** Adapted from Wendell L. French and Cecil H. Bell, Jr., *Organization Development: Behavioral Science Interventions for Organization Improvement,* 2d ed., © 1978, p. 166. Adapted by permission of Prentice-Hall, Inc., Englewood Cliffs, N.J.

acteristics from the middle of the scale to the right-hand side tend to be associated with organizational excellence and high morale. Some techniques, such as work simplification or traditional use of attitude surveys, can readily be redesigned to include some of the characteristics on the right-hand side of the scale. Survey feedback, for example, involves using attitude surveys in a participative and group way.

SO WHAT? IMPLICATIONS FOR YOU

Understanding what is being changed through the use of various improvement strategies and the ramifications of those changes is important in selecting, managing, and participating in improvement efforts. Some implications to consider are:

As a Member in an Organization

Generalizations	Implications
1. Some individual-, group-, and organization improvement strategies use the expert concept; some the facilitator concept.	1. You are more likely to be asked to participate in the approaches that use facilitators.

Generalizations	Implications
2. Group participative improvement strategies are typically enhanced by employee and supervisory training in communications, leadership, and group dynamics.	2. These strategies may provide you with an opportunity for learning skills that can be useful to you in your subsequent career and in your participation in other organizational meetings.
3. MBO programs frequently feature a high-control element and typically reinforce a one-on-one form of leadership style.	3. If you assess the extent that your supervisor is willing for you to influence the setting of objectives, you may have extensive control over your own work in contrast to goals being set for you.
4. T-groups, involving "strangers" from different organizations, are essentially educational interventions in which a person develops interpersonal and group insights and skills. Translation of these skills into the organizational setting requires the support of peers and the supervisor.	4. Skills and insights learned in the T-group may be very helpful to you in the organization and in other settings. However, utilization of the insights gained may be frustrated if others have not had similar training; try to get others interested.
5. In quality circles, participants identify quality, production, and other problems, help in problem diagnosis and gathering information, and in making action plans.	5. As a participant, you will have an opportunity to engage in challenging problem diagnosis and problem solving. In addition to assisting your unit in solving significant problems, participation gives you an opportunity to practice your interpersonal, group, and leadership skills.
6. Team building involves a collaborative examination of the functional and dysfunctional aspects of the way a group works together as well as a joint addressing of problems	6. As a participant, you will have the opportunity to engage in an examination of both emergent and causal phenomena, particularly those seen as dysfunctional to optimal group ef-

Generalizations	Implications
not previously solved well by the group.	fectiveness. You should consciously assess the risks of being open and candid and gauge your openness to the level of trust in the group. Some risks, however, must be taken if the group is to improve its functioning.

As a Current or Future Manager

Generalizations	Implications
1. Different improvement strategies vary in terms of the extent to which they focus initially on causal in contrast to emergent variables, the implicit time frame involved to accomplish significant results, and the number of subsystems and variables changed.	1. As a manager, you will want to be aware of the complexities involved, and realize that you can't just install a change program. If it is to be successful, it needs to be managed carefully and, in many cases, over a long period of time. Furthermore, you need to be aware of the ramifications for the system of any change-directed effort.
2. Group, participative improvement strategies typically require employee and supervisory training in communications, leadership, and group dynamics.	2. This means investments of time and resources, and a commitment on your part to develop and enhance your skills in these areas.
3. Job-enrichment programs frequently result in the elimination of a layer of supervision or a restructuring of the role of the supervisor.	3. What will happen to your job is a legitimate concern. Ideally, the organization will assure supervisors of job security, and your role will be to help your subordinates with the changes and probably to assume more training, planning, and expediting functions. If a group approach is used, your role is likely to include leading group problem-solving sessions.

Generalizations	Implications
4. Positive reinforcement programs emphasize praise for good performance and the avoidance of punishment for substandard work.	4. If involved in such a program, watch for side effects, such as higher expectations in terms of financial rewards if the program is successful, or the fading of the effectiveness of praise. If there is no formal program, think through whether you are providing sufficient praise for work that is done well. Organizations are notoriously deficient in dispensing praise, and deserved praise is a morale builder as well as a motivator.
5. MBO programs vary a great deal in terms of real participation between subordinate and superior in setting goals.	5. It is important to examine your own style in working with subordinates on goal setting. Is there real give and take, or are you being autocratic in your approach? Have you tried setting some goals as a team? Have you encouraged subordinates to react to your goals?
6. Sensing is a quick way for a manager to skip several layers of supervision and obtain information directly from employees.	6. The effective use of this technique depends a good deal upon the supervisors at the different levels being adequately informed as to the purpose of the intervention, and upon the top manager not making commitments that undermine the effectiveness of intermediate layers of supervision.
7. The establishment of semiautonomous work groups requires the cooperation of the union, and involves changes in each person's job and in the role of the supervisor.	7. If your organization is going to use semiautonomous teams, understand the changes that will be required in your role, and use the situation as an opportunity to upgrade your skills.
8. The role-analysis technique can be a helpful approach to	8. This technique can be somewhat threatening, and it is im-

Generalizations	Implications
clarifying mutual expectations between members of a work team, but it needs to be used with care.	portant that it be used in a supportive environment and that people volunteer to participate in the exercise. Ideally, several people participate, including you. The outcomes can be useful, agreed-upon job prescriptions and improved work cooperation and interaction.
9. The confrontation meeting is a quick way for a total management group to identify and address significant issues pertaining to the performance of an organization. To be successful, it requires a number of conditions to be present.	9. The more you understand this technique, the more you will be in a position to give sound advice to higher management about the relevance of its use. If you are involved in such a meeting, this will provide you with an unusual opportunity for practicing your group skills and your knowledge of functional and dysfunctional phenomena in your organization. It will require hard work subsequent to the meeting to correct some of the problems that have been identified. The confrontation meeting can be the start of a long-range organizational-improvement effort.
10. Third-party peacemaking, intergroup team building, and the organization mirror rely on the sharing of perceptions in a controlled setting and on the desire of the parties to improve the relationship.	10. It is important for you to assess the favorableness of the situation for the effective use of these interventions. Intergroup team building, for example, is usually more effective if both groups have been involved in their own team building prior to the two groups coming together.
11. Quality-of-work-life programs may be very broad and may include union cooperation, quality circles, team building, skill training, and changes in	11. Again, be aware of the complexity of the changes being proposed or underway. You may be in a position to point out to higher management

Generalizations	Implications
personnel policies and practices.	some of the variables that need to be managed that are not being given adequate attention.
12. Survey feedback is much more than the administration of a questionnaire; it is an intervention in the psychosocial subsystem and may be an intervention in the other subsystems as well.	12. Again, be aware of the complexities. You may want to try to influence the content of the questionnaire to include items you think are important. The real payoff of such a process will come when you and your subordinates, with the help of a facilitator, explore the underlying meaning of the responses to the questionnaire and collaboratively make plans to solve problems.
13. Grid OD starts with the use of the *Managerial Grid* in diagnosing and examining one's leadership style.	13. Such a program can be an opportunity for you to examine your style of leadership and to practice new modes of leadership.
14. Comprehensive OD focuses on intact work teams, task forces, and intergroup relationships, uses a participant action research model and facilitators, and requires a long-range perspective and the management of system ramifications.	14. Be aware of the implications, including the knowledge that comprehensive OD is a long-term strategy to shift organizational culture toward a more participative, team-oriented, open, supportive yet confrontive developmental mode. Such a shift will be both an opportunity and a challenge to learn more effective interpersonal, group, intergroup, and leadership behaviors as well as more effective problem-solving processes.

LEARNING APPLICATIONS ACTIVITIES

1. Write a vignette based on your experience that describes, in part at least, a planned, systematic organization-improvement effort. If you have not worked in an organization where such a program was undertaken, team up with someone in the class who had such an experience, perhaps assisting with the write-up by interviewing the person and taking notes.

2. With two colleagues, make contact with some organization that has been involved in a major improvement effort. Interview three key people in the organization with regard to their views of the goals of the improvement effort, the techniques used, and the results to date. Write a short report and present it to the class.

3. Individually analyze the vignette *A Data-Gathering, Feedback Process* in terms of the dimensions shown on Figure 16.2. Discuss, in a group of four to six, what conditions are likely to be needed for the process described to succeed. Present your conclusions to the total class for discussion.

4. In a group of four to six, compare and contrast (a) the T-group, (b) team building, and (c) quality circles. Report your analysis to the total class for discussion.

5. Review the discussion of intergroup team building in this chapter and the research on groups in conflict presented in Chapter 8. Explain how the intergroup intervention probably solves some of the dysfunctional aspects of intergroup conflict.

6. *Step 1:* Describe, in your own words, organization development (OD) and Quality of Work Life (QWL).

Step 2: Share your description with two or three colleagues. Note similarities and differences between OD and QWL.

Step 3: Report the main similarities and differences between OD and QWL to the class and discuss.

7. As a follow-up to Assignment 6, have each member in your subgroup list the conditions that he or she believes would be necessary for (a) OD efforts to succeed and (b) QWL efforts to succeed.

REFERENCES

Beckhard, Richard, *Organization Development: Strategies and Models*. Reading, Mass.: Addison-Wesley, 1969.

Beckhard, Richard. "The Confrontation Meeting." *Harvard Business Review* 45 (March-April 1967): 149–155.

Blake, Robert, H. A. Shepard, and J. S. Mouton. *Managing Intergroup Conflict in Industry.* Houston: Gulf, 1964.

Blake, Robert R., and Jane S. Mouton. "An Overview of the Grid." *Training and Development Journal* 29/5 (May 1975): 29–37.

———. *Building a Dynamic Corporation Through Grid Organization Development*. Reading, Mass.: Addison-Wesley, 1969.

Bluestone, Irving. "How Quality of Worklife Projects Work for the United Auto Workers." *Monthly Labor Review* 103 (July 1980): 39–41.

Cole, Robert C. "Made in Japan—Quality-Control Circles." *Across the Board* 16 (November 1979): 72–78.

Dayal, I., and J. M. Thomas. "Operation KPE: Developing a New Organization." *Journal of Applied Behavioral Science* 4/4 (1968): 473–506.

Ford, Robert N. "Job Enrichment Lessons From AT&T." *Harvard Business Review* 51 (January-February 1973): 96–106.

Fordyce, Jack K., and Raymond Weil. *Managing With People*. Reading, Mass.: Addison-Wesley, 1971.

French, Wendell L., and Cecil H. Bell, Jr. *Organization Development: Behavioral Science Interventions for Organization Improvement*. 3d ed. Englewood Cliffs, N.J.: Prentice-Hall, 1984.

French, Wendell L., Cecil H. Bell, Jr., and Robert A. Zawacki. *Organization Development: Theory, Practice, Research*. rev. ed. Plano, Texas: Business Publications, 1983.

French, Wendell L., and Robert W. Hollman. "Management by Objectives: The Team Approach." *California Management Review* 17 (Spring 1975): 13–22.

Fuller, Stephen H. "How Quality-of-Worklife Projects Work for General Motors." *Monthly Labor Review* 103 (July 1980): 37–39.

Goodman, Paul S. *Assessing Organizational Change*. New York: Wiley, 1979.

Hackman, J. Richard, and Greg R. Oldham. *Work Redesign*. Reading, Mass.: Addison-Wesley, 1980.

Hamner, W. Clay, and Ellen P. Hamner. "Behavior Modification on the Bottom Line." *Organizational Dynamics* 4 (Spring 1976): 8–9.

Hayes, J. P., and G. C. Swanson. "Quality Circles at Lockheed Shipbuilding." Mimeographed. Seattle, Wash. 1982.

Iman, Stephen C. "The Development of Participation by Semiautonomous Work Teams: The Case of Donnelly Mirrors." In Louis E. Davis and Albert L. Cherns (Eds.), *The Quality of Working Life*, vol. 2. New York: Free Press, 1975.

Levinson, Harry. "Management by Whose Objectives?" *Harvard Business Review* 48 (July-August 1970): 128–129.

Likert, Rensis, and M. Scott Fisher. "MBGO: Putting Some Team Spirit into MBO." *Personnel* 54 (January-February 1977): 40–47.

Mann, Floyd C. "Studying and Creating Change." In Warren Bennis, Kenneth Benne, and Robert Chin (Eds.). *The Planning of Change*. New York: Holt, Rinehart & Winston, 1961.

Miles, Raymond E., and Howard R. Rosenberg. "The Human Resources Approach to Management: Second-Generation Issues." *Organizational Dynamics* 10/3 (Winter 1982): 26–41.

Mills, Ted. "Altering the Social Structure in Coal Mining." *Monthly Labor Review* 99 (October 1976): 3–10.

Myers, M. Scott. *Every Employee a Manager*. New York: McGraw-Hill, 1970.

Paul, William, Keith Robertson, and Frederick Herzberg. "Job Enrichment Pays Off." *Harvard Business Review* 47 (March-April 1969): 61–78.

Walton, Richard E. "Criteria for Quality of Working Life." In Louis E. Davis and Albert B. Cherns (Eds.), *The Quality of Working Life*, vol. 1. New York: Free Press, 1975.

———. "Work Innovations in the United States." *Harvard Business Review*, 57 (July-August) 1979: 98.

———. *Interpersonal Peacemaking: Confrontations and Third-Party Consultation*. Reading, Mass.: Addison-Wesley, 1969.

Walton, Richard E. "Work Innovations at Topeka: After Six Years." *The Journal of Applied Behavioral Science* 13/3 (July-August-September 1977): 422–433.

Yager, Ed. "Examining the Quality Control Circle." *Personnel Journal* 58 (October 1979): 682–684.

Zippo, Mary. "Productivity and Morale Sagging? Try the Quality Circle Approach." *Personnel* 57 (May-June 1980): 43–45.

17 Career Development

LEARNING OBJECTIVES

After reading this chapter you should be able to:

1. Define a career and describe the career development perspective.
2. Recognize some career transitions and choices that you will face.
3. Identify your career goals and begin to develop action plans for accomplishing them.
4. Understand adult life cycles and career stages and how they can affect attitudes and behavior.
5. Describe various career paths.
6. Identify and give examples of typical career problems in organizations.

A MAJOR DECISION

Sandra was jotting down some notes to take with her to an appointment with her academic advisor. She had narrowed her considerations of majors to nursing, recreation administration, social welfare, or business administration. She was trying to think about the advantages and disadvantages of each, but it wasn't easy. Her father, an account representative for Burroughs, had told her before school started that it was about time she made up her mind. He seemed to encourage her interest in business, but she sensed that her mother tended to nudge her toward a more traditional career in one of the helping professions.

Sandra felt she was qualified for any of her four alternatives, but she was a little leery of the math/stat requirements for business and some of the science prerequisites for nursing. She was an avid participant in team sports—soccer, slowpitch, and volleyball. It would really be neat to combine vocation and avocation. But jobs in the recreation-administration field were scarce. She enjoyed the two sociology courses she took last year and felt she would be good at counseling—maybe on the staff of a prison or halfway house. Peter, her friend, told her that an M.B.A. would be more valuable in the long run than a B.A. in business or any other field. He said he had read that technical training and work experience would be helpful in getting into a good graduate school of business administration. Sandra wondered if nursing might be the best bet (even though she became squeamish at the sight of blood) because it might lead to a long-run career in health-care administration.

DISILLUSIONMENT

John Wilkenson received his undergraduate degree in accounting. All during his university career, John had heard the virtues of public accounting extolled by his accounting professors and fellow students. Many of them felt that the public-accounting profession was the best possible career, where all the action, pay, and prestige could be found for an accountant. There was even greater prestige to working with one of the "Big Eight" multinational accounting firms. John was a top student and he was strongly encouraged by his professors and fellow students to aspire to be a partner in one of the Big Eight.

John's major goal was to be hired by a Big Eight firm. He made certain that he had excellent recommendations from the professors and took the courses that would have the most appeal. He was very successful in the interview game, asking all the right questions and giving the right answers. He was offered a position by several Big Eight firms and selected the one that offered the best opportunity for growth and advancement. He was excited about his future career and very confident of success. Several partners indicated their pleasure with his decision by taking him and his wife to dinner.

After a year of working with the firm, John's perceptions had changed significantly. He now recognized that it would be many years, if ever, before he would be able to attain the organizational level he desired. In fact, since he joined the firm, the partners had lengthened the years of service required before promotion at every level, and made the policy retroactive to apply to all personnel. For John, the possibility of becoming a national partner seemed as remote as a fairy tale.

Another factor that bothered John was the large number of friends and co-workers who had left the organization. Through the grapevine, John learned that the firm hired its personnel with the full expectation of losing 60 percent of them. John felt that this implied a lack of concern for the individual.

John performed his functions competently. He was assigned to many special projects and made suggestions for improvement that were accepted. In spite of some interesting assignments, John became increasingly dissatisfied with the work, the organization, and the tremendous pressure. It was not unusual for him to put in 16 hours a day for six or seven days a week during the busy season. This put quite a strain on his family life.

John discussed his career problems with his boss, George Thompson, without much satisfaction. George's response was, "We all suffer under these conditions, and you knew coming in that the sacrifice would be necessary. All I can say to you now is that we can try to find you a different place in the firm, but the only way to rid yourself of these problems is to leave." In response to his questions regarding slow progress and the new policy requiring more time in rank before promotion, George said, "John, you must understand that the expertise required to manage an audit, given the present legal and accounting environment, is substantial. We feel that it is no longer feasible to allow personnel with less work experience than our new guidelines recommend to advance to higher management positions. It isn't just for you; it is for the entire firm. We just don't dare bend the rules when the problems are so great. Remember, this is for your own benefit ultimately."

John reviewed his earlier career decisions. He realized that his original perceptions, formed while at the university, were drastically wrong. He now realized that the areas of tax, private industry, and governmental accounting all required special expertise and offered good career opportunities. And working in public accounting for one of the Big Eight was not all that great. He began looking for new and different career opportunities.

THE PROPOSAL

Hitoshi Yamamoto was a graduate of Tokyo University with a degree in law. In Japan, the law degree is conferred at the undergraduate level and students are encouraged to become generalists by studying economics, political sciences, and other subjects in addition to law. Very few law students practice law after graduation.

Tokyo University stands at the apex of Japanese educational institutions. It is not far from reality to say that the Japanese society is run by generations of Tokyo University graduates. As a Tokyo University graduate, particularly the law school, one is considered to have made it in life. Like many other of the top-half graduates that year, Hitoshi could pick his job from a number of opportunities. After weighing the various offers, he was attracted to two alternatives that meant quite different careers for the rest of his life. In the rather immobile Japanese society, there is very little exchange of personnel between the government and private sector or other types of job changing. One choice was to join the Ministry of International Trade and Industry (MITI), the powerful organization that formulates all the key policies for trade and industrial activity in Japan. The other was the Nippon Steel Company, one of the largest steel companies in Japan. MITI promised more challenge in later years, but the initial pay was lower and there was some danger of being made a scapegoat as a lower level manager in the event of a government scandal. Nippon Steel, on the other hand, hired over a dozen Tokyo University graduates each year, so the competition for future executive positions would be strong. Hitoshi also felt that his lower-middle-class background might be a drawback among some graduates with good family ties in influential business circles in Japan. He finally decided on Nippon Steel. Like many Japanese corporations, Nippon trains its future executives in a four- to five-year program by first rotating them within headquarters and then sending them to one of the operations located throughout Japan. Hitoshi was assigned to the corporate planning and research department, a good position in which to start his career. He learned a great deal and enjoyed good relationships with his co-workers.

After a year in this position, he was expecting to be transferred to another job. Strangely enough, it was not his immediate boss, but the department head, Kozo Otami, who called him into his office for a conference. A department head in the company is equivalent to an executive vice president position in a major American corporation. After complimenting Hitoshi on his work as a trainee, Otami suddenly switched his inquiries into personal matters such as his family, his hobbies, his goals in the company and the like. Hitoshi felt the boss was beating around the bush, but he didn't know exactly what to expect.

"I was wondering if you would like to come to my house for dinner sometime and meet our daughter," said Otami. It took a few seconds for the message to sink into Hitoshi's mind. The boss was essentially urging him to marry his daughter. His mind raced trying to come up with a safe and diplomatic answer. Meeting her even once meant no option but to marry her. Turning down the offer might be a fatal blow to his future advancement in the company.

He finally murmured that he was still so young that he never gave a serious thought to marriage and that he would like to give it further thought. He hastily thanked the boss and hurried out the door. Back at his own office he realized the dilemma facing him. Was he going to abandon his private life for promotion or would he give up his powerful connection, which he had always wished to have?

A CAREER DILEMMA

Gordon Pollard had worked as an engineer for United Aerospace Corporation for 20 years. He had joined the company in 1962, immediately after receiving his B.S. degree in aeronautical engineering. He was fortunate to get in on the ground floor with the inauguration of the jet age and the development of commercial and military aircraft. The company had been very successful in designing, producing, and marketing jet aircraft and was one of the world's leaders in this field. In his early career, Gordon had held a variety of engineering jobs in different divisions. After a few years he became more specialized in working on navigational systems. He could trace his career with the company through the development of many new aircraft models. He was proud of his own and the company's accomplishments.

Recently, the aircraft industry had been jolted by a number of adversities. First, the oil embargos and the continuing crisis in the Middle East had raised jet-fuel prices significantly. The dramatic increase in interest rates severely limited the ability of airlines to purchase new aircraft. The aircraft controllers strike in the summer of 1981 certainly didn't help the industry, nor did deregulation and subsequent rate wars. Many airlines were in severe financial straits and several, including Braniff, were forced into bankruptcy.

The entire aircraft industry was affected by these conditions and the United Aerospace sonnel with the full expectation of losing 60 percent of them. John felt that this implied a lack of concern for the individual.

John performed his functions competently. He was assigned to many special projects and made suggestions for improvement that were accepted. In spite of some interesting assignments, John became increasingly dissatisfied with the work, the organization, and the tremendous pressure. It was not unusual for him to put in 16 hours a day for six or seven days a week during the busy season. This put quite a strain on his family life.

John discussed his career problems with his boss, George Thompson, without much satisfaction. George's response was, "We all suffer under these conditions, and you knew coming in that the sacrifice would be necessary. All I can say to you now is that we can try to find you a different place in the firm, but the only way to rid yourself of these problems is to leave." In response to his questions regarding slow progress and the new policy requiring more time in rank before promotion, George said, "John, you must understand that the expertise required to manage an audit, given the present legal and accounting environment, is substantial. We feel that it is no longer feasible to allow personnel with less work experience than our new guidelines recommend to advance to higher management positions. It isn't just for you; it is for the entire firm. We just don't dare bend the rules when the problems are so great. Remember, this is for your own benefit ultimately."

John reviewed his earlier career decisions. He realized that his original perceptions, formed while at the university, were drastically wrong. He now realized that the areas of tax, private industry, and governmental accounting all required special expertise and offered good career opportunities. And working in public accounting for one of the Big Eight was not all that great. He began looking for new and different career opportunities.

THE PROPOSAL

Hitoshi Yamamoto was a graduate of Tokyo University with a degree in law. In Japan, the law degree is conferred at the undergraduate level and students are encouraged to become generalists by studying economics, political sciences, and other subjects in addition to law. Very few law students practice law after graduation.

Tokyo University stands at the apex of Japanese educational institutions. It is not far from reality to say that the Japanese society is run by generations of Tokyo University graduates. As a Tokyo University graduate, particularly the law school, one is considered to have made it in life. Like many other of the top-half graduates that year, Hitoshi could pick his job from a number of opportunities. After weighing the various offers, he was attracted to two alternatives that meant quite different careers for the rest of his life. In the rather immobile Japanese society, there is very little exchange of personnel between the government and private sector or other types of job changing. One choice was to join the Ministry of International Trade and Industry (MITI), the powerful organization that formulates all the key policies for trade and industrial activity in Japan. The other was the Nippon Steel Company, one of the largest steel companies in Japan. MITI promised more challenge in later years, but the initial pay was lower and there was some danger of being made a scapegoat as a lower level manager in the event of a government scandal. Nippon Steel, on the other hand, hired over a dozen Tokyo University graduates each year, so the competition for future executive positions would be strong. Hitoshi also felt that his lower-middle-class background might be a drawback among some graduates with good family ties in influential business circles in Japan. He finally decided on Nippon Steel. Like many Japanese corporations, Nippon trains its future executives in a four- to five-year program by first rotating them within headquarters and then sending them to one of the operations located throughout Japan. Hitoshi was assigned to the corporate planning and research department, a good position in which to start his career. He learned a great deal and enjoyed good relationships with his co-workers.

After a year in this position, he was expecting to be transferred to another job. Strangely enough, it was not his immediate boss, but the department head, Kozo Otami, who called him into his office for a conference. A department head in the company is equivalent to an executive vice president position in a major American corporation. After complimenting Hitoshi on his work as a trainee, Otami suddenly switched his inquiries into personal matters such as his family, his hobbies, his goals in the company and the like. Hitoshi felt the boss was beating around the bush, but he didn't know exactly what to expect.

"I was wondering if you would like to come to my house for dinner sometime and meet our daughter," said Otami. It took a few seconds for the message to sink into Hitoshi's mind. The boss was essentially urging him to marry his daughter. His mind raced trying to come up with a safe and diplomatic answer. Meeting her even once meant no option but to marry her. Turning down the offer might be a fatal blow to his future advancement in the company.

He finally murmured that he was still so young that he never gave a serious thought to marriage and that he would like to give it further thought. He hastily thanked the boss and hurried out the door. Back at his own office he realized the dilemma facing him. Was he going to abandon his private life for promotion or would he give up his powerful connection, which he had always wished to have?

A CAREER DILEMMA

Gordon Pollard had worked as an engineer for United Aerospace Corporation for 20 years. He had joined the company in 1962, immediately after receiving his B.S. degree in aeronautical engineering. He was fortunate to get in on the ground floor with the inauguration of the jet age and the development of commercial and military aircraft. The company had been very successful in designing, producing, and marketing jet aircraft and was one of the world's leaders in this field. In his early career, Gordon had held a variety of engineering jobs in different divisions. After a few years he became more specialized in working on navigational systems. He could trace his career with the company through the development of many new aircraft models. He was proud of his own and the company's accomplishments.

Recently, the aircraft industry had been jolted by a number of adversities. First, the oil embargos and the continuing crisis in the Middle East had raised jet-fuel prices significantly. The dramatic increase in interest rates severely limited the ability of airlines to purchase new aircraft. The aircraft controllers strike in the summer of 1981 certainly didn't help the industry, nor did deregulation and subsequent rate wars. Many airlines were in severe financial straits and several, including Braniff, were forced into bankruptcy.

The entire aircraft industry was affected by these conditions and the United Aerospace

Corporation was particularly hard pressed. It had recently lost a major air force contract for a military transport plane and was finding competition very stiff in the commercial aircraft market from the European aircraft builder, Airbus Industries. It had lost a number of large sales from airlines in other countries to Airbus and it looked as if it might lose even more. Gordon had been with the company through many ups and downs but nothing quite like this. The company had already had a significant reduction in employment and things looked very bleak for the future. There were rumors that several other airlines might cancel their orders and Gordon knew that this would have continuing repercussions. A number of his engineering co-workers had already been laid off and he knew that the project he was currently working on was very likely to be terminated if things got any worse. Gordon had talked the situation over with his boss, Peter Miller, who assured him of the company's high regard for his abilities and performance. However, there were no guarantees that they would continue to have a position for him.

Gordon began quietly looking for other career opportunities. He didn't want to leave the area because his two children were in school and his wife had a good job with a local bank. However, due to the general economic recession, there was considerable unemployment in the area and good jobs were not easy to find. Besides, Gordon had been involved in highly specialized work and there really weren't many demands for his skills. He was 44 years old and had never really looked for a job.

Finally, he was able to line up another opportunity with a fledgling electronics firm. The position didn't pay as much as his current job and opportunities for further advancement were uncertain. There were risks involved in taking the new position, but there were certainly risks in trying to tough it out at United Aerospace. Gordon was in a dilemma. He had always enjoyed his work with United and was loyal to the company. Had things gone well, he would have been satisfied to complete his career there. But, now that there was a strong likelihood that he might be laid off and he had the other offer, he faced a major career choice.

THE INVENTOR

BY TERRY BIVENS

The Philadelphia Inquirer

Lightning, again in the form of a multimillion-dollar bolt from above, has struck twice for Howard Head.

Head, 67, the inventor of the revolutionary Head metal skis and, more recently, the oversized tennis racket, sold his second company in 13 years Tuesday. Chesebrough-Pond's Inc. of Greenwich, Conn., announced Tuesday it would pay $62 million in stock for Head's Prince Manufacturing Inc. in Princeton, N.J.

For Chesebrough-Pond's, a cosmetic and health-care products conglomerate that had sales of $1.17 billion last year, the purchase amounted to a relatively modest foray into the sporting-goods business. Prince manufactures and sells the oversized tennis racket that Head designed.

For Head, a 6-foot-4-inch man whose shaved pate has become a beacon for entrepreneurial dreamers, the transaction meant roughly $37 million, because he owned about 60 percent of the stock of the privately held Prince.

That bonanza, of course, came on top of the $4 million he received as part of a $16 million buyout of his ski-making company by AMF Inc. in 1969.

"It's a lot better the second time around," Head, a Baltimore resident, said in a telephone interview from his Princeton office. "It's a nice feeling. I'm feeling very soft and pleasant toward the company and life in general."

And why not? For Head, a colorful Harvard graduate who first wanted to become a newspaper writer, life has been very good, indeed.

Now, it shapes up as an uncluttered stretch of time for him to indulge his love of tennis and scuba diving at Caneel Bay on the Caribbean island of St. John.

But it wasn't always that way.

Head, the son of a Philadelphia dentist, veered from a career in newspapering after noticing that no one offered him any encouragement while he worked as a copy boy in the summertime.

He turned to scriptwriting, but was fired from his first job after his supervisors noticed he was spending more time fiddling with the film-splicing machines.

Head's mechanical aptitude, however, served him better once he shifted his attention to skiing. After becoming frustrated by his inability to swoop gracefully down the slopes, Head decided that it was the skis' fault—not his—and set about to build a better ski.

With about $6,000 in poker winnings and some loans from his friends, he worked his way through about 40 versions in three years.

The result was the Head ski, a wood-cored runner with an aluminum-and-plastic-alloyed outer surface. The metal skis proved so maneuverable that they were dubbed "cheaters."

Head sold his highly profitable Head Ski Co., which also included a line of sportswear, in 1969. Then, at age 55, he took up tennis.

Once again, the sport proved difficult. Better players, for example, often knocked his racket out of his hand.

Head, using the same logic that resulted in the Head ski, believed that the solution lay in an improved racket.

Noting that tennis rules said nothing about the size of a racket, he designed a model that was about 2 inches longer and 3½ inches wider. Those changes increased the strung area of the racket by 50 percent and quadrupled the size of the "sweet spot," the strung area where the ball rebounds best.

Ignoring the protests of purists who derided the racket as a coal shovel or fly swatter, Head began mass-producing them at the Prince plant in Princeton in 1976.

The first year sales were about $3 million. However, by last year sales had grown to $35 million, he said, with projections of $60 million for this year.

The rackets, which are available in six models ranging from $82 to $320 each, are now used by professional players such as Gene Mayer, Peter McNamara and Pam Shriver. The use of Prince-size racquets is approaching 30 percent in the sport "and that landslide is moving at a faster and faster rate," Head said.

Despite an additional $37 million in his pocket, Head is not inclined to chant "I told you so" at his early critics.

"Oh, I have nothing but a nice feeling," said Head, who will become a consultant for Chesebrough-Pond's at a retainer he termed nominal.

"I decided to sell the company because it had reached maturity, and it was time for me to move into a more relaxed way of life," he said. "Right now, I'm going to move very slowly. I don't expect to change my lifestyle much at all.

"I certainly have no plans for a third business," he said. "But then again, I had no plans for a second. It just happened, and I'm very content about it.

"The company (Prince) has fulfilled my best possible dreams," he said.

Source: Terry Bivens, "A Big Racket's Inventor Nets Profit on Firm," *The Philadelphia Inquirer,* 23 June 1982.

INTRODUCTION

These incidents involve people facing important personal issues revolving about their own career development. You have been (and may always be) involved in your own career planning and development. You have decided to go to college and may have selected a degree major. You have had various work-related experiences and have probably formed images of what you want to do in your life's work. You will always be facing some issue of career planning and development; you probably won't make decisions that will remain in force throughout your working life. Many of us are faced with various types of career decisions at different stages. Notice that in your conversations with others you rarely find a person who is not facing some sort of career question.

The vignettes illustrate a wide variety of career issues, ranging from Sandra's decision on which major to pursue in college to Gordon Pollard's decision on whether or not to leave the company for which he had worked for 20 years. You may have experienced situations similar to several of the vignettes. Hitoshi Yamamoto faced a career decision less familiar to us because of cultural and interpersonal differences in Japan as compared to the United States. But, the dilemma concerning life and career was very real to him. This illustrates a key point in this discussion of career development: A career is something that is very personal to each of us. It is based on our unique experiences in the world of work. We cannot look at it as a separate entity; it is a fundamental part of our existence.

Considering career issues can be very exciting because they are so personal and important to each of us. Careers can also be very unpredictable as the incident concerning Howard Head illustrates. He started on a short-lived career in newspapering and ended up with two innovative products and companies—Head metal skis and Prince tennis racquets. We should not be surprised to learn that he has started another enterprise.

In this chapter we will look at issues of individual career planning as well as how organizations can provide the climate appropriate for individual growth and development. The following topics will be covered:

The Concept of a Career
A Career-Development Perspective
Profile of Managers
What People Want in Their Careers
Adult Life Cycles
Different Career Paths
Career Problems
Individual Strategies for Career Development
Organizational Strategies for Career Development
So What? Implications for You

THE CONCEPT OF A CAREER

What is a career? This question often leads to confusing and ambiguous answers. In choosing a career, is it the job or the work or the profession you are embracing? Is a career determined by the functional requirements of an organization, or is it something that the individual experiences? As a concept, does it have only short-term applicability or does it speak of something that spans a lifetime? Is a career something that can be separated from family relationships and other nonwork activities? When does one start a career?

Traditionally, only a few professions—doctor, lawyer, minister, statesman, and the like—were considered to have careers. More recently however, the concept of career has been extended to include many other work-related roles. A distinction can be made between a job or occupation and a career. The concept of a job focuses on aspects external to the individual; it can be described separately from the person. A career includes these external aspects. However, it simultaneously demands consideration of internal (to the individual) or subjective aspects including individual attitudes and self-concepts. A career, then, is experienced by a person and, like any other experience, is both similar to the experiences of others but also different because of individual variations.

Using these ideas, we can state that *a career consists of the sequence of work-related activities and adventures that an individual experiences, perceives, and acts on during a lifetime*. A career is individually perceived and experienced and is associated with work-related activities. However, it is influenced by, and it exercises influence on, all other life activities—familial and social included. It cannot be observed at a single point in time; rather it is a process that covers the lifetime of the individual.

There are a number of commonly held views that are not necessarily associated with the concept of a career. A career need not imply upward mobility. There are linear careers, to be sure, but also other types—doctor, lawyer, or professor—that do not necessarily lead to progression up a hierarchy. Careers are not associated with a particular occupation but refer to any work-related experiences that extend over a relatively long period. Careers are not necessarily associated with one organization. Although some people spend their entire working life in one company, many others are highly mobile and will pursue their careers in many different organizations. Finally, career success cannot be externally measured by such things as rank, salary, and speed of promotion. Although these factors may affect an individual's self-perception of career success, there are many other factors that might affect individual perceptions. For example, one person may see her career primarily as the means to provide money to have a particular life style while another person may view success as an end in itself. These two individuals would likely evaluate career events differently.

The concept of a career being individually perceived and experienced raises the idea of free choice. Fortunately, in our society we have many opportunities for making career and life-style choices. This right of choice, however, also carries the responsibility for accepting the consequences of these decisions. It will be a basic theme throughout this chapter that you, as an individual, have the opportunity and responsibility for career and life choices. Using external criteria as a measurement of career success and waiting for someone else to plan and chart your career is inappropriate. The concept of personal choice suggests that you and you alone can take this responsibility.

A CAREER-DEVELOPMENT PERSPECTIVE

Emphasis on the individual's choice regarding career decisions does not mean that these take place in isolation. In career development, there is a continual matching process between the organization and the individual. The organization needs to recruit, train, motivate, manage, and develop human resources in order to maintain its effectiveness through survival and growth. At the same time, people need to find work situations that provide challenge, security, and opportunities for development throughout their entire life cycles. As discussed in Chapter 2, a psychological contract is developed and continually renegotiated throughout the career of the individual in the organization. Figure 17.1 provides an illustration of this matching process. The outcomes for the organization are drawn in terms of productivity, creativity, and effectiveness. Individual outcomes can be measured by satisfaction, security, personal development, and integration of work with other aspects of life. Ideally, this matching process leads to a mutually beneficial relationship.

It is useful to think of *investing* your career in a work organization. It is said that the largest investment most Americans make is in a home and the second largest is in an automobile. This is incorrect; your major investment is in your career. The amount of money spent preparing for a useful and productive career is substantial. Life-time earnings as a result of this career are even more significant. You should be a great deal more careful about this investment decision than any other. Many people adopt a passive stance regarding career development. We suggest that you should take an active approach to planning and developing your own career.

Career Transitions and Choices

Career development is not a one-shot process of deciding on a job and work organization in your early twenties and then sitting back to let nature take its course. It is a lifelong endeavor that requires substantial self-assessment and analysis and, in turn, provides challenges and opportunities. Most of us face many career transitions or breakpoints. "It is a *breakpoint* in which established relationships are severed and new ones forged, old behavior patterns forgotten and new ones learned, former responsibilities abandoned and new ones taken on. In short, breakpoints require the individual to discover or reformulate certain everyday assumptions about their working life" (Van Maanen, 1977, p. 16).

In our mobile society, people are facing many career transitions. They are changing their professions, organizations, and geographic locations. We also face career transitions because of changes in ourselves—our attitudes, values, motivations, and preferred life styles. For example, a young adult may have a different

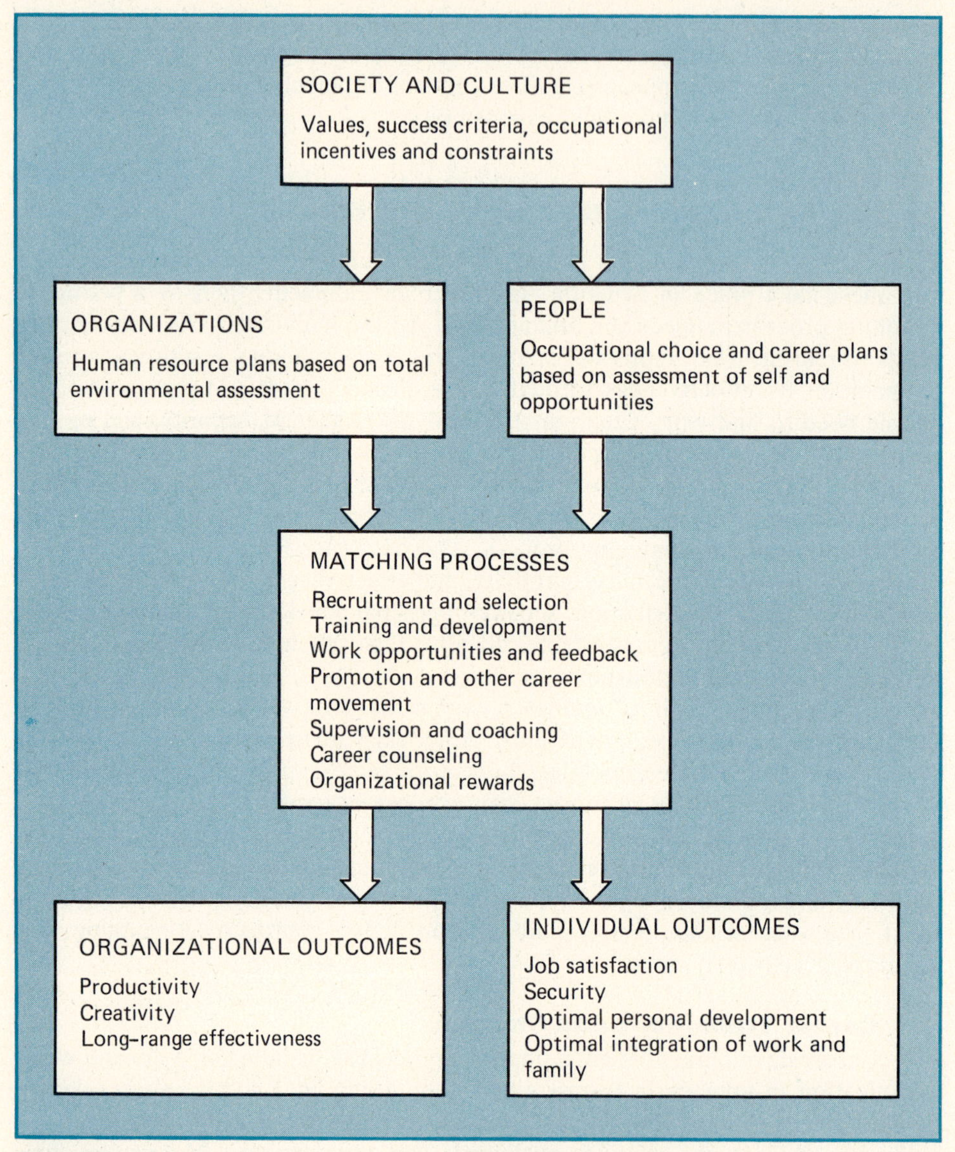

FIGURE 17.1 Components of the Career Development Perspective. **Source:** Edgar H. Schein, *Career Dynamics:* Matching Individual and Organizational Needs (Reading, Mass.: Addison-Wesley, 1978), p. 3. Reprinted with permission.

internal orientation toward his career than the long-term middle-aged employee. External forces, such as economic adversities, changing technologies, and company takeovers or reorganizations may force individuals to make career changes.

Each transition requires career decisions. These are perhaps some of the most important and difficult decisions facing people during their lifetime. Here is a sampling:

1. Deciding on career to pursue.
2. Obtaining education and training necessary for career.
3. Selecting a beginning job to fulfill career plans.
4. Developing a strategy for obtaining a specific position in an appropriate organization.
5. Selecting job offer from among alternatives.
6. Deciding the assignments and tasks to pursue within the organization.
7. Developing a career path, such as technical or managerial.
8. Obtaining a position in another location or with another organization.
9. Preparing for the next position. Strategies for continuing education and development.
10. Continuing self-appraisal and development of career goals.
11. Deciding to step down or move laterally during latter part of career.
12. Selecting the time for retirement and strategy of disengagement.

In career-development seminars it is interesting to note the large number and great diversity of career decisions. No one seems to have difficulty in coming up with at least one issue and most have many. This is apparent regardless of the level or function in the organization. The president may be concerned with when he should retire and how to disengage smoothly. The young engineer is concerned with her next project assignment and how this will affect her future promotions.

You will face many career transitions and choices, and you need to manage the decision-making process. These choices should be made in the context of long-range career plans. This does not mean that you cannot take advantage of good luck and chance opportunities. However, it is our observation that good fortune in careers seems to come most frequently to those who *position themselves* to take advantage of opportunities. In golf, a hole-in-one certainly involves luck; but the greater the number of times the ball goes on the green ending up close to the pin, the greater the chance for luck to take its course. It is not too early to recognize that you will make many career choices and that your lifetime satisfactions will likely be enhanced if you develop long-range career plans.

PROFILE OF MANAGERS

Since the turn of the century there have been profound changes in the jobs that Americans perform. In your grandparents' generation, most people worked on farms and as blue-collar workers in factories and mines. Even since your parent's generation there have been significant changes in the makeup of jobs. Since 1950 there has been a proportionate decline in agricultural, mining, basic-transportation, and manufacturing employment. More and more workers have moved into wholesale and retail trade, services, and especially the professions. The most significant increase has been in the number of professional and technical personnel, managers, and administrators. These are the occupational categories where you will likely find your career.

There have been a number of other major shifts in the size and composition of the nation's labor force. Since 1950 there has been a trend toward higher participation in the labor force—more of the population are working. Between 1950 and 1980 there was a 44 percent increase in the nation's population but a 64 percent increase in the labor force. Part of this increased participation is due to an aging population, but the most significant cause is the growing number of women in the labor force. The number of males in the labor force increased by 35 percent, while the number of females increased by 136 percent. Women now make up over 42 percent of the total labor force. Although they are still overrepresented in the lower-level clerical and service occupations, a large number have entered professional, technical, and managerial occupations. For both sexes, the shifts have been toward occupations requiring high levels of education. A much higher proportion of the population has received college and postgraduate educations in various fields.

Various studies of the profiles of current managers reflect these underlying trends. A study published in *Fortune* magazine of the profiles of 800 chief executives indicates that most of them came from middle-class backgrounds and had parents who were businessmen or professionals (Burck, 1976). This study found a significant increase in the level of formal education. Currently, 95 percent of the surveyed executives have attended college compared to less than 40 percent in 1900 and 75 percent in 1950. The survey results also suggest that job jumping did not seem to be a factor in promotion to the top. Nearly two-thirds of the CEOs switched employers no more than once and many had started their careers in the organization they later headed.

A survey of 11,227 executives, taken at the time they were promoted to vice president or president of a major U.S. company, suggests similar profiles for executives (Swinyard & Bond, 1980). The newly appointed executive was well educated, with most being college graduates and a large number possessing graduate degrees. Their most common field in undergraduate education was business administration (27 percent), followed by engineering (26 percent), and social and behavioral science (which includes economics) (22 percent). The most common graduate degree was in business administration, followed by law and engineering. Currently 25 percent of the newly appointed executives hold MBA degrees.

These studies describe the characteristics of the top executives in the nation's major companies, but how about the millions of managers and professionals who work at lower levels in many different types of work organizations? Although it is impossible to draw any exact profile of these managers, there are some characteristics and trends:

Managers come from a wide spectrum of family backgrounds and social classes.

They have a much higher level of education than in the past. Most have college degrees and an increasing proportion have graduate degrees.

An increasing proportion have been trained in business administration, engineering, and law rather than in the liberal arts.

Managerial positions have become more open to diverse ethnic groups. However, most minority managers are still at the lower and middle levels in their organizations.

The number of women who have college degrees in business administration and management has increased significantly. This has led to more women in lower and middle levels of managerial positions who will be working their way to higher executive positions in the future.

There are more specialized jobs in management requiring specialized training such as accountants, financial analysts, systems designers, human resource systems specialists, and market researchers.

Career mobility is highest at the beginning of an individual's career and decreases gradually over time.

More people trained in management are finding careers in not-for-profit organizations such as hospitals, educational institutions, and other public agencies.

Job-hopping pays off for some but not for most. A high proportion of job-hopping occurs at a relatively young age—30 to 35.

There is evidence to suggest that successful managers have substantial intracompany job mobility. They have taken on a wide variety of departmental, project, and other assignments. Their career paths have not generally followed a straight hierarchical path but rather have many horizontal and diagonal movements that have broadened their managerial experiences.

The primary conclusion from this discussion of profiles of managers is one of diversity. There are no strict paths to follow to managerial success nor are there a limited number of managerial roles. Rather, there are many career paths to a variety of managerial positions. Many possibilities are open to individuals. What are their expectations regarding these career options?

WHAT PEOPLE WANT IN THEIR CAREERS

We have stressed the importance of matching individual needs with job opportunities. A fundamental question is "What do I really want from my career?" Traditionally, jobs were thought of as the means for making money and earning a living. Although money and fringe benefits are still important, many people have developed new expectations about their work life. A challenging position that provides for personal development and achievement seem to be the goal of many.

In a survey 23,008 readers of *Psychology Today* magazine responded to a job satisfaction questionnaire. This sample of respondents tended to be younger, better educated, higher paid, and with a higher concentration of professional managers compared to the national work force. They represented the type of people that many college graduates of today will be like five to twenty years from now.

"How satisfied are you with each of the following aspects of your job? And how important to you is each of them?"

Respondents were asked to choose among different degrees of importance and satisfaction for each job feature. Based on averages of their responses, the numbers below rank each from 1 (most important to the group or most often satisfying) to 18 (least important or least often satisfying).

	Importance	Satisfaction
Chances to do something that makes you feel good about yourself	1	8
Chances to accomplish something worthwhile	2	6
Chances to learn new things	3	10
Opportunity to develop your skills and abilities	4	12
The amount of freedom you have on your job	5	2
Chances you have to do things you do best	6	11
The resources you have to do your job	7	9
The respect you receive from people you work with	8	3
Amount of information you get about your job performance	9	17
Your chances for taking part in making decisions	10	14
The amount of job security you have	11	5
Amount of pay you get	12	16
The way you are treated by the people you work with	13	4
The friendliness of people you work with	14	1
Amount of praise you get for job well done	15	15
The amount of fringe benefits you get	16	7
Chances for getting a promotion	17	18
Physical surroundings of your job	18	13

FIGURE 17.2 Importance and Satisfaction with Various Aspects of Jobs. **Source:** Patricia A. Renwick, Edward E. Lawler, and the *Psychology Today* staff, "What You Really Want from Your Job," *Psychology Today,* May 1978, p. 56. Reprinted from *Psychology Today Magazine*. © 1978, American Psychological Association.

Figure 17.2 shows two rankings: (1) the importance of various characteristics of their jobs and (2) the degree of satisfaction for each job characteristic. The striking impression from these responses is the importance attached to self-growth and development and the low importance attached to job security, fringe benefits, physical surroundings, and pay. These responses seem to reinforce the view that status and self-actualization are the dominant needs for people in managerial and professional positions. It is also interesting that people are most satisfied with their social relationships on the job, security, autonomy, and fringe benefits. They were least satisfied with the chances of getting a promotion, feedback on performance, and pay.

What factors do college graduates think are most important in their career choices? A review of responses from graduates of business schools concerning

Job Choice Factor	Rank in Importance
Intellectual Challenge	1
Opportunity for Advancement	2
Early Chance for Responsibility	3
Location, Living Conditions	4
Transferability of Experience	5
Compatibility with People in Company	6
Firm's Reputation	7
Independence/Autonomy	8
Salary or Other Compensation	9
Family Considerations (dual careers, etc)	10
Travel Requirement	11

FIGURE 17.3 Key Factors Affecting Job Choices for M.B.A. Graduates, 1982

their reasons for choosing a particular job, suggest an interesting and consistent pattern. We have reviewed a number of these surveys and they reflect similar responses. Figure 17.3 shows the response of MBAs from one school, the University of Washington. The students were asked to rank factors that influenced their job choice. The strongest factors were an intellectually stimulating job that provided an opportunity for advancement and challenging responsibilities in the beginning. The initial salary of the job was far down the list of importance. Commitment to work is different than in the past. It is less directed toward working for a particular organization or even in a particular occupation. People seem to be more interested in their own personal career development. They are more concerned with challenge, advancement, autonomy, and decision-making opportunities than the young people of the 1960s. They have higher expectations and consequently will make greater demands for career satisfaction. No longer will fair pay and good working conditions be enough.

Career Anchors

As a result of education, early organizational socialization, and work experience, an individual develops certain knowledge about the match between self and job. Schein (1978, p. 125) uses the term *career anchors* to explain this concept.

> The early career can therefore be viewed as a time of *mutual discovery* between the new employee and the employing organization. Through successive trials and new job challenges, each learns more about the other. Even more significantly, however, the new employee gradually gains *self-knowledge* and develops a clearer *occupational self-concept*. This self-concept has three components, which together make up what I will call the person's "*career anchor*."
>
> 1. *Self-perceived talents and abilities* (based on actual successes in a variety of work settings);

2. *Self-perceived motives and needs* (based on opportunities for self-tests and self-diagnosis in real situations and on feedback from others);
3. *Self-perceived attitudes and values* (based on actual encounters between self and the norms and values of the employing organization and work setting).

Schein developed this concept of career anchors after a longitudinal study of alumni of the Sloan School of Management at the Massachusetts Institute of Technology. He interviewed students when they graduated and then again 10 to 12 years later after they had established definite occupational self-concepts. The career anchor functions in the individual's work life as a way of organizing experience and identifying one's area of contribution over the long run. It determines those types of activities where the individual feels competent. Schein identified five distinct categories of career anchors:

Anchor 1—Managerial Competence. The individual seeks and values opportunities to manage. There is a strong motivation to rise to positions of managerial responsibility.

Anchor 2—Technical/Functional Competence. The individual seeks and values opportunities to exercise various technical talents and areas of competence. Interested primarily in the technical content of the job—whether the work is finance, engineering, marketing, or some other functional area.

Anchor 3—Security. The individual is motivated by the need to stabilize the career situation. This person will do whatever is required to maintain job security, a decent income, and the potential of a good retirement program.

Anchor 4—Creativity. The individual has an overarching need to build or create something that is entirely his or her own. It is self-extension—through the creation of a new product, process, or theory, a company of their own, a personal fortune as an indication of achievement—that seems to be the career objective of these people.

Anchor 5—Autonomy and Independence. The individual seeks work situations that will be maximally free of organizational constraints to pursue their professional competence. Freedom from constraints and the opportunity to pursue one's own life and work style appears to be a primary need.

You should read these descriptions carefully and try to assess your own values in terms of these career anchors. How do you see yourself in the future? Do you anticipate a highly specialized career based on technical/functional competence, as in accounting, financial analysis, or computer systems? Or, will you develop general managerial competence? Perhaps you will seek autonomy and independence, in which case you might opt for a career as a management consultant or entrepreneur. Schein's research and other findings suggest that, in order to have a successful career, there needs to be an effective match between the career anchor—an individual's abilities, motivation, and self-perceived attitudes and values—and the requirements of the job.

It is worth noting the three specific areas in which successful managers feel a high level of competence (Schein, 1978, pp. 135–136):

1. Analytical competence: the ability to identify, analyze, and solve problems under conditions of incomplete information and uncertainty.
2. Interpersonal competence: the ability to influence, supervise, lead, manipulate, and control people at all levels of the organization toward the more effective achievement of organizational goals.
3. Emotional competence: the capacity to be stimulated by emotional and interpersonal crises rather than exhausted or debilitated by them, the capacity to bear high levels of responsibility without becoming paralyzed, and the ability to exercise power without guilt or shame.

Schein makes the point that we do not firmly develop career anchors until after we have been involved in a work situation for an extended period. His respondents had been working for 10 to 12 years. "Career anchors clearly *reflect* the underlying needs and motives which the person brings into adulthood, but they also reflect the person's values and, most important, *discovered talents*. By definition there cannot be an anchor until there has been work experience, even though motives and values may already be present from earlier experience" (Schein, 1978, p. 171). You probably already have some indications concerning your possible career anchors. This has been reflected in the major you choose in college, in how you respond to different courses, and in what you do and enjoy as outside activities.

ADULT LIFE CYCLES

In recent years there has been a growing interest in adult development and in the concept of adult life cycles, particularly as they relate to the occupational experiences. Throughout life we go through a series of developmental and transition periods. The general nature of development and change is seen as a succession of periods of tranquility and self-assuredness followed by stressful transition periods. A review of the literature concerning adult life cycles suggests the following phases and characteristics (Erickson, 1963; Levinson, 1978; Gould, 1972; Vaillant, 1977):

AGE	PHASE
18–22	Early Adult Transition: Striking Out
	Leaving family Educational and occupational choices Dependence on support of peer group Developing self-identity First jobs seen as means of self-support
23–28	Moving into the Adult World: Search for Identity

	Building career and family Developing intimacies—marriage, family, togetherness Period of high energy, enthusiasm, idealism Formation of one's "dreams" Very sure of oneself Career success becomes a goal
29–34	The Developing Crisis: Questions, Questions
	The first sobering period—time of reappraisal Assurance waivers Life and work become less rosy Marital and family satisfaction may decline Idealism of the 20s turns to the harsher realities of the 30s Marriage and career shifts are common Questions of who am I and where am I going Job changes likely
35–40	Becoming One's Own Person
	Getting act together. Seeking order, stability, security and control Reaffirming one's commitments—putting down roots Learning acceptance of self, spouse, and children Striving for upward achievement For career-oriented people a major concentration on work and advancement
41–48	Midlife Transition: A Period of Adjustment
	Emotional awareness of impending death and shortness of time Changing family relationship—growing independence of children Facing the disparity between one's dreams and actual accomplishments Uneasy sense of obsolescence Less mobility, more concern for job security Values open to question. Was the striving worth it? A return to experimentation and uncertainty of adolescent behavior New choices in terms of family, marriage, life style May be last time for evaluation and change of career
49–62	Settling Down and Mellowing
	A stable time—the die is cast Optimistic stabilization and contentment of relationships

	Decisions must be lived with and life settles down Turning to family and close friends Money and material welfare less important, social relationships more so Accepting oneself for what one is and not blaming others May take a mentoring role with others For most people fewer job, organization, and career changes
63 and after	Retirement and Old Age Period of major transition Finding substitutes for work as a major part of life Loss of work associates—developing new friends and relationships Evidently a wide degree of variability as to individuals ability to make adjustments and find satisfaction in later life.

It is important to understand these phases in the adult life cycle when looking at career issues. As individuals evolve and change over their life their relationships with their jobs and careers also change. What might be a successful career for a young adult might be intolerable for the middle-aged person. Many people who have become locked into deadening jobs are in this position.

Stages in the adult life cycle suggest certain things regarding jobs and careers: (1) the first job is likely to be taken because it provides income with little thought to long-term career issues; (2) people often enter their first jobs after college with a high degree of enthusiasm and ambition; (3) this is frequently followed by a period of disillusionment and frequent job changes; (4) the 30–40 period is one of maximum career development; (5) the midlife crisis will again result in frequent job changes and midcareer adjustments; (6) once this transition is past there is much less job mobility; and (7) the final career crisis is one of adapting to the absence of a job.

DIFFERENT CAREER PATHS

Our society and its work organizations have a wide variety of task requirements and this leads to many diverse career opportunities. People move in and out of organizations and often change their occupations. The concept of career paths must deal with many diverse routes.

The most obvious career path for most people is one of vertical mobility up the hierarchy. There are different skill requirements at different levels in the hierarchy. At the lowest level, the primary job skills are technical: understanding the equipment, technology, procedures, processes, and other techniques. A variety of technical careers are available in most organizations, whether in engineering, accounting, financial analysis, marketing research, or production. These jobs require specialized education, often acquired in business schools or schools of engineering. It is quite likely that you will start at this specialized-training level in your first permanent position. In some organizations that have a dual ladder for promotion—technical and managerial—it is possible to move up the hierarchy while retaining a technical orientation. However, in most organizations, moving up requires a shift in career interests. The primary skills for first-line and middle management are leadership and effective interpersonal relationships. The functions are less technical and deal more with relationships among people. Movement into a managerial position is likely to be one of your most important career transitions and will require you to display or develop new skills. Even the best of training in technical skills will not be sufficient in making this transition.

The transition from middle to upper management requires another major shift—from interpersonal to conceptual skills. The top manager needs to develop broad conceptual skills that help in relating the organization to its environment, to develop broad strategic plans, and to design the organization for effective implementation of strategies. Effective leadership skills are important in establishing the general organizational climate. Here, right-brain thinking, emphasizing innovation and creativity, tends to be more important than left-brain technical thinking.

This movement up the hierarchy may be the appropriate path for some; it cannot be achieved by most people. Organizations have a pyramidal structure with many more positions at the bottom than at the top. There are many opportunities for technical and middle management careers, but few spaces at the top. If this were the only career path available, there would be many dissatisfied and disillusioned people.

Driver (1979) cites four basic career paths:

1. *Transitory*—no clear pattern
2. *Steady State*—lifetime occupation
3. *Linear*—steady progression in a career ladder
4. *Spiral*—planned search for increasing self-development

The *transitory pattern* is typical of young people when they enter the job market. There is no clear pattern and the emphasis is on finding a job to provide income. The individual typically has a number of different jobs, and career moves are typically lateral. There is frequently little loyalty to the job or to the occupation. Although many people start their work life in this transitory phase, most people move on in their development into other patterns. However, there are some people who spend their entire work lives in the transitory stage. This pattern can be highly successful for some. The transitory entrepreneurial type thrives on starting new ventures, and as soon as activities become stabilized moves on to something else. A transitory entrepreneurial career can be highly unstable with many successes and failures. The classic example is the entrepreneur who has made and lost millions a number of times. A few of you may follow this career pattern.

The *steady-state pattern* is typical of many professional- and craft-type occupations, such as physician, dentist, electrician, and carpenter. It frequently takes a long training period to attain a steady state. In a craft or profession, years of training and upward movement from apprentice to craftsman may be needed, but once the desired role is attained, it is held for life. The steady-state person may have to work hard for long periods to attain this role. The steady-state pattern may also develop later in life for the individual who has had upward mobility but is now blocked from further advancement. The term *plateaued* is used to describe this pattern.

The *linear pattern* is typically thought of in career development. This pattern involves a steady upward advancement through managerial, professional, or political levels. A critical factor separating this pattern from steady state maintenance is the nearly insatiable upward striving that is manifested. The linear pattern is characteristic of high achievers and usually requires significant sacrifices of other interests to career advancements. Family and other activities may often be orchestrated to support this upward career drive. Linear-type careers are most subject to disruption, particularly at midcareer. The pyramidal nature of most organizations means that increasingly smaller numbers of people can move upward. Many linear careers stabilize or plateau and the individual is blocked from further advancement. For the aggressive, achievement-oriented, upwardly mobile individual this can result in a career crisis. The individual has been forced to change from a linear to a steady-state career.

The *spiral career pattern* is most interesting. It offers the greatest opportunity for diversity of experiences. It may involve many lateral and diagonal as well as vertical moves. The project-organization form offers the opportunity for employees to be associated with a particular project task for a period of time and then to move back onto a linear track. This pattern seems to be internally driven by a desire for self-growth that moves the individual toward greater self-development and awareness. Driver (p. 95) suggests that there are at least two types of spiral patterns: (1) an internal spiral—who stays within an organization or professional field, yet moves around creatively in search of self-development and (2) an external spiral—who more dramatically switches organizations and fields. There is substantial evidence to suggest that the internal spiral pattern is more appropriate for reaching top executive levels than is a strict linear path.

Different career concepts are appropriate for various types of organizations. For example, both the linear and the steady state career patterns fit well with the traditional bureaucratic organization, where positional roles are well-defined and career paths are definite. In contrast, the transitory and spiral career concepts fit more appropriately with the more organic, less-structured organization. The entrepreneurial organization is an example. The spiral pattern seems to fit with many high-technology and artistic organizations. It is also appropriate where organizations use the project, program, and matrix forms.

There is also evidence that organizations are changing. Many organizations are developing more adaptive/organic forms that permit and even encourage spiral-career patterns. New forms of work, such as flextime, job sharing, and working at home appeal to the transitory career pattern. The spiral pattern is evident when people change organizations and careers later in their work lives.

In our society it is important that there are a wide variety of jobs that fit in with these various career concepts in order to more effectively utilize human resources. The traditional concepts of a steady-state career, a craft or profession for a lifetime, or a linear path are still with us, but increasingly we are developing alternative job designs that appeal to the transitory and spiral-career patterns. With a decline in the growth of the labor force, organizations will have to be much more creative in designing work to fit the career patterns of the available people.

CAREER PROBLEMS

Success in a career is just one part of your overall life. Many professionals and managers have had what might be described as highly successful careers, but apparently with great sacrifices to family and personal life. Some people hold the view that a successful management career demands that the individual sacrifice personal and family relationships. This idea presents a dilemma—you can have one or the other, but not both. There has been little real evidence to indicate a pattern. There are many so-called war-stories of the sacrifices that are necessary to be successful, but there are also many examples of successful managers and professionals who lead rewarding and fulfilling family and outside work lives. We support the view expressed by Bartolomé and Evans (1980) in Box 17.1 that what happens in one's work life can have a profound effect on family and other relationships. It is difficult to shake off major job dissatisfactions at 5:00 P.M. and not have them carry over into private life. We cannot segment our lives into work and nonwork segments; there is a strong synergistic effect.

You will face career issues and problems throughout your lifetime. At the current stage you may be preoccupied with obtaining an education or finding a job. You may discount the potential for future career problems and presume that a clear track lies ahead. People who have moved into middle- and top-management positions continue to experience career problems. It may be of interest to note what a group of 811 top managers and 383 middle managers saw as the factors most likely to impede their future career advancement as shown in Figure 17.4. The top managers saw the lack of communicative and other interpersonal skills as the chief factors impeding future career advancement. In contrast, middle

BOX 17.1
MUST SUCCESS COST SO MUCH?

After countless exchanges with managers and their wives and after careful analysis of research data, we concluded that the major determinant of work's impact on private life is whether negative emotional feelings aroused at work spill over into family and leisure time. When an executive experiences worry, tension, fear, doubt, or stress intensely, he is not able to shake these feelings when he goes home, and they render him psychologically unavailable for a rich private life. The manager who is unhappy in his work has a limited chance of being happy at home—no matter how little he travels, how much time he spends at home, or how frequently he takes a vacation.

When individuals feel competent and satisfied in their work—not simply contented, but challenged in the right measure by what they are doing—negative spillover does not exist. During these periods executives are open to involvement in private life; they experience positive spillover. When work goes well, it can have the same effect as healthy physical exercise—instead of leading to fatigue, it is invigorating.

Source: Reprinted by permission of the *Harvard Business Review.* Excerpt from "Must Success Cost So Much?" by Fernando Bartolomé and Paul A. Lee Evans [March-April 1980].

managers felt that the factors impeding their career advancement were the fewer higher managerial jobs available, inadequate career planning and guidance, and being too closely identified with a particular organizational faction. Interestingly, top executives seemed to attribute lack of career advancement to personal factors, such as skills and talents, while middle managers generally attributed lack of advancement to external factors.

Certain problem areas stand out such as those of the young manager, the plateaued manager, and couples pursuing dual careers. Job stress and its effect on performance and satisfaction has also become an increasingly important issue. While it is impossible to cover all possible career problems, we will discuss some of the more pervasive ones.

Career Problems of the Young Manager or Professional

Organizational socialization is the process of becoming an accepted member in an organization (see Chapter 2). The individual learns new values and appropriate ways of behaving and what is expected by the organization. As the employee moves from entry levels into the managerial hierarchy new career issues and problems develop. The exact timing of this move varies greatly. Most college graduates and MBAs do not go directly into managerial positions. There is some

Factor	Ranking by Top Management (N=811)	Ranking by Middle Management (N=383)
Lack of adequate managerial talents and/or professional skills	1	4
Lack of adequate communicative and other interpersonal skills	2	5
Being too closely identified with a particular organization faction or power group	3	2
Inadequate career planning and guidance	4	3
Fewer managerial jobs resulting from organizational streamlining	5	1
Factors such as sex, age, race, or matter involving private life or personal habits	6	6
Retirement practices	7	9
Competition from better-educated managers	8	7
Competition from younger or more aggressive managers	9	8

FIGURE 17.4 Factors Most Likely to Impede Future Career Advancement. **Source:** Adapted, by permission of the publisher, from *Manager to Manager II: What Managers Think of Their Managerial Careers,* an AMA Survey Report, by Robert F. Pearse, p. 31.

time spent in a learning, training, and technical role. In many organizations it is likely to be two to five years before they move into the lower levels of management. For example, MBAs entering General Electric Company will likely spend three to four years on jobs of the individual-responsibility type before being considered for first-line management positions.

There has been substantial research concerning career problems of young managers and professionals (Hall, 1976; Webber, 1976; Dalton, Thompson, & Price, 1977). One key observation is that the most important individual in the career development of the young manager is his or her own immediate manager. The "boss" does a great deal to set the climate for the young manager. It is the boss who most typically makes the assignments and evaluates performance. If your manager is highly respected in the organization and seen as powerful by others, she can have a major influence. The skilled and supportive manager can provide excellent coaching and guidance. Most successful executives have had mentors who provided primary support during their careers. In most organizational situations the mentoring relationship is more likely to be man-to-man than woman-to-woman or mixed genders. This is the current reality of not having sufficient numbers of women in higher executive positions and is one of the subtle forces making it more difficult for women to advance. Mentors are important and women have more difficulty in developing a mentoring relationship.

Rarely does the young professional or manager find the perfect boss. Developing an effective relationship with your superior is not just his or her responsibility. Too often we feel that the superior should lead, motivate, reward, coach, and generally support us as subordinates. Too infrequently, we recognize that the relationship is mutual and that we also can manage the boss. Reflect for a minute about your last work situation. Did you think consciously about managing your boss? Did you look for ways that would support and motivate your boss to act according to your expectations? Did you look for ways to reward your boss for effective performance? It is vitally important that you understand your manager and yourself. What are your boss's strengths and weaknesses and how can you complement these? As a subordinate, you also have equal responsibility to manage the relationship with your boss if it is to be successful.

Even with support from a mentor and a good interpersonal relationship with your superior, you are likely to find a number of career problems typical of younger managers and professionals:

Underutilization of potential. The major complaint of young managers and professionals in organizations is the feeling that their talents and skills are not being effectively utilized. Hall calls this "the syndrome of unused potential" (Hall, 1976, p. 66). College graduates, and particularly business school students, are often trained to think like top managers and to solve strategic problems. They are frequently highly motivated and have high expectations for a challenging job and early advancement. However, existing managers have often spent years working up the ladder and feel that younger employees should prove themselves before they are given more important jobs.

Insufficient performance evaluation and feedback. This is associated with the syndrome of unused potential. Many younger managers report a lack of feedback on their performance; they want to know where they stand and how they are doing on the job. As discussed in Chapter 4, one of the characteristics of people with high achievement motivation is the need for feedback on performance. Lack of feedback can cause anxiety and frustration. Too frequently, higher managers assume that newer employees have a good sense of their performance and contributions and don't see the need to be redundant in providing information. This feeling is not limited to new workers but is characteristic of all employees. We know that good feedback on performance can help any individual learn and develop. It is important for every organization to design effective systems to provide feedback, particularly to their younger managers and professionals.

Political aspects of organizations. By their very nature organizations are political systems. The new manager and professional often has difficulty in coming to terms with this reality. Much of his or her background and training has assumed rational solving of technical problems in artificial and nonpolitical settings. When faced with the realities of a political system, many young managers are insensitive or hypersensitive. They don't want to play the power game but want to be evaluated purely on their technical merits, failing to recognize that the ability to exert influence is behind every effective organizational activity. As a manager you cannot remain outside the political arena. The new manager must face these political realities and learn to use them.

Feelings of dependence. Young managers must also come to grips with dependency relationships. They typically are dependent on superiors for support and guidance; at the same time they may represent a threat to the established manager. The bright young newcomers may have many concepts and ideas unfamiliar to their managers. The young manager is also dependent on his or her subordinates. It is unlikely that the young manager will have the technical skills and local knowledge possessed by subordinates.

This dependence on others may create problems for the young manager. He or she has been engaged in a life-long struggle to gain independence from parents, teachers, and school systems and has developed a strong desire for autonomy and independence. It is vitally important for effective managers to manage these dependencies through the acquisition and skillful use of power.

> The primary reason power dynamics emerge and play an important role in organizations is not necessarily because managers are power hungry, or because they want desperately to get ahead, or because there is an inherent conflict between managers who have authority and workers who do not. It is because the dependence inherent in managerial jobs is greater than the power or control given to the people in those jobs. Power dynamics, under these circumstances, are inevitable and are needed to make organizations function well (Kotter, 1979, pp. 16–17).

Loyalty issues and ethical dilemmas. Many young managers are confronted with issues of loyalty—to themselves, their superiors and colleagues, and the organization. Most superiors and organizations expect loyalty from employees and particularly from managers. The issue of loyalty frequently creates ethical dilemmas. Unfortunately, there is no single guideline to follow. Does ethical behavior mean economic self-interest, obeying the law, adhering to religious principles, being loyal to a superior, supporting the organization, or obtaining the greatest good for the most people? The young manager frequently faces conflict and must choose the particular ethical principle to be followed. Younger employees are most vulnerable to these issues of loyalty and ethical dilemmas. It is easy, as the Watergate incident showed, for an aspiring professional to go along with actions of others without bringing to bear his or her own critical judgments.

Plateauing and Obsolescence

After a number of years of advancement many individuals will come up against the inevitable; in hierarchical organizations there are fewer positions at the next level. It is inevitable that many managers will be plateaued at a certain level with further advancements difficult, at best.

Many factors contribute to this plateauing. In periods of steady growth, such as our society experienced between 1946 and the early 1970s, there were many opportunities for advancement. Many people had excellent careers by growing with the organization. In periods of slow growth or decline, this career strategy is less likely to be fruitful.

Basic demographic factors have also influenced the number of qualified people competing for higher positions in organizations. The high birth-rate period between 1945 and 1965 produced a bumper crop of people in the 25–40 age group who are competing for better positions. The increased number of women who have the education and aspirations to move higher in organizations has contributed to more competition. There is evidence that many people are feeling plateaued and blocked off from further advancement. Survey results indicate that one of the major dissatisfactions among managerial and clerical employees is the lack of opportunity for advancement (Cooper, Morgan, Foley, & Kaplan, 1979).

Obsolescence is frequently associated with plateauing although they are not the same. Plateauing refers to the lack of further advancement because of limited personal, managerial, or technical skills or because of limited opportunity. Obsolescence is related to the failure to learn and develop new knowledge and skills necessary to perform the job effectively. Obsolescence occurs when office managers fail to keep up with computer developments and resist the introduction of new technologies into their operations. Obsolescence may occur for the engineer or scientist who is assigned to a specialized project and fails to keep up with other developments in the field. The specter of obsolescence faces all of us. The only answer is a continual educational- and career-development program. Fortunately, as one moves up the hierarchy, less emphasis is generally placed on technical skills and more on human relations, interpersonal, and conceptual skills. However, with rapid changes in attitudes and values, the manager may become obsolete in human-relations skills as well as technical skills. The manager (or coach, teacher, or counselor) who tries to deal with people the same way that he did twenty or thirty years ago is likely to experience great difficulties.

There are several alternative outcomes to the process of leveling off in career advancements. It is inevitable for most people to reach a level in the organization where their likelihood of further advancement is limited. This is natural and not necessarily a problem. What is bad is the possibility of becoming obsolete, obstructionist, and ineffective. There are at least two types of plateauees: the solid citizens who remain effective performers and those ineffective plateauees who do not meet expectations (Ference, Stoner, & Warren, 1977). A key managerial challenge is to prevent solid citizens from gradually losing motivation to perform effectively and slipping into the ineffective category.

In many organizations the solid citizens are neglected. Their loyalty, motivation, and interest in the organization are often taken for granted. Managers often fail to provide them feedback and rewards for their performance. If there is no perceived consequence of good behavior, that behavior gradually becomes extinct. By not providing positive feedback and rewards for effective performance, we may drive people into the ineffective category.

> Comparable attention is not focused on maintaining the performance of the solid citizens who constitute the greater bulk of the management group. Organizations need solid citizens to maintain stability, provide continuity, and keep the level of competition for higher level jobs within manageable bounds. But interviews reported a tendency to treat solid citizens passively. They may be denied access to development programs and challenging assignments. Such practices may starve solid citizens of exactly the types of stimulation and opportunity they require to remain effective (Ference, Stone, & Warren, 1977, p. 607).

In many organizations it is difficult to get rid of ineffective plateauees because of contractual obligations, tenure, and seniority. Besides, dismissal of the long-term employee is often distasteful. It is important that organizations develop means for identifying people who are likely to be ineffective plateauees, and to create effective career guidance and development program. Prevention of low performance is much easier than correcting it.

It is also important to recognize how organizational norms can affect behavior and performance. The idea that one goes *up* or *out* leaves little room for the effective plateauee. Leveling out is not failing in one's career and it should be given more respectability. It seems to us somehow that an organization is wrong if it makes the majority of its people feel like failures.

Job Stress

One of the potential career problems is job-related stress. It is a significant part of the stress that stems from modern life. Many current newspaper and magazine articles reflect the growing concern about the effect of stress on our productivity, sense of well-being, and physical and emotional health. Within this context we are becoming more aware of the cost, in both financial and human terms, of high pressure and stress in our daily work lives.

What is stress? It is difficult to define and even more difficult to measure. Events that might cause anxiety, frustration, and even physical manifestations in one individual might go unnoticed by another. Generally, stress results from any external situation that requires behavioral adjustments. It is the response that a stressor evokes in the individual's body/mind. More specifically stress is an adaptive response, mediated by individual characteristics and/or psychological processes, that is a consequence of any external action, situation, or event that places special physical and/or psychological demands upon a person (Ivancevich and Matteson, 1980, p. 8–9).

The physiological consequences of stress are readily measurable; increased heart rate, blood pressure, adrenalin levels, respiratory rate, blood glucose, serum cholesterol levels, perspiration, and blood flow to muscles. These responses to stressors are functional to most animals. They were the physiological preparations for *fight or flight* as discussed in Box 17.2. For early man, these were the two basic responses to a stressor and they were functional. Once the stressors were encountered the stress response prepared the individual to either physically meet the challenge or run away. Fortunately (or perhaps unfortunately) today's world requires many other types of stress responses. "The problem that we encounter today is that the human nervous system still responds the same way to environmental stressors, although the environment is radically different. The tigers are gone and with them the appropriateness of the fight-or-flight response. Yet it is that response for which the body is prepared" (Ivancevich & Matteson, 1980, p. 10).

In your life you have faced many stressors where the fight-or-flight response is not appropriate. The professor gives you a low grade, you are passed over for a promotion, or your boss gives you a disagreeable assignment. You usually can neither flee nor fight these stressors; you are expected to respond in a calm and civilized way. The problem is that your body has already prepared for the fight-or-flight response. Enacting either of these responses typically alleviates the stress. But in not acting, the body has prepared for something that doesn't happen. If there are a continuing series of stressors, the body remains in a stress alert or fight-or-flight stage, and this continuing stress response can have detrimental effects on physical and mental health and on performance.

Dr. Hans Selye (1956) first conceptualized the *General Adaptation Syndrome* into three phases:

1. The *alarm stage* is the body's response to a threat from the environment. The alarm is sounded and almost every major organ in the body responds to make ready for "flight-or-fight." In many cases this is short-lived as when you are startled by a stranger at night.
2. The *resistance stage* is when the stressor is more long-lived and is dealt with physiologically or mentally. The person adapts to the stressor and the symptoms usually disappear.
3. The *exhaustion stage* is when physical and psychological resources are overcome. Prolonged exposure to stressors may eventually overcome the adaptive energy and the system becomes exhausted. The alarm stage symptoms reappear and result in many other physical manifestations such as fatigue, disease, and disability, and even death. It is in the exhaustion stage that the adverse consequences of stress become apparent in terms of productivity and physical and mental well-being.

This general adaptation syndrome provides a general model of responses to stress but it does not explain individual differences. The effects of environmental

BOX 17.2
'FIGHT OR FLIGHT'

Stress is difficult to define and even more difficult to quantify. We believe that stress results from environmental situations that require behavioral adjustment—ranging from petty daily annoyances to such events as significant illness, death of a spouse, and divorce. The behavioral adjustments necessitated by stress are, in turn, related to specific physiological changes, including increased blood pressure and heart rate, sweating, faster breathing, and markedly increased blood flow to the muscles. These changes frequently occur in an integrated, coordinated pattern called the "fight-or-flight response."

First described by Dr. Walter B. Cannon of the Harvard Medical School, this response has had great evolutionary significance. When used appropriately, it enables an animal to escape a threatening or dangerous situation by fighting or running. Many scientists contend that the long-term survival of human beings was made possible because of this response.

In our everyday lives, the elicitation of the fight-or-flight response is often associated with increased performance. Before an athletic event, competitors involuntarily elicit this response. Before an examination, students exhibit increased heart rate and blood pressure. Similarly, in today's business environment, the stimulus of the fight-or-flight response is often essential to success.

The same response, however, can also have undesirable effects. If the response is elicited frequently in a person who cannot fight or run—that is, cope in some appropriate way—the resulting stress is believed to be an underlying cause of high blood pressure, heart attacks, and strokes. High blood pressure affects about 60 million Americans. Related diseases of the heart and brain account for about 50% of the deaths each year in the United States, and during 1979 they cost society an estimated $35.1 billion.

Source: Reprinted by permission of the *Harvard Business Review*. Excerpt from "How Much Stress is Too Much?" by Herbert Benson and Robert L. Allen [September-October 1980].

stressors are mediated by individual characteristics. Some people tolerate stressful conditions better than others and are more effective in coping with stressors. There is substantial research evidence to suggest that different personality types both respond and deal with stressors differently (Friedman & Rosenman, 1974). People with Type-A behavior patterns tend to be competitive, hard driving, aggressive, hyperalert, impatient with people and situations that hinder accomplishments, achievement oriented, and continually under time pressure. They often react to stressors with hostility and anger. Type A people also seem to be the major sufferers from the prolonged effects of stress—heart disease, alcoholism, and other manifestations.

Type-B behavior individuals tend to respond differently to stress; they have better coping mechanisms. It should be emphasized that Type-B individuals still may be highly motivated and goal oriented. They are not at all necessarily blasé, lazy, or lacking in ambition (although Type A's may see them this way). They may be just as desirous of success and accomplishments as Type A's. The difference is that they seek satisfaction of these needs and behave in ways that do not create the adverse physical and mental consequences that affect the Type-A person. The Type-B person seems to have natural or learned immunities to the impact of stressors just as some people are immune to bacterial invaders.

What are job stressors? In a sense, any situation, person, or event that we encounter might be a source of stress. Fortunately most of these are not stressors. We cope with them without invoking undue response. Many factors outside the work organization may contribute to individual stress, such as family crises or major life changes. These stressors can result in behavior that has a detrimental impact on job performance and satisfaction.

Many forces in the organizational environment have been identified as sources of stress. *Physical environmental factors*—improper lighting, excessive noise, extreme temperatures, air pollution, noxious working materials—can certainly be stressors. These physical environmental stressors generally affect people in factories and production lines more than clerical, professional, and managerial workers. Many *job qualities* have been associated with stress such as the pace of the work, work underload or underutilization, work overload, and too little or too much variety. *Role conflicts* can be highly stressful where the individual may have ambiguous responsibilities or may be subject to conflicting requirements. *Relationships on the job,* difficulties with supervisor, peers, or subordinates, may also be sources of stress. As a corollary to this, we can note that responsibility for things—equipment, budgets, and the like—is less stressful than responsibility for people (Ivancevich & Matteson, 1980, pp. 114–115).

Of particular interest here are what might be called *career development stressors,* which are related to the individual's perception of the quality of his or her career progress. "Career variables may serve as stressors when they become sources of concern, anxiety, or frustration to the individual. This can happen if an employee feels a lack of job security, is concerned about real or imagined obsolescence, feels that promotion progress is inadequate, and/or is generally dissatisfied with the match between career aspirations and the current level of attainment" (Ivancevich & Matteson, 1980, p. 115). Stress brought on by career stressors often manifests itself in the form of decreased job satisfaction and lower performance. It may help to explain the ineffective plateauees discussed earlier.

This has been called the Age of Anxiety. We are becoming aware of the adverse consequences of excessive stress and are developing individual and organizational programs for dealing with it. Throughout your work career you will be subject to a wide variety of stressors and how you handle them will be a prime determinant of your mental and physical well-being, as well as your performance.

Jick and Payne (1980) suggest that there are three basic ways for dealing with stress in organizations: (1) treat the symptoms of stress; (2) change the person; and (3) change or remove the stressor. Treating the symptoms of stress helps individuals who are already suffering from its effects. Providing people with health-care and counseling services is an example. Physical and psychological examinations to help identify people who are adversely affected by stress-related diseases is another example.

The second approach seeks to change the individual, to reduce the vulnerability and develop better resistance and coping responses to stress. Adams (1977) calls this the "self-management of stress." Better nutrition, more exercise, effective time management, meditation, relaxation, and biofeedback are examples of this approach. They are aimed at changing the person's psychological and physical condition. A key element in helping an individual withstand stress is the development of social support systems. Support from family, colleagues, and important others can be a key factor in buffering the individual from excessive stress.

The third basic strategy attacks the causes of stress by eliminating, ameliorating, or changing the stressors in the work environment. Many things can be done to reduce the stressors in the physical environment, such as reducing noise and pollution. Dealing with psychological and social stressors is more difficult. Altering an organization's climate (Chapter 15) or its managerial style (Chapter 18) to provide a more productive and satisfying environment can go a long way toward reducing the ill effects of stress.

Ultimately, each of us needs to develop means for the self-management of stress. We should understand our limitations and recognize the factors that are our major stressors. Throughout your career it is better to recognize the early warning symptoms of stress and not wait until it reaches the third stage—exhaustion of resistance. It is easier to modify one's life style and environment to prevent undue stress than it is to cure the adverse consequences.

Dual Career Families

Over the past twenty years there has been significant increase in two-career families. The number of women in the labor force has increased dramatically and, even more important than the numbers alone, there are more opportunities for women to have professional and managerial careers. A generation ago women worked, but their careers were almost always subordinated to family concerns. Most life and career decisions were based on the enhancement of the man's career. Today the situation is changing rapidly. With women receiving more education and professional training and entering a wider variety of occupations, career opportunities for women and men are becoming more equalized. Today many couples are striving to maximize the career opportunities for both members.

Planning is much more difficult for the dual career than the single career family. For example, what happens when there is an opportunity to move to a different geographic area for a significant advancement? In a dual career family this decision is very difficult. It takes more effective career planning, mutual understanding, and maturity on the part of both partners. Hall and Hall (1978) suggest several critical factors in successful dual-career relationships:

1. There is a mutual commitment to both careers. In many cases the couple's self-concept is built around themselves as a working team.
2. Flexibility is important. Both partners need to have personal flexibility to shift gears, revise plans, and to consider new opportunities when career opportunities develop. It is very helpful if at least one of the partners has a flexible or high-autonomy job.
3. Coping mechanisms are essential for the viable career couple. The couple needs to develop some means for dealing with the potential conflicts in pursuing their careers. They generally need to establish better guidelines concerning mutual expectations and also be better in planning, scheduling, and organizing shared activities.
4. Energy commitment and time management are two very important coping mechanisms. Both parties must be committed to *make it work*. This has to be top priority in their entire relationship. Time management, particularly to insure time for togetherness and time for self as well as for career, is vitally important.

It is evident that a two-career family is particularly subject to the problems and stresses discussed in this chapter. But, it also is possible to achieve an enhanced level of satisfaction, a greater sense of accomplishment, and greater joys of sharing experiences.

Women and Minorities

Women and minorities face many of the same career problems already discussed in this chapter, but probably with greater intensity than the white male population. Traditionally, women and minorities held lower-level, less prestigious, more routine, and lower-paying jobs. Although this is changing somewhat, this historical pattern continues. These groups have the additional problems of obtaining the necessary educational preparation for managerial careers and then maneuvering in the organizational hierarchy.

In many areas considered in this chapter, women and minorities are at a career disadvantage. For example, they are less likely to have mentors and a good social support system. They are also subject to a number of additional stressors, both from their work environment and from outside situations. Although there have been improvements in career opportunities for women and minorities, advancements are slow.

It is even more important now that some progress is being made to renew the efforts within business and other organizations to provide equal career opportunities for all: not just in name but in terms of the total organizational climate and the entire support system. To do less would certainly not be maximizing the use of available human resources nor providing opportunities for enhancing individual satisfaction.

INDIVIDUAL STRATEGIES FOR CAREER DEVELOPMENT

Early in this chapter we suggested that careers result from the matching of the individual with the organization. Sometimes people sit back passively and wait for the organization to make all the moves. Although organizations should take more responsibility for the development of human resources, they cannot take full responsibility for each individual's career development. If you are willing to let the organization totally determine your work life, it will do so. But this will create too much organizational control and restrict your autonomy. The self-management of your career will help you determine your own destiny and increase your independence. In many career decisions, the individual is the only one with appropriate information. You know what you want from life and work and the price you will pay to achieve this. You know what tradeoffs you will be willing to make. You know under what circumstances you are likely to be effective and ineffective. You have a substantial amount of personal information, but, it is essential in managing your career not to deceive yourself. In all cases you should be honest and realistic. For example, if you are not willing to pay the price in terms of the time and energy that it takes to get to the top in a certain organization, don't kid yourself into thinking that other factors are holding you back. With this in mind there are certain steps in a successful self-management of careers program.

1. *Start now.* You have already made decisions that will have an impact on your career. Don't make the mistake of thinking, "I will develop career plans after I finish my education and things get settled down." You will always have uncertainties concerning your career and self-management can actually help to reduce these uncertainties.
2. *Know thyself.* The central concept in self-management of careers is self-appraisal and awareness—knowing yourself. You should take a personal skills inventory to determine your strengths and weaknesses. You should clearly assess your own values and beliefs.
3. *Analyze career opportunities.* You are now ready to look at the other side of the match: What are the career opportunities? There are many sources of official information concerning occupations such as the U.S. Department of Labor's *Occupational Outlook Handbook, The Dictionary of Occupational Titles,* and *The College Placement Annual.*
   You can pick up useful information from friends and relatives concerning occupations. Don't wait until your last term to visit the campus-placement office. Spend a few hours browsing to determine what it is potential employers are seeking.
4. *Establish career goals.* Armed with information about yourself and about organizations and occupations, you are now ready to develop more specific career goals. As we discussed in Chapter 3, the process of

establishing goals can have an important effect on performance. Career goals should be measurable and should be both short and long term. Goals should stretch your performance but be achievable. Success in meeting career goals leads to even higher aspirations and improved performance.

5. *Obtain feedback*. It is important to think about how you will obtain feedback on performance and goal attainment. While you are in school you usually get definite and precise feedback on your academic performance through the grading system. In many jobs, it is more difficult to obtain feedback. You can begin now by obtaining feedback from others concerning your self-analysis and current career planning.
6. *Manage your career*. Self-management of your career is not a one-shot operation, it should occur continually over your entire working life. You should be looking for and taking advantage of opportunities and developing relationships with others, particularly potential mentors. There should be a continual process of evaluating and modifying career goals and plans over time. For many people it is useful to set aside a certain date each year to thoroughly review past performance and develop new career goals and plans. It is important to seek out projects and jobs that are challenging and provide high exposure. There is danger in becoming competent in a narrow job and being so indispensable that there are no replacements. It is also important to retain flexibility and not be tied completely to a particular job, department, or organization.

ORGANIZATIONAL STRATEGIES FOR CAREER DEVELOPMENT

Business and other organizations have become more aware of the importance of career-development programs in the effective management of human resources. Many practical issues are directly related to career issues, such as reducing turnover of newly hired employees, developing high-potential candidates for managerial positions, minimizing the problems of ineffective plateauees, and providing opportunities for many upward aspiring employees. Planning and counseling activities can do a great deal to provide early identification of career-related problems. Many organizations have established career counseling workshops and career guidance specialists.

Van Maanen and Schein (1977, pp. 84–93) suggest a number of specific things that organizations can do for more effective career development programs:

Improve Manpower Planning and Forecasting Systems. Careful manpower planning will help in the recruiting of the right number and type of new employees and identify the developmental needs of present employees to fill future positions.

Improve Dissemination of Career Option Information. There should be good information concerning the career paths that employees may follow. What are the options for career development within the organization?

Initial Career Counseling in Connection with Performance Appraisal. One of the key aspects of periodic performance appraisal is career counseling. In addition to appraising past performance this is an excellent time to discuss employee's goals and expectations regarding his or her career and for the manager to discuss the opportunities available and to establish development plans.

Support of Education and Training Activities for All Levels of Employees. As employees gain experience they will identify areas where they need additional education that is prerequisite for further career growth. It is important that the organization have clearly defined policies concerning time off and financial support. Supporting these activities is a growing trend and is becoming an important part of the reward system of many organizations.

Job Posting. It is important, particularly in larger organizations, to make special efforts to provide all employees with information concerning job openings. If people know about these openings, more qualified people will likely apply and the selection will be more appropriate. In addition, this procedure provides workers with information concerning what is necessary for advancement. It also stimulates employees' interest in career planning and development.

Special Assignments and Job Rotation. Providing special assignments and job rotation allows the individual to experience new situations and test competencies. It also allows the organization to learn firsthand how the individual will perform in a different setting. These special assignments can be of particular importance for the plateaued employee who may need the stimulation and challenge of a different assignment.

Career Development Workshops. An increasing number of organizations are formalizing their career-development activities in workshops and seminars. These workshops are clear indications that the organization cares about individuals' careers. A central assumption of these workshops is the joint responsibility of the individual and the organization for career development.

Sabbaticals, Flexible Working Hours, and Other Off-Work Activities. The traditional concept of a 40-hours-per-week job continuing for 40 years with two to three weeks' annual vacation is becoming obsolete. Organizations need to develop greater flexibility in the utilization of human resources. Some organizations are experimenting with the idea of giving employees longer periods of time off to pursue personal interests. The sabbatical leave to get away from the job and to develop new life interests may be a possible answer to the boredom and apathy of middle-aged, plateaued managers. Flexible working hours may help the two-career family cope with job requirements and personal needs. Job sharing has been tried in a number of organizations and has worked effectively.

Flexible Reward and Promotional Systems. Organizations are too limited in their thinking about rewards and success criteria. In the financial area, there is a growing trend toward giving employees a choice among several forms of financial reward. It is clear that organizations need to develop multiple ladders for promotion and rewards; not all people want to be in the line hierarchy. The promotional system should reflect the desires for spiral as well as linear careers. Above all, people should be rewarded for effective performance in current-level jobs. If the organization only holds out the reward of promotion for the few who can make it up the hierarchy, there are going to be a number of dissatisfied, poorly motivated, and low-performing individuals.

Development of Assessment Centers. A number of organizations have developed formal assessment centers that are used to evaluate the potential for advancement of employees. In recent years it has become a more common practice to use assessment centers not only for selection of people for advancement but also for career planning and development purposes (Hart & Thompson, 1979). For example, the 3M Company has a two day *management assessment program* that is geared to identifying career goals, developmental needs, and placement opportunities. One of the pioneering programs was developed at American Telephone & Telegraph that combines the selection process with a more comprehensive career-development program. General Electric Company has developed an *assessment center approach* for college graduates and MBAs who have been in task oriented work situations to assess their potential for moving into management. Career counseling and planning is a basic part of GE's approach. Individuals are brought to a centralized assessment center facility for two to seven days, where they are observed in simulated managerial roles. These people have proven performance at the technical level but their managerial potential is unknown. The assessment center attempts as nearly as possible to simulate the kinds of situations and elicit the kinds of behavior that are typical in managerial positions. Usually a number of observers, including line managers and trained observers, serve as assessors. A wide variety of simulated situations, such as role playing, business games, in-basket exercises, leaderless group discussions, conflict resolving sessions, and problem-solving exercises, can be used. The primary purposes of these programs is to see how the individual might perform in a managerial role.

Not all experiences with assessment centers have been successful. There have been problems when too much emphasis is placed on the results for promotion to managerial positions. Predictions of managerial potential from assessment-center results are not infallible and should not be used as the exclusive basis for selection and promotion. There is danger that potentially effective people might be written off and labeled as not fit for promotion. Effective assessment centers emphasize career-development aspects. Individuals should be provided feedback on their performance, followed by career counseling and planning that focuses on how the employee and the organization can alleviate any deficiencies and develop action steps.

The assessment-center approach reemphasizes the point made at the start of this chapter. Career planning and development is the responsibility of both the individual and the organization. The assessment center is an effective way of bringing together resources to facilitate this individual and organizational activity.

SO WHAT? IMPLICATIONS FOR YOU

Knowledge about career development is important from both the individual and organizational perspectives. This developmental process is a key factor in understanding human behavior in organizations. The next step is applying this knowledge either as an individual participant or as a manager in an organization.

As a Member in an Organization

Generalizations	Implications
1. A career consists of the sequence of work-related activities and adventures that an individual experiences, perceives, and acts on during a lifetime. You will always be facing some issues of career development and planning.	1. Recognize that a career is experienced by you as an individual and that you will continue to face a number of important career decisions.
2. Career development is a continual matching process between the organization and the individual. Organizations need to recruit, train, motivate, manage, and develop human resources in order to maintain their survival, effectiveness, and growth. At the same time, people need to find work situations that provide challenge, security, and opportunities for development throughout their entire life cycles.	2. Be aware of this continuing matching process in your own career development. It is useful to think of *investing* your career in a work organization. Recognize that this is one of the most important decisions you will make.
3. Career development is not a one-shot process of deciding on a job and then letting nature take its course. Most of us face many career transitions throughout our work life. In our mobile society, people face many career transitions. They	3. Create a personal career-development program. Recognize that this is a lifelong endeavor that requires substantial self-assessment and analysis and has many challenges and opportunities. Good fortune in careers come most

Generalizations	Implications
are changing their professions, organizations, and geographic location.	frequently to those who position themselves to take advantage of opportunities.
4. Managers come from a wide variety of family backgrounds, have diverse college majors, and have been educated in a large number of different colleges and universities. The one most significant trend is the increasing levels of formal educations; most executives have college degrees and an increasing number have attended graduate school.	4. Do not assume that most managers come from wealthy backgrounds. Most come from the middle class and a fairly large number from blue-collar families. Each of you has an opportunity to compete for these positions.
5. There have been important changes in what people want in their careers. Traditionally, jobs were thought of as the means for making money and earning a living. People have developed new expectations about their work life. Most people want jobs to provide for personal growth and development as well as money and security.	5. Assess what you want from your career. If you are like most college graduates you will place a high value on an intellectually stimulating job that involves meaningful responsibility and provides opportunities for advancement.
6. Career anchors function in the individual's work life as a way of organizing experience and identifying one's areas of contribution over the long run. They determine those types of activities where the individual feels competent. There are five categories of career anchors: (1) managerial competence; (2) technical competence; (3) security; (4) creativity; and (5) autonomy.	6. Reread the descriptions of career anchors on page 638 and try to assess your occupational self-concept in terms of these descriptions. Daydream a bit and visualize your career in the future. Which career anchor will be most significant for you?
7. The process of adult development involves a series of developmental and transition	7. Consider your own adult life cycle development. What stage are you currently in? Consider

Generalizations	Implications
periods. We are continually adjusting to biological and physical changes and also to social and environmental forces.	other significant people in your life and where they are in their development. You may want to discuss this with others to obtain their perceptions.
8. There are various types of career patterns: (1) the transitory with no clear pattern; (2) the steady state with a lifetime occupation; (3) the linear with steady progression up a career ladder; and (4) the spiral with planned search for self-development and increased diversity.	8. Recognize that each of these career patterns is a viable alternative. No single pattern is best for everyone; each offers advantages and disadvantages. Determine which pattern is likely to be best for you.
9. Young managers and professionals face a particular set of career problems: finding a mentor; developing relationships with the boss; feeling that potential is not being utilized; needing feedback on performance; adapting to political pressures; feeling dependent; and dealing with issues of loyalty and ethical dilemmas.	9. Be prepared to face these issues and do not be surprised to find these problems in organizations. How you react to these dilemmas will affect your performance, advancement, and satisfaction in the organization.
10. One of the potential career problems is dealing with job stress. The stress response is the psychological and physiological chain of events triggered by some external event or disruption. Continued job stress can create many adverse consequences.	10. Be aware of those stressors to which you are especially subject. While a moderate amount of stress can be beneficial, continued high stress can be dysfunctional to your performance and health. You may need to adapt your life style to reduce stressors or to help you cope with the stress response when it comes.
11. While the organization may provide some help, it is important for the individual to develop a program of career self-management. Individuals	11. Recognize that the person most concerned with your career is *you*. Develop an individual strategy for career development that includes: (1)

Generalizations

should take active rather than passive roles.

Implications

starting now; (2) knowing yourself through self appraisal; (3) analyzing career opportunities; (4) establishing career goals; (5) developing long-range plans for career development; and (6) reviewing your career progress periodically.

As a Current or Future Manager

Generalizations

1. The career development perspective suggests that there is a continual matching process between the individual and the organization. The outcomes for the organization of this matching process can be seen in terms of effectiveness, productivity, and creativity. Individual outcomes can be measured by satisfaction, security, personal development, and integration of work and other aspects of life. Ideally, this matching process leads to a mutually beneficial relationship.

Implications

1. As a manager you should be continually aware of this matching process. People are investing their careers in your organization and have expectations about what they should receive in return. Their performance is related to how these expectations are met over their entire work life.

Generalizations

2. People in an organization face many career transitions and decisions. These decisions start from the day they enter the organization and are only completed with retirement.

Implications

2. Recognize that you have a responsibility to help your subordinates with their career transitions and decisions. You should provide appropriate information and be a good sounding board in helping them cope with related issues.

Generalizations

3. People have high expectations for their careers. Younger people attach high importance to self-growth and development, an intellectually stimulating job, early responsibilities, and advancement.

Implications

3. Consider what your potential jobs have to offer in terms of these expectations. Don't look only at the salary and security but consider all aspects of the job.

Generalizations	Implications
4. Throughout life we go through a series of developmental and transition periods. Adult life cycles are directly related to work experiences and career issues.	4. Be aware of how phases in the adult life cycle can affect the attitudes and behavior of your employees.
5. There are a number of career paths: transitory; steady state; linear; and spiral. Different paths are appropriate for different people.	5. Try to provide opportunities within your organization for alternative career paths. Not all people want the linear path up the hierarchy, so other routes should be available.
6. People face a number of career problems throughout their work life. Young managers and professionals are particularly subject to these problems.	6. Be aware of the likely types of career problems faced by your subordinates during their career stages. In your mentoring role you should help them deal with these problems.
7. Many individuals will come up against the inevitable. In hierarchical organizations there are fewer positions at the next level up. It is inevitable that most people will be plateaued at some level with further advancement difficult.	7. Be alert to the problems of plateauing. It is vitally important to maintain a climate favorable for effective plateauees. Don't neglect long-term subordinates who are doing a good job but will not likely advance further.
8. There is evidence of the high cost, in both financial and human terms, of pressure and stress in our daily work lives. There are many job stressors affecting behavior that have a detrimental impact on performance and satisfaction.	8. Be alert to those stressors in the work environment that adversely affect your employees. These may be physical environmental factors as well as psychological stressors. Carefully evaluate your own behavior. You may be a *stress carrier.*
9. The dollar costs of stress are very high. Adverse consequences of stress may be such things as accident proneness, drug and alcohol use, aggressiveness, antagonism at work, and job dissatisfaction. Many	9. If these stress related problems are prevalent in your organization, it may be useful to consider some formal stress-management programs. Providing people with health-planning and counseling services, phys-

Generalizations	Implications
of these consequences lower productivity.	ical and psychological examinations, exercise programs, training in time management, and meditation, relaxation, and biofeedback training may be helpful.
10. Business and other organizations have become more aware of the importance of career-development programs in the effective management of human resources. Planning and counseling activities can do a great deal to provide early identification of career related problems.	10. Evaluate how well your organization is doing in helping employees to deal with career related issues. Check to make certain that you use existing opportunities, such as the annual performance evaluation, to discuss and counsel on career issues.

LEARNING APPLICATION ACTIVITIES

1. Write a vignette based on your own experience (or the experience of a friend or relative) that illustrates an issue of career development.

2. a. Review the vignette *Disillusionment*. What were some of the factors that contributed to John Wilkenson's dissatisfaction with his career progress?
   b. If possible, interview a recent college graduate who has taken a similar position with an accounting firm to obtain his or her observations and feelings about the job.

3. a. Review the vignette *A Career Dilemma*. What do you think Gordon Pollard should do?
   b. Share your analysis and recommendations with three or four colleagues.

4. *Step 1:* With one or two colleagues who have similar career interests, interview an individual in a position you aspire to in 10 or 15 years. Ask about his or her major career problems and personal development strategies.
   Step 2: Based on this interview, reevaluate your own career planning. Share your ideas with the group.

5. *Step 1:* Based on readings, interviews of others, or personal observations, describe a person who has followed each of the four basic types of career paths: (1) transitory; (2) steady state; (3) linear; and (4) spiral.
   Step 2: Share these descriptions with three or four colleagues.

6. Review the descriptions of the five types of career anchors. Assess your values in terms of these career anchors. Which one is most likely to determine your primary career anchor?

7. Review those factors most likely to impede career advancement as suggested in Figure 17.4. Think about how you will deal with each of them.
8. Meet in mixed-gender groups of four and discuss issues of dual career families. Each person should list career expectations and any problems anticipated as a two-career couple. List and discuss ways of dealing with these problems.
9. *Step 1:* With two or three colleagues, interview a manager and discuss the organizational strategies for career development used in his or her company.

   Step 2: Share your findings with the entire class.

REFERENCES

Adams, John D. "A Program for Improving the Management of Stress." *Exchange: The Organizational Behavior Teaching Journal* 2/4 (1977): 17–22.

Bartolemé, Fernando, and Paul A. Lee Evans. "Must Success Cost So Much?" *Harvard Business Review* 58/2 (March-April 1980): 137–148.

Benson, Herbert, and Robert L. Allen. "How Much Stress Is Too Much?" *Harvard Business Review* 58/5 (September-October 1980): 86–92.

Bivens, Terry. "Head Strikes It Rich Again in Racket Firm Sale." *Philadelphia Inquirer,* 24 June 1982.

Burck, Charles G. "A Group Profile of the Fortune 500 Chief Executives." *Fortune* 93/5 (May 1976): 173–177.

Cooper, Michael R., Brian S. Morgan, Patricia M. Foley, and Leon B. Kaplan. "Changing Employee Values: Deepening Discontent?" *Harvard Business Review* 57/1 (January-February 1979): 117–125.

Dalton, Gene W., Paul H. Thompson, and Raymond L. Price. "The Four Stages of Professional Careers—A New Look at Performance by Professionals." *Organizational Dynamics* 6/1 (Summer 1977): 19–42.

Driver, Michael J. "Career Concepts and Career Management in Organizations." In Gary L. Cooper (Ed.), *Behavioral Problems in Organizations*. Englewood Cliffs, N.J. Prentice-Hall, 1979.

Erickson, Erik H. *Childhood and Society,* 2d ed. New York: W. W. Norton, 1963.

Ference, Thomas P., James A. F. Stoner, and E. Kirby Warren. "Managing the Career Plateau." *Academy of Management Review* 2 (October 1977): 602–612.

Friedman, Meyer, and Ray Rosenman. *Type A Behavior and Your Heart*. New York: Knopf, 1974.

Gould, Roger. "The Phases of Adult Life: A Study in Development Psychology." *American Journal of Psychiatry* 129 (November 1972): 521–531.

Hall, Douglas T. *Careers in Organization*. Santa Monica, Calif.: Goodyear, 1976.

Hall, Francine S., and Douglas T. Hall. "Dual Careers—How Do Couples and Companies Cope with the Problems?" *Organizational Dynamics* 6/4 (Spring 1978): 57–77.

Hart, Gary L., and Paul H. Thompson. "Assessment Centers: For Selection or Development?" *Organizational Dynamics* 7/4 (Spring 1979): 63–77.

Ivancevich, John M., and Michael T. Matteson. *Stress and Work*. Glenview, Ill.: Scott, Foresman, 1980.

Jick, Todd D., and Roy Payne. "Stress at Work." *Exchange: The Organizational Behavioral Teaching Journal* 5/3 (1980): 50–55.

Kotter, John P. *Power in Management*. New York: American Management Association, 1979.

Levinson, Daniel J. *The Seasons of a Man's Life*. New York: Knopf, 1978.

Pearse, Robert F. *Manager to Manager II: What Managers Think of Their Managerial Careers*. New York: American Management Association, 1977.

Renwick, Patricia A., Edward E. Lawler, and the *Psychology Today* staff. "What You Really Want from Your Job." *Psychology Today* 11/12 (May 1978): 53–65.

Schein, Edgar H. *Career Dynamics: Matching Individual and Organizational Needs*. Reading, Mass.: Addison-Wesley, 1978.

Selye, Hans. *The Stress of Life*. New York: McGraw-Hill, 1956.

Swinyard, Alfred W., and Floyd A. Bond. "Who Gets Promoted?" *Harvard Business Review* 58/5 (September-October 1980): 6–18.

Vaillant, George E. *Adaptation to Life*. Boston: Little, Brown, 1977.

Van Maanen, John, ed. *Organizational Careers: Some New Perspectives*. New York: Wiley, 1977.

Van Maanen, John, and Edgar H. Schein. "Career Development." In J. Richard Hackman and J. Lloyd Suttle (Eds.), *Improving Life at Work*. Santa Monica, Calif.: Goodyear, 1977.

Webber, Ross, A. "Career Problems of Young Managers." *California Management Review* 18/4 (Summer 1976): 19–33.

18

Managerial Philosophy and Style

LEARNING OBJECTIVES

After reading this chapter you should be able to:

1. Explain how a person's managerial philosophy and style affects his or her behavior in an organization.
2. List and discuss a number of guidelines—based on your values, beliefs, knowledge, and skills—that affect your behavior. (You should be able to write a meaningful essay entitled: "My Philosophy of Management.")
3. Describe the concept of self-fulfilling prophecies and illustrate (with examples from your own experience, if possible) how they can have both negative and positive consequences.
4. Compare and contrast managing and leading, showing how philosophy and style affect behavior in these roles.
5. Demonstrate how participation, change, and quality of work life are related by describing an example with positive results and another with negative results.
6. Identify several personal goals for improvement (in terms of your behavior as a manager or potential manager) and outline action plans for achieving them.

ARTESIAN INSURANCE COMPANY

Tom, Edith, Vicky, and Alan were seated at a corner table in the employees' lounge having coffee and cake as part of the centennial celebration. Special events had been scheduled all through the year, most of them directed at Artesian's customers and the community where its headquarters was located. C. R. (Robbie) Robinson III, the current president, was a grandson of the founder. This particular afternoon he had made a stirring speech to all employees over the intercom about the history of the company, its 100-year milestone, and the important role that all employees had played in the company's growth and development. He had urged them to continue to improve in order to meet the challenges of the future for their industry. Then, he had encouraged them to take extra time at the break for free coffee, punch, cookies, and cake. This startled some employees because Artesian was known for its emphasis on punctuality. Time clocks were a rule; all employees punched in and out. Moreover, a bell rang at 12 noon and 1:00 P.M. to signal the beginning and ending of the lunch hour. Morning and afternoon breaks were also signaled by a bell. To extend the break period for even 15 minutes was unusual, but maybe once every 100 years did not indicate the company was becoming overly lax.

Vicky and Alan, both of whom had been with the company less than three years, were joking about the president's sudden magnanimity. They, along with many other employees, went along with relatively strict rules and regulations because the company paid well and was a major employer in an area they chose to live in. They grumbled from time to time about codes of conduct that covered how to dress, how to be well groomed, and how to present a businesslike image. For example, all men wore plain white shirts and ties with conservative suits. No slacks and sport coats were allowed.

Tom and Edith had been with the company more than 25 years, evolving with the data-processing department from punch cards and calculators to sophisticated electronic computers. They defended the company and its personnel policies, stating that "it was necessary to regulate the behavior of a large organization. Otherwise, we might have chaos." They told stories of how C. R. II helped needy employees over the rough spots. He kept Nell on the payroll for three years until she reached retirement age, even though her poor eyesight made her ineffective in her job. The Robinson family had been pillars in the Methodist church in the community for over a century. Charles R. Robinson founded the company on principles taken from the Bible. He approached business with a religious fervor and expected the same kind of zeal from his employees. The golden rule was paramount: "Do unto others as you would have them do unto you." He believed in hard work, sobriety, family, and church. As the company grew over a period of 100 years from a handful of employees to more than 5000, it obviously became difficult for any one person to control the behavior of everyone in the organization—both on and off the job. Not that they didn't try. C. R. II continued in his father's footsteps and tried to maintain control via his messages in the company newsletter and by serving as an example for employees to emulate. Older employees like Tom and Edith were steeped in Artesian's approach and seemed to thrive in it. They couldn't understand why some of the new employees seemed to chafe and rebel. Rules meant coordination to some people; to others they meant regimentation.

Artesian had enjoyed success and was a leader in the insurance industry. It would be interesting to see if that position of leadership could be maintained.

AFTER JFR RETIRES

It happened during a workshop involving the top 25 people in the finance organization. The vice president of finance, John F. (Jack) Roberts had invited the president, Stan Davis, to spend a couple of hours with the group and respond to their questions. Davis was new on the job and the managers were eager to get his view from the top. As a means of structuring the session to some degree, the participants were asked to write their questions on five- by eight-inch cards that could then be sorted into categories.

President Davis responded to a number of general questions and then, in the middle of the stack, he came to this one: "Do you plan any major changes, such as restructuring the organization, after JFR retires?" Roberts looked startled and flushed a bit around the collar. The president said, "I didn't know you called him JFR; I'll have to remember that. I also didn't know he was going to retire." Jack muttered, "Neither did I." The president continued, "In any case, I think the answer is no. Jack and your entire organization are doing a fine job, and I see no reason to upset things. When we were searching for a vice president for administration, we did discuss some possible changes. But Jack convinced me that the current arrangement should be kept intact, and I agreed."

Later, after the president had left, Jack said he wanted to speak to that "ringer" question in order to clear the air. "Undoubtedly I will retire sometime, but it is not imminent. In any case, I think we should strive for an organization that would function 'as usual' with or without me. I don't consider this *my* organization. Our purpose is to serve our internal and external clients to the best of our ability in order to help achieve the goals of the total organization. I think you folks are doing a hell of a job, and I see no need for major changes. Of course, we're not perfect; we need to keep alert and to look for ways to improve."

EASTERN AIR LINES: FROM ACE TO ASTRONAUT

Picture, if you will, an art deco ballroom in a second-rate Miami Beach hotel in the fall of 1961. Squirming on little gilt folding chairs are 500 men, all acutely uncomfortable. But it is not the chairs that make them so; it is the torture they are witnessing.

On the dais there sits a gaunt, craggy-faced, elderly man, his famous crumpled felt hat on the table in front of him, his bushy eyebrows knit in a frown of displeasure. He is Edward Vernon (Captain Eddie) Rickenbacker, high-school dropout, auto mechanic, racing car driver, World War I ace of aces, self-taught businessman, and, for more than 28 years, chief executive of Eastern Air Lines Inc. And he is engaged in his favorite management technique.

One by one each member of the audience—250 city sales managers and 250 airport operations managers—mounts the dais and reads a report on his performance during the previous six months: how many tickets sold, how many phone calls answered, how many reservations made, how many passengers enplaned, how many meals and bags handled, and all at what cost. If the performance does not live up to the forecast made six months earlier, an explanation is demanded—and it had better be good.

Rickenbacker is playing with a loaded deck. He has had an advance copy of each man's report to study for weeks. Consequently, he interrupts continually with a barrage of questions. One man argues back. Although events later prove the man right, no one tells the captain he is wrong anymore. The man is off the payroll the next morning. At the meeting another man nervously pleads for money to help him reach more prospective customers. The brutal public humiliation continues.

"Son," inquires Rickenbacker, "do you know how much profit we make on every passenger in your city?"

"No, but I guess it isn't very much."

"Well, you damn well ought to know we lose money on every one of your passengers. The fact that you want Eastern to pour money we don't have into your operation so it can lose still more money tells me you're not very good at your job."

Crestfallen and beet red, the man resumes reading his report.

In his book *From the Captain to the Colonel,* the story of Eastern Air Lines, author Robert J. Serling quotes Wayne Parrish, a longtime editor and publisher of aviation publications, as saying that no outsider ever stayed the course at one of these management meetings. Parrish is probably right. I tried in October, 1961, at the meeting I've just described and lasted barely two hours. The meeting lasted a week.

In Eastern's early days, when the airline was small and everyone knew everyone else, these meetings—which Rickenbacker always considered "give-and-take sessions"—may well have been a useful management tool. Everyone got involved; everyone was able to understand the problems of the whole airline, and the reasons for choosing to solve some problems before tackling others could be understood firsthand by everyone. But by the 1960s the management meetings were no longer give and take. Rickenbacker's autocratic and erratic behavior at these sessions caused Eastern to lose many good people.

The tragedy was that Rickenbacker could not—or at least, did not—change with the times. Every policy that had worked so well for him in the beginning was set in concrete. His notorious philosophy of "never mind the pennies, watch the mills" made Eastern the first airline to get off federal subsidy and the only airline during World War II to have to pay an excess profit tax.

Eastern had been a monument to brilliant piston-engine-age thinking. It had also been a money machine, superbly planned, situated, and organized for the short-range airplanes of its early years and for an existence without any real competition. When jets and competition came, Rickenbacker drove Eastern almost to the edge of bankruptcy.

At first Eastern's board did not act forcefully enough. It brought in an heir-designate, Malcolm A. MacIntyre, a brilliant lawyer and former Rhodes scholar whom Rickenbacker neither liked nor trusted. And it watched helplessly while Rickenbacker stayed at his post, demanding from the ranks at Eastern the same loyalty and subservience they had shown him in the past.

Poor MacIntyre. He never had a chance. At Eastern he developed a "personal failing that is painful to relate," to quote Serling. "He had, to put it as bluntly as possible, a drinking problem in those tense days. It must be added quickly that he didn't have one when he came to Eastern. Virtually every former associate of his who was interviewed in the course of the research for this history is convinced that Rickenbacker's persistent second-guessing, interference, and sniping literally drove MacIntyre to drink."

And so, in 1963, MacIntyre had to go, leaving behind almost no trace of his passing except Eastern's now famous Boston-New York-Washington air shuttle which he, more than anyone, fathered. At this time the board decided that Rickenbacker had to retire. Serling offers a poignant description of the night Captain Eddie agreed to go.

For its next chief executive, Eastern's board chose Floyd Hall, vice-president and general manager of Trans World Airlines. Undoubtedly, Hall's greatest achievement was to rescue Eastern financially, lifting it up, to use his own phrase, by its own bootstraps. He had caused an outside study of Eastern's cash flow to be made and was appalled to learn that Eastern, the fourth largest domestic airline in the U.S., would not be able to meet its payroll eight months later. He lured away from other carriers a group of young executives whom Serling correctly characterizes as probably the brightest team ever assembled in one airline company. So long as these men were confronted with the awesome challenge of turning Eastern around, they worked as a team. But when they succeeded, the unity disappeared. Since each team member was roughly the same age, ambitious, and entirely capable of being—as well as wanting to be—Eastern's president, the group squabbled incessantly. Finally it fell apart. Hall did not help matters by vacillating between wanting to be an aloof elder statesman of the industry and Eastern's day-to-day chief executive. And so, Eastern plunged into another financial abyss.

Eastern's board realized it would lose the brightest star in its management diadem, its chief operating officer, ex-astronaut Colonel Frank Borman, if it did not put him in complete charge. In December, 1975, Borman became Eastern's chairman, president, and chief executive. "His earliest moves," writes Serling, "jolted Eastern to its roots." It is characteristic of Borman's style that after years of struggling with Eastern's equipment, balance sheet, route, and passenger disaffection—problems that had their origin in the philosophies of the captain—he will say only: "At last Eastern is headed in the right direction."

To the recounting of Eastern's history author Serling has brought the enormous authority that comes from more than 20 years of distinguished aviation reporting. He is respected for his encyclopedic knowledge of aviation and admired for his integrity and objectivity by more pilots, mechanics, flight attendants, airline officers—including presidents past, present, and future—than any living aviation historian. Consequently, when Serling sets out to do research for a book, all aviation is glad to down tools and submit to his interviews.

From the Captain to the Colonel is head and shoulders above Serling's 11 earlier books. He tells the story of Eastern's first 50 years with a novelist's skill (Serling is the author of *The President's Plane is Missing,* a best-selling suspense novel) and a historian's insight. Probably because the story of Eastern has so many elements of a Greek tragedy, this is Serling's most mature work. One comes away from reading it with far more than the feeling of understanding the life story of an airline in human terms, although that dimension alone would ensure this work an important niche in the literature of aviation. One also understands how and why things happened, and how and why so many admirable people were fated to do so many things wrong. In short, this is superb history.

Source: Brenton Welling. Reprinted from the March 3, 1980 issue of *Business Week* by special permission, © 1980 by McGraw-Hill, Inc.

IF YOU WANT IT DONE RIGHT

Lou Gordon was general manager of Walker's Department Store in Laramie, Wyoming. The store had been in business for 80 years; it had grown with Laramie and was recognized as *the* place to shop. A new branch was under construction in the shopping center being built south of town. Walker's would be a main unit there along with Penny's and Grant's.

The construction project and the prospects of opening a new store were major concerns for Lou. However, his primary concern was Don Nolte, the manager of the sporting-goods department. More specifically, his concern was that Greg Alberts had just resigned as assistant manager in sporting goods. Greg was the third assistant to work for Don Nolte in the past two years. John Gary had been developing quite nicely when he suddenly quit to take a lower-paying job in a similar operation in Denver. Carol Sunden had moved over from housewares to become assistant manager in sporting goods, but she lasted only three months. She had practically begged Lou to let her move back to her old position "before I go crazy or do something foolish." Lou had reluctantly agreed because he felt she was a valuable asset for Walker's over the long run.

He had been hoping that the various assistant managers would be developing to the point that they could staff the new store, or the old departments if the department heads chose to move to the new unit. In most cases, his development program was working; most of the department managers had capable assistants, usually two or three to cover the seven-day week and long hours that Walker's maintained. But sporting goods was a dilemma. Don Nolte was obviously the most knowledgeable, technically proficient, and hard-working manager that Lou had ever known. He ran a tight ship and his department was extremely successful. He had little mottos stuck on the wall in his cubbyhole office like:

> Plan your work and work your plan.
> A place for everything and everything in its place.
> When the going gets tough, the tough get going.

The one that wasn't on the wall, but should have been, according to Greg during his exit interview, was "If you want anything done right, do it yourself." From the point of view of the assistants, Don just could not bring himself to delegate anything of real consequence. Whenever he involved subordinates in decision making, it related to issues that really didn't make much difference. Greg kept asking for more responsibility in order to learn, as had his predecessors, but to no avail. Don always seemed to agree but never got around to it. The straw that broke the camel's back came when Greg was given responsibility for taking the midyear inventory. He and several others in the department worked late three nights in order to finish it. The following Monday he learned from the custodian that Don had spent all day Sunday checking the inventory to make sure they had done it accurately.

Lou had a real dilemma. He needed back-up people for key spots. However, he believed in delegation as a key means of developing talent. Therefore he felt very uncomfortable about interfering with Don Nolte's management of the sporting goods department. He had been dropping subtle hints during their performance-review sessions. But he hadn't confronted Don directly on this specific issue of not being able to keep and develop potential replacements.

COMPLEMENTARY DIFFERENCES

A man whose father was a railroad cook and whose first home in the Savannah area was a low-income housing project became Chatham County's highest-appointed officer after an extensive search process. Harry Johnson, 40, won out over 70 other candidates. He was chosen by County Executive Ruth Tavelli for the $55,000-a-year job as her deputy, responsible for day-to-day operation of the county government.

In announcing the appointment, Tavelli—daughter of a superior court judge and member of a prominent local family—said the differences in the backgrounds and life experiences between her and her new deputy would bring great strength to the county's executive suite. Tavelli is an attorney by training and spent her early professional life as an assistant attorney general and then as a Chatham County deputy prosecutor. For the past 13 years, Harry Johnson has been executive director of Neighborhood House, a local private nonprofit social service agency. He received a master's degree in social work from the University of Georgia. He began his career as a supervisor of delinquent boys at Edison School. After that he became assistant supervisor of a group home in Atlanta and then joined Neighborhood House as a group worker. He also served as director of Terrace Community Center.

Johnson will take over his new job next month, succeeding Mary Bonini, who will return to private law practice. Bonini and Tavelli were classmates at Emory Law School; both were honor students and worked on the law review together. Bonini was filling in on an interim basis only, after turning down an offer to take the position on a permanent basis.

Tavelli said several other candidates had backgrounds similar to her own. "But that would be the same as having another Ruth around and some would say that one Ruth is enough," the county executive quipped.

Asked if he thought his appointment would have meaning to the local minority community, Johnson said, "I hope it has meaning for everybody, the message being that this will be an open government, responsive to people from various backgrounds." Tavelli said, "The appointment reflects the human diversity of Chatham County. It is important that we in the administration understand that diversity and manage accordingly. Harry and I may disagree at times because we see things from different points of view based on our backgrounds and experiences. That may be uncomfortable at times, but in the long run it will be the best for the county and its people."

By executive order, Johnson will have virtually complete authority to govern the county in Tavelli's absence, such as later in the year when Tavelli takes a month's vacation with her family on the French Riviera. Under the county charter, however, only the elected executive can veto an ordinance passed by the county council.

INTRODUCTION

The foregoing vignettes illustrate the managerial philosophy and style of various managers. A person's *managerial philosophy* is a system of principles for guiding managerial behavior. Behavior is guided by values, beliefs, and attitudes. *Style* refers to the way in which anything is done: the manner of one's thinking and acting. Taken together, managerial philosophy and style is the distinctive manner in which a manager behaves (thinks and acts) as constrained by knowledge and skill and guided by values and beliefs.

Jack Roberts expressed a particular philosophy in telling his subordinates that no one was indispensable and that together they were doing a fine job, but there was still room for improvement. The book review describes Eddie Rickenbacker as autocratic and tough on subordinates who did not meet their goals. It also describes his failure to *grow,* to adapt to changing conditions over time. *Artesian Insurance Company* and *If You Want It Done Right* are vignettes that describe typical situations in work organizations. Paternalism (maybe even benevolent autocracy) can be effective and efficient. This managerial approach may also satisfy many people. However, it can also be stifling for self-starters and free spirits. Don Nolte, *Walker's Department Store,* is a type of manager we have all been exposed to: extremely competent technically and unwilling to delegate to others for fear that they might make a mistake (*mistake* equals "not exactly the way I would do it myself"). By contrast Ruth Tavelli's selection of a person with significantly different background and experience to be her deputy is unusual. We typically hire and promote in our own image. This tends to result in organizations (or major units of organizations) with a managerial philosophy and style that outsiders can recognize. As Tavelli suggested, differences of opinion may make the job more complex but also more in tune with the times and ultimately more rewarding.

We will approach our consideration of managerial philosophy and style within the general framework of this book. Our primary concern is understanding human behavior in organizations. In this "summary" chapter we are concerned with managerial behavior and the effect that it has on the behavior of others in work organizations. In some cases, particularly in organizations where an owner/manager is forceful in perpetuating a particular philosophy and style, the organization tends to reflect the ideas of that one person. In other cases, a variety of influences are involved. Work organizations are part of an external environment wherein cultural mores affect behavior. The organizational context also provides guidelines for behavior (see Figure 1.1). These environmental and contextual influences affect human behavior in organizations that lead to results/outputs/performance. Performance is measured in terms of effectiveness, efficiency, and participant satisfaction. Current performance is tempered by giving attention to individual, group, and organizational improvement. That is, we are concerned with future as well as current capabilities.

A contingency view has been emphasized throughout the book, and it is part of managerial philosophy and style. Flexibility and adaptability are important. Thomas Peters (1981) writes about "a style for all seasons," but a key

ingredient in his prescription is the importance of concentrating on a few basics and modifying one's behavior according to the specifics of a particular situation. A contingency view focuses on the need to find the most appropriate behavior somewhere between *it all depends* and *the one best way.*

Philosophy and style are grounded in the way we think about the world around us. Our thought processes lead to decisions and behavior that become patterns over time. Managerial philosophy and style are reflected in the goals (what results are desirable) and actions (what means are appropriate) that organizations use on a day-to-day basis. In this chapter, we will consider these general issues and the basic elements that comprise one's managerial philosophy and style. As we do so, you the reader, can begin to develop your own guidelines and determine the way you behave or would like to behave in a managerial role. We will consider the following topics:

Guidelines for Behavior
View of Human Nature
Managerial Role
Leading and Following
Power and Participation
Productivity and Quality of Work Life
Change and Improvement
So What? Implications for You

GUIDELINES FOR BEHAVIOR

A number of factors are involved in guiding human behavior in general and managerial behavior in work organizations in particular. Formal guidelines come about in laws, regulations, and ordinances that are established by legislative bodies and interpreted by the judicial system. Another source of guidelines is religious doctrine that may coincide with a nation or culture. In mosaic cultures, such as the United States, a number of sets of shalts and shalt nots are available. Two major threads run through these pluralistic guidelines: The Calvinistic or Protestant Ethic, which supports a laissez faire, survival-of-the-fittest, profit-maximization view, and the Judeo-Christian Ethic that supports a humanistic, social-responsibility, and multiple-objectives view. There is some indication of a shift from a relatively simple to a more complex ideology, as indicated in Box 18.1. Codes of ethics are sources of guidance for professional groups such as lawyers and public accountants. Such codes have not been formalized for professional managers, but there is continuing concern for, and debate about, appropriate behavior for managers of work organizations. While laws, religious tenets, and professional codes of ethics are reasonably useful in guiding behavior, it is important to recognize the role of informal cultural mores and organizational norms, as well as individual values and beliefs.

Values and beliefs provide implicit guidance for managerial behavior. *Values* underlie our notions of what should or ought to be, with regard to both ends (goals) and means (action plans for achieving goals). Sets of attitudes—predispositions to respond in favorable or unfavorable ways to objects, persons, or concepts—make up a person's general values. *Beliefs* reflect an individual's convictions that certain things are true or real. They include opinions, expectations, or judgments that have some factual basis (often assumed) but not absolute certainty.

Societal and Organizational Norms

Individual and organizational guidelines are based on societal norms or standards of conduct (preferred ways of behaving according to shared sentiments). For example, our society was founded on independence, self-reliance, and entrepreneurship. However, once two or more people are engaged in a joint effort to achieve a common goal, independence must be tempered with interdependence. Individualism must be blended with cooperation. Thus, we have these overriding polar views about designing and managing organizational endeavor. Within this broad framework, shared sentiments on key issues shape the way the organization operates in general and the way its people behave in specific situations. For example, Deal and Kennedy (1982, pp. 107–108) describe four culture types based on the degree of risk associated with organization activities:

Tough Guy/Macho. Individualists who take high risks and get quick feedback on their actions. Example: advertising.

Work Hard/Play Hard. Fun and action. Employees take moderate risks, all with quick feedback. Example: computers.

Bet Your Company. Companies with big-stake decisions where years pass before employees know if the risks pay off. Example: aerospace.

Process Culture. A world of little or no feedback. Employees find it hard to measure what they do. Example: government.

These generic types, like any model, tend to be extreme; they stereotype and caricature organizational cultures. But they do illustrate tendencies and differences. And to some extent people select themselves into cultures wherein they will be comfortable: public or private; manufacturing or retailing; computers or cosmetics; small or large; new or old; stable or dynamic; and secure or opportune.

BOX 18.1
IDEOLOGICAL PREFERENCES AND PREDICTIONS

Ideology I

The first ideology, enunciated by philosopher John Locke 300 years ago, is the nucleus of the traditional "American way" extolling the values of individualism, private property, free competition in an open marketplace, and limited government. This is the way we stated Ideology I in the survey:

"The community is no more than the sum of the individuals in it. Self-respect and fulfillment result from an essentially lonely struggle in which initiative and hard work pay off. The fit survive and if you don't survive, you are probably unfit. Property rights are a sacred guarantor of individual rights, and the uses of property are best controlled by competition to satisfy consumer desires in an open market. The least government is the best. Reality is perceived and understood through the specialized activities of experts who dissect and analyze in objective study."

Ideology II

The second ideology defines the individual as an inseparable part of a community in which his rights and duties are determined by the needs of the common good. Government plays an important role as the planner and implementer of community needs. We expressed Ideology II this way in the survey:

"Individual fulfillment and self-respect are the result of one's place in an organic social process; we 'get our kicks' by being part of a group. A well-designed group makes full use of our individual capacities. Property rights are less important than the rights derived from membership in the community or a group—for example, rights to income, health, and education. The uses of property are best regulated according to the community's need, which often differs from individual consumer desires. Government must set the community's goals and coordinate their implementation. The perception of reality requires an awareness of whole systems and of the interrelationships between and among the wholes. This holistic process is the primary task of science."

Significant Findings

More than two thirds of the respondents prefer Ideology I. However, many readers sense its replacement by a new set of value definitions based on the communitarian principles of Ideology II. Some 62% of the readers regard Ideology I as the more dominant ideology in the United States today, whereas 73% anticipate that Ideology II will dominate in 1985.

Many readers think that the transformation from Ideology I to II could lead to social disaster, with burdensome government interference causing the disintegration of business and loss of personal freedom. A minority accept the change with cautious optimism, acknowledging that many perplexing problems—including resource shortages, explosive population growth, and environmental degradation—can be resolved only within the framework of Ideology II.

The U.S. and non-U.S. responses differed sharply. Two thirds of the Americans regard Ideology I as the more effective ideological framework for solving future problems, while the same proportion of foreign respondents believe Ideology II is more desirable.

Source: Reprinted by permission of the *Harvard Business Review.* Excerpt from "Our Society in 1985—Business May Not Like It," by William F. Martin and George Cabot Lodge [November-December 1975]. © 1975 by the President and Fellows of Harvard College; all rights reserved.

Once in a particular industry or corporate culture, one becomes acclimated or attuned to the common sentiments that guide behavior. The same is true in the public sector, where differences may occur depending on the particular agency or line of work involved and whether it falls into the municipal, state, or federal-government category. For example, local police organizations (paramilitary) may have more in common with state police and the U.S. Army than with the local public works or social welfare departments.

Organizational culture is often captured in slogans that indicate degree of emphasis in areas such as research, production, or marketing. For example:

Continental Insurance: "You'll never outgrow us"
Delta Airlines: "The Delta family feeling"
Digital Equipment: "We change the way people work"
General Electric: "Progress is our most important product"
W.R. Grace: "One step ahead of a changing world"

Such slogans may never permeate all subsystems in an organization nor every individual in every situation. However, they do give an indication of what goals are important and what behavior is preferred.

More elaborate guidelines are often set forth in advertisements such as the following (Fortune, 1982, inside front cover):

≪ Bankers Trust Company Philosophy ≫

Excellence is achieved only through consistency and innovation. And teamwork.

Excellence, in any endeavor, is based on superior performance, day in and day out. And success is achieved only when like-minded profession-

> als combine their experience and ingenuity in such a manner as to set them apart.
>
> It is an accomplishment which requires common purpose sparked with rare determination. A drive that provides the ability to perform consistently under pressure. Teamwork. These are parts of a real-life philosophy. A philosophy which yields handsome rewards.

Many organizations might be characterized by a guideline such as "Never be responsible for making a mistake." You may have participated in an organization where "Cover your own a--" is a basic managerial philosophy. Contrast this to the approach reported for 3M Company: "Never be responsible for killing an idea" ("Corporate Culture," 1980, p. 151). These two philosophies engender significantly different attitudes and behavior. In a high-technology company, progress, survival, and profitability depend on new ideas that can be translated into marketable products. Such organizations cannot afford to stifle creativity for the sake of neatness and control. Long-run success depends on how well organizations fit their niche in the environment. Appropriate organizational behavior is a composite of appropriate behavior of its individuals and subgroups.

Contrasting philosophies and their effects can be seen in other examples. Think about the following two slogans:

> The customer is always right.
> Let the buyer beware (caveat emptor).

These two philosophies provide rationales for quite different behavior in any exchange process, particularly client-customer relations. A competitor once described J.C. Penney's business style, set by the company's founder, as "avoiding taking unfair advantage of anyone the company did business with" ("Corporate Culture," 1980, p. 148). Parallel policies that relate to internal relationships are exemplified by the company's avoiding layoffs at all costs and finding easier jobs for those who cannot handle more demanding ones (see Box 18.2). Such policies lead to long-term loyalty from customers, suppliers, and employees. Penney's average executive tenure is 33 years, while PepsiCo's is 10.

> A new employee at PepsiCo quickly learns that beating the competition whether outside or inside the company is the surest path to success. In its soft-drink operation, for example, Pepsi's marketers now take on Coke directly, asking customers to compare the taste of the two colas. That direct confrontation is reflected inside the company as well. Managers are pitted against each other to grab more market share, to work harder, and to wring more profits out of their businesses. Because winning is the key value at Pepsi, losing has its penalties. Consistent runners-up find their jobs gone. Employees know they must win in order to stay in place—and must devastate the competition to get ahead ("Corporate Culture," 1980, p. 148).

BOX 18.2
THE PENNEY IDEA
Adopted 1913

–1–
To serve the public, as nearly as we can, to its complete satisfaction.

–2–
To expect for the service we render a fair remuneration, and not all the profit the traffic will bear.

–3–
To do all in our power to pack the customer's dollar full of value, quality and satisfaction.

–4–
To continue to train ourselves and our associates so that the service we give will be more and more intelligently performed.

–5–
To improve constantly the human factor in our business.

–6–
To reward the men and women in our organization through participation in what the business produces.

–7–
To test our every policy, method and act in this wise: 'Does it square with what is right and just?''

Source: Reprinted with permission by J. C. Penney Company Inc., New York, NY.

Differences, such as those between PepsiCo and J.C. Penney, occur across sectors of the economy, industries, companies, and subgroups within organizations.

Within organizations, individual behavior is affected by characteristics, values, and beliefs. Actual behavior results from the interplay of individual propensities and corporate culture. The most widely discussed example in the last several decades is Whyte's *organization man:* a person who avoids risk, conforms readily to assumed norms, doesn't "make waves," and makes progress slowly by perseverence and longevity. This caricature was rejected by many managers because it is not a reflection of "the American way." However, there is enough evidence for the significant presence of such characteristics and behavior to warrant keeping it in mind. The typical AT&T manager has been described as "the traditional Bell-shaped man" ("Corporate Culture," 1980, p.

150). AT&T is now faced with competition in once-captive markets. Therefore, it needs new ideas in order to develop an appropriate strategy for the future. Such a strategy must encompass human-resource development as well as the marketing and production of products and services. Changing the way people think and behave may be the more difficult. It requires a change in culture.

Maccoby (1978) provides a framework of managerial characteristics and behavior that includes the organization man (he uses the term company man) in a set of types. The overall model is described succinctly on the cover of his book, *The Gamesman.*

> *The Craftsman:* An independent perfectionist whose passion is for quality and for doing things better.
>
> *The Jungle Fighter:* A power-hungry predator who likes to be feared. Will fail where success depends on teamwork.
>
> *The Company Man:* A courteous, loyal careerist who believes in performance and people—but wants security even more than success.
>
> *The Modern Gamesman:* A fast-moving, flexible winner who loves change. Competes for the pleasure of the contest and for the sheer exhilaration of victory.

The jungle fighters, who add survival of the fittest to caveat emptor, are comprised of two subgroups—foxes and lions. "Foxes operate by seduction, manipulation, and betrayal. The lions are also wily but . . . they dominate through their superior ideas, courage, and strength" (pp. 77–78).

The ideal role model, according to Maccoby, is a creative gamesman—a lion with heart. The creative, lion-hearted gamesman is flexible enough to behave appropriately in a variety of situations. This calls for a reasonable degree of balance between cognitive (thinking) and affective (feeling) abilities. One would need to be mentally tough but also compassionate. Maccoby describes a specific creative gamesman (a manager with high potential) as follows:

> He brought energy, verve, and originality to his work. He was a person who could motivate others to go beyond themselves. Furthermore, he was one of the rare young managers who expressed real social concern, as well as interest in his own self-development. He was one of the few managers who saw the threat of corporate life to his own human development and worried how he would maintain his integrity as a corporate winner. . . .
>
> He is extremely likable and seems open, yet one always feels in danger of being tripped or slightly conned. He is very seductive. He seems gregarious, yet when one knows him better, he is introverted and a little lonely. Like the typical gamesman, he is a collection of seeming paradoxes. He is idealistic, yet shrewd and pragmatic: cooperative yet highly

competitive; enthusiastic yet detached; earnest yet evasive; graceful yet restless; energetic yet itchy. Serious on the one hand, he is also boyish and playful, with a twinkle in his eye (pp. 124–125).

Integrity

Integrity—the quality or state of being complete, unimpaired, of sound moral principles, sincere, and honest—may be the most important aspect of a person's managerial philosophy. "Integrity rather than genius is the basic requirement" (Drucker, 1977, p. 28). Does the manager adhere to sound moral principles? Does actual behavior reflect expressed values? Do espoused theories (what managers say is important) and theories-in-use (the ones that really guide their behavior) coincide? (Argyris & Schon, 1974, p. 21). Integrity requires congruence between espoused theory and actual behavior.

Attitudes and beliefs can be inferred from behavior. Individuals may "talk a better game than they play." As Father Divine said, "I have a lot of theorizers in the church; what I need is more tangibilitators." And Mark Twain said, "It is noble to be good. It is even nobler to tell others how to be good, and a whole lot less trouble." Thus, there may be a gap between attitudes and behavior of individuals and organizations. Operating tactics may not reflect the mission statements set forth in the company's annual report. The president's message may not permeate the behavior of everyone in the organization. Thus, explicit guidelines must be tempered with implicit guidelines that are a reflection of actual behavior.

Knowledge and Skill

Within the guidelines stemming from values and beliefs, behavior is affected by knowledge. We think it is important that managers are reasonably knowledgeable about the technical aspects of the business they are in. They need to know the terms and be able to speak the language in order to communicate effectively with other managers and nonmanagers. There have been suggestions that good managers can manage anything. We don't believe it; it is important to know the technical aspects well enough to be able to evaluate the ideas and actions of peers and subordinates. Knowledge and experience can lead to wisdom—enlightened common sense. Wisdom is garnered when we learn from experience: the experience of others in the form of recorded knowledge; our own experience in terms of recognizing the reasons for success and failure.

Another factor in guiding behavior is skill. It is not enough to know the business or the theory of managing. One has to be able to use such knowledge to accomplish tasks, including coordinating the work of other people. Lack of skill development constrains managerial behavior because people hesitate to do things that they can't do very well. This phenomenon highlights the need for continuing growth and development through experience, coaching, and training. It is important to *learn how to learn* because knowledge and skills may be obsolete in a short time.

Figure 18.1 shows the mix of activities and skills that tend to be appropriate

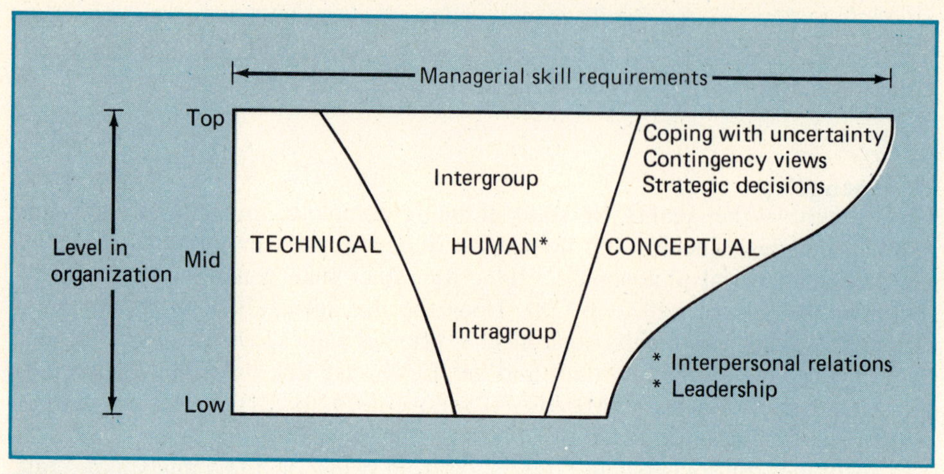

FIGURE 18.1 Skill Mix of Effective Managers—By Organizational Level. **Source:** Reprinted by permission of the *Harvard Business Review.* Adapted from "Skills of an Effective Administrator," by Robert L. Katz (September-October 1974): 90–102. © 1974 by the President and Fellows of Harvard College; all rights reserved.

at different levels in an organizational hierarchy. That is, to be effective, managers must adjust their behavior to fit different roles in the organization. For example, many managers continue to do the technical part of their job—be it accounting or engineering or marketing—when coordinating the activity of others has become more important in their middle manager role. Few managers seem to develop the conceptual skills required at top levels in organizations. Recall our discussion of job design; enriched jobs have an increased amount of planning (both what to do and how to do it) relative to doing. Enriched jobs are particularly important for people with a strong need to grow and develop their managerial skills. Those without such a need will tend not to take advantage of the opportunity to emphasize planning and leading more than doing (Don Nolte, in *If You Want It Done Right,* for example). This approach, of course, is less complex and more comfortable. An unenriched job is safer and requires little or no change in a manager's behavior.

The reason it is so important to understand human behavior in organizations is that knowledge and skill in this area is crucial for moving up in organizations. A typical approach in organizations is to promote people with technical skills into positions of management where interpersonal relations and leadership become more important for success than technical knowledge and ability. First-line supervisors may need technical skills, and, indeed, may join in doing the task. However, facilitating intragroup relations becomes quite important also. A manager must plan the work, assign responsibility, and coordinate the efforts of others in order to achieve goals. As one moves to higher organizational levels, one's managerial philosophy and style affect more people. The emphasis becomes one of coordinating groups as well as individuals. A great deal of time is taken up in resolving conflict between, and coordinating efforts of, interdependent departments or divisions. Recall our discussion of structure and the complex role played by top management in coordinating functional and project managers that are aligned in a matrix organization.

As one moves toward the top in any organization, strategic planning becomes relatively more important. It is not that technical and human skills are unimportant (they are still important parts of the mix), it is just that new skills must be added. Being able to cope with uncertainty and maintain a contingency view of the organization and its environment is important for long-run success. Without this ability, managers tend to have tunnel vision, to do what they have always done, and to wonder in retrospect what went wrong. Past experience and limited knowledge become a strait jacket for behavior and increase the likelihood that that behavior is inappropriate for a specific situation (like Eddie Rickenbacker in the vignette *Eastern Air Lines*). The problem is not too severe in a stable environment with unchanging technology. However, as the pace of change accelerates throughout our society, such an approach is likely to be inappropriate.

At this point it is useful to recall Chapter 6, "Leadership," and particularly Figure 6.4. Leading is a part of managing—the people part. It is a skill that must be developed in order to achieve results and develop human resources simultaneously. Emphasis on people and relationships must be coupled with emphasis on accomplishing the task and being productive. And the organization should improve on all of these dimensions over time. One's behavior as a leader (style) is affected by one's managerial philosophy, particularly one's view of human nature.

VIEW OF HUMAN NATURE

Basic beliefs about people affect our approach to designing work organizations and managing them. Assumptions about basic human nature range from *good, industrious, responsible,* and *smart* to *evil, lazy, irresponsible,* and *dumb*. Such summary statements reflect polar positions which, admittedly, are unrealistic. Human beings are neither completely good nor completely evil. There are obvious ranges for behavior in terms of cooperation-competition, love-hate, friendship-emnity, or harmony-discord. Given a particular issue, an individual's behavior will reflect a position on one or more of these continua. However, the basic assumption one makes can have a significant effect on organizations and management. Relationships are structured in certain ways; compensation systems are designed; communication patterns are established; authority-responsibility relationships are identified; planning and control processes are established; and many other pertinent organizational considerations are affected by managers' assumptions about the nature of people.

Alternative Views

McGregor (1960) set forth two alternative views of people, which he termed Theory X and Theory Y.

Theory X

The average human being has an inherent dislike of work and will avoid it if possible.

Because of this human characteristic of dislike of work, most people must be coerced, controlled, directed, or threatened with punishment to get them to put forth adequate effort toward the achievement of organizational objectives.

The average human being prefers to be directed, wishes to avoid responsibility, has relatively little ambition, and wants security above all.

Theory Y

The expenditure of physical and mental effort in work is as natural as play or rest.

External control and the threat of punishment are not the only means of inducing effort toward organizational objectives.

People will exercise self-direction and self-control in the service of objectives to which they are committed.

Commitment to objectives is a function of the rewards associated with their achievement.

The average human being learns, under proper conditions, not only to accept but to seek responsibility.

The capacity to exercise a high degree of imagination, ingenuity, and creativity in the solution of organizational problems is widely, not narrowly, distributed in the population.

Under the conditions of modern industrial life, the intellectual potentialities of the average human being are only partially utilized.

These theories can be related to the need hierarchy (Chapter 4) in the sense that the traditional view of direction and control relies on the assumption that lower-level needs are dominant in motivating people to perform organizational tasks. Theory Y, on the other hand, assumes that people will exercise self-direction and self-control in working toward objectives to which they are committed.

Based on extensive research in contemporary organizations, Likert (1967) concluded that a managerial system paralleling Theory Y makes significantly better use of human resources and enhances both effectiveness and efficiency of organizational endeavor. He evolved several models of management systems, which he designated by number, one through four (see Chapter 14).

System 1: Exploitive Autocratic
System 2: Benevolent Autocratic
System 3: Consultative
System 4: Participative Group

System 4 incorporates the basic assumptions and approaches of Theory Y and seems to lead to improvement in organizational performance (Likert, 1967). The conclusions may not be completely generalizable, but they apply to many industries, companies, and subunits within organizations (Bowers, 1976; Ouchi, 1981). Moving toward such a managerial system is often a slow process that requires reeducation and reorientation of all organizational participants (Schein, 1975). However, there does seem to be a trend in this direction.

Football and Computers

A basic view of human nature is reflected in the coaching/managing philosophies of two successful football coaches: Don James, University of Washington Huskies, and Bill Walsh, San Francisco 49ers. James says, "I don't like to have any coaches swearing at players, or yanking them around during practice." He believes in delegating to assistants and not interfering. "How much credibility does a position coach have with his players if he's catching hell on the practice field? . . . I decided when I finally headed a program I'd coach coaches" (Owen, 1978, p. D–4). Walsh says, "I believe human dignity is vital. You can only succeed when people are communicating, not just from the top down but in complete interchange. Communication comes from fighting off my ego and listening. . . . Leadership is by example, not talk" (Moore, 1982, p. 63).

A similar view is reflected in the philosophy of Tandem Computers (Magnet, 1982, p. 87).

1. All people are good.
2. People, workers, management, and company are all the same thing.
3. Every single person in a company must understand the essence of the business.
4. Every employee must benefit from the company's success.
5. You must create an environment where all of the above can happen.

The company's founder, Jim Treybig, stresses ideology and incentives, the convergence of capitalism and humanism. Delegation is encouraged and control is maintained informally through widespread understanding of the basic concept and philosophy. Says Treybig, "You never have the right at Tandem to screw a person or mistreat them. It's not allowed. . . . No manager mistreats a human without fear of their job" (Magnet, 1982, p. 82).

Another basic element of the Treybig/Tandem philosophy is that most people need less management than most managers think. Managing less requires a positive view of human nature and a tolerance for different approaches and methods, something that Don Nolte couldn't seem to do in the *If You Want It Done Right* vignette. In an experiment conducted in England, the researchers set up three teams with different managerial strategies: (1) structured hierarchy; (2) participative management; and (3) total anarchy. The "unmanaged" team produced more products at a lower unit cost and with the fewest rejects. It made twice as much profit as the participative team and ten times as much as the hierarchical team. Based on these results and feedback from participants concerning what happened and how they felt, the researchers suggest the following:

People like to be inventive in the way they do their work.

Managers tend to overmanage; they can usually achieve more by standing back and intervening only when employees cannot solve a problem by themselves (Clutterback, 1980, p. 32).

Delegating without hovering is an important skill that requires a positive view of human nature and practice. Tolerance of mistakes is essential because perfection is impossible. Moreover, subordinates can learn from mistakes; effective management can facilitate the fusion of knowledge and experience into wisdom.

Direct and Indirect Effects

Within our overall view of human nature, all of us tend to sterotype subgroups in society and in work organizations. Sex, age, and race stereotypes are part of one's philosophy and affect managerial decisions and actions. For example, a belief that women won't work for a woman boss could lead to precluding a qualified woman applicant from consideration in a promotion/selection process. Or, a man might be precluded because he is considered too young to be a manager. In both cases, people are discriminated against on the basis of irrelevant criteria. The aim should be to discriminate on relevant criteria and to have our views of people coincide with facts and experience, not unfounded beliefs or myths.

Our view of basic human nature has a direct effect on behavior in terms of policies, procedures, and rules that are designed to guide behavior. For example, time clocks reflect a low level of trust that people will put in a day's work for a day's pay. And, punching in at eight and out at five does not ensure a day's work. The flextime system (Chapter 13) is an indication of a high level of trust that people will put in a day's work sometime between 6:00 A.M. and 6:00 P.M., at their discretion.

An indirect effect on behavior comes from participants modeling the behavior of key people in the organization. Obviously, the person most fitting the description is the chief executive officer, but a number of others are always evident as role models. People assume that past and current behavior is effective because it has obviously led to success. Moreover, key people may make their managerial philosophy public, thus providing overt guidelines for behavior.

The values and beliefs of ten "tough" top managers are illustrated in Box 18.3. In some cases their philosophies are stated explicitly; in other cases they have to be inferred from behavior as described by subordinates and former colleagues. Whether being tough is the cause of success or not, many people will emulate the behavior of those top managers. Some managers are successful in spite of their own ineffective leadership because of a favorable environment or a unique market niche. Or, they may be successful in the short run but fail in the long run because human resources are used up in the process. Toughness may be an asset if it is focused on challenging, realistic goals and people are evaluated on the degree to which those goals are accomplished. It may be a liability (at least in the long run) if it is applied capriciously and focused on means—how to do it—rather than goals. Even worse, toughness may be equated with enforcing arbitrary rules or codes of conduct that may in fact be insignificant or irrelevant.

A poll of the CEO's of the Fortune 500 companies was used to identify the best top managers as seen by their peers (Morrison, 1981, pp. 133–136). A glimpse of the philosophies and styles of the first three are indicated on page 689:

> The leader of a company has to develop entrepreneurial spirit through the organization. Developing that spirit at GE means giving young managers freedom to operate within a few policy guidelines, involving such matters as antitrust and minority hiring. *Reginald Jones, General Electric*

> It's important for people to be able to spend a certain amount of money on their own, and be answerable for it after the fact. *John Swearingen, Standard Oil of Indiana*

> People would ask me if I got the jitters because I didn't know what the units were doing. I always figured I'd get more jitters if I did know. *Henry Singleton, Teledyne*

A common thread in the philosophies of these managers is the importance of delegating authority and responsibility for decision making to the lowest possible level. Delegating without hovering over subordinates has two advantages: (1) the people directly affected are involved in making decisions; and (2) people develop their managerial skills by dealing with relevant, important issues.

The CEOs also selected the companies with the best overall management. At the top of the list were General Electric, IBM, Exxon, and Emerson Electric. "Leaders of the six companies that were winners in either category have one thing in common: all are continually looking for ways of improving their operations" (Morrison, 1981, p. 136). The best managers and organizations often use each other as models of effective behavior. Thus, the philosophy and style of a successful manager can have an indirect effect on people in many organizations.

Self-Fulfilling Prophecies

Assumptions about people—basic human nature or specific stereotypes—tend to become self-fulfilling prophecies. If we assume the worst, something bad will happen. If we assume the best, something good will happen. Organizations that are managed on a positive note tend to be more satisfying for participants and they can be more effective and efficient as well. As a rule, optimistic, positive managers tend to do the following:

1. Believe in themselves and have confidence in what they are doing.
2. Believe in their ability to develop the talents of their employees—to select, train, and motivate them. Their great faith in their ability to pick the right person makes them reluctant to give up on their choice and to admit that the person might be the wrong choice. Thus, they try that much harder to make sure the worker succeeds.
3. Are able to communicate to workers that their expectations are realistic and achievable. If employees are encouraged to strive for unattainable goals, they eventually give up trying and settle for results that are lower than they are capable of achieving.
4. Believe that workers can learn to make decisions and to take the initiative

(Theory Y). They thus encourage and allow their employees to do so, assuming the best rather than the worst from them.

5. Prefer rewards that come from the success and increased skill of their subordinates over the rewards they get from their own supervisors (Phillips, 1975, p. 7).

BOX 18.3
OH, WHAT THEY SAY ABOUT THE BOSS

•How others see him

■How he sees himself

Robert Abboud, Chairman and C.E.O.
First Chicago Corp.

•Known as "Idi" Abbound . . . bright, abrasive, aggressive, extremely ambitious . . . very tough on people . . . used to dress down his peers as well as subordinates . . . likes to make decisions solo.

■Declined to be interviewed.

Thomas Mellon Evans
Chairman and C.E.O.
Crane

•No question he is a genius . . . has his own ideas and pursues them . . . doesn't listen well, so he is frustrating to work for . . . most glaring trait is his lack of feeling for people.

■Declined to be interviewed.

Maurice Greenberg, President and C.E.O.
American International Group

•Extremely blunt . . . accomplished at belittling people in front of others . . . You haven't achieved any standing if you haven't experienced his wrath.

■I like running a winning ball club . . . that calls for total commitment . . . If you consider that a sacrifice, you are in the wrong company . . . I look for discipline in people.

Richard Jacob, Chairman and C.E.O.
Dayco

●Do something wrong and he lands on you, all 300 pounds of him . . . uses rough language . . . but he's fair, cares about his people . . . you either love him or hate him.

■I am very demanding . . . won't tolerate laziness . . . If you aren't prepared to bust your ass, you had better find another job.

David Mahoney, Chairman and C.E.O.
Norton Simon

●Presents a smooth front but more explosive than he seems . . . Irish temperament with short fuse . . . becomes enamored of someone but that wears off . . . made Norton Simon known for executive turnover.

■I insist that, goddammmit, we do our best every day . . . I'm intense in everything I do and I expect that others will be too.

Alex Massad, Executive Vice President
Mobil

●Creates a lot of sparks . . . thinks nothing of putting in eighteen hours, seven days a week . . . always a hard driver and impatient . . . He's antagonized a lot of people and they've stayed that way.

■I just work hard . . . I don't know what my management style is . . . Ask my superiors if they think I'm tough.

Andrall Pearson, President
PepsiCo

●Everyone has to be a superperformer . . . presenting a marketing plan is like going through the third degree . . . If you're insecure, don't work for him . . .

■We flushed out a bunch of people not digging deeply enough—people should think about why they are here. That is one reason I am tough to deal with.

BOX 18.3 (continued)
OH, WHAT THEY SAY ABOUT THE BOSS

●How others see him

■How he sees himself

Don Rumsfeld, President and C.E.O.
G.D. Searle

●Fast-paced, urgent . . . when people argue with him—God it can be tough . . . demolishes anyone who blows smoke at him.

■You not only let someone who has not been obeying you go, you do it publicly so everyone knows that breaking the rules brings immediate punishment . . . We got rid of a bunch for the good of the rest.

Robert Stone, Executive Vice President
Columbia Pictures

●Known as Captain Queeg when he ran Hertz . . . A galley master who, hearing that the rowers would die if the beat were raised to 40, would say, "Make it 45."

■I'm a hands-on manager. At Hertz I put in a business review that was painful if you didn't know the answers. Professionals never have a problem with Bob Stone.

William Ylvisaker, Chairman and C.E.O.
Gould

●Uses Marine Corps boot-camp approach . . . creates aura of power and wealth and reminds people it all flows from him . . . They won't go to the bathroom without his permission.

■Tough means unfair and unreasonable. This company is managed objectively . . . I don't think you have to be tough anytime.

Source: Hugh D. Menzies, "The Ten Toughest Bosses," *Fortune*, 21, April 1980, p. 65.

Pessimistic, negative managers, on the other hand, do not do any of these things. They tend to keep tight control, tend not to delegate, and often preclude the development of subordinates. Assuming a person is irresponsible will preclude that person's opportunity to practice being responsible. Thus, the prophecy is fulfilled. If it is assumed a person cannot learn, he or she will not be afforded training opportunities or be coached and encouraged. Thus, it is almost inevitable that the person will be seen as lacking knowledge and skill.

Given the effects of pessimistic, negative assumptions about people and based on the phenomenon of self-fulfilling prophecy, we think it is imperative for managers to be as optimistic and positive as possible—until they are convinced otherwise. At least, a manager should keep an open mind with regard to peers and subordinates in order that opportunities for their growth and development are not foreclosed prematurely. It is very difficult for subordinates to work themselves out of a hole; that is, to overcome resistance stemming from negative stereotypes. At the same time it must be recognized that some individuals are indeed lazy and irresponsible and that they may lack not only the requisite knowledge skill to do the job, but the desire. It is only fair that they be dealt with accordingly and perhaps dismissed. However, assuming the worst without empirical evidence does not make good sense.

MANAGERIAL ROLE

Individuals bring their values, beliefs, and skills to their task (see Figure 18.1). Another phenomenon that shapes and guides behavior is the role expectation. Some expectations are set forth explicitly in job descriptions; others are negotiated periodically in performance-planning sessions between bosses and subordinates; and still others are implicit but *understood* by those involved. In the global sense the managerial role is the same regardless of type of organization or one's level in it. Managers plan and control organizational endeavor to achieve goals. In specific settings more detailed expectations and prescriptions can be developed for the managerial role. Before doing that, however, it may be useful to look at what managers do.

What Do Managers Do?

On the basis of his own observations of managers and a review of other related research, Mintzberg (1975; pp. 49–61) suggests that the top manager's job can be described in terms of various roles or organized sets of behaviors that are identified with that position.

Interpersonal roles:—figurehead, leader, liaison
Informational roles:—monitor, disseminator, spokesperson
Decisional roles:—entrepreneur, disturbance handler, resource allocation, negotiator

These various roles can be illustrated from everyday experience. The petrochemical plant manager (*figurehead*) greets the high school contemporary problems class to discuss water-pollution problems. The airline president (*leader*) exhorts all employees to increase sales and decrease costs in order to forestall bankruptcy. The executive vice president (*liaison*) meets with several project managers and the director of manufacturing in order to sort out scheduling priorities. The mayor *monitors* federal and state legislation in order to determine what effect it will have on local funding. She also *disseminates* such information at staff meetings so that it will reach appropriate subordinates. The union president (*spokesperson*) testifies before a congressional committee to lobby for legislation that will benefit his members. Top managers, regardless of the size of the organization, are often involved in *entrepreneurial* endeavors that result in new products or services. Although managers may try to plan and control activities in a reasonably logical and straightforward manner, much of their time is spent in *handling disturbances,* reacting to crises, and fending off external pressures. When a former employee, who has recently been fired, sets a fire that destroys half of the plant, the manager must react by finding substitute space and coordinating the activities that are necessary in implementing a revised plan. The dean is a *resource allocator* as she attempts to balance the programs proposed by department heads and program directors with the anticipated budget for the coming year. The *negotiating* role is broadly construed to include more than labor-management relations. For example, the senior vice president can be involved in negotiations among several product managers and the vice president for marketing over the amount and type of advertising to be used.

These various roles are carried out to some extent by all managers. However, the amount of time spent may vary with levels or functions. A top manager, for example, is likely to spend relatively more time being a figurehead, spokesperson, or entrepreneur than is a production supervisor. Mintzberg's research indicated that sales managers spend relatively more of their time in interpersonal roles; production managers emphasize decisional roles; and staff managers spend the most time in informational roles (p. 59).

Note that Mintzberg observed and described top managers and that the roles identified have a heavy flavor of human and conceptual skills (see Figure 18.1). It is in those areas that managerial philosophy and style are most apparent. Interpersonal and leadership skills are evident in everyday behavior. Conceptual skills are evident if strategic and operational plans are explicit and communicated throughout the organization.

What Should Managers Do?

Prescriptions for managerial behavior make it seem to be a logical, sequential, straightforward process. Managers coordinate human and material resources in order to achieve objectives. They plan and control activities. Two basic functions—setting goals and implementing action steps—are sometimes missing from the model of what managers do. This is because doing or implementing is assumed to take place. In many organizations emphasis is on activities rather than results, and goals are assumed. That is, the goals or the rationale for the organization's existence have been accepted and become traditional. Another way to look at a managerial role is to suggest that managers should be involved in sensing problems/opportunities and in solving them. They should identify and work on high-priority issues. In a sense this way of looking at the managerial role suggests that what managers do (description) may be what managers should do (prescription). Mintzberg and others have observed effective managers reacting to problems/opportunities and coping with them effectively and efficiently (Kotter, 1982). How comfortable a manager is with this approach is a function of her philosophy and style. This includes characteristics such as cognitive complexity, openmindedness, and tolerance for ambiguity. Some managers may prefer a step-by-step, straightforward approach to managing. Others may find such an approach uninteresting and stifling.

Box 18.4 reflects the managerial philosophy and style of Frederick Crawford of TRW Incorporated. His guidelines, based on years of experience, cover both the what and how of managing. His suggestions include several themes that are consistent with the CEOs cited previously. One is that creative ideas should be encouraged and people ought to have a chance to fail. A manager should be genuinely interested in people, encourage a trusting relationship, and develop commitment on the part of participants. He stresses the need for a sense of urgency in solving problems or taking advantage of opportunities. Finally, he emphasizes the importance of the chief executive as a role model for all members of the organization. It is not enough to espouse a particular corporate and personal philosophy; one has to live it on a day-to-day basis. Actions speak louder than words.

LEADING AND FOLLOWING

Managerial philosophy and style becomes most evident when one is carrying out a leadership role. How effective one is as a follower is also an indication of values and beliefs. We have discussed leadership in some detail (Chapter 6). Therefore, in this chapter we are interested here in noting specifically how philosophy affects behavior and style.

Facilitating Motivation

Many managers talk as if they motivate their subordinates. We don't believe it. It may be a subtle difference, but we think that effective leaders facilitate their subordinates' becoming motivated. Motivation is an internal phenomenon that energizes, directs, and sustains effort toward some end. The key is inducing effort, which, coupled with skill, ability, and other organizational resources, results in desired performance. The effective leader creates conditions within which followers become motivated, expend effort, and perform well.

How we look at motivation is, again, related to our basic view of human nature. A positive view attributes motivation to the follower and assumes that good things will happen if the conditions are right. A negative view attributes motivation to something the leader does in spite of the poor raw material evidenced in the followers.

Text continued on page 699.

BOX 18.4
TEN THINGS I HAVE LEARNED ABOUT MANAGEMENT

Frederick C. Crawford
TRW Incorporated

People who make the tired old criticism that business is a vast bureaucracy devoid of leadership have never talked to Frederick C. Crawford. Mr. Crawford used his natural gift for leadership and straight talk to build Thompson Products, a small Cleveland-based autoparts maker, into TRW Incorporated, a diversified giant. At ninety, he still serves as honorary chairman and as a consultant.

Crawford was recently inducted into Fortune magazine's National Business Hall of Fame. His business peers—from Alfred P. Sloan to William M. Allen, from Charles M. Schwab to Lammot du Pont—have marveled at what has been described as Crawford's "uncanny feel for human relations, for the hopes and worries of the common man." During his tenure, TRW never had a work stoppage, and productivity and profits flourished.

Crawford believes that today, as never before, management must be sensitive to the human problems in business. "There are only two organizations that can operate irrespective of the quality of their leadership—the Army and the Catholic Church," he quips. He offers the following ten views on business management as lessons gleaned during his sixty-five years at TRW.

1. **Always run your business lean and hungry.** Benjamin Franklin said it best: "There is no cure for affluence." Small businesses struggle, grow and become rich. Management then looks around and starts thinking, "We can get mahogany desks now. We can raise the ceiling on expense accounts now." It's human nature, but bad business. There's a saying: A businessman should always remember that someone, somewhere, is making a product that will make his product obsolete. Always assume that there's a disaster around the corner. Look askance at every fancy expense that doesn't contribute to your business. Seemingly invincible businesses do fail. Consider the list of the top twenty-five industrial corporations in 1900: only two on that list enjoy that status today. Business leaders must remember that corporations are expendable and that success is at best an impermanent phenomenon.
2. **Never depend on luck in business; prepare to win, whatever happens.** Most good business decisions result not from luck, but from getting the facts and having the foresight to plan well.

   For example, at one point Thompson Products was very dependent on the aircraft-valve market. Aircraft designers began specifying a new kind of valve, a sleeve valve, that we didn't make. So it was clear we had to jump into the sleeve-valve business. We discovered that the technology for producing sleeve valves was very similar to the technology for truck cylinders. Aha—two markets for the price of one, we thought. So we began to make truck cylinders, partly to learn how to make sleeve valves. When World War II broke out, the sleeve-valve business virtually disappeared. But by then we had a thriving truck-cylinder business. No matter which way the situation went, we were covered. It's remarkable—the more attention you pay to details at work, the more luck you seem to have.

3. **Education and intelligence are not synonymous with good judgment.** You need common sense more than brilliance or college degrees to be a good manager. I believe in the Persian poverb: One pound of learning requires ten pounds of common sense to apply it.
4. **Every company reflects the character and personality of its leader.** If the CEO is an inventor, everybody in the company is inventing things. If the CEO is frugal, subordinates mind their budgets. If the CEO has integrity, the company has integrity. People take their cues from the top person; he or she explicitly and implicitly sets the tone for the organization.
5. **People with ideas are the people who build a business.** Cherish them. Remember that creative people are generally the most sensitive. When they offer ideas that you must reject, don't do it heavy-handedly. Creative people often leave companies because management is forever trampling on their ideas.

   When our creative people would submit a proposal about which I wasn't enthusiastic, I took pains not to shoot it down immediately. I would think, "Well, maybe they've got something here. It's better to let them run with their idea; maybe they'll make a mistake, but let them run with it."
6. **The gulf between management and labor is often unnecessarily wide.** To bridge it, management must gain the trust of the worker. Management almost reflexively thinks that workers want higher pay and less work. But that's not so. Basically, workers have three concerns. The first concern is job security, especially in these tough times. Their second concern is to feel needed, to know they are members of a team. Employees' third concern is money, the desire to receive the best salaries available, consistent with the other two concerns.

   So once you know these concerns, it makes sense to communicate in terms of these concerns. For example, talking to workers about productivity per se won't be effective, but talking

BOX 18.4 (continued)
TEN THINGS I HAVE LEARNED ABOUT MANAGEMENT

to them about productivity in terms of their job security might. Put yourself in their places. It sounds oversimplified, but interest in people does solve problems. Chief executives should get the message out that every supervisor should take a genuine interest in his own people. In the end, the Golden Rule and communication are the keys to labor harmony.

7. **Strive to produce new developments rather than commodities.** There are only two types of products: new developments and commodities. A new development—something innovative that provides an exclusive benefit—is what makes a company highly profitable. A commodity is a product that has marketing features that can be applied equally to a competing product. Steel, for instance, is by and large a commodity now; a major domestic producer can't obtain a higher price for its steel than a Japanese producer can. Clearly, it pays to strike out on new paths rather than travel the traditional routes.
8. **As a good management exercise, imagine that you've been fired and replaced by a new CEO.** Imagine you go across the street, rent a second-story room and observe what the new CEO is doing. Upon observing, you'll find yourself saying, "I could have done that. The new guy isn't doing anything that *I* couldn't have done." Then, do it yourself. I don't know of a better way of assessing the state of your business.
9. **Average Americans, teaming up under inspirational leadership, rise above the average.** Management's chief job is to provide that inspirational leadership. I like to think I never gave an order in my life. I can't ever remember telling a manager, "Now, you do it this way." Instead, I might say, "If I were doing it, I would do it this way. But my way may not be the only way." Too many top-level executives lose sight of the fact that there isn't just one right way of doing something.
10. **Cultivate a sense of urgency.** Invariably, it's better to do something—even if it proves to be not the best possible thing—than to do nothing at all. Every action you take will have its trade-offs; perfection is for the gods of Olympus, not for CEOs. But do something. When you don't instill a sense of urgency, lethargy tends to spread in the organization.

Source: "Ten Things I Have Learned About Management," by Frederick C. Crawford. Reprinted courtesy of *United Mainliner,* carried aboard United Airlines. © 1981. East/West Network, publisher.

Using Group Dynamics

Group dynamics, based on communication and interaction, can be functional or dysfunctional in achieving group and organizational goals. As indicated in Chapter 11, groups can be assets or liabilities in solving problems, depending on the effectiveness of leadership. We think of leadership as a function that all group members should be involved in. However, the most typical situation is for group members to look to the formal or positional leaders to run routine meetings or facilitate the meetings of ad hoc groups. In such situations it is difficult to know exactly when to be a follower, according to tradition, and when to help fill the leadership role. Group effort has such a bad reputation that even a little improvement stemming from effective leadership pays big dividends.

As was indicated in Figure 6.5, good leadership involves recognizing people and facilitating relationships. Whether in a temporary task force or a permanent work group, one of the basic skills is facilitating interaction among members that has a synergistic effect. That is, by tapping the ideas and abilities of everyone, the composite result is greater than the sum of individual accomplishments. Effective leaders are able to draw people out, check for meaning, use conflict constructively, achieve mutual understanding, and reach agreement.

Active Listening

We suggested in Chapter 5 that the goal of communication can be a form of mutual understanding that is not necessarily agreement. This means that communication involves a recognition of diverse opinions within an overall framework of consensus and mutuality of interests sufficient to achieve common goals. Active listening is a crucial skill and, in many settings, a lost art. We all need considerable practice in order to be more effective listeners. To become an integral part of a person's style it must be based on basic values and a part of one's managerial philosophy. If your view of human nature is pessimistic and negative (evil, lazy, irresponsible, and dumb), you will tend not to be an active listener. It is only when we project positive energy toward others that we tend to watch them closely and listen to them attentively. In work organizations, there is a tendency to listen to one's superiors but not subordinates (or peers). This tendency leads to frustration on the part of participants who want to contribute ideas and opinions about the job and the work place. Indeed, managers' tendency not to listen to subordinates was a primary finding in a study of *Work in America:*

> The most consistent complaint reported to our task force has been the failure of bosses to listen to workers who wish to propose better ways of doing their jobs. Workers feel that their bosses demonstrate little respect for their intelligence. Supervisors are said to feel that workers are incapable of thinking creatively about their jobs (p. 37).

It is important to recognize individuals and their ideas. All of the knowledge, ability, and creativity is not concentrated at the top in work organizations. Therefore, it is important to tap these resources at every level. And, the complaints are heard from vice presidents as well as first-line operators—"The boss never asks me what I think." A first step is recognizing people by name as a small indication of respect and consideration. Following a workshop on memory (including how to remember names), participants wrote these comments:

1. "The highlight was finding out that *I was known by name* by upper administration and others, and talking with them in small groups on important issues."
2. "The highlight was when Vice President Dunn made an effort to meet me *as a person*."
3. "The best part was working with immediate superiors *as peers* in problem solving."

The next step is respect for ideas as well as people. Listening actively and positively reinforcing good ideas will increase the probability that more will be forthcoming. On the other hand, inattention and lack of response will tend to dampen or stifle participation and creativity.

Active listening requires skill as well as a positive attitude and respect for others. We need to be able to override the tendency for marshalling our own thoughts rather than attending to what others are saying. We need to be able to check for meaning (paraphrase what another person has said; express our understanding; ask whether we have got the message) fairly often rather than waiting until the end of a long, complex message. If too much time elapses, we are not able to remember the ideas that need to be clarified.

Inspiring Performance

Leaders that make the headlines of the daily papers or weekly periodicals are often described as inspiring. They are singled out in business and other areas (particularly sports) for doing the most with the least. They have been able to tap the latent human capability of their followers and achieve performances that require individuals to give 110 percent of capacity. These individual efforts were molded to achieve outstanding group results. Brute persistence has been the primary common thread when significant improvements have been made in ailing organizations (Peters, 1981). Within this overall theme, effective leaders have concentrated on basic goals, communicated simple ideas, encouraged experimentation, and positively reinforced good performance. For every success story reported in *Sports Illustrated* and *Business Week,* there are many other unsung heroes who have done an outstanding job of inspiring performance in subparts of obscure organizations. They are able to influence behavior by using rewards and punishments where appropriate. Many different styles (philosophies, characteristics, and behaviors) can be effective.

We feel that over the long run the best results are gained by downplaying punishment and emphasizing positive reinforcement. As a general approach to motivation, there is a worldwide shortage of positive reinforcement. Human beings seem prone to evaluate, criticize, and punish one another. Such an environment is demotivating. Why the shortage of positive reinforcement? First of all, punishment seems to, work, at least in the short run. Undesired behavior stops. However, there may be unintended consequences such as bad feelings toward the punisher, scheming to get even, and continuing the undesired behavior covertly. The effects of positive reinforcement are more subtle and may take longer. Many of us find it difficult to compliment others; it appears to be more natural to ignore good points and concentrate on faults. Parenting and bossing often have a lot in common. Children and subordinates often lament, "The only time we ever talk is when I am in trouble." Another factor may be that people in our culture are not particularly good at receiving positive reinforcement. It may be so rare that we are embarrassed by it. In turn, such an episode may be embarrassing for the supervisor and hence become less likely in the future.

Many managers, when asked about why positive reinforcement is not used more often, say that it shouldn't be necessary. "We pay employees to do a good job; why should we have to tell them when they do so?" On the other hand, positive reinforcement in the form of recognition and praise does not cost anything. If it is warranted and sincere, it can be effective in shaping behavior in desired directions and in creating conditions that are beneficial for both individuals and organizations (Hamner & Hamner, 1976).

A leader's power and effectiveness depend on the zone of acceptance maintained by followers. That is, if there is a high degree of trust, followers are prone to accept the orders or suggestions of a leader and carry them out with enthusiasm. A narrow zone of acceptance, on the other hand, can result in reluctant compliance or outright refusal to carry out proposed action steps. *Charisma* is a phenomenon that widens the zone of acceptance significantly. A leader is charismatic when her qualities are admired and respected to the point that followers suspend their own judgment, modify their beliefs, and maybe even adjust their values in order to fall into line. A charismatic personality can foster commitment and effort that leads to success, even though the planning is poor and the environment hostile. The most evident examples of charisma and action come from military and sports settings. However, it can play a role in work organizations as well.

POWER AND PARTICIPATION

We discussed the concept of power in Chapter 6, "Leadership." We also discussed participation in decision making in Chapter 11. In this chapter we are interested in how attitudes toward power and participation are an integral part of one's managerial philosophy. And, one's view of human nature affects one's view of power and participation. A positive, optimistic view leads to increased participation on the basis that everyone has something to contribute. A negative, pessimistic view leads to less participation; it also leads to centralizing power and authority on the assumption that sharing power means to give up something and to lose power. Let us discuss some of the issues involved and see why sharing power does not necessarily mean losing it.

Sources and Uses of Power

Power, being the ability to influence behavior, can stem from formal or legal authority. Other sources of power include technical competence, persuasive abilities, and personal charisma.

Power is often used to control the behavior of people in work organizations. Complete power allows a manager to control both ends and means; to decide what the goals are and how to go about accomplishing them. An alternative view of power—to enable the accomplishment of goals—results in a significantly different organizational atmosphere. Emphasis is on encouraging participation, unleashing power, and facilitating creative problem solving.

Competence and Influence

Competence and influence are closely related. We tend to be influenced by others who are knowledgeable and skillful, or (in the case of confidence artists) who appear to be. A basic desire is to be and appear competent and thereby be influential. To be able to influence one's co-workers and superiors is rewarding. This basic desire is thwarted if power is closely held in an organization and participation is minimal.

> Traditional management theory and practice have done more than just ignore human competence by assuming quite the opposite—that people in general are not competent and have no desire to excel. This unflattering view is evident in traditional management's attempt to reserve all planning, directing, and controlling in the organization for itself—as if sharing power with "workers" would be disastrous (Hall, 1980, book jacket).

Again, assumptions about human beings—competent or incompetent—can be self-fulfilling prophecies. If we assume that people are not competent and don't want to become so, we will give them little opportunity to demonstrate their knowledge or ability. Unused capacity will atrophy and people will indeed become incompetent. Thus, it is important to assume the best until we know otherwise and hence provide opportunities for people to demonstrate their capabilities and improve.

Power of the System

Figure 18.2 shows the effect of traditional assumptions about power and how it might be. If it is assumed, as in the top tier (A), that power is a fixed amount in a paired relationship or system, then for Person 1 (P_1) to give up power or delegate responsibility to P_2 results in a decrease for P_1 and an increase for P_2. However, the bottom tier (B) indicates how power is not necessarily fixed. If we move away from the concept of power as the ability to control others toward the concept of power as the ability to accomplish results, sharing power can mean an increase in the total amount of power in the system. For example, the bottom tier indicates how person P_1 can delegate responsibility to one or more others and thus have a smaller share of the power pie. However, because

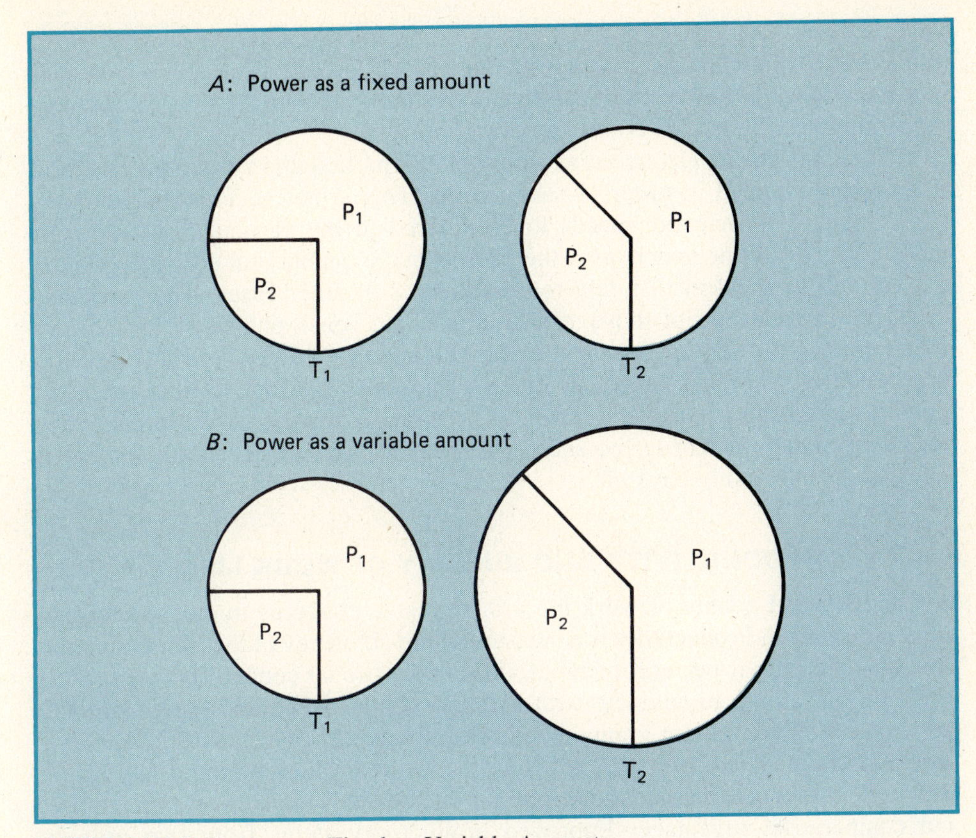

FIGURE 18.2 Power as a Fixed or Variable Amount

the total amount of power in the system has increased, P_1's power has increased. The more we get people involved and committed, the more they are able to demonstrate their competence in solving problems and taking advantage of opportunities. Thus, the total system becomes more competent and powerful in terms of its ability to accomplish the desired ends.

Efficacy of Participation

Participation is a key lever in improving individual and organizational performance. And, it is a simple process. A manager needs only to internalize a positive and optimistic view that underlies the tendency to ask others what they think and to involve them in both planning and doing important tasks. There is a tendency to try to do everything (as Don Nolte did in the vignette) on the assumption that no one can do it as well as you can. This is crucial for first-line supervisors who tend to keep doing their technical job as well as their new managerial responsibilities. Better results are obtained if they are able to adjust their activities to fit the new role. Allowing people to become involved and committed will pay off over the long run even if there are a few mistakes or glitches along the way. One has to have some tolerance for ambiguity and a willingness to allow things to be done somewhat differently from their own tried-and-true ways. The key is to concentrate on results and allow considerable leeway concerning how people go about achieving them.

There may be an erroneous assumption that participation requires a meeting of everyone affected in order to take a vote. This is not necessarily the case. The degree of participation needs to be tailored to the particular situation. In some cases, everyone may expect the boss to make a unilateral decision. Maybe it is enough to check with a few representatives in other cases. The particular issue, the expectations of those affected, and time constraints are all important in determining the appropriate degree of participation. The key here is to develop an attitude of involving people as much as possible in order to draw upon as much potential competence and power as possible. A participative approach may not be the most efficient in the short run, but, in terms of developing potential managers, it inevitably pays off.

PRODUCTIVITY AND QUALITY OF WORK LIFE

Productivity and quality of work life are pervasive concerns in our society and around the world. Productivity is a measure of the efficiency of the transformation process—the output per unit of input. This is a national concern because of its effect on our ability to compete with nations such as Japan and West Germany for markets. If we cannot compete successfully, we lose sales and jobs. Some protection is afforded for markets within the United States by imposing tariffs. However, this is not the ultimate solution if one believes in one world, free trade, and comparative advantage. Improved productivity stems from two primary sources: (1) technological improvement and (2) human effort. Our focus as a society for nearly a century has been on technological advances that make productivity less dependent on human effort, knowledge, and ability. But this approach can go only so far; at some point attention must turn to productivity improvements through people. This is our focus in this section. One's managerial philosophy includes some ideas about the relative importance of productivity and quality of work life. Are they mutually exclusive, or can progress be made in both areas simultaneously?

Quantity and Quality of Results

The issue of productivity is more complex than the number of widgets per work hour. It includes an element of quality: whether we are referring to a manufactured item or a service such as banking or health care. In some cases we may be interested in higher quality of service (government agencies) for a given amount of resources (tax dollars).

The key concept is value added during the transformation process. How much more worth is created by people combining available resources and their own efforts to produce a product or service? Quality of results is often more dependent on human factors than the quantity of output. For example, the number of cars produced by an automobile plant may be a function of the speed of the assembly line. The quality of each automobile that rolls off the end of that line is highly dependent on the commitment of workers to be thorough and careful in carrying out their functions. Achieving such results is a challenge for managers in modern organizations.

Making a Better Workplace

Quality of work life is often thought of in terms of physical aspects of the plant or office. Perhaps this is because the workplace is the most visible part of the job. Such considerations are not unimportant (Steele, 1973), but other aspects may be more important. The organization's structure, its processes, and its characteristic leadership style may determine the quality of work life. A number of elements that together (sometimes subtly) determine the quality of work life are listed in Chapter 16.

A broad view includes changing the entire organizational milieu by humanizing work, individualizing organizations, and fundamentally changing the structural and managerial systems. In addressing the issue of improving quality of work life, managers need to address questions such as these below (Suttle, 1977, pp. 1–2):

How can individuals be helped to develop careers that allow them to realize the full range and extent of their capabilities and interests, while at the same time meeting both the short-term and the long-term manpower needs of the organizations that employ them?

How can jobs be designed so that effective performance is linked with meaningful, interesting, and challenging work?

Under what conditions do various types of rewards (such as pay, promotion, and fringe benefits) and reward systems (such as job-based versus skill-based pay, hourly versus salary payment, and individual versus group-incentive plans) prove most effective for encouraging workers to join an organization, come to work regularly, and perform effectively?

What are the dynamics of group and intergroup relations that must be taken into account in any attempt to understand the behavior and improve the quality of work life of group members?

What are the key supervisory strategies that produce the highest quality of work life for people in organizations? What are the structural and other constraints that influence a supervisor's behavior?

How can the desired organizational changes, once identified, actually be brought about?

By finding answers to most or all of these questions, we can make organizations better places to work. In doing so, what happens to productivity? If one assumes that work is basically an onerous duty, the thought of improving its quality may be a contradiction in terms. On the other hand, there is reason to believe that both ends can be achieved simultaneously with certain shifts in perspective and changes in methodology. This view is supported by the notion (Chapter 4) that job satisfaction, a critical element in the quality of work life, follows performance that is recognized and rewarded. Thus, challenging, realistic goals that are accepted and achieved can go a long way toward maintaining a positive tone. We have now come full circle to reemphasize the influence of optimistic views in creating and maintaining a subtly positive aura in work organizations.

Doing the Job Better

A key element in doing the job better—becoming more productive—is working smarter rather than harder (Burck, 1981). The focus is effective utilization of time, energy, and ingenuity to achieve more and better results. Unnecessary activities can be eliminated; procedures can be streamlined; and dull, uninteresting tasks can be enriched. Doing the job can become challenging and intrinsically rewarding. Doing the job better and knowing the results (feedback) can lead to continued improvement, particularly if good performance is positively reinforced (Blanchard & Johnson, 1982).

In a study of 62 large U.S. companies that have sustained excellent performance for many years, the researchers concluded that eight basic attributes seem to account for success. They are simple-sounding ideas, but difficult to carry out. At the core is the phenomenon of shared values: a widespread acceptance of the following basic managerial practices as keys to success (Peters & Waterman, 1982, pp. 13–15):

1. *A bias for action,* for getting on with it. Even though these companies may be analytical in their approach to decision making, they are not paralyzed by that fact (as so many others seem to be).
2. *Close to the customer.* These companies learn from the people they serve. They provide unparalleled quality, service, and reliability.
3. *Autonomy and entrepreneurship.* These companies foster many leaders and many innovators throughout the organization.
4. *Productivity through people.* The excellent companies treat the rank and file as the root source of quality and productivity gain. They do not foster we/they labor attitudes or regard capital investment as the fundamental source of efficiency improvement.
5. *Hands-on, value driven.* The basic philosophies of the excellent companies have much to do with their achievements. Top management keeps in touch by visiting the "front line."
6. *Stick to the knitting.* While there were a few exceptions, the odds for excellent performance seem strongly to favor those companies that stay reasonably close to businesses they know.
7. *Simple form, lean staff.* The underlying structural forms and systems in the excellent companies are elegantly simple. Top-level staffs are lean.
8. *Simultaneous loose-tight properties.* The excellent companies are both centralized and decentralized. They have pushed autonomy down to the shop floor of product development. On the other hand, they are fanatic centralists around the few core values they hold dear.

The research involved extensive in-depth interviews and much on-sight observation. Peters and Waterman sum up their experience as follows:

> Above all, the *intensity itself,* stemming from strongly held beliefs, marks these companies. During our first round of interviews, we could "feel it." The language used in talking about people was different. The expectation of regular contributions was different (p. 16).

An obvious common thread in these findings is the optimistic view of human nature and an assumption that competent people are the key to productivity, success, and excellence. Intensity and *controlled chaos* may be a stressful environment for some managers and nonmanagers. However, many people seem to thrive in such a challenging culture as long as there is a positive tone plus ample communication, feedback, and recognition.

Managing Stress

Considerable attention is being focused on the concept of stress in work organizations and its negative consequences in terms of ill health and poor performance (see Chapter 17). Acute problems such as accidents, heart attacks, or confining illnesses are evident and their costs are tremendous. Chronic problems, such as alcoholism, anxiety, and high blood pressure, are less noticeable, but may have more overall detrimental effects on individual and organizational performance.

Although we cannot say with certainty that stress *causes* ill health or poor performance, there seems to be enough evidence to warrant continuing efforts to understand the relationships among stress, health, and performance. At the very least, stress has an effect on a person's physical and psychological ability to resist diseases: both those that are infectious and acute, and those that are chronic and stem from maladaptation of the body's systems.

The concepts *stress* and *stressor* have received considerable attention from researchers in many disciplines and a variety of definitions have been put forth depending on the researcher's point of view. We like the notion that there is an interactive process between individuals and their environment. Stressors in a particular situation act as stimuli that are mediated by individuals (thinking and feeling) and result in physical, physiological, psychological, and emotional responses. As long as the response remains within some normal or tolerable range for an individual, the level of stress is appropriate. Figure 18.3 shows the concept of an appropriate range within which the positive aspects significantly outweigh the negative aspects. There is enough so that people don't rust out, but there is not so much stress that people burn out.

The term *stress* can be considered neutral with the words *distress* and *eustress* used for designating bad and good effects. Thus, eustress can indicate a situation where the individual is in balance or within tolerable limits. Distress would connote effects that are out of balance or outside the tolerable limits.

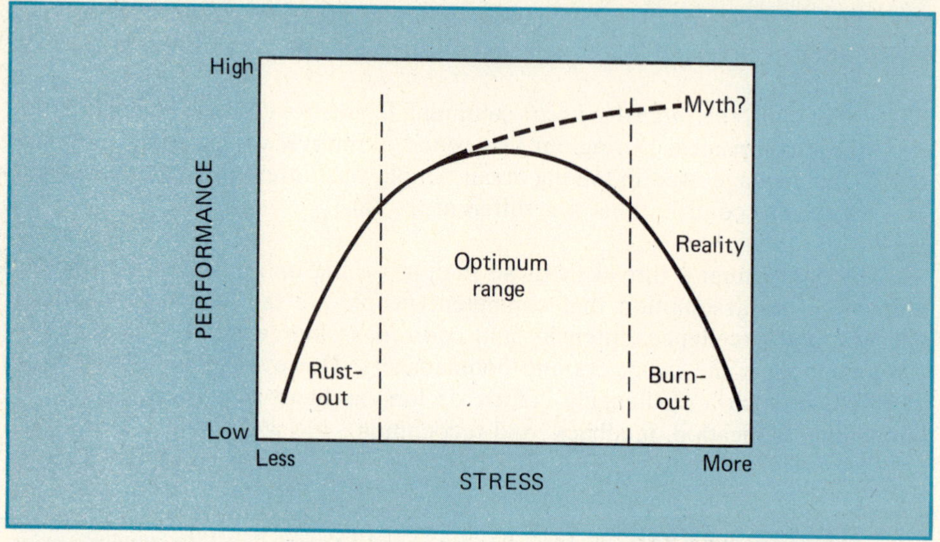

FIGURE 18.3 Stress and Performance

Several key ideas emerge from various definitions of stress: (Shuler, 1980, p. 189; Ivancevich & Matteson, 1980, p. 239; and McGrath, 1970, p. 17):

1. Stress is a response within an individual, stemming from an interactive process with stressors in the environment.
2. Given individual differences, potentially stressful situations will lead to distress for some individuals but not for others.
3. Stress is not all bad; within tolerable limits eustress is functional and facilitates good performance.
4. Distress occurs when imbalance or disequilibrium get beyond tolerable limits; that is, when the gap between where a person is and where one should be or wants to be is too wide for comfort or the path is blocked.

The concept of an appropriate amount of stress is extremely important. Much of the literature implies that the goal is to reduce stress. It may be, but not necessarily. For some people, the level of stimulation is too low; they are bored and need more challenge. If stress is a neutral concept, then the goal is to reduce distress and maintain eustress. Thus, we are concerned with maintaining balance and equilibrium, recognizing that it is a dynamic process. A number of organization-design and management-practice issues can be related to the idea of balance. For example:

1. Uncertainty can lead to distress, but so can certainty or overcontrol.
2. Pressure can lead to distress, but so can limbo or lack of contact.
3. Responsibility can lead to distress, but so can lack of responsibility or insignificance.
4. Performance evaluation can lead to distress, but so can lack of feedback concerning performance.

5. Role ambiguity can lead to distress, but so can job descriptions that constrain individuality.

For these and other dimensions of organization design and management practice, the key is providing an appropriate amount for the organization in general and each individual in particular.

Out of all the potential stressors, the primary causes of distress in work organizations are these: confusion or conflict in expectations; role incongruity or role overload; nature of the work (occupations); performance evaluation; physical environment; interpersonal problems/conflicts. Organizations can help manage stress—that is, maintain an appropriate level—by doing a good job in areas such as performance planning, role analysis, work redesign/job enrichment, continuing feedback, ecological considerations, and interpersonal skills training.

Enlightened managers can design organization structures and processes that maintain stress at appropriate levels and thus facilitate individual and organizational performance. However, it is difficult to ensure such results for everyone, given the differential effects of stressors on individuals. Therefore, some attention needs to be paid to individual means for coping with distress in organizations and thereby restoring or maintaining a tolerable quality of work life.

CHANGE AND IMPROVEMENT

The managerial role typically emphasizes *accomplishing the task*. Less emphasis is put on the process used or *how we did it*. And yet, no person or organization or process is ever exactly the same in two time periods. Change is inevitable (see Chapters 15 and 16). And the pace of change in modern society is accelerating. "Change is often closely tied to conflict. Sometimes change breeds conflict; sometimes conflict breeds change" (Brown, 1983, p. v).

Perceptible change highlights the difference (possibly the conflict) between the new and the old. The word improvement has an inherently good ring to it. It is difficult to be against improvement. On the other hand, change is a more controversial concept. Change might mean improvement; or it might not. "Things may go pretty badly for a while, but then they'll take a turn for the worse." Of course, whether or not change is seen as improvement depends on one's point of view and degree of comfort with the current situation. Resistance to change stems from vested interests in the current status or processes, lack of understanding of new goals and methods, and uncertainty with regard to intended and unintended effects in the future.

Dynamic Equilibrium

Managers are responsible for maintaining a dynamic equilibrium in organizations. Whatever the endeavor, it is important to diagnose the situation to determine what's going well (what we should keep doing or do more of) and what's not going well (what we should stop doing or do less of). Such a continuing diagnosis can lead to adjustments that are appropriate for coping with current conditions. Tex Schramm, general manager of the Dallas Cowboys expresses the coaching staff's philosophy as follows:

> We get the best people and, if for some reason the job isn't getting done, then we look at our methods, the way we're doing things, rather than changing people around. Your people have to have a certain feeling of permanence. They have to be able to make decisions not only regarding the present, but the future. If you have somebody who doesn't know how long he's going to be around, he'll do things for the present and sacrifice the future (Owen, 1982, p. D–1).

A dynamic equilibrium for an organization would include the following (Kast & Rosenzweig, 1979, p. 565):

1. Enough stability to facilitate achievement of current goals.
2. Enough continuity to ensure orderly change in either ends or means.
3. Enough stability to react appropriately to external opportunities and demands as well as changing internal conditions.
4. Enough innovativeness to allow the organization to be proactive (initiate changes) when conditions warrant.

Balancing stability and continuity with adaptation and innovation is obviously a delicate process. But all of these dimensions are important for long-run success and maybe even survival. The accelerating pace of change in some industries suggests that relatively more emphasis be put on adaptation and innovation. For other industries and organizations an emphasis on stability and continuity will better fit the environmental milieu. As a manager, one should devote considerable time and attention to diagnosing personal and organizational situations. It is only with a solid foundation of diagnosis that an appropriate strategy for coping can be developed.

Renewal

Organizational change and improvement is often termed *renewal*. Many changes are unplanned; they occur inadvertently and, if they work out, we attribute it to luck or serendipity. From a managerial perspective *planned change* is a primary focus of attention that indicates the importance of improvement or renewal. The basic process involves continual diagnosis and action planning to make sure the organization is as effective, efficient, and satisfying for participants as possible. The *as possible* in the phrase calls attention to the situational nature of good managerial decision making. Changes will be improvements if they are appropriate to the circumstances. Widespread involvement of organizational participants in the renewal process increases the probability that appropriate (from the point of view of the participants) action steps will be designed and implemented enthusiastically. Involvement increases the probability that participants will grow as organizational members and potential managers.

The notion that organization renewal and improvement is a fundamental part of the managerial role means that every manager is an agent change. It suggests the need for a program of self-help in making renewal a part of the everyday process of managing. Some managers will be better change agents than others. Effective leadership is needed to facilitate constructive conflict and related changes. If a manager lacks the relevant skills or is unsure in the change agent role, he or she may find the use of consultants helpful. The consultants may be internal or external, and they may be either experts or facilitators.

Expert consultants are most appropriate when the issues at hand are complex and technical, when changes are irrevocable and costly, or when there is just no time for organization members to do what needs to be done. Legal and accounting advice are two examples of such situations. The in-between approach—that is, in between doing it yourself and relying on experts—is to use a facilitator to help the organization help itself. A facilitator's role is primarily one of getting a formal renewal process started and keeping it rolling. It includes helping the organization identify problems/opportunities, facilitating analysis, decision making, and action planning, and reminding key organization members to follow up as part of the never-ending renewal (improvment) process.

The use of a facilitator preserves the integral role of the manager (and all or most members) in the renewal process. Active involvement should lead to both accomplishing the task at hand and improving the process at the same time. In other words, the organization learns by doing. It not only solves problems but it gets better at the problem-solving process. Without introspection and critique, this organizational learning does not occur. Facilitating such a critique is the key role. It is a difficult one for participants to do on their own without considerable practice. However, it can be done with help in the initial stages. Once the key people gain some experience they are able to continue a process on their own with periodic help for fine-tuning or dealing with particularly sticky issues.

SO WHAT? IMPLICATIONS FOR YOU

The material in this chapter is offered as food for thought—on the subject of managing. Knowledge and skill are important for long-run success, but your philosophy and style are also basic ingredients. They will affect your decisions and guide your behavior. You should address the issues in this chapter explicitly. What is your view of human nature? Can you be an effective leader and follower? What do you think about power? About participation? Can you balance productivity and quality of work life? Will you encourage organization improvement? Or resist change? Are you committed to self-renewal?

Learning how to learn may be the most important goal for you as a manager, or in any role (Zemke, 1980). In our society with its accelerated pace of change, technical knowledge or skill become obsolete rather quickly. Thus, self-renewal should have a high priority in your personal planning. As for the organization as a whole, or any of its subunits, individual managers need a strategy and tactics for achieving success (Steiner, 1976). Personal and organizational success are intertwined in most situations. However, it is important for you to develop personal goals and action plans for achieving them. This will relate in large measure to your role in a work organization. On the other hand, it can and should include other aspects of your life. Each person plays many roles. Performance in each one contributes to an overall sense of success and well being. Progress in a professional association is closely related to work and can often have organizational as well as personal payoffs. Other roles (e.g., recreational groups, fraternal orders, or political affiliations) may not be closely related to your role in a work organization, but the experience can be relevant and does contribute to the total picture or mosaic of your life space.

Self-renewal calls for managing your time and your life (Lakein, 1973). An oft-heard lament is, "I don't have enough time." But the reality is that each of us has all of the time there is. It is a unique resource that is irreplaceable. Therefore, the real question is how to use time. Managers spend millions of dollars every year in workshops entitled *time management* or *managing your time*. But the real issue is *not time* management, it is *self* management. According to Drucker (1966, p. 25) effective executives do not start with their tasks. Moreover, they do not start with planning. They start with their time and allocate it to high priority tasks and issues. They know how to cut back unproductive use of time and consolidate their discretionary time into fairly large blocks in order to facilitate work on things that require thought and creativity. They eliminate unnecessary activities and delegate to others where possible. They engage in a continual process of diagnosis and action planning that is focused on their most precious resource—time.

Within this framework, managers behave differently based on personal preferences and organizational situations. The main idea is for you to take control, keeping in mind emotional, psychological, and physical needs. Good nutrition and proper exercise are important to maintain one's health and well-being. Otherwise, there is no energy to apply during the time that may be available. In other words, good health (physical, psychological, and emotional well-being) is a necessary foundation for achieving short-run goals and maintaining a process of self-renewal that enhances the probability of long-run success regardless of the specific situation.

As indicated in the previous section, management's responsibility includes maintaining an appropriate level of stressors to facilitate individual and organizational performance. Assuming that doesn't happen, or assuming that individuals react differently to stressors, you need some personal means of coping with life and work organization stressors. The basic human approach to crises or stress is to fight or flee (see Chapter 17). Both responses increase physiological activity, such as pulse rate, blood pressure, and adrenalin flow. This was appropriate when the caveman was trying to elude the saber-toothed tiger. It is probably less appropriate when you are going into a performance-evaluation session with your boss. In such a context, the fight or flight response may inhibit your ability to think clearly and to come across as calm, cool, and collected.

You can cope by means of adaptive self-statements that mediate between stressors in the situation and emotional responses. For example, you could talk to yourself before an oral presentation in terms of:

> "I won't die if it flops."
> "I probably won't even get fired."
> "Even if I get fired, I could probably find another job. I've done it before."
> "This is no big deal; I've done it a hundred times and it always seems to work out."

Another approach is deep muscle relaxation, perhaps coupled with deep breathing. Whereas adaptive self-statements are focused on emotional responses, deep muscle relaxation focuses on physiological responses and the autonomic nervous system.

Simultaneous with the fight-or-flight response is a relaxation response that is also part of the autonomic nervous system. However, this part of our physiological system either has not developed as fully or it has withered from disuse. Meditation is designed to rehabilitate the relaxation response and use it as a way to mediate between stressors and stress (Benson, 1976). Deep breathing, muscle relaxation, and meditation are means of gaining a "pause that refreshes." In all three cases the key element is a change of pace. Whether it is ten minutes, one minute, or ten seconds, the key is a relatively short period of rest and rehabilitation. In a sense, it is a very short cycle of self-renewal folded into an overall strategy that covers months and years.

"He who knows others is learned; he who knows himself is wise." These words from the Chinese philosopher Lao-tse are appropriate to close a book on understanding human behavior in organizations. First, you need to understand people one at a time—why they behave the way they do. Second, you need to understand the behavior of people in interacting roles and in groups of various sizes. Then you need to understand what effects formal structures and processes have on individual behavior in organizations.

Knowledge and understanding is a foundation. Skillful application of knowledge comes with experience. A more difficult achievement is wisdom gained by judiciously tempering knowledge with experience. It involves a contingency view that facilitates coupling thorough diagnosis with implementation of appropriate action steps. All of this is important for personal success. But basic to everything is knowing yourself—your managerial philosophy and style—and either becoming comfortable with who you are or designing strategies that will bring you to your goals. It is important to set challenging but realistic goals in personal planning, just as in organizational planning. Rewards are crucial. If you are not careful, you can become dependent on extrinsic rewards that are under the control of others. A fundamental step is to select a kind of work that has intrinsic rewards for you—work that, *in the doing,* is rewarding in and of itself. Of course, some jobs can be doubly rewarding: the work itself being interesting and inviting effort naturally; there being, as well, a reasonably high probability of performing well and being rewarded for doing so.

Many means of organizational and individual renewal seems commonsensical, but somehow our culture has managed to override common sense and build work organizations that are simply no fun at all. Your most crucial task as a future manager may be to balance the dual needs in any work organization—quality of work (productivity) and quality of work life.

LEARNING APPLICATION ACTIVITIES

1. Write a vignette based on your experience that illustrates the effect of managerial philosophy and style on human behavior in a work organization.

2. Write an essay (500–750 words) entitled ''My Philosophy of Management.'' Share your essay with a colleague; invite feedback; and note similarities and differences.

3. *Step 1:* Find an example of managerial philosophy and style as described in a current newspaper or magazine article. Summarize the key concepts in a short paragraph or list three to five guidelines for behavior that are stated or implied in the article.

Step 2: Share your example with three or four colleagues. Compare and contrast the key concepts or guidelines.

Step 3: Report common threads to the total class.

4. *Step 1:* Illustrate the phenomenon of self-fulfilling prophecy (either positive or negative) with an example from your experience.

Step 2: Share your example with three or four colleagues. Note common elements in (a) positive examples and (b) negative examples.

Step 3: Report your group findings to the total class and discuss their relevance for managerial philosophy.

5. Relate the term productivity to quality of services (rather than quantity) and illustrate the concept with an actual example. Share your example with the class.

6. Write down the *things* (events, situations, people, etc.) at work that are most stressful for you. Next, list the emotional and physiological indicators of stress for you. Now, note some action steps that you might take to cope with either (a) the *sources* of stress for you or (b) their *effects* on you.

7. Write out two goals for personal improvement with particular reference to your potential as a manager. For each goal list the action steps necessary to achieve it. Reflect on the feasibility of each step; refine them if necessary; and arrange them in an appropriate sequence. Share your plans with a friend and invite comments.

8. *Step 1:* Browse through current newspapers or magazines for articles dealing with the issues of productivity and quality of work life in the U.S. or other countries.

Step 2: Share your findings with three or four colleagues and develop a composite list of important issues.

Step 3: Share your results with the class and discuss.

REFERENCES

Argyris, Chris and Donald A. Schon. *Theory in Practice*. San Francisco: Jossey-Bass, 1974.

Benson, Herbert, M.D., (with Miriam Z. Klipper). *The Relaxation Response*. New York: Avon Books, 1976.

Blanchard, Kenneth, and Spencer Johnson. *The One Minute Manager.* New York: William Morrow & Company, 1982.

Bowers, David G. *Systems of Organization*. Ann Arbor: University of Michigan Press, 1976.

Brown, L. David. *Managing Conflict at Organizational Interfaces*. Reading, Mass.: Addison-Wesley, 1983.

Burck, Charles G. "Working Smarter." *Fortune,* 15 June, 1981, pp. 68–73.

Clutterback, David. "Management by Anarchy." *International Management* 35/5 (May 1980): 30–32.

"Corporate Culture: The Hard-to-Change Values that Spell Success or Failure." *Business Week,* 27 October, 1980, pp. 148–160.

Crawford, Frederick C. "Ten Things I Have Learned About Management." *United Mainliner,* May 1981, pp. 148–150.

Deal, Terrance E., and Allen Kennedy. *Corporate Cultures—The Rites and Rituals of Corporate Life*. Reading, Mass.: Addison-Wesley, 1982.

Drucker, Peter. *An Introductory View of Management*. New York: Harper & Row, 1977.

Drucker, Peter. *The Effective Executive*. New York: Harper & Row, 1966.

Fortune, 12 July, 1982, inside front cover.

Hall, Jay. *The Competence Process*. The Woodland, Tex.: Teleometrics International, 1980.

Hamner, W. Clay, and Ellen P. Hamner. "Behavior Modification on the Bottom Line." *Organizational Dynamics* 4/4 (Spring 1976): 3–21.

Ivancevich, John M., and Michael T. Matteson. *Stress and Work: A Managerial Perspective*. Glenview, Ill.: Scott, Foresman, 1980.

Kast, Fremont E., and James E. Rosenzweig. *Organization and Management: A Systems and Contingency Approach*. New York: McGraw-Hill, 1979.

Katz, Robert L. "Skills of an Effective Administrator." *Harvard Business Review* 52/5 (September-October 1974): 90–102.

Kotter, John P. "What Effective General Managers Really Do." *Harvard Business Review* 60/6 (November-December 1982): 156–167.

Lakein, Alan. *How to Get Control of Your Time and Your Life*. New York: New American Library (Signet), 1973.

Likert, Rensis. *The Human Organization*. New York: McGraw-Hill, 1967.

Maccoby, Michael. *The Gamesman*. New York: Bantam, 1978.

Magnet, Myron. "Managing by Mystique at Tandem Computers." *Fortune,* 28 June, 1982, pp. 84–91.

Martin, William F., and George Cabot Lodge. "Our Society in 1985—Business May Not Like It." *Harvard Business Review* 53/6 (November-December 1975): 143–150.

McGrath, Joseph E., ed. *Social and Psychological Factors in Stress*. New York: Holt, Rinehart & Winston, 1970.

McGregor, Douglas. *The Human Side of Enterprise*. New York: McGraw-Hill, 1960.

Menzies, Hugh D. "The Ten Toughest Bosses." *Fortune,* 21 April, 1980, pp. 62–72.

Mintzberg, Henry. "The Manager's Job: Folklore and Fact." *Harvard Business Review* 53/4 (July-August 1975): 49–61.

Morrison, Ann M. "C.E.O.s Pick the Best C.E.O.s." *Fortune,* 4 May, 1981, pp. 133–136.

Moore, Kenny. "To Baffle and Amaze." *Sports Illustrated,* 26 July, 1982, pp. 60–72.

Ouchi, William G. *Theory Z.* Reading, Mass.: Addison-Wesley, 1981.

Owen, John. "Man Behind the Whistle." *Seattle Post-Intelligencer,* 2 April, 1978, p. D–4.

———. "Seahawks Taking Lessons from Cowboys." *Seattle Post-Intelligencer,* 25 April, 1982, p. D–1.

Peters, Thomas J. "Putting Excellence into Management." *Business Week,* 21 July, 1980, pp. 196–205.

———. "A Style for All Seasons." *The Best of Business* 3/1 (Spring 1981): 23–26.

Peters, Thomas J., and Robert H. Waterman, Jr. *In Search of Excellence*. New York: Harper & Row Publishers, 1982.

Phillips, Linda L. *Productivity and the Self-Fulfilling Prophecy: The Pygmalion Effect*. Film guide. New York: McGraw-Hill Films, 1975.

Schein, Edgar H. "In Defense of Theory Y." *Organizational Dynamics* 4/1 (Summer 1975): 17–30.

Schuler, Randall S. "Definition and Conceptualization of Stress in Organizations." *Organizational Behavior and Human Performance* 25 (1980): 184–215.

Steele, Fritz. *Physical Settings in Organizational Development*. Reading, Mass.: Addison-Wesley, 1973.

Steiner, George A. "Invent Your Own Future." *California Management Review* 19/1 (Fall 1976): 29–33.

Suttle, J. Lloyd. "Improving Life at Work—Problems and Prospects." In J. Richard Hackman and J. Lloyd Suttle (Eds.), *Improving Life at Work*. Santa Monica, Calif.: Goodyear, 1977.

Work in America. Report of a Special Task Force to the Secretary of Health, Education, and Welfare. Cambridge, Mass.: MIT Press, 1973.

Zemke, Ron. "Survival Skill for the '80s Manager." *Training/HRD,* November 1980, p. 6.

Welling, Brenton. "Eastern Airlines: From Ace to Astronaut." *Business Week,* 3 March 1980, p. 3.

SUBJECT INDEX

A

B

C

D

E

F

G

J

K

L

M

N

O

P

Q

R

S

T

U

V

W

X

Z

AUTHOR INDEX

F

G

H

I

J

K

L

M

N

O

P

R

S

T

U

V